# COST ACCOUNTING

(For B.Com., M.Com., B.B.A. and M.B.A. of all Universities of India)

**Dr. M. Wilson,**

***M.Com., M.B.A., D.B.A., M.Phil. Ph.D.***

*Reader in Commerce,*

*Scott Christian College (Autonomous)*

*Nagercoil*

Himalaya Publishing House

ISO 9001:2015 CERTIFIED

| | | | | | |
|---|---|---|---|---|---|
| **First Edition** | : | **2007** | **Fifth Edition** | : | **2014** |
| **Second Revised Edition** | : | **2008** | **Edition** | : | **2015** |
| **Third Revised Edition** | : | **2011** | **Edition** | : | **2017** |
| **Fourth Edition** | : | **2012** | **Edition** | : | **2019** |
| | | | **Edition** | : | **2020** |

**Published by** : Mrs. Meena Pandey for **Himalaya Publishing House Pvt. Ltd.,** "Ramdoot", Dr. Bhalerao Marg, Girgaon, **Mumbai - 400 004.** Phone: 022-23860170/23863863, Fax: 022-23877178 **E-mail:** himpub@bharatmail.co.in; **Website:** www.himpub.com

**Branch Offices** :

**New Delhi** : "Pooja Apartments", 4-B, Murari Lal Street, Ansari Road, Darya Ganj, New Delhi - 110 002. Phone: 011-23270392, 23278631; Fax: 011-23256286

**Nagpur** : Kundanlal Chandak Industrial Estate, Ghat Road, Nagpur - 440 018. Phone: 0712-2738731, 3296733; Telefax: 0712-2721216

**Bengaluru** : Plot No. 91-33, 2nd Main Road Seshadripuram, Behind Nataraja Theatre, Bengaluru - 560020. Phone: 08041138821, Mobile: 09379847017, 09379847005.

**Hyderabad** : No. 3-4-184, Lingampally, Besides Raghavendra Swamy Matham, Kachiguda, Hyderabad - 500 027. Phone: 040-27560041, 27550139

**Chennai** : New No. 48/2, Old No. 28/2, Ground Floor, Sarangapani Street, T. Nagar, Chennai - 600 012. Mobile: 09380460419

**Pune** : First Floor, "Laksha" Apartment, No. 527, Mehunpura, Shaniwarpeth (Near Prabhat Theatre), Pune - 411 030. Phone: 020-24496323/24496333; Mobile: 09370579333

**Lucknow** : House No 731, Shekhupura Colony, Near B.D. Convent School, Aliganj, Lucknow - 226 022. Phone: 0522-4012353; Mobile: 09307501549

**Ahmedabad** : 114, "SHAIL", 1st Floor, Opp. Madhu Sudan House, C.G. Road, Navrang Pura, hmedabad - 380 009. Phone: 079-26560126; Mobile: 09377088847

**Ernakulam** : 39/176 (New No: 60/251) 1st Floor, Karikkamuri Road, Ernakulam, Kochi - 682011. Phone: 0484-2378012, 2378016 Mobile: 09387122121

**Cuttack** : New LIC Colony, Behind Kamala Mandap, Badambadi, Cuttack - 753 012, Odisha. Mobile: 9338746007

**Kolkata** : 108/4, Beliaghata Main Road, Near ID Hospital, Opp. SBI Bank, Kolkata - 700 010, Phone: 033-32449649, Mobile: 07439040301

**DTP by** : **Sri Siddhi Softtek**

**Printed by** : M/s. Sri Sai Art Printer. Hyderbad. On behalf of HPH.

## PREFACE

The subject Cost Accounting is an important tool for management to plan and control the cost. It provides various methods to reduce the cost right from the purchase of raw material to the final production. It operates the cost in small elements to reduce the cost of production. In competitive market it is a must for the business units, to reduce the cost of production. It also helps for the quality output through various management decisions.

This book written by me is an additional contribution in the existing vast number of books of this kind. This book explains the concepts and theories in a systematic and organised manner through fourteen chapters. This book contains a lot of illustrations to explain the concepts and theories in all chapters. It also contains multiple choice questions, theory question and problems with answers in sufficient number. Hence, it will satisfy the academic community concerned with commerce and management to the maximum extent.

I express my thanks to God Almighty for giving me strength and vision to write this textbook. I express my thanks to the management, principal, Dr.E. James Reynold Daniel and all the members of the staff of Scott Christian College (Autonomous) for their encouragement and moral support. My sincere thanks are due to Mr. Niraj Pandey and Mr. Vijay Pandey, Partners of Himalaya Publishing House for publishing the textbook. I also thank the representatives of Himalaya Publishing House. My thanks are also due to my parents **Mr. K. Muthiah (Rtd. D.F.O.) and Mrs. G. Rosamma,** relatives and to my family members Joy and Doyle for their encouragement in writing this textbook.

**M. WILSON**

# CONTENTS

# CHAPTER - I

# INTRODUCTION

Cost Accounting emerged as a subject in order to provide information to management to take various managerial decisions. The business at present is highly competitive. In order to withstand competition the concerns have to supply goods at low prices. Low prices may affect the basic concept of the profit maximisation of business. To overcome this problem the only alternative for a concern is to reduce the cost of production. Cost Accounting as a subject is designed to provide many methods and techniques to reduce the cost of production through various stages of production.

## Definitions of Costing, Cost Accounting and Cost Accountancy

### Costing

The Institute of Cost and Management Accountants (ICMA) London defined, costing as the ascertainment of costs. It includes the technique and process of ascertainment of costs. The technique means the principles and rules required for ascertainment of cost of production of products and services. The process refers to the procedure for the ascertainment of cost.

### Cost Accounting

ICMA London defined Cost Accounting as "the process of accounting for cost from the point at which expenditure is incurred or committed to the establishment of its ultimate relationship with cost centres and cost units. In its widest usage, it embraces the preparation of statistical data, the application of cost control methods and the ascertainment of the profitability of activities carried out or planned". Hence, the Cost Accounting is the process of determining cost of activities of a concern and the ascertainment of the profitability from the activities.

### Cost Accountancy

ICMA London defined Cost Accountancy as "the application of costing and cost accounting principles, methods and techniques to the science, art and practice of cost control and ascertainment of profitability as well as presentation of information for the purpose of managerial decision - making". Hence, it is clear that Cost Accountancy includes costing, cost accounting, budgetary control, cost control and cost audit.

## Cost Accounting and Financial Accounting

The following are the differences between Cost Accounting and Financial Accounting.

1. Cost Accounting includes only operating activities. Financial accounting is concerned with both operating and non-operating activities (like dividend received, interest received and paid etc.)
2. Cost Accounting aims at providing information for the management. Financial Accounting aims at providing information external to the management, like shareholders, debentureholders, creditors, government etc.
3. Cost Accounting has no time limit in the preparation of accounts. It may be prepared for 15 days or for 1 month, 2 months,3 months like that. But, Financial Accounting is prepared only for one year. TheProfit and Loss Account and the Balance sheet are prepared at the end of the financial year which cover the activities for one year.
4. There is no compulsion for the preparation of Cost Accounting. Financial Accounting is compulsory according to the Companies Act of 1956.
5. Cost Accounting reports are not circulated to external parties. It is only for the management personnels to take managerial decisions. Financial Accounting report including the Profit & Loss Account and Balance Sheet are prepared for circulation to the external parties also.

**Cost Accounting and Management Accounting**

The important differences between Cost Accounting and Management Accounting are as follows.

1. The purpose of Cost Accounting is the ascertainment of cost at each stages of production. The purpose of Management Accounting is to provide information to the management for decision making.
2. Cost Accounting is prepared mainly on the basis of past and less emphasis is given for the future. Management Accounting purely aims at the future based on the past information.
3. Cost Accounting is prepared on the basis of some rules and regulations prescribed by the ICWAI. Management Accounting is prepared without adopting any speicific and rigid rules. It may be prepared according to the will of the managerial personnels.
4. The reports of the Cost Accounting are subject to statutary audit. The reports of the Management Accounting are not subject to statutary audit.
5. The reports of the Cost Accounting are useful both to the internal and external parties. The reports of the Management Accounting are useful only for the internal parties.

## Objectives of Cost Accounting

The important objectives of Cost Accounting are as follows.

1. Ascertainment of cost.
2. Planning and control of cost.
3. Providing information for managerial decision making.

### 1. Ascertainment of Cost

One of the important objectives of cost accounting is the ascertainment of cost at different stages of production. The cost incurred for each department and activities are to be calculated. The Standard cost for all types of costs are also to be calculated in order to compare the actual cost with the standard cost.

### 2. Planning and Control of Cost

The expenses in each stages of production for all departments should be well planned in advance. It helps the management to take steps to control the cost, in case the actual costs are more than already planned one.

### 3. Providing information for managerial decision making

Cost Accounting provides information to management which will help the management to take various managerial decisions. The decision regarding the fixation of price, quantity and type of production are taken on the basis of costing information.

## Advantages of Cost Accounting

The advantages of Cost Accounting are as follows.

1. In cost accounting, cost can be ascertained on departmental-wise , process-wise and functional-wise.
2. It helps to identify the departments which are performing well and which are not performing well. Hence, suitable action can be taken by the management against the non-performing departments.
3. The standard cost for all activities are fixed in cost accounting. Hence, it is possible to identify the area where the performance is falling below standard.
4. The material consumed is properly checked with the help of the Stores Ledger.
5. Cost accounting provides information to determine the cost well in advance before the commencement of production.
6. It provides information to the management for planning and controlling of cost.
7. It helps for reduction in cost to sell the products at low price.

**Limitations of Cost Accounting**

The limitations of Cost Accounting are as follows.

1. The estimation based on the cost incurred on the past, may not be correct always.
2. If the standard fixed, for various activities are not accurate, then the comparision with actual will not be correct.
3. The classification of costs by different types may lead to more confusion.
4. The classification of costs done for one purpose, may not be relevant for other purposes.
5. Calculation of cost on the basis of departments, functions and processes involves more clerical work.
6. Cost accounting excludes some items of expenses like dividend, interest etc. Hence, it will not give the accurate cost of production.

## INSTALLATION OF A COST ACCOUNTING SYSTEM

There are various methods of cost accounting system for a manufacturing company. The selection of a suitable cost accounting system depends upon number of factors like size, nature of business etc. Hence, the management should take utmost care in the selection and installation of a good cost accounting system.

**Factors influencing the installation of Cost Accounting System**

The important factors which influence the installation of a Cost Accounting System are stated as follows.

**1. Size of the business**

The requirement of cost data is more for a big business when compared to the requirement for the small business. Hence, different type of cost accounting systems need to be adopted by these two types of companies.

**2. Nature of raw materials**

Nature of raw materials used in the business also influences the cost accounting system. The degree of wastage of raw materials is not same for all type of raw materials. Hence, the cost accounting system with respect to raw materials also changes.

**3. Number of products**

The costing system adopted for a single product is different from the costing system adopted for multiple products.

**4. Manufacturing Process**

The costing system adopted for a single process is not suitable for the costing system adopted for a product with many processes of manufacturing.

**5. Needs of the Management**

The cost accounting system selected must be suitable to provide the necessary information required by the management.

**6. Efficiency of the Staff.**

The cost accounting system adopted must be suitable according to the efficiency of the staff of the company.

**7. Structure of the Organisation.**

The structure of the organisation also influences the selection of the suitable method of cost accounting system.

**Essentials of a good Cost Accounting System**

The essentials of a good cost accounting system are stated as follows.

1. The cost accounting system selected should be accurate one. It should not misguide the management. It should provide correct information for managerial decision making.
2. The system adopted should be simple to operate and easy to understand.
3. The cost accounting system adopted should be flexible, so that it should accomodate the changes in the company.
4. The system adopted should be one which would facilitate for easy comparision of the result of one period with other periods.
5. The system adopted should be of economical. The expenses involved in the adoption of the system should be very minimum.
6. The cost accounting system selected is one which should facilitate for the preparation of the reports in time. The timely preparation of accounts would facilitate the management to take necessary managerial decisions at the earliest.

**Difficulties in the installation of Cost Accounting System**

The difficulties in the installation of a cost accounting system are as follows.

1. The existing staff members may object for the introduction of a cost accounting system since they feel that it is an additional work for them.
2. It is difficult for inexperienced and inefficient staff members to handle the cost accounting system.
3. It involves additional expenses to the management.

4. The heads of various departments may not like the introduction of the cost accounting system since they are accountable to their superiors for any variations in the actual cost with standard cost.

## METHODS, TECHNIQUES AND SYSTEMS OF COSTING

### (a) Methods of Costing

The methods of costing adopted by various companies are as follows.

1. Job Costing
2. Batch Costing
3. Contract Costing
4. Process Costing
5. Operation Costing
6. Single or output Costing
7. Operating Costing

**1. Job Costing**

The costing adopted by concerns which produce goods according to the specific order of the customer is called Job Costing.

(Eg) Printing, Machine tools, Repair shops, Job foundries, Ship building etc.

**2. Batch Costing**

Batch costing is a method of costing adopted to concerns which produces group of identical or similar product in large units.

(Eg) Medicines, Ready-made garments, Toys, Spare parts etc.

**3. Contract Costing**

Contract costing is adopted by the concerns which produce product of constructions type. It is just like job costing, but the period of completion of the work is long when compared to the job costing.

(Eg) Construction of building, bridges, road, dams etc.

**4. Process Costing**

Process costing is adopted by concerns which produce products of mass scale with two or more processes.

(Eg). Sugar, chemical, paper, cement industries etc.

**5. Operation Costing**

Operation costing is a method of costing adopted for the concerns, producing products with number of processes or operations' where costs are collected, accumulated and ascertained for each operation separately.

(Eg) Engineering, Toy making etc.

**6. Single or Output Costing**

Single or output costing is a method of costing adopted by concerns which produce one product with identical and standard units through two or more processes. Under this method the total cost is ascertained and divided with the number of units produced , in order to find out the cost per unit.

(Eg) Mines, Quarries, Brick works, Steel works etc.

**7. Operating Costing**

The method of costing adopted by concerns which render services, is called operating costing.

(Eg) Railways, Airways, Road Transport, Hospital, Canteen, Power house etc.

**(b) Techniques (or Types of Costing)**

The manner in which cost of a product is ascertained is known as Technique of Costing. The important techniques of costing are as follows.

1. Historical Costing
2. Standard Costing
3. Absorption Costing
4. Marginal Costing
5. Uniform Costing

**1. Historical Costing**

The determination of cost after the costs have been incurred is called Historical Costing.

**2. Standard Costing**

The determination of cost before the costs are incurred for the production is called standard costing. In standard Costing the cost of each stages of production are determined well in advance. It helps the management to control the cost in all stages of production.

**3. Absorption Costing**

The Absorption Costing is also known as Full Costing. In absorption costing, different costs incurred for manufacturing a product are charged to the product. Direct costs are charged directly and indirect costs are apportioned and then charged.

**4. Marginal Costing**

Marginal Costing is also called variable costing. It helps the management to take decisions on the basis of variable cost and fixed cost.

**5. Uniform Costing**

Uniform Costing is an adoption of similar costing principles and practices.

## COSTING SYSTEM

Costing System is a system adopted for the ascertainment of cost.There are two costing systems i.e., Job order costing system and Process costing system. The different costing techniques are within the two systems of costing.

## COST CENTRES AND COST UNIT

### COST CENTRES

According to the Institute of Cost and Management Accountants, London "cost centre means a location, person or item of equipment (or group of these) for which cost may be ascertained and used for the purpose of cost control". On the basis of the definition Cost Centre may be classified as follows.

1. Personnel Cost Centre
2. Impersonnel Cost Centre
3. Operation Cost Centre
4. Process Cost Centre

**1. Personnel Cost Centre**

A cost centre which consists of a person or group of persons for which costs may be ascertained and used for the purpose of cost control, is called Personnel Cost Centre.

**2. Impersonnel Cost Centre**

A cost centre which consists of a location or item of equipment or group of these, for which cost may be ascertained and used for the purpose of cost control, is called Impersonnel Cost Centre.(Eg.) Cost incurred for a machine, department etc.

**3. Operation Cost Centre**

A cost centre which consists of the machines and/or person carrying out similar operations, for which cost may be ascertained and used for the purpose of cost control, is called Operation Cost Centre.

**4. Process Cost Centre**

A cost centre which consists of a specific process or a continuous sequence of operations, for which cost may be ascertained and used for the purpose of cost control, is called Process Cost Centre.

### COST UNITS

According to the Institute of Costs and Management Accountants, London a cost unit is, "a unit of quantity of product, service or time (or combination of these), in relation to which cost may be ascertained or expressed". Hence, cost unit is a unit of quantity of a product or service. On the basis of suitable cost units the cost of production and sales per unit are ascertained.Examples of cost units are tonne, number, kgm.,etc. The cost unit depends upon the type of product or service. The following are the important types of cost units on the basis of the nature and type of product or service.

**Types of Industries and Cost Units**

| Types of Industries | Cost Unit | Method of Costing |
|---|---|---|
| 1. Construction | Each contract | Contract costing |
| 2. Cement | Tonne | Process costing |
| 3. Sugar | Tonne, Kgm | Process Costing |
| 4. Chemical | Tonne, Kgm | Process Costing |
| 5. Steel | Tonne | Process Costing |
| 6. Automobile | Number | Process Costing |
| 7. Transport | Tonne Kilometre / Passenger Kilometre | Operating Costing |
| 8. Paper | Ream | Process Costing |
| 9. Bicycle | Number | Multiple Costing |
| 10. Textiles | Metres | Process Costing |
| 11. Flour | Tonne | Process Costing |
| 12. Hospital | Per bed occupied / Out-patient visit | Operating Costing |
| 13. Soft Drinks | Cases | Process Costing |
| 14. Ice Cream | Per gallon | Process Costing |
| 15. Readymade garments | Number | Batch Costing |
| 16. Timber | Cubic Feet | Process Costing. |

## CLASSIFICATION OF COSTS

Costs may be classified on the following basis

1. Element wise classification
2. Functional - wise classification
3. On the basis of identifiability
4. Behaviour - wise classification
5. On the basis of Controllability.
6. On the basis of Time.
7. On the basis of Relevancy.

### 1. Element-wise classification

On the basis of element-wise, costs may be classified into (a) Material Cost (b) Labour Cost and (c) Expenses.

#### (a) Material Cost

The cost incurred for the purchase and storage of material is called material cost. Material Cost is classified into (i) Direct material cost and (ii) Indirect material cost. Direct Material costs are those material cost which can be easily identified in a product. It can be easily allocated to the process of prodution. Indirect material costs are those material costs which cannot be easily identified in the product. It cannot be allocated but apportioned, to the process of production.

**(b) Labour Cost**

The cost incurred in the form of wages and salaries to the employees of a concern is called labour cost. Labour cost may be classified into (i) Direct Labour cost and (ii) Indirect Labour cost. Direct labour costs are those labour costs which can be easily identified in a product. It can be easily allocated to the process of production. Indirect Labour costs are those labour costs which cannot be easily identified in the product. It cannot be allocated, but apportioned, to the process of production.

**(c) Expenses**

The costs other than the material cost and labour cost are called expenses. Expenses are also classified into (i) Direct Expenses and Indirect Expenses. Direct expenses are those expenses which can be easily identified in a product and can easily be allocated to the process of production. Indirect expenses are those expenses which cannot be easily identified but apportioned, to the process of production.

**2. Functional-wise Classification**

Classification of costs on the basis of the functions of an organisation is called functional-wise classification. It may be classified into (a) Production Cost (b) Administration Cost and (c) Selling and Distribution Cost.

**(a) Production Cost**

The cost incurred in the factory or work place of a concern is called production cost. It includes the cost of direct material, direct labour, direct expenses and factory indirect expenses (factory overhead). The total of direct material, direct labour and direct expenses is called "Prime Cost". When factory overhead is added with Prime cost it is called Production Cost or Factory Cost.

**(b) Administration Cost**

The cost of administration of an organisation is called Administration cost. It includes indirect material, indirect labour and indirect expenses.(Eg) Stationery,salary,travelling expenses, refreshment expenses etc., incurred for the administration department.

**(c) Selling and Distribution Cost**

The costs incurred for selling and distribution of a product are called Selling and Distribution costs. It includes indirect material, indirect labour and indirect expenses.(Eg) Stationery,salary,travelling,refreshment expenses etc., incurred for the selling and distribution department.

### 3. On the basis of Identifiability

On the basis of Identifiability costs are classified into (a) Direct Costs, and (b) Indirect Cost.

**(a) Direct Costs**

Direct Costs are those costs which can easily be identified in a product. It can easily be allocated to the cost centre. It includes Direct Material, Direct Labour and Direct Expenses.

**(b) Indirect Costs**

Indirect costs are those costs which cannot easily be identified in a product. It cannot be allocated to the cost centre and it should be apportioned. It includes Indirect Material, Indirect Labour and Indirect Expenses.

### 4. Behaviour-wise Classification of Costs

On the basis of behaviour, cost may be classified into (a) Fixed Cost, (b) Variable cost and (c) Semi Variable Cost.

**(a) Fixed Cost**

The cost which remains constant upto a certain level of activity is called fixed cost. It may also be stated that the cost which would not change due to the changes in the volume of production. This cost should be incurred irrespective of the number of units manufactured. This cost should be incurred eventhough the company do not produce any units. Fixed cost per unit is variable.(Eg) Salary to staff, Rent, Insurance etc.

**(b) Variable cost**

The cost which changes according to the changes in the volume of production is called variable cost. It varies in direct proportion to the volume of production. Variable cost per unit remains fixed.

(Eg) Direct material, Direct labour, Direct expenses.

**(c) Semi-variable Cost**

The cost which is partly fixed and partly variable is called semi-variable cost.

(Eg) Salary to salesman based on monthly salary plus commission, Telephone charges etc.

### 5. On the basis of controllability

On the basis of controllability cost may be classified into (a) Controllable cost and (b) Uncontrollable cost.

**(a) Controllable costs**

The costs which can be influenced by the action of the management of a concern are called controllable costs.

(Eg) Salary and wages, Electricity, Telephone charges etc.

**(b) Uncontrollable Costs**

The costs which cannot be influenced by the action of the management of a concern are called uncontrollable costs.

(Eg) Price of raw material, Freight charges etc.

**6. On the basis of Time**

On the basis of time costs are classified into (a) Historical cost and (b) Pre-determined cost.

**(a) Historical Costs**

Costs which have already been incurred are called Historical costs. It is otherwise called as Actual Cost incurred for the production.

**(b) Pre-determined Costs**

Costs which are estimated in advance before the commencement of production are called Pre-determined Costs. It is also known as Estimated Cost or Standard Cost.

**7. On the basis of Relevancy**

On the basis of Relevancy costs are classified into (a) Relevant Costs and (b) Irrelevant Costs.

**(a) Relevant Costs**

Relevant Costs are those costs which are reliable for taking managerial decision. These costs are not subject to immediate changes. But relevant costs are subject to change in future due to the changes in the decision of management.

**(b) Irrelevant Costs**

Irrelevant costs are those costs which are not relevant for taking managerial decision. These costs may change often and also it is difficult to estimate these costs.

## DEFINITIONS OF RELATED CONCEPTS

The definitions of important related concepts of Cost Accounting are stated as follows.

**1. Cost**

Cost is the amount of expenditure incurred for the activites like production of product or for providing services. Costs are in the form of deferred cost and expired cost. Deferred costs are also known as capitalised cost which provide benefit in the future period. (Eg) Cost incurred for the purchase of Fixed Assets. Expired costs are those cost incurred for the present period only.(Eg) Salary, Electricity, Rent etc.

**2. Expenses**

Expenses means expired cost. It is the cost meant for the present period. Hence, expenses are the cost incurred for the generation of revenue for the present period and not for the future. Therefore, the deferred costs are not called as expenses.

**3. Loss**

When the revenue is less than the expense, it is called loss. If a fixed asset is sold for less than the present cost, it is also called loss.

**4. Opportunity Cost**

The cost connected with the loss of an opportunity is called opportunity cost. Opportunity Cost normally arises in the selection of one alternative from the various alternatives, for an action. If the alternative selected is not the best, then the loss of not selecting the best alternative is called the opportunity cost.

**5. Sunk Cost**

Sunk Cost is the difference between the purchase price of a fixed asset and the realised value of the asset, if sold. It may also be stated that it is the difference between the book value and scrap value of an asset.

**6. Differential Cost**

The difference in the total cost between any two alternatives is called Differential Cost. If there is an increase in cost from one alternative to another, the differential cost is called 'Incremental cost'. If there is decrease in cost from one alternative to another, then the differential cost is called 'Decremental Cost'.

**7. Imputed Cost**

Imputed costs are the cost which are measured or estimated for managerial decision-making. Hence, the costs actually incurred are not called as imputed costs.(Eg) Rent value of the own building, interest on own capital, interest on internally generated funds etc.

**8. Out-of-Pocket Cost**

Out-of-Pocket cost means the cost actually spent for manufacturing a product. Hence, the cost of depreciation is not included in the out-of pocket cost.

**9. Shut Down Cost**

Shut-down costs are those costs which are incurred even after the stoppage of production or closing of a department. Variable costs need not be incurred after the stoppage of production. Hence,shut-down cost includes only the fixed cost.

## EXERCISE

**I. Choose the correct answer for the following**

1. The accounting which provides the methods and techniques to reduce the cost of production is called
   (i) Profit & Loss Accounting (ii) Balance Sheet
   (iii) Cost Accounting (iv) Financial Accounting
2. Cost Accounting includes only the activities of
   (i) Non - Operating (ii) Operating
   (iii) Operating and Non-operating (iv) Cost auditing
3. Cost incurred even after the stoppage of production is called
   (i) Shut down cost (ii) Sunk cost
   (iii) Historical cost (iv) Relevant cost
4. The difference between the purchase price of a fixed asset and its realised value, from sales is known as
   (i) Relevant Cost (ii) Inputed Cost
   (iii) Sunk Cost (iv) Opportunity Cost
5. If there is an increase in cost from one alternative to another, the differential cost is called
   (i) Incremental Cost (ii) Decremental Cost
   (iii) Sunk Cost (iv) Imputed Cost
6. The differene in the total cost between two alternatives is called
   (i) Sunk Cost (ii) Fixed Cost(iii) Variable Cost (iv) Differential Cost
7. The method of costing adopted for the production of identical products is called
   (i) Job Costing (ii) Batch Costing
   (iii) Contract Costing (iv) Output Costing
8. The method of costing adopted in specific order is known as
   (i) Fixed Cost (ii) Variable Cost(iii) Job Costing (iv) Batch Costing
9. The method of costing adopted when the period of a job is long, is called
   (i) Contract Costing (ii) Fixed Cost
   (iii) Sunk Cost (iv) Historical Costing
10. The cost which is partly fixed and partly variable is known as
    (i) Fixed Cost (ii) Marginal Cost
    (iii) Semi-variable Cost (iv) Contract Cost
11. Determination of cost before the cost is incurred is called
    (i) Historical Costing (ii) Variable Cost
    (iii) Marginal Costing (iv) Standard Costing
12. The location or person for which cost is ascertained and used is
    (i) Cost Centre (ii) Cost Unit(iii)Costing method (iv) Uniform Cost

13. Costs which can easily be identified in a product is called
    (i) Indirect Cost (ii) Direct Cost
    (iii) Variable Cost (iv) Differential cost
14. The cost which remains constant upto a certain level of activity is known as
    (i) Semi-variable cost (ii) Variable Cost
    (iii) Marginal Cost (iv) Fixed Cost
15. Marginal Costing is otherwise called as
    (i) Variable costing (ii) Operation costing
    (iii)Process costing (iv) Operating costing

[Ans : 1. (iii) 2. (ii) 3. (i) 4. (iii) 5. (i) 6. (iv) 7. (ii) 8. (iii) 9. (i) 10. (iii) 11. (iv) 12. (i) 13. (ii) 14. (iv) 15. (i) ]

## II. Answer the following

16. Define Cost Accounting. State the differences between Cost Accounting and Financial Accounting.
17. Define Cost Accounting. State the differences between Cost Accounting and Management Accounting.
18. Distinguish between Costing, Cost Accounting and Cost Accountancy.
19. What is Cost Accounting? Explain the advantages and limitations of Cost Accounting.
20. What is installation of cost accounting system? Explain the factors influencing the installation of cost accounting system.
21. State the essentials and difficulties in the installation of cost accounting system.
22. Explain the different methods of Costing.
23. Explain the different techniques of Costing.
24. Give an account of Cost Centres and Cost Unit.
25. Explain briefly, the different methods of classfication of costs.
26. Distinguish between cost, expenses and loss.
27. Write short notes of the following.
    (i) Opportunity Cost (ii) Sunk Cost (iii) Relevant Cost
    (iv) Differential Cost (v) Imputed Cost (vi) Shut Down Cost.
28. Write short notes of the following:
    (i) Direct cost and Indirect cost
    (ii) Historical Cost and Estimated Cost
    (iii) Fixed cost and Variable Cost
    (iv) Controllable Cost and Uncontrollable Cost.

# CHAPTER II

# MATERIAL

Material means substance of which a thing is made. It is also defined as commodity supplied to manufacturing industry for further processing to get a product which has utility. Material in raw form has utility only for manufacturing industry. It assumes utility only when it is converted into some other product. The term "material" and "stores" are often used interchangeably. But stores is wider term used to mean raw materials, (like factory supplies, jigs, fixtures, component parts, equipments, tools, maintenance and repair item), partly finished goods and finished goods.

## I. Material Control

Material constitutes prime part in a product. Material cost assumes a major portion of the cost of the product. Hence, a control in the material cost reduces the cost of production. Material cost can be controlled in two ways. (i) By economical purchase and (ii) By economical utilisation of the material in the production process. Economical purchase means buying raw material at right quantity, at right time and at right price. Purchase of too much quantity means locking up of working capital in the store room. At the same time purchase of too little quantity may not be sufficient for the smoothful production activity. Hence, it is advisable to purchase optimum quantity. Purchasing of material at right time indicates purchasing when the price of the material is at low level. Right price indicates the good bargaining and also selecting the right source where the price is comparatively low.

Economical utilisation means preventing wastage, spoilage and theft of material. It can be done with the help of sophisticated machines, efficient techniques and by good store-house. Hence, the material control ultimately aims at reducing the cost of production. It is the duty of the managers in charge of the Purchase Department, Finance Department and Production Department to control the cost of material and achieve the low cost of production.

The effective control of material involves the following requirements.

1. The investment in material would be at optimum level.
2. Minimum stock of material should be maintained for uninterrupted production.

3. Material purchased should be of good quality at reasonable price.
4. Proper storage facilities should be provided to prevent fire, theft and spoilage.
5. Store-room should be near to the production centre to minimise the cost of transfer of material.
6. Stores ledger should be maintained to record the receipt, issue and balance of material.
7. Vouchers regarding purchase and material requisition should be maintained properly.
8. There should be proper coordination between the Finance Department, Purchase Department, Production Department and Department of Store-keeping.
9. Standard printed forms should be used for material requisition for purchase and for issue of material.
10. Internal check system should be adopted in the material requisition, purchase and issue.
11. Bin cards should be maintained, if the materials are of different varities and types.

## II. Procedures related to Planning and Control of Material

Planning and Control of material are needed right from the purchase of material to the final production.It involves the following steps.

1. Purchasing of material
2. Receiving and inspection of material
3. Payment for the material purchased
4. Storing of material
5. Classification and codification of material
6. Issuing of material
7. Accounting of material
8. Preparation and maintenance of Stores Ledger

### 1. Purchasing of Material

It is the duty of the Purchase department to purchase the material. The Purchase department must know the type and quantity of material to be purchased. Hence, it is the duty of the Production department to inform about their requirement to the purchase department. Most of the companies have a standard form for making purchase requirement.

A model of the Purchase Requisition Form is stated as follows.

**XYZ COMPANY LIMITED**
**PURCHASE REQUISITION**

Department : ..........................
No. : ..........................
Cost Centre : ..........................
Date : ..........................

Please purchase the following:

| Item | Code No. | Description of material | Qty. | Required Date | Remarks |
|---|---|---|---|---|---|
| | | | | | |

| Requested by | Checked by | Approved by |
|---|---|---|
| .................... | ................ | .................. |

The purchase department, after receiving the purchase requisition from the production department, must take necessary steps for the purchasing of the material. Purchase department should identify the right source of the material where good quality material is available at reasonable price. Some companies are having the practice of making order through a standard purchase order form. A specimen of Purchase Order Form is given below.

**XYZ COMPANY LIMITED**
**PURCHASE ORDER**

Date Required : ................... Purchase Order No. :....................
To Requisition No. :...................
.................... Date :..................
.....................
.....................

Please supply the following items according to the term and condition mentioned herewith:

| Item No. | Description | Qty. | Rate Rs. | Total cost Rs. | Remarks |
|---|---|---|---|---|---|
| | | | | | |

Purchase Manager

Terms and conditions

| |
|---|
| ........................................................................................ |
| ........................................................................................ |
| ........................................................................................ |

The purchase manager must fill up the purchase order and send it to the source of purchase.

**2. Receiving and Inspection of Material**

The receiving department should unload and inspect the material received. The person responsible for receiving the material should inspect the material with regard to the quantity, quality and type of material. If the material received is not according to the order placed proper steps should be taken to replace the material. If the material received are not upto the satisfaction of the purchasing department, the material may be returned to the supplier. If the material received is as per the order, then material received report should be prepared.

A model of the Material Received Report is stated below:

**XYZ COMPANY LIMITED**
**MATERIALS RECEIVED REPORT**

Received from : ........................ Purchase Order No.: ..................
Date : ..................

| Item No. | Description | Qty Received | Remarks |
|---|---|---|---|
| | | | |

Counted by ............... Inspected by .................. Approved by ..................

The copies of the Material Received Report should be sent to Purchase, Store and Accounting Departments.

**3. Payment for the Material purchased**

Purchase of material may be either by cash or on credit basis. If purchase is on cash basis payment may be done either at the time of ordering the material or after receiving the material. Sometimes the payment should be made at the time of taking delivery of the material. The method of payment depends upon the terms and conditions of the purchase.

**4. Storing of Material**

Material received by the company should be kept in store-room. The purpose of store-keeping is to prevent damages, loss and theft; and also to control the movement of material from the store. Perishable type of materials and chemicals require artificial climate. The cold or hot climate required for these materials should be maintained in the store-room.

**5. Classification and Codification**

The store-room contains different types of materials. Each type of material is kept in seperate places. Hence, the materials should be properly classified and code number should be given for all the types of materials. Codification means assigning code numbers to materials.

**6. Issuing of Material**

The process of sending the material from the store-room to the production centre is called issuing of material. Materials are mostly required by the production department. Administration and selling departments are also in need of materials like stationery.

Normally materials are issued by the store-keeper after receiving the Material Requisition Note. It contains the date,quantity required, type of material and signature of the authorised person. A model of the Material Requisition Note is stated below.

**XYZ COMPANY LIMITED**
**MATERIAL REQUISITION NOTE**

Job No. : ..........................
Serial No. : ..........................
Bin Card No.: ..........................

| Code No. | Description | Qty. | Rate Rs. | Amount Rs. | Stores Ledger |
|---|---|---|---|---|---|
| | | | | | |

Authorised by ...................... Store-keeper ...................
Received by ......................
Cheked by ......................

Three copies of the Material Requsition Notes should be prepared. Two copies should be sent to the store-keeper and one copy should be kept in file by the material requisition department. The store-keeper on receiving the requisition note, send the two requisition note along with the material to get signature of the receipient of material. One copy of the note should be kept by the store-keeper and one copy should be send to the Accounting department. Store-keeper should pass necessary entries in the Bin card about the issue of materials.

## 7. Accounting of Material

Accounting of material is the process of recording the receipt of material and issue of material. When it is received, it should be recorded in the Bin Card. The date, type, rate and quantity of materials received should be entered in the Bin Card. At the time of issue of material also, proper entries should be made in the Bin card with regard to date, type, quantity and rate. Since materials are purchased at different rates, it is a complicated process to charge the issue price of the material. There are different methods for calculating issue price. They are First-in-First Out (FIFO), Last-in-First Out (LIFO), Average price, Highest-in-Last Out (HILO) and Base Stock methods. A suitable method should be adopted for charging the issue price of the material.

**8. Preparation and maintenance of Stores Ledger**

Stores ledger is a ledger for recording the receipts and issue of material from the store. It also records the balance of material. Stores Ledger is prepared to know the stock position of various materials. Separate Ledger accounts should be prepared for each type of material. Stores ledger is a record of receipt, issue and balance of material. It shows the quantity of material purchased and issued during a period and the balance of material available in the store-room.

A model of Stores Ledger is stated below.

**XYZ COMPANY LIMITED**
**STORES LEDGER**

Name of the material :.............. Maximum stock level.................
Code No. ............................... Minimum stock level .................
Re-order stock level .................
Re-order quantity .................

| Receipts | | | | | Issues | | | Balance | | |
|---|---|---|---|---|---|---|---|---|---|---|
| Date | Source of Receipt | Qty | Rate Rs. | Amt. Rs. | Qty | Rate Rs. | Amt. Rs. | Qty | Rate Rs. | Amt. Rs. |
| | | | | | | | | | | |

The Stores Ledger contains separate columns for recording Receipt, Issue and Balance of material. It also contains details regarding the Maximum, Minimum and Re-order stock levels.

## III. Meaning and Definitions of related concepts

### 1. Direct Material and Indirect Material

Direct materials are those materials which can easily be identified in the product. (Eg) wood in furniture, steel in car, etc. Indirect materials are those material which cannot be easily identified in the product.(Eg) Tools, Jigs, Fixture, consumable stores used in operation, Lubricating oil, Grease, Fuel oil, Broom stick, Cotton waste etc.

### 2. Centralised and Decentralised Purchasing

Centralised purchasing means purchasing by a separate department for all the requirements of the concern. Thc separate department called purchase department which will purchase on behalf of all other departments. Purchase department in some concerns, purchase the material for the requirements of the branches also. The purchase department purchases the material on the basis of the Purchase Requisition received from other departments.

Decentralised purchasing means purchasing by all the departments. Each department purchase the materials by themselves without depending on other department. In decentralised purchasing, there will not be a separate purchasing department.

### 3. Store-keeping

Store-keeping is the process of receiving and maintaining of material in a place callcd storchouse. The material will be maintained so that there will be no damage, theft or loss of material. Material should be kept in storehouse with proper classification and codification, so that it can easily be identified.

### 4. Centralised store-keeping and Decentralised store-keeping

In centralised store-keeping all the materials of the concern are kept at one place. A store-keeper is in charge of the storehouse. He receives the material purchased and keeps it in concerned places. He also issues the material to various departments on the basis of the authorised Material Requisition Note. It is the duty of the store-keeper to maintain proper records for the material receipt, material issue and the balance of materials.

Decentralised store-keeping means keeping the material at various places of material requirement centres of the concern. It avoids unnecessary delay in getting the material from one place.

**5. Store-keeper**

Store-keeper is the person in charge of the storehouse. It is the duty of him to receive the material, inspect the material, classify and assign code number and keeping them in concerned places, He also issues the material to various departments,particularly the production department on the basis of the material requisition note. He has to maintain records for the receipt, issue and balance of the materials; and to make entries in the Bin Cards.

**6. Bin Card**

Bin card is a card maintained by the store-keeper to record the quantitative data of receipt, issue and balance of the material. It also contains details regarding maximum,minimum and re-order stock level. It is kept at the bin where the material is kept. Each type of material has separate Bin cards. A model of the Bin Card is stated below.

**XYZ LIMITED**

**BIN CARD**

Bin No .................. Maximum Stock level ...........
Description .................. Location........... Minimum Stock level..............
Code No .................. Re-ording Stock level...........
Unit .................. Re-ording Quantity................

| Date | Receipt | | Issue | | Balance | Physical Verification |
|---|---|---|---|---|---|---|
| | MRN/No | Qty | M.R.N.No. | Qty | Balance Qty | |
| | | | | | | |

**7. Difference between Bin card and Stores Ledger**

The important differences between Bin Card and Stores Ledger are as follows.

1. Bin Card is a record of quantities only. Stores Ledger is a record of both quantities and value.
2. Bin Card is maintained, by store-keeper while Stores Ledger is maintained by Cost Accountant.
3. In Bin Card, transactions are recorded immediately after the receipt or issue of material. In Stores Ledger, transactions are not recorded immediately.
4. In Bin Card all transactions are recorded, but in Stores Ledger transactions are summarised and posted periodically, say once in a month.

## 8. Stock Verification

Stock Verification is the process of comparing the physical quantity or weight of materials in the store with the records. The balance of materials recorded in the stores ledger, should be available in the store-room. The physical units of material as well as its quality should be examined in the stock verification process. By Stock verification, the frauds by manipulating stores ledger can be identified and rectified.There are two methods of stock verification. They are (a) Periodic stock verification and (b) Perpectual stock verification.

### (a) Periodic Stock Verification

Periodic stock verification is a method of verifying the stock periodically like once in a month, quarterly, half-yearly or yearly. The stock verification should be done without affecting the production process. This method is normally adopted when the quantity and types of materials are large. Different verification periods may be adopted for different materials. Costly material requires verification often than low cost materials.

The details of the verification should be recorded in inventory records and kept with the respective bins or racks. After verifying all the stocks a report should be prepared by the investigators.

### (b) Perpectual Stock Verification

This method is otherwise called as continuous stock verification. In this method the verification of stock is done continuously. Whenever the materials are purchased and issued to the production centre, stock should be verified. This method is normally adopted when the materials are of high value. There is a need for a team of staff to check the stock if the quantity and type of materials are large. The investigators should compare the records with the physical quantity of material. If any difference is identified then it should be recorded in the remark column, of the respective Bin Cards.

## IV. Maintenance of Stock Level

The optimum purchase of material depends upon the requirement of the material and the financial commitment of the concern. The requirement of material and financial commitment determine the stock level to be maintained in the concern. On the requirement side too small quantities purchased will disturb the smoothful production process. Hence, it favours large quantity purchase. On the other hand, the financial commitment favours for small quantity purchase. When huge quantity of material is purchased, there would be unnecessary blocking of working capital in store-room without any return. Hence, there should be a balance between large and small quantity of materials purchased at a time.This balance is called optimum quantity of purchase. This optimum quantity of purchase mostly determines the various stock levels in a concern. These stock levels are stated as follows,

1. Maximum Stock Level
2. Minimum Stock Level
3. Recorder Stock Level
4. Danger Stock Level

### 1. Maximum Stock Level

Maximum stock level means the maximum quantity of material kept as stock at any time. The stock level should not raise beyond the maximum level.

The maximum stock level depends upon the following factors.

(i) The demand for the product
(ii) The capacity of the store house
(iii) The nature of the raw material
(iv) The nature of the production process
(v) Availability of the material
(vi) Source of the raw material
(vii) The capacity of the company to invest in raw material
(viii) The financial policy of the company.

The maximum level can be ascertained through the following formula.

Maximum level = Re-order Level + Re-order quantity-(Minimum Consumption x Minimum Re-order period)

## 2. Minimum Stock Level

Minimum Stock level is a level below which the quantity of material should not be allowed to fall. If the stock level falls below the minimum level, it will hamper the production due to non-availability of material. Hence, this level should be determined by taking into account of the requirement of material for production for a particular period and the time span between the ordering and receipt of material. The minimum level can be calculated through the following formula.

Minimum Level = Re-order level - (Normal Consumption x Normal Re-order period)

If Normal consumption and Normal Re-order period are not given in the problem it can be calculated as,

Normal consumption = (Maximum Consumption + Minimum Consumption) / 2

Normal Re-order period = (Maximum Re-order period + Minimum Re-order period) / 2

## 3. Re-order Level

Re-ordering level is a level at which the order for material should be placed so that the level of stock should not go below the minimum level when the material received. It means when the material is received the stock level should not fall below minimum level. Moreover, the stock level should not be above the maximum level when the material received. The formula for Re-order level is as follows.

Re-order level = Maximum Re-order period x Maximum consumption per day or week.

## 4. Danger Level

Danger level is a level below the Minimum level. If the stock level reached the danger level, emergency steps should be taken to purchase the material. Otherwise the complete stock would be exhausted and the production will be stopped. Danger level can be calculated as follows.

Danger level = Minimum consumption x Maximum Re-order period for emergency purchase.

**Illustration: 1**

Material A and B are used in a company on the following basis.

Maximum Usage - 200 units per week each
Minimum Usage - 80 units per week each
Normal Usage - 140 units per week each
Re-order quantity - A: 900 units; B: 1100 units

Re-order period - A: 3 to 6 weeks; B: 2 to 4 weeks.

Calculate (a) Maximum level (b) Minimum level and (c) Re-order level.

***Solution:***

(i) Re-order level = Maximum consumption x Maximum Re-order period

Material A = 200 x 6 = 1,200 units

Material B = 200 x 4 = 800 units

(ii) Maximum level = Re-order level + Re-order quantity - (Minimum consumption x Minimum Re-order period)

Material A = 1,200 + 900 - (80 x 3)

= 2,100 - 240 = 1860 units

Material B = 800 + 1,100 - (80 x 2)

= 1,900 - 160 = 1,740 units

(iii) Minimum level = Re-order level - (Normal consumption x Normal Re-order period)

Material A = 1,200 - [140 x (3 + 6)/2]

= 1,200 - 630 = 570 units

Material B = 800 - [140 x (2 + 4)/2]

= 800 - 420 = 380 units

**Illustration: 2**

Material X and Y are used in a company as follows.

| | | | |
|---|---|---|---|
| Maximum usage per month | - | X : 1000 units; | Y : 1500 units |
| Minimum usage per month | - | X : 400 units; | Y : 900 units |
| Normal usage per month | - | X : 800 units; | Y : 1100 units |
| Re-order quantity | - | X : 2100 units; | Y : 3800 units |
| Re-order period | - | X : 1 to 3 months; | Y : 2 to 4 months |

Calculate for each material (a) Maximum level, (b) Minimum level, (c) Re-order level and (d) Average stock level.

***Solution:***

(i) Re-order level = Maximum consumption x Maximum Re-order period

Material X = 1,000 x 3 = 3,000 units

Material Y = 1,500 x 4 = 6,000 units

(ii) Maximum level = Re-order level + Re-order quantity - (Minimum consumption x Minimum Re-order period)

Material X = 3,000 + 2,100 - (400 x 1)
= 5,100 - 400 = 4,700 units

Material Y = 6,000 + 3,800 - (900 x 2)
= 9,800-1,800 = 8,000 units

(iii) Minimum level = Re-order level-(Normal consumption x Normal Re-order period)

Material X = 3,000-[800 x (1 + 3)/2]
= 3,000-1,600 = 1,400 units

Material Y = 6,000-[1,100 x (2 + 4)/2]
= 6,000 - 3,300 = 2,700 units

(iv) Average stock level = (Maximum level + Minimum level) / 2

Material X = (4,700 + 1,400)/2 = 3,050 units

Material Y = (8,000 + 2,700)/2 = 5,350 units

## V. Economic Ordering Quantity (EOQ)

Economic Ordering Quantity is the optimum quantity at which the material ordering cost is equal to the material carrying cost. Material ordering cost is the cost connected with the ordering and receiving of material. When small quantity of material is purchased ordering cost will increase, since many orders have to be placed in a year. When huge quantity of material is purchased, number of orders will be reduced and thereby it reduces the ordering cost in a year. Hence, ordering cost favours large quantity of purchase at a time, to reduce the cost. Carrying cost is the cost for maintaining the material. It includes the storehouse rent, interest for the value of material kept in the storehouse etc. When huge quantity of material is purchased carrying cost will increase. Hence, carrying cost favours for the small quantity of purchase at a time, to reduce the cost. So there should be a balance between the huge quantity and small quantity of purchase. This is called the optimum quantity which can be determined where the material ordering cost equals to material carrying cost.

The EOQ is calculated through the following formula,

$$EOQ = \sqrt{(2AO)/C}$$

Where, A = Annual consumption
O = Ordering cost per order
C = Inventory carrying cost per unit per year.

**Illustration: 3**

The annual requirement of material in a factory is 5000 units. The interest and carrying cost is 10% of the cost of material. Cost per unit is Rs.20. Cost of placing an order is Rs.50. Find out the Economic ordering quantity and prove the result through a table.

***Solution:***

$$EOQ = \sqrt{(2AO)/C}$$

A = 5000 units.

O = Rs 50 per order.

C = 10%of Rs.20 = Rs.2

$$EOQ = \sqrt{(2 \times 5000 \times 50)/2}$$

= 500 Units.

**Verification of EOQ**

| Unit of order at a time | Value of order at Rs.20 per Unit | No. of order per year | Average Inventory Rs. | Carrying Cost @ 10% | Ordering Cost @Rs.50 per order | Total Cost Rs. |
|---|---|---|---|---|---|---|
| 5,000 | 100,000 | 1 | 50,000 | 5,000 | 50 | 5,050 |
| 2,500 | 50,000 | 2 | 25,000 | 2,500 | 100 | 2,600 |
| 1,250 | 25,000 | 4 | 12,500 | 1,250 | 200 | 1,450 |
| 1,000 | 20,000 | 5 | 10,000 | 1,000 | 250 | 1,250 |
| 625 | 12,500 | 8 | 6,250 | 625 | 400 | 1,025 |
| 500 | 10,000 | 10 | 5,000 | 500 | 500 | 1,000 |
| 250 | 5,000 | 20 | 2,500 | 250 | 1,000 | 1,250 |
| ˙100 | 2,000 | 50 | 1,000 | 100 | 2,500 | 2600 |
| 50 | 1,000 | 100 | 5,00 | 50 | 5,000 | 5,050 |

It is clear from the table that at 500 units, the total cost is low. When the ordering quantity is increased or decreased from 500 units the total cost will increase. Hence, it is proved that EOQ is 500 units.

**Graphical representation of Economic Ordering Quantity:**

The Economic Ordering Quantity can be graphically determined. In order to determine the EOQ the material ordering cost and material carrying cost should be plotted in the graph corresponding to the different quantities of material. The two curves would intersect at a point.A perpendicular line from the point to the X axis should be drawn and the point in the X axis should be identified.EOQ is the distance from the orgin to the point at X axis.The graphical representation of the EOQ is presented as follows.

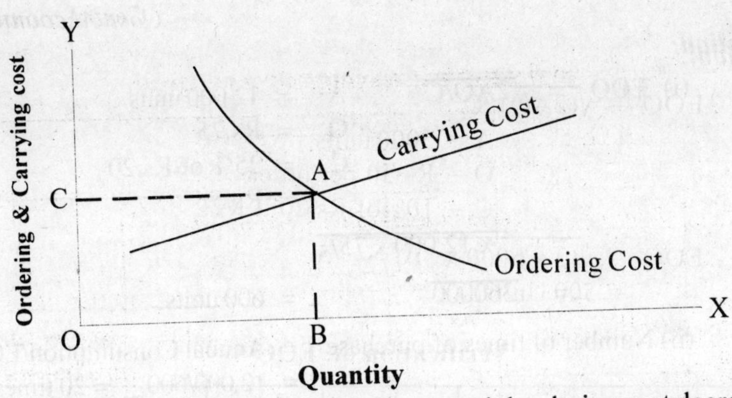


It is clear from the graph that the material ordering cost decreases due to the increase in the quantity of purchase at a time. But the material carrying cost increases due to the increase in the quantity of purchase at a time. These curves cut each other at a point. This point helps to find out Economics Ordering Quantity. In this graph the curves cut at point 'A'. Hence, the EOQ is OB units or OC in value.

**Illustration: 4**

Calculate Economic Ordering Quantity where annual consumption is 1,00,000 units, ordering cost is Rs.100 and carrying cost is 20% of the cost of material. Total annual cost of consumption is Rs. 2,50,000.

***Solution:***

EOQ $= \sqrt{2AO/C}$

A = Rs.100,000

O = Rs.100

C = 20% of $\frac{2,50,000}{1,00,000}$ = Rs.0.5

$$EOQ = \sqrt{2 \times 100000 \times 100 / .5}$$

$$= \sqrt{400000000} = 20,000 \text{ units}$$

**Illustration: 5**

A factory requires 12,000 units per annum. The cost of material is @ Rs.20 per unit. The ordering cost is Rs.75 per order. The material carrying cost is 25% of the average inventory.

Calculate (i) Economic ordering quantity, (ii) the total inventory cost for the year (iii) the number of time of purchase in the year. (iv) If the purchase price per unit is reduced by 5% for the same quantity,whether the material can be purchased in lots of 1000 units.

***Solution:***

(i) EOQ $= \sqrt{2AO/C}$    A = 12,000 units
O = Rs.75
C = 25% of Rs.20
= Rs.5

$= \sqrt{2 \times 12{,}000 \times 75/5}$

$= \sqrt{360000}$ = 600 units.

(ii) Number of times of purchase = Annual Consumption/EOQ
= 12,000/600 = 20 times

(iii) Total cost of inventory = Purchase price + Ordering cost + Carrying cost
= (12000 x 20)+(20 x 75) +(5 x 600 / 2)
= 2,40,000 + 1,500 + 1,500
= Rs.2,43,000
(Ordering cost = Carrying cost at EOQ)

(iv) When the purchase price is reduced by 5% and number of units ordered at a time is 1000,

Total inventory cost = Purchase price + Ordering cost + Carrying cost
Total number of order = 12,000 / 1000 = 12 times
Carrying cost per unit = 19 x 25% = Rs.4.75
(Material cost = 20 - 5% of 20 = Rs.19)
Total Inventory cost = (12000 x 19) + (12 x 75) + (4.75 x 1000 / 2)
= 228,000 + 900 + 2,375= Rs.231,275

It is advisable to buy 1000 units per order at 5% reduction in price,since the profit in such purchase is 243000-231,275 = Rs.11,725

**VI. Inventory Turnover Ratio**

Inventory turnover ratio is otherwise called as stock turnover ratio or stock velocity. It is the ratio between the cost of raw material consumed in a year and the average stock of material in a year. It shows the rate of movement of materials for production. Inventory turnover ratio can be calculated as follows:

Inventory Turnover Ratio = Cost of raw material consumed during the year/Average stock of raw material

Cost of raw material consumed during the year = Opening stock of material + Purchase of material - Closing stock of material

Average stock of raw material = (Opening stock+Closing stock)/2

Average material holding or Turnover period can be calculated as follows:

Average Material Holding = 365 days / Inventory Turnover Ratio

For Example, the material purchased is Rs.45,000, opening stock of material Rs.15,000 and closing stock of materials Rs.20,000.

Material consumed = 15,000 + 45,000 - 20,000
= Rs.40,000

Average stock of material = (15,000 + 20,000) / 2
= Rs.17500

Inventary turnover ratio = 40,000 / 17,500
= 2.29

Average material Holding = 365 / 2.29
= 159 days

**Illustration: 6**

Calculate Stock turnover ratio and Turnover period from the following:

| | Material X | Material Y |
|---|---|---|
| | Rs. | Rs. |
| Opening Stock | 6,000 | 12,000 |
| Purchases | 44,000 | 56,000 |
| Closing Stock | 10,000 | 8,000 |

***Solution:***

Calculation of Stock Turnover Ratio and Turnover period.

| | Material X | Material Y |
|---|---|---|
| | Rs. | Rs. |
| Opening Stock | 6,000 | 12,000 |
| **Add:** Purchases | 44,000 | 56,000 |
| | 50,000 | 68,000 |
| **Less:** Closing stock | 10,000 | 8,000 |
| Material consumed | 40,000 | 60,000 |

Average Stock = (6000+10000)/2 ;(12000+8000)/2
= Rs.8,000 = Rs.10,000

Stock Turnover Ratio = Material consumed /Average stock

Material X = 40,000 / 8,000 = 5 times

Material Y = 60,000 / 10,000 = 6 times

Turnover period = 365 days / Turnover Ratio

Material X = 365 / 5 = 73 days.

Material Y = 365 / 6 = 61 days

## VII. ABC Analysis

ABC analysis is otherwise called as Always Better Control (ABC) analysis. This is a method of inventory control. Under this method, the materials are grouped into high priced, medium priced and low priced materials, for controlling the materials. High priced material is termed as A; medium priced material is termed as B and low priced material is termed as C. According to this method, the high priced material (A) constitutes high value say, 70-75% of the total value of material; and low quantity say 5-10% of the total quantity of material. The medium priced material (B) constitutes 15-20% of quantity as well as value of the total material. The low priced material (C) constitutes low value say, 5-10% of the total value of material and high quantity i.e., 70-75% of the total quantity of material. This concept states that high priced materials (A) need comparatively greater control measures, medium priced materials (B) need medium control measures and low priced materials need low control measures.

ABC analysis may be graphically presented as follows:

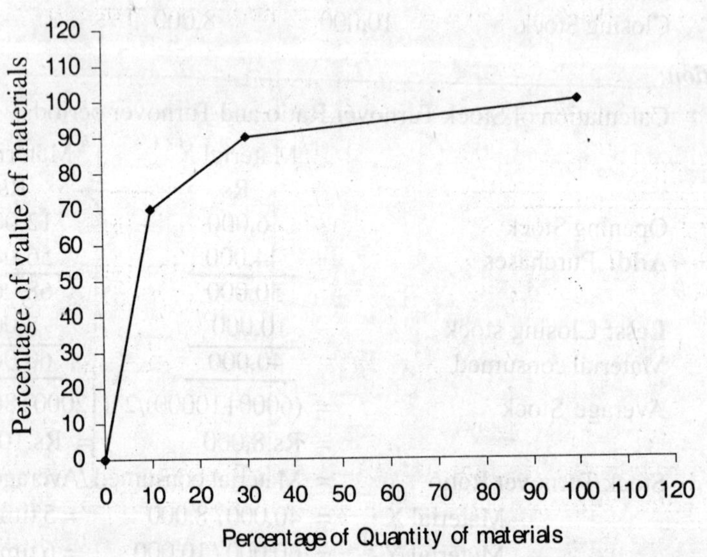

**Illustration: 7**

Classify the following materials according to ABC Analysis method.

| Code No. | Annual Consumption (units) | Price per unit Rs. |
|---|---|---|
| 425 | 2,000 | 15 |
| 426 | 1,000 | 110 |
| 427 | 4,000 | 2.10 |
| 428 | 3,500 | 2.20 |
| 429 | 1,500 | 14 |
| 430 | 1,300 | 127 |
| 431 | 3,800 | 2 |
| 432 | 3,200 | 2.50 |
| 433 | 1,800 | 15 |
| 434 | 4,000 | 1.80 |

***Solution:***

**Statement showing the cost and rank of materials**

| Code No | Quantity | Price per unit Rs. | Annual Consumption Rs. | Rank |
|---|---|---|---|---|
| 425 | 2,000 | 15 | 30,000 | 3 |
| 426 | 1,000 | 110 | 110,000 | 2 |
| 427 | 4,000 | 2.10 | 8,400 | 6 |
| 428 | 3,500 | 2.20 | 7,700 | 8 |
| 429 | 1,500 | 14 | 21,000 | 5 |
| 430 | 1,300 | 127 | 165,100 | 1 |
| 431 | 3,800 | 2 | 7,600 | 9 |
| 432 | 3,200 | 2.50 | 8,000 | 7 |
| 433 | 1,800 | 15 | 27,000 | 4 |
| 434 | 4,000 | 1.80 | 7,200 | 10 |

On the basis of the price of different raw materials the materials are classified as follows:

**Statement showing the ABC Analysis**

| Code No | Annual Consumption Value (Rs) | Percentage value of Consumption | Annual Quantity Consumed | Percentage of Quantity | Category |
|---|---|---|---|---|---|
| 430 | 165,100 | 42.12 | 1,300 | 4.98 | |
| 426 | 110,000 | 28.06 | 1,000 | 3.83 | A |
| | | 70.18 | | 8.81 | |
| 425 | 30,000 | 7.65 | 2,000 | 7.66 | |
| 433 | 27,000 | 6.89 | 1,800 | 6.90 | |
| 429 | 21,000 | 5.36 | 1,500 | 5.75 | B |
| | | 19.90 | | 20.31 | |
| 427 | 8,400 | 2.14 | 4,000 | 15.33 | |
| 432 | 8,000 | 2.04 | 3,200 | 12.26 | |
| 428 | 7,700 | 1.96 | 3,500 | 13.40 | |
| 431 | 7,600 | 1.94 | 3,800 | 14.56 | |
| 434 | 7,200 | 1.84 | 4,000 | 15.33 | C |
| | | 9.92 | | 70.88 | |
| Total | 392,000 | 100 | 26,100 | 100 | |

## VIII. VED Analysis

VED Analysis is otherwise called as Vital, Essential and Desireable Analysis. This analysis is used for classifying and controlling the spare parts according to their importance. The spare parts which are more essential and the absence of it even for a very short period, may stop the production is called vital spare parts. The spares which are essential and the absence of which for few hours or a day may be tolerated is called essential spares. The spares which are not much essential and the absence of which even for a week will not affect the production is called desireable parts. The degree of the control needed for Vital spare parts is more than the Essential and Desireable spare parts. The degree of control needed for the Essential spare parts is more than the Desireable spare parts.

## IX. Input - Output Analysis

Input – Output ratio is the ratio between Standard Cost of Actual Quantity Consumed and Standard Cost of Standard Quantity of output.

The Formula for this ratio is as follows.

$$\text{Input – Output Ratio} = \frac{\text{Input of material}}{\text{Output of material as final product}}$$

This ratio helps to find out the performance of a company with respect to the economical consumption of raw material.

**Illustration: 8**

Calculate input-output ratio from the following:

| Particulars | Standard | Actual |
|---|---|---|
| Input of material (Units) | 500 | 700 |
| Output of material (Units) | 400 | 600 |
| Material Cost is Rs.20 per unit. | | |

***Solution:***

$$\text{Input – Output Ratio} = \frac{\text{Input of material}}{\text{Output of material as final product}}$$

$$\text{Standard input – output ratio} = \frac{500}{400} = 1.25$$

$$\text{Actual input – output ratio} = \frac{700}{600} = 1.17$$

Standard cost of raw material for finished output = 1.25 x 20 = Rs.25

Actual cost of raw material for finished output = 1.17 x 20 = Rs.23.40

## X. Methods of Pricing Material Issues

In order to carry the production without break the materials are purchased in advance and kept in stores. Materials are purchased by keeping in mind of the minimum stock level and maximum stock level. The materials may be purchased from different sources. Purchase price may be different due to different time and different source of purchase. Hence, the material available in the store are at different prices. If all the materials are at one price there is no problem in charging the price of issue of material. If materials available in the store are at different prices, then the problem is at what price the material will be issued to the production centre.For example, material purchased are 1st January 500 units @ Rs.12 per unit, 5th January 400 units @ Rs.10 per unit. 7th January 600 units @ Rs.15 per unit, 15th January 700 units @ Rs.11 per unit. Suppose material issued is 600 units on 9th January and 350 units on 14th January, it is to be decided on what price the material should be charged. It depends upon the policy of the management.

There are different methods for calculating issue price of materials. The following are the important methods of pricing of material issues.

**A. Actual Cost Price Methods:**

1. First-in-First-Out method (FIFO)
2. Last-in-First-Out method (LIFO)
3. Highest-in-First-Out method (HIFO)
4. Base stock price method

**B. Average Price Methods**

1. Simple Average price method
2. Weighted Average price method
3. Periodic Simple Average price method
4. Periodic Weighted Average price method
5. Moving Simple Average price method
6. Moving Weighted Average price method

**C. Notional Price Methods**

1. Standard Price method
2. Inflated Price Method
3. Replacement or Market Price Method

**A. Actual Cost Method**

**1. First-in-First-Out Method (FIFO)**

This method of pricing is based on the principle that the material purchased first are issued to the production centre, first. The material issue price is charged as per the price of the first consignment. If the quantity of the first consignment is exhausted completely then the price at which the next consignment purchased is taken into account for the issue price of material.

**Advantages**

(i) This method is simple to understand and easy to calculate.
(ii) Since the actual cost of material is taken into account the profit will not be unduly inflated or deflated.
(iii) The value of closing stock would be at the latest market price.

**Disadvantages**

(i) Since same material is issued at different prices, it may complicate the calculations.
(ii) If the price of material is increasing, then the cost of production for one period is greater than the next period. This affects the

market price of the final product.

(iii) It is difficult to decide the issue price, if the materials are purchased at different prices at a time from different or same source.

## 2. Last-in-First-Out Method (LIFO)

In this method, the price of the last purchase is taken into account for the issue price of the material. When the quantity of last batch is exhausted completely then, the next previous purchase price is considered for the issue price. In the mean time a new purchase is made then, the price of that purchase is considered for the issue price. When the price of recent purchase is taken into consideration, it does not mean that only the quantity of material recently purchased should be used first, for production purpose.

**Advantages**

1. Under this method, the current revenues are more related with the current cost.
2. This method does not result is unrealised profit or loss, since the current market price of the material is charged to find out the cost of production.
3. In the event of rising prices, the value of closing stock is less than the market price. It helps to reduce the cost of production in future.

**Disadvantages**

1. The closing stock will not represent the current market price.
2. When the price of material is decreasing, this method of pricing increases the cost of production in future.
3. Current revenues will not be matched with current costs if the re-order period is long and irregular.

## 3. Highest-in-First-Out Method (HIFO)

Under this method the material purchased at the highest price will be issued first. It means that the issue price of the material is at higher price among the different prices for which material is purchased. When the quantity of material at the highest price is completely issued, then the next highest price should be charged for the material issues.

For example the material purchased on 1st January 500 units @ Rs.20 per unit, 4th January 600 units @ Rs.22 per unit, 8th January 400 units @ Rs.25 per unit. Issue of material on 6th January 400 units, 9th

January 500 units. The issue prices calculated as 6th January @ Rs.22 per unit and 9th January @ Rs.25 for 400 units and @ Rs.22 for 100 units.

**4. Base Stock Price Method**

Under this method a minimum stock is kept as base stock to meet emergency situation. These stock is valued at the cost price. The remaining stock of the material is issued on the basis of First-in-First-Out method or Last-in-First-Out method. The quantity of base stock depends upon the size, nature and policy of the concerns. The base stock need not be the old stock. The latest purchase is kept as base stock, but the price of the base stock material should be the price on the date of adoption of base stock method.

For example, the base stock is 500 units for a company and the date of adoption of base stock is 1st January 2006. The purchase of material is 700 units @ Rs.30 per unit on 1st January. The base stock of 500 units should be valued only @ Rs.30 per unit throughout the period. Suppose the material purchased is 1000 units @ Rs.33 per unit on 20th January and the issue of material is 600 units on 5th January and 800 units on 22nd January, in all situations price of base stock should be valued @ Rs.30 only.

**Illustration: 9**

A manufacturing company is producing product X with the help of raw material A. The details regarding the receipts and issues of materials in a factory during January and February 2011 are stated as follows:

| | |
|---|---|
| January 1 | Opening Balance 600 units @ Rs.20 per unit |
| January 6 | Received 400 units @ Rs.22 per unit |
| January 10 | Issued 700 units |
| January 18 | Issued 200 units |
| January 20 | Received 500 units @ Rs.25 per unit |
| February 1 | Issued 400 units |
| February 5 | Issued 100 units |
| February 10 | Received 400 units @ Rs.30 per units |
| February 15 | Issued 300 units |

Prepare Stores Ledger Account on the basis of First-in-First-out method.

***Solution:***

**Stores Ledger Account (FIFO)**

| Date | Particulars | Receipts | | | Issue | | | Balance | | |
|---|---|---|---|---|---|---|---|---|---|---|
| | | Qty | Rate Rs. | Amt. Rs. | Qty | Rate Rs. | Amt. Rs. | Qty | Rate Rs. | Amt. Rs. |
| Jan 1 | Balance | | | | | | | 600 | 20 | 12,000 |
| Jan 6 | Receipts | 400 | 22 | 8,800 | | | | 600}<br>400} | 20<br>22 | 20,800 |
| Jan 10 | Issued | | | | 600}<br>100} | 20<br>22 | 14,200 | 300 | 22 | 6,600 |
| Jan 18 | Issued | | | | 200 | 22 | 4,400 | 100 | 22 | 2,200 |
| Jan 20 | Received | 500 | 25 | 12,500 | | | | 100}<br>500} | 22<br>25 | 14,700 |
| Feb1 | Issued | | | | 100}<br>300} | 22<br>25 | 9,700 | 200 | 25 | 5,000 |
| Feb5 | Issued | | | | 100 | 25 | 2,500 | 100 | 25 | 2,500 |
| Feb10 | Received | 400 | 30 | 12,000 | | | | 100}<br>400} | 25<br>30 | 14,500 |
| Feb15 | Issued | | | | 100}<br>200} | 25<br>30 | 8,500 | 200 | 30 | 6,000 |

**Illustration: 10**

Prepare Stores Ledger Account on the basis of FIFO Method of pricing issue of material, from the following particulars:

| | |
|---|---|
| March 1 | Balance 200 units @ Rs 15 per unit |
| March 5 | Received 400 units @ Rs.18 per unit |
| March 10 | Issued 300 units |
| March 15 | Issued 200 units |
| March 16 | Received back from production centre, 50 units (Issued on 10th March) |
| March 18 | Received 500 units @ Rs.20 per unit |
| March 20 | Returned to vendor 100 units (Purchased on 5th March) |
| March 25 | Issued 200 units |
| March 30 | Issued 150 units |

On verification at 31st March it was found out that a shortage of 60 units of material.

**Solution:**

**Stores Ledger Account (FIFO)**

| Date | Particulars | Receipts | | | Issues | | | Balance | | |
|---|---|---|---|---|---|---|---|---|---|---|
| | | Qty | Rate Rs. | Amt. Rs. | Qty | Rate Rs. | Amt. Rs. | Qty | Rate Rs. | Amt. Rs. |
| Mar 1 | Balance | | | | | | | 200 | 15 | 3,000 |
| Mar 5 | Received | 400 | 18 | 7,200 | | | | 200}<br>400} | 15<br>18 | 10,200 |
| Mar 10 | Issued | | | | 200<br>100 | 15<br>18 | 4,800 | 300 | 18 | 5,400 |
| Mar 15 | Issued | | | | 200 | 18 | 3,600 | 100 | 18 | 1,800 |
| Mar 16 | Issued back from Production centre | 50 | 18 | 900 | | | | 100}<br>50} | 18}<br>18} | 2,700 |
| Mar 18 | Received | 500 | 20 | 10,000 | | | | 150}<br>500} | 18<br>20 | 12,700 |
| Mar 20 | Returned to Vendor | | | | 100 | 18 | 1,800 | 50}<br>500} | 18<br>20 | 10,900 |
| Mar25 | Issued | | | | 50}<br>150} | 18<br>20 | 3,900 | 350 | 20 | 7,000 |
| Mar 30 | Issued | | | | 150 | 20 | 3,000 | 200 | 20 | 4,000 |
| Mar 31 | Shortage | | | | 60 | 20 | 1,200 | 140 | 20 | 2,800 |

[Note: Returned from production centre should be priced on the assumption that the goods first sent has been consumed first.]

**Illustration: 11**

The following information are related to material purchase and issue of a manufacturing company for the month of April 2011.

| | |
|---|---|
| April 1 | Balance 600 units @ Rs.50 per unit |
| April 4 | Purchased 300 units @ Rs.45 per unit |
| April 5 | Issued 400 units |
| April 7 | Purchased 500 units @ Rs.60 per unit |
| April 12 | Issued 600 units |
| April 15 | Issued 200 units |
| April 19 | Purchased 400 units @ Rs.65 per unit |
| April 25 | Issued 200 units |

*Material*

April 26 Returned to store 50 units (Issued on 12th April)
April 28 Issued 200 units
April 29 Purchased 300 units @ Rs.55 per unit
April 30 Issued 450 units.

Prepare Stores Ledger Account on the basis of Last-in-First-Out method.

***Solution:***

**Stores Ledger Account (LIFO)**

| Date | Particulars | Receipts | | | Issues | | | Balance | | |
|---|---|---|---|---|---|---|---|---|---|---|
| | | Qty | Rate Rs. | Amt. Rs. | Qty | Rate Rs. | Amt. Rs. | Qty | Rate Rs. | Amt. Rs. |
| Apr 1 | Balance | | | | | | | 600 | 50 | 30,000 |
| Apr 4 | Received | 300 | 45 | 13,500 | | | | 600}<br>300} | 50<br>45 | 43,500 |
| Apr 5 | Issued | | | | 300}<br>100} | 45<br>50 | 18,500 | 500 | 50 | 25,000 |
| Apr 7 | Received | 500 | 60 | 30,000 | | | | 500}<br>500} | 50<br>60 | 55,000 |
| Apr 12 | Issued | | | | 500}<br>100} | 60<br>50 | 35,000 | 400 | 50 | 20,000 |
| Apr 15 | Issued | | | | 200 | 50 | 10,000 | 200 | 50 | 10,000 |
| Apr 19 | Received | 400 | 65 | 26,000 | | | | 200}<br>400} | 50<br>65 | 36,000 |
| Apr 25 | Issued | | | | 200 | 65 | 13,000 | 200}<br>200} | 50<br>65 | 23,000 |
| Apr 26 | Returned to store | 50 | 60 | 3,000 | | | | 200}<br>200}<br>50 | 50<br>65<br>60 | 26,000 |
| Apr 28 | Issued | | | | 50}<br>150} | 60<br>65 | 26,000<br>12,750 | 200}<br>50} | 50<br>65 | 13,250 |
| Apr 29 | Received | 300 | 55 | 16,500 | | | | 200}<br>50}<br>300} | 50<br>65<br>55 | 29,750 |
| Apr 30 | Issued | | | | 300}<br>50}<br>100} | 55<br>65<br>50 | 24,750 | 100 | 50 | 5,000 |

**Illustration: 12**

Prepare Stores Ledger Account on the basis of Base stock method (on the basis of FIFO method) from the following information.(Base stock 200 units)

| | | |
|---|---|---|
| 2011 October | 1 | Balance 400 units @ Rs.22 per unit |
| | 7 | Purchased 300 units @ Rs.25 per unit |
| | 10 | Issued 200 units |
| | 15 | Purchased 250 units @ Rs.18 per unit |
| | 17 | Issued 500 units |
| | 20 | Purchased 350 units @ Rs.30 per unit |
| | 25 | Issued 350 units |
| | 27 | Purchased 400 units @ Rs.24 per unit |
| | 29 | Issued 300 units |

***Solution:***

**Stores Ledger Account (Base Stock-FIFO)**

| Date | Particulars | Receipts | | | Issue | | | Balance | | |
|---|---|---|---|---|---|---|---|---|---|---|
| | | Qty | Rate Rs. | Amt. Rs. | Qty | Rate Rs. | Amt. Rs. | Qty | Rate Rs. | Amt. Rs. |
| 2011 Oct 1 | Balance | | | | | | | 400 | 22 | 8,800 |
| 7 | Received | 300 | 25 | 7,500 | | | | 400} | 22 | |
| | | | | | | | | 300} | 25 | 16,300 |
| 10 | Issued | | | | 200 | 22 | 4,400 | 200} | 22 | |
| | | | | | | | | 300} | 25 | 11,900 |
| 15 | Received | 250 | 18 | 4,500 | | | | 200} | 22 | |
| | | | | | | | | 300} | 25 | |
| | | | | | | | | 250} | 18 | 16,400 |
| 17 | Issued | | | | 300} | 25 | | 200} | 22 | |
| | | | | | 200} | 18 | 11,100 | 50 } | 18 | 5,300 |
| 20 | Received | 300 | 30 | 9,000 | | | | 200} | 22 | |
| | | | | | | | | 50 } | 18 | |
| | | | | | | | | 300} | 30 | 14,300 |
| 25 | Issued | | | | 50} | 18 | | | | |
| | | | | | 300} | 30 | 9,900 | 200 | 22 | 4,400 |
| 27 | Received | 400 | 24 | 9,600 | | | | 200} | 22 | |
| | | | | | | | | 400} | 24 | 14,000 |
| 29 | Issued | | | | 300 | 24 | 7,200 | 200} | 22 | |
| | | | | | | | | 100} | 24 | 6,800 |

**llustration: 13**

Prepare Stores Ledger Account on the basis of Base stock method (both on the basis of FIFO and LIFO) from the following information:

2011 May 1 Purchased 600 units @ Rs.30 per unit
11 Purchased 200 units @ Rs.35 per unit
16 Issued 300 units
18 Purchased 500 units @ Rs.40 per unit
22 Issued 300 units
25 Purchased 400 units @ Rs.45 per unit
28 Issued 200 units
30 Issued 500 units

The base stock to be maintained is 300 units.

***Solution:***

**(a) Stores Ledger Account (Base Stock-FIFO)**

| Date | Particulars | Receipts | | | Issues | | | Balance | | |
|---|---|---|---|---|---|---|---|---|---|---|
| | | Qty | Rate Rs. | Amt. Rs. | Qty | Rate Rs. | Amt. Rs. | Qty | Rate Rs. | Amt. Rs. |
| May 1 | Purchased | 600 | 30 | 18,000 | | | | 600} | 30 | 18,000 |
| May 11 | Purchased | 200 | 35 | 7,000 | | | | 600}<br>200} | 30<br>35 | 25,000 |
| May16 | Issued | | | | 300} | 30 | 9,000 | 300}<br>200} | 30<br>35 | 16,000 |
| May 18 | Purchased | 500 | 40 | 20,000 | | | | 300}<br>200}<br>500} | 30<br>35<br>40 | 36,000 |
| May22 | Issued | | | | 200<br>100 | 35<br>40 | 11,000 | 300}<br>400} | 30<br>40 | 25,000 |
| May 25 | Purchased | 400 | 45 | 18,000 | | | | 300}<br>400}<br>400} | 30<br>40<br>45 | 43,000 |
| May28 | Issued | | | | 200 | 40 | 8,000 | 300}<br>200}<br>400} | 30<br>40<br>45 | 35,000 |
| May30 | Issued | | | | 200<br>300 | 40<br>45 | 21,500 | 300}<br>100} | 30<br>45 | 13,500 |

**(b) Stores Ledger Account (Base Stock-LIFO)**

| Date | Particulars | Receipts | | | Issues | | | Balance | | |
|---|---|---|---|---|---|---|---|---|---|---|
| | | Qty | Rate Rs. | Amt. Rs. | Qty | Rate Rs. | Amt. Rs. | Qty | Rate Rs. | Amt. Rs. |
| May 1 | Purchased | 600 | 30 | 18,000 | | | | 600 | 30 | 18,000 |
| May 11 | Purchased | 200 | 35 | 7,000 | | | | 600 | 30 | |
| | | | | | | | | 200 | 35 | 25,000 |
| May16 | Issued | | | | 200} | 35 | | | | |
| | | | | | 100} | 30 | 10,000 | 500 | 30 | 15,000 |
| May 18 | Purchased | 500 | 40 | 20,000 | | | | 500 | 30 | |
| | | | | | | | | 500 | 40 | 35,000 |
| May22 | Issued | | | | 300 | 40 | 12,000 | 500 | 30 | |
| | | | | | | | | 200 | 40 | 23,000 |
| May 25 | Purchased | 400 | 45 | 18,000 | | | | 500 | 30 | |
| | | | | | | | | 200 | 40 | |
| | | | | | | | | 400 | 45 | 41,000 |
| May28 | Issued | | | | 200 | 45 | 9,000 | 500 | 30 | |
| | | | | | | | | 200 | 40 | |
| | | | | | | | | 200 | 45 | 32,000 |
| May30 | Issued | | | | 200 | 45 | | | | |
| | | | | | 200 | 40 | | | | |
| | | | | | 100 | 30 | 20,000 | 400 | 30 | 12,000 |

## B Average Price Methods

### 1. Simple Average Price Method

In this method, the average of the prices of previous purchases should be considered as the issue price of the material. If the quantity of material issued for a period exceeds the earlier purchase, then the price of that purchases should not be considered for calculating the average price.

### 2. Weighted Average Price Method

Under this method, the issue price of material is calculated by dividing the total cost of available material in the store with the total quantity of material. This price should be calculated every time of purchase of material. This method fairly represents the cost of the stock and cost of issue of material.

**3. Periodic Simple Average Price Method**

In this method, the average purchase price of a particular period is considered as the issue price of the material. Hence, the issue price during a period for all issues should be the same. For example, if the purchase prices during the period are Rs 12, Rs 14 and Rs 19 then the issue price for all the issues during the period is Rs 15 per unit [(12+14+19) / 3].

**4. Periodic Weighted Average Price Method**

Under this method the weighted average price of the purchase of the material for a period is calculated to charge the issue price for all the issues of the period. Weighted average price is the value of all the purchase of a period divided by the total quantity of material purchased during the period.

**5. Moving Simple Average Price Method**

This method is based on the Periodic Simple Average Price Method. Under this method the moving averages of various periodic simple average prices should be calculated to charge the material issue price for various periods. The issue price of a period will be the average price of the few previous periods and the current period price. The average price for the next period includes the price of all the previous periods and the current period price. The periods may either be a week, 2 weeks, 3 weeks etc., or 1 month or 2 months etc.

**6. Moving Weighted Average Price Method**

Under this method material issue price is calculated by taking the average of the periodic weighted average price. This method is like the moving simple average price method. In this method average of periodic weighted average price is calculated instead of average of periodic simple average price.

**Illustration: 14**

The following information are provided by a manufacturing company.

| | | |
|---|---|---|
| 2011 March | 1 | Balance of material 400 units @ Rs.15 per unit |
| | 3 | Purchased 300 units @ Rs.20 per unit |
| | 5 | Issued 300 units |
| | 6 | Issued 100 units |
| | 15 | Purchased 500 units @ Rs.18 per unit |
| | 20 | Issued 200 units |
| | 25 | Purchased 300 units @ Rs.22 per unit |
| | 27 | Issued 200 units |

Prepare Stores Ledger Account on the basis of Simple Average Price method.

***Solution:***

**Stores Ledger Account (Simple Average Price Method)**

| Date | Particulars | Receipts | | | Issue | | | Balance | | |
|---|---|---|---|---|---|---|---|---|---|---|
| | | Qty | Rate Rs. | Amt. Rs. | Qty | Rate Rs. | Amt. Rs. | Qty | Rate Rs. | Amt. Rs. |
| Mar 1 | Balance | | | | | | | 400 | 15 | 6,000 |
| 3 | Purchased | 300 | 20 | 6,000 | | | | 700 | - | 12,000 |
| 5 | Issued | | | | 300 | 17.5 | 5,250 | 400 | - | 6,750 |
| 6 | Issued | | | | 100 | 17.5 | 1,750 | 300 | - | 5,000 |
| 15 | Purchased | 500 | 18 | 9,000 | | | | 800 | - | 14,000 |
| 20 | Issued | | | | 200 | 19 | 3,800 | 600 | - | 10,200 |
| 25 | Purchased | 300 | 22 | 6,600 | | | | 900 | - | 16,800 |
| 27 | Issued | | | | 200 | 20 | 4,000 | 700 | - | 12,800 |

**Note:**

(i) Issue price for 5 & 6 March = (20+15)/2 = Rs.17.50

(ii) Issue price for 20th March = (20+18)/2 = Rs.19

(iii) Issue price for 27th March = (20+18+22)/3 = Rs.20

**Illustration: 15**

The following information are provided by a manufacturing company for the month of January, 2011 with respect to the purchase and issue of materials.

| | | |
|---|---|---|
| January | 1 | Balance of material 500 units @ Rs.20 per unit |
| | 4 | Purchased 400 units @ Rs.25 per unit |
| | 5 | Issued 600 units |
| | 7 | Purchased 500 units @ Rs.22 per unit |
| | 10 | Issued 400 units |
| | 18 | Purchased 300 units @ Rs.26 per unit |
| | 25 | Issued 500 units |
| | 28 | Purchased 500 units @ Rs.30 per unit |
| | 30 | Issued 600 units |

Prepare Stores Ledger Account on the basis of Weighted Average Price method of charging the issue price.

***Solution:***

**Stores Ledger Account (Weighted Average Price Method)**

| Date | Particulars | Receipts | | | Issues | | | Balance | | |
|---|---|---|---|---|---|---|---|---|---|---|
| | | Qty | Rate Rs. | Amt. Rs. | Qty | Rate Rs. | Amt. Rs. | Qty | Rate Rs. | Amt. Rs. |
| Jan 1 | Balance | | | | | | | 500 | 20 | 10,000 |
| 4 | Purchase | 400 | 25 | 10,000 | | | | 900 | 22.2 | 20,000 |
| 5 | Issued | | | | 600 | 22.2 | 13,320 | 300 | 22.2 | 6,680 |
| 7 | Purchase | 500 | 22 | 11,000 | | | | 800 | 22.1 | 17,680 |
| 10 | Issued | | | | 400 | 22.1 | 8,840 | 400 | 22.1 | 8,840 |
| 18 | Purchase | 300 | 26 | 7,800 | | | | 700 | 23.77 | 16,640 |
| 25 | Issued | | | | 500 | 23.77 | 11,885 | 200 | 23.77 | 4,755 |
| 28 | Purchase | 500 | 30 | 15,000 | | | | 700 | 28.22 | 19,755 |
| 30 | Issued | | | | 600 | 28.22 | 16,932 | 100 | 28.22 | 2,823 |

**Workings:**

Issue price for 5th January = 20000/900 = Rs.22.20 per unit

Issue price for 10th January = 17680/800 = Rs.22.10 per unit

Issue price for 25th January = 16640/700 = Rs.23.77 per unit

Issue price for 30th January = 19755/700 = Rs.28.22 per unit

**Illustration: 16**

Prepare Stores Ledger Account on the basis of Periodic Simple Average Price Method (for each month) from the following particulars.

| | | |
|---|---|---|
| March | 1 | Stock in hand 300 units @ Rs.12 per unit |
| | 4 | Purchased 400 units @ Rs.16 per unit |
| | 12 | Issued 500 units |
| | 15 | Purchased 600 units @ Rs.17 per unit |
| | 22 | Issued 400 units |
| | 25 | Purchased 300 units @ Rs.21 per unit |
| April | 5 | Issued 200 units |
| | 7 | Purchased 400 units @ Rs.16 per unit |
| | 15 | Issued 500 units |
| | 20 | Purchased 300 units @ Rs.18 per unit |
| | 25 | Issued 400 units |

***Solution:***

**Stores Ledger Account (Periodic Simple Average Price Method)**

| Date | Particulars | Receipts | | | Issues | | | Balance | | |
|---|---|---|---|---|---|---|---|---|---|---|
| | | Qty | Rate | Amt. | Qty | Rate | Amt. | Qty | Rate | Amt. |
| Mar 1 | Balance | 300 | 12 | 3,600 | | | | 300 | 12 | 3,600 |
| 4 | Purchase | 400 | 16 | 6,400 | | | | 700 | | 10,000 |
| 12 | Issued | | | | 500 | 18 | 9,000 | 200 | | 1,000 |
| 15 | | 600 | 17 | 10,200 | | | | 800 | | 11,200 |
| 22 | - | | | | 400 | 18 | 7,200 | 400 | | 4,000 |
| 25 | | 300 | 21 | 6,300 | | | | 700 | | 10,300 |
| | Total | 1,600 | | 26,500 | 900 | 18 | 16,200 | 700 | - | 10,300 |
| Apr 1 | Balance | 700 | | 10,300 | | | | 700 | | 10,300 |
| 5 | | | | | 200 | 17 | 3,400 | 500 | | 6,900 |
| 7 | | 400 | 16 | 6,400 | | | | 900 | | 13,300 |
| 15 | | | | | 500 | 17 | 8,500 | 400 | | 4,800 |
| 20 | | 300 | 18 | 5,400 | | | | 700 | | 10,200 |
| 25 | | | | | 400 | 17 | 6,800 | 300 | | 3,400 |
| | | 1,400 | | 22,100 | 1,100 | | 18,700 | 300 | | 3,400 |

Working: (i) (16+17+21) /3 = Rs.18 (ii) (16+18) /2 = Rs.17

**Illustration: 17**

Prepare Stores Ledger Account on the basis of Periodic Weighted Average Price method from the following particulars:

2011 September 1 Opening Stock 300 units @ Rs.12 per unit
5 Purchased 200 units @ Rs.14 per unit
8 Issued 400 units
13 Purchased 350 units @ Rs.18 per unit
15 Issued 300 units
20 Purchased 450 units @ Rs.16 per unit
24 Issued 300 units
27 Purchased 200 units @ Rs.13 per unit
October 5 Purchased 600 units @ Rs.11 per unit
10 Issued 700 units
17 Purchased 500 units @ Rs.10 per unit
20 Issued 600 units
25 Purchased 400 units @ Rs.14 per unit
29 Issued 300 units

***Solution:***

**Stores Ledger Account (Periodic Weighted Average Price Method)**

| Date | Particulars | Receipts | | | Issues | | | Balance | | |
|---|---|---|---|---|---|---|---|---|---|---|
| | | Qty | Rate Rs. | Amt. Rs. | Qty | Rate Rs. | Amt. Rs. | Qty | Rate Rs. | Amt. Rs. |
| 2011 | | | | | | | | | | |
| Sep.1 | Op.Stock | 300 | 12 | 3,600 | | | | 300 | 12 | 3,600 |
| 5 | Received | 200 | 14 | 2,800 | | | | 500 | | 6,400 |
| 8 | Issued | | | | 400 | 15 | 6,000 | 100 | | 400 |
| 13 | Received | 350 | 18 | 6,300 | | | | 450 | | 6,700 |
| 15 | Issued | | | | 300 | 15 | 4,500 | 150 | | 2,200 |
| 20 | Received | 450 | 16 | 7,200 | | | | 600 | | 9,400 |
| 24 | Issued | | | | 300 | 15 | 4,500 | 300 | | 4,900 |
| 27 | Received | 200 | 13 | 2,600 | | | | 500 | | 7,500 |
| | | 1,500 | 15 | 22,500 | 1000 | 15 | 15,000 | 500 | 15 | 7,500 |
| Oct 1 | Op.Stock | 500 | 15 | 7,500 | | | | 500 | 15 | 7,500 |
| 5 | Received | 600 | 11 | 6,600 | | | | 1,100 | | 14,100 |
| 10 | Issued | | | | 700 | 12.35 | 8,645 | 400 | | 5,455 |
| 17 | Received | 500 | 10 | 5,000 | | | | 900 | | 10,455 |
| 20 | Issued | | | | 600 | 12.35 | 7,410 | 300 | | 3,045 |
| 25 | Received | 400 | 14 | 5,600 | | | | 700 | | 8,645 |
| 29 | Issued | | | | 300 | 12.35 | 3,705 | 300 | | 4,940 |
| | | 2,000 | 12.35 | 24,700 | 1600 | 12.35 | 19,760 | 400 | 12.35 | 4,940 |

**Illustration: 18**

Calculate the method of charging the issue price of material by Moving Simple Average Price method for the period starting from May 2011 from the following particulars:

| Period | Price per unit |
|---|---|
| 2011 | |
| January | 11.50 |
| February | 13.00 |
| March | 12.50 |
| April | 12.40 |
| May | 11.70 |
| June | 13.20 |
| July | 12.80 |
| August | 10.40 |
| September | 13.50 |
| October | 14.80 |
| November | 15.90 |
| December | 16.10 |

***Solution:***

**Statement of the issue price of material**
**(Moving Simple Average Price Method)**

| Period | Periodic Simple Average Price per unit (Rs.) | Five monthly Total (Rs.) | Five monthly Moving Simple Average Price per unit (Rs.) |
|---|---|---|---|
| 2011 | | | |
| January | 11.50 | | |
| February | 13.00 | | |
| March | 12.50 | | |
| April | 12.40 | | |
| May | 11.70 | 61.10 | 12.22 |
| June | 13.20 | 62.80 | 12.56 |
| July | 12.80 | 62.60 | 12.52 |
| August | 10.40 | 60.50 | 12.10 |
| September | 13.50 | 61.60 | 12.32 |
| October | 14.80 | 64.70 | 12.94 |
| November | 15.90 | 67.40 | 13.48 |
| December | 16.10 | 70.70 | 14.14 |

**Illustration: 19**

Calculate the 3 monthly Moving Weighted Average Prices for charging the material issues from following particulars:

| Period | Quantity | Prices per unit Rs. |
|---|---|---|
| 2011 | | |
| January 4 | 500 | 20 |
| 15 | 300 | 24 |
| 17 | 400 | 26 |
| 20 | 300 | 21 |
| February 5 | 400 | 22 |
| 15 | 600 | 25 |
| March 6 | 300 | 22 |
| 12 | 200 | 20 |
| 25 | 300 | 24 |
| April 5 | 300 | 33 |
| 15 | 200 | 30 |
| May 10 | 600 | 28 |
| 15 | 400 | 25 |
| 18 | 500 | 26 |
| June 1 | 400 | 32 |
| 11 | 600 | 35 |

***Solution:***

**Calculation of Perodic Weighted Average Prices**

$$\text{2011 January} = \frac{(500 \times 20) + (300 \times 24) + (400 \times 26) + (300 \times 21)}{500 + 300 + 400 + 300}$$

$$= \frac{33{,}900}{1500} = \text{Rs.22.60 per unit}$$

$$\text{February} = \frac{(400 \times 22)+(600 \times 25)}{400 + 600} = \frac{23{,}800}{1000} = \text{Rs.23.80 per unit}$$

$$\text{March} = \frac{(300 \times 22) + (200 \times 20) + (300 \times 24)}{300 + 200 + 300}$$

$$= \frac{17{,}800}{800} = \text{Rs 22.25 per unit}$$

$$\text{April} = \frac{(300 \times 33)+(200 \times 30)}{300+200} = \frac{15{,}900}{500} = \text{Rs.31.80 per unit}$$

$$\text{May} = \frac{(600 \times 28) + (400 \times 25) + (500 \times 26)}{600 + 400 + 500}$$

$$= \frac{39{,}800}{1{,}500} = \text{Rs.26.53 per unit}$$

$$\text{June} = \frac{(400 \times 32) + (600 \times 35)}{400 + 600} = \frac{33{,}800}{1{,}000}$$

$$= \text{Rs.33.80 per unit}$$

**Statement of the issue price of material by 3 yearly Moving Weighted Average Price Method**

| Period | Periodic Weighted Average Price per unit | Three Monthly Total | Three Monthly Moving Weighted Average Price per unit (Rs.) |
|---|---|---|---|
| 2011 | | | |
| January | 22.60 | - | - |
| February | 23.80 | - | - |
| March | 22.25 | 68.65 | 22.88 |
| April | 31.80 | 77.85 | 25.95 |
| May | 26.53 | 80.58 | 26.86 |
| June | 33.80 | 92.13 | 30.71 |

## C. Notional Price Method

Notional price is normally a fixed price decided by the management. Hence, there may not be any difficulty in the identification of the issue price. The important types of notational price methods are as follows:

1. Standard Price Method
2. Inflated Price Method
3. Replacement or Market Price Method

## 1. Standard Price Method

Standard price is the predetermined price by taking into account of the highest and lowest prices. This price is fixed on the basis of the past and expected future prices. It helps to find out to what extent the purchase price varies with the standard price. All the issues are priced on the basis of standard price and the difference in the actual price and standard price will be adjusted in the closing stock.

## 2. Inflated Price Method

Inflated price is the actual price. It includes carrying cost and cost of normal loss due to evaporation amd shrinkage. Inflated price is calculated at the time of issue of material to production centre.

## 3. Replacement or Market Price Method

In this method the issue price of a material is, the market price of the material at the time of issue of material to the production centre. It is the price required to replace the material due to the issue to the production centre.

**Illustration: 20**

X Ltd. is manufacturing a product with the help of raw material K. The purchases and issues of materials in the month of July 2011 are as follows:

| | | |
|---|---|---|
| July 6 | Purchase | 600 units @ Rs.30 per unit |
| July 8 | Purchase | 800 units @ Rs.27 per unit |
| July 12 | Issued | 500 units |
| July 15 | Issued | 700 units |
| July 18 | Purchase | 900 units @ Rs.29 per unit |
| July 20 | Purchase | 600 units @ Rs.32 per unit |
| July 25 | Issued | 400 units |
| July 31 | Issued | 600 units |

The standard price per unit of material is Rs.30 fixed for the year. Prepare Stores Ledger on the basis of Standard Price method.

***Solution:***

**Stores Ledger Account (Standard Price Method)**

| Date | Parti-culars | Receipts | | | Issue | | | Balance | | |
|---|---|---|---|---|---|---|---|---|---|---|
| | | Qty | Rate Rs. | Amt. Rs. | Qty | Rate Rs. | Amt. Rs. | Qty | Rate Rs. | Amt. Rs. |
| 2011 | | | | | | | | | | |
| July 6 | Purchase | 600 | 30 | 18,000 | | | | 600 | 30 | 18,000 |
| July 8 | Purchase | 800 | 27 | 21,600 | | | | 1,400 | | 39,600 |
| July 12 | Issued | | | | 500 | 30 | 15,000 | 900 | | 24,600 |
| July 15 | Issued | | | | 700 | 30 | 21,000 | 200 | | 3,600 |
| July 18 | Purchase | 900 | 29 | 26,100 | | | | 1,100 | | 29,700 |
| July 20 | Purchase | 600 | 32 | 19,200 | | | | 1,700 | | 48,900 |
| July 25 | Issued | | | | 400 | 30 | 12,000 | 1,300 | | 36,900 |
| July 31 | Issued | | | | 600 | 30 | 18,000 | 700 | | 18,900 |

**Note:**

In this method the issue price is same for all the issues. The price is fixed as Rs.30 per unit by the management.The balance is at different values since the purchase at different periods are at different values.

**Illustration: 21**

XYZ Ltd, a manufacturing company is providing the following particulars for January and February of 2011.

| | | |
|---|---|---|
| Purchases | Jan 3 | 1100 units @ Rs.15 per unit |
| | Jan 15 | 1500 units @ Rs.17 per unit |
| | Jan 20 | 1000 units @ Rs.12 per unit |
| | Jan 25 | 1200 units @ Rs.14 per unit |
| | Jan 31 | 1000 units @ Rs.13 per unit |
| Issues | Jan 17 | 1200 units @ Rs.18 |
| | Jan 27 | 2000 units @ Rs.16 |
| | Feb 1 | 1000 units @ Rs.13 |
| | Feb 20 | 500 units @ Rs.15 |
| | Feb 25 | 600 units @ Rs.10 |

Prepare a Stores Ledger on the basis of Market Price method.

***Solution:***

**Stores Ledger Account (Market Price Method)**

| Date | Parti-culars | Receipts | | | Issues | | | Balance | | |
|---|---|---|---|---|---|---|---|---|---|---|
| | | Qty | Rate Rs. | Amt. Rs. | Qty | Rate Rs. | Amt. Rs. | Qty | Rate Rs. | Amt. Rs. |
| 2011 | | | | | | | | | | |
| Jan 3 | Purchase | 1,100 | 15 | 16,500 | | | | 1,100 | 15 | 16,500 |
| Jan 15 | Purchase | 1,500 | 17 | 25,500 | | | | 2,600 | | 42,000 |
| Jan 17 | Issued | | | | 1,200 | 18 | 21,600 | 1,400 | | 20,400 |
| Jan 20 | Purchase | 1,000 | 12 | 12,000 | | | | 2,400 | | 32,400 |
| Jan 25 | Purchase | 1,200 | 14 | 16,800 | | | | 3,600 | | 49,200 |
| Jan 27 | Issued | | | | 2,000 | 16 | 32,000 | 1,600 | | 17,200 |
| Jan 31 | Purchase | 1,000 | 13 | 13,000 | | | | 2,600 | | 30,200 |
| Feb 1 | Issued | | | | 1,000 | 13 | 13,000 | 1,600 | | 27,200 |
| Feb 20 | Issued | | | | 500 | 15 | 7,500 | 1,100 | | 19,700 |
| Feb 25 | Issued | | | | 600 | 10 | 6,000 | 500 | | 13,700 |

## EXERCISE

**I. Choose the correct answer for the following:**

1. If purchasing is done at one central place, it is called
   (i) Decentralised purchasing (ii) Optimum purchasing
   (iii) Centralised purchasing (iv) Economical Purchasing
2. The process of assigning numbers or symbols to materials is called
   (i) Store- Keeping (ii) Codification(iii) Store (iv) Bin Card
3. Maximum consumption x Maximum re-order period is called
   (i) Re-ordering level (ii) Maximum level
   (iii) Minimum level (iv) Re-ordering quantity
4. Cost of storage of materials is known as
   (i) Ordering Cost (ii) EOQ (iii) Carrying Cost (iv) Total Cost
5. The quantity at which material ordering cost and carrying cost are equal is called
   (i) Maximum Quantity (ii) Economic Ordering Quantity
   (iii) Minimum Quantity (iv) Re-ordering Quantity
6. A quantitative record of receipts, issues and closing balances of a particular item of stores is known as
   (i) Material Order (ii) Wage Card (iii) Material Card (iv) Bin Card

7. The physical movement of receipts and issues of material is recorded in
   (i) Stores Ledger (ii) Pay Roll (iii) Cost Sheet (iv) Wage Sheet
8. The analysis based on the concept of selective inventory management is known as
   (i) EOQ Analysis (ii) VED Analysis
   (iii) B.E.P. Analysis (iv) ABC Analysis
9. The analysis used primarily for the control of spare parts is called
   (i) ABC Analysis (ii) VED Analysis
   (iii) B.E.P. Analysis (iv) EOQ Analysis
10. Inventory Turnover Ratio is a ratio between cost of material consumed and
    (i) Average Stock (ii) Base Stock
    (iii) Opening Stock (iv) Closing Stock
11. When the issue price is based on the price of oldest materials, it is called
    (i) LIFO (ii) FIFO (iii) HIFO (iv) Average Price
12. When the issue price is based on the price of latest material, it is called
    (i) HIFO (ii) FIFO (iii) LIFO (iv) Average Price

[Ans: 1. (iii) 2. (ii) 3. (i) 4. (iii) 5. (ii) 6. (iv) 7. (i) 8. (iv) 9. (ii) 10.(i) 11. (ii) 12. (iii)]

**II. Answer the following questions:**

13. Distinguish between direct material and indirect material.
14. State the requirements for the effective control of material.
15. Define Material. Explain briefly the procedures related to planning and control of material.
16. Distinguish between classification and codification of material.
17. Distinguish between Centralised and Decentralised purchasing of material.
18. What is Store-keeping?
19. Define Store-keeping. Distinguish between Centralised Store-keeping and Decentralised Store-keeping.
20. Define Bin Card. Distinguish between Bin Card and Stores Ledger.
21. What is Stores Ledger?
22. Define Stores Ledger. Distinguish between Stores Ledger and Bin Card.
23. What is Stock Verification?

24. Distinguish between Perpectual inventory system and Periodic inventory system.
25. What is Stock level? Explain briefly the different types of Stock levels.
26. Distinguish between Maximum Stock level and Minimum Stock level.
27. Write Short notes on (i) Re-order level (ii) Re-order quantity and (iii) Danger level.
28. Write short notes on (i) Bin Card (ii) Stores Ledger (iii) Direct Material and (iv) Indirect Material.
29. What is Economic Ordering Quantity?
30. Distinguish between Material Ordering cost and Material Carrying cost.
31. Explain the graphical representation of Economic Ordering Quantity.
32. What is Inventory Turnover Ratio?
33. What is ABC Analysis?
34. What is VED Analysis?
35. Explain briefly the Actual Cost methods of pricing material issues.
36. Explain briefly the Average Cost methods of pricing material issues.
37. Explain briefly the Notional price methods of pricing material issues.
38. Write short notes on (i) FIFO (ii) LIFO (iii) HIFO (iv) Base Stock Method.
39. Write short notes on (i) Simple Average Price Method (ii) Weighted Average Price Method (iii) Moving Average Price Method.
40. Write short notes on (i) Standard Price Method (ii) Inflated Price Method (iii) Market Price Method.
41. Write short notes on (i) VED Analysis (ii) EOQ and (iii) ABC Analysis.
42. State the merits and demerits of FIFO and LIFO methods.
43. The usage of material X,Y and Z in a company are as follows:

    Maximum usage - 500 units per week each
    Minimum usage - 200 units per week each
    Normal usage - 350 units per week each
    Re-order quantity - X: 2200 units; Y: 2000 units; Z: 2500 units
    Re-order period - X 2 to 4 weeks; Y3 to 6 weeks; Z1to3 weeks.

    Calculate for each material (i) Maximum level (ii) Minimum level (iii) Re-order level and (iv) Average stock level.

    [Ans: (i) 3800; 4400; 3800; (ii) 950; 1425; 800; (iii) 2000; 3000; 1500; (iv) 2375; 2913; 2300]
44. Material A and B are used in a company as follows:

    Maximum usage per week- A: 2000 units; B: 2500 units
    Minimum usage per week - A: 800 units; B: 1000 units

Normal usage per week - A: 1500 units; B: 1700 units
Re-order quantity - A: 4000 unis; B: 5500 units
Re-order period - A: 2 to 4 weeks B: 1 to 3 weeks

Calculate for each material (a) Maximum level (b) Minimum level (c) Re-order level and (d) Average stock level.

[Ans: (a) 10400; 12000; (b) 3500; 4100; (c) 8000; 7500; (d) 6950; 8050]

45. The annual requirement of material in a factory is 30,000 units. The interest and carrying cost is 10 % of the cost of material. Cost of placing an order is Rs.100. Cost of material is Rs.60 per unit. Find out the Economic Ordering Quantity and prove the result through tabulation. (Ans: 1000 units)

46. Calculate Economic Ordering Quantity when annual consumption is Rs.9,00,000, cost of placing and receiving an order is Rs.200 and annual carrying cost is 10 %.Price Rs10 per unit (Ans: 6,000 units)

47. A factory requires 50,000 units per annum. The cost of material is @ Rs.5 per unit. The ordering cost is Rs.250 per order. The material carrying cost is 20% of the average inventory. Calculate (a) EOQ, (b) The total inventory cost (c) The number of times of purchase in the year and (d) If the purchase price per unit is reduced by 2% for the same quantity, whether the material can be purchased in lots of 10,000 units.

(Ans: (a) 5,000 units (b) Rs.255,000 (c) 10 times (d) Yes, since total cost is Rs.2,51,150).

48. Calculate Stock turnover ratio and Turnover period from the following.

| | Material A | Material B |
|---|---|---|
| | Rs. | Rs. |
| Opening Stock | 5,000 | 11,000 |
| Sales | 60,000 | 74,000 |
| Closing Stock | 8,000 | 9,000 |

(Ans: 8.7; 7.6; 41.62; 48.03)

49. The information regarding the receipts and issue of materials in a factory during April and May 2011 are stated below.

| | | |
|---|---|---|
| April 2 | Opening Balance | 750 units @ Rs.15 per unit |
| ,, 5 | Received | 500 units @ Rs.17 per unit |
| ,, 10 | Issued | 800 units |
| ,, 17 | Issued | 300 units |
| ,, 20 | Received | 600 units @ Rs.18 per unit |
| May 1 | Issued | 500 units |

| | | |
|---|---|---|
| ,, 4 | Issued | 100 units |
| ,, 10 | Received | 700 units @ Rs.20 per units |
| ,, 20 | Issued | 600 units |

Prepare Stores Ledger Account on the basis of First-in-First-out method.

(Ans: Stock 250 units @ Rs.20, Rs.5000 )

50. Prepare Stores Ledger Account on the basis of FIFO method of pricing the issue of material, from the following particulars.

| | | |
|---|---|---|
| July 1 | Balance | 400 units @ Rs.24 per unit |
| 4 | Received | 600 units @ Rs.25 per unit |
| 9 | Issued | 500 units |
| 12 | Issued | 200 units |
| 13 | Material returned from production centre 100 units (issued on 9[th] July) | |
| 17 | Received | 400 units @ Rs.22 per unit |
| 20 | Returned to suppliers 200 units (purchased on 4[th] July) | |
| 26 | Issued | 250 units |
| 30 | Issued | 200 units |

On verification at 31st July, it was found out a shortage of 70 units of material.

(Ans: Cl. Stock 800 units @ Rs.22, Rs.1760; Loss 70 @ Rs.22, Rs.1540)

51. Prepare Stores Ledger Account on the basis of Last-in-First-out, from the following information:

| | | |
|---|---|---|
| August 1 | Balance | 500 units @ Rs.40 per unit |
| 4 | Purchased | 400 units @ Rs.42 per unit |
| 5 | Issued | 400 units |
| 8 | Purchased | 600 units @ Rs.44 per unit |
| 10 | Issued | 700 units |
| 12 | Issued | 200 units |
| 18 | Purchased | 500 units @ Rs.45 per unit |
| 22 | Issued | 400 units |
| 27 | Purchased | 300 units @ Rs.50 per unit |
| 30 | Issued | 400 units |

(Ans: Cl. Stock 200 units @ Rs.40, Rs.8000)

52. Prepare Stores Ledger Account on the basis of Highest-in-First-out method, from the following information:

| | | |
|---|---|---|
| 2011 September 1 | Balance | 300 units @ Rs.30 per unit |

| | | |
|---|---|---|
| 6 | Purchased 400 units @ Rs.35 per unit | |
| 9 | Issued 400 units | |
| 14 | Purchased 500 units @ Rs.28 per unit | |
| 17 | Issued 600 units | |
| 21 | Purchased 400 units @ Rs.37 per unit | |
| 25 | Issued 300 units | |
| 27 | Purchased 400 units @ Rs.40 per unit | |
| 30 | Issued 600 units | |

(Ans: Cl. Stock 100 units @ Rs.30, Rs.3000)

53. Prepare Stores Ledger Account on the basis of Base Stock method (both on the basis of FIFO and LIFO) from the following information. The base stock to be maintained is 200 units.

| | | | |
|---|---|---|---|
| 2011 November | 1 | Purchased | 500 units @ Rs.50 per unit |
| | 7 | Purchased | 300 units @ Rs.45 per unit |
| | 8 | Issued 400 units | |
| | 15 | Purchased | 200 units @ Rs.40 per unit |
| | 17 | Issued 400 units | |
| | 21 | Purchased | 300 units @ Rs.44 per unit |
| | 25 | Issued 200 units | |
| | 30 | Issued 200 units | |

(Ans: Cl. Stock 200 units @ Rs.50, Rs.10000)

54. Prepare Stores Ledger Account on the basis of Simple Average Price method, from the following information:

| | | |
|---|---|---|
| 2011 April 1 | Balance of material | 300 units @ Rs.12 per unit |
| 4 | Purchased | 400 units @ Rs.10 per unit |
| 6 | Issued | 400 units |
| 12 | Purchased | 500 units @ Rs.15 per unit |
| 15 | Issued | 200 units |
| 17 | Issued | 300 units |
| 22 | Purchased | 300 units @ Rs.18 per unit |
| 30 | Issued | 400 units |

(Ans: Cl. Stock 200 units; Rs.3,250)

55. The following information are provided by a manufacturing company for the month of October 2011.

| | | |
|---|---|---|
| October 1 | Balance of material | 900 units @ Rs.5 per unit |
| 4 | Purchased | 600 units @ Rs.6 per unit |
| 6 | Issued | 1,000 units |
| 8 | Purchased | 800 units @ Rs.7 per unit |
| 12 | Issued | 700 units |
| 17 | Purchased | 500 units @ Rs.4 per unit |

| | | |
|---|---|---|
| 20 | Issued | 900 units |
| 25 | Purchased | 800 units @ Rs.8 per unit |
| 27 | Issued | 600 units. |

Prepare the Stores Ledger Account on the basis of Weighted Average Price method.

(Ans: Cl. Stock 400 units @ Rs.7.46, Rs.2,988)

56. Prepare Stores Ledger Account on the basis of Periodic Simple Average Price method (for each month) from the following information:

| | | |
|---|---|---|
| May | 1 | Balance 400 units @ Rs.10 per unit |
| | 3 | Purchased 600 units @ Rs.12 per unit |
| | 10 | Issued 500 units |
| | 17 | Purchased 500 units @ Rs.16 per unit |
| | 24 | Issued 700 units |
| | 27 | Purchased 400 units @ Rs.17 per unit |
| June | 5 | Issued 300 units |
| | 7 | Purchased 600 units @ Rs.13 per unit |
| | 11 | Issued 700 units |
| | 20 | Purchased 800 units @ Rs.10 per unit |
| | 27 | Issued 900 units. |

(Ans: Cl.Stock 200 units; Rs.1,950)

57. Prepare Stores Ledger Account on the basis of Periodic Weighted Average Price method from the following particulars:

| | | |
|---|---|---|
| 2011 October | 1 | Opening Stock 600 units @ Rs.60 per unit |
| | 4 | Purchased 700 units @ Rs.55 per unit |
| | 7 | Issued 800 units |
| | 14 | Purchased 900 units @ Rs.62 per unit |
| | 17 | Issued 1000 units |
| | 21 | Purchased 800 units @ Rs.65 per unit |
| | 25 | Issued 700 units |
| | 30 | Purchased 300 units@ Rs.70 per unit |
| 2011 November | 5 | Issued 600 units |
| | 7 | Purchased 800 units @ Rs.58 per unit |
| | 12 | Issued 500 units |
| | 17 | Purchased 600 units @ Rs.68 per unit |
| | 20 | Issued 800 units |
| | 24 | Purchased 700 units @ Rs.64 per unit |
| | 30 | Issued 600 units |

(Ans: Cl. Stock 700 units @ Rs.61.61; 300 units @ Rs.62.55)

58. Calculate the cost of charging the issue price of material by Moving Simple Average Price method for the period starting from May 2006 from the following particulars:

| Period | Price per unit (Rs.) |
|---|---|
| 2011 | |
| January | 24.50 |
| February | 22.00 |
| March | 26.00 |
| April | 28.00 |
| May | 30.50 |
| June | 29.50 |
| July | 31.50 |
| August | 32.50 |
| September | 34.00 |
| October | 28.00 |
| November | 26.00 |
| December | 24.00 |

(Ans: Rs.21.12; 26.20; 26.75; 27.43; 28; 28.72; 28.65; 28.41; 28.04)

59. Calculate 4 yearly Moving Weighted Average Prices for charging the material issues from the following particulars:

| Period | Quantity | Price per unit (Rs.) |
|---|---|---|
| 2011 June 5 | 200 | 12 |
| 7 | 300 | 11 |
| 11 | 500 | 10 |
| 22 | 400 | 13 |
| July 6 | 600 | 12 |
| 11 | 400 | 15 |
| 21 | 300 | 17 |
| August 2 | 700 | 14 |
| 17 | 500 | 13 |
| September 4 | 300 | 12 |
| 7 | 200 | 11 |
| 9 | 100 | 10 |
| October 6 | 600 | 13 |
| 12 | 200 | 14 |
| November 7 | 300 | 15 |
| 15 | 400 | 11 |
| December 2 | 300 | 10 |

| 4 | 500 | 12 |
|---|---|---|
| 20 | 200 | 11 |

(Ans: Rs.12.59; 12.72; 12.72; 12.50)

60. The purchases and issues of material A during December 2006 are as follows:

| | | |
|---|---|---|
| December | 4 | Purchased 500 units @ Rs.40 per unit |
| | 7 | Purchased 400 units @ Rs.45 per unit |
| | 13 | Issued 300 units |
| | 17 | Issued 500 units |
| | 20 | Purchased 700 units @ Rs.42 per unit |
| | 23 | Purchased 400 units @ Rs.46 per unit |
| | 25 | Issued 500 units |
| | 30 | Issued 600 units |

The standard price per unit of material A is Rs.42 fixed for the year. Prepare Stores Ledger Account on the basis of Standard Price method.

(Ans: Cl. Stock 100 units @ Rs.42 , Rs.4200)

61. Prepare a Stores Ledger on the basis of Market Price method from the following particulars:

Purchases:

| | | |
|---|---|---|
| December | 2 | 900 units @ Rs.8 per unit |
| | 12 | 800 units @ Rs.12 per unit |
| | 17 | 1000 units @ Rs.11 per unit |
| | 20 | 600 units @ Rs.13 per unit |
| | 25 | 500 units @ Rs.10 per unit |

Issues:

| | | |
|---|---|---|
| December | 4 | 700 units @ Rs.9 per unit |
| | 13 | 600 units @ Rs.11 per unit |
| | 19 | 1100units @ Rs.12 per unit |
| | 24 | 700 units @ Rs.8 per unit |
| | 30 | 400 units @ Rs.13 per unit |

(Ans: Cl.Stock 300 units Rs.3,700)

62. Calculate the cost of charging the issue price of material by Moving Simple Average Price method for the period starting from May 2011 from the following particulars:

| **Period** | **Price per unit (Rs.)** |
|---|---|
| 2011 | |
| January | 35.50 |

| | |
|---|---|
| February | 33.00 |
| March | 54.00 |
| April | 45.00 |
| May | 37.50 |
| June | 39.50 |
| July | 49.50 |
| August | 57.50 |
| September | 55.00 |
| October | 60.00 |
| November | 51.00 |
| December | 40.00 |

(Ans: Rs.41; 40.75; 42; 43.94; 45.17; 46.65; 47.05; 46.46)

63. The purchases and issues of material A during November 2011 are as follows:

| | | |
|---|---|---|
| November | 3 | Purchased 1500 units @ Rs.20 per unit |
| | 8 | Purchased 500 units @ Rs.25 per unit |
| | 15 | Issued 1300 units |
| | 19 | Issued 200 units |
| | 21 | Purchased 1000 units @ Rs.26 per unit |
| | 25 | Purchased 700 units @ Rs.30 per unit |
| | 27 | Issued 900 units |
| | 30 | Issued 800 units |

The standard price per unit of material A is Rs.25 fixed for the year. Prepare Stores Ledger Account on the basis of Standard Price method.

(Ans: Cl.Stock 500 units @ Rs.19, Rs.9,500)

64. The purchases and issues of material X during December 2011 are as follows:

| | | |
|---|---|---|
| December | 1 | Purchased 2000 units @ Rs.40 per unit |
| | 5 | Purchased 1000 units @ Rs.44 per unit |
| | 10 | Issued 1700 units |
| | 17 | Issued 800 units |
| | 20 | Purchased 1100 units @ Rs.39 per unit |
| | 25 | Purchased 900 units @ Rs.45 per unit |
| | 29 | Issued 1200 units |
| | 31 | Issued 700 units |

The standard price per unit of material A is Rs.43 fixed for the year. Prepare Stores Ledger Account on the basis of Standard Price method.

(Ans: Cl.Stock 600 units @ Rs.30.33, Rs.18,200)

# CHAPTER - III
# LABOUR

Labour is one of the important factors of production. The success of a concern mostly depends on the efficiency and contribution of the labour. The quality of a product and economical production depend on the efforts of the labour. Hence, utmost care should be given for the management of the labour. Management of labour starts from recruitment and placement. Efficient and experienced persons should be selected by the company. They should be appointed in suitable jobs. The labourers should be given adequate training often for better performance of their job. Payment of wage is an important factor to motivate the workers. If the workers are paid well they will be motivated to contribute more in the production activities. Payment of wage should include monetary and non-monetary incentives. Efficient workers should be motivated by paying more wages and promotion.

## I. LABOUR COST CONTROL

Control of labour cost is the prime concern of a management in order to reduce the cost of production. Labour cost control is a co-ordinated effort of the following departments.

1. Personnel Department
2. Engineering Department
3. Time-Keeping Department
4. Payroll Department
5. Cost Accounting Department

### 1. Personnel Department

It is the duty of the personnel department to meet the requirement of personnel in the organisation. The personal department has to execute the policies of Board of Directors, in connection with the appointment, placement, training, fixation of wages and promotion. Personnel Manager should assess the requirement of personnels in all the departments of the organisation. The departmental heads in the organisation should inform their requirement of labour force to the Personnel Manager.

### 2. Engineering Department

The functions of Engineering Department are formulating production methods and working conditions for the production process. Hence, the department has to prepare the production plan and specifications for each job; supervise the production process; inspect the parts manufactured; and supervise research and experiment work.

**3. Time - Keeping Department**

Time-keeping department has to maintain records with regard to the time spent by each worker in the factory. The record should contain details regarding the total hours worked, number of days worked, leave availed for each worker. The wages of the workers are calculated on the basis of the records maintained by this department.

**4. Payroll Department**

Payroll department acts as an intermediary between the Time-keeping department and Cost Accounting department. It receives information from Time-keeping department and prepare payroll for each worker. This information are then given to the Cost Accounting department. It is the duty of this department to maintain pay roll records to calculate wages and deductions for employees and to prepare departmental payroll summaries.

**5. Cost Accounting Department**

Cost Accounting department has to collect details about all costs incurred in various departments in order to find out the total cost for each job and to prepare Costing profit & loss account. Since labour is an important element of cost of production, the department needs the labour cost incurred in each job which can be obtained from the Time-keeping and Payroll departments. Hence, Cost accounting department maintains records related to the wages paid for each worker and for each job.

## II. TIME-KEEPING

Time-Keeping is recording of the time spent by each worker in an organisation. Recording of time is required for preparing payrolls; meeting the statutory requirements; calculating wages, pension, gratuity, provident fund etc. Time-keeping department can follow any of the following methods to record the attendance of workers.

1. Manual Methods
   (i) Attendance Register Method
   (ii) Disc Method
2. Mechanical Methods
   (i) Time-recording Clock
   (ii) Dial Time Recorder

## 1. Manual Methods

### (i) Attendance Register Method

In this method, an attendance register is kept at the entrance of the factory. The attendance register contains columns for name, identity number, arrival and departure time, and signature. The workers has to record the time of arrival and time of departure, against their name. In some organisations, a person may be in charge of the register to record the time. Entries are made in the individual attendance records of the workmen, from this Attendance Register.

### (ii) Disc Method

This method is otherwise called asToken Method. In this method each worker is allotted a metal disc, bearing the name and employee number. These discs are kept on hooks on a board. The board is placed either at the gate or at the entrance of the department. When the workers enter the factory they have to remove the disc bearing their name and number, and put it in a box meant for it. The box is taken away when the reporting time is over. After that, another box is kept for late comers. This box may be changed every half an hour till the maximum late time is over.

Absence of a worker can be identified through the non-removal of disc from the board. On the basis of the discs collected from different boxes, the time-keeper records the attendance of workers in the register.

## 2. Mechanical Methods

### (i) Time-recording Clock

Time-recording clock records the time of entering and leaving of the workers. Each worker is given a time card. This card is usually meant for a week. It contains columns to record the arrival and departure time. The cards are kept in a tray near the time recording clock. When the worker enters the factory they will insert the card in the time-recording clock which will record the time in the card. This process is repeated when the workers leave the factory. The hours spent by the workers in a week can easily be calculated from the time cards.

### (ii) Dial Time Recorder

Dial Time Recorder is a machine to record the time of entering and leaving of the workers in the factory. It contains number of holes, (ie, about 160 holes) around a dial. Each hole is marked with a number which represents the number assigned to a worker. It contain a radial arm at the centre. The worker has to press the radial arm into the hole corresponding to his number. Then the time is automatically recorded in the roll of paper inside the Recorder, corresponding to his number. This process can be repeated when the workers leave the factory.. The time spent by each worker in the factory for a week can easily be calculated with the help of the roll of paper kept inside the Recorder.The total time spent by all the workers can be calculated from the roll papers meant for the respective workers.

## III. TIME BOOKING

Time-booking means recording of the time spent by a worker on each job, process or operation. The purpose of Time-booking is to calculate the wages and bonus for the workers; to ascertain the quantity and value of work completed; and to calculate the cost of the product or job. The following are the methods of Time-booking.

(i) Job Ticket or Job Card
(ii) Labour Cost Card
(iii) Daily Time Sheets
(iv) Weekly Time Sheets
(v) Time and Job Card

### (i) Job Ticket or Job Card

Job Card is a card given to each worker to record the time spent by him in a job. The workers have to record the actual time spent by him in the job. After completing the job, he will be given another card meant for another job. Job card helps to ascertain the labour cost meant for a job. If one job is carried on by more workers then, each of them will be given a job card related to that job.

### (ii) Labour Cost Card

When the job involves many operations or stages, labour cost card is issued by the concern. Each worker is not given a separate card. Each job has one card. The workers have to pass the card after recording his time on the job. Total hours spent by all the workers can be computed from the job card after the job is completed.

### (iii) Daily Time Sheets

This sheet is meant for recording the daily time spent by the workers in different jobs. Each worker is given Daily Time Sheet. The workers have to record the time spent by him in different jobs. The sheet contains columns to record the description and number of the jobs. These sheets are given when the workers have to perform number of different jobs in a day. These sheets should be handed over daily, to the foreman or supervisor.

**(iv) Weekly Time Sheets**

Weekly Time Sheets contain columns to fill the time spent by workers for a week. The workers should fill the sheets daily and hand them over to the supervisor or foreman at the end of the week. Each workers will be given a weekly time sheet.It helps to calculate the wages for the workers.

**(v) Time and Job Card**

This card contains columns to record the attendance time and job work time of the workers for one week. Each worker has a separate Time and Job Card. At the end of the week, time spent by workers in the factory and in a job can easily be calculated.

## IV. IDLE TIME AND OVERTIME

### IDLE TIME

Idle time is the difference between the time spent by the worker in the factory and the time spent in a job for productive purpose. For example, the workers may spend 8 hours in a factory and may spend 6 hours in the job.Then the 2 hours during which the worker remains idle, without productive work is called Idle Time. Normally, wages is paid for 8 hours including the idle time.

Idle time is of two types. They are

1. Normal Idle Time and 2. Abnormal Idle Time

**1. Normal Idle Time**

Normal Idle time arises due to unavoidable circumstances. It may arise due to the following reasons.

(i) Time lost due to moving of workers from factory gate to place of work

(ii) Time lost in moving from one job to another

(iii) Time lost in moving from one machine to another machine

(iv) Time lost due to normal fatigue, minor accidents, and personal needs

(v) Time lost due to delay in the supply of material and instruction.

**2. Abnormal Idle Time**

Idle time arises due to abnormal situation is called Abnormal Idle Time. The following are the reasons of Abnormal Idle Time.

(i) Machine breakdown

(ii) Excessive waiting time for material and instruction

(iii) Strikes, lockout, fire, floods etc.

(iv) Excessive power failure

(v) Non availability of materials.

**Control of Idle Time**

Normal Idle time could not be controlled. The expenses connected with normal idle time are unavoidable. Abnormal Idle Time can be controlled to some extent. Proper planning and control can minimise the cost of Abnormal Idle Time. It can be controlled through the following steps.

(i) Proper maintenance of machine can prevent the machine break down.

(ii) Timely purchase of material.

(iii) Avoiding delay in the supply of material from store and delay in the instruction.

(iv) Power failure can be prevented through internal power generators.

**Treatment of the Cost of Idle Time**

Expenses connected with Normal Idle Time is unavoidable and hence they should be treated as cost of production. It forms part of the factory cost.

The expenses or loss arising due to Abnormal Idle Time cannot be considered as part of the cost of production. It should be treated as an Abnormal Loss and transferred to the Costing Profit and Loss Account.

**OVERTIME**

Overtime is the time spent by workers over and above the normal working hours. According to the Factories Act 1948, the normal working hour is 8 hours per day or 48 hours per week. Hence, if the worker worked more than 8 hours in a day or 48 hours in a week the extra hours worked are called overtime. Overtime is paid normally at double the rate of the normal time. If the Factories Act is not applied in an organisation then the overtime premium is double the rate or one and half the rate or reasonably high rate.

Overtime premium is an additional expenditure for a concern. Hence, it should be discouraged. Since overtime is a gain for the workers, they may postpone the normal work to be done as overtime. Overtime can be controlled through proper planning, supervision and control of the work.The workers should be instructed to do the minimum work in a day.In addition to this, effective supervision should be carried on to get quality work.

**Treatment of Overtime Premium**

Treatment of overtime premium is based on the reasons for the overtime. The different treatments of overtime are stated as follows.

(i) Overtime premium is charged to the particular job order for which overtime is paid.

(ii) Overtime premium is treated as a factory overhead if it is paid due to increase in production to meet a seasonal demand.

(iii) Overtime premium is charged to capital work order account, if it is paid for capital order like maintenance and fabrication of machines for internal use.

(iv) Overtime premium is charged to Costing Profit and Loss account, if the overtime is due to abnormal situations like, fire, flood, strike or lockout.

(v) If overtime is caused due to the fault of any particular department, such overtime premium should be charged to that particular department.

## V. WORK STUDY, TIME STUDY AND MOTION STUDY

### 1. WORK STUDY

Work study is a study of the job, its methods and techniques to decide the best method and technique. While conducting the work study the time and motion studies should be taken into consideration. Work study is conducted through (i) Method Study and (ii) Work measurement.

**(i) Method Study**

Method study is a study of the different methods of doing a work. It helps to develop a new method or to improve the existing method of doing the work. For a method study a detailed study about the work, machines, locations, procedures of different operations etc should be conducted. After analysing the merits and demerits of different methods, the best method should be selected. The selected method should be applied for doing the work and corrective measures can be taken if there is any defect in this method.

**(ii) Work Measurement**

Work measurement is the measurement of work to be completed in a particular time. In the process of work measurement, actual time taken for a work and wastage of time in doing the work can be found out.

## 2. TIME STUDY

Time study is a study about the requirement of time to complete a work by an average worker. Efficient worker may complete a work quickly but an inefficient worker takes more time to complete the work. Hence a time should be determined to balance the high and low time taken by efficient and inefficient workers. This time is called Standard Time. Standard time varies according to the nature and type of work. To determine the standard time the works should be well defined by dividing it into small elements. Time study helps to fix the wages and incentives to workers.

## 3. MOTION STUDY

Motion study is a study about the movement of workers in a factory in order to prevent the unnecessary movement. Workers have to move from one job to another. The movement of the workers can be studied, while they are doing the work. Then the unnecessary movements can be prevented by proper instructions and by proper arrangement of machines.

## VI. JOB EVALUATION AND MERIT RATING

## JOB EVALUATION

Job evaluation is a process of assessment and analysis of each job. In this process of assessment, the relative merits and demerits of each job can be ascertained. Hence, it is easy to determine the wages and salary to each job according to the relative merits of each job. Job evaluation also helps to determine the qualification and experience required for each job. It facilitates the personnel department for recruitment, training and placement of workers. Job evaluation should be conducted by well-qualified persons. The following are the important methods of Job evaluation.

(i) Ranking Method
(ii) Grading Method
(iii) Point Rating Method

### (i) Ranking Method

In this method, different jobs in an organisation should be arranged in an order either from the lowest to the highest or from the highest to the lowest. This arrangement should be done according to the relative importance and merits of each job over the other job. Before ranking the job, each job should be evaluated properly through efficient and qualified persons.

**(ii) Grading Method**

In this method, a number of grades are determined in advance. After determining the grades, each job in the organisation should be well analysed and then suitable grades should be given to the jobs. Each grade should be fixed with separate pay scales. The grading and fixing of salary for each grade should be done by well qualified and experienced persons.A model of the Grading and Pay Scale table is stated as follows:

**GRADING AND PAY SCALE**

| Points | Grade | Pay Scale (Monthly) Rs |
|---|---|---|
| 25 - 50 | VII | 1000-1500 |
| 50 -75 | VI | 1500-2000 |
| 75 - 100 | V | 2000-3000 |
| 100-125 | IV | 3000-4000 |
| 125-150 | III | 4000-5000 |
| 150-175 | II | 5000-6000 |
| 175-200 | I | 6000-7000 |

This method is easy to calculate. The main defect of this method is that it is difficult to assign points for each factor, accurately.

**(iii) Point Rating Method**

In this method, job factors which are common to all jobs should be used to analyse each job. The job factors are like education, skill required, training and experience, working conditions and physical factors. Each job should be analysed and given points according to the importance in the job factors. Finally all the points with regard to each job should be added to know the individual score. On the basis of this score, each job should be graded. A model of the Point Rating is stated as follows.

**POINT RATING CHART**

| Factors | Jobs | | | |
|---|---|---|---|---|
| | A | B | C | D |
| Education | 10 | 15 | 10 | 5 |
| Experience | 45 | - | 30 | 5 |
| Efforts | 30 | 25 | 20 | 10 |
| Skill | 30 | 20 | 35 | 15 |
| Working condition | 35 | 35 | 30 | 20 |
| Responsibility | 40 | 20 | 25 | 5 |
| Total Points | 190 | 115 | 150 | 60 |

The chart shows the rating of 4 jobs.But in general, organisations have to do rating for many jobs. According to this chart, A scored high points and D scored low points.

## MERIT RATING

Merit Rating is a systematic evaluation of the performance of the employees, by his superior. Normally, the superior evaluates the complete performance of each worker who is working on a similar job. The objectives of merit rating are (i) to find out the suitability of an employee in the job, (ii) to determine the wage and incentives, (iii) to give promotion, increment, reward and other benefits (iv) to create competitive and competence in the job among the workers.

The merit rating is conducted on the basis of the following characteristics.

(i) Attendance and discipline.
(ii) Education, training and experience.
(iii) Quality of work done.
(iv) Cooperation.
(v) Character and Integrity.
(vi) Initiative and aptitude in doing the work.

### Advantages of Merit Rating

The following are the advantages of merit rating .

(i) It improves the performance of the workers.
(ii) It creates a competitive spirit among the workers.
(iii) It improves the employees - management relations.
(iv) Production and productivity will improve due to merit rating.

### Drawbacks of Merit Rating

The following are the drawbacks of merit rating.

(i) It creates tension and dissatisfication among the workers.
(ii) The superior may be biased towards some workers and may assign more merit points to them.
(iii) It affects the relationship between the superiors and subordinates.

### Difference between Job Evaluation and Merit Rating

The following are the differences between Job evaluation and Merit Rating.

(i) Job evaluation is the assessment of the different jobs and Merit Rating is the assessment of the performance of workers in a job.

(ii) Job evaluation aims at uniform wage and salary for different jobs. But, Merit rating aims at different wages and salary according to the relative performance of each worker.

(iii) Job evaluation helps to fix wages and salary according to different grades of job. Merit rating helps in fixing the wages and salary according to the performance of workers in a job.Hence job evaluation advocates one wage for one job while merit rating advocates different wages for one job according to the performance of employees.

## VII. LABOUR TURNOVER

Labour turnover is defined as the rate of change of labour force in an organisation during a specific period. It is otherwise called replacement of labour force during a period. Labour turnover cannot be prevented completely. Since labour turnover is an expensive one high labour turnover should be avoided. The expenses in labour turnover arises due to recruitment, training and placement of new workers.

### Causes of Labour Turnover

Causes of labour turnover are classified into 1. Avoidable Causes 2. Unavoidable Causes and 3. Personal Causes.

#### 1. Avoidable Causes

The following are the avoidable causes.

(i) Low wages when compared to other concerns.

(ii) Poor working conditions

(iii) Dissatisfaction about the job

(iv) Unsatisfactory relationship with superiors and colleagues.

(v) Lack of job guarantee and promotion.

(vi) Inadequate medical and recreation facilities

(vii) Lack of transport and accommodation facilities.

#### 2. Unavoidable Causes

The following are the unavoidable causes.

(i) Dismissal from service due to indiscipline

(ii) Retrenchment due to low demand for the product in the market.

(iii) Retrenchment due to shortage of finance, material, power etc.

### 3. Personal Causes

The following are the personal causes

(i) Dissatisfaction with the job

(ii) Retirement due to old age and ill health

(iii) Death

(iv) Due to better job opportunity in other concerns

(v) Marriage

(vi) Dissatisfaction about the environment.

## Effect of Labour Turnover

The high labour turnover leads to increase in cost of production, due to the following reasons.

(i) Cost of recruitment, training and placement of workers.

(ii) The performance of inexperienced workers is very low and due to this labour productivity will decrease.

(iii) The cost of maintenance of plant and machinery increases due to inefficient handling by new workers.

(iv) Losses due to increase in wastage, spoilage and defectives.

## Cost of Labour Turnover

The cost of labour turnover can be classified into

1. Preventive Costs and 2. Replacement Costs.

### 1. Preventive Costs

Preventive costs are those costs which are incurred to reduce the rate of labour turnover. The important preventive costs are as follows,

(i) Cost of providing recreation facilities

(ii) Cost of providing retirement benefits.

(iii) Cost of providing medical,housing and recreation facilities.

(iv) Cost of educational facilities provided to children of the employees.

### 2. Replacement Costs

Replacement costs are those costs incurred due to labour turnover. The following are the important replacement costs.

(i) Cost of recruitment, training and placement of new workers

(ii) Cost of excessive defectives and spoilage

(iii) Loss due to low-productivity of the new workers

(iv) Cost of rectifying the abnormal breakage of machine and equipments by the new workers

**Treatment of the cost of Labour Turnover**

The cost of labour turnover is normally treated as factory overhead. The preventive costs should be shared by all the departments, according to the number of workers in each departments. But the replacement costs should be shared only by those departments affected by labour turnover. These departments should share the replacement cost according to the number of workers replaced.

**Measurement of Labour Turnover**

The important methods of measurement of labour turnover are, as follows,

1. Separation Method
2. Replacement or Net Labour Turnover Method
3. Flux or Separation-cum-Replacement Method

**1. Separation Method**

$$\text{Labour Turnover} = \frac{\text{Number of Separation in the period}}{\text{Average number of workers in the period}} \times 100$$

**2. Replacement or Net Labour Turnover Method**

$$\text{Labour Turnover} = \frac{\text{Number of workers replaced during the period}}{\text{Average number of workers during the period}} \times 100$$

**3. Flux or Separation-cum-Replacement Method**

$$\text{Labour Turnover} = \frac{\text{Number of Separations} + \text{Number of Replacements}}{\text{Average number of workers during the period}} \times 100$$

Average number of workers during the period

$$= \frac{\text{Number of workers at the begining} + \text{Number of workers at the end of the period}}{2}$$

**Illustration: 1**

Calculate labour turnover rate and equivalent rate under (i) Separation method (ii) Replacement method and (iii) Flux method from the following particulars:

Number of workers as on 1st March 2011 is 800, and as an 31st May 2011 is 950. During the period, 40 workers were terminated and 15 left the factory. The company recruited 150 new workers. Among the 150 workers, 30 were appointed to replace the vacancy caused by the labour turnover and the remaining were appointed due to the high demand for the product of the company.

***Solution:***

$$\text{Average number of workers} = \frac{800+950}{2} = 875$$

**(i) Separation method**

$$\text{Labour turnover rate} = \frac{\text{Number of separation in the period}}{\text{Average number of workers in the period}}$$

$$= \frac{55 \times 100}{875} = 6.29\%$$

$$\text{Equivalent rate} = \frac{12 \times 6.29}{3} = 25.16\%$$

**(ii) Replacement method**

$$\text{Labour turnover rate} = \frac{\text{Number of workers replaced during the period}}{\text{Average number of workers during the period}} \times 100$$

$$= \frac{30 \times 100}{875} = 3.43\%$$

$$\text{Equivalent rate} = \frac{12 \times 3.43}{3} = 13.72\%$$

**(iii) Flux method**

$$\text{Labour turnover rate} = \frac{\text{Number of Separations + Number of Replacements}}{\text{Average number of workers during the period}} \times 100$$

$$= \frac{(55+30) \times 100}{875} = 9.71\%$$

$$\text{Equivalent rate} = \frac{12 \times 9.71}{3} = 38.84\%$$

**Note:** In Flux method only number of separations and number of replacement should be taken into considerstion

## VIII. METHODS OF WAGE PAYMENT

The following are the methods of wage payment.

A. Time wage system
B. Piece wage system
C. Incentive methods of wage payment
D. Group Bonus plans
E. Indirect Incentive method

### A. TIME WAGE SYSTEM

Under Time Wage system wages are paid to workers on the basis of time worked, irrespective of their production. It may be paid daily, weekly, fortnightly or monthly. In this method, wages can be calculated as

Wage = Number of hours worked x Rate per hour

**Example:** If the wage rate per hour is Rs.20 and the worker X worked for 7 hours, then the wage for X = 7 x 20 = Rs.140.

**Application of Time Wage System**

This system is most suitable for the following circumstances.

(i) Where quality of work is more important than the output
(ii) Where the contribution or services of the workers cannot be easily measured.
(iii) Where the output is not repetitive in nature
(v) Where close supervision is required for the work.

**Advantages**

The advantages of time wage system are as follows,

(i) It is easy to calculate
(ii) It is easy to understand and operate
(iii) This method is good for average and below average workers
(iv) This method satisfies the workers and their union.

**Disadvantages**

The disadvantages of time wage system are as follows,

(i) The workers are not given any incentive to increase the production.
(ii) There is no distinction between efficient and inefficient workers, in this method.
(iii) This system increases the labour cost.
(iv) This method requires costly supervision.

(v) It encourages overtime work.

(vi) The workers are not properly motivated in this system

(vii) It is difficult to know the labour cost per unit well in advance.

## B. PIECE WAGE SYSTEM

Under this system, the wage is paid on the basis of number of units produced by the workers. Piece wage is calculated as,

Wage = Number of units produced x Rate per unit

**Example:** If the piece rate per unit is Rs.10 and worker X produced 30 units, then wage for X = 30 x 10 = Rs.300.

Rate per unit of production is determined on the basis of standard hours required for producing one unit of the product. Hence, the rate is fixed so that the wage for an average worker will not be less than the normal time wage per day.

### Advantages

The advantages of piece wage system are as follows.

(i) It is easy to calculate and simple to understand

(ii) It increases the production and thereby reduces the overhead cost per unit.

(iii) It helps to know the labour cost per unit in advance, for the purpose of fixation of price of the product.

(iv) It improves the competitive spirit among the workers

(v) Efficient workers can easily be identified so that they can be given incentives and promotion.

### Disadvantages

The disadvantages of piece wage system are as follows.

(i) It is difficult to fix the standard rate per unit.

(ii) Quality of work may be affected, in this system.

(iii) It leads to damage of tools and machines, loss of material and it increases in spoilage and defectives.

(iv) It may affect the health of workers due to overstrain, and thereby creates more absentees.

(v) It is not suitable if the quality of production is more important.

(vi) This method requires more supervision and thereby increases the cost of supervision.

(vii) It increases the misunderstanding among the workers due to different wages for the same group of workers.

## C. INCENTIVE METHODS OF WAGE PAYMENT

Incentive methods of wage payment are based on the efficiency of the workers. The important incentive methods of wage payment are as follows.

1. Halsey Premium Plan
2. Halsey-Weir Premium Plan
3. Rowan Plan
4. Taylor's Differential Piece Rate Plan
5. Merrick's Multiple Piece Rate System
6. Gnatt Task and Bonus Plan
7. Bedaux Point Premium Plan
8. Emerson's Efficiency Plan

### 1. Halsey Premium Plan

This method is developed by an american engineer named F.A.Halsey in the year 1891. Under this method, standard time is fixed for every job. If the worker completes the job at standard time or more than the standard time he will be paid according to the standard time. His wage would be standard time multiplied by time rate. If the worker completes the job less than the standard time, he will be paid wage for actual hours taken plus bonus at the rate of 50% of the wage for the time saved. These workers can do some other work in the time saved and earn from that work also.

**Illustration: 2**

Standard time for completing a job in a company is fixed as 42 hours. Wage rate is Rs. 8 per hour. Worker A completed the work by 30 hours; B completed it by 48 hours and C completed the work by 42 hours. Calculate wage of the workers on the basis of Halsey Premium Plan.

***Solution:***

| | | |
|---|---|---|
| Standard time | = | 42 hours |
| Standard rate | = | Rs.8 per hour |
| Wage for worker A | = | 30 x 8 + 50% (42-30) x 8 |
| | = | 240 + 50% of 96 |
| | = | 240 + 48 = Rs.288 |
| Wage for worker B | = | 42 x 8 = Rs.336 |
| Wage for worker C | = | 42 x 8 = Rs.336 |

### 2. Halsey-Weir Premium Plan

This method is based on Halsey Premium Plan. In this method, the premium paid to the worker is 33 1/3% of the time saved instead of 50%. Time saved is excess of the standard time over actual time. If the worker completes the job at or after the standard time, he is guaranteed wage at standard time.

**Illustration: 3**

Calculate wages for workers A, B and C by Halsey-Weir Premium Plan from the following particulars.

Standard time 45 hours; Standard Rate Rs.9 per hour. Actual time taken by A 50 hours; B 45 hours; and C 38 hours.

***Solution:***

Wage for worker A = 45 x 9 = Rs.405

Wage for worker B = 45 x 9 = Rs.405

Wage for worker C = 38 x 9 + 33 1/3 % (45 - 38) x 9

= 342 + 1/3 x 7 x 9

= 342 + 21 = Rs.363

**3. Rowan Plan**

This method, was developed by James Rowan during 1898. This method is based on Halsey Premium Plan. In this method also wage is paid on the basis of time wage system. Standard wage is paid to the worker who completes the work by the standard time or after the standard time. If the worker completes the work before the standard time, he should be paid time wage for the time taken and a bonus for the time saved. The bonus is calculated as follows.

$$\text{Bonus} = \frac{\text{Standard Time - Time taken}}{\text{Standard time}} \times (\text{Time taken} \times \text{Rate})$$

$$\therefore \text{Wage} = T \times R + \frac{(S - T)}{S} \times T \times R$$

Where T = Acual time (Time taken)

S = Standard time

R = Rate per hour

**Illustration: 4**

Calculate wage for workers X, Y and Z from the following, by Rowan Method.

Standard time 8 hours; Hourly Rate Rs.10

Actual time X 12 hours;

Y 8 hours and Z 5 hours.

***Solution:***

Workers X and Y are not eligible for bonus, since they completed the job at and above the standard time.

Wage for X = 8 x 10 = Rs.80

Wage for Y = 8 x 10 = Rs.80

$$\text{Wage for Z} = T \times R + \frac{(S - T)}{S} \times T \times R$$

$$= 5 \times 10 + \frac{(8 - 5)}{8} \times 5 \times 10$$

$$= 50 + (3 \times 50) / 8$$

$$= 50 + 18.75 = \text{Rs.}68.75$$

**4. Taylor's Differential Piece Rate System**

This system was introduced by F.W. Taylor. In this system, two piece rates i.e., low piece rate and high piece rate should be fixed. High piece rate is given to efficient workers who produce more than the standard output and low piece rate is given to inefficient workers who produce less than the standard output. For example, if the standard output per day is 12 units, those who produces 12 units and above are called efficient workers and those who produce less than 12 units are called inefficient workers.

**Illustration: 5**

Calculate weekly wages of two workers by Taylor's Differential Piece Rate system from the following:

Standard output per week 150 units

Piece rates are Rs.4 and Rs.6 per unit

Worker I produced 170 units and

Worker II produced 140 units

***Solution:***

Since worker I produced above the standard units, he is called efficient worker. Worker II produced less than the standard units and hence, he is called inefficient worker.

∴ Wage for worker I = 170 x 6 = Rs.1,020

Wage for worker II = 140 x 4 = Rs.560

**Illustration: 6**

Calculate wages for workers X and Y by Piece Rate method and Taylor's differential piece rate method from the following.

Standard time per unit is 15 minutes

Normal rate per hour is Rs.9

Differential piece rate are that 75% of piece rate for below standard workers and 125% of piece rate for above standard workers.

In a day X produced 30 units and Y produced 40 units. Normal working hours per day is 8.

***Solution:***

Standard production per hour $= \frac{60}{15} = 4$ units

Standard production per day $= 4 \times 8 = 32$ units

Normal rate per hour (for 4 units) = Rs.9

Normal piece rate per unit $= \frac{9}{4} =$ Rs.2.25

Low piece rate $= \frac{75 \times 2.25}{100} =$ Rs.1.69

High piece rate $= \frac{125 \times 2.25}{100} =$ Rs.2.81

**(i) Piece Rate Method**

Wage for worker X $= 30 \times 2.25 =$ Rs.67.50

Wage for worker Y $= 40 \times 2.25 =$ Rs.90

**(ii) Taylor's Differential Piece Rate Method**

Since worker X produced (30 units) less than the standard units (32) he is an inefficient worker and worker Y produced (40 units) more than the standard units (32). Hence, he is an efficient worker.

$\therefore$ Wage for X $= 30 \times 1.69 =$ Rs.50.70

Wage for Y $= 40 \times 2.81 =$ Rs.112.40

**5. Merrick's Multiple Piece Rate System**

This method is based on the Taylor's Differential Piece Rate system. Under Taylor's method, two piece rates are adopted, but in Merrick's method, three piece rates are adopted. Normal piece rate is paid for efficiency upto 83%. For efficiency above 83% upto 100% the piece rate is 10% above the normal rate. For efficiency above 100%, the piece rate is 20% above the normal rate.

**Illustration:7**

Calculate wages for workers X, Y and Z from the following by Merrick's Piece Rate method and Normal Piece Rate method.

Standard output of the worker per week is 45 units. Normal piece rate is Rs.8 per unit.

Output of X is 35 units, Y is 42 units and Z is 48 units.

***Solution:***

Efficiency of workers,

$$X = \frac{35 \times 100}{45} = 78\%$$

$$Y = \frac{42 \times 100}{45} = 93.3\%$$

$$Z = \frac{48 \times 100}{45} = 106.7\%$$

| | |
|---|---|
| Wage rate - upto 83% Efficiency | = Rs.8 per unit |
| 83% to 100% Efficiency | = Rs.8 + 10% of 8 |
| | = Rs.8.80 per unit |
| Above 100% Efficiency | = Rs.8 + 20% of 8 |
| | = Rs.9.60 per unit |

**(i) Merrick's Piece Rate System**

| | | | |
|---|---|---|---|
| Wage for X | = | 35 x 8 | = Rs.280.00 |
| Y | = | 42 x 8.80 | = Rs.369.60 |
| Z | = | 48 x 9.60 | = Rs.460.80 |

**(ii) Normal Piece Rate System**

| | | | |
|---|---|---|---|
| Wage for X | = | 35 x 8 | = Rs.280 |
| Y | = | 42 x 8 | = Rs.336 |
| Z | = | 48 x 8 | = Rs.384 |

**6. Gnatt Task and Bonus Plan**

This method combines a guaranteed time rate and piece rate. Daily time wage is guaranteed to all the workers. In this system, wages to workers are calculated as (i) Guaranteed time rate for output below standard (ii) Time wage plus bonus @ 20% on time wage for standard output and (iii) High piece rate or time wage plus bonus @ 20% on time wage is paid for output above standard.

**Illustration: 8**

Calculate wages for 3 workers X, Y and Z under Gnatt Task and Bonus Plan.

Standard production 60 units per week

Time Rate : Rs.12 per hour

Working hours : 42 hours per week

Piece Rate above standard output: Rs.10 per unit

Output of the week for the three workers X: 55 units; Y: 60 units, and Z: 68 units.

***Solution:***

Time wage is paid to worker X since his performance is below standard. For worker Y time wage plus 20% bonus is paid since his performance is 100% of the standard. High piece rate is paid to Z, since his performance is above 100%.

$\therefore$ Wage for X = 42 x 12 = Rs.504

Wage for Y = 42 x 12 + 20% of (42 x 12)

$$= 504 + \frac{20}{100} \times 504$$

= 504 + 100.80 = Rs.604.80

Wage for Z = 68 x 10 = Rs.680

**7. Bedaux Point Premium Plan**

Under this system, standard time allowed for a job is mentioned in points or Bs. The standard performance of an hour is denoted as 60 Bs. In addition to the wages as per the time worked, a bonus of 75% of time saved is given to the worker. Bonus is calculated as 75% of the time wage for the time saved. In this method, the bonus for the remaining 25% time saved should be given to supervisors and indirect labourers. Since the scheme became unpopular, later on 100% bonus was adopted instead of 75% bonus. Wages for the workers in this method are calculated as follows.

$$\text{Wages} = (\text{Actual hours} \times \text{Time Rate}) + \frac{75}{100} \times \frac{\text{Points Saved}}{60} \times \text{Time Rate}$$

[ For 75% of bonus ]

= (Actual hours x Time Rate ) + (100% of Time Saved x Time Rate)

[ For 100% of bonus ]

**Illustration: 9**

Calculate wages by Bedaux point premium plan from the following information.

Standard Time allowed 720 Bs.

Time taken 540 Bs.

Time Rate Rs.10 per hour

***Solution:***

**(i) If 75% of the time saved is paid as bonus**

$$\text{Wages} = (\text{Actual hours} \times \text{Time Rate}) + \frac{75}{100} \times \frac{\text{Points Saved}}{60} \times \text{Time Rate}$$

$$= (540/60 \times 10) + \frac{75}{100} \times \frac{720 - 540}{60} \times 10$$

= 90 + 22.5 = Rs.112.50

**(ii) If 100% of the time saved is paid as bonus**

Wage = ( 540/60 x 10 ) + ( 100% of 180/60 x 10 )

= 90 + 30 = Rs.120

## 8. Emerson's Efficiency Plan

In this method, workers are eligible to get bonus only when his efficiency reached 66 2/3%. The efficiency is measured according to their production in their alloted hours. For example, if standard production is 120 units in 10 standard hours and actual production is 96 units in 10 hours, then the efficiency is calculated as $\frac{96 \times 100}{120} = 80\%$ In addition to the time wage for hours worked, bonus is paid as a percentage of time wage according to the efficiency of the workers. But the efficiency should be more than 66 2/3% to get bonus. Emerson suggested different rates of bonus for different efficiencies. For 66 2/3% of efficiency bonus is 0.01%; For 80% efficiency bonus is 3.27%; For 90% efficiency bonus is 9.91 %; For 100% efficiency bonus is 20%; For above100% efficiency, additional 1% of bonus for every one percent increase in efficiency in addition to the 20% bonus. Hence, for 110% efficiency bonus is 30%.

**Illustration: 10**

Calculate wages for workers A, B, C and D from the following information, by Emerson's Efficiency Plan.

Standard Production in 10 hours is 150 units; Actual production in 10 hours by A 120 units, B 75 units, C 165 units and D 150 units.

Time Rate is Rs.8 per hour.

***Solution:***

Efficiency of worker A $= \frac{120 \times 100}{150} = 80\%$

Efficiency of worker B $= \frac{75 \times 100}{150} = 50\%$

Efficiency of worker C $= \frac{165 \times 100}{150} = 110\%$

Efficiency of worker D $= \frac{150 \times 100}{150} = 100\%$

Worker B is not eligible for bonus since he has not reached 66 2/3% of efficiency.

Bonus for 80% efficiency = 3.27%; Bonus for 100% efficiency = 20%; Bonus for 110% of efficiency = 30%

Wage for A = $(10 \times 8) + (10 \times 8 \times \frac{3.27}{100})$

= 80 + 2.62 = Rs.82.62

Wage for B = 10 x 8 = Rs.80

Wage for C = (10 x 8) + (10 x 8 x 30/100)

= 80 + 24 = Rs.104

Wage for D = (10 x 8) + (10 x 8 x 20/100)

= 80 + 16 = Rs.96

## D. GROUP BONUS PLANS

In Group Bonus plans, incentive is paid in the form of bonus in uniform to all the workers. The worker in a particular group are not discriminated according to the efficiency. The incentive is paid when the performance of the group exceeds the expected standard. This system is applied in the following situations.

(i) When the performance of individual workers are difficult to assess

(ii) When all the workers in the group are collectively responsible for the production.

(iii) To encourage and motivate all the workers for better contribution in the production.

**Advantages**

The advantages of group bonus plan are as follows.

(i) It encourages co-operation and team spirit

(ii) It is easy to calculate and simple to understand

(iii) It requires less clerical work.

(iv) It increases the productivity of labour.

**Disadvantages**

The disadvantages of group bonus plan are as follows.

(i) There is no difference between efficient and inefficient workers in this system.

(ii) Performance of inefficient workers will decrease further due to this system.

**Types of Group Bonus Plans**

The important types of Group Bonus Plans are as follows.

1. Towne Gain Sharing Plan
2. Rucker Plan
3. Scanlon Plan
4. Priestman's Production Bonus Plan

**1. Towne Gain Sharing Plan**

Under this plan, the group bonus is paid if there is gain in labour cost. Gain in labour cost is calculated deducting the standard cost with the actual cost. 50% of the gain so calculated is distributed as bonus to all the workers. This bonus is shared by the foreman and workers in proportion to their time wage.

**2. Rucker Plan**

Under this plan bonus is calculated on the basis of 'value added'. Value added can be calculated either by (i) Sales value less cost of all materials and services like power and fuel or (ii) Direct labour plus production overheads plus gross profit. After calculating the value added, standard direct labour cost is determined as a percentage of the value added. If the percentage of actual cost is less than the standard percentage of direct labour cost, bonus is paid as per the rate of the difference in the percentages.

(Eg) If the standard direct labour cost is 65% of the value added and the actual direct labour cost is 61% of the value added then 4% is distributed as bonus.

In this method, the 2/3 of the bonus is distributed in the same month and the balance is transferred to a revenue fund so that it can be used for the month during which performance is below the standard.

**3. Scanlon Plan**

This plan is a modification of the Rucker plan. In this plan ratio of direct labour cost to 'sales value of production' is followed instead of the ratio of direct labour cost to 'value added'. Other calculations are similar to those of the Rucker Plan.

**4. Priestman's Production Bonus Plan**

In this method, bonus is paid in the same proportion of the excess of performance over the standard. The standard performance is fixed in terms of number of units or points. Suppose the performance exceeds 30% of standard, then the workers get bonus equal to 30% of their wage. (Eg) If the standard production is 500 units and the actual production is 625 units, then the increase in performance above standard is 25% (i.e., 125/500 x 100). Hence, the workers will get bonus equal to 25% of their wages.This system encourages the workers to increase their performance.

**E. INDIRECT INCENTIVE METHODS**

The following are the important indirect incentive methods of wage payment.

1. Profit Sharing
2. Co-partnership
3. Non- Monetary Incentives

## 1. PROFIT - SHARING

Profit sharing is an extra payment to the workers from the profit of the company in addition to their normal wages and incentives. It may either be paid in the form of cash or in the form of shares of the company. It is usually given on a percentage basis, on the wages or salaries, of the employees. The percentage is usually determined through negotiation between the employer and the union of the employees. According to the Payment of Bonus Act 1965 the minimum and maximum bonus to be paid is fixed at 8 1/3% and 20% respectively of the Net Profit. While distributing the bonus, the procedures of the Payment of Bonus Act should be strictly followed.

## 2. CO-PARTNERSHIP

Co-partnership is a scheme adopted by some concerns to share the capital and profit of the company. This scheme creates a sense of cooperation and understanding among the employer and the employees. In this system, the employees will work with maximum effort as if they are working in their own concern. They will work jointly to earn more profit in order to share the profit in addition to the wages.

## 3. NON-MONETARY INCENTIVES

Non-monetary incentives are incentives provided by the employees in non-monetary form. These incentives are given in the form of free of cost or subsidised rate.Non-monetary incentives are like, free accomodation, training, education to the children of workers, canteen and recreation facilities.The non-monetary incentives are much attractive in large scale business units than in small scale business units.

# IX. DEFINITIONS OF RELATED CONCEPTS

## 1. Pay Rolls

Payroll is otherwise called as wage sheets. It is the duty of Payroll Department to prepare the payroll. Payroll is a record of the details about the Gross wages and Net wages earned. The gross wages are computed in the payroll in separate columns by normal hours worked, overtime worked and hourly rate. The Net wages are computed by the various deductions like, Provident Fund, Insurance, Income Tax, Loan recoveries etc.

Pay roll is prepared with the help of Time card if wages are paid on time basis; or piece rate cards if wages are paid on piece rate basis. For monthly salaries payroll is prepared, with the help of Attendance Register.

Separate Payrolls are prepared for different departments. In the payroll, the employees name and ticket number should clearly be recorded corresponding to their gross wages and net wages. A model of payroll is stated as follows.

**PAYROLL (WAGE SHEET)**

Department:

| SI.No. | Workers Name | Workers Number | Total hour or units | Rate per hour or per unit (Rs.) | Wages (Rs.) | Overtime hours | Overtime wages | Leave & Holiday pay (Rs.) | D.A. & other allowances (Rs.) | Gross Wages (Rs.) | Deductions | | | | Total Deduction | Net Wages (Rs.) |
|---|---|---|---|---|---|---|---|---|---|---|---|---|---|---|---|---|
| | | | | | | | | | | | Provident Fund | Income Tax | ESI | Others | | |
| | | | | | | | | | | | | | | | | |

Prepared by : Verified by :

It is clear from the wage sheet that the complete details about the wages of a department relating to a period, are recorded in the sheet. The wage sheets for all the departments concerned with all the periods should be maintained in the payroll department.

**2. Pay Slip**

Pay Slip is a slip containing the details of wages paid to each employee. It contains the gross wages, all deductions and net wages. It is prepared from the wage sheet. It should be given to each employee at the time of payment of wages. A model of Pay Slip is stated as follows.

**XYZ COMPANY LTD**
**PAY SLIP**

| Name of the worker ............. | Department.................. |
| --- | --- |
| Ticket No .............................. | For the period .............. |
| | Rs |
| Normal Wages | ................ |
| Overtime Wages | ................ |
| Dearness Allowance | ................ |
| Leave Pay | ................ |
| Other Allowances | ................ |
| GROSS WAGES | ................ |
| **Deductions** | |
| P.F. Contribution | ................ |
| Income Tax | ................ |
| Insurance | ................ |
| Other Recoveries | ................ |
| Total Deductions | ................ |
| NET WAGES | ................ |
| Prepared by .................. | |
| Date ............................ | Signature of Pay Officer ............. |

Pay slip is a record to verify the actual work done and the calculations of the wages. If any worker got doubt in the calculations, then they can complain to the concerned authorities for verification and rectification of the mistakes, if any.

**3. Disbursement of wages**

The cashier usually makes payment of wages to the workers. The wage sheets are signed by the responsible officer and handed over to the cashier. The net amount payable to workers, is drawn from the bank. Wages are paid by the cashier to workers in a separate envelope. The envelope contains the exact net wages and the Pay slip.

**4. Direct Labour and Indirect Labour**

The labour directly involved in the conversion of raw material into finished products is called direct labour. (Eg) Workers in the manufacturing and assembling units. Indirect labour is those labour who is not directly involved in the process of production. (Eg) Foremen, Supervisors and Office staff. Direct labour cost is those labour cost which can easily be identified in the product and can be allocated to cost centre. Indirect labour cost is those labour cost which cannot be easily identified and allocated to the cost centre. It should be apportioned to cost centre.

### 5. Wage Abstract and Wage Analysis

The Financial Accounting department calculate the total wages paid, with the help of Payroll or (Wage Sheet). For financial accounting purpose, total wages paid for the accounting year is enough. But for the cost accounting purpose the wages paid should be classified into direct and indirect. The indirect wages paid should be allocated to production, administration, and selling and distribution departments. Wages paid for different work or job should also be calculated. To meet all the requirements Costing Department prepares two statements called Wage Abstract and Wage Analysis.

#### (a) Wage Abstract

Wage Abstract is a statement which shows the classification of wages according to different jobs or different works. Total wages paid should be apportioned for different jobs or works on the basis of time spent or the cost of job or any other basis. A model of Wage Abstract is stated below.

**XYZ & CO. LTD**
**WAGE ABSTRACT**

Period ending ........................

| Serial Number | Depart-ment | Production Order No. | Job Card No. | Hours worked or units produced | Rate per hour or Rate per unit Rs | Total Labour Cost Rs |
|---|---|---|---|---|---|---|
| | | | | | | |
| Prepared by .................... | | | | | | |

#### (b) Wage Analysis

Wage Analysis is a statement to classify the wages into direct and indirect. The indirect wage is further classified for the purpose of Production, Administration and Selling & Distribution Departments. A model of the Wage Analysis is stated as follows.

**XYZ & Co. LTD.**

**WAGES ANALYSIS**

Period ending ..........................

| Depart-ment | Total Wages (Direct & Indirect) | Direct Wages | Production Department (Factory Overhead) | Administration Department (Ad. Overhead) | Selling & Distribution department (Sell.&Dis. Overhead) |
|---|---|---|---|---|---|
| | | | | | |
| Prepared by .................... | | | | | |

## MISCELLANEOUS ILLUSTRATIONS

**Illustration: 11**

The wage sheet of a manufacturing company contains the following details

Basic salary is Rs.50 per day. Dearness Allowance is Rs.2 for every point over 100 cost of living index. Present cost of living index is 600 points.

Leave salary is 12% of the Basic salary and Dearness Allowance.

Employer's contribution to provident fund is 8% of the basic, dearness allowance and leave salary.

Employer's contribution to ESI is 2% of the basic, dearness allowance and leave salary.

Entertainment allowance to labour is Rs.120 per month.

Number of working days in a month is 20 days of 8 hours each.

Calculate labour cost per man-day of 8 hours.

***Solution:***

**Statement of Labour cost**

| | | Rs. |
|---|---|---|
| Basic Salary | | 50.00 |
| Dearness Allowance | $\frac{2 \times 500}{100}$ | 10.00 |

| | | |
|---|---|---|
| Leave Salary | $\frac{12}{100} \times 60$ | 7.20 |
| Employer contribution to P.F | $67.20 \times \frac{8}{100}$ | 5.38 |
| Employer's contribution to ESI | $67.20 \times \frac{2}{100}$ | 1.34 |
| Amenities to worker | $\frac{120}{20}$ | 6.00 |
| Total | | 79.92 |

**Illustration: 12**

A manufacturing company provides the following information related to wages for workers during May 2011.

| **Employees** | **Wages** (Rs.) |
|---|---|
| Foreman | 3,000 per month |
| Technician | 80 per day |
| Mechanic | 70 per day |
| Workman | 60 per day |

The employer's contribution of provident fund is 8% and employees contribution of provident fund is 8% of the basic wages. The employer contributes 2.5% and employee contributes 3% of the monthly wages for Employees State Insurance.

The working days of the company is 6 days in a week @ 8 hours per day. Sundays are treated as paid holidays.

Calculate (i) Net wages paid for the month (ii) Total labour cost to the employer for the month and (iii) Total job cost when the material consumed is Rs.15,000 and overhead is 40% of prime cost.

(Adapted: ICWA Inter )

***Solution:***

(i) Calculation of Net Wages

| | | Rs. |
|---|---|---|
| Foreman | | 3,000.00 |
| Technician (31 x 80) | | 2,480.00 |
| Mechanic (31 x 70) | | 2,170.00 |
| Workman (31 x 60) | | 1,860.00 |
| Gross wages | | 9,510.00 |
| **Less:** Contribution by employees: PF | | |
| $\frac{8}{100} \times 9510$ | 760.80 | |

| | | |
|---|---|---|
| ESI Contribution $\frac{3}{100} \times 9510$ | 285.30 | 1,046.10 |
| Net wages paid | | 8,463.90 |

(ii) Calculation of Total Labour Cost for the employer

| | Rs. |
|---|---|
| Gross wages payable | 9,510.00 |
| P.F. Contribution by employer $\frac{8}{100} \times 9510$ | 760.80 |
| ESI Contribution by employer $\frac{2.5}{100} \times 9510$ | 237.75 |
| | 10,508.55 |

(iii) Calculation of Total Job cost

| | Rs. |
|---|---|
| Material Consumed | 15,000.00 |
| Labour Cost | 10,508.55 |
| Prime Cost | 25,508.55 |
| **Add:** Overhead $\frac{40}{100} \times 25508.55$ | 10,203.42 |
| | 35,711.97 |

**Illustration: 13**

Calculate the monthly wages of 3 workers X, Y and Z, from the following data:

Standard production per month for each worker is 2000 units. Actual production: X 1,900 units, Y 1,840 units and Z 1,600 units. Piece wage is Rs.1 per unit.

The workers are paid a bonus @ Rs.25 for each percentage of increase in the production above 90% of the standard production. In addition to this, Dearness Allowance for each worker is paid as Rs.300 per month.

(Adapted: ICWAI Inter)

***Solution:***

Standard production = 2,000 units

Production X = 1,900 units; Y = 1,840 units; Z = 1,600 units

X' s efficiency $= \frac{1900 \times 100}{2000} = 95\%$

Y's efficiency $= \frac{1840 \times 100}{2000} = 92\%$

Z's efficiency $= \frac{1,600 \times 100}{2,000} = 80\%$

X's Increase in efficiency above 90% is 5%

Y's Increase in efficiency above 90% is 2%

Z's Increase in efficiency above 90% is nil

∴ Bonus for X = 5 x 25 = Rs.125

Bonus for Y = 2 x 25 = Rs.50

Bonus for Z = Nil

**Statement of wages**

| Particulars | Workers | | |
|---|---|---|---|
| | X (Rs.) | Y (Rs.) | Z (Rs.) |
| Basic wages @ Rs.1 per unit | 1,900 | 1,840 | 1,600 |
| Dearness Allowance | 300 | 300 | 300 |
| Bonus | 125 | 50 | - |
| Total | 2,325 | 2,190 | 1,900 |

**Illustration: 14**

A job is undertaken by a technician, 2 mechanics and 3 assistants for a piece rate of Rs.11,200. Each of them worked for 150 hours to complete the job. The workers are eligible for time rate as Technician @ Rs.12 per hour, Mechanic @ Rs.10 per hour and Assistants @ Rs.8 per hour.

The piece work premium of the work is shared by the workers in the proportion of their wages.

Calculate (i) The wages for each type of workers. (ii) The selling price of the job if the cost of material is Rs.13,500, Factory overhead is 15% of Prime cost, Selling & Distribution overhead is 10% of Works cost and Profit is 20% of Sales.

***Solution:***

**(i) Time wage for the workers:**

| | | | Rs. |
|---|---|---|---|
| Technician | 150 hour x Rs.12 | = | 1,800 |
| Mechanics | 150 hour x Rs.10 x 2 | = | 3,000 |
| Assistants | 150 hour x Rs.8 x 3 | = | 3,600 |
| | Total Time wage | = | 8,400 |

| | | |
|---|---|---|
| Total piece wage | = | 11,200 |
| ∴ Piece work premium | = | 2,800 |
| Ratio of time wage | = | 1800 : 3000 : 3600 |
| | = | 3 : 5 : 6 |

Share of piece work premium:

| | | Rs. |
|---|---|---|
| Technician | = $\frac{3}{14}$ x 2,800 = | 600 |
| Mechanics | = $\frac{5}{14}$ x 2,800 = | 1,000 |
| Assistants | = $\frac{6}{14}$ x 2,800 = | 1,200 |
| | | 2,800 |

| | | |
|---|---|---|
| Wage for Technician | = 1800 + 600 | = Rs.2,400 |
| Wage for Mechanics | = 3000 + 1000 | = Rs.4,000 |
| Wage for Assistants | = 3600+1,200 | = Rs.4,800 |
| | | Rs.11,200 |

**(ii) Statement of Cost:**

| | | Rs. |
|---|---|---|
| Direct material | = | 13,500 |
| Direct wages | = | 11,200 |
| Prime Cost | = | 24,700 |
| Factory Overhead (15% of 24700) | = | 3,705 |
| Works Cost | = | 28,405 |
| Selling & Distribution Overhead (10% of 28405) | = | 2,841 |
| Cost of Sales | = | 31,246 |
| Profit $\frac{20}{80}$ x 31,246 | = | 7,812 |
| Sales | = | 39,058 |

**Illustration: 15**

In a factory, the standard time allowed for producing 25 units of a product is 1 hour. The hourly rate is Rs.11. Workers A, B and C produced 275 units, 200 units and 325 units respectively in a day.

Calculate (i)Wages for each worker on that day. (ii) Effective rate of earnings per hour for each worker under (a) Halsey Premium Bonus (bonus @ 50% of time saved) Plan (b)Rowan Premium method (c) Straight piece rate method.

(Adapted: ICWAI Inter)

***Solution:***

**(i) Wages for each worker for one day**

Time Rate = Rs.11 per day

Wages for A = $\frac{1}{25}$ x 275 x 11 = Rs.121

Wages for B = $\frac{1}{25}$ x 200 x 11 = Rs.88

Wages for C = $\frac{1}{25}$ x 325 x 11 = Rs.143

**(ii) Calculation of Effective rate of earnings per hour**

**(a) Halsey Premium Plan:**

Wage = Hours worked x Rate per hour + (50% of time saved x Rate per hour)

Actual time for A, B, C = 8 hours each.

Standard Time for A = $\frac{275}{25}$ = 11 hours

B = $\frac{200}{25}$ = 8 hours

C = $\frac{325}{25}$ = 13 hours

Wages for A = 8 x 11 + 50% of (11 - 8) x 11
= 88 + 16.50 = Rs.104.50

B = 8 x 11 + 50% of (8 - 8) x 11
= Rs.88

C = 8 x 11 + 50% of (13 - 8 ) x 11
= 88 + 27.50 = Rs.115.50

Effective Rate per hour for A = $\frac{104.50}{8}$ = Rs.13.06

B = $\frac{88}{8}$ = Rs.11

C = $\frac{115.50}{8}$ = Rs.14.44

**(b) Rowan Premium Method**

Wage = Hours worked x Hourly Rate + $\frac{\text{Time Saved}}{\text{Time Allowed}}$ x Hours worked x Hourly Rate

A = 8 x 11 + $\frac{3}{11}$ x 8 x 11
= 88 + 24 = Rs.112

B = 8 x 11 + $\frac{0}{8}$ x 8 x 11
= Rs.88

$$C = 8 \times 11 + \frac{5}{13} \times 8 \times 11$$

$$= 88 + 33.85 = \text{Rs.}121.85$$

Effective hourly rate, $A = \frac{112}{8} = \text{Rs.}14$

$B = \frac{88}{8} = \text{Rs.}11$

$C = \frac{121.85}{8} = \text{Rs.}15.23$

**(c) Straight Piece Rate**

Piece Rate $= \frac{11 \times 8}{25 \times 8} = \text{Rs.}0.44$

Wage for A = 275 x .44 = Rs.121

B = 200 x .44 = Rs.88

C = 325 x .44 = Rs.143

Effective hourly rate for each worker would be Rs.11 per hour.

i.,e., $A = \frac{121}{11} = \text{Rs.}11$

$B = \frac{88}{8} = \text{Rs.}11$

$C = \frac{143}{13} = \text{Rs.}11$

**Illustration: 16**

In a factory, the standard output of a product is 50 units per day of 8 hours. The normal wage is Rs.80 per day. Calculate the wages on the basis of (i) Time Rate (ii) Piece Rate (iii) Halsey Plan (iv) Rowan Plan and (v) Taylor's Differential Piece Rate method, if the output is 40, 60 and 70 units per day. Also calculate labour cost per unit. Differential piece rates are 80% and 120% of the normal piece rate.

***Solution:***

Normal Time wage per day = Rs.80

Hourly Time Rate $= \frac{80}{8} = \text{Rs.}10$

Piece rate for 50 units = Rs.80

Piece rate for one unit $= \frac{80}{50} = \text{Rs.}1.60$

**(i) Wage as per Time Rate:**

| Output | Time Wage (Rs.) | Cost per unit (Rs.) |
|---|---|---|
| 40 | 80 | 2.00 |

| | | |
|---|---|---|
| 60 | 80 | 1.33 |
| 70 | 80 | 1.14 |

**(ii) Wage as per Piece Rate:**

| Output | Piece Wage (Rs.) | Cost per Unit (Rs.) |
|---|---|---|
| 40 | 40 x 1.60 = 64 | 1.60 |
| 60 | 60 x 1.60 = 96 | 1.60 |
| 70 | 70 x 1.60 = 112 | 1.60 |

**(iii) Halsey Plan:**

Standard hours for 50 units = 8

Standard hours for 40 units $= \frac{8}{50} \times 40 = 6.4$

Standard hours for 60 units $= \frac{8}{50} \times 60 = 9.6$

Standard hours for 70 units $= \frac{8}{50} \times 70 = 11.2$

Wages by Halsey Plan = Actual hour x Hourly Rate + (50% of Time saved x Hourly Rate)

| Output | Wages (Rs.) | Cost per unit (Rs.) |
|---|---|---|
| 40 | 8 x 10 + (50% of 0 x 10) = 80 | 2.00 |
| 60 | 8 x 10 + (50% of 9.6-8 x 10) = 80 + 8 = 88 | 1.47 |
| 70 | 8 x 10 + (50% of 11.2-8 x 10 ) = 80 + 16 = 96 | 1.37 |

**(iv) Wages as per Rowan Plan:**

$$\text{Wages} = \text{Actual Time} \times \text{Hourly Rate} + \left[\frac{\text{Time saved}}{\text{Standard Time}} \times \text{Actual Time} \times \text{Hourly Rate}\right.$$

| Output | Wages (Rs.) | Cost per unit (Rs.) |
|---|---|---|
| 40 | $= 8 \times 10 + \frac{0}{8} \times 8 \times 10 = 80$ | 2.00 |
| 60 | $= 8 \times 10 + \frac{1.6}{9.6} \times 8 \times 10$ <br> $= 80 + 13.33 = 93.33$ | 1.56 |
| 70 | $= 8\times10 + \frac{3.2}{11.2} \times 8 \times 10$ <br> $= 80 + 22.86 = 102.86$ | 1.47 |

**(v) Wage as per Taylor's Differential Piece Rate:**

Wage = Piece Rate x Output

Differential Piece rate for

Below Standard performance $= \frac{80}{100} \times 1.60 =$ Rs.1.28

Above Standard performance $= \frac{120}{100} \times 1.60 =$ Rs.1.92

| Output | Wage Rs. | Cost per unit Rs. |
|---|---|---|
| 40 | 40 x 1.28 = 51.20 | 1.28 |
| 60 | 60 x 1.92 = 115.20 | 1.92 |
| 70 | 70 x 1.92 = 134.40 | 1.92 |

**Illustration: 17**

Calculate Capacity ratio, Activity ratio and Efficiency ratio from the following particulars:

The man-hours required for producing products M and N are 1.5 and 4 hours respectively. In a month 4,000 units of product M and 2000 units of product N are produced. Number of working days in the month is 22 of 8 hours per day. The company employed 70 workers. The budgeted man-hours are 132,000 for the year.

***Solution:***

Standard hours for actual production:

Product M = 4000 x 1.5 = 6,000

Product N = 2000 x 4 = 8,000

14,000

Budgeted Hours = 1,32,000 for one year

or $\frac{1,32,000}{12} =$ 11,000 for one month

Maximum possible hours = 22 x 8 x 70 = 12,320

Actual hours are assumed as 12,320

(i) Capacity Ratio:

(a) Standard Capacity Usage Ratio $= \frac{\text{Budgeted Hours}}{\text{Max. possible Hours}} \times 100$

$= \frac{11,000}{12,320} \times 100 = 89\%$

(b) Actual Capacity Usage Ratio $= \frac{\text{Actual Hours Worked}}{\text{Max. Possible Hours}} \times 100$

$$= \frac{12,320}{12,320} \times 100 = 100\%$$

(ii) Activity Ratio = $\frac{\text{Actual Production in terms of Std. Hours} \times 100}{\text{Budgeted Hours}}$

$$= \frac{14,000}{11,000} \times 100 = 127\%$$

(iii) Efficiency Ratio = $\frac{\text{Actual Production in terms of Std. Hours} \times 100}{\text{Actual Hours worked}}$

$$= \frac{14,000}{12,320} \times 100 = 114\%$$

## EXERCISE

**I. Choose the correct answer for the following:**

1. The cost of labour which cannot be easily identified in the product is called
   (i) Indirect labour Cost (ii) Direct labour cost
   (iii) Total labour cost (iv) Fixed labour cost
2. The method of recording the time spent by each worker in a company is known as
   (i) Pay-roll (ii) Time-keeping (iii)Time study (iv) Motion Study
3. The recording of the time spent by a worker on each job or operation is called
   (i) Time management (ii) Pay-roll
   (iii) Personnel Department (iv) Time booking
4. The card given to each worker to record the time spent by him in a job is called
   (i) Job card (ii) Bin card (iii) Wage card (iv) Salary card
5. The difference between the time spent in the factory and in the job is known as
   (i) Real time (ii) Work time (iii) Job time (iv) Idle time
6. The time spent by workers over and above the normal working hours is called
   (i) Idle time (ii) Over time (iii)Actural time (iv) Job time
7. A study about the job and its method is known as
   (i) Work study (ii) Time study (iii) Motion study (iv) Idle time study
8. A study about the movement of workers in a factory is called
   (i) Motion study (ii) Time study
   (iii) Work measurement (iv) Work study
9. The process of assessment and analysis of each job is known as
   (i) Merit Rating (ii) Time Keeping
   (iii) Work study (iv) Job evaluation

10. The systematic evaluation of the performance of the employee is called
    (i) Job evaluation (ii) Merit rating (iii) Work study (iv) Time study
11. The rate of change of labour force in an organisation is known as
    (i) Material turnover (ii) Debtors turnover
    (iii) Labour turnover (iv) Work assessment
12. The payment of wages on the basis of time spent by the workers is called
    (i) Piece wage (ii) Time wage (iii) Indirect wage (iv) Direct wage
13. The payment of wages on the basis of the number of units produced is called
    (i) Time wage (ii) Direct wage (iii) Indirect wage (iv) Piece wage
14. The payment of wages according to the efficiency of the workers is called
    (i) Incentive wage (ii) Time wage (iii) Picce wage (iv) Direct wage
15. When the incentive is shared by all the workers in a job, it is known as
    (i) Time wage (ii) Bonus (iii) High piece rate (iv) Group bonus

[Ans: 1. (i) 2. (ii) 3. (iv) 4. (i) 5. (iv) 6. (ii) 7. (i) 8. (i) 9. (iv) 10.(ii) 11. (iii) 12. (ii) 13.(iv) 14. (i) 15.(iv)]

**II. Answer the following questions:**

16. Distinguish between direct labour and indirect labour.
17. Explain the role of various departments in labour cost control.
18. What is time-keeping? Briefly explain the different methods of time-keeping.
19. What is time-booking? Briefly explain the different methods of time booking.
20. Define Idle time. Distinguish between Normal Idle time and Abnormal idle time.
21. What is Idle time? Explain the method of control and treatment of idle time.
22. Define Overtime. Explain the method of treatment of overtime.
23. What is work study?
24. Distinguish between Time Study and Motion Study.
25. Distinguish between Work Study and Time Study.
26. Distinguish between Work Study and Motion Study.
27. Define Job Evaluation. Explain different methods of job evaluation.
28. What is merit rating?
29. Define merit rating. Distinguish between job evaluation and merit rating.

30. What is Labour Turnover? State the causes of labour turnover.
31. Explain the cost of labour turnover and its treatment.
32. State the equation for the measurement of labour turnover.
33. Distinguish between time wage system and piece wage system.
34. What is incentive wage system?
35. Define incentive wage system. Briefly explain the different methods of incentive wage system.
36. Write short notes of (i) Halsey Premium plan (ii) Rowan plan (iii) Taylor's Differential Piece Rate System.
37. Define Group Bonus plan. State the merits and demerits of Group Bonus plan.
38. Define Group Bonus plan. Briefly explain the different methods of Group Bonus plan.
39. Explain the different indirect incentive methods of wage payment.
40. Distinguish between profit - sharing and co-partnership.
41. State the procedures of preparing Pay Rolls.
42. Distinguish between pay rolls and pay slips.
43. Calculate labour turnover rate and equivalent rate under (a) Separation method (b) Replacement method and (c) Flux method from the following particulars.

    The number of workers as on 1st April 2011 is 500 and as on 1st October 2011 is 700. During the period 30 workers were terminated and 20 left the factory. The company recruited 200 new workers. Among the 200 workers, 25 were appointed to replace the vacancy caused by the labour turnover, and the remaining were appointed due to the expansion of the company.

    (Ans: (a) 8.33%; 16.67 (b) 4.17%; 8.34 (c) 12.5%; 25%)
44. The standard time required for a job in a company is 40 hours. Wage rate is Rs.10 per hour. Worker X completed the job by 35 hours.Calculate wage of the worker on the basis of Halsey Premium plan. (Ans: Rs.375)
45. The standard time required for a job is 35 hours; standard rate is Rs.11 per hour. Actual time taken by A is 30 hours; B is 35 hours and C is 38 hours. Calculate wages on the basis of Halsey-Weir premium plan. (Ans: Rs.348.33; Rs.385; Rs.385)
46. Calculate wage for workers A, B and C from the following by Rowan method. Standard time 8 hours, Hourly rate is Rs.12. Actual time for worker A is 13 hours B is 8 hours and C is 5 hours.

    (Ans: Rs.96; Rs.96; Rs.82.50)

47. Calculate weekly wages of 3 workers by Taylor's Differential Piece Rate system from the following. Standard output per week is 200 units. Differential piece rates are Rs.5 and Rs.7 per unit. X produced 240 units, Y produced 200 units and Z produced 160 units. (Ans: Rs.1,680; Rs.1,400; Rs.800)

48. Calculate wage for workers A, B and C by piece rate method and Taylor's differential piece rate method, from the following: Standard time per unit is 10 minutes, Normal rate per hour is Rs.12. Production by A, B and C are 60, 48 and 40 units respectively. Differential piece rates are 75% of piece rate for workers of below standard and 125% of piece rate for workers of above standard.Normal working hours per day is 8. (Ans: (i) Rs.720; Rs.576; Rs.480 (ii) Rs.900; Rs.720; Rs.360)

49. Calculate wages for workers A, B and C from the following by Merrick Piece Rate Method and Normal Piece Rate Method.

Standard output per week is 60 units Normal Piece rate is Rs.12 per unit. Output of A is 43 units, B is 55 units and C is 65 units.

(Ans: (i) Rs.516; Rs.726; Rs.936; (ii) Rs.516; Rs.660; Rs.780)

50. Calculate wages for X, Y and X under Gnatt Task and Bonus Plan from the following:

Standard output is 80 units per week. Time Rate is Rs.20 per hour. Working hours- 40 hours per week. Piece rate above standard output is Rs.15 per unit. Output of X is 75 units, Y 80 units and Z 90 units. (Ans: Rs.800; Rs.960; Rs.1,350)

51. Calculate wages by Bedaux point premium plan from the following information:

| | |
|---|---|
| Standard time allowed | 240 Bs. |
| Time taken by X | 204 Bs. |
| Y | 264 Bs. |
| Time Rate | Rs.30 per hour |

(Ans: Rs.92; Rs.141)

52. Calculate wages for workers A, B and C from the following by Emerson's Efficiency Plan.

Standard production in 8 hours is 200 units. Actual production in 8 hours A 200 units, B 170 units and C 240 units. Time Rate is Rs.12 per hour. (As per Emerson's Bonus percentage table, percentage of bonus are 6.17, 20 and 40 for efficiencies 85%, 100% and 120% respectively).

(Ans: Rs.115.20; Rs.102; Rs.134.40)

53. The Wage Sheet of a manufacturing company contains the following details:

Basic salary- Rs.80 per day. Dearness Allowance is Rs.3 for every point over 100 cost of living index. Present cost of living index is 600 points.

Leave salary is 10% of the Basic Salary and Dearness Allowance.

Employer's contribution to Provident Fund is 9% of the basic, dearness allowance and leave salary.

Employer's contribution to ESI is 3% of the basic, dearness allowance and leave salary.

Expenditure on amenities of labour is Rs.154 per month.

Number of working days in a month is 22 of 8 hours per day.

Calculate labour cost per man-day of 8 hours. (Ans: Rs.129)

54. X Ltd provides the following information related to wages of workers for June 2011.

Wages for Foreman Rs.3500 per month; Technncian Rs.90 per day; Mechanic Rs.80 per day; Workmen Rs.70 per day.

The employer's contribution to Provident Fund is 9% and employees contribution to Provident Fund is 9% of the basic wage. The employer contributes 4% and employee contributes 3% of the monthly wages for Employees State Insurance.

The company worked for 6 days in a week @ 8 hours per day. Sundays are treated as holidays with full pay.

Calculate (a) Net wage paid for the month (b) Total labour cost to the employer for the month and (c) Total job cost when the material consumed is Rs.21,500 and overhead is 50% of Prime cost. (Ans: Rs.9,416 ; Rs.12,091; Rs.50,386.50)

55. Calculate monthly wages of workers A, B and C from the following

Standard production per month for each worker is 3,000 units Actual production: A 2,760 units, B 2,910 units and C 2,400 units. Piece wage is Rs.1.20 per unit.

The workers are paid a bonus @ Rs.20 for each percentage of increase in the production above 80% of the standard production. In addition to this, Dearness Allowance for each worker is paid as Rs.400 per month. (Ans: Rs.3,942; Rs.4,232; Rs.3,280)

56. A job is undertaken by one foreman, 2 technicians and 4 workmen for a piece rate of Rs.12,720. Each of them worked for 120 hours to complete the job. The persons are eligible for time rate on the basis as Foreman @ Rs.15 per hour. Technician @ Rs.13 per hour and workman @ Rs.10 per hour. The piece work premium of the work is shared by the workers in the proportion of their wages.

    Calculate (a) Wages for each type of workers (b) The selling price of the job if the cost of material is Rs.9,500. Factory overhead is 30% of prime cost, administration overhead is 15% of factory cost, selling and distribution overhead is 10% of cost of production and profit is 25% on cost of sales.

    (Ans: (a) Rs.2,356; Rs.4,083; Rs.6,281 (b) Rs.4,8721)

57. The standard time allowed for producing 20 units of a product in a factory is 1 hour. The hourly rate is Rs.12 per hour. Workers X, Y and Z producd 200 units, 160 units and 300 units respectively in a day. Working hours per day is 8.

    Calculate (i) Wage for each worker on that day (ii) Effective rate of earnings per hour for each worker under (a) Halsey Premium Bonus plan (bonus 50% of time saved) (b) Rowan Premium method and (iii) Straight Piece rate method. (Ans: (i)Rs.120; Rs.96; Rs.180; (ii) (a)Rs.108;Rs.96; Rs.138; (b) Rs.139.20; Rs.96; Rs.140.80 (iii) Rs.120; Rs.96; Rs.180)

58. In a factory the standard output of a product is 40 units per day of 8 hours. The normal wage is Rs.120 per day. Calculate the wage on the basis of (i) Piece Rate (ii) Halsey Plan (iii) Rowan Plan and (iv) Taylor's Differential Piece rate method, if the output is 35, 40, 55 and 60 units per day. Differential Piece rates are 90% and110%of the normal piece rate.(Ans: (i) Rs.105; Rs.120; Rs.165; Rs.180 (ii)Rs.120; Rs.120; Rs.142.50; Rs.150 (iii) Rs.120; Rs.159.73; Rs.160 (iv) Rs.94.50; Rs.132; Rs.181.50; Rs.198)

59. Calculate Capacity ratio, Activity ratio and Efficiency ratio from the following particulars:

    The man-hours required for producing products K and M are 2 and 3 hours respectively. In a month 5,000 units of product K and 3,000 units of product M are produced. Number of working days in the month is 25 of 8 hours per day. The company employed 90 workers.The budgeted man-hours are 2,10,000 for the year.

    (Ans: 97.22%; 108.57%; 105.56%)

# CHAPTER-IV

# OVERHEADS

Overhead is otherwise called as indirect cost. Indirect costs are those cost which cannot easily be identified in the cost centre. It could not be allocated to a particular cost centre. It would be apportioned to the cost centre since these costs are commonly incurred for two or more cost centres .On the other hand direct cost can easily be identified in a cost centre.It should be allocated to the respective cost centres. Direct cost constitutes direct meterial, direct labour and direct expenses. Like that, indirect cost constitutes indirect material, indirect labour and indirect expenses.

## I. CLASSIFICATION OF OVERHEADS

Overheads can be classified on the following basis

1. Element -wise classification
2. Functional -wise classification
3. Behaviour -wise classsification

### 1. Element -wise classification

Overhead is classified on the basis of element-wise as follows.

a) Indirect Material cost; b) Indirect Labour cost
c) Indirect expenses

#### *a) Indirect Material cost*

Indirect material cost is those material cost which could not be easily identified in the product. It cannot be allocated and it can be apportioned to the cost centre.*Example:*Lubricating oil, fuel,cotton waste, stores spent for repair and maintenance, wax, nails etc.

#### *b) Indirect Labour cost*

Indirect labour cost is those labour cost which could not be easily identified in the product. It cannot be allocated and it can be apportioned to the cost centre by a common basis of apportionment. *Example :* Salary paid to store keeper, foreman, supervisors, workman compensation , holiday pay, allowances to employees etc.

#### *c) Indirect Expenses*

Indirect expenses are those expenses which could not be identified in the product. This expenses could not be allocated and can be apportioned to the cost centre.*Example :* Insurance, Depreciation for fixed assets, Taxes, Canteen expenses,Rent and rates, Lighting and heating, Hospital expenses, etc.

**2. Functional-wise classification**

According to the functions performed in an organisation overheads can be classified as follows.

a) Manufacturing overhead
b) Administration overhead
c) Selling and Distribution overhead

***a) Manufacturing Overhead***

Manufacturing overhead is otherwise called as Factory overhead.It is the indirect cost incurred in the manufacturing of the product (i.e, in the factory or manufacturing division of the organisation) It includes indirect material, indirect labour and other indirect expenses connected with the factory. These cost should be apportioned to the relevant cost centre on the suitable basis of apportionment. Factory overhead is added with direct material, direct labour and direct expenses to ascertain the prime cost. Hence, factory overhead constitutes some portion of the prime cost.

***b) Administration Overhead***

Administration overhead is the indirect cost incurred for the performance of the administrative function of an organisation. It includes indirect material (Eg : Stationary), indirect labour (Eg : Salary to the staff of the administrative department) and indirect expenses (Eg : Conveyance expenses, Entertainment, Refreshments etc.)

***c) Selling and Distribution Overhead***

Selling and Distribution overhead are the indirect costs incurred for the Selling and Distribution Department. Payment of salary to sales manager, salesmen and other expenses are included in the Selling and Distribution overhead. It includes indirect material (Eg: Stationary) indirect labour (Eg: Salary to the staff of the Selling and distribution department)and indirect expenses (Eg: Conveyance expenses, Refreshments etc.)

**3.Behaviour-wise classification**

Overhead may be classified on the basis of behaviour, as follows.

a) Fixed Overhead
b) Variable Overhead
c) Semi-Variable Overhead

***a) Fixed Overhead***

Fixed overhead are those indirect expenses which remain constant upto certain level of activity .It will not change due to the changes in the volume of production upto certain level. These expenses should be incurred even though there is no production in a period. Since total fixed overhead remains constant, fixed cost per unit of production will vary according to the variation in the units of output. The fixed cost per unit will increase due to the decrease in the volume of production and it will decrease due to the increase in the volume of production. Examples for fixed overhead are rent, salary, interest etc.

***b) Variable Overhead***

Variable overhead are those indirect expenses which varies according to the variation in the unit of production. Hence, the total variable overhead increases due to the increase in the unit of production and decreases due to the decrease in the unit of production. The variable overhead per unit remains constant irrespective of the units of production. Examples for variable overheads are electricity, canteen expenses, consumable stores etc.

***c) Semi-variable Overhead***

Semi-variable overhead are those indirect expenses which are partly fixed and partly variable. It contains fixed element and variable element of indirect expenses.(Eg) Telephone charges, Eletricity charges, Remuneration for salesman with monthly salary plus commission based on sales etc.

## Segragation of Semi-variable overhead into Fixed and Variable overheads

Semi-Variable overhead should be seperated into fixed overhead and variable overhead for the purpose of cost ascertainment, cost planning and cost control. Hence, each semi variable overhead should be classified into two parts namely fixed and variable. It is a complicated process and requires some techniques to be adopted. The following are the important methods for segragating the semi- variable overhead into fixed and variable overheads.

1. Graphic method
2. High-low points method
3. Average method
4. Simultaneous equation method
5. Least square method

### *1.Graphic method*

Under this method semi-variable overhead at various level of activities should be plotted on a graph paper. The X axis of the graph should represent quantity and Y axis should represent cost. The plotted points at the graph represents the semi variable overhead at different level of activities. From the plotted points a straight line of best fit which pass through most of the plotted points should be drawn. The straight line touches a point at Y axis. The point represents the fixed portion of the semi-variable overhead. Hence the remaining amount of the semi-variable overhead is called the variable overhead.

**Illustration: 1**

Find out the fixed overhead from the following information by graphic method.

| Months | Production (in units) | Semi-variable overhead (Rs.) |
|---|---|---|
| January | 700 | 2,900 |
| February | 500 | 2,500 |
| March | 1,200 | 3,900 |
| April | 1,000 | 3,500 |
| May | 800 | 3,100 |
| June | 600 | 2,700 |

***Solution:***

**Segregation of fixed overhead from semi - variable overhead**

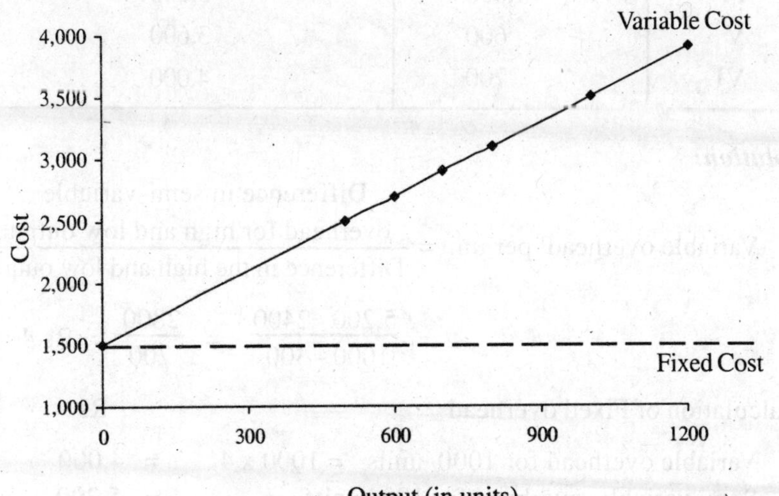

It is clear from the graph that the line drawn through the plotted points representing the different level of activities cuts the Y axis at a point. The point measures the Y axis as 1,500. Hence, the fixed overhead portion of the semivariable overhead is Rs1,500.

### *2. High- low points method*

Under this method the two level of activities (i.e, the low level and high level) should be ascertained. Then the semi-variable overhead for these two levels of activities should be noted. The variable overhead per unit can easily be ascertained from these values .The variable overhead per unit is the ratio between the difference in the cost to the difference in output units between the two level of activities.

$$\text{i.e, Variable overhead per unit} = \frac{\text{Difference in semi-variable overhead}}{\text{Difference in output units}}$$

**Illustration: 2**

Find out the Fixed overhead and Variable overhead from the following particulars by high- low point method.

| Period | Output (units) | Semi-variable overheads (Rs) |
|---|---|---|
| I | 500 | 3,200 |
| II | 300 | 2,400 |
| III | 800 | 4,400 |
| IV | 1,000 | 5,200 |
| V | 600 | 3,600 |
| VI | 700 | 4,000 |

***Solution:***

$$\text{Variable overhead per unit} = \frac{\text{Difference in semi-variable overhead for high and low output}}{\text{Difference in the high and low output}}$$

$$= \frac{5{,}200 - 2400}{1000 - 300} = \frac{2800}{700} = \text{Rs.}4$$

| Calculation of Fixed overhead | | Rs. |
|---|---|---|
| Variable overhead for 1000 units | = 1000 x 4 | = 4,000 |
| Semi variable overhead for 1000 units | | = 5,200 |
| Fixed overhead = 5200 - 4000 | | = 1,200 |

**Fixed and variable overhead for different levels of activities**

| Period | Output (units) | Semi-variable overhead Rs. | Fixed overhead Rs. | Variable overhead Rs. |
|---|---|---|---|---|
| I | 500 | 3,200 | 1,200 | 2,000 |
| II | 300 | 2,400 | 1,200 | 1,200 |
| III | 800 | 4,400 | 1,200 | 3,200 |
| IV | 1,000 | 5,200 | 1,200 | 4,000 |
| V | 600 | 3,600 | 1,200 | 2,400 |
| VI | 700 | 4,000 | 1,200 | 2,800 |

### 3. *Average method*

Under this method the semi-variable overheads for different level of activities should be grouped into two or three sets. Then the average for the grouped output units and semi-variable overheads should be calculated. These data are to be plotted in a graph and the plotted points should be joined so that the line cuts at a point in the Y axis. The distance from the origin to the point measures the Fixed Overhead.

**Illustration: 3**

Find out the fixed overhead by Average Method from the data in data given below:

| Period | Output (units) | Semi-variable overhead (Rs.) |
|---|---|---|
| I | 500 | 4,500 |
| II | 400 | 4,000 |
| III | 800 | 6,000 |
| IV | 1,000 | 7,000 |
| V | 900 | 6,500 |
| VI | 700 | 5,500 |

***Solution:***

The data can be grouped into two categories as follows:

| | | |
|---|---|---|
| Output units | = 500 + 400 + 800 | = 1,700 |
| | = 1000 + 900 + 700 | = 2,600 |
| Average output units | = 1,700 / 3 | = 567 |
| | = 2,600 / 3 | = 867 |
| Semi-variable overhead | = 4500 + 4000 + 6000 | = Rs.14,500 |
| | = 7000 + 6500 + 5500 | = Rs.19,000 |
| Average semi- variable overhead | = 14,500 / 3 | = Rs.4,833 |
| | = 19,000 / 3 | = Rs.6,333 |

**Graph**

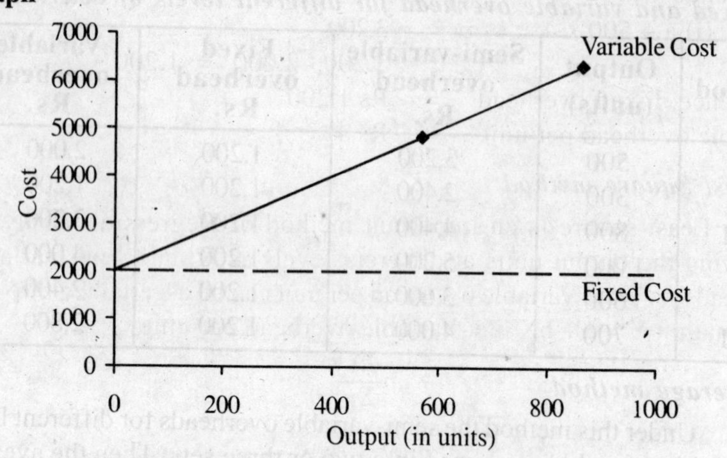


It is clear from the graph that the straight line cuts a point in the Y axis at 2000. Hence, the fixed overhead is Rs.2,000.

### *4. Simultaneous Equation method*

In this method, the straight line equation Y = a+bX should be applied. In this equation Y represents total cost; a represents fixed overhead; b represents variable overhead per unit and X represents output (units). Semi-variable overheads for any two periods should be selected to apply in the simultaneous equations.

**Illustration: 4**

Find out the fixed overhead and variable overhead from the following information by simultaneous equation method.

| Months | Output (Units) | Semi-variable overhead (Rs.) |
|---|---|---|
| January | 500 | 3,200 |
| March | 800 | 4,400 |

***Solution:***

**Calculation of fixed and variable overheads.**

| | | | |
|---|---|---|---|
| Y | | = | a + bX |
| 3200 | | = | a + b500 |
| 4400 | | = | a + b 800 |
| a+ 500b | | = | 3,200 ........... (i) |
| a+ 800 b | | = | 4,400 ........... (ii) |
| (ii) - (i) | 300 b | = | 1,200 |
| | b | = | 1,200 / 300 = 4 |

(i) a + 500 x 4 = 3,200

a = 3,200 - 2,000 = 1,200

Hence, Fixed overhead = Rs.1,200

Variable overhead per unit = Rs.4

***5. Least Square method***

Least square is an important method of Regression Analysis. By taking the output units at different levels as X; and semi-variable overheads as Y the Variable overhead per unit can be ascertained through the equation Y = a + bX i.e, Variable overhead per unit,

$$b = \frac{\Sigma xy}{\Sigma x^2}$$

Where $x = X - \overline{X}$ and $y = Y - \overline{Y}$

**Illustration: 5**

Calculate the fixed overhead and variable overhead per unit by least square method from the following:

| Period | Output (units) | Semi - variable overhead (Rs.) |
|---|---|---|
| I | 700 | 5,500 |
| II | 800 | 6,000 |
| III | 300 | 3,500 |
| IV | 1,000 | 7,000 |
| V | 1,200 | 8,000 |

***Solution:***

**Calculation of fixed and variable overheads.**

| Period | Output (units) X | Semi - variable overhead Y (Rs.) | x $(X-\overline{X})$ (X - 800) | y $(Y-\overline{Y})$ (Y - 6,000) | xy | $x^2$ |
|---|---|---|---|---|---|---|
| I | 700 | 5,500 | -100 | -500 | 50,000 | 10,000 |
| II | 800 | 6,000 | 0 | 0 | 0 | 0 |
| III | 300 | 3,500 | -500 | -2500 | 12,50,000 | 2,50,000 |
| IV | 1,000 | 7,000 | 200 | 1000 | 2,00,000 | 40,000 |
| V | 1,200 | 8,000 | 400 | 2000 | 8,00,000 | 1,60,000 |
| | 4,000 | 30,000 | | | Σxy = 23,00,000 | $\Sigma x^2$ = 4,60,000 |

$\overline{X} = 4{,}000 / 5 = 800$

$\overline{Y} = 30{,}000 / 5 = 6000$

$Y = a + bx$

$$b = \frac{\Sigma xy}{\Sigma x^2} = \frac{23{,}00{,}000}{4{,}60{,}000} = 5$$

Apply any value to the equation, $Y = a + bX$

In units - 1,000, Semi - variable overhead Rs.7,000 is applied as,

$7{,}000 = a + (1{,}000 \times 5)$

$a + 5{,}000 = 7{,}000$

$a = 7{,}000 - 5{,}000 = 2{,}000$

Hence, Fixed overhead = Rs.2,000

Variable overhead = Rs.5 per unit

## FACTORY OVERHEADS

Factory overhead is otherwise called as production overhead or manufacturing overhead. Factory overhead consists of indirect material, indirect labour and indirect expenses. It could not be easily identified in a product and it cannot be allocated but can be apportioned in the cost centre.Examples of factory overheads are consumable store, salary of supervisors and foremen, transport cost of materials,etc. The apportionment of factory overhead is a complicated task and requires special skill.It should be apportioned on some suitable basis of apportionment.

### Accounting of Factory overhead

The following steps are required for the apportionment of factory overhead to the cost centres.

1. Collection and Codification of Factory Overheads
2. Departmentalisation
3. Apportionment of Factory Overheads.
4. Absorption of Factory Overheads

### 1. Collection and Codification of Factory overheads:

Collection and codification are the first step in the distribution of overhead to various cost centres. The factory overhead incurred during the period should be collected from various records and it should be grouped according to the common nature. Then the grouped data should be codified for easy identification.

Codification is the process of assigning numbers, letters or symbols to the grouped factory overheads.

***Methods of Codifications***

Following are the important methods of codification

(i) Numerical codes
(ii) Decimal codes
(iii) Codes with a combination of numbers and alphabets.

***(i) Numerical Codes***

Numerical code is the assignment of numbers to the factory overheads.

(Eg) 6666 Factory Rent
1171 Power expenses
7333 Repairs and Maintenance

***(ii) Decimal Codes***

Decimal code is the assignment of decimals to the factory overheads.

(Eg) 1.1. Indirect material
1.1.1 Lubricating oil
1.1.2 Cotton waste
1.2. Indirect labour
1.2.1 Supervisor's salary
1.2.2. Overtime wage.

***(iii) Codes with a combination of Numbers and Alphabets***

In this type of codification both numbers and alphabets are used.

(Eg) XY 22 Foremen's salary
IM 23 Lubricating oil
IM 54 Wax
IL 25 Supervisor's salary

**2. Departmentalisation**

Departmentalisation is the division of the factory into production cost centres and service cost centres. These two centres are called production departments and service departments.The number of production departments and service departments depend upon the nature and size of the business. The purpose of departmentalisation is for easy apportionment of factory overheads.

**3. Apportionment of Factory Overheads**

Overheads cannot be allocated normally to vaious cost centres. In rare cases the overhead like indirect material, spend for each department can be identified which can be directly allocated to the relevant cost centres. Mostly overheads should be apportioned since it is difficult to identify and allocate the overheads for each department. Overheads are commonly spend for all the departments.It should be apportioned on some common basis.

**Basis of apportionment of Factory overheads**

The following are some common basis of apportionment of factory overheads:

| | Factory overheads | Basis of Apportionment |
|---|---|---|
| 1. | Rent; Rates; Lighting; Depreciation; Repairs and maintenance and Insurance of building | Area occupied |
| 2. | Canteen expenses; Welfare expenses Time-keeping and pay-roll expenses; Medical expenses ; Recreation; Supervisorvising expenses. | Number of employees |
| 3. | Lighting | Light points |
| 4. | Depreciation, Insurance, Repairs and Maintenance of Plant & Machinery | Book value of the Plant & Machinery |
| 5. | Repairs & Maintenance of Plant & Machinery | Machine hours |
| 6. | Heating; Electric power; Steam consumption | Horse power, Kwh |
| 7. | Salary of Supervisors, Factory Manager's salary | Direct labour hours |
| 8. | Audit fees | Sales, Total cost |
| 9. | Delivery vans | Weight, Volume, Kms. |

**Steps in the apportionment of Factory Overhead**

The following are the steps in the apportionment of factory overhead.

1. PRIMARY DISTRIBUTION
2. SECONDARY DISTRIBUTION

**1. PRIMARY DISTRIBUTION**

Primary distribution means the apportionment of overheads to the production departments and service departments. Factory overheads commonly incurred should be apportioned by suitable basis of apportionment to all the departments. Overheads incurred for the individual departments can directly be allocated to the respective departments. Total overhead for the individual departments including the Production and Service Departments can be ascertained after the apportionment.

**Illustration: 6**

Doyle & Co.Ltd has three production departments namely, Assembling , Painting and Finishing; and two service departments namely, Store- keeping and Canteen. The following expenses are incurred for these departments in March 2011.

| | | Rs. |
|---|---|---|
| Indirect Material: | | |
| Production Departments | Assembling | 11,500 |
| | Painting | 9,500 |
| | Finishing | 5,000 |
| Service Departments | Store Keeping | 4,000 |
| | Canteen | 3,500 |
| Indirect Labour | | |
| Production Departments | Assembling | 9,000 |
| | Painting | 7,500 |
| | Finishing | 6,000 |
| Service Departments | Store Keeping | 3,800 |
| | Canteen | 2,600 |
| Rent | | 5,000 |
| Power | | 4,000 |
| Depreciation for machinery | | 4,500 |
| Supervisor's salary | | 6,000 |
| Lighting | | 2,400 |
| Insurance for plant & machinery | | 2,000 |
| Insurance for employees | | 1,200 |

The following further information are also given:

| Particulars | Assem-bling | Painting | Finishing | Storekeeping | Canteen |
|---|---|---|---|---|---|
| No.of workers | 20 | 15 | 10 | 8 | 7 |
| Total wages(Rs.) | 15,000 | 12,000 | 8,000 | 3,000 | 2,000 |
| Value of Plant & Machinery(Rs) | 2,00,000 | 150,000 | 50,000 | - | - |
| Area (Sq.ft) | 600 | 500 | 400 | 300 | 200 |
| Light points | 12 | 10 | 8 | 6 | 4 |

Prepare a departmental distribution summary.

**Solution:**

**Primary (Departmental) Distribution summary**

| Expenses | Basis | Total Rs. | Production Departments | | | Service Departments | |
|---|---|---|---|---|---|---|---|
| | | | Assembling Rs. | Painting Rs. | Finishing Rs. | Store keeping Rs. | Canteen Rs. |
| Indirect - Material | Allocation | 33,500 | 11,500 | 9,500 | 5,000 | 4,000 | 3,500 |
| Indirect - Labour | Allocation | 28,900 | 9,000 | 7,500 | 6,000 | 3,800 | 2,600 |
| Rent | Area | 5,000 | 1,500 | 1,250 | 1,000 | 750 | 500 |
| Power | Plant - Value | 4,000 | 2,000 | 1,500 | 500 | - | - |
| Depreciation | Plant - Value | 4,500 | 2,250 | 1,688 | 562 | - | - |
| Insurance- Plant | Plant - Value | 2,000 | 1,000 | 750 | 250 | - | - |
| Insurance- Worker | Wages | 1,200 | 450 | 360 | 240 | 90 | 60 |
| Supervision | No.of Workers | 6,000 | 2,000 | 1,500 | 1,000 | 800 | 700 |
| Light | Light - Points | 2,400 | 720 | 600 | 480 | 360 | 240 |
| Total | | 87,500 | 30,420 | 24,648 | 15,032 | 9,800 | 7,600 |

## 2. SECONDARY DISTRIBUTION

Secondary distribution is otherwise known as 'Re-apportionment' or 'Re-distribution'. It means distribution of service department costs to all the production departments. The secondary distribution is done on the basis of some common basis of apportionment. The secondary distribution can be done only after the primary distribution. In primary distribution only the cost of the individual service departments can be ascertained. The types and importance of service departments depends upon the nature and size of the business.

The basis of apportionment of service department costs to the production departments are stated as follows:

| Service Departments | Basis of Apportionment |
|---|---|
| 1. Personal, Canteen, Factory office, Recreation, Medical, Payroll, Time-keeping departments | Number of employees, Labour hours, Labour cost |
| 2. Engineering,Maintenance and Repairs Departments | Machine hours, Labour hours, Labour cost |
| 3. Purchasing, Receiving departments | Cost of material, Number of units, Number of orders |
| 4. Store-keeping department | Cost of Material, Number of units, Number of requisitions |

The following are the important methods of Secondary Distribution.

a) Direct Re-apportionment Method
b) Step Ladder Method
c) Reciprocal Distribution Method

***(a) Direct Re-apportionment Method***

In this method the service department costs are directly apportioned to all the prodution departments. The re-apportionment is done on the basis of some suitable basis of apportionment. The service rendered by one service department to another service department is not taken into account under this method.

**Illustration: 7**

The primary distribution statement of KM& Co. Ltd for the month January 2011 shows the following details:

| | Rs. |
|---|---|
| Production departments | |
| X | 32,000 |
| Y | 19,500 |
| Z | 21,500 |
| Service departments | |
| M | 12,000 |
| N | 5,500 |

The cost of service department M is apportioned in the ratio 3 : 2 : 1 and of N is apportioned in the ratio 2 : 2 : 1 for the production departments X, Y and Z respectively.

Prepare a statement showing the apportionment of the expenses by direct distribution method.

***Solution:***

**Secondary Distribution Summary(Direct Distribution Method)**

| Particulars | Total Rs. | X Rs. | Y Rs. | Z Rs. |
|---|---|---|---|---|
| Expenses as per primary distribution | 73,000 | 32,000 | 19,500 | 21,500 |
| Service departments | | | | |
| M (3 : 2 : 1) | 12,000 | 6,000 | 4,000 | 2,000 |
| N (2 : 2 : 1) | 5,500 | 2,200 | 2,200 | 1,100 |
| Total | 90,500 | 40,200 | 25,700 | 24,600 |

**Illustration: 8**

Prepare a departmental distribution summary from the following details:

| Particulars | Production departments | | | Service departments | |
|---|---|---|---|---|---|
| | A | B | C | X | Y |
| Direct Material(Rs) | 18,000 | 12,000 | 10,000 | 6,000 | 4,000 |
| Direct Wages(Rs) | 11,000 | 8,000 | 7,000 | 4,000 | 2,000 |
| Direct Expenses(Rs) | 4,000 | 3,000 | 2,000 | 1,230 | 1,220 |
| Area Sq.ft | 300 | 400 | 200 | 200 | 100 |
| Plant & Mach.(Rs) | 80,000 | 70,000 | 60,000 | 20,000 | - |
| No. of workers | 40 | 35 | 25 | 20 | 10 |
| Light points | 25 | 20 | 15 | 10 | 10 |
| Horse power | 200 | 150 | 100 | 50 | - |

The expenses incurred by the company for the period are as follows:

| | Rs. |
|---|---|
| General overhead | 16,000 |
| Rent | 6,000 |
| Lighting | 800 |
| Power | 1,500 |
| Store-keeping | 1,000 |
| Amenities to workers | 1,300 |
| Depreciation of plant | 6,900 |
| Repairs of plant | 2,300 |

The Company decided to apportion the expenses of service department X in the ratio of direct wages and of Y in the ratio 5 : 3 : 2 to departments A,B and C respectively.

***Solution:***

**Statement of Primary Distribution**

| Particulars | Basis | Total Rs. | Production Departments | | | Service Depts. | |
|---|---|---|---|---|---|---|---|
| | | | A Rs. | B Rs. | C Rs. | X Rs. | Y Rs. |
| Direct Material | Actual | 50,000 | 18,000 | 12,000 | 10,000 | 6,000 | 4,000 |
| Direct Wages | Actual | 32,000 | 11,000 | 8,000 | 7,000 | 4,000 | 2,000 |
| Dirct Expenses | Actual | 11,450 | 4,000 | 3,000 | 2,000 | 1,230 | 1,220 |
| General Overhead | Direct Wages (11:8:7:4:2) | 16,000 | 5,500 | 4,000 | 3,500 | 2,000 | 1,000 |
| Rent | Area (3:4:2:2:1) | 6,000 | 1,500 | 2,000 | 1,000 | 1,000 | 500 |
| Lighting | Light Points (5:4:3:2:2) | 800 | 250 | 200 | 150 | 100 | 100 |
| Power | Horse Power (4:3:2:1) | 1,500 | 600 | 450 | 300 | 150 | - |
| Store-Keeping | Direct Material (9:6:5:3:2) | 1,000 | 360 | 240 | 200 | 120 | 80 |
| Amenities to Workers | No. of Workers (8:7:5:4:2) | 1,300 | 400 | 350 | 250 | 200 | 100 |
| Depreciation of Plant | Value of Plant (8:7:6:2) | 6,900 | 2,400 | 2,100 | 1,800 | 600 | - |
| Repairs of Plant | Value of Plant (8:7:6:2) | 2,300 | 800 | 700 | 600 | 200 | - |
| Total | | 1,29,250 | 44,810 | 33,040 | 26,800 | 15,600 | 9,000 |

**Statement of Secondary Distribution**

| Particulars | Basis of Apportion-ment | Total Rs. | Production Departments | | |
|---|---|---|---|---|---|
| | | | A Rs. | B Rs. | C Rs. |
| As per primary distribuation | Direct | 1,04,650 | 44,810 | 33,040 | 26,800 |
| Service Department X | Direct Wages (11:8:7) | 15,600 | 6,600 | 4,800 | 4,200 |
| Service Department Y | 5:3:2 | 9,000 | 4,500 | 2,700 | 1,800 |
| Total | | 1,29,250 | 55,910 | 40,540 | 32,800 |

***(b) Step Ladder Method***

This method is also known as Step Method.In this method the service departments are classified according to their importance. The cost of most important service department is apportioned first to other remaining service departments and to all the production departments. Like that, the cost of the next important service departments are taken for apportionment. Hence, least important service department cost is apportioned at the end only to all the production departments.

**Illustration: 9**

A Ltd has 3 production departments namely X,Y and Z and 4 service departments namely,Maintenance, Store-keeping, Time- Keeping and Canteen. The expenses of these departments for the month January 2011 as per primary distribution are as follows:

| | | Rs. |
|---|---|---|
| Production departments: | X | 18,500 |
| | Y | 14,500 |
| | Z | 12,000 |
| Service departments: | | |
| | Maintenance | 4,300 |
| | Store-keeping | 10,200 |
| | Time-keeping | 9,500 |
| | Canteen | 16,000 |

The following additional information are also given:

| Departments | No. of employees | Direct material consumed Rs. | Plant & Machinery Rs. |
|---|---|---|---|
| Production Depts: X | 30 | 15,000 | 80,000 |
| Y | 20 | 13,000 | 70,000 |
| Z | 10 | 12,000 | 50,000 |
| Service Depts: | | | |
| Maintenance | 15 | 4,000 | 20,000 |
| Store-keeping | 10 | - | - |
| Time-keeping | 5 | - | - |
| Canteen | 10 | 1,000 | - |

Prepare a statement showing the apportionment of Service department costs to the Production departments by Step Ladder method.

***Solution:***

**Statement of Distributiuon of Overhead**

| Particulars | Service Departments | | | | Production Departments | | |
|---|---|---|---|---|---|---|---|
| | Time-keeping Rs. | Canteen Rs. | Store-keeping Rs. | Maintenance Rs. | X Rs. | Y Rs. | Z Rs. |
| As per primary distribution | 9,500 | 16,000 | 10,200 | 4,300 | 18,500 | 14,500 | 12,000 |
| Time-keeping (Basis- No. of workers- 2:2:3:6:4:2) | (9,500) | 1,000 | 1,000 | 1,500 | 3,000 | 2,000 | 1,000 |
| Canteen (Basis- No.of workers- 2 : 3 : 6 :4 : 2) | | (17,000) | 2,000 | 3,000 | 6,000 | 4,000 | 2,000 |
| Store-keeping (Basis- Direct material 4 : 15 : 13 :12) | | | (13,200) | 1,200 | 4,500 | 3,900 | 3,600 |
| Maintenance (Basis- Plant & Machinery 8 : 7 : 5) | | | | (10,000) | 4,000 | 3,500 | 2,500 |
| Total | | | | | 36,000 | 27,900 | 21,100 |

### (c) Reciprocal Distribution method

The service rendered by one service department to another service department is not taken into account in the Direct Distribution method and is not fully taken into account in the Step Ladder method. Reciprocal Distribution method is a method of secondary distribution which takes into account of the inter service department costs while reapportionment of it to all the production departments. There are three important methods of apportionment in Reciprocal Distribution method. They are

(i) Repeated Distribution method
(ii) Trial and Error method
(iii) Simultaneous Equation method

#### *(i) Repeated Distribution Method*

In this method each service department expenses are repeatedly apportioned to other service departments and all the production departments. The basis for apportionment of the service departments is the percentage (or ratio) of services rendered by each service department to other service departments and all the production departments.

For example, A company has 3 production departments namely, A, B and C and 2 service departments namely X and Y. The service department X renders service to A, B and C and also to Y. Hence, expenses of X should be shared by A, B, C and Y. Like that the expesnses of Y should be shared by A, B, C and X. This kind of distribution should be done to the respective departments repeatedly till the single digit value of the service department exists for distribution. Then the single digit value of a service department should be distributed only to the production departments.

**Illustration: 10**

A manufacturing company has 3 production departments namely X, Y and Z and 2 service departments namely A and B. The departmental distribution summary shows the following details:

| Departments | | Rs. |
|---|---|---|
| Production Depts. | X | 32,000 |
| | Y | 45,000 |
| | Z | 62,000 |
| Service Depts. | A | 15,000 |
| | B | 12,000 |

The basis of apportionment of service department costs to the production departments are stated as follows:

| Depts. | X | Y | Z | A | B |
|---|---|---|---|---|---|
| A | 30% | 10% | 40% | - | 20% |
| B | 20% | 40% | 30% | 10% | - |

Prepare a statement showing the distribution of the service department expenses to the production departments on the basis of repeated distribution method.

***Solution:***

**Statement of Secondary Distribution**

| **Particulars** | **Basis of apportion-ment** | **Production Departments** | | | **Service Departments** | |
|---|---|---|---|---|---|---|
| | | **X Rs.** | **Y Rs.** | **Z Rs.** | **A Rs.** | **B Rs.** |
| As per primary distribution | | 32,000 | 45,000 | 62,000 | 15,000 | 12,000 |
| Service Dept. A. | 3:1: 4:2 | 4,500 | 1500 | 6,000 | (15,000) | 3,000 |
| Service Dept. B | 2:4:3:1 | 3,000 | 6,000 | 4,500 | 1,500 | (15,000) |
| A | 3:1:4:2 | 450 | 150 | 600 | (1,500) | 300 |
| B | 2:4:3:1 | 60 | 120 | 90 | 30 | (300) |
| A | 3:1:4:2 | 9 | 3 | 12 | (30) | 6 |
| B | 2:4:3:1 | 1 | 3 | 2 | - | (6) |
| Total | | 40,020 | 52,776 | 73,204 | - | - |

***(ii) Trial and Error Method***

In this method, each service department costs are apportioned repeatedly to other service departments on the basis of the inter services performed by them.The basis for apportionment is the percentage of service rendered to other service departments. Then the total cost of the service departments, after the repeated apportionment should be calculated. This total cost of each service department would be apportioned to all the production departments on the basis of the percentage of services rendered by them.

**Illustration: 11**

A manufacturing company has 3 production departments namely A,B and C and 2 service departments namely X and Y. The departmental distribution summary of the company for the month December 2011 shows the following details:

| | | Rs. |
|---|---|---|
| Production Departments | A | 27,500 |
| | B | 32,500 |
| | C | 21,500 |
| Service Departments | X | 22,000 |
| | Y | 14,000 |

The basis of apportionment of service department costs to production departments are as follows:

| Departments | A | B | C | X | Y |
|---|---|---|---|---|---|
| X | 40% | 30% | 20% | - | 10% |
| Y | 35% | 20% | 25% | 20% | - |

Prepare a statement showing the apportionment of service department expenses to the production departments on the basis of Trial and Error Method.

***Solution:***

**Statement of total cost of Service Departments**

| Particulars | Service Departments | |
|---|---|---|
| | X (Rs.) | Y (Rs.) |
| Expenses as per primary distribution | 22,000 | 14,000 |
| 10% of Rs.22,000 to Y | - | 2,200 |
| 20% of Rs.16,200 to X | 3,240 | |
| 10% of Rs.3,240 to Y | | 324 |
| 20% of Rs.324 to X | 65 | |
| 10% of Rs.65 to Y | | 7 |
| 20% of Rs.7 to X | 1 | |
| Total | 25,306 | 16,531 |

**Secondary Distribution summary**

| Particulars | Production Departments | | | Total Rs. |
|---|---|---|---|---|
| | A Rs. | B Rs. | C Rs. | |
| Expenses as per primary distribution | 27,500 | 32,500 | 21,500 | 81,500 |
| Service Department X (Rs. 25,306) -Basis 40%, 30%, 20% | 10,122 | 7,592 | 5,061 | 22,775 |
| Service Department Y (Rs. 16.531) -Basis 35%, 20%, 25% | 5,786 | 3,306 | 4,133 | 13,225 |
| Total | 43,408 | 43,398 | 30,694 | 117,500 |

Note: Total expenses of production departments and service departments is same as Rs.1,17,500.

***(iii) Simultaneous Equation Method***

In this method, the total cost of each service departments, after taking into account of the inter departmental service cost, is ascertained by solving the simultaneous equations. The simultaneous equations are formed on the basis of the percentage of services rendered by them to other service departments. The total cost of service departments calculated through the simultaneous equations would be apportioned to all the production departments on the basis of the percentage of service rendered by the service departments.

**Illustration: 12**

K Ltd has 3 production departments namely X,Y and Z and 2 service departments namely A and B. The expenses incurred to these departments for 3 months ending March 2011 are stated as follows:

| | | Rs. |
|---|---|---|
| Production Departments: | X | 52,500 |
| | Y | 47,000 |
| | Z | 41,500 |
| Service Departments: | A | 18,000 |
| | B | 22,000 |

The basis of apportionment of the service department expenses to production departments are as follows:

| Departments | X | Y | Z | A | B |
|---|---|---|---|---|---|
| A | 35% | 25% | 30% | - | 10% |
| B | 40% | 30% | 10% | 20% | - |

Prepare a statement showing the distribution of service department expenses to the production departments on the basis of Simultaneous Equation method.

***Solution:***

**Calculation of total expenses of the Service Departments.**

Let x be the total expense of the service department A and y be the total expenses of the service department B.

Hence, x = 18,000 +.2y

y = 22,000 +.1x

i.e, 10x - 2y = 18,0000..................................(i)

-x +10y = 22,0000.................................(ii)

(ii)x10; -10x +100y = 2200000................................(iii)

10x - 2y = 180000....................................(i)

(iii) + (i) 98y = 2380000

$$y = \frac{2380000}{98} = 24,286$$

(i) 10x - 2(24,286) = 1,80,000

10x = 1,80,000 + 48,572

10x = 2,28,572

$$x = \frac{2,28,572}{10} = 22,857$$

**Secondary Distribution Summary**

| **Particulars** | **Production Departments** | | | **Total Rs.** |
|---|---|---|---|---|
| | **A Rs.** | **B Rs.** | **C Rs.** | |
| As per primary distribution | 52,500 | 47,000 | 41,500 | 141,000 |
| Service Department A (Rs.22,857) | | | | |
| Basis: 35%, 25%, 30% | 8,000 | 5,714 | 6,857 | 20,571 |
| Service Department B (Rs.24286) | | | | |
| Basis: 40%, 30%, 10% | 9,714 | 7,286 | 2,429 | 19,429 |
| Total | 70,214 | 60,000 | 50,786 | 181,000 |

## ABSORPTION OF OVERHEAD

Absorption of overhead is a process of apportionment of overheads of the production departments according to the number of units of production, or machine hours or labour hours etc. The total overhead of each production department is known through the primary and secondary distribution.

The overhead of each departments may need to be apportioned when portion of the production is sold or giving quotation for a specified quantity of the product.The apportionment of the overheads is done with the help of overhead rates.

### *Overhead Absorption Rates*

Overhead Absorption Rate is the rate at which the overheads are apportioned. It is calculated by dividing the total overhead by a suitable base. The base may be number of units, machine hours, labour hours etc. The selection of suitable base depends upon the nature of business, nature of production and the types of requirement.

### *Kinds of Overhead Absorption Rates*

The important types of overhead absorption rates are as follows

1. Actual Overhead Rate
2. Predetermined Overhead Rate
3. Blanket Overhead Rate
4. Multiple Overhead Rate

### 1. Actual Overhead Rate

Actual Overhead Rate is calculated by dividing the actual overhead incurred for a period with the actual quantum of the basis (value of quantity) of the period

$$\text{(i.e.) Actual Overhead Rate} = \frac{\text{Actual Overhead of the period}}{\text{The total quantum of basis ( value or quantity)}}$$

The period of the actual overhead rate may either be a month or 3 months or 6 months or one year etc. The quantum of basis may be number of units, weight, machine hour, labour hour etc.

### 2. Predetermined Overhead Rate

Predetermined Overhead Rate is otherwise called as Budgeted Overhead Rate. The predetermined overhead rate is calculated by dividing the budgeted overhead for the period with budgeted total quantum of basis (value or quantity).

i.e., Predetermined Overhead Rate = $\frac{\text{Budgeted overhead for the period}}{\text{Budgeted base of the period}}$

Budgeted overhead and the base are determined on the basis of the actual overheads of the previous periods. Budgeted base may be number of units, weight, machine hours, labour hours etc.

**3. Blanket Overhead Rate**

Blanket overhead rate is also known as single overhead rate or Plant wide rate. Blanket overhead rate is a single overhead rate for the factory as a whole. This is possible for a small factory which provides single product where the overhead rates for different operations are uniform.

**4. Multiple Overhead Rate**

Multiple overhead rate means different overhead rates for different cost centres. It may be calculated for different production departments and different service departments.

## METHODS OF ABSORPTION OF PRODUCTION OVERHEADS

The following are the important methods of absorption of production overheads

1. Percentage of Direct Material cost
2. Percentage of Direct Wages
3. Percentage of Prime cost
4. Direct Labour Hour Rate
5. Machine Hour Rate.

The overheads may also be apportioned on the basis of (i) Rate per unit of production and (ii) Selling Price method.

***1. Percentage of Direct Material Cost***

In this method overhead rate is calculated by dividing the total overhead for a period with Direct material cost for the period

i.e., Overhead Rate = $\frac{\text{Overhead for the period x 100}}{\text{Direct Meterial cost}}$

(Eg) If Overhead for a month is Rs.60,000 and the direct material cost for the month is Rs.2,00,000 then the overhead

$$\text{Rate} = \frac{60{,}000 \times 100}{2{,}00{,}000} = 30\%$$

It means that Overhead is 30% of direct material cost.

This method is suitable for concerns (i) where the raw material cost is an important factor which influences the overheads and (ii) the price of raw material is stable for a period.

***2. Percentage of Direct Labour Cost***

In this method overhead rate is calculated by dividing the total overhead for a period with the Direct labour cost for the period

$$\text{i.e., Overhead Rate} = \frac{\text{Overhead for the period}}{\text{Direct Labour Cost}} \times 100$$

(Eg) If Overhead for a month is Rs.20,000 and the direct labour cost is Rs.80,000 then,

$$\text{the Overhead Rate} = \frac{20{,}000}{80{,}000} \times 100 = 25\%$$

It means that overhead is 25% of the direct labour cost

This method is suitable when the direct labour cost is the major factor which influences the overhead. This method is advisable for concerns where the total wages remains stable. It is advisable for concerns which follow piece rate system of wage payment.

***3. Percentage of Prime Cost***

Under this method overhead rate is calculated by dividing the total overhead for a period by the prime cost of the period

$$\text{i.e., Overhead Rate} = \frac{\text{Overhead for the period} \times 100}{\text{Prime Cost}}$$

Prime cost is the total cost of direct material, direct labour and direct expenses. If direct expense is not available then the total of direct material cost and direct labour cost would be taken into account. (Eg)If the overhead is Rs.40,000, direct material cost is Rs.1,10,000, direct labour cost is Rs.80,000 and direct expense is Rs.10,000

$$\text{then the Overhead Rate} = \frac{40{,}000}{(110{,}000+80{,}000+10{,}000)} \times 100 = 20\%$$

It means the Overhead is 20% on Prime cost.

***4. Direct Labour Hour Rate***

In this method overhead Rate is calculated by dividing the total overhead for a period with direct labour hours involved for the period

$$\text{i.e., Overhead Rate} = \frac{\text{Overhead for the period}}{\text{Direct Labour Hours}}$$

This method is suitable for concerns where labour is an important factor of production.

**Illustration: 13**

M Ltd has three production departments namely X,Y and Z and a service department namely A.The expenses for these departments for the month September 2011 are as follows:

| Particulars | Total (Rs) | Departments | | | |
|---|---|---|---|---|---|
| | | X | Y | Z | A |
| Time Keeping | 6,000 | - | - | - | - |
| Rent | 12,000 | - | - | - | - |
| Welfare | 4,000 | - | - | - | - |
| Lighting & Power | 3,000 | - | - | - | - |
| Supervisors Salary(Rs) | 11,000 | 4,000 | 3,000 | 2,000 | 2,000 |
| Others (Rs) | 2,000 | 800 | 400 | 600 | 200 |
| Time-keeping | | 30% | 30% | 20% | 20% |
| Number of workers | | 40 | 30 | 20 | 10 |
| Area in sq. feet | | 400 | 600 | 700 | 300 |
| Light Points | | 20 | 15 | 10 | 5 |
| Service rendered by service department | | 60% | 25% | 15% | - |

The working days in September 2011 are 25 days of 8 hours each. Assume that all the departments work with full attendance.

Calculate Labour hour rate for all the three production departments.

(Adapted: C.A. Inter)

***Solution:***

**Calculation of Labour Hour Rate**

| Particulars | Basis of Apportion-ment | Total | Production Depts | | | Service Depts |
|---|---|---|---|---|---|---|
| | | | X(Rs.) | Y(Rs.) | Z (Rs.) | A (Rs.) |
| Time-keeping | 3:3:2:2 | 6,000 | 1,800 | 1,800 | 1,200 | 1,200 |
| Rent | Area (4:6:7:3) | 12,000 | 2,400 | 3,600 | 4,200 | 1,800 |
| Welfare | No.of workers (4:3:2:1) | 4,000 | 1,600 | 1,200 | 800 | 400 |
| Lighting and power | Light Points (4:3:2:1) | 3,000 | 1,200 | 900 | 600 | 300 |
| Supervisor's Salary | Direct | 11,000 | 4,000 | 3,000 | 2,000 | 2,000 |
| Others | Direct | 2,000 | 800 | 400 | 600 | 200 |
| | | 38,000 | 11,800 | 10,900 | 9,400 | 5,900 |
| Allocation of Service Dept. Cost | 60%,25%,15% (12:5:3) | - | 3,540 | 1,475 | 885 | (5,900) |
| Total | | 38,000 | 15,340 | 12,375 | 10,285 | - |
| Labour Hours | @200 hours for 40, 30, 20 | - | 8,000 | 6,000 | 4,000 | - |
| Labour Hour Rate | - | | 1.92 | 2.06 | 2.57 | |

### 5. *Machine Hour Rate*

In this method overhead Rate is calculated by dividing the overhead for a period with the number of machine hours.

$$\text{i.e., Overhead Rate} = \frac{\text{Overhead for the period}}{\text{Number of Machine Hours}}$$

The overhead for Machine Hour Rate is classified into two catagories. They are (a) Fixed charges and (b) Variable or machine expenses.

**(a) Fixed or Standing charges**

Expenses like Rent and Rate, Supervision, Insurance, Heating and Lighting, Lubricating oil and Consumable Stores and Miscellaneous expenses are called standing charges.

Rent and Rates are apportioned on the basis of floor area occupied by each machine; Supervision is apportioned on the basis of the value of Machine; Heating and Lighting is apportioned on the basis of horse power.

**(b) Variable or Machine Expenses**

Expenses like Depreciation, Power and Repairs are called Variable expenses.

Depreciation is apportioned on the basis of value of machines; Power is apportioned on the basis of meter reading or horse power of machines; Repair is apportioned on the basis of value of machine.

**Illustration: 14**

Calculate machine hour rate for machine X from the following data:

| | |
|---|---|
| Cost of Machine | Rs.80,000 |
| Effective working life | 12,000 hours |
| Estimated scrap value | Rs.6000 |
| Running time per week | 40 hours |
| Repair and maintenance charges per week | Rs.100 |
| Standing charges allocated for the week | Rs.500 |
| Power used by the machine | 2 units per hour @ Rs.2.50 per hour |

***Solution:***

**Calculation of Machine Hour Rate**

| Particulars | Per hour Rs. |
|---|---|
| Standing Charges (500/40) | 12.50 |
| Machine Expenses | |
| Depreciation $\left(\frac{80{,}000-6{,}000}{12{,}000}\right)$ | 6.17 |
| Repairs and Maintenance $\frac{100}{40}$ | 2.50 |
| Power (2x2.50) | 5.00 |
| Machine Hour Rate | 26.17 |

**Illustration: 15**

Compute the Machine Hour Rate from the following:

| | |
|---|---|
| Cost of Machine | Rs.200,000 |
| Other Charges (Freight and Installation) | Rs.30,000 |
| Working life | 12 years |
| Working hours | 2,400 per year |
| Scrap value | Rs.5,000 |
| Electric power | 5 units per hour @ Rs.1.50 per hour |
| Steam | 30 paise per hour |
| Water | 10 paise per hour |
| Repairs | 10% of the depreciation |
| Rent per annum | Rs.12,000 |
| Lubricating oil and consumable stores | @ Rs.16 per day of 8 hours per day |
| Wages of Machine operator | @ Rs.32 per day. |

***Solution:***

**Calculation of Machine Hour Rate**

| **Particulars** | **Per hour Rs.** |
|---|---|
| Standing Charges: | |
| Rent (12,000/2,400) | 5.00 |
| Lubricating oil & Consumable stores (16/8) | 2.00 |
| Wages of Operators (32/8) | 4.00 |
| Total standing charge | 11.00 |

| | |
|---|---|
| **Machine expense:** Depreciation $\left(\frac{200,000+30,000-5,000}{12 \times 2,400}\right)$ | 7.81 |
| Repairs (10% of 7.81) | 0.78 |
| Power | 1.50 |
| Steam | .30 |
| Water | .10 |
| Machine Hour Rate | 21.49 |

**Illustration: 16**

Calculate comprehensive Machine hour rate from the following:

| | |
|---|---|
| Cost of Machine | Rs.280,000 |
| Estimated scrap value | Rs.10,000 |
| Life of the machine | 9 years |

Depreciation is calculated on straight line basis

| | |
|---|---|
| Departmental overhead | Rs. |
| (i) Supervision per annum | 60,000 |
| (ii) Rent per annum | 48,000 |
| (iii) Heat and Light per annum | 24,000 |
| Reserve equipment cost per annum | 10,000 |

Power cost per hour of running time Rs.2

Hours run on production for the year - 2,000

Setting and adjusting time for the year - 300 hours

Cost of labour Rs.10 per hour

For setting and adjusting full labours are required and for running the machine one worker can manage 4 machines.

Total area occupied by the company is 1,50,000 sq.feet.

Area occupied by the machine is 5,000 sq.feet. There are 20 machines in the department.

***Solution:***

**Calculation of Comprehensive Machine Hour Rate**

| **Particulars** | **Rs.** |
|---|---|
| **Standing charges:** | |
| Supervision $\left(\frac{60,000}{20}\right)$ | 3,000 |
| Rent $\left(\frac{48,000 \times 5,000}{150,000}\right)$ | 1,600 |
| Heat and Light $\left(\frac{24,000 \times 5,000}{150,000}\right)$ | 800 |

| | |
|---|---|
| Depreciation $\left(\frac{280,000 - 10,000}{9}\right)$ | 30,000 |
| Reserve Equipment $\left(\frac{10,000}{20}\right)$ | 500 |
| Labour cost for setting and adjustment (300x10) | 3,000 |
| Total standing chaιges for 2000 hours | 38,900 |
| Standing charges for one hour $\left(\frac{38,900}{2000}\right)$ | 19.45 |
| **Machine Charges:** | |
| Power | 2.00 |
| Labour for running the machine (1/4x10) | 2.50 |
| Comprehensive Machine Hour Rate | 23.95 |

**Illustration: 17**

The particulars related to a machine in a manufacturing company are stated as follows:

| | |
|---|---|
| Cost of the machine | Rs.5,00,000 |
| Estimated life of the machine | 12 years |
| Scrap Value | Rs.20,000 |
| Running time for the year 40 weeks @ 45 hours per week | |
| Setting up time for the year | 180 hours |
| Setting up cost for 5 machines was Rs.80 per hour | |
| Maintenance of the machine for the year | 200 hours |
| Maintenance cost per year | Rs.2,000 |
| Requirement of chemical per week | Rs.240 |
| Electricity consumed is 5 units per hour @ Rs.2 per unit | |
| Electricity is required only for running the machine. | |
| Departmental overhead allocated to the machine for the year | Rs.32,000 |
| Wages for the 3 operators per week | Rs.1,200 |

The operators operate 4 more machines of this kind in addition to this machine.

Calculate machine hour rate with the assumption that

(i) setting up time is productive and

(ii) setting up time is unproductive.

***Solution:***

**Calculation of Machine Hour Rate**

**(i) When Setting up cost is productive**

| Particulars | | Rs. |
|---|---|---|
| **Standing Charges:** | | |
| Depreciation | $\frac{(500,000 - 20,000)}{12}$ | 40,000 |
| Chemical | 240 x 40 | 9,600 |
| Overhead | | 32,000 |
| Setting up Cost | $\frac{180 \times 80}{5}$ | 2,880 |
| Standing charges for 40 x 45 hours | | 84,480 |
| Standing charges for one hour | $\frac{84,480}{1,800}$ | 46.93 |
| **Machine Charges for one hour:** | | |
| Wages | $\frac{3 \times 1,200}{5 \times 45}$ | 16.00 |
| Electricity | (5 x 2) | 10.00 |
| Maintenance | $\frac{2000}{200}$ | 10.00 |
| Machine Hour rate | | 82.93 |

**(ii) When Setting up cost is unproductive.**

| Particulars | | Rs. |
|---|---|---|
| **Standing Charges:** | | |
| Depreciation | $\frac{(500,000 - 20,000)}{12}$ | 40,000 |
| Chemical | 240 x 40 | 9,600 |
| Overhead | | 32,000 |
| Standing charges for (1800 - 180) hours | | 81,600 |
| Standing charges for one hour | $\frac{81,600}{1,620}$ | 50.37 |
| **Machine Charges for one hour:** | | |
| Wages | $\frac{3 \times 1200}{5 \times 45}$ | 16.00 |
| Electricity | (5 x 2) | 10.00 |
| Maintenance | $\frac{1800}{180}$ | 10.00 |
| Machine Hour rate | | 86.37 |

**Illustration: 18**

The estimated expenses for a manufacturing company are on the following basis:

| | |
|---|---|
| Number of machines | 10 |
| Normal working hours in a week | 38 hours |
| Number of weekly loss of hours on maintenance | 3 hours per machine |
| Estimated annual overhead | Rs.70,000 |
| Estimated direct wage rate per hour per machine | Rs.10 |
| Number of weeks worked | 40 |
| Actual expenses incurred for 4 weeks are as follows | |
| Machine hours produced | 1,500 |
| Overhead incurred | Rs.7,000 |
| Wages incurred | Rs.1,59,000 |

Calculate overhead rate per machine hour and under or over absorption of wages and overheads.

(Adapted: C.A)

***Solution:***

(i) Estimated effective hours per year for 10 machine = 40 x (38-3) x 10 machines
= 40 x 35 x 10 = 14,000 hours

Estimated overhead per year = Rs.70,000

Overhead absorption rate per machine hour = $\frac{70,000}{14,000}$ = Rs.5

(ii) (a) Overhead absorbed = 1,500 x 5 = Rs.7,500
Overhead incurred = Rs.7,000
Over-absorption of overhead = 7,500-7,000 = Rs.500

(b) Wages absorbed = 38 hours x 4 weeks x Rs.10 x 10 machines
= Rs.1,52,000

Wages incurred = Rs.1,59,000

Under absorbed wages = 1,59,000-1,52,000
= Rs.7,000

## ADMINISTRATION OVERHEAD

The Institute of Cost and Management Accountants (ICMA) London defined administration cost as the cost of formulating the policy, direct the organisation, and controlling the operation of an undertaking, which is not related direct to a production, selling, research or development activity or function.

It is clear from the definition that administration costs are those costs which are not directly related to the production or distribution. Hence, the costs are indirect in nature.The administration overhead consists of the following indirect cost.

1. Indirect Material cost, like printing and stationary and other office supplies.
2. Indirect Labour cost, like salary and allowance for Chairman, Managing Directors, Directors and other administrative staff.
3. Other Indirect expenses like, Rent, Rates and Insurance for the office, Electricity, Depreciation for office building, Legal charges etc.

Administrative overhead is an important item of cost for a concern. It is a part of the cost of production. Hence, it should be added with the cost of production. Normally the Administration overhead is added with the Factory cost to ascertain the cost of production. In the case of estimation of administration overhead, it may be given either on the basis of value or on the basis of percentage to works cost.

## SELLING AND DISTRIBUTION OVERHEADS

Selling and distribution overheads are the indirect expenses incurred for selling and distribution of a product. Since selling and distribution are related activities, it has been treated as a single item for the ascertainment of the cost of sales.

Selling and distribution overhead consists of the following indirect cost:

1. Indirect Material cost like, printing, stationary equipments for the selling department.
2. Indirect Labour cost like, salary, commision and allowances for the staff of the selling and distribution department.
3. Other indirect expenses like advertisement and sales promotion expenses, transport cost, warehousing and storage rent etc.

### *Accounting of Selling and Distribution Overheads*

Selling and Distribution overheads are part of the total cost of production. It is treated after treating the direct cost and administrative overhead. In the cost sheet selling and distribution overhead are added with the cost of production to ascertain the cost of sales.

**Illustration: 19**

A manufacturing company provides the following information from its books under the head 'Establishment'.

| | Rs. |
|---|---|
| Director's remuneration | 4,000 |
| Travelling expenses for Sales Manager | 1,750 |
| Commission to agents | 7,500 |
| Warehouse wages | 1,900 |
| Warehouse repairs | 600 |
| Office Lighting | 1,100 |
| Office Salaries | 5,500 |
| Lighting of warehouse | 900 |
| Rent, Rate and Insurance of warehouse | 1,800 |
| Rent, Rate and Insurance of office | 2,000 |
| Bad debts | 1,200 |
| Discount allowed | 3,500 |
| Donation | 1,000 |
| Bank charges | 700 |
| Printing and stationery for selling department | 2,300 |
| Trade Magazine | 500 |

Prepare an overhead analysis statement

(Adapted: ICWAI)

***Solution:***

**Overhead Analysis Statement**

| Particulars | Rs. | Rs. |
|---|---|---|
| (i) Selling Overhead: | | |
| Commision to agents | 7,500 | |
| Printing and stationery | 2,300 | |
| Travelling expenses | 1,750 | |
| Discount allowed | 3,500 | |
| Bad debts | 1,200 | |
| Trade magazine | 500 | |
| | | 16,750 |
| (ii) Distribution Overhead: | | |
| Rent, Rate and Insurance of warehouse | 1,800 | |
| Lighting of warehouse | 900 | |
| Warehouse wage | 1,900 | |
| Warehouse repair | 600 | |
| | | 5,200 |

| | | |
|---|---|---|
| (iii) Administration Overhead: | | |
| Director's remuneration | 4,000 | |
| Rent Rate and Insurance of office | 2,000 | |
| Office salaries | 5,500 | |
| Office lighting | 1,100 | |
| | | 12,600 |
| (iv) Others: | | |
| Bank charges | 700 | |
| Donation | 1,000 | |
| | | 1,700 |
| Total | | 36,250 |

## OVER ABSORPTION AND UNDER ABSORPTION OF OVERHEADS

Over-absorption or under- absorption of overheads arises when the company has predetermined rate for absortption of overhead. If the amount of overhead absorbed is higher than the overhead incurred, it is called over-absorption of overhead. (Eg.) If the overhead recovered (absorbed) is Rs.24,000 and the actual overhead is Rs.21,000, then the over-absorbed overhead is Rs.3,000. Over-absorption of overhead is a profit for the company. If the amount of overhead absorbed is less than the overhead incurred, it is called under-absorption of overhead. (Eg.) If the overhead rcovered is Rs.20,000 and the actual overhead is Rs.25,000, then the under-absorbed overhead is Rs.5,000. Under-absorption of overhead is a loss for the company.

**Treatment of over-absorption or under-absorption of overhead**

There are three important methods for treating over-absorption and under-absorption. They are,

1. Use of supplementary Overhead Absorption Rates
2. Write off to Costing Profits & Loss Account
3. Carry Forward to the Accounts of Next Period.

***1. Use of supplementary Overhead Absorption Rates***

This method is applied when the over or under absorption of overhead is of greater value. In this method a supplementary Overhead Absorption rate is calculated by dividing the over or under absorbed overhead with the Actual value of the base. For over-absorbed overhead, the supplementary overhead rate is called Negative supplementary Overhead rate. Over-absorbed overhead should be deducted on the basis of the rate. For under-absorbed overhead the supplementary overhead rate is called Positive Supplementary overhead rate.

Under-absorbed overhead should be added on the basis of the rate.

***2. Write off to Costing Profit & Loss Account***

This method is applied when the over or under absorbed overhead is of low value. In this method over or under absorbed overhead is transferred to the Costing Profit and Loss Account. i.e., over-absorbed overhead is credited and under-absorbed overhead is debited in the Costing Profit and Loss Account.

***3. Carry Forward to the account of next period***

In this method the over or under absorbed overhead is transferred to the account of the next period.

## EXERCISE

### I. Choose the Correct answer for the following:

1. Indirect cost is known as
   (i) Overhead (ii) Expenses (iii) Cost centre (iv) Cost unit
2. Indirect cost incurred for the production department is called
   (i) Administration Overhead (ii) Factory Overhead
   (iii) Selling Overhead (iv) Works Cost
3. The division of factory into production cost centres and service cost centres is called
   (i) Codification (ii) Centralisation (iii) Departmentalisation (iv) Stores
4. Electricity expense is allocated on the basis of
   (i) Area occupied (ii)No.of workers (iii)Horse power (iv) Light points
5. Rent is allocated on the basis of
   (i) Horse power (ii) Area occupied (iii) Light points(iv)Labour hours
6. Apportionment of overheads to the production and service departments is called
   (i) Secondary distribution (ii) Repeated distribution
   (iii) Primary distribution (iv) Trial and Error distribution
7. Apportionment of service department costs to the production departments is called
   (i) Secondary distribution (ii) Primary distribution
   (iii) Repeated distribution (iv) None of the above
8. The basis of apportionment of store-keeping department cost to various production departments is
   (i) Wages paid (ii) Material cost
   (iii) No.of employees (iv) Factory overhead
9. When the service rendered byone service department to other service

departments are not taken into account, the method of secondary distribution is called

(i) Direct Re-apportionment method (ii) Reciprocal method

(iii) Primary distribution method (iv) Step ladder method

10. Inter services rendered by the service depar.ments are taken into consideration in

(i) Primary distribution (ii) Step ladder method

(iii) Repeated distribution method (iv) Cost Sheet

11. Depreciation is apportioned on the basis of the value of

(i) Fixed Assets (ii) Total Assets (iii) Current Assets (iv) Fictitious Assets

12. Canteen cost is apportioned on the basis of

(i) Material cost (ii) Factory overhead

(iii) Adminstration overhead (iv) Number of employees

[Ans: 1. (i) 2. (ii) 3. (iii) 4. (iv) 5. (ii) 6. (iii) 7. (i) 8. (ii) 9. (i) 10.(iii) 11. (i) 12. (iv)]

**II. Answer the following:**

13. Define Overhead. Explain briefly the different functional types of overhead.
14. What is Overhead? Explain the types of overhead on the basis of element of cost.
15. What is Overhead? Explain the types of overhead on the basis of behaviours.
16. Explain briefly the different methods of segragation of semi-variable overhead into fixed overhead and variable overhead.
17. Define Codification. Explain the different methods of codification of factory overhead
18. Distinguish between primary and secondary distribution of factory overhead.
19. What is secondary distribution? Explain the different methods of secondary distribution.
20. Explain the different methods of secondary distribution under Reciprocal distribution method.
21. What is overhead absorption rate? Explain the different kinds of overhead absorption rates.
22. Explain briefly the different methods of absorption of production overhead.
23. Find out the fixed overhead from the following information by graphic method.

| Months | Production (in units) | Semi-variable overhead (Rs) |
|---|---|---|
| January | 1000 | 4000 |
| February | 1200 | 4400 |
| March | 2000 | 6000 |
| April | 1500 | 5000 |
| May | 1600 | 5200 |
| June | 2200 | 6400 |
| July | 2500 | 7000 |

(Ans: Fixed overhead Rs.2,000, Variable overhead Rs.2 per unit)

24. Find out the fixed overhead and variable overhead from the following particularls by High-low point method.

| Period | Output (units) | Semi-variable Overhead (Rs.) |
|---|---|---|
| I | 2000 | 13,000 |
| II | 3000 | 17,000 |
| III | 3500 | 19,000 |
| IV | 4000 | 21,000 |
| V | 5000 | 25,000 |
| VI | 6000 | 29,000 |

(Ans: Fixed overhead Rs.5000; Variable overhead Rs.4 per unit)

25. Find out the fixed overhead and variable overhead from the following particulars by Average Method:

| Period | Output (units) | Semi-variable Overhead (Rs.) |
|---|---|---|
| I | 5,000 | 35,000 |
| II | 6,000 | 40,000 |
| III | 7,500 | 47,500 |
| IV | 9,000 | 55,000 |
| V | 10,000 | 60,000 |
| VI | 12,000 | 70,000 |

(Ans:Fixed overhead Rs 10,000;Variable overhead Rs 5 per unit)

26. Calculate fixed overhead and variable overhead by simultaneous equation methods from the following data:

| Month | Output (units) | Semi-variable Overhead (Rs.) |
|---|---|---|
| January | 1,200 | 13,200 |
| April | 2,000 | 18,000 |

(Ans: Fixed overhead Rs.6,000;Variable overhead Rs.6 per unit)

27. Calculate fixed overhead and variable overhead by simultaneous equation method from the following data

| Period | Output (units) | Semi-variable Overhead (Rs.) |
|---|---|---|
| I | 4,000 | 25,000 |
| II | 2,000 | 17,000 |

(Ans: Fixed Overhead Rs.9,000; Variable overhead Rs.4 per unit)

28. Calculate the fixed overhead and variable overhead by least square method from the following data.

| Period | Output (units) | Semi-variable Overhead (Rs.) |
|---|---|---|
| I | 500 | 3,000 |
| II | 800 | 3,600 |
| III | 1000 | 4,000 |
| IV | 1500 | 5,000 |
| V | 2000 | 6,000 |

(Ans: Fixed overhead Rs.2,000; Variable overhead Rs.2 per unit)

29. X & Co. Ltd. has three production department namely Assembly, Painting and Finishing, and two service departments namely, Store-keeping and Power House. The following expenses were incurred for these departments for three months ending March 2011. Prepare a departmental distribution summary.

| | | Rs. |
|---|---|---|
| **Indirect Material:** | | |
| Production Departments: | Assembly | 22,000 |
| | Painting | 12,500 |
| | Finishing | 6,000 |
| Service Departments: | Store-keeping | 5000 |
| | Power House | 4,000 |
| **Indirect Labour:** | | |
| Production Departments: | Assembly | 11,000 |
| | Painting | 8,000 |
| | Finishing | 8,000 |
| Service Departments: | Store-keeping | 6,000 |
| | Power House | 3,000 |
| Rent | | 7,000 |
| Canteen | | 6,000 |
| Depreciation for machinery | | 5,000 |
| Supervision | | 8,000 |
| Lighting | | 3,000 |
| Insurance for Plant & Machinery | | 4,000 |
| Insurance for employees | | 2,000 |

The following further information are also given.

| Particulars | Assembly | Painting | Finishing | Store-keeping | Power House |
|---|---|---|---|---|---|
| No. of workers | 30 | 25 | 20 | 15 | 10 |
| Total wages (Rs.) | 10,000 | 8,000 | 7,000 | 3,000 | 2,000 |
| Value of Plant & Machinery (Rs.) | 30,000 | 20,000 | 60,000 | - | 40,000 |
| Area (sq.feet) | 700 | 500 | 400 | 200 | 200 |
| Light Points | 20 | 15 | 10 | 2 | 3 |

(Ans: Rs.42,950; Rs.28,150; Rs.22,200; Rs.14,220; Rs.11,480)

30. The primary distribution statement of K Ltd for the month January 2011 shows the following details:

| Production Departments: | Rs. |
|---|---|
| A | 60,000 |
| B | 45,000 |
| C | 30,000 |
| Service Departments: | |
| X | 18,000 |
| Y | 16,000 |

The cost of service department X is apportioned in the ratio 2:3:1 and of Y is apportioned in the ratio 4:3:1 for the production departments A, B and C respectively. Prepare a statement showing the apportionment of the expenses by direct distribution method.

(Ans: Rs.74,000; Rs.60,000; Rs.35,000)

31. Prepare a departmental distribution summary from the following details:

| Particulars | Productions Depts | | | Service Depts. | |
|---|---|---|---|---|---|
| | X | Y | Z | A | B |
| Direct material Rs. | 20,000 | 17,000 | 13,000 | 8,000 | 2,000 |
| Direct Wages Rs. | 18,000 | 13,000 | 9,000 | 5,000 | 3,000 |
| Direct Expenses Rs. | 6,000 | 4,000 | 3,000 | 2,000 | 1,000 |
| Area (sq.ft) | 500 | 400 | 300 | 200 | 100 |
| Plant & Machinery | 200,000 | 150,000 | 100,000 | 50,000 | - |
| No. of workers | 60 | 50 | 40 | 30 | 20 |
| Light Points | 40 | 20 | 20 | 10 | 10 |
| Horse Power | 300 | 200 | 100 | 100 | - |

The expenses incurred by the company for the period are as follows:

| | Rs. |
|---|---|
| General overhead | 20,000 |
| Rent | 12,000 |
| Lighting | 5,000 |
| Power | 3,000 |
| Store-keeping | 2,000 |
| Amenities to workers | 1,500 |
| Depreciation of Plant | 20,000 |
| Repairs of Plant | 5,000 |

The company decided to apportion the expenses of Service Department A in the ratio of direct wages and of B in the ratio 2:2:1 to Departments X,Y and Z.

(Ans: Rs.83,243; Rs.64,286; Rs.45,971)

32. JD&Co. Ltd has 3 production departments namely A,B and C and 4 service departments namely Maintenance, Store-keeping, Time-keeping and Canteen. The expenses allocated to these departments for the month January 2011 as per primary distribution are stated as follows:

| | | Rs. |
|---|---|---|
| Production departments: | A | 26,000 |
| | B | 20,000 |
| | C | 15,000 |
| Service departments: | | |
| Maintenance | | 6,000 |
| Store-keeping | | 10,000 |
| Time-keeping | | 8,000 |
| Canteen | | 12,000 |

The following additional information are also given:

| Departments | No. of Employees | Direct Material consumed Rs. | Plant & Machinery Rs |
|---|---|---|---|
| Production Depts: A | 50 | 20,000 | 300,000 |
| B | 40 | 17,000 | 200,000 |
| C | 20 | 13,000 | 100,000 |
| Service Depts: | | | |
| Maintenance | 10 | 10,000 | 50,000 |
| Store-keeping | 18 | - | - |
| Time-keeping | 6 | - | - |
| Canteen | 22 | 5,000 | - |

Prepare a statement showing the apportionment of service department costs to the production departments by Step Ladder method.

(Ans: Rs.40,753; Rs.32,553; Rs.23,694)

33. A manufacturing company has 3 production departments namely, A,B and C and 2 service departments namely X and Y. The departmental distribution summary shows the following details:

| | | Rs. |
|---|---|---|
| Production Depts: | A | 40,000 |
| | B | 55,000 |
| | C | 75,000 |
| Service Depts: | X | 18,000 |
| | Y | 15,000 |

The basis of apportionment of service deptartment costs to the production departments are stated as follows:

| Depts | A | B | C | X | Y |
|---|---|---|---|---|---|
| X | 40% | 30% | 20% | - | 10% |
| Y | 25% | 35% | 20% | 20% | - |

Prepare a statement showing the distribution of the service department expenses to the production departments on the basis of repeated distribution method.

(Ans: Rs.52,857; Rs.67,429; Rs.82,714)

34. GC & Co.Ltd. has three production departments namely, J, K and L and two service departments namely A and B. The primary distribution for a period shows the following details:

| | | Rs. |
|---|---|---|
| Production Depts: | A | 70,000 |
| | B | 60,000 |
| | C | 50,000 |
| Service Depts: | A | 30,000 |
| | B | 20,000 |

The basis of apportionment of service department costs to the production departments are stated as follows:

| Depts. | J | K | L | A | B |
|---|---|---|---|---|---|
| A | 30% | 20% | 40% | - | 10% |
| B | 20% | 30% | 30% | 20% | - |

Prepare a statement showing the distribution of the service department expenses to the production departments on the basis of Trial and Error method.

(Ans: Rs.85,102; Rs.73,980; Rs.70,918)

35. GT & Co. Ltd. has three production departments namely X, Y and Z and two service departments namely A and B. The primary distribution for February 2011 shows the following details:

| | | Rs. |
|---|---|---|
| Production Depts: | X | 1,20,000 |
| | Y | 1,00,000 |
| | Z | 80,000 |
| Service Depts: | A | 70,000 |
| | B | 60,000 |

The basis of apportionment of service departments costs to production departments are stated as follows:

| Depts. | X | Y | Z | A | B |
|---|---|---|---|---|---|
| A | 20% | 40% | 10% | - | 30% |
| B | 40% | 30% | 20% | 10% | - |

Prepare a statement showing the distribution of the service department expenses to the production departments on the basis of Simultaneous Equation method.

(Ans: Rs.1,69,070; Rs. 1,56,390; Rs.1,04,535

36. Calculate Fixed overhead and variable overhead by simultaneous equation method for the following data:

| Period | Output (units) | Semi-variable Overhead (Rs) |
|---|---|---|
| I | 5,000 | 35,000 |
| II | 3,000 | 25,000 |

(Ans: Fixed Overhead Rs.10,000; Variable overhead Rs.5 per unit)

37. Calculate the fixed overhead and variable overhead by least square method, from the following data:

| Period | Output (units) | Semi-variable Overhead (Rs.) |
|---|---|---|
| I | 1,000 | 8,000 |
| II | 1,500 | 9,500 |
| III | 2,000 | 11,000 |
| IV | 2,500 | 12,500 |
| V | 3,000 | 14,000 |

(Ans: Fixed overhead Rs.5,000; Variable overhead Rs.5 per unit)

# CHAPTER V

# SINGLE OR OUTPUT COSTING

Single or output costing is a method of costing adopted by the concerns which produce a single product. The single article may be in two or three grades. The total cost of production for these type of articles will be uniform for all the units produced in a period. Hence, the cost per unit of the product can be known by dividing the total cost by the number of units produced in a period. Examples of concerns which produce single product are brick kiln, mines, quarries, collieries, flour mills, cement factories, sugar factories etc. The cost unit in single or output costing depends on the nature of the business. It may be tonne, kgm, number of units etc.

## Procedures of preparing Single or Output Costing

### 1. *Classification of Costs*

All costs incurred for the production for a period will be classified into direct costs and indirect costs.The direct costs include direct material direct labour and direct expenses. Indirect costs (otherwise called as overheads) includes indirect material, indirect labour and indirect expenses.It can be classified according to the functions performed in the organisation. Accordingly, the indirect costs are classified into Factory overhead, Administration overhead and Selling & Distribution overhead. These indirect costs would be apportioned for production during a period on the basis of suitable basis of apportionment.

### 2. *Treatment of stock of raw material*

There may be opening as well as closing stock of material during a period. It will be adjusted with the purchase during the period. In order to know the material consumed opening stock will be added with purchase of material and then the closing stock will be deducted from it.

i.e., Material Consumed = Opening Stock + Purchase - Closing Stock.

### 3. *Treatment of Work-in-progress*

Work-in-progress is otherwise called as partly finished goods or incomplete product. When the accounts are prepared for a specific period of time, the incomplete product will exist. There may be both opening and closing work-in-progress. The cost of opening and closing work-in-progress will be treated after adding the Direct cost with the Factory Overhead. The value of opening work-in-progress will be added and closing work-in-progress will be deducted from it.

### 4. *Treatment of Stock of Finished Goods*

There may be stock of finished goods in the process of production and sales for a concern. Stock of finished goods may be in the form of opening and closing stock. In order to know the correct cost of goods sold and the costing profit, the stock of finished goods should be adjusted after the direct cost, factory overhead and administration overhead (cost of production). Opening stock will be added with it and closing stock will be deducted from it.

i.e., Cost of Goods sold = Opening Stock of Finished Goods + Cost of Production - Closing Stock of Finished Goods.

### 5. *Preparation of Cost Sheet*

Cost sheet is a statement of cost incurred for the production during a period. There is no time basis for the cost sheet. It may be for 15 days 1 month, 2 months or 3 months etc. All the costs incurred in the production of the product during a period should be systematically stated in the cost sheet. The direct cost like direct material, direct labour and direct expenses will be stated first. The total of these cost is called 'Prime Cost'. Adjustment of opening and closing stock of material will be done before calculating the Prime Cost. Then the factory overhead will be added with the cost. This is called the 'Works Cost'. If there is any work-in-progress then the opening and closing work-in-progress should be adjusted before calculating the Works Cost. The administration overhead will be added with the work cost to find out the 'Cost of Production'. If there is any opening and closing stock of finished goods, then it will be adjusted to find out the 'Cost of Goods Sold'. Selling and Distribution overhead will be added with the cost of Goods sold to know the 'Cost of sales'.

**(i) Cost sheet without Stock and Work-in-progress**

**COST SHEET**

| **Particulars** | **Rs.** |
|---|---|
| Direct Material | x x x x |
| Direct Wages | x x x x |
| Direct Expenses | x x x x |
| Prime Cost | x x x x |
| Add: Factory Overhead | x x x x |
| Works Cost (or Factory cost) | x x x x |
| Add: Administration overhead | x x x x |
| Cost of Production | x x x x |
| Add: Selling & Distribution Overhead | x x x x |

| | |
|---|---|
| Cost of Sales | x x x x |
| Costing Profit | x x x x |
| Sales | x x x x |

**(ii) Cost Sheet with Stock and Work-in-progress**

**COST SHEET**

| Particulars | Rs. |
|---|---|
| Opening Stock of material | x x x x |
| Add: Purchase | x x x x |
| | x x x x |
| Less: Closing stock of material | x x x x |
| Direct material consumed | x x x x |
| Direct Wages | x x x x |
| Direct Expenses | x x x x |
| Prime Cost | x x x x |
| Add: Factory overhead | x x x x |
| Opening work-in-progress | x x x x |
| | x x x x |
| Less: Closing work-in-progress | x x x x |
| Works Cost | x x x x |
| Add: Administration Overhead | x x x x |
| Cost of Production | x x x x |
| Add: Opening stock of Finished Goods | x x x x |
| | x x x x |
| Less: Closing stock of Finished Goods | x x x x |
| Cost of Goods sold | x x x x |
| Add: Selling and Distribution Overhead | x x x x |
| Cost of Sales | x x x x |
| Costing Profit | x x x x |
| Sales | x x x x |

**Illustration: 1**

Prepare a cost sheet and find out the cost of production and costing profit from the following information for the month June 2011.

| | |
|---|---|
| Direct material consumed | Rs.40,000 |
| Direct wages | Rs.14,000 |
| Direct expenses | Rs.4,000 |
| Factory overhead | Rs.5,000 |
| Adminstration overhead | Rs.7,000 |
| Selling and Distribution overhead | Rs.9,000 |

The profit for the company is estimated as 20% on cost of sales.

***Solution:***

**Cost Sheet for the month ended 30th June 2011**

| Particulars | Rs. |
|---|---|
| Direct material consumed | 40,000 |
| Direct wages | 14,000 |
| Direct expenses | 4,000 |
| Prime Cost | 58,000 |
| Factory Overhead | 5,000 |
| Works Cost | 63,000 |
| Adminsitration overhead | 7,000 |
| Cost of Production | 70,000 |
| Selling and Distribution overhead | 9,000 |
| Cost of Sales | 79,000 |
| Costing Profit | 19,750 |
| Sales | 98,750 |

Profit = 20% on Sales

i.e., Sales = 100; Profit = Rs.20

Cost = 100-20 = Rs.80

Hence, Profit = $\frac{20}{80}$ x 79,000 = Rs.19,750

**Illustration: 2**

X Ltd is providing the following information related to the month of July 2011, in order to prepare Cost sheet and to find out the cost per unit.

| | |
|---|---|
| Direct Material | Rs.37,000 |
| Direct Wages | Rs.30,000 |
| Direct Expenses | Rs.13,000 |

Factory overhead absorbed is 60% of direct wages. Administration overhead absorbed is 30% of factory cost. Selling and distribution overhead absorbed is 20% on cost of production. Profit earned is 20% on cost of sales. Number of units produced is 1,000.

***Solution:***

**Cost Sheet of X Ltd. for the month July 2011**

| Particulars | Rs. |
|---|---|
| Direct Material | 37,000 |
| Direct Wages | 30,000 |
| Direct Expenses | 13,000 |
| Prime Cost | 80,000 |

| | |
|---|---|
| Factory Overhead $\left[\frac{60}{100} \times 30{,}000\right]$ | 18,000 |
| Factory Cost | 98,000 |
| Administration Overhead $\left[\frac{30}{100} \times 98{,}000\right]$ | 29,400 |
| Cost of Production | 1,27,400 |
| Selling and Distribution Overhead $\left[\frac{20}{100} \times 127{,}400\right]$ | 25,480 |
| Cost of Sales | 1,52,880 |
| Costing Profit $\left[\frac{20}{100} \times 1{,}52{,}880\right]$ | 30,576 |
| Sales | 1,83,456 |

Production = 1,000 units

Cost of Production per unit $= \frac{127400}{1000} =$ Rs.127.40

Cost of Sales per unit $= \frac{152{,}880}{1000} =$ Rs.152.88

Selling price per unit $= \frac{183456}{1000} =$ Rs.183.46

**Illustration: 3**

ABC & Co. Ltd provides the following information from its costing records for the month of July 2011.

| | Rs. |
|---|---|
| Stock of raw materials as on 1st July 2011 | 11,500 |
| Stock of raw materials as on 31st July 2011 | 12,800 |
| Purchase of material | 27,500 |
| Direct wages paid | 17,500 |
| Direct Expenses | 8,700 |
| Factory overhead | 6,400 |
| Adminstration overhead | 10,300 |
| Selling and distribution overhead | 12,300 |
| Work-in-progress as on 1st July 2011 | 14,500 |
| Work-in-progress as on 31st July 2011 | 11,200 |
| Stock of finished goods as on 1st July 2011 | 17,500 |
| Stock of finished goods as on 31st July 2011 | 13,000 |
| Sales | 95,000 |

Prepare a cost sheet and find out the costing profit.

***Solution:***

**Cost Sheet for the month July 2011**

| Particulars | Rs. | Rs. |
|---|---|---|
| Op. Stock of material | 11,500 | |
| Add: Purchase | 27,500 | |
| | 39,000 | |
| Less: Cl. Stock of material | 12,800 | |
| Direct Material consumed | | 26,200 |
| Direct Wages | | 17,500 |
| Direct Expenses | | 8,700 |
| Prime Cost | | 52,400 |
| Add: Factory overhead | 6,400 | |
| Opening work-in-progress | 14,500 | |
| | 20,900 | |
| Less: Closing work-in-progress | 11,200 | 9,700 |
| Works Cost | | 62,100 |
| Add: Administration Overhead | | 10,300 |
| Cost of Production | | 72,400 |
| Add: Opening stock of finished goods | | 17,500 |
| | | 89,900 |
| Less: Closing stock of finished goods | | 13,000 |
| Cost of goods sold | | 76,900 |
| Add: Selling and Distribution Overhead | | 12,300 |
| Cost of sales | | 89,200 |
| Costing profit | | 5,800 |
| Sales | | 95,000 |

**Illustration: 4**

KMW & Co Ltd provides the following information from its costing records related tothe month of August 2011.

| | As on 1st August 2011 Rs. | As on 31st August 2011 Rs. |
|---|---|---|
| Stock of Raw Material | 18,600 | 14,100 |
| Stock of Work-in-progress | 11,400 | 10,200 |
| Stock of Finished goods | 22,600 | 20,300 |

| | Rs. |
|---|---|
| Direct material consumed | 37,700 |
| Direct wages | 41,300 |
| Direct expenses | 7,700 |
| Indirect wages | 3,200 |

| | |
|---|---|
| Freight for purchase of material | 700 |
| Factory supervisor's salary | 2,500 |
| Repairs and maintenance of plant | 1,700 |
| Power | 1,500 |
| Electricity | 1,600 |
| Selling commission | 3,000 |
| Selling expenses | 2,600 |
| Travelling expenses to salesmen | 1,800 |
| Salary for salesmen | 5,700 |
| Rent paid | 2,400 |
| Salary for office staff | 6,000 |
| Stationery purchased for office | 500 |
| Travelling allowance for office manager | 800 |
| Sales | 1,73,000 |

Rent and electricity are shared in the ratio 2:2:1 for factory, office and selling departments respectively.

Prepare a cost sheet and find out the costing profit.

***Solution:***

**Cost Sheet for the month August 2011**

| **Particulars** | **Rs.** | **Rs.** |
|---|---|---|
| Opening stock of material | 18,600 | |
| Add: Purchase of material (calculated) | 32,500 | |
| Freight paid | 700 | |
| | 51,800 | |
| Less: Closing stock of material | 14,100 | |
| Direct material consumed | | 37,700 |
| Direct wages | | 41,300 |
| Direct expenses | | 7,700 |
| Prime Cost | | 86,700 |
| Add: Factory Overhead: | | |
| Indirect wages | 3,200 | |
| Supervisor's salary | 2,500 | |
| Repairs and maintenance | 1,700 | |
| Power | 1,500 | |
| Electricity (2/5x1600) | 640 | |
| Rent paid (2/5x2400) | 960 | |
| | 10,500 | |
| Add: Op. work-in-progress | 11,400 | |
| | 21,900 | |

| | | |
|---|---|---|
| Less: Cl. work-in-progress | 10,200 | 11,700 |
| Works cost | | 98,400 |
| Add: Administration Overhead: | | |
| Salary | 6,000 | |
| Stationery | 500 | |
| Travelling allowance | 800 | |
| Electricity (2/5x1600) | 640 | |
| Rent (2/5x2400) | 960 | |
| | | 8,900 |
| Cost of production | | 1,07,300 |
| Add: Op. Finished goods | | 22,600 |
| | | 1,29,900 |
| Less: Cl. Finished goods | | 20,300 |
| Cost of goods sold | | 1,09,600 |
| Add: Selling and Distribution overhead | | |
| Salary for salesman | 5,700 | |
| Selling commission | 3,000 | |
| Selling expenses | 2,600 | |
| Travelling expenses | 1,800 | |
| Electricity (1/5x1600) | 320 | |
| Rent (1/5x2400) | 480 | |
| | | 13,900 |
| Cost of sales | | 1,23,500 |
| Costing profit | | 49,500 |
| Sales | | *1,73,000* |

**Illustration: 5**

The costing information related to the year ended 31st March 2011, of XYZ Ltd are as follows:

| Inventory position | 31st March 2010 | 31st March 2011 |
|---|---|---|
| | Rs. | Rs. |
| Raw materials | 7,400 | 4,500 |
| Work-in-progress | 19,200 | 17,500 |
| Finished Goods | 32,500 | 35,000 |

| | Rs. |
|---|---|
| Purchase of materials | 42,000 |
| Direct wages paid | 39,500 |
| Indirect wages | 11,800 |
| Direct expenses | 13,500 |

| | |
|---|---|
| Power | 3,700 |
| Electricity | 6,000 |
| Indirect wages paid in advance | 1,500 |
| Salary for foremen | 18,000 |
| Salary for office staff | 42,000 |
| Salary for Selling department | 31,500 |
| Sales promotion | 7,200 |
| Selling commission | 4,500 |
| Interest on Loan | 14,500 |
| Dividend paid | 23,500 |
| Rates and Taxes | 8,400 |
| Income Tax paid | 7,400 |
| Value of Building | 3,00,000 |
| Value of Plant & Machinery | 2,40,000 |
| Value of Office Equipment | 60,000 |
| Repairs & Maintenance of Plant | 4,200 |
| Repairs & Maintenance of Office Equipment | 1,700 |
| Outstanding salary for foreman | 2,100 |

Provide 12% depreciation on Plant & Machinery, 10% depreciation for Office Equipment and 8% depreciation for Building. Share the Electricity and Rates & taxes in the ratio 3:2:1 and depreciation for building in the ratio 4:3:1 for factory, office and selling departments respectively. The company earned a profit of 10% on sales.

Prepare a cost sheet and find out the costing profit.

***Solution:***

**Cost Sheet of XYZ & Co Ltd as on 31st March 2011**

| Particulars | | Rs. | Rs. |
|---|---|---|---|
| Op. Stock of material | | 7,400 | |
| Add: Purchase | | 42,000 | |
| | | 49,400 | |
| Less: Closing stock of material | | 4,500 | |
| Direct material consumed | | | 44,900 |
| Direct wages | | | 39,500 |
| Direct expenses | | | 13,500 |
| Prime Cost | | | 97,900 |
| Add: Factory overhead | | | |
| Indirect wages | 11,800 | | |
| Less: Paid in advance | 1,500 | 10,300 | |
| Power | | 3,700 | |

| Particulars | | | |
|---|---|---|---|
| Salary for foreman | 18,000 | | |
| Add: Outstanding | 2,100 | 20,100 | |
| Repairs & Maintenance of Plant | | 4,200 | |
| Depreciation for Plant (12/100) x 2,40,000 | | 28,800 | |
| Depreciation for Building (24000 x 4/8) | | 12,000 | |
| Electricity (6000 x 3/6) | | 3,000 | |
| Rates (8400 x 3/6) | | 4,200 | |
| | | 86,300 | |
| Add: Op. Work-in-progress | | 19,200 | |
| | | 1,05,500 | |
| Less: Closing work-in-progress | | 17,500 | 88,000 |
| Works Cost | | | 185,900 |
| Add: Administration Overhead | | | |
| Salary | | 42,000 | |
| Depreciation for Office equipment | | 6,000 | |
| Depreciation for Building (24,000 x 3/8) | | 9,000 | |
| Maintenance of Office equipment | | 1,700 | |
| Electricity (6000 x 2/6) | | 2,000 | |
| Rates (8400 x 2/6) | | 2,800 | 63,500 |
| Cost of Production | | | 2,49,400 |
| Add: Op. stock of Finished goods | | | 32,500 |
| | | | 2,81,900 |
| Less: Closing stock of Finished goods | | | 35,000 |
| Cost of goods sold | | | 2,46,900 |
| Add: Selling & Distribution overhead | | | |
| Salary to salesman | | 31,500 | |
| Sales promotion | | 7,200 | |
| Selling commission | | 4,500 | |
| Depreciation for building (24,000 x 1/8) | | 3,000 | |
| Electricity (6000 x 1/6) | | 1,000 | |
| Rates (8,400 x 1/6) | | 1,400 | 48,600 |
| Cost of Sales | | | 2,95,500 |
| Costing Profit (10/90)x2,95,500 | | | 32,833 |
| Sales | | | 3,28,333 |

(Note: Income tax, Interest on loan and Dividend paid are purely financial transactions. Hence, it could not be treated in the cost sheet.)

**Illustration: 6**

The Costing information of a NLtd shows the following information for the month of August 2011.

| Inventory Accounts | 1st August Rs. | 31st August Rs. |
|---|---|---|
| Finished goods | 16,400 | 17,900 |
| Work-in-progress | 9,700 | 7,200 |
| Raw material | 4,200 | 5,600 |

| | Rs. |
|---|---|
| Direct labour | 19,200 |
| Direct expenses | 2,000 |
| General and administration expenses | 11,400 |
| Selling expenses | 7,500 |
| Sales | 92,000 |
| Cost of goods sold | 80,000 |

Direct labour cost is 120% of factory overhead. Calculaté the cost of sales and costing profit.

***Solution:***

Since direct material purchased is not given it should be calculated on the following basis:

| Particulars | Amount Rs. |
|---|---|
| Cost of goods sold | 80,000 |
| Add: Closing stock of finished goods | 17,900 |
| | 97,900 |
| Less: Opening stock of finished goods | 16,400 |
| Cost of Production | 81,500 |
| Less: Administration Overhead | 11,400 |
| Works Cost | 70,100 |
| Add: Closing stock of work-in-progress | 7,200 |
| | 77,300 |
| Less: Opening stock of work-in-progress | 9,700 |
| | 67,600 |
| Less: Factory Overhead (100/120 x 19,200) | 16,000 |
| Prime cost | 51,600 |
| Less: Direct wages | 19,200 |
| | 32,400 |
| Less: Direct expenses | 2,000 |
| Material consumed | 30,400 |
| Add: Closing stock of material | 5,600 |
| | 36,000 |
| Less: Opening stock of material | 4,200 |
| Purchase of Material | 31,800 |

**Cost Sheet of N Ltd for the month of August 2011**

| Particulars | Rs. | Rs. |
|---|---|---|
| Opening stock of material | 4,200 | |
| Add: Purchases | 31,800 | |
| | 36,000 | |
| Less: Closing stock of material | 5,600 | |
| Direct material consumed | | 30,400 |
| Direct wages | | 19,200 |
| Direct Expenses | | 2,000 |
| Prime Cost | | 51,600 |
| Add: Factory Overhead | 16,000 | |
| Opening work-in-progress | 9,700 | |
| | 25,700 | |
| Less: Closing work-in-progress | 7,200 | 18,500 |
| Works Cost | | 70,100 |
| Add: Administration Overhead | | 11,400 |
| Cost of Production | | 81,500 |
| Add: Opening finished goods | | 16,400 |
| | | 97,900 |
| Less: Closing finished goods | | 17,900 |
| Cost of goods sold | | 80,000 |
| Add: Selling & Distribution Overhead | | 7,500 |
| Cost of Sales | | 87,500 |
| Costing Profit | | 4,500 |
| Sales | | 92,000 |

**Illustration: 7**

The following are the costing information related to Joyce & Co. Ltd. for three months ending 31st March 2011.

| Inventory Account | 1st January 2011 | | 31st March 2011 |
|---|---|---|---|
| | Rs. | | Rs. |
| Raw Material | 5,500 | | 4,000 |
| Work-in- progress | 14,200 | Rs. | 15,000 |
| Purchase of raw material | | 39,500 | |
| Direct wages | | 31,200 | |
| Rent, rates and works on cost | | 17,500 | |
| Carriage inwards | | 2,000 | |
| Factory supervision cost | | 12,000 | |
| Administration cost | | 31,000 | |
| Sales | | 1,80,000 | |

Selling cost @ Rs.0.80 per unit sold

The stock of finished goods as on 1st January 2011 is 2,000 units and on 31st March 2011 is 2,500 units. The company sold 39,500 units during the period.

Prepare a cost sheet and find out the costing profit, cost per unit and selling price per unit.

***Solution:***

**Statement of Cost for 3 months ending 31st March 2011**

| Particulars | Rs. | Rs. |
|---|---|---|
| Opening stock of material | 5,500 | |
| Add: Purchases of material | 39,500 | |
| Carriage inwards | 2,000 | |
| | 47,000 | |
| Less: Closing stock of material | 4,000 | |
| Material consumed | | 43,000 |
| Direct wages | | 31,200 |
| Prime cost | | 74,200 |
| Add: Factory Overhead: | | |
| Rent, Rates and works on cost | 17,500 | |
| Factory supervision cost | 12,000 | 29,500 |
| Add: Opening work-in-progress | | 14,200 |
| | | 1,17,900 |
| Less: Closing work-in-progress | | 15,000 |
| Works Cost | | 1,02,900 |
| Add: Administration Overhead | | 31,000 |
| Cost of Production (40,000 units) | | 1,33,900 |
| Add: Opening stock of finished goods (2000 x 3.35) | | 6,700 |
| | | 1,40,600 |
| Less: Closing stock of finished goods (2500 x 3.35) | | 8,375 |
| Cost of goods sold | | 1,32,225 |
| Add: Selling & Distribution Overhead (39500 x 0.80) | | 31,600 |
| Cost of sales | | 1,63,825 |
| Costing Profit | | 16,175 |
| Sales (39,500 units) | | 1,80,000 |

***Workings*:**

| | | units |
|---|---|---|
| | Sales | 39,500 |
| Add | Closing stock | 2,500 |
| | | 42,000 |
| Less | Opening stock | 2,000 |
| | Production of finished goods | 40,000 |

$$\text{Cost of finished goods} = \frac{\text{Cost of production}}{\text{No. of units}}$$

$$= \frac{1{,}33{,}900}{40{,}000} = \text{Rs.}3.35 \text{ per unit}$$

$$\text{Selling price per unit} = \frac{\text{Sales}}{\text{No. of units sold}}$$

$$= \frac{180{,}000}{39{,}500} = \text{Rs.}4.56 \text{ per unit}$$

**Illustration: 8**

A manufacturing company provides the following information for the month 30th June, 2011.

| | Rs. |
|---|---|
| Direct material consumed | 30,000 |
| Direct wages paid | 24,000 |
| Direct expenses | 6,000 |
| Factory Overhead | 8,000 |
| Administration expenses | 12,000 |
| Selling expenses | 9,000 |

The company produced 2,000 units during the period and earned a profit @ 20% on sales.

The company wants to produce 2,500 units during July 2011. The company estimated that the cost of raw material and direct wages will increase by 10% and 15% respectively.

It is estimated that the cost of factory overhead (variable) will reduce by 10%. In the factory overhead, 60% is fixed and 40% is variable. In administration overhead, 75% is fixed and 25% is variable.

Prepare the statement of cost for the months June and July 2011.

***Solution:***

**Statement of cost for the month June 2011**

| Particulars | Per unit Rs. | Total Rs. |
|---|---|---|
| Direct material | 15 | 30,000 |
| Direct wages | 12 | 24,000 |
| Direct expenses | 3 | 6,000 |
| Prime Cost | 30 | 60,000 |
| Add: Factory overhead | | |
| Fixed 60% of Rs.4,800 | | |
| Variable 40% of Rs.3200 | 1.60 | 8,000 |
| Works Cost | | 68,000 |
| Add: Administration overhead | | |
| Fixed 75% of Rs.9,000 | | |
| Variable 25% of Rs.3,000 | 1.50 | 12,000 |
| Cost of production | | 80,000 |
| Add: Selling and distribution overhead | 4.50 | 9,000 |
| Cost of sales | | 89,000 |
| Costing profit (20/80 x 89,000) | | 22,250 |
| Sales | 55.63 | 1,11,250 |

**Calculation of Estimated Costs:**

| | | | Rs. |
|---|---|---|---|
| Material cost per unit | = 15 + 10% of 15 | = | 16.50 |
| Labour cost per unit | = 12 + 15% of 12 | = | 13.80 |
| Direct expenses per unit | | = | 3.00 |
| Variable Factory overhead per unit | = 1.60 - 10% of 1.60 | = | 1.44 |
| Variable Administration overhead per unit | | = | 1.50 |
| Selling and distribution overhead per unit | | = | 4.50 |

**Estimated statement of cost for the month of July 2011**
**(2,500 units)**

| Particulars | Per unit Rs. | Total Rs. |
|---|---|---|
| Direct Material | 16.50 | 41,250 |
| Direct wages | 13.80 | 34,500 |
| Direct Expenses | 3.00 | 7,500 |
| Prime Cost | | 83,250 |

| | | | |
|---|---|---|---|
| Add: Factory overhead | | | |
| Fixed | 4,800 | | |
| Variable (1.44 x 2500) | 3,600 | 1.44 | 8,400 |
| Works Cost | | | 91,650 |
| Add: Administration overhead | | | |
| Fixed | 9,000 | | |
| Variable (1.50 x 2500) | 3,750 | 1.50 | 12,750 |
| Cost of Production | | | 1,04,400 |
| Add: Selling and distribution ovehead (4.50 x 2500) | | 4.50 | 11,250 |
| Cost of Sales | | | 1,15,650 |
| Costing Profit (20/80 x 115,650) | | | 28,912 |
| Sales | | | 1,44,562 |

**Illustration: 9**

Calculate selling price per unit from the following costing information:

| | Rs. |
|---|---|
| Estimated Costs | |
| Direct material | 3 per unit |
| Direct wages | 1.20 per unit |
| Factory expenses | 32,000 |
| Administration expenses | 46,000 |

Selling expenses 10% of sales

Estimated annual sales 50,000 units and the profit per unit is Rs.0.90

(Adapted: I.C.W.A.)

***Solution:***

**Statement of Cost**

| Particulars | Rs. |
|---|---|
| Direct material (50,000 x 3) | 1,50,000 |
| Direct wages (50,000 x 1.20) | 60,000 |
| Prime Cost | 2,10,000 |
| Add: Factory overhead | 32,000 |
| Works Cost | 2,42,000 |
| Add: Administration overhead | 46,000 |
| Cost of Production | 2,88,000 |

Assume total sales as x

Profit = 50,000 x 0.90 = Rs.45,000

Selling Overhead = 10% of sales = 0.1 x

Cost of Sales = Cost of Production + Selling Overhead

$= 288{,}000 + 0.1\,x$

Sales $= $ Cost of Sales + Profit

$x = 288{,}000 + 0.1\,x + 45{,}000$

$X - 0.1x = 288{,}000 + 45{,}000$

$0.9\,x = 333{,}000$

$$x = \frac{3{,}33{,}000}{0.9} = 370{,}000$$

$$\text{Selling price per unit} = \frac{3{,}70{,}000}{50{,}000} = \text{Rs.}7.40$$

## WASTAGE, SCRAP AND SPOILAGE

It is natural to get wastage, scrap or spoilage during the production. Strict control measures may reduce this kind of losses. It could not be prevented completely. Hence, it will be adjusted in the cost of production. If these loss do not realise anything then it will inflate the cost per unit. The method of treatment is to reduce the units lost and calculate the cost per unit by taking into account of the number of actual units produced. If these loss realise any value, then reduce it from the total cost of production and calculate the cost per unit by taking into account of the good units produced. The defective units will be deducted from the total units produced, to calculate the cost of good units produced. If the realised value is due to sale of scrap it will be deducted from the direct material consumed. If the realised value is due to sale of defective product, it may be deducted from the total cost of production or cost of sales or it may be added with the sales without deducting from the cost.

**Illustration: 10**

A manufacturing company is providing the following information from the costing books and accounts for 3 months ending 30th June, 2011.

Direct material:

Material A 1,200 units @ Rs.8 per unit

Material B 800 units @ Rs.15 per unit

Direct Wages:

Grade I workers 20 workers @ Rs.30 per day for 60 days

Grade II workers 15 workers @ Rs.22 per day for 60 days

Direct Expenses - Rs.14,500; Factory overhead - Fixed Rs.17,000 and Variable 20% of direct wages.

Administration overhead -

Fixed Rs.10,000 and variable @ 12% on works cost.

Selling and Distribution Overhead @ 8 % on cost of production.

The company earned a profit of 20% on sales.

The company manufactured 1,500 units. In the process of manufacturing, the company realised Rs.2,400 due to the sale of scraps.

Prepare a statement of cost and find out the cost per unit and selling price per unit.

(Adapted:C.A.)

***Solution:***

**Statement of Cost for 3 months ending 30th June 2011**

| Particulars | Per unit Rs. | Total Rs. |
|---|---|---|
| Direct Material: | | |
| Material A (1200 x 8) | 6.40 | 9,600 |
| Material B (800 x 15) | 8.00 | 12,000 |
| | 14.40 | 21,600 |
| Less: Sale of scrap | 1.60 | 2,400 |
| | 12.80 | 19,200 |
| Direct wages: | | |
| Grade I workers (20 x 30 x 60) | 24.00 | 36,000 |
| Grade II workers (15 x 22 x 60) | 13.20 | 19,800 |
| Direct Expenses | 9.67 | 14,500 |
| Prime Cost | 59.67 | 89,500 |
| Add: Factory Overhead | | |
| Fixed | 11.33 | 17,000 |
| Variable [20% of (36000 + 19800)] | 7.44 | 11,160 |
| Works Cost | 78.44 | 1,17,660 |
| Add: Administration Overhead | | |
| Fixed | 6.67 | 10,000 |
| Variable (12% of 117,660) | 9.41 | 14,119 |
| Cost of Production | 94.52 | 1,41,779 |
| Add: Selling and Distribution Overhead (8% of 141779) | 7.56 | 11,342 |
| Cost of Sales | 102.08 | 1,53,121 |
| Costing Profit (20/80 x 153,121) | 25.52 | 38,280 |
| Sales | ***127.60*** | ***1,91,401*** |

**Illustration: 11**

The following information are provided by a manufacturing company related to the production of 1,000 kgms of a product.

| | Rs. |
|---|---|
| Direct Material | 27,500 |
| Direct Wages | 22,000 |
| Direct Expenses | 10,500 |

Factory overhead absorbed is 100% of direct wages. Administration overhead absorbed is 20% on works cost and Selling and distribution overhead absorbed is 10% on cost of production. Profit earned is 25% on sales.

Out of the total productioon 20% became defective. The defective product was sold at a discount of 15% on the normal price. During the process of production the company realised Rs.4,000 due to sale of scrap.

Prepare a statement of cost and find out the selling price for normal units of production and defective units of production.

(Adapted: ICWAI)

***Solution:***

**Statement of Cost**

| Particulars | Rs. |
|---|---|
| Direct Material | 27,500 |
| Less: Sale of scrap | 4,000 |
| | 23,500 |
| Direct Wages | 22,000 |
| Direct Expenses | 10,500 |
| Prime Cost | 56,000 |
| Add: Factory Overhead | 22,000 |
| Works Cost | 78,000 |
| Add: Administration Overhead (20% of 78,000) | 15,600 |
| Cost of Production | 93,600 |
| Add: Selling and Distribution Overhead (10% of 93,600) | 9,360 |
| Cost of Sales | 1,02,960 |
| Costing Profit (25/75 x 1,02,960) | 34,320 |
| **Sales** | **1,37,280** |

**Calculation of selling price per unit**

| | | | Kgrams |
|---|---|---|---|
| | Total Production | | 1,000 |
| Less: | Defective Production (20%) | | 200 |
| | Good Production | | 800 |
| | Equivalent units of good production (85% of 200) | | 170 |
| | Equivalent units of good production | | *970* |
| | Price per kgm of good production | = | 1,37,280 / 970 |
| | | = | Rs.141.525 |
| | | = | Rs.141.53 |
| | Price per kgm of defective production | = | 141.53 - 15% of 141.525 |
| | | = | 141.53 - 21.23 |
| | | = | Rs.120.30 |

| | | | |
|---|---|---|---|
| Proof: | Sales of good production 800 x 141.525 | = | Rs.1,13,220 |
| | Sale of defective production 200 x 120.30 | = | Rs.24,060 |
| | | = | ***Rs.1,37,280*** |

## PRODUCTION ACCOUNT

Production account is the presentation of cost sheet in T-form. Left side of the T form is called debit side and right side is called the credit side. Expenses of every stages of production are debited and the sales is credited in the account. Prime Cost, Works Cost, Cost of Production and Cost of Sales are respectively shown in the Production Account.

**Illustration: 12**

Prepare a production account from the following information for XYZ & Co Ltd. for the year ending 31st March 2011.

| Inventory Account: | As on 1st April 2010 | As on 31st April 2011 |
|---|---|---|
| | Rs. | Rs. |
| Raw material | 7,250 | 9,500 |
| Work-in-progress | 29,500 | 32,200 |
| Finished goods | 33,000 | 29,500 |

| | Rs. |
|---|---|
| Direct material purchased | 52,750 |
| Direct wages paid | 63,500 |
| Direct expenses paid | 29,000 |
| Factory overhead | 47,500 |
| Administration overhead | 75,400 |
| Selling and distribution overhead | 52,500 |

The company earned a profit @ 25% on cost of sales.

**Production Account of XYZ & Co Ltd as on 31st March 2011**

| **Particulars** | **Rs.** | **Particulars** | **Rs.** |
|---|---|---|---|
| To Op. stock of material | 7,250 | By Closing stock of material | 9,500 |
| To Purchase of material | 52,750 | By Prime Cost c/d | 1,43,000 |
| To Direct wages | 63,500 | | |
| To Direct expenses | 29,000 | | |
| | *1,52,500* | | *1,52,500* |
| To Prime Cost b/d | 1,43,000 | By Closing Work-in-progress | 32,200 |
| To Factory overhead | 47,500 | By Works Cost c/d | 1,87,800 |
| To Op. Work-in- progress | 29,500 | | |
| | *2,20,000* | | *2,20,000* |
| To Works Cost b/d | 1,87,800 | By Cost of Production c/d | 2,63,200 |
| To Administration overhead | 75,400 | | |
| | *2,63,200* | | *2,63,200* |
| To Cost of production b/d | 2,63,200 | By Closing stock of finished goods | 29,500 |
| To Opening stock of finished goods | 33,000 | By Cost of Goods Sold c/d | 2,66,700 |
| | *2,96,200* | | *2,96,200* |
| To Cost of Goods Sold b/d | 2,66,700 | By Cost of Sales c/d | 3,19,200 |
| To Selling & Distribution overhead | 52,500 | | |
| | *3,19,200* | | *3,19,200* |
| To Cost of Sales b/d | 3,19,200 | By Sales | 3,99,000 |
| To Costing Profit (25% of 3,19,200) | 79,800 | | |
| | **3,99,000** | | **3,99,000** |

## EXERCISE

### I. Choose the correct answer for the following:

1. The method of costing adopted by concerns which produce a single product is called
   (i) Marginal costing (ii) Standard costing (iii) Output costing (iv) Process costing
2. Partly finished goods are otherwise known as
   (i) Semi-variable overhead (ii) Work-in-progress (iii) Raw material (iv) Finished goods
3. Statement of cost is called
   (i) Cost sheet (ii) Wage sheet (iii) Overhead sheet (iv) P&L A/c
4. Direct cost plus factory overhead is called
   (i) Works cost (ii) Prime cost (iii) Cost of sales (iv) Cost of production
5. Prime cost is the sum of all the
   (i) Indirect costs (ii) Factory costs
   (iii) Administration costs (iv) Direct costs
6. Works cost plus Administration overhead in known as
   (i) Cost of sales (ii) Cost of production
   (iii) Costing profit (iv) Factory cost
7. Cost of goods sold is calculated by adjusting the cost of production with stock of
   (i) Raw material (ii) Work-in-progress
   (iii) Finished goods (iv) None of the above
8. Costing profit is the difference between the sales and
   (i) Cost of sales (ii) Prime cost (iii) Factory cost (iv) Fixed cost
9. The cost sheet in account form is called
   (i) Cost of sales A/c (ii) Production A/c
   (iii) Sales A/c (iv) Factory cost A/c
10. If the rate of costing profit is 25% on cost, and the sales is Rs.2,40,000, then the costing profit is
    (i) Rs.25,000 (ii) Rs.48,000 (iii) Rs.60,000 (iv) Rs.70,000
11. If the rate of costing profit is 20% on sales, and the cost of sales is Rs.320,000, then the costing profit is
    (i) Rs.80,000 (ii) Rs.50,000 (iii) Rs.64,000 (iv) Rs.26,667
12. If the rate of costing profit is 10% on cost, the cost of production is Rs.2,50,000 and selling & distribution overhead is Rs.25,000, then the costing profit is
    (i) Rs.25,000 (ii) Rs.30,000 (iii) Rs.40,000 (iv) Rs.27,500

[Ans: 1. (iii) 2. (ii) 3. (i) 4. (i) 5. (iv) 6. (ii) 7. (iii) 8. (i) 9. (ii) 10.(ii) 11. (i) 12. (iv)]

**II. Answer the following:**

13. Define Single or output costing. State the procedures of preparing single or output costing.
14. Define single or output costing. Give a specimen of Cost Sheet.
15. What is single or output costing? State how the stock of material, work-in-progress and stock of finished goods are treated in the Cost Sheet.
16. State the treatment of wastage, scrap and spoilage in the cost sheet.
17. Distinguish between production account and cost sheet.
18. Explain Factory overhead and Administration overhead with suitable examples.
19. The following information have been extracted from the books of a manufacturing company.

| | Rs. |
|---|---|
| Stock of raw materials as on 1st January 2011 | 29,500 |
| Stock of raw materials as on 31st March 2011 | 35,000 |
| Direct material purchased | 62,000 |
| Direct expenses paid | 17,500 |
| Work-in-progress as on 1st January 2011 | 39,000 |
| Work-in-progress as on 31st March 2011 | 34,500 |
| Indirect wages | 15,500 |
| Supervision for factory | 25,000 |
| Carriage inwards | 2,000 |
| Depreciation on Plant & Machinery | 6,500 |
| Rent for factory | 4,000 |
| Rent for office | 5,000 |
| Rent for selling department | 2,000 |
| Carriage outwards | 2,500 |
| Salary for the staff of office | 14,500 |
| Salary for the sales department | 12,300 |
| Commission paid to salesman | 6,500 |
| Sales | 2,40,000 |
| Stock of finished goods as on 1st January 2011 | 42,500 |
| Stock of finished goods as on 31st March 2011 | 45,000 |

Prepare a statement of cost

(Adapted: M.K.University M.Com)

(Ans: Profit Rs.5,40,200)

20. Prepare a cost statement and find out the costing profit and sales from the following particulars:

| Stock | As on 1st January | As on 31st January |
|---|---|---|
| | Rs. | Rs. |
| Raw material | 3,400 | 5,000 |

| | | |
|---|---|---|
| Work-in-progress | 6,500 | 4,000 |
| Finished goods | 10,000 | 9,000 |

Factory overhead absorbed is 80% on direct wages, administration overhead absorbed is 20% on works cost and selling expenses absorbed is 10% on cost of production. Direct material purchased is Rs 21,500, Direct wages paid Rs.18,500, Direct expenses Rs 5,500. Credit on account of sale of scrap is Rs.3,500. The company earned a profit @ 20% on sales.

(Ans: Sales Rs.1,01,125)

21. XYZ & Co Ltd provides the following information from its costing records related to the month of August 2011.

| Stock | As on 1st August 2011 | As on 31st August 2011 |
|---|---|---|
| | Rs. | Rs. |
| Raw material | 16,600 | 12,500 |
| Work-in-progress | 10,400 | 13,000 |
| Finished goods | 20,500 | 19,000 |

| | Rs. |
|---|---|
| Purchase of direct material | 32,400 |
| Direct wages | 39,500 |
| Direct expenses | 6,000 |
| Indirect wages | 9,500 |
| Freight for purchase of material | 2,700 |
| Selling commission | 4,000 |
| Selling expenses | 6,500 |
| Travelling expenses to sales man | 4,500 |
| Factory supervisor's salary | 3,500 |
| Repairs and maintenance of plant | 1,500 |
| Power | 1,700 |
| Electricity | 800 |
| Rent paid | 2,000 |
| Salary for office staff | 7,000 |
| Stationery purchased for office | 400 |
| Travelling allowances for office manager | 700 |
| Sales | 1,70,000 |

Rent and electricity are to be shared in the ratio 2:2:1 for factory, office and selling department respectively.

Prepare a cost sheet and find out the costing profit

(Ans: Rs.44,400)

22. The costing information of ABC & Co Ltd shows the following information for the month of August 2011:

| Stock | 1st August (Rs) | 31st August (Rs) |
|---|---|---|
| Raw material | 3,400 | 2,500 |
| Work-in-progress | 5,000 | 4,000 |
| Finished goods | 7,500 | 8,000 |

| | Rs |
|---|---|
| Direct wages paid | 18,000 |
| Direct expenses | 4,700 |
| Administrative expenses | 9,800 |
| Factory overhead 70% of Direct wages | |
| Selling expenses | 6,500 |
| Cost of goods sold | 75,000 |
| Sales | 90,000 |

Calculate the cost of sales and costing profit

(Adapted: ICWAI)

(Ans: Rs.60,600)

23. The following are the costing information related to W.D & Co Ltd for 6 months ending 30th June 2011.

| Inventory | 1st January 2011 Rs. | 30th June 2011 Rs. |
|---|---|---|
| Work-in-progress | 22,000 | 20,000 |
| Raw material | 11,500 | 13,500 |

| | Rs. |
|---|---|
| Purchase of material | 65,000 |
| Direct wages | 59,000 |
| Rent,Rates and works on cost | 24,000 |
| Supervisors salary for factory | 20,000 |
| Administration cost | 47,000 |
| Carriage inwards | 2,300 |
| Sales | 2,30,000 |

Selling expenses @ Rs.0.70 per units sold.

The stock of finished goods as on 1st January is 3,000 units and on 30th June 2011 is 3,500 units. The company produced 50,000 units during the period.

Prepare a statement of cost and find out the costing profit, cost per unit and selling price per unit.

(Ans: Rs.1,10,355)

24. A manufacturing company provides the following information for the month August, 2011. Prepare a statement of cost for the month August 2006 and estimated cost sheet for September 2011.

| | Rs. |
|---|---|
| Direct material | 25,000 |
| Direct wages | 18,000 |
| Direct expenses | 4,000 |
| Factory expenses | 12,000 |
| Administrative expenses | 15,000 |
| Selling expenses | 10,000 |

The company produced 25,000 units during the period and earned a profit @ 25% on sales.

The company decided to produce 3,000 units during September 2011. The company estimated that the cost of the raw material and direct wages will increase by 10% and 12% respectively.

It is estimated that the cost of factory overhead (variable) will reduce by 20%, 60% of factory overhead is fixed and 40% is variable. 70% of administration overhead is fixed and 30% is variable.

(Adapted: ICWAI)

(Ans: Rs.1,32,000; Rs.1,36,480)

25. A manufacturing company provides the following costing information.

| Estimated costs: | Rs. |
|---|---|
| Direct material | 2.50 per unit |
| Direct wages | 1.10 per unit |
| Factory expenses | 35,000 |
| Administration expenses | 50,000 |

Selling expenses 8% of sales

Estimated annual sales 40,000 units and profit per unit is Rs.1.20. Calculate selling price per unit.

(Adapted: ICWAI)

(Ans: Rs.5.77)

26. ABC & Co Ltd provides the following costing information for the year ended 31st March 2011.

| Stock | 31st March 2010<br>Rs. | 31st March 2011<br>Rs. |
|---|---|---|
| Finished goods | 47,500 | 50,000 |
| Work-in-progress | 19,500 | 17,500 |
| Raw material | 7,800 | 4,500 |

| | Rs. |
|---|---|
| Purchase of material | 76,000 |
| Direct wages | 47,500 |
| Direct expenses | 19,000 |
| Indirect wages | 17,000 |
| Salary for foreman | 21,500 |
| Salary for office staff | 65,000 |
| Salary for sales department | 49,000 |
| Power | 8,500 |
| Electricity | 9,000 |
| Dividend paid | 22,000 |
| Rates and taxes | 12,000 |
| Income tax paid | 11,000 |
| Repairs & Maintenance of Plant | 7,000 |
| Repairs & Maintenance of Office equipment | 6,000 |
| Interest on loan | 14,000 |
| Outstanding direct wages | 7,500 |
| Salary for office staff paid in advance | 4,000 |
| Advertisement | 13,000 |
| Selling commission | 9,500 |
| Value of Plant & Machinery | 2,75,000 |
| Value of Office equipment | 1,20,000 |
| Value of Building | 2,00,000 |

Provide 10% depreciation for Plant & Machinery, 8% depreciation for Office Equipment and 6% depreciation for Building. Share the Electricity and Rates & taxes in the ratio 2:2:1 and depreciation for building in the ratio 3:2:1 for factory, office and selling department respectively. The company earned a profit of 10% on Sales.

Prepare a cost sheet and find out the costing profit.

(Ans: Rs.81,322)

27. A manufacturing company is providing the following information from the costing records for the month ending August 2011.

Direct material:

| | |
|---|---|
| Material X | 1500 units @ Rs.10 per unit |
| Material Y | 800 units @ Rs.12 per unit |
| Material Z | 700 units @ Rs.8 per unit |

Direct wages:

Grade I workers, 25 workers @ Rs.35 per day for 22 days

Grade II workers, 20 workers @ Rs.30 per day for 22 days

Direct expenses - Rs.21,000; Factory Overhead - Fixed Rs.10,000 and variable 30% of direct wages; Administration overhead, fixed Rs.15000 and variable @ 15% on works cost. Selling and distribution overhead @ 10% on cost of production. The profit of the company is 20% on sales.

The company manufactured 20,000 units. In the process of manufacturing the company realised Rs.3000 due to the sale of scrap.

Prepare a statement of cost and find out the cost per unit and selling price per unit.

(Adapted: C.A.)

(Ans: Rs.7.16; Rs.8.95)

28. X Ltd is providing the following information related to the production of 200 units of a product.

| | Rs. |
|---|---|
| Direct material | 32,000 |
| Direct wages | 30,000 |
| Direct expenses | 6,000 |

Factory overhead absorbed is 80% on direct wages. Administration overhead absorbed is 25% on works cost. Selling and distribution overhead absorbed is 10% on cost of production. The company earned a profit @ 20% on sales.

Prepare a Production Account and find out the costing profit.

(Ans: Rs.28,750)

29. AB Ltd is providing the following information related to the production of a product named X.

| | Rs. |
|---|---|
| Direct material | 90,000 |
| Direct wages | 50,000 |
| Direct expenses | 17,000 |

Factory overhead absorbed is 70% on direct wages. Administration overhead absorbed is 30% on works cost. Selling and distribution overhead absorbed is 10% on cost of production.The company earned a profit @ 10% on sales.

The company manufactured 5,000 units. In the process of manufacturing the company realised Rs.4,000 due to the sale of scrap.

Prepare a Production Account and find out the costing profit.

(Ans: Rs.29,871)

# CHAPTER-VI

# JOB COSTING, BATCH COSTING AND CONTRACT COSTING

The system of costing adopted for the production of goods according to the specification of customer is called Job Order Costing or Specific Order Costing. Job Costing, Batch Costing and Contract Costing are the different types of the Specific Order Costing. Though the treatment of costs and the nature of the terms and conditions of the work are same in job costing and contract costing, they are differing with the period of completion of the work. Usually the work of contract will go for more than one year. But in job costing the work was limited with fifteen or thirty days or to the maximum a year. Batch Costing is also a modified form of the specific order costing. In this method annual demand is determined and accordingly the goods are manufactured. Each lot should be combined as one unit and costs are allocated to that batch number. Manufacturing concerns using Job order Costing are machine tool manufacturing concerns, printing presses, ship-building, construction work, furniture shops etc. The non-manufacturing undertakings are Auto repair shops, Work shops, Auditing works etc.

## I JOB COSTING

### Meaning

Job costing is a method of costing in the category of Specific Order Costing. In Job Costing size of the job is relatively small. It requires very short period for completing the work. Job costing is distinct from contract costing in two respects. In contract costing the job is very big in terms of money value.Exception to this is the job costing performed by goldsmiths. Another point of disinction is in the duration of work. Contract works usually go for more than one year, even 5 years or 10 years.

### Objectives of Job Costing

The objectives of Job Costing are as follows.

1. In Job Costing, profit or loss of each job can be ascertained. It facilitates the management to know the different types of cost incurred for different jobs to take appropriate actions for the future period.
2. It facilitates the management to estimate the costs for the future period for the similar jobs. Hence, it would be easy for the management to quote prices for orders.
3. It helps for cost control techniques to be adopted by comparing the actual costs with the estimated costs.

**Ascertainment of Job Costs**

The cost of a job is determined on the basis of the requirement of direct material cost,direct labour cost, direct expenses and overheads.

***1. Direct material cost***

The requirement of direct material for a job can easily be determined and the cost is directly charged to the job.

***2. Direct labour cost***

The direct labour cost required for a job can be determined on the basis of the past data. Hence, this cost can also be directly charged to the job.

***3. Direct expenses***

Like the direct material cost and direct labour cost, direct expenses can be determined well in advance. All direct costs except direct material cost and direct labour cost is called the direct expenses.This cost is also directly charged to the job.

***4. Overheads***

Overheads are the indirect expenses which could not be easily identified for a job. These costs are commonly incurred for all jobs. Hence, it should be apportioned on a suitable basis of apportionment for respective jobs.

***Illustration: 1***

The following particulars are extracted from the books of Beta & Co Ltd. in respect of production of Order No.807

| | | |
|---|---|---|
| Material issued | | Rs.14,000 |
| Direct Labour | - Dept. A 700 hours | @ Rs.7 per hour |
| | Dept. B 900 hours | @ Rs.11 per hour |
| | Dept. C 1200 hours | @ Rs.12 per hour |
| Direct Expenses | | Rs.7,000 |

Factory overhead absorbed is 40% on direct wages.Administration overhead absorbed is 20% on works cost and Selling&Distribution overhead absorbed is 10% on works cost.

Material worth Rs.1,000 was returned to store after the work. Calculate the cost of production for the Job and find out the slling price if 20% profit is charged on selling price.

***Solution:***

**Job Cost Sheet of Beta & Co. Ltd for Job No 807**

| Particulars | Rs. | Rs. |
|---|---|---|
| Direct material | 14,000 | |
| Less: Returns | 1,000 | |
| | | 13,000 |
| Direct Wages - Dep. A 700 x 7 | 4,900 | |
| Dep. B 900 x 11 | 9,900 | |
| Dep. C 1200 x 12 | 14,400 | 29,200 |
| Direct Expenses | | 7,000 |
| PRIME COST | | 49,200 |
| Factory Overhead (40% of 29,200) | | 11,680 |
| WORKS COST | | 60,880 |
| Administration Overhead (20% of 60,880) | | 12,176 |
| COST OF PRODUCTION | | 73,056 |
| Selling and Distribution overhead (10% 0f 60,880) | | 6,088 |
| COST OF SALES | | 79,144 |
| PROFIT (20/80 x 79144) | | 19,786 |
| SELLING PRICE | | *98,930* |

**Illustration: 2**

The information given below have been extracted form the costing records of a company in respect of Job order No 555.

| | | | |
|---|---|---|---|
| Material | Rs.7,200 | | |
| Wages | Dept I | 120 hours | @ Rs.4 per hour |
| | Dept II | 300 hours | @ Rs.5 per hour |
| | Dept III | 500 hours | @ Rs.6 per hour |

Factory overhead are

| | |
|---|---|
| Dept I | 40% of wages |
| Dept II | 20% of wages |
| Dept III | 60% of wages |

Administration overhead absorbed was 20% on factory cost, and selling and distribution overhead absorbed was 25% on factory cost.

20% of the production will have to be scrapped and sale proceeds of the scrapped output was only 10% of the cost of sales.

Find out the cost of production and selling price to give a profit of 30% on cost.

***Solution:***

**Cost sheet for Job No: 555**

| Particulars | Rs. | Rs. |
|---|---|---|
| Direct Material | | 7,200 |
| Direct Wages Dept I 120 x 4 | 480 | |
| Dept II 300 x 5 | 1,500 | |
| Dept III 500 x 6 | 3,000 | 4,980 |
| PRIME COST | | 12,180 |
| Factory overhead Dept I 40% of 480 | 192 | |
| Dept II 20% of 1,500 | 300 | |
| Dept III 60% of ,3000 | 1,800 | 2,292 |
| WORKS COST | | 14,472 |
| Administration overhead (20% on Rs.14,472) | | 2,894 |
| COST OF PRODUCTION | | 17,366 |
| Selling and Distribution overhead (25% on Rs.14,472) | | 3,618 |
| COST OF SALES | | 20,984 |
| Less: Sale proceeds of scrap (10% of 20% of Rs.20,984) | | 420 |
| Cost of sales of the work order | | 20,564 |
| PROFIT (30% on cost) | | 6,169 |
| SALES | | 26,733 |

**Illustration: 3**

The cost incurred for 4 different jobs namely Job I, Job II, Job III and Job IV for the month of October 2011, by a manufacturing company are stated as follows:

| | Job I | Job II | Job III | Job IV |
|---|---|---|---|---|
| | Rs. | Rs. | Rs. | Rs. |
| Direct Material | 1,400 | 1,000 | 800 | 1,500 |
| Direct Wages | 1,100 | 700 | 900 | 700 |
| Direct Expenses | 500 | 400 | 350 | 250 |

Factory overhead absorbed is 60% of prime cost and Administration overhead absorbed is 20% on works cost. Calculate the total cost of each job.

***Solution:***

**Job Cost Sheet**

| Particulars | JobI Rs. | Job II Rs. | Job III Rs. | Job IV Rs. |
|---|---|---|---|---|
| Direct material | 1,400 | 1,000 | 800 | 1,500 |
| Direct wages | 1,100 | 700 | 900 | 700 |
| Direct expenses | 500 | 400 | 350 | 250 |
| Prime Cost | 3,000 | 2,100 | 2,050 | 2,450 |
| Factory overhead (60% on Prime cost) | 1,800 | 1,260 | 1,230 | 1,470 |
| Works Cost | 4,800 | 3,360 | 3,280 | 3,920 |
| Administration overhead (20% on works cost) | 960 | 672 | 656 | 784 |
| Total Cost | 5,760 | 4,032 | 3,936 | 4,704 |

**Illustration: 4**

Calculate the work cost for a Job No: 28466 for a manufacturing company, from the following particulars:

Direct material consumed Rs.1,500; Direct wages Rs.450; Direct expenses Rs.150

Indirect wages - Salary for foremen is Rs.4,000 and the Job No 28466 consumed 10% of their labour hours. Machine A and B are used for completing the work. Machine A is used for 30 hours and its machine hour rate is Rs.5.50. Machine B is used for 35 hours and its machine hour rate is Rs.4 per hour. Other factory overhead is 100% on direct labour.

***Solution:***

**Job Cost Sheet**

| Particulars | Rs. | Rs. |
|---|---|---|
| Direct Material | | 1,500 |
| Direct Wages | | 450 |
| Direct Expenses | | 150 |
| Prime Cost | | 2,100 |
| Factory overhead: | | |
| Machine A (30 x 5.50) | 165 | |
| Machine B (35 x 4) | 140 | |
| Salary for foremen (10% of 4,000) | 400 | |
| Other factory overhead (100% on Direct wages) | 450 | 1,155 |
| | | 3,255 |

**Illustration: 5**

KMW Co. Ltd is providing the following information in order to prepare a cost estimate.

The costs incurred by the company in a normal year are as follows:

| | Rs. |
|---|---|
| Direct Material | 95,500 |
| Direct Wages:- Manufacturing Section (12,000 hours) | 32,000 |
| Assembling section (9000 hours) | 36,000 |
| Factory overhead - Manufacturing section | 30,000 |
| and Assembling Section | 18,000 |
| Administration overhead | 14,500 |
| Selling overhead | 12,500 |
| Distribution overhead | 9,000 |

Calculate the overhead rates and also find out the cost estimate for a Job No.2132. The job requires Direct material 30Kg @ Rs.15 per Kg and 20Kg @ Rs.12 per Kg; Direct wages - Manufacturing section 18 hours @ Rs.9 per hour and Assembling section 22 hours @ Rs.10 per hour.

***Solution:*** **Cost Sheet**

| Particulars | Rs. | Rs. |
|---|---|---|
| Direct material | | 95,500 |
| Direct Wages | | |
| Manufacturing section | 32,000 | |
| Assembling section | 36,000 | |
| | | 68,000 |
| Prime cost | | 1,63,500 |
| Add: Factory overhead | | |
| Manufacturing section | 30,000 | |
| Assembling section | 18,000 | 48,000 |
| Works cost | | 2,11,500 |
| Add: Administration overhead | | 14,500 |
| Cost of Production | | 2,26,000 |
| Add: Selling overhead | 12,500 | |
| Distribution overhead | 9,000 | 21,500 |
| Cost of Sales | | 2,47,500 |

**Calculation of Overhead Rates:**

Factory Overhead Rate

$$\text{Manufacturing section} = \frac{30{,}000}{12{,}000} = \text{Rs.2.5 per hour}$$

$$\text{Assembling section} = \frac{18{,}000}{9000} = \text{Rs.2 per hour}$$

$$\text{Administration Overhead Rate} = \frac{\text{Administration Overhead}}{\text{Works cost}}$$

$$= \frac{14{,}500 \times 100}{2{,}11{,}500} = 6.86\%$$

Selling and Distribution Overhead Rate

$$= \frac{\text{Selling \& Distribution Overhead}}{\text{Cost of production}} \times 100$$

$$= \frac{21{,}500 \times 100}{2{,}26{,}000} = 9.51\%$$

**Estimated Cost for Job No: 2132**

| Particulars | | Rs. | Rs. |
|---|---|---|---|
| Direct Material: (30 x 15) | 450 | | |
| (20 x12) | 240 | 690 | |
| Direct wages: | | | |
| Manufacturing Section (18 x 9) | 162 | | |
| Assembling Section (22 x 10) | 220 | 382 | |
| **Prime Cost** | | | 1,072 |
| Factory overhead: | | | |
| Manufacturing Section (18 x 2.5) | 45 | | |
| Assembling Section (22 x 2) | 44 | | 89 |
| **Works cost** | | | 1,161 |
| Administration overhead (1161x 6.86/100) | | | 80 |
| **Cost of production** | | | 1,241 |
| Selling and Distribution Overhead (1241x 9.51/100) | | | 118 |
| **Cost of Sales** | | | 1,359 |

## II. BATCH COSTING

Batch costing is a method of costing practiced in industries which manufacture articles in definite batches or lots. The production should involve limited repetitive work. Hence, Batch costing may otherwise be called as 'lot costing'.

ICMA London defines batch costing as that form of specific order costing which applies where similar articles are manufactured in batches either for sale or use within the company.

Examples of business establishment using batch costing are brick manufacturing concerns, bakeries, toys manufacturing companies, shoe making concerns etc.

***Job Costing and Batch Costing***

Job Costing is similar to Batch Costing in most respects. Batch Costing is a modified form of Job Costing. The treatment of costs under Job Costing and Batch Costing are the same. Under batch costing the unit of cost, is a batch. Each batch should be given a batch number. Cost spent for direct material and direct labour for batch numbers should be identified and charged to respective batch numbers. Similarly overhead should be apportioned on suitable basis and charged to the respective batch number. The total of direct material, direct labour, direct expenses and overheads would be the total batch cost for respective numbers. Cost of production per unit in a batch can be calculated by dividing the total cost in the respective batch number by the total number of units under the batch.

The basic difference between the Batch costing and Job costing is that under batch costing, goods are manufactured as stock for sales to customers, but under job costing work will be performed in accordance with the specification of the customers. In Batch costing, Economic Batch Quantity can be determined but it is not possible to determine Economic Batch Quantity under the Job-Order Costing System.

***Determination of Economic Batch Quantity.***

The important task in batch costing is determination of the size of the batch, i.e., the optimum number of units in each batch. The cost of mainting of large batch and the cost of mainting of small batch should be balanced so as to derive an optimum batch size. The optimum batch size can be called as Economic Batch Quantity. In Economic Batch Quantity, Setting - up cost and Carrying cost are equal.

***Setting - up cost***

It is a cost incurred for setting - up the plant & machinery before production commences. This cost will normally remain constant for each batch. Increase in batch size means reduction in number of batches to be manufactured in a year. Hence the setting - up cost for one year will diminish due to the increase in the size of the batch. Therefore, increase in batch size means decrease in setting - up cost and decrease in batch size means increase in setting- up cost.

***Carrying Costs***

Carrying cost consists of costs for maintaining the stocks

in the storehouse. (Eg) Storage rent, salaries to store - keeper, other storage costs, interest on capital blocked in large stocks and the risk of obsolesence etc. Carrying cost will increase in proportion to the increase in batch size and decrease with the decrease in batch size.

Hence, increase in batch size means economy in setting up cost but disadvantage in carrying cost; decrease in batch size means economy in carrying cost but disadvantage in setting - up cost. So, a balance should be maintained to get maximum economy from both setting up cost and carrying cost. This can be determined through a mathematical formula.

***Formula for Economic Batch Quantity***

The information required for the calculation of Economic Batch Quantity are,

(i) The setting - up cost
(ii) The cost of storage
(iii) Rate of interest on the capital blocked in the stock of goods.
(iv) Cost of production, and
(v) Annual requirement of articles.

Economic Batch Quantity can be determined through the following formula.

$$E.B.Q = \sqrt{2AS / C}$$

Where, A - referes to Annual demand for the product
S - refers to Setting - up cost per batch
C - refers to Carrying cost per unit.

If monthly demand was given then

$$E.B.Q. = \sqrt{24DS / C}$$

Where D refers to monthly demand

When the rate of interest on Capital and the cost of production per unit is given, Carrying cost per unit can be ascertained by multiplying the Rate of interest with the cost per unit. The formula would be

$$E.B.Q. = \sqrt{2AS / IC}$$

where I refers to Rate of Interest of capital
C refers to cost of production per unit.

If monthly demand was given then

$$E.B.Q = \sqrt{24DS / IC}$$

The formula for E.B.Q should be modified by multiplying with 12 if monthly demand is given in the problem. Hence it is stated as 24 DS instead of 2 AS.

**Graphical representation of Economic Batch Quantity**

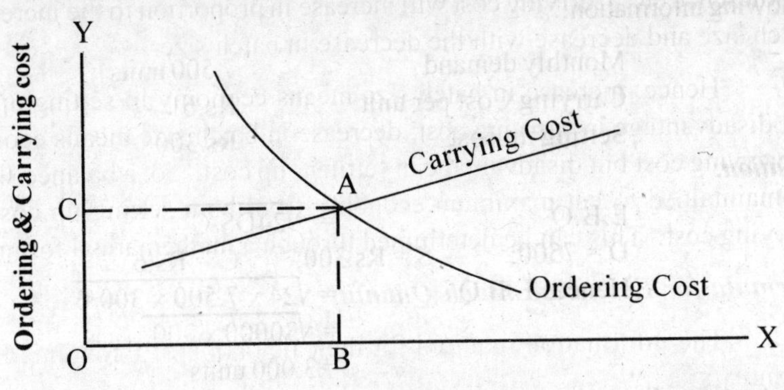


In the above graph X axis represents Batch size and Y axis represents cost per unit. Carrying cost curve indicates that the increase in batch size will increase the cost and vice versa. But the set up cost decreases due to the increase in batch size. The two curves intersect at a point 'A' where both carrying cost and setting up cost are equal. A parellel line of Y axis should be drawn from 'A' touching the X axis at B. OB is called as Economic Batch Quantity.

**Illustration: 6**

Compute the economic batch quantity with the information given below:

| | |
|---|---|
| Annual demand for the product | 40,000 units |
| Setting up cost | Rs.100 |
| Cost of production per unit | Rs.20 |
| Rate of interest per annum | 10% |

***Solution:***

Economic batch quantity = $\sqrt{2AS/IC}$

A = 40,000 units S = Rs.100

I = 10% C = Rs.20

$$\text{Hence, E.B.Q.} = \sqrt{\frac{2 \times 40,000 \times 100}{20 \times 10\%}}$$

$$= \sqrt{40,000 \times 100}$$

$$= 2,000 \text{ units}$$

**Illustration: 7**

Calculate the economic batch quantity of a company from the following information:

| | |
|---|---|
| Monthly demand | 7,500 units |
| Carrying Cost per unit | Rs.6 |
| Setting up cost | Rs.300 |

***Solution:***

E.B.Q $= \sqrt{24DS/C}$

D = 7500; S = Rs 300; C = Rs.6

Hence, E.B.Q $= \sqrt{24 \times 7,500 \times 300/6}$

$= \sqrt{30000 \times 300}$

= 3,000 units

**Illustration: 8**

Compute Economic Batch Quantity through E.B.Q formula and prove the result by tabular form.

| | |
|---|---|
| Annual demand | 2,000 units |
| Setting up cost | Rs.200 |
| Cost of production per unit | Rs.200 |
| Rate of interest per annum | 10% |

***Solution:***

E.B.Q. = $\sqrt{2AS/IC}$

A = 2000 units

S = Rs.200

I = 10%

C = Rs.200

$$E.B.Q. = \sqrt{\frac{2 \times 2000 \times 200}{200 \times 10\%}}$$

= 200 units

**Calculation of EBQ**

| Size of the batch Units | No. of times in a year | Setting up Cost @ Rs.200 Rs. | Average Size Units | Carrying Cost @ Rs.20 Rs. | Total Cost Rs. |
|---|---|---|---|---|---|
| 2000 | 1 | 200 | 1,000 | 20,000 | 20,200 |
| 1000 | 2 | 400 | 500 | 10,000 | 10,400 |
| 500 | 4 | 800 | 250 | 5,000 | 5,800 |
| 200 | 10 | 2,000 | 100 | 2,000 | 4,000 |
| 100 | 20 | 4,000 | 50 | 1,000 | 5,000 |
| 50 | 40 | 8,000 | 25 | 500 | 8,500 |
| 20 | 100 | 20,000 | 10 | 200 | 20,200 |

It is proved from the above tabulation that the E.B.Q is 200 units. At 200 units of production, carrying cost equals with setting-up cost. Also the total cost is the minimum at the E.B.Q. level.

## III. CONTRACT COSTING

Contract costing is just like job costing. The principles adopted in job costing is also adopted in contract costing. Normally, the value of work adopted in contract costing is huge amount whereas, in job costing the value of work is very small. The work adopted in job costing requires very short period. But the work adopted in contract costing is long period and even it may be more than one year. The type of work requires contract costing are construction of buildings, dams, bridges, road, railway lines, etc. The person who undertakes the contract is called the contractor and the person who gives the contract is called contractee.

### *Types of contract*

There are two types of contract. They are,

1. Fixed Price Contract and 2. Cost Plus Contract.

### *1. Fixed Price Contract:*

Under the fixed price contract, the contract is given to the contractor on fixed price basis. The contractor has to complete the work within the fixed price in order to earn profit. This profit is the difference between fixed price and the expenses incurred for the contract.

### *2. Cost Plus Contract:*

Under the cost plus contract, the contractor is allowed to do the work wthout fixing the price. The contractor is paid on the basis of the total expenses for the work plus a profit on the total cost.

### *Accounting of Contract Cost and Revenue*

In order to find out the profit or loss on contract, the contractor prepares an account called Contract Account. If a contractor undertook more than one contract, then separate Contract Accounts should be maintained for each contract. The Contract Account is prepared in a T form, where the left hand side is called debit and right hand side is called credit. The expenses incurred for the period is debited and the contract price is credited in the Contract Account. The difference in the debit side and credit side is called the profit or loss. If credit is more than debit, it is called profit and if debit is more than credit, then, it is called loss on contract.

Hence, the accounting procedures of Contract costing is classified into

I Treatment of Cost and
II Treatment of Revenue.

## I. Treatment of cost

The different types of costs involved in a contract are stated as follows.

### *1. Direct Material Cost*

Material is an important cost in the contract. Cost of material consumed during the period is debited in the contract account. The cost of material consumed is calculated by taking into account of opening stock of material and closing stock of material. i.e., Cost of material consumed = Opening stock of material + Purchase of material - Closing stock of material. If material is returned from the work place then it should also be deducted.

### *2. Direct Labour Cost*

The remuneration paid to the employees engaged in a contract is treated as direct labour cost. The nature of work is not a factor in contract account since there is no need for apportionment of the labour cost. In case, the labourers are engaged in different contracts of the contractor, then the labour cost should be apportioned on the basis of time spent by them in different contract work.

### *3. Direct Expenses*

The expenses other than the direct material and direct labour are called Direct Expenses. (Eg) Architects Fees, Cost of designs, transport cost etc.

### *4. Indirect Expenses*

Normally, all expenses are treated as direct when there is one contract . If the contractor is doing more than one contract work then the expenses commonly incurred are called indirect expenses or overhead. These expenses should be apportioned for different contracts on suitable basis of apportionment.

### *5. Depreciation of Plant and Machinery*

There are two methods of treating depreciation for plant & machinery. The value of the plant in the beginning should be debited and the value of the plant at the end of the contract period or accounting period should be created in the contract account. Another method of treating the depreciation is debiting the contract account with depreciation of plant.It is calculated on percentage basis. If the plant is hired for rent, then the hire charges should be debited in the contract account.

### *6. Cost of Sub-contract*

Sometimes, the contractor may do some portion of the contract work, with the help of another contractor. The expenses paid for the work is treated as a direct expense and debited in the contract account.

### *7. Cost of Maintenance periods*

Sometimes, even then the work of contract is completed, the contractor has to maintain the work for a specific period of time. The expenses of the maintenance are debited in the contract account.

## II. Treatment of Revenue

The treatments of Revenue in a contract account are stated as follows.

### *1. Revenue of a Completed Contract*

The contract account is credited for the contract price if the contract work is completed. The same procedure is adopted whether the period of contract is one year or more than one year. The difference between the debit side and credit side is called profit or loss of contract. If the credit side is more than the debit side,the difference is called profit and if the debit side is more than the credit the difference is called loss.

### *2. Revenue of an Incomplete Contract*

Normally the period of contract is extended for more than one year. In this case, it is difficult to find out the revenue for the accounting period. Hence, the revenue is ascertained on the basis of the certificate issued by the architect about the work completed. This value is called "work certified" and is credited in the contract account by an account called ".Work-in-progress account". If the contractor feels that some portion of the work is not certified by the architect, then that portion of the work is also included in the Work- in- progress Account in the name 'work uncertified'. But before transferring the profit of incomplete contracts some portion of the profit is kept as reserve by debiting the contract account with Work-in-progress account. The portion of reserve depends upon the percentage of work completed.

### *Work-in-progress Account*

This account is opened in a Contract Account to treat the profit of incomplete contracts. This account is credited in the contract account for work certified and work uncertified. It is required for the contractors to keep certain amount of profit as reserve before transferring the profit on incomplete contract to the Profit & Loss Account. It is done through debiting the contract account with work-in-progress account. The amount of reserve, depends on the percentage of work completed. The calculation of reserve for different stages of completion of the work are as follows.

(i) When less than 25% of the work is completed, then entire profit is transferred to reserve in the name of WIP account.

(ii) When more than 25% but less than 50% work is completed, then the reserve is calculated as,

$$\frac{1}{3} \text{ x Notional Profit x } \frac{\text{Cash received}}{\text{Work certified}}$$

(iii) When more than 50% but less than 90% work is completed, then the reserve is calculated as,

$$\frac{2}{3} \text{ x Notional Profit x } \frac{\text{Cash received}}{\text{Work certified}}$$

(iv) When more than 90% but less than 100% work is completed, then the reserve is calculated as

$$\text{Notional Profit x } \frac{\text{Work certified}}{\text{Contract price}}$$

If estimated profit is known then the reserve is calculated as

$$\text{Estimated Profit x } \frac{\text{Cash received}}{\text{Work certified}}$$

### *Meaning of Related Terms*

#### *1. Notional Profit*

Notional profit is the difference between the work certified (and work uncertified) and the expenses incurred for the contract during the period.

#### *2. Retention Money*

The difference between the work certified and the cash received is called the 'Retention Money'.

#### *3. Escalation Clause*

Sometimes the contract entered by the parties contains a clause called Escalation Clause, in order to safeguard the contractor from the raising cost of production due to increase in price. According to this clause, the contractee will compensate the contractor when the contractor suffered loss due to rising price of material, labour cost and other expenses.

**Illustration: 9**

The following information are related to a contract of X Ltd. for the year ending 31st March 2011.

| | |
|---|---|
| Direct Material | Rs.3,00,000 |
| Direct Wages | Rs.2,20,000 |
| Direct Expenses | Rs.1,70,000 |
| Indirect Expenses | Rs.50,000 |

The contract price was Rs.12,00,000. The cash received on 31st March, 2011 amounted to Rs.6,00,000 being 75% of work certified. The work uncertified was valued at Rs.40,000. Prepare Contract Account and find out the profit to be credited to Profit and Loss Account.

***Solution:***

**Contract Account**

| Date | Particulars | Amount Rs. | Date | Particulars | Amount Rs. |
|---|---|---|---|---|---|
| 2011 | | | 2011 | | |
| Mar 31 | To Direct material | 3,00,000 | Mar 31 | By Work-in-progress: | |
| | To Direct wages | 2,20,000 | | Work certified | 8,00,000 |
| | To Direct expenses | 1,70,000 | | (6,00,000 x100/75) | |
| | To Indirect expenses | 50,000 | | Work uncertified | 40,000 |
| | To Notional Profit c/d | 1,00,000 | | | |
| | | 8,40,000 | | | 8,40,000 |
| Mar 31 | To Profit & Loss A/c $(100,000 \times 2/3 \times \frac{75}{100})$ | 50,000 | Mar 31 | By Notional Profit | 1,00,000 |
| | To Work-in-progress A/c (Reserve) | 50,000 | | | |
| | | 1,00,000 | | | 1,00,000 |
| 2011 | | | 2011 | | |
| April 1 | To Work-in-progress: | | April 1 | By Work-in-progress A/c (Reserve) | 50,000 |
| | Work certified | 8,00,000 | | | |
| | Work uncertifed | 40,000 | | | |

**Illustration: 10**

The following information relates to a contract of Rex Construction Ltd for the financial year 2011.

| | Rs. |
|---|---|
| Direct material sent to site | 1,86,000 |
| Direct wages | 1,14,000 |
| Direct expenses | 48,500 |
| Plant | 2,00,000 |
| Material returned to store | 16,000 |
| Establishment charges | 37,500 |
| Wages outstanding for the year 2011 | 7,250 |
| Expenses outstanding for the year 2011 | 4,750 |
| Value of plant as on 31st March 2011 | 1,86,000 |
| Material at site as on 31st March 2011 | 20,000 |
| Work certified | 4,70,000 |
| Work uncertified | 39,000 |

The contract price is Rs.17,00,000. The cash received from contractee is 70% of the value of work certified.

Prepare the Contract Account and Contractee's Account and find out the profit to be credited to the Contractor's Profit and Loss Account.

***Solution:***

**Contract Account**

| Date | Particulars | Amount Rs. | Date | Particulars | Amount Rs. |
|---|---|---|---|---|---|
| 2011 Mar 31 | To Material | 1,86,000 | 2011 Mar 31 | By Material returned to store | 16,000 |
| | " Wages 1,14,000 | | | " Material at site | 20,000 |
| | Add: Outstanding 7250 | 1,21,250 | | " Plant at site | 1,86,000 |
| | " Direct Expenses 48,500 | | | " Work-in-progress | |
| | Add: Outstanding 4,750 | 53,250 | | Work certified | 4,70,000 |
| | " Establishment charges | 37,500 | | Work uncertified | 39,000 |
| | " Plant | 2,00,000 | | | |
| | " Notional Profit | 1,33,000 | | | |
| | | *7,31,000* | | | *7,31,000* |
| Mar 31 | To Profit & Loss A/c (133,000 x 1/3 x 70/100) | 31,033 | Mar 31 | By Notional Profit | 1,33,000 |
| | " Work-in-progress (Reserve) | 1,01,967 | | | |
| | | *1,33,000* | | | *1,33,000* |
| 2011 April 1 | To Work-in-progress | | 2011 April 1 | By Work-in-progress (Reserve) | 1,01,967 |
| | Work certified | 4,70,000 | | | |
| | Work uncertified | 39,000 | | | |

**Contractee's Account**

| | Particulars | Rs. | | Particulars | Rs. |
|---|---|---|---|---|---|
| 2011 Mar 31 | To Balance c/d | 3,29,000 | 2011 Mar 31 | By Cash | 3,29,000 |
| | | | 2011 April 1 | By Balance c/d | 3,29,000 |

**Illustration: 11**

The Rose Builders Ltd, provides the following information relating to a contract for Rs.10,00,000

| | 2009 Rs. | 2010 Rs. | 2011 Rs. |
|---|---|---|---|
| Materials | 80,000 | 75,000 | 1,05,000 |
| Wages | 70,000 | 65,000 | 80,000 |
| Direct Expenses | 17,000 | 4,000 | 3,600 |
| Indirect Expenses | 2,800 | 3,500 | 5,000 |
| Plant | 20,000 | - | - |
| Work certified | 1,70,000 | 5,00,000 | 10,00,000 |
| Work uncertified | | 20,000 | - |

The value of the plant at the end of 2009, 2010 and 2011 are Rs.18,000, Rs.14,000 and Rs.10,000 respectively. The cash received being 80% of the value of work done as certified by the architect.

Prepare Contract Account.

***Solution:***

**Contract Account**

| Date | Particulars | Amount Rs. | Date | Particulars | Amount Rs. |
|---|---|---|---|---|---|
| 2009 Mar 31 | To Materials | 80,000 | 2009 Mar 31 | By Work-in-progress: | |
| | " Wages | 70,000 | | Work certified | 1,70,000 |
| | " Direct expenses | 17,000 | | Work uncertified | - |
| | " Indirect expenses | 2,800 | | " Plant | 18,000 |
| | " Plant | 20,000 | | " Loss trasferred to Costing P&L A/c | 1,800 |
| | | *1,89,800* | | | *1,89,800* |
| 2010 Mar 31 | To Work-in-progress: | | 2010 Mar 31 | By Work-in-progress: | |
| | Work certified | 1,70,000 | | Work certified | 5,00,000 |
| | Work uncertified | - | | Work uncertified | 20,000 |
| | " Materials | 75,000 | | " Plant | 14,000 |

| Date | Particulars | Rs. | Date | Particulars | Rs. |
|---|---|---|---|---|---|
| | " Wages | 65,000 | | | |
| | " Direct expenses | 4,000 | | | |
| | " Indirect expenses | 3,500 | | | |
| | " Plant | 18,000 | | | |
| | " Profit & Loss A/c (198500x $^2/_3$x80/100) | 1,05,867 | | | |
| | " Work-in-progress (Reserve) | 92,633 | | | |
| | | *5,34,000* | | | *5,34,000* |
| 2011 Mar 31 | To Work-in-progress | | 2011 Mar 31 | By Work-in-progress (Reserve) | 92,633 |
| | Work certified | 5,00,000 | | " Contractee's Personal A/c | 10,00,000 |
| | Work uncertified | 20,000 | | " Plant | 10,000 |
| | " Material | 1,05,000 | | | |
| | " Wages | 80,000 | | | |
| | " Direct expenses | 3,600 | | | |
| | " Indirect expenses | 5,000 | | | |
| | " Plant | 14,000 | | | |
| | " Profit & Loss A/c | 3,75,033 | | | |
| | | *11,02,633* | | | *11,02,633* |

**Illustration: 12**

Joyce Construction Company undertook three contracts, the work of which commenced on 1st April, 1st July and 1st October 2010 respectively. The accounts of the three contracts as on 31st March, 2011 showed the following details.

| | Contract I Rs. | Contract II Rs. | Contract III Rs. |
|---|---|---|---|
| Materials | 84,000 | 76,000 | 54,000 |
| Wages paid | 67,000 | 57,000 | 45,000 |
| Direct expenses | 11,000 | 13,000 | 14,000 |
| Overhead | 19,000 | 18,000 | 21,000 |
| Materials on hand | 7,000 | 4,000 | 6,000 |
| Plant installed | 75,000 | 85,000 | 70,000 |
| Wages accrued | 2,000 | 4,000 | 1,000 |
| Work certified | 2,40,000 | 2,10,000 | 1,80,000 |
| Work finished but not certified | 30,000 | 20,000 | 20,000 |
| Cash received | 2,00,000 | 1,40,000 | 1,20,000 |
| Contract Price | 12,00,000 | 7,00,000 | 4,00,000 |

Prepare Contract Account and Balance Sheet as on 31st March 2011. Assume that the plant was installed on the date of commencement of each contract and the depreciation is to be charged @ 10% per annum.

***Solution:***

**CONTRACT No:I ACCOUNT**

| Particulars | Rs. | Particulars | Rs. |
|---|---|---|---|
| To Material | 84,000 | By Materials at site | 7,000 |
| " Wages | 67,000 | " Plant (75,000 - 7,500) | 67,500 |
| " Direct expenses | 11,000 | (Dep: 75,000 x 10/100) | |
| " Overhead | 19,000 | " Work-in-progress: | |
| " Wages accrued | 2,000 | Work certified | 2,40,000 |
| " Plant | 75,000 | Work uncertified | 30,000 |
| " Work-in-progress (Reserve) | 86,500 | | |
| | 3,44,500 | | 3,44,500 |

**CONTRACT No.II ACCOUNT**

| Particulars | Rs. | Particulars | Rs. |
|---|---|---|---|
| To Material | 76,000 | By Material at site | 4,000 |
| " Wages | 57,000 | " Plant (85,000 - 6,375) | 78,625 |
| " Direct expenses | 13,000 | (Dep:85,000x10/100x9/12) | |
| " Overhead | 18,000 | " Work-in-progress: | |
| " Wages accrued | 4,000 | Work certified | 2,10,000 |
| " Plant | 85,000 | Work uncertified | 20,000 |
| " Profit & Loss A/c | 13,250 | | |
| " Work-in-progress (Reserve) | 46,375 | | |
| | 3,12,625 | | 3,12,625 |

**CONTRACT No. III ACCOUNT**

| Particulars | Rs. | Particulars | Rs. |
|---|---|---|---|
| To Material | 54,000 | By Material at site | 6,000 |
| " Wages | 45,000 | " Plant (70,000 - 3,500) | 66,500 |
| " Direct expenses | 14,000 | (Dep:70,000x10/100x6/12) | |
| " Overhead | 21,000 | " Work-in-progress: | |
| " Wages accrued | 1,000 | Work certified | 1,80,000 |
| " Plant | 70,000 | Work uncertified | 20,000 |
| " Profit & Loss A/c | 30,000 | | |
| " Work-in-progress (Reserve) | 37,500 | | |
| | 2,72,500 | | 2,72,500 |

**BALANCE SHEET as on 31ST MARCH 2011**

| Assets | | Amount Rs. | Rs. |
|---|---|---|---|
| | Work-in-progress | 5,29,625 | |
| Less: | Contractee's A/c (Advance Received) | 4,60,000 | 69,625 |
| | Plant | 2,30,000 | |
| Less: | Depreciation | 17,375 | 2,12,625 |
| | Materials in hand | | 17,000 |

***Note:***

1. Since less than ¼th of the contract was completed in the contract No: I all the profit should be taken as Work-in-progress reserve.
2. Profit & Loss A/c for contract No: II is
$59,625 \times {}^1/_3 \times \frac{1,40,000}{2,10,000} = $ Rs.13,250
3. Profit & Loss A/c for Contract No: III is
$67,500 \times {}^2/_3 \times \frac{120,000}{80,000} = $ Rs.30,000
4. Work-in-progress in Balance Sheet
270,000 + 230,000 + 200,000 - (86,500 + 46,375 + 37,500)
= 700,000 - 170,375 = Rs.5,29,625

## EXERCISE

**I. Choose the correct answer for the following:**

1. The system of costing adopted for specific job order is called
(i) Batch costing (ii) Job costing
(iii) Contract costing (iv) Process costing
2. Batch costing is adopted in concerns which produce articles in definite
(i) Lots (ii) Contract (iii) Job (iv) Quantity
3. In Economic Batch Quantity, Setting-up cost and Carrying cost are
(i) Not equal (ii) Fixed cost (iii) Equal (iv) Neither equal nor unequal
4. EBQ is applied in
(i) Contract costing (ii) Job costing
(iii) Process costing (iv) Batch costing
5. The period of completion of a job is normally more than one year in
(i) Batch costing (ii) Contract costing
(iii) Marginal costing (iv) Process costing

6. Work certified in a contract account is treated in
   (i) Work-in-progress A/c (ii) Prime cost
   (iii) Direct expense (iv) Indirect expense
7. The differece between work certified and cash received in a contract account is called
   (i) Revenue (ii) General Revenue
   (iii) Retention Money (iv) Works cost
8. The difference between revenue and expenses in contract costing without crediting for reserve is called
   (i) Net profit (ii) Notional profit (iii) Gross profit (iv) Net loss
9. Machine set up cost and carrying cost are equal in
   (i) EBQ (ii) EOQ (iii) XOQ (iv) AOQ
10. When number of units in a batch increase the machine set up cost will proportionately
    (i) Increase (ii) Remains constant
    (iii) Neither increase nor decrease (iv) Decrease

[Ans: 1. (ii) 2. (i) 3. (iii) 4. (iv) 5. (ii) 6. (i) 7. (iii) 8. (ii) 9. (i) 10. (iv)]

**II. Answer the following:**

11. Define Job Costing and state the objectives of Job Costing.
12. What is Job Costing? State the procedure of calculating the cost for Job costing.
13. Define Batch Costing. State the procedures of determination of Economic Batch Quantity.
14. Distinguish between Job Costing and Batch Costing.
15. Define Economic Batch Quantity. State the graphical representation of Economic Batch Quantity.
16. Define Contract costing. State the treatment of costs in Contract Account.
17. What is contract costing? State the treatment of Revenue in Completed and Incompleted contract.
18. Define Contract Costing. State the purpose and methods of treatment of Work-in-progress account in Contract costing.
19. Distinguish between Job costing, Batch costing and Contract costing.
20. Write short notes of the following:

| | | | |
|---|---|---|---|
| (i) | Escalation Clause | (ii) | Retention Money |
| (iii) | Notional Profit | (iv) | Cost-plus Contract |
| (v) | E.B.Q | (vi) | Carrying Cost |
| (vii) | Machine set-up cost | | |

21. The following particulars have been extracted from the books of XY & Co Ltd with respect of production Order No. 105

| | | |
|---|---|---|
| Material issued | | Rs.1,17,000 |
| Direct Labour | Dept A | 800 hours @ Rs.8 per hour |
| | Dept B | 1,000 hours @ Rs.10 per hour |
| | Dept C | 900 hour @ Rs.9 per hour |
| Direct Expenses | | Rs.10,000 |

Factory overhead absorbed is 50% on Direct wages, Adminstration overhead absorbed is 30% on Factory cost,and Selling and distribution overhead absorbed is 20% on Cost of production.

Material worth Rs.1,500 was returned to store after the work. Calculate the cost of production and find out the selling price if 25% profit is charged on selling price.

(Ans: Rs.129,480)

22. The information related to the cost for Job order No:333 are as follows:

| | | |
|---|---|---|
| Material | | Rs.12,000 |
| Wages | Dept I | 200 hours @ Rs.5 per hour |
| | Dept II | 150 hours @ Rs.4 per hour |
| | Dept III | 300 hours @ Rs.6 per hour |
| Factory overhead: | | |
| | Dept I | 50% of wages |
| | Dept II | 30% of wages |
| | Dept III | 40% of wages |

Administration overhead absorbed is 30% on Factory cost, and Selling and distribution overhead absorbed is 20% on Factory cost.

25% of the production will have to be scrapped and sales proceeds of the scrapped output is only 15% of the cost of sales.

Find out the cost of production and selling price when the profit is 25% on cost.

(Ans: Rs.30,319)

23. The cost incurred for 4 different jobs by a manufacturing company are as follows:

| | Job I | Job II | Job III | Job IV |
|---|---|---|---|---|
| | Rs. | Rs. | Rs. | Rs. |
| Direct material | 5,000 | 4,000 | 6,000 | 7,000 |
| Direct wages | 6,000 | 5,000 | 4,000 | 5,000 |
| Direct expenses | 4,000 | 3,000 | 2,000 | 4,000 |

Factory overhead is 50% of prime cost and Administration overhead is 25% on works cost.

Calculate the total cost of each job

(Ans: Job I Rs.28125; Job II Rs.12,500; Job III Rs.12,500; Job IV Rs.30,000)

24. Calculate the work cost for a Job No. 4746 for a manufacturing company, from the following particulars:

Direct material consumed Rs.6,000; Direct wages Rs.5,500; Direct expenses Rs.2,000

Indirect wages - Salary for foremen Rs.7,000 and the Job No. 4746 consumed 20% of their labour hours

Machines X and Y are used for completing the work. Machine X is used for 50 hours and the machine hour rate is Rs.5 per hour. Machine Y is used for 40 hours and the machine hour rate is Rs.6 per hour. Other factory overhead is 80% on direct labour.

(Ans: Rs.20,890)

25. XYZ Ltd is providing the following information in order to prepare a cost estimate.

The cost incurred by the company in normal year are as follows:

| | | |
|---|---|---|
| Direct material | | Rs.80,000 |
| Direct wages - | Manufacturing Section (15,000 hours) | Rs.45,000 |
| | Assembly Section (10,000 hours) | Rs.60,000 |
| Factory overhead - | Manufacturing Section | Rs.50,000 |
| | Assembly section | Rs.30,000 |
| Administration overhead | | Rs.40,000 |
| Selling overhead | | Rs.25,000 |
| Distribution overhead | | Rs.15,000 |

Calculate the overhead rates and also find out the cost estimate for a Job No: 777. The job requires Direct material 50 kgm @ Rs.60 per kgm and 40 kgm @ Rs.30 per kgm; Direct wages - Manufacturing section 20 hours @ Rs.15 per hour and Assembly section 15 hours @ Rs.20 per hour.

(Ans: Rs.3.30 & Rs.3; Rs.15, Rs.11.40; Rs.6,330)

26. Compute the economic batch quantity for X Ltd. with the information given below:

| | |
|---|---|
| Annual demand for the product | 50,000 units |
| Setting up cost | Rs.120 |
| Cost of production per unit | Rs.30 |
| Rate of interest per annum | 20% |

(Ans: 1414 units)

27. Calculate the economic batch quantity of a company from the following information.

Monthly demand 8,000 units; Carrying cost Rs.7 per unit; Setting up cost Rs.350

(Ans: 3098 units)

28. Compute Economic Batch Quantity through E.B.Q formula and prove the result by tabular form.

Annual demand 2,500 units; Setting up cost Rs.250; Cost of production per unit Rs.250; Rate of interest per annum 20%

(Ans: 158 units)

29. The following information are related to a contract of X Ltd for the year ending 31st March 2011.

Material Rs.4,00,000; Direct wages Rs.2,75,000; Direct expenses Rs.1,50,000; Indirect expenses Rs.75,000.

The contract price is Rs.14,00,000. The cash received on 31st March 2006 amounted to Rs.7,00,000 being 60% of work certified. The work uncertified is valued as Rs.30,000.

Prepare Contract Account and find out the profit to be credited to Profit & Loss Account.

(Ans: Rs.59,333)

30. The following information are related to the cost incurred for a contract of ABC & Co Ltd, for the year ending 31st March 2011.

| | Rs. |
|---|---|
| Direct material sent to site | 2,10,000 |
| Direct wages | 1,80,000 |
| Direct expenses | 60,000 |
| Plant | 4,00,000 |
| Material returned to store | 20,000 |
| Establishment charges | 40,000 |
| Wages outstanding for the year 2011 | 8,000 |
| Expenses outstanding for the year 2011 | 6,000 |
| Value of plant as on 31st March 2011 | 3,60,000 |
| Material at site as on 31st March 2011 | 25,000 |
| Work certified | 7,00,000 |
| Work uncertified | 40,000 |

The contract price is Rs.27,00,000. The cash received from the contractee is 80% of the value of work certified.

Prepare the Contract Account and Contractee's Account and find out the profit to be credited to the Contractor's Profit & Loss Account.

(Ans: Rs.1,28,533)

31. XYZ Ltd is providing the following information related to a contract for Rs.13,00,000.

| | 2009 | 2010 | 2011 |
|---|---|---|---|
| | Rs. | Rs. | Rs. |
| Material | 1,20,000 | 80,000 | 1,35,000 |
| Wages | 90,000 | 85,000 | 1,00,000 |
| Direct Expenses | 20,000 | 7,000 | 5,000 |
| Indirect Expenses | 7,000 | 5,000 | 6,000 |
| Plant | 2,00,000 | - | - |
| Work certified | 2,30,000 | 7,00,000 | 13,00,000 |
| Work uncertified | - | - | |

The value of the plant at the end of 2009, 2010 and 2011 are Rs.1,80,000, Rs.1,50,000 and Rs.1,30,000 respectively. The cash received being 75% of the value of work done as certified by the architect and rest on completion of the contract.

Prepare the Contract Account.

(Ans: Profit Rs.3,65,500)

32. Joyce & Co undertook three contracts, the work of which commenced on 1st April, 1st July and 1st October 2010 respectively. The account of the three contracts as on 31st March 2011 showed the following position.

| | Contract I | Contract II | Contract III |
|---|---|---|---|
| | Rs. | Rs. | Rs. |
| Material | 90,000 | 85,000 | 50,000 |
| Wages | 65,000 | 70,000 | 64,000 |
| Direct expenses | 10,000 | 15,000 | 20,000 |
| Overhead | 22,000 | 20,000 | 23,000 |
| Material in hand | 8,000 | 6,000 | 5,000 |
| Plant installed | 1,20,000 | 1,00,000 | 1,50,000 |
| Wages accrued | 5,000 | 6,000 | 3,000 |
| Work certified | 2,70,000 | 2,50,000 | 2,40,000 |
| Work finished but not certified | 20,000 | 30,000 | 25,000 |
| Cash received | 2,40,000 | 2,00,000 | 1,80,000 |
| Contract Price | 13,00,000 | 6,50,000 | 3,50,000 |

Prepare Contract Account and Balance Sheet as on 31st March 2011. Assume that the plant was installed on the date of commencement of each contract and the depreciation is to be charged @ 10% per annum.

(Ans: I WIP Rs.94,000; II P&L Rs.23,333; III P & L Rs.1,55,000)

# CHAPTER - VII

# PROCESS COSTING

Process costing is a method of costing to find out the cost of production when the product undergoes different stages or process of production. The characteristics of process costing is that the finished product of one process is used as the raw material of another process. Apart from this each process has its own expenses like, material cost, labour cost and other expenses. This costing method helps to ascertain the cost of production and the cost per unit in each stages of production. Process costing can be prepared for any span of time, say one month, 3 months or one year. It depends upon the nature of the product and policy of the management. The product to which process costing is applied is of uniform and standardised one. It should be produced with large volume with continuous production flow. Examples of products applied for process costing are petroleum, chemicals, steel, cement,rubber, textiles, plastic, sugar, etc. The assembly type of industries like automobiles, television, radios etc. and service industries like water, gas, electric power etc. also apply process costing to ascertain the cost of production.

## I. Difference between Process Costing and Job Costing

The following are the differences, between process costing and job costing.

1. Job costing is applied where different products are produced to specific order but, process costing is applied to mass production of a uniform product with different processes.
2. The product applied for job costing may change in size, design and quality according to the specific order of customers. But the product applied for job costing won't often change and it remains uniform with regard to quality, design and size.
3. The cost of production in job costing is ascertained when the job is completed. In process costing the cost of production is ascertained at each stages of production.
4. The period of costing differs from product to product (job to job) in job costing. The period of costing is uniform for process costing. The period of costing for process costing is either one month or three months or 1 year etc.
5. One work-in-progress account is maintained for job costing. But different works-in-progress accounts are

maintained for different process in process costing.

6. Normally there is no transfer from one job to another except when there is surplus or excess production. In process costing the transfer from one process to another is a usual one.
7. In job costing the cost per unit is calcuated by dividing the total cost of the job by the number of units produced. In process costing the cost per unit is calculated for each process by dividing the total process cost by the number of units produced in the respective process.

## II. PROCEDURES FOR PREPARING PROCESS COSTING

The following procedures may be applied to the process costing.

1. The process costing is prepared in 'T' form containing debit side and credit side. All expenses are debited in the process account. The opening stock in each process is also debited. The transfer of completed work to next process and the closing stock in the process are credited.If the process is a last one then instead of crediting the completed work to next process, it is credited to the Finished Stock account. The number of process account prepared depends upon the number of processes.
2. The expenses debited in the process account contain direct material cost, direct labour cost, direct expenses and factory overhead. The material is usually debited only in the first process account. But in some cases, the second and subsequent processes also require some material. This material cost is also debited in the respective process accounts.
3. The factory overhead debited in the process account may be incurred commonly for all the processes. This will be apportioned on the basis of some predetermined overhead rates.
4. The work of each process is to supply its output as an input to the next process. Hence, each process account is closed by transferring to the next process account. Transfer to next process account is credited to close the accounts. But the last process account is closed by finished goods account instead of transfer to next process account.
5. Normal process loss will not be shown in the process account and it will automatically be adjusted in the

process cost. Due to this, per unit cost of the process increases to the extent of normal loss. But any realisation due to sale of scrap of normal loss is credited in the process account. It reduces the normal loss.

6. If the output in the process is less than the input of material, after making adjustment of the normal loss, opening stock and closing stock then it is called abnormal loss. Abnormal loss is calculated just as the units produced and transfered to the next process. Abnormal loss is credited in the process costs, so that it is transferred (debited) to the profit and loss account.
7. If the output in a process is greater than the input of material after making the adjustment of the normal loss, opening stock and closing stock, then it is called Abnormal gain. Abnormal gain is calculated just as the units produced and transferred to the next process. Abnormal gain is debited in the process account so that it is transferred (credited) to the profit and loss account.

**Illustration: 1**

A product manufactured by a company undergoes three different processes. Prepare process accounts and find out the cost of each process of manufacture, from the following particulars. Also calculate the cost per unit of the product.

| | Process I | Process II | Process III |
|---|---|---|---|
| | Rs. | Rs. | Rs. |
| Material consumed | 28,500 | 19,500 | 15,000 |
| Direct wages | 22,000 | 20,000 | 18,000 |
| Direct expenses | 7,500 | 12,000 | 9,000 |

The indirect expenses amounted to Rs.36,000 which should be apportioned on the basis of wages. The total quantity produced was 500 units.

***Solution:***

Ratio of Direct wages = 22 : 20 : 18

Indirect expense for process I = (22/60) x 36,000
= Rs.13,200

Indirect expense for process II = (20/60) x 36,000
= Rs.12,000

Indirect expense for process III = (18/60) x 36,000
= Rs.10,800

**Process I Account**

| Particulars | Rs. | Particulars | Rs. |
|---|---|---|---|
| To Direct material | 28,500 | By Process II A/c | 71,200 |
| To Direct wages | 22,000 | (Transfer) | |
| To Direct expenses | 7,500 | | |
| To Indirect expenses | 13,200 | | |
| (22/60x36000) | | | |
| | 71,200 | | 71,200 |

**Process II Account**

| Particulars | Rs. | Particulars | Rs. |
|---|---|---|---|
| To Process I A/c | 71,200 | By Process III A/c | 134,700 |
| To Direct material | 19,500 | (Transfer) | |
| To Direct wages | 20,000 | | |
| To Direct expenses | 12,000 | | |
| To Indirect expenses | 12,000 | | |
| (20/60x36000) | | | |
| | 134,700 | | 134,700 |

**Process III Account**

| Particulars | Rs. | Particulars | Rs. |
|---|---|---|---|
| To Process II A/c | 134,700 | By Finished StockA/c | 187,500 |
| To Direct material | 15,000 | | |
| To Direct wages | 18,000 | | |
| To Direct expenses | 9,000 | | |
| To Indirect expenses | 10,800 | | |
| (18/60x36,000) | | | |
| | 187,500 | | 187,500 |

$$\text{Cost of production per unit} = \frac{187500}{500} = \text{Rs.}375$$

**Illustration: 2**

Prepare process cost accounts from the following data.

| | Process X | Process Y | Process Z |
|---|---|---|---|
| Direct material (Rs.) | 41,500 | 32,400 | 24,600 |

| | | | |
|---|---|---|---|
| Direct wages (Rs.) | 29,700 | 27,400 | 24,100 |
| Factory overhead (Rs.) | 14,300 | 17,700 | 12,300 |
| Number of units produced | 25,000 | 30,000 | 32,000 |
| Stock as on 1st August 2011 (units) (From preceeding process) | | 6,000 | 3,000 |
| Stock as on 31st August 2011 (units) (From preceeding process) | | 4,000 | 5,000 |

Assume that the increase of output in subsequent process is due to additional material.

***Solution:***

**Process X Account**

| Particulars | Rs. | Particulars | Rs. |
|---|---|---|---|
| To Direct material<br>To Direct wages<br>To Factory overhead | 41,500<br>29,700<br>14,300 | By Process Y A/c<br>(Transfer @ Rs.3.42 per unit) | 85,500 |
| | 85,500 | | 85,500 |

**Process Y Account**

| Particulars | Rs. | Particulars | Rs. |
|---|---|---|---|
| To Op.stock (of process X) (6000 x 3.42) | 20,520 | By Cl.stock (of processX) (4000 x 3.42) | 13,680 |
| To Process X A/c | 85,500 | By Process Z A/c (Transfer @ Rs.5.66 per unit)- 30,000 units | 169,840 |
| To Direct material | 32,400 | | |
| To Direct wages | 27,400 | | |
| To Factory overhead | 17,700 | | |
| | 183,520 | | 183,520 |

**Process Z Account**

| Particulars | Rs. | Particulars | Rs. |
|---|---|---|---|
| To Op. stock (of process Y) (3000 x 5.66) | 16,980 | By Cl. stock (of process Y) (5000 x 5.66) | 28,300 |
| To Process Y A/c | 169,840 | (Transfer @ Rs.6.86 per unit) - 32,000 units | 219,520 |
| To Direct material | 24,600 | | |
| To Direct wages | 24,100 | | |
| To Factory overhead | 12,300 | | |
| | 247,820 | | 247,820 |

## III. TREATMENT OF PROCESS LOSSES AND GAINS

### Process Losses

Process Losses are of two types. They are (1) Normal loss (2) Abnormal loss

#### (1) Normal loss

Normal loss is a loss which arises due to unavoidable and uncontrollable situations. It could not be prevented. It forms part of the manufacturing process. Normal loss may be in the form of (a) Scrap (b) Normal wastage and (c) Normal spoilage.

#### Treatment of Normal loss

The amount of normal loss should not be transferred to the Profit and Loss account. It should be adjusted with the cost in the process account.For example, if the units introduced in the process are 1000 and the normal loss is 100 units. Then it should be assumed that the units introduced are 900. i.e., the cost incurred for 1000 units would be treated as the cost incurred for 900 units. If the normal loss units realised some amount by way of sale of scrap, then the amount should be credited in the process account in the name of Normal Loss account (or sale of scrap account). Otherwise, the normal loss account will not be shown in the process account.

#### (2) Abnormal Loss

Abnormal loss is a loss which arises due to abnormal and unexpected situations. This loss can be controlled and avoided. Abnormal loss may be due to abnormal wastage, abnormal spoilage, negligence, accident, fire, theft etc. Abnormal wastage and Abnormal Spoilage arise due to the loss over and above the permitted standard normal wastage and normal spoilage.

#### Treatment of Abnormal Loss

The value of abnormal loss should be shown in the process account. It should be credited in the process account in the name of Abnormal Loss account.

The value of abnormal loss is just like the value of cost of units produced (the value of closing stock). The value of abnormal loss can be calculated as,

Value of Abnormal Loss

$$= \frac{\text{Cost of production (excluding the realisation of normal loss)} \times \text{Abnormal loss units}}{\text{Number of units produced (including the Abnormal loss units}}$$

and excluding the Normal loss units if any, from the input units)

Number of units produced = Units introduced -Units of normal loss

Abnormal loss account should be closed by transferring it to Costing Profit & Loss Account. If there is any realisation due to normal loss than abnormal loss account should be credited to the proportionate amount, before transfering to the costing profit and loss account.

**Process Gain**

Process Gain is otherwise called as Abnormal Gain. Abnormal gain arises when the actual normal loss is less than the standard or expected normal loss. For example if the input of material is 1000 units, the normal loss is 100 units and the output is 950 units, then the abnormal gain is 50 units.

**Treatment of Abnormal Gain**

The value of Abnormal gain should be debited in the process account. The value is calculated just like the calculatation of the value of Abnormal loss. It can be calculated as,

Value of Abnormal gain

$$= \frac{\text{Cost of production (excluding the realisation of normal units)} \times \text{Number of Abnormal gain units}}{\text{Number of units produced}}$$

Number of units produced = Units introduced - Units of normal loss

Abnormal gain account should be closed by transferring to the Costing Profit and Loss account. If there is any realisation due to normal loss then the Abnormal gain account should be debited with the proportionate amount, before transferring to the Costing Profit and Loss account.

**Illustration: 3**

A manufacturing company provides the following information related to its process I.

Material consumed 1,500 units @ Rs.6 Direct wages Rs.7,500, Direct expenses, Rs.6,210. The normal loss is 12% of input. The scrap in the process was sold @ Rs.1.50 per unit. The net production in the process is 1,100 units.

Prepare process I Account and find out the cost per unit of Transfer to process II.

***Solution:***

**Process I Account**

| Particulars | No.of Units | Rs. | Particulars | No.of Units | Rs. |
|---|---|---|---|---|---|
| To Material | 1,500 | 9,000 | By Normal loss | 180 | 270 |
| To Wages | | 7,500 | By Abnormal loss @ Rs.17 | 220 | 3740 |
| To Direct expenses | | 6,210 | By Process II A/c (Transfer) @ Rs.17 | 1100 | 18700 |
| | 1500 | 22,710 | | 1,500 | 22,710 |

Normal Loss = 1,500 x 12/100 = 180 units

Sale of scrap (Realisation of normal loss)

= 180 x 1.50 = Rs.270

Abnormal loss = 1,500-(1100+180) = 220 units

Total Cost = 22,710 - 270 = Rs.22,440

No. of units = 1,500-180 = 1,320

Cost per unit = 22,440/1,320 = Rs.17

**Illustration: 4**

Prepare Process A Account from the following information. 2000 units were introduced @ Rs.50 per unit to the Process A. Material cost Rs.32,000, Labour Cost Rs.28,000 Factory Overhead Rs.17,800.

The net output is 1,900 units. The normal process loss is @ 8% of the input. The normal loss realised Rs.3,000 by sale of scrap.

***Solution:***

**Process A Account**

| Particulars | No.of Units | Rs. | Particulars | No.of Units | Rs. |
|---|---|---|---|---|---|
| To Units introduced | 2000 | 100,000 | By Normal loss | 160 | 3,000 |
| To Materials | | 32,000 | By Process B A/c (Transfer) @ Rs.95 per unit | 1900 | 80,500 |
| To Labour cost | | 28,000 | | | |
| To Factory overhead | | 17,800 | | | |
| To Abnormal Gain | 60 | 5,700 | | | |
| | 2,060 | 18,3500 | | 2,060 | 183,500 |

Normal Loss = 200 x 8/100 = 160 units

Abnormal gain = (2,000-160) - 1,900= 60 units

Cost per unit $= \frac{(100,000 + 32,000 + 28000 + 17800) - 3000}{2000 - 160}$

$= \frac{177800 - 3000}{1,840} = \frac{174800}{1,840} = \text{Rs.}95$

Value of Abnormal gain = 60 x 95 = Rs.5,700

Value of Net output = 1900 x 95 = Rs.1,80,500

**Illustration: 5**

The product manufactured by XYZ Co.Ltd. passes through three different processes. The details of the expenses incurred in these processes are as follows:

| | Process I | Process II | Process III |
|---|---|---|---|
| Direct Material consumed (Kgm) | 15,000 | 11,000 | 10,000 |
| Material cost per Kgm (Rs.) | 5 | 7 | 4 |
| Direct wages paid (Rs.) | 32,000 | 34,500 | 30,500 |
| Manufacturing expenses (Rs.) | 16,300 | 12,892 | 21,084 |
| Production (in Kgm) | 13,000 | 19,000 | 26,000 |

The following further information are also given.

(i) In the process of production, 2% of the total weight in each process is lost and 8%, 9% and 10% of Process I , II and III respectively became scrap.

(ii) The scrap of Process I, II and II are sold @ Rs.1.50, Rs.1.00 and Rs.2.00 per kgm respectively.

Prepare the process accounts.

(Adapted: M.K. University, M.Com.)

***Solution:***

**Process I Account**

| Particulars | No. of Units | Rs. | Particulars | No.of Units | Rs. |
|---|---|---|---|---|---|
| To Material | 15,000 | 75,000 | By Loss in weight | 300 | - |
| To Wages | | 32,000 | By Normal loss realised @ Rs.1.50 | 1200 | 1,800 |
| To Manufacturing expenses | | 16,300 | By Abnormal loss @ Rs.9 per unit | 500 | 4500 |
| | | | By Transfer to Process II @ Rs.9 per unit | 13,000 | 117,000 |
| | 15,000 | 123,300 | | 15,000 | 123,300 |

## Process II Account

| Particulars | No. of Units | Rs. | Particulars | No.of Units | Rs. |
|---|---|---|---|---|---|
| To Process I A/c | 13,000 | 117,000 | By Loss in weight | 480 | - |
| To Material | 11,000 | 77,000 | By Normal loss -realised Rs.1 | 2,160 | 2,160 |
| To Wages | | 34,500 | ByAbnormal loss @ Rs.11.20 per unit | 2,360 | 26,432 |
| To Manufacturing expenses | | 12,892 | By Process III A/c (Transfer) @ Rs.11.20 per unit | 19,000 | 212,800 |
| | 24,000 | 241,392 | | 24,000 | 241,392 |

## Process III Account

| Particulars | No. of Units | Rs. | Particulars | No.of Units | Rs. |
|---|---|---|---|---|---|
| To Process II A/c | 19,000 | 212,800 | By Loss of weight | 580 | - |
| To Material | 10,000 | 40,000 | By Normal Loss realised Rs.2 | 2,900 | 5,800 |
| To Wages | | 30,500 | By Finished Goods A/c @ Rs.11.70 per unit | 26,000 | 304,200 |
| To Manufacturing expenses | | 21,084 | | | |
| To Abnormal Gain @ Rs.11.70 per unit | | 5,616 | | | |
| | 29,480 | 310,000 | | 29,480 | 310,000 |

**Illustration: 6**

W.D & Co. Ltd produces a product with the help of three processes. The following are the information available in the cost records of the company:

| | Process A | Process B | Process C |
|---|---|---|---|
| Materials (Rs.) | 5,500 | 3,220 | 3,000 |
| Wages (Rs.) | 4,500 | 5,000 | 5,500 |
| Normal Loss as a percentage of input | 10 % | 20 % | 15 % |
| Value of scrap per kgm (Rs.) | Nil | 4 | 5 |
| Output (Kgm) | 650 | 600 | 450 |

In the Process A, 800 Kgm are introduced @ Rs.10 per kgm. Factory overhead absorbed is 80 % on direct wages.

Prepare process accounts, abnormal loss account and abnormal gain account.

***Solution:***

**Process A Account**

| Particulars | No.of Units | Rs. | Particulars | No.of Units | Rs. |
|---|---|---|---|---|---|
| To Units introduced | 800 | 8,000 | By Normal loss | 80 | - |
| ,, Material | | 5,500 | ,, Abnormal loss @ Rs.30 | 70 | 2,100 |
| ,, Wages | | 4,500 | ,, Process B A/c (Transfer) @ Rs.30 | 650 | 19,500 |
| ,, Factory overhead (80% of wages) | | 3,600 | | | |
| | 800 | 21,600 | | 800 | 21,600 |

**Process B Account**

| Particulars | No.of Units | Rs. | Particulars | No.of Units | Rs. |
|---|---|---|---|---|---|
| To Process A A/c | 650 | 19,500 | By Normal loss | 130 | 520 |
| ,, Material | | 3,220 | ,, Process C A/c (Transfer) @ Rs.60 | 600 | 36,000 |
| ,, Wages | | 5,000 | | | |
| ,, Factory Overhead (80% of wages) | | 4,000 | | | |
| ,, Abnormal gain @ Rs.60 | 80 | 4,800 | | | |
| | 730 | 36,520 | | 730 | 36,520 |

**Process C Account**

| Particulars | No.of Units | Rs. | Particulars | No.of Units | Rs. |
|---|---|---|---|---|---|
| To Process C A/c | 600 | 36,000 | By Normal loss | 90 | 450 |
| ,, Material | | 3,000 | By Abnormal loss @ Rs.95 | 60 | 5,700 |
| ,, Wages | | 5,500 | ,, Finished Goods A/c @ Rs.95 | 450 | 42,750 |
| ,, Factory Overhead (80% of wages) | | 4,400 | | | |
| | 600 | 48,900 | | 600 | 48,900 |

**Abnormal Loss Account**

| Particulars | No.of units | Rs. | Particulars | No.of units | Rs. |
|---|---|---|---|---|---|
| To Process A A/c | 70 | 2,100 | By Sale of scrap in Process A A/c | 70 | - |
| ,, Process C A/c | 60 | 5,700 | ,, Sale of scrap in Process C A/c | 60 | 300 |
| | | | ,, Costing P & L A/c | | 7,500 |
| | 130 | 7,800 | | 130 | 7,800 |

**Abnormal Gain Account**

| Particulars | No.of units | Rs. | Particulars | No.of units | Rs. |
|---|---|---|---|---|---|
| To Sale of scrap (due to Normal Loss) @ Rs.4 | 80 | 320 | By Process B A/c | 80 | 4,800 |
| ,, Costing P & L A/c | | 4,480 | | | |
| | 80 | 4,800 | | 80 | 4,800 |

**Workings :**

(i) Cost per unit in Process A A/c $= \frac{21600}{600 + 70}$

$= \text{Rs.}30$

(ii) Cost per unit in Process B A/c $= \frac{(19500+3220+5000+4000)-520}{650-130}$

$= \frac{31720 - 520}{520} = \frac{31200}{520}$

$= \text{Rs.}60$

(iii) In the Abnormal Gain and Abnormal Loss A/c the sale of scrap due to normal loss should be adjusted.

## IV. TREATMENT OF STOCK IN THE PROCESS ACCOUNT

Some manufacturing companies keep some stock of each process, without transferring the entire production of the process to the next process. Opening stock is debited in the process account. The value of the opening stock of the process is decided by the company. Hence, the value of the opening stock is normally given, for the preparation of process accounts.The closing stock is calculated just like the calculation of the process transfer account.

Closing stock = No of units of opening stock + Units introduced in the process - Normal Loss units (if any) - Units transferred to the next process.

The value of closing stock is calculated as follows.

$$\text{Value of closing stock} = \frac{\text{Cost of production (excluding the realisation of Normal Loss) x No.of units of closing stock}}{\text{Number of units produced.}}$$

The number of units produced = No.of units of opening stock + Units introduced-Units of Normal Loss

The value of closing stock is credited in the process account.

**Illustration: 7**

A Ltd. manufactured a product namely, DE. The product manufactured by the company is processed by two different processes. The following are the expenses and other costing information connected with the two processes.

The wastage in the process of manufacturing is 6% in Process X and 10% in Process Y. The wastage of material is calculated as a percentage to the input of material in each process. The wastage was sold @ Rs.1.50 per unit and @ Rs.1.00 per unit for Process X and Y respectively.

The input of material in Process X is 50,000 units valued at Rs.1,80,000. The other expenses are,

| | **Process X** | **Process Y** |
|---|---|---|
| Other materials (Rs.) | 65,000 | 35,000 |
| Direct Wages (Rs.) | 25,000 | 20,000 |
| Manufacturing expenses (Rs.) | 16,500 | 12,000 |
| Output (in units) | 45,000 | 43,400 |
| Stock of Finished Product (in units) | | |
| 1st September 2011 | 7,000 | 4,000 |
| 30th September 2011 | 5,000 | 5,000 |

The Stock as an 1st September 2011 is valued @ Rs.5.50 and Rs.6.50 per unit for Process X and Y respectively.

Prepare Process Accounts and Process Stock Accounts. Assume that the stock and the Transfer are valued on the basis of weighted average stock method.

***Solution:***

**Process X Account**

| Particulars | No.of units | Rs. | Particulars | No.of units | Rs. |
|---|---|---|---|---|---|
| To Units introduced | 50,000 | 180,000 | By Normal Loss -Realised @ Rs.1.50 | 3,000 | 4,500 |
| ,, Other material | | 65,000 | ,, Abnormal Loss @ Rs.6 | 2,000 | 12,000 |
| ,, Direct wages | | 25,000 | ,, Process X Stock A/c @ Rs.6 | 45,000 | 270,000 |
| ,, Manufacturing expenses | | 16,500 | | | |
| | 50,000 | 286,500 | | 50,000 | 286,500 |

**Process X Stock Account**

| Particulars | No.of units | Rs. | Particulars | No.of units | Rs. |
|---|---|---|---|---|---|
| To Op. Stock @ Rs.5.50 | 7,000 | 38,500 | By Closing Stock @ Rs.5.9327 | 5,000 | 29,663 |
| ,, Process X A/c | 45,000 | 270,000 | ,, Process Y A/c (Transfer) @ Rs.5.9327 | 47,000 | 278,837 |
| | 52,000 | 308,500 | | 52,000 | 308,500 |

**Process Y Account**

| Particulars | No.of units | Rs. | Particulars | No.of units | Rs. |
|---|---|---|---|---|---|
| To Process X stock A/c | 47,000 | 278,837 | By Normal Loss | 4,700 | 4,700 |
| ,, Other materials | | 35,000 | ,, Process Y stock A/c (Transfer) @ Rs.8.0647 | 43,400 | 350,008 |
| ,, Direct wages | | 20,000 | | | |
| ,, Manufacturing expenses | | 12,000 | | | |
| ,, Abnormal gain @ Rs.8.0647 | 1,100 | 8,871 | | | |
| | 48,100 | 354,708 | | 48,100 | 354,708 |

**Process Y Stock Account**

| Particulars | No.of units | Rs. | Particulars | No.of units | Rs. |
|---|---|---|---|---|---|
| To Opening Stock @ Rs.6.50 | 4,000 | 26,000 | By Closing stock @ Rs.7.9327 | 5000 | 39,663 |
| ,, Process Y A/c (Transfer @ Rs.8.064) | 43,400 | 350,008 | ,, Finished Stock A/c @ Rs.7.9327 | 42,400 | 336,345 |
| | 47,400 | 376,008 | | 47,400 | 376,008 |

**Workings:**

$$\text{Cost per unit of Process X} = \frac{286500 - 4{,}500}{50{,}000 - 3000}$$

$$= \frac{282000}{47{,}000} = \text{Rs. } 6$$

$$\text{Cost per unit of Process Y} = \frac{(278837+35000+20000+12000)-4700}{47000 - 4700}$$

$$= \frac{345837 - 4700}{42{,}300}$$

$$= \text{Rs } 8.0647$$

$$\text{Cost per unit of Process X Stock A/c} = \frac{308500}{52{,}000} = \text{Rs } 5.9327$$

$$\text{Cost per unit of Process Y Stock A/c} = \frac{376008}{47{,}400} = \text{Rs.}7.9327$$

## V TREATMENT OF PARTLY SALES OF OUTPUT OF A PROCESS

The output of a process may be sold apart from the transfer to the next process. If companies can get profit and there is demand they may sell the output of the process before they are converted into finished goods. Hence, they can produce morc in order to meet the sales as well as the need for the next process. If there is partial sales of the output of the process then the output should be transferred to 'Process Stock Account'. (Process Stock Account is debited). For sales the Process Stock Account is credited. The profit from sales is debited in the Process Stock Account to Costing Profit and Loss Account (For loss, the Process Stock Account is credited). The cost of goods sold is calculated just like the cost of transfer to next process. The Process Stock Account is closed by crediting with Transfer to Next Process Account.

**Illustration: 8**

MW & Co. Ltd manufactures a product named 'X'. The product X passes through three different processes namely A,B and C.

20% of the output of Process A, 40% of the output of Process B and the entire output of Process C are sold. The expenses incurred for these processes are as follows:

| | Process A | Process B | Process C |
|---|---|---|---|
| Input of material @ Rs.12 (units) per unit | 5,000 | - | - |
| Other material cost (Rs.) | 20,500 | 13,120 | 12,000 |
| Direct wages (Rs.) | 12,500 | 10,000 | 8,500 |
| Loss of weight (as a percentage to input) | 10% | 15% | 10% |
| Sale of scrap (due to loss of weight) per unit (Rs.) | 4 | 5 | 6 |
| Selling price per unit (Rs.) | 25 | 40 | 70 |

Manufaturing expense is 100% of direct wages. The general management expense is Rs.7,500 and selling expense is Rs.7,000. Prepare the Process Accounts, Process Stock Accounts and Profit & Loss Account.

***Solution:***

**Process A Account**

| Particulars | No.of units | Rs. | Particulars | No.of units | Rs. |
|---|---|---|---|---|---|
| To Input of material | 5,000 | 60,000 | By Normal Loss-Realised @ Rs.4 | 500 | 2,000 |
| ,, Other materials | | 20,500 | ,, Process A Stock A/c @ Rs.23 | 4,500 | 103,500 |
| ,, Direct wages | | 12,500 | | | |
| ,, Manufactuing expenses | | 12,500 | | | |
| | 5,000 | 105,500 | | 5,000 | 105,500 |

**Workings:**

Process A stock = 105,500 - 2,000
= Rs.103,500

Good Units = 5,000 - 500
= 4,500

Process A stock per unit = 103,500 / 4,500
= Rs.23

## Process A Stock A/c

| Particulars | No.of units | Rs. | Particulars | No.of units | Rs. |
|---|---|---|---|---|---|
| To Process A A/c (Transfer@ Rs.23) | 4,500 | 103,500 | By Sales @ Rs.25 | 900 | 22,500 |
| ,, Profit & Loss A/c (profit) | | 1,800 | ,, Process B A/c @ Rs.23 | 3,600 | 82,800 |
| | 4,500 | 105,300 | | 4,500 | 105,300 |

## Process B Account

| Particulars | No.of units | Rs. | Particulars | No.of units | Rs. |
|---|---|---|---|---|---|
| To Process A Stock A/c @ Rs.23 | 3,600 | 82,800 | By Normal Loss Realised @ Rs.5 | 540 | 2,700 |
| ,, Other Materials | | 13,120 | ,, Process B Stock A/c @ Rs.37 (Transfer @ Rs.37) | 3,060 | 113,220 |
| ,, Direct Wages | | 10,000 | | | |
| ,, Manufacturing expenses | | 10,000 | | | |
| | 3,600 | 115,920 | | 3,600 | 115,920 |

## Process B Stock Account

| Particulars | No.of units | Rs. | Particulars | No.of units | Rs. |
|---|---|---|---|---|---|
| To Process B A/c (Transfer @ Rs.37) | 3,060 | 113,220 | By Sales @ Rs.40 | 1,224 | 48,960 |
| ,, Profit & Loss A/c (Profit) | | 3,672 | ,, Process C A/c @ Rs.37 | 1,836 | 67,932 |
| | 3,060 | 116,892 | | 3,060 | 116,892 |

**Workings:**

Process B stock = 115,920 - 2,700
= Rs.113,220

Good Units = 3,600 - 540 = 3,060

Process B stock per unit = 113,220 / 3,060
= Rs.37

## Process C Account

| Particulars | No.of units | Rs. | Particulars | No.of units | Rs. |
|---|---|---|---|---|---|
| To Process B A/c @ Rs.37 | 1,836 | 67,932 | By Normal Loss- Realised @ Rs.6 | 184 | 1,104 |
| ,, Other Materials | | 12,000 | ,, Process C Stock A/c @ Rs.58.007 | 1,652 | 95,828 |
| ,, Direct Wages | | 8,500 | | | |
| ,, Manufacturing expenses | | 8,500 | | | |
| | 1,836 | 96,932 | | 1,836 | 96,932 |

## Process C Stock Account

| Particulars | No.of units | Rs. | Particulars | No.of units | Rs. |
|---|---|---|---|---|---|
| To Process C A/c | 1,652 | 95,828 | By Sales @ Rs.70 | 1,652 | 115,640 |
| ,, Profit & Loss A/c (Profit) | | 19,812 | | | |
| | 1,652 | 115,640 | | 1,652 | 115,640 |

## Costing Profit and Loss Account

| Particulars | Rs | Particulars | Rs. |
|---|---|---|---|
| To Management expenses | 7,500 | By Process A Stock A/c | 1,800 |
| ,, Selling expenses | 7,000 | ,, Process B Stock A/c | 3,672 |
| ,, Net Profit | 10,784 | ,, Process C Stock A/c | 19,812 |
| | 25,284 | | 25,284 |

**Workings:**

Process C stock = 96,932 - 1104
= Rs.95,828

Good Units = 1836 - 184
= 1,652

Process C stock per unit = 95,828 / 1,652
= Rs.58.007

The Profit & Loss Account may also be shown in statement form as follows:

**Statement of Profit**

| Particulars | Rs. | Rs. |
|---|---|---|
| Profit as per Process A Stock A/c | | 1,800 |
| Profit as per Process B Stock A/c | | 3,672 |
| Profit as per Process C Stock A/c | | 19,812 |
| Total Profit | | 25,284 |
| **Less:** Management expenses | 7,500 | |
| Selling expenses | 7,000 | 14,500 |
| Net Profit | | 10,784 |

## VI. FURTHER PROCESSING OF BY - PRODUCT

Companies may sometimes produce a by - product apart from the main product at the end of the last process. The by - product may require further processing before selling it to customers. The value of by - product is credited in the Final Process account by Further Process account. The value credited in the Final Process account = (Selling price per unit - cost per unit of further processing ) x Number of units of the by-product. Further Processing account is debited with the cost of processing the by-product. This account is closed by transferring to Finished Stock Account.

**Illustration: 9**

Joyce & Co.Ltd is producing Product X by three processes namely A, B and C. Process C produces a by - product in addition to the product X. The by- product is further processed in Process D to get a new product called by - product 'CX'. The information available in the costing records of the company for the month January 2011 are as follows:

| | Process A | Process B | Process C |
|---|---|---|---|
| Direct material introduced 20,000 units @ Rs.4 (Rs.) | 80,000 | - | - |
| Direct materials added (Rs.) | 21,000 | 13,170 | 12,460 |
| Direct wages (Rs.) | 13,000 | 11,000 | 10,000 |
| Direct expenses (Rs.) | 5,000 | 4,000 | 6,000 |
| Standard normal loss as a percentage of input | 5% | 10 % | 10% |
| Realisation of normal loss by sale of | | | |

| | | | |
|---|---|---|---|
| Scrap per unit (Rs.) | 2 | 4 | 5 |
| Output (in units) | 18,500 | 17,200 | 14,000 |

Production Overhead amounted to Rs.17,000 which was absorbed as a percentage on direct wages. The processing cost of by - product 'CX' is Rs.4 per unit. The output of the by-product is 1,200 units. Selling expenses for product CX is @ Rs.1.50 per unit. The selling price per unit of product CX is Rs.15.50.

Prepare Process A, B, C and D accounts.

(Adapted: ICWAI)

***Solution:***

**Process A Account**

| Particulars | No.of units | Rs. | Particulars | No.of units | Rs. |
|---|---|---|---|---|---|
| To Materials introduced | 20,000 | 80,000 | By Normal loss -Realised @ Rs.2 | 1,000 | 2,000 |
| ,, Direct material | | 21,000 | ,, Abnormal loss @ Rs.6.50 | 500 | 3,250 |
| ,, Direct wages | | 13,000 | | | |
| ,, Direct expenses | | 5,000 | ,, Process B A/c (Transfer @ Rs.6.50) | 18,500 | 120,250 |
| ,, Production overhead | | 6,500 | | | |
| | 20,000 | 125,500 | | 20,000 | 125,500 |

**Process B Account**

| Particulars | No.of units | Rs. | Particulars | No.of units | Rs. |
|---|---|---|---|---|---|
| To Process A A/c (Transfer @ Rs.6.50) | 18,500 | 120,250 | By Normal loss (Realised @ Rs.4) | 1,850 | 7,400 |
| | | | ,, Process C A/c (Transfer @ Rs.8.80) | 17,200 | 151,360 |
| ,, Direct material | | 13,170 | | | |
| ,, Direct wages | | 11,000 | | | |
| ,, Direct expenses | | 4,000 | | | |
| ,, Production overhead | | 5,500 | | | |
| ,, Abnormal gain A/c @ Rs.8.80 | 550 | 4,840 | | | |
| | 19,050 | 158,760 | | 19,050 | 158,760 |

**Process C Account**

| Particulars | No.of units | Rs. | Particulars | No.of units | Rs. |
|---|---|---|---|---|---|
| To Process B A/c (Transfer @ Rs.8.80) | 17,200 | 151,360 | By Normal loss (Realised @ Rs.5) | 1,720 | 8,600 |
| ,, Direct material | | 12,460 | ,, Abnormal loss @ Rs.11.50 | 280 | 3,220 |
| ,, Direct wages | | 10,000 | ,, Finished goods A/c (Transfer @ Rs.11.50) | 14,000 | 161,000 |
| ,, Direct expenses | | 6,000 | ,, Process D A/c (15.50 - 5.50) @ Rs.10 | 1,200 | 12,000 |
| ,, Production overhead | | 5,000 | | | |
| | 17,200 | 184,820 | | 17,200 | 184,820 |

**Process D Account**

| Particulars | No.of units | Rs. | Particulars | No.of units | Rs. |
|---|---|---|---|---|---|
| To Process C A/c (Transfer from Process C A/c) | 1,200 | 12,000 | By Finished Stock A/c | 1,200 | 18,600 |
| ,, Processing Cost @ Rs 4 | | 4,800 | | | |
| ,, Selling & Distribution expenses @ Rs 1.50 | | 1,800 | | | |
| | 1,200 | 18,600 | | 1,200 | 18,600 |

**Workings:**

(i) Production Overhead = Rs.17,000

Shared in the ratio of Direct Wages

i.e., 13,000 : 11,000 : 10,000 for A, B & C

$$A = \frac{13000 \times 17,000}{34000} = \text{Rs.}6,500$$

$$B = \frac{11000 \times 17,000}{34000} = \text{Rs.}5,500$$

$$C = \frac{10,000 \times 17,000}{34,000} = \text{Rs.}5,000$$

(ii) Cost per unit in Process A $= \frac{125,500 - 2000}{20,000-1000} =$ Rs.6.50

(iii) Cost per unit in Process B $= \frac{(1,20,250 + 13,170 + 11,000 + 4,000 + 5500) - 7400}{18500 - 1850}$

= Rs.8.80

(iv) Cost per unit in Process C $= \frac{184820 - 8600 - 12,000}{17200 - 1720 - 1200}$

= Rs.11.50

(v) Process cost for by-product CX = 15.50 - (4 + 1.50)

= Rs.10 per unit

## VII. EQUIVALENT PRODUCTION

Equivalent production is otherwise called as equivalent performance units, equivalent units or effective performance units. When the process accounts are prepared for the specific period of time there arises the work-in-progress in any of the process or all the processes. The units which completed in the process are eligible to transfer to the next process for further processing. The units partly completed which are called work-in-progress would remain in the process accounts as on the date of preparation of the process account. The work-in-progress in the process account may either be opening work-in-progress or closing work-in-progress or both opening and closing work-in-progress. Since the work-in-progress consumes part of the expenses it should be valued accordingly. It is difficult to identify the actual cost incurred for the work-in-progress. Hence, it should be converted into equivalent units (i,e., reduced) on the basis of the estimated percentage of expenses incurred in the work-in-progress.

### Procedures for calculating Equivalent Production

The following statements should be prepared before the preparation of Process Account, when there is equivalent production.

(i) Statement of Equivalent production

(ii) Statement of Cost

(iii) Statement of Apportionment of Cost

### (i) Statement of Equivalent Production

This is a statement to convert the units of work-in-progress into equivalent units. The units of work-in-progress would be converted into equivalent units with respect to material, labour and overhead.

For example; If the units of work-in-progress is 100 and the material consumed is 80%, labour consumed is 60% and overhead consumed is 50%, then the equivalent units are 80,60 and 50 respectively with regard to material, labour and overhead. To find out the cost per unit the units completed and transferred is added with the equivalent units.Hence, different equivalent units existed for material, labour and overhead.

**(ii) Statement of Cost**

This is a statement to find out the cost per unit of material, labour and overhead. In this statement the equivalent units of material, labour and overhead should be divided with the cost of material, labour and overhead.

**(iii) Statement of Apportionment of Cost**

In this statement the cost of units completed and transferred to next units and the cost of work-in-progress should be calculated. Cost of units completed and transferred is the total cost per unit multiplied with the units completed. Cost of work-in-progress is the total cost of the material, labour and overhead calculated respectively by multiplying the cost per unit with respective equivalent units.

## Types of Equivalent Production (work-in-progress) in Process Account

The existence of Equivalent production (work-in-progress) may be in any of the following ways

1. Process costing with closing work-in-progress and without process loss or gain.
2. Process costing with closing work-in-progress and with process loss or gain.
3. Process costing with opening and closing work-in-progress and without process loss or gain.
4. Process costing with opening and closing work-in-progress and with process loss or gain.

### 1. Process costing with closing work-in-progress and without process loss or gain

If the process contains closing work-in-progress, the cost of work-in-progress should be calculated by preparing the statement of equivalent units, statement of cost and statement of apportionment of cost. The cost so calculated should be credited in the process account by closing work-in-progress account. The process account is also credited with the Process Transfer Account for the units completed and transferred to next process.

**Illustration: 10**

The cost information related to process X are as follows:

Material introduced in the process (units) 10,000

Units completed and Transferred 8,000

**Process Cost:** Material Rs.13,720

Labour Rs.24,000

Overhead Rs.15,980

Degree of completion of closing work-in-progress

Material 90%

Labour 80%

Overhead 70%

Prepare Statement of equivalent production, Statement of cost and Process X Account.

(For M.Com)

***Solution:***

**Statement of Equivalent Production**

| Input | Output | | Equivalent Production | | | | | | |
|---|---|---|---|---|---|---|---|---|---|
| | Units | Particulars | Total Units | Material Units | % | Labour Units | % | Overhead Units | % |
| Material Introduced | 10,000 | Units Completed & Transferred | 8,000 | 8,000 | 100 | 8,000 | 100 | 8,000 | 100 |
| | | Cl.work-in Progress | 2,000 | 1,800 | 90 | 1,600 | 80 | 1,400 | 70 |
| | 10,000 | | 10,000 | 9,800 | | 9,600 | | 9,400 | |

**Statement of Cost**

| Element of Cost | Cost (Rs.) | Equivalent Production (units) | Cost per completed units (Rs.) |
|---|---|---|---|
| Material | 13,720 | 9,800 | 1.40 |
| Labour | 24,000 | 9,600 | 2.50 |
| Overhead | 15,980 | 9,400 | 1.70 |
| | 53,700 | | 5.60 |

**Statement of Apportionment of Cost**

| | | |
|---|---|---|
| Output Transferred | 8,000 x 5.60 = Rs.44,800 | |
| Cl. Work-in-progress: | Rs. | |
| Material | 1,800 x 1.40 = 2,520 | |
| Labour | 1,600 x 2.50 = 4,000 | |
| Overhead | 1,400 x 1.70 = 2,380 | = Rs.8,900 |

**Process X Account**

| Particulars | No.of units | Rs. | Particulars | No.of units | Rs. |
|---|---|---|---|---|---|
| To Material | 10,000 | 13,720 | By Output Transferred to Next process | 8,000 | 44,800 |
| ,, Labour | | 24,000 | ,, Cl.Work-in-progress | 2,000 | 8,900 |
| ,, Overhead | | 15,980 | | | |
| | 10,000 | 53,700 | | 10,000 | 53,700 |

**Illustration: 11**

XYZ & Co. Ltd manufactures a product with the help of two processes. The Costing information related to these two processes for the month September 2011 are as follows:

| | Process A | Process B |
|---|---|---|
| Direct material (Rs.) | 150,000 | 70,000 |
| Direct wages (Rs.) | 105,000 | 60,000 |
| Factory Overhead (Rs.) | 74,250 | 56,000 |
| Input (units) | 75,000 | 50,000 |

The following further information are also given:

(i) The incompleted units in Process A at the end of the month are 25,000 units.

(ii) The incompleted units constitute 100% of material, 80% of labour and 75 % of factory overheads.

Assume that the input received by the Process B is consumed completely and there is no closing work-in-progress. Completed units of Process A are transferred to Process B Account.

Prepare necessary Cost statements and find out the Cost per unit in Process B Account.

(Adapted: ICWAI)

***Solution:***

**Statement of Equivalent Production**

| Particulars | Materials | | Wages | | Factory Overhead | |
|---|---|---|---|---|---|---|
| | Percentage | Units | Percentage | Units | Percentage | Units |
| **Process A:** | | | | | | |
| Completed Units | 100 | 50,000 | 100 | 50,000 | 100 | 50,000 |
| Incompleted Units (25,000) (Closing work -in-progress) | 100 | 25,000 | 80% | 20,000 | 70% | 17,500 |
| Total | | 75,000 | | 70,000 | | 67,500 |

**Statement of cost per unit of Process A**

| Element of Cost | Cost (Rs.) | Equivalent Production (Units) | Cost Per unit (Rs.) |
|---|---|---|---|
| Direct Material | 150,000 | 75,000 | 2.00 |
| Direct Wages | 105,000 | 70,000 | 1.50 |
| Factory Overhead | 74,250 | 67,500 | 1.10 |
| | 329,250 | | 4.60 |

**Statement of Total Cost**

| Particulars | | Rs. |
|---|---|---|
| **Cost of Process A:** | | |
| Direct Material | | 150,000 |
| Direct Wages | | 105,000 |
| Factory Overheads | | 74,250 |
| | | 3,29,250 |
| **Less:** Closing work-in-progress | | |
| Direct Material 25,000 x 2.00 = 50,000 | | |
| Direct Wages 20,000 x 1.50 = 30,000 | | |
| Factory Overhead 17,500 x 1.10 = 19,250 | | 99,250 |
| Cost of Finished Output from Process A | | 230,000 |
| **Add:** Cost of Process B: | | |
| Direct Material | 70,000 | |
| Direct Wages | 60,000 | |
| Factory Overhead | 56,000 | 186,000 |
| Total Cost of production (for 50,000 units) | | 416,000 |
| Cost per unit (416,000/50,000) | | 8.32 |

**Note:**

The material consumed is 100 percentage for completed units as well as incompleted units. Wages incurred is 100 percentage for completed units and 80 percentage for incompleted units. Factory overhead absorbed is 100 percentage of completed units and 70 percentage for incompleted units. On this basis the equivalent units for material are 7,500; wages 70,000;and overhead 67,500.

## 2. Process Costing with Closing Work-in-progress and with process loss or gain

If the process contains abnormal loss then the abnormal loss units should be added to the units produced for transfer and the equivalent units of work-in-progress. This will give the total equivalent units for material, labour and overhead.

If the process contains closing work-in-progress and abnormal gain, then the abnormal gain units should be deducted from the units produced for transfer to next process and the equivalent units of work-in-progress with respect to material, labour and overhead. If there is normal loss also in both the above situations , the units of normal loss should not be included in the calculation of equivalent units.

**Illustration: 12**

The product manufactured by a company undergoes two processes, namely I & II. The expenses incurred for the month August 2011, related to process I are as follows:

| | Rs. |
|---|---|
| Input of material (5,000 units) | 60,000 |
| Additional direct material | 15,780 |
| Direct Labour | 24,120 |
| Works Overhead | 19,700 |

The normal loss is estimated as 10% of the input. The units produced and transferred to process II is 3,000. The incomplete units are 800. The stages of completion of incomplete units are Material 80%, Labour 40% and Overhead 30%. The scrap in the process are sold @ Rs.4 per unit.

Prepare a statement of equivalent production, Statement of cost, Statement of apportionment and Process I Account.

**Solution:**

### Statement of Equivalent Production

| Particulars | Units | Equivalent Production | | | | | |
|---|---|---|---|---|---|---|---|
| | | Material | | Labour | | Work Overhead | |
| | | % of Completion | Units | % of Completion | Units | % of Completion | Units |
| Normal Loss | 500 | - | - | - | - | - | - |
| Abnormal Loss | 700 | 100 | 700 | 100 | 700 | 100 | 700 |
| Completed and Transferred to Process II | 3,000 | 100 | 3,000 | 100 | 3,000 | 100 | 3,000 |
| Cl. work-in-progress | 800 | 80 | 640 | 40 | 320 | 30 | 240 |
| | 5,000 | | 4,340 | | 4,020 | | 3,940 |

### Statement of Cost

| Element of Cost | Cost (Rs.) | Equivalent Production (units) | Cost per unit (Rs.) |
|---|---|---|---|
| Material Introduced | 60,000 | | |
| Additional material | 15,780 | | |
| | 75,780 | | |
| Less: Sale of Scrap | 2,000 | | |
| (500 x 4) | 73,780 | 4,340 | 17.00 |
| Direct Labour | 24,120 | 4,020 | 6.00 |
| Works Overhead | 19,700 | 3,940 | 5.00 |
| Total | 117,600 | | 28.00 |

### Statement of Apportionment of Cost

| Particulars | | Rs. |
|---|---|---|
| Abnormal Loss | 700 x 28 = 19,600 | |
| Output produced and Transferred | 300 x 28 = 84,000 | |
| | | 103,600 |
| Cl. Work-in-progress: | | |
| Material | 640 x 17 = 10,880 | |
| Labour | 320 x 6 = 1,920 | |
| Overhead | 240 x 5 = 1,200 | |
| | | 14,000 |
| | Total | 117,600 |

## Process I Account

| Particulars | No.of units | Rs. | Particulars | No.of units | Rs. |
|---|---|---|---|---|---|
| To Units introduced | 5,000 | 60,000 | By Normal loss | 500 | 2,000 |
| ,, Direct material | | 15,780 | ,, Abnormal loss | 700 | 19,600 |
| ,, Direct labour | | 24,120 | ,, Process II A/c (Transfer) | 3,000 | 84,000 |
| ,, Works overhead | | 19,700 | ,, Cl. Work-in -progress | 800 | 14,000 |
| | 5,000 | 119,600 | | 5,000 | 119,600 |

**Note:**

Abnormal loss is 700 units which is calcuated by deducting 5000 units introduced with normal loss of 500 units, completed and transfered units of 3000 and closing incompleted units of 800. Abnormal loss is considered as consuming 100 percentage of material, 100 percentage of labour and 100 percentage of works overhead.

**Illustration: 13**

The cost data related to the manufacturing of product 'JW' by a manufacturing company, XYZ & Co.Ltd for the month April, 2011 are as follows:

| | Process A | Process B |
|---|---|---|
| Direct Material (Rs.) | 87,000 | - |
| Direct Labour (Rs.) | 57,520 | 39,000 |
| Factory Overhead (Rs.) | 22,720 | 17,780 |
| Units received in process (units) | 30,000 | 27,000 |
| Completed and transferred | 27,000 | 24,800 |
| Remaining in process at the end | 1,200 | 2,000 |
| Normal Loss in process | 1,000 | 600 |

Production remaining in the process is completed to the extent of Direct material 100% Direct Labour 80% and Factory overhead 50%.

Prepare necessary ledger accounts and find out the cost per unit in each process.

**Solution:**

**Statement of Equivalent Production**

| Particulars | Units | Material | | Labour | | Works Overhead | |
|---|---|---|---|---|---|---|---|
| | | % | Units | % | Units | % | Units |
| **Process: A** | | | | | | | |
| Normal Loss | 1000 | - | - | - | - | - | - |
| Abnormal Loss | 800 | 100 | 800 | 100 | 800 | 100 | 800 |
| Completed & Transferred | 27,000 | 100 | 27,000 | 100 | 27,000 | 100 | 27,000 |
| Cl. Work-in-progress | 1,200 | 100 | 1200 | 80 | 960 | 50 | 600 |
| | 30,000 | | 29,000 | | 28,760 | | 28,400 |
| **Process: B** | | | | | | | |
| Normal Loss | 600 | - | - | - | - | - | - |
| Abnormal Gain | (400) | 100 | (400) | 100 | (400) | 100 | (400) |
| Completed and Transferred | 24,800 | 100 | 24,800 | 100 | 24,800 | 100 | 24,800 |
| Cl.Work-in-progress | 2,000 | 100 | 2,000 | 80 | 1,600 | 50 | 1,000 |
| | 27,000 | | 26,400 | | 26,000 | | 25,400 |

**Statement of Cost**

| Element of Cost | Cost (Rs.) | Equivalent Production (units) | Cost per unit (Rs.) |
|---|---|---|---|
| **Process: A** | | | |
| Material | 87,000 | 29,000 | 3.00 |
| Labour | 57,520 | 28,760 | 2.00 |
| Overhead | 22,720 | 28,400 | 0.80 |
| | 167240 | | 5.80 |
| **Process: B** | | | |
| Transfer from Process A (27,000x5.80) | 156,600 | 26,400 | 5.9318 |
| Labour | 39,000 | 26,000 | 1.50 |
| Overhead | 17,780 | 25,400 | 0.70 |
| | 213,380 | | 8.1318 |

Note: Abnormal loss in Process A Account = 30000-(1000+27000+1200)

Abnormal gain in Process B Account = 27000-(600+24800+2000)

**Statement of Apportionment of Cost**

| Particulars | | | | Rs. |
|---|---|---|---|---|
| **Process A** | | | | |
| Abnormal Loss | 800 x 5.80 | = | 4,640 | |
| Produced & Transferred | 27,000 x 5.80 | = | 156,600 | 161,240 |
| Work-in-progress: | | | | |
| Material | 1200 x 3.00 | = | 3,600 | |
| Labour | 960 x 2.00 | = | 1,920 | |
| Overhead | 600 x 0.80 | = | 480 | 6,000 |
| | | | | 167,240 |
| **Process B** | | | | |
| Produced & Transferred | 24,800 x 8.1318 | | | 201,669 |
| Work-in-progress: | | | | |
| Material | 2000 x 5.9318 | = | 11,864 | |
| Labour | 1,600 x 1.50 | = | 2,400 | |
| Overhead | 1000 x 0.70 | = | 700 | 14,964 |
| | | | | 216,633 |
| **Less :** Abnormal gain 400 x 8.1318 | | | | 3,253 |
| | | | | 213,380 |

**Process A Account**

| Particulars | Units | Rs. | Particulars | Units | Rs. |
|---|---|---|---|---|---|
| To Material | 30,000 | 87,000 | By Normal Loss | 1000 | - |
| ,, Labour | | 57,520 | ,, Abnormal loss @ Rs 5.80 | 800 | 4,640 |
| ,, Overhead | | 22,720 | ,, Process B A/c - Transfer @ Rs 5.80 | 27,000 | 156,600 |
| | | | ,, Cl. Work-in-Progress A/c | 1,200 | 6,000 |
| | 30,000 | 167,240 | | 30,000 | 167,240 |

**Note:**

The normal loss units of 1,000 is inflated with the cost of production. Abnormal loss units consumed are100 percentage of material, labour and overhead. The closing work- in- progress consumed 100 percentage of materials 80 percentage of labour and 50 percentage of overhead. On this basis, the equivalent units of closing work-in-progress are material 1200, labour 960 and overhead 600.

## Process B Account

| Particulars | Units | Rs. | Particulars | Units | Rs. |
|---|---|---|---|---|---|
| To Process A A/c Transfer | 27,000 | 156,600 | By Normal Loss | 600 | - |
| ,, Labour | | 39,000 | ,, Finished Goods A/c @ Rs.8.1318 | 24,800 | 201,669 |
| ,, Overhead | | 17,780 | ,, Cl. Work-in-progress A/c | 2,000 | 14,964 |
| ,, Abnormal gain A/c | 400 | 3,253 | | | |
| | 27,400 | 216,633 | | 27,400 | 216,633 |

## Abnormal Loss Account

| Particulars | Units | Rs. | Particulars | Units | Rs. |
|---|---|---|---|---|---|
| To Process A A/c | 800 | 4,640 | By Costing Proft & Loss A/c | 800 | 4,640 |
| | 800 | 4,640 | | 800 | 4,640 |

## Abnormal Gain Account

| Particulars | Units | Rs. | Particulars | Units | Rs. |
|---|---|---|---|---|---|
| To Costing Profit & Loss A/c | 400 | 3,253 | By Process B A/c | 400 | 3,253 |
| | 400 | 3,253 | | 400 | 3,253 |

## Costing Profit and Loss Account

| Particulars | Rs. | Particulars | Rs. |
|---|---|---|---|
| To Abnormal Loss Account | 4,640 | By Abnormal Gain Account | 3,253 |

**Note:**

Abnormal Loss and Abnormal Gain should be tranferred to Costing Profit and Loss Account. Abnormal Loss is debited and Abnormal Gain is credited in Costing Profit and Loss Account. The cost per unit of Abnormal Loss and Abnormal Gain is equal to the cost of production in the respective processes.

**Illustration: 14**

K Ltd., a manufacturing company is producing product A with the help of 3 processes. The information regarding the first process namely, X are stated as follows:

| | |
|---|---|
| Opening Work-in-progress | Nil |
| Units introduced | 15,000 units @ Rs.5 per unit |
| Direct material | Rs.44,400 |
| Direct labour | Rs.26,940 |
| Overheads | Rs.23,850 |

The following further information are also given.

(i) Normal Loss is 6% of the input.

(ii) Closing Work-in-progress is 1,100 units. The Work-in-progress completed to the extent of material 100%, Labour 70%, and Overhead 50%.

(iii) The degree of completion of abnormal loss is material 80% and labour and overhead 40%.

(iv) The output of the process is 12,500 units.

(v) Normal Loss realised @ Rs.2 per unit due to the sale of scrap.

(vi) The units of abnormal loss are sold @ Rs.3 per unit.

Prepare Process X Account, Statement of Equivalent Production, Statement of Cost and Abnormal Loss account from the available information.

***Solution:***

**Statement of Equivalent units**

| Particulars | Units | Material | | Labour | | Works Overhead | |
|---|---|---|---|---|---|---|---|
| | | % | Units | % | Units | % | Units |
| Normal Loss | 900 | - | - | - | - | - | - |
| Abnormal Loss | 500 | 80 | 400 | 40 | 200 | 40 | 200 |
| Completed & Transferred | 12,500 | 100 | 12,500 | 100 | 12,500 | 100 | 12,500 |
| Work-in-progress | 1,100 | 100 | 1,100 | 70 | 770 | 50 | 550 |
| | 15,000 | | 14,000 | | 13,470 | | 13,250 |

**Statement of Cost**

| Element of Cost | Cost (Rs.) | Equivalent Production (units) | Cost per unit (Rs.) |
|---|---|---|---|
| Material introduced (15000 x 5) | 75,000 | | |
| **Add:** Direct material | 44,400 | | |
| | 119,400 | | |
| **Less:** Sale of scrap (900 x 2) | 1,800 | | |
| | 117,600 | 14,000 | 8.40 |
| Direct labour | 26,940 | 13,470 | 2.00 |
| Overhead | 23,850 | 13,250 | 1.80 |
| | 168,390 | | 12.20 |

**Statement of Apportionment of Cost**

| Particulars | | | Rs. |
|---|---|---|---|
| Produced and Transferred | 12,500 x 12.20 | | 152,500 |
| **Abnormal Loss:** | | | |
| Material | 400 x 8.40 = | 3,360 | |
| Labour | 200 x 2.00 = | 400 | |
| Overhead | 200 x 1.80 = | 360 | 4,120 |
| **Closing Work-in-progress:** | | | |
| Material | 1,100 x 8.40 = | 9,240 | |
| Labour | 770 x 2.00 = | 1,540 | |
| Overhead | 550 x 1.80 = | 990 | 11,770 |
| | | Total | 168,390 |

**Note:**

The abnormal loss may not normally realise any value. In rare situations abnormal loss may be identified as scrap units. Hence, it may realise some revenue through sales. In this example the scrap units of 500 realised at the rate of Rs.3 per unit. It should be treated only in the abnormal loss account. In the process account the cost of abnormal loss is treated on the basis of the equivalent units. The difference of revenue and cost is tranferred to Costing Profit and Loss account.The abnormal loss is given that it consumed 80 percentage of material, 40 percentage of labour and 40 percentage of overhead. Hence, the equivalent units for abnormal loss is 400 units of material, 200 units of labour and 200 units of overhead.

**Process X Account**

| Particulars | Units | Rs. | Particulars | Units | Rs. |
|---|---|---|---|---|---|
| To Material Introduced | 15,000 | 75,000 | By Normal loss @ Rs.2 | 900 | 1,800 |
| ,, Direct Material | | 44,400 | ,, Abnormal loss A/c | 500 | 4,120 |
| ,, Direct Labour | | 26,940 | ,, Produced and Transferred to next process @ Rs.12.20 | 12,500 | 152,500 |
| ,, Overhead | | 23,850 | ,, Work-in-progress A/c | 1,100 | 11,770 |
| | 15,000 | 170,190 | | 15,000 | 170,190 |

**Abnormal Loss Account**

| Particulars | Units | Rs. | Particulars | Units | Rs. |
|---|---|---|---|---|---|
| To Process X A/c | 500 | 4,120 | By Normal Loss -Realised (500x2) | 500 | 1,000 |
| | | | ,, Sale @ Rs.3 (of abnormal units) | | 1,500 |
| | | | ,, Costing Profit & Loss A/c | | 1,620 |
| | 500 | 4,120 | | 500 | 4,120 |

**3. Process Costing with Opening and Closing Work-in-progress and without Process Loss or Gain**

In the process of manufacturing, any one or more processes may contain opening and closing work-in-progress and without process loss or gain. The closing work-in-progress is converted into equivalent units by multiplying the units with the percentage of work completed with respect to each element of cost.For example, if the closing work-in-progress is 500 units and the material consumed is 70%, then the equivalent units of material is 350 units.This equivalent units are added to the units completed and transferred in order to find out per unit cost of various elements of cost. But the treatment of opening work-in-progress depends upon the policy of the management which can be known from the nature of the problem. The following are the methods of treatment of opening work-in-progress.

(a) First-in-First-out (FIFO) Method

(b) Average Cost Method

(c) Last-in-First-out (LIFO) Method.

**(a) First-In-First-Out (FIFO) Method**

In this method, the incompleted portion of each element of cost of the Opening Work-in-progress is treated as equivalent units. For example, if the Material completed is 80% Labour completed is 40% and Overhead completed is 30% and the units of opening work-in-progress are 500, then the equivalent units of the opening work-in-progress is material 500 x 20% = 100 units, Labour 500 x 60% = 300 units and Overhead 500 x 70% = 350 units. The equivalent units should be added with the units completed for transfer and in the equivalent units of closing work-in-progress, to find out the cost per unit. Only when the units and the percentage of work completed of opening work-in-progress are given then this method can be applied.

**(b) Average Cost Method**

When the units of opening work-in-progress and the value of each element of cost are given and the percentage of work completed is not given then this method can be applied. In this method equivalent units of opening work-in-progress cannot be calculated. The units of opening work-in-progress are added to the units completed for transfer and the equivalent units of each element of cost. While calculating the average cost for each element of cost the value of each element of cost of the opening work-in-progress is added to the cost of the process.

**(c) Last-In-First-Out (LIFO) Method**

When the value of each element of cost and the percentage of the cost of the opening work-in-progress is given, then this method can be applied. In this method, the closing work-in-progress units are considered as it contains the opening work-in-progress also. In the calculation of equivalent units only incompleted portion of the opening-work-progress is added to the units completed for transfer and the units of closing work-in-progress are not treated for equivalent units. The value of opening work-in-progress is not taken into account for calculating the per unit cost of each element of cost.

**(a) FIFO METHOD**

**Illustration: 15**

The costing information of a manufacturing company for the month August 2011 are as follows:

| | |
|---|---|
| Material | Rs.14,322 |
| Labour | Rs. 7,776 |
| Overhead | Rs. 6,870 |
| Opening Work-in-progress 500 units @ Rs.8 | |
| Units introduced to the process | 4,500 |
| Transfer to next process (Units) (3,700 + 500) | 4,200 |
| Closing Work-in-progress (Units) | 800 |

Degree of completion of opening WIP:

| | |
|---|---|
| Material | 100% |
| Labour | 40% |
| Overhead | 20% |

Degree of completion of closing WIP:

| | |
|---|---|
| Material | 80% |
| Labour | 40% |
| Overhead | 60% |

Assume the FIFO method of valuation of material.

Prepare the Statement of equivalent production, Statement of apportionment of cost and Process Account.

***Solution:***

**Statement of Equivalent Production**

| Input | Output | Units | Material | | Labour | | Overhead | |
|---|---|---|---|---|---|---|---|---|
| | | | % | Units | % | Units | % | Units |
| 500 | Opening Work-in-progress | 500 | - | - | 60 | 300 | 80 | 400 |
| 4,500 | Completed & Transferred | 3,700 | 100 | 3,700 | 100 | 3,700 | 100 | 3,700 |
| | Closing Work -in-progress | 800 | 80 | 640 | 40 | 320 | 60 | 480 |
| 5,000 | | 5000 | | 4,340 | | 4,320 | | 4,580 |

**Statement of Cost**

| Element of Cost | Cost (Rs.) | Equivalent Production (units) | Cost per unit (Rs.) |
|---|---|---|---|
| Material | 14,322 | 4,340 | 3.30 |
| Labour | 7,776 | 4,320 | 1.80 |
| Overhead | 6,870 | 4,580 | 1.50 |
| | 28,968 | | 6.60 |

### Statement of Apportionment of Cost

| Particulars | | | Rs. |
|---|---|---|---|
| Completed and Transferred (3,700 x 6.60) | | | 24,420 |
| **Opening Work-in-progress:** | | | |
| Material | | | |
| Labour | 300 x 1.80 = | 540 | |
| Overhead | 400 x 1.50 = | 600 | 1,140 |
| **Closing work-in-progress:** | | | |
| Material | 640 x 3.30 = | 2112 | |
| Labour | 320 x 1.80 = | 576 | |
| Overhead | 480 x 1.50 = | 720 | 3,408 |
| | | Total | 28,968 |

### Process Account

| Particulars | Units | Rs. | Particulars | Units | Rs. |
|---|---|---|---|---|---|
| To Opening WIP | 500 | 4,000 | By Transfer to next process (3700 x 500) | 4,200 | 29,560 |
| ,, Material | 4,500 | 14,322 | | | |
| ,, Labour | | 7,776 | ,, Cl.WIP | 800 | 3,408 |
| ,, Overhead | | 6,870 | | | |
| | 5,000 | 32,968 | | 5,000 | 32,968 |

**Workings:**

Transfer to next process = Opening Stock + Units completed in the process

| Cost of Transfer to next process: | | Rs. |
|---|---|---|
| Cost of Opening Stock | = 4000 +1140 = | 5,140 |
| Cost of Units Completed | = | 24,420 |
| Total | = | 29,560 |

## (b) AVERAGE PRICE METHOD

**Illustration: 16**

The costing information of a manufacturing company related to Process A for the month September 2011 are as follows:

| | |
|---|---|
| Opening WIP | 12,000 units |
| Units Introduced | 52,000 units |
| Units Completed for Transfer | 54,000 units |
| Closing WIP | 10,000 units |

Cost incurred for the month are

| | Rs. |
|---|---|
| Material | 28,000 |
| Labour | 20,000 |
| Overhead | 16,000 |

The Opening WIP constitutes the following expenses:

| | Rs. |
|---|---|
| Material | 3,000 |
| Labour | 3,200 |
| Overhead | 1,400 |

The closing work-in-progress consumed 80% of material, 40% of labour and overhead.

Prepare a Statement of equivalent production, Statement of cost, and Process A account by Average costing method.

***Solution:***

**Statement of Equivalent Production**

| Input | Units | Output | Units | Material | | Labour | | Overhead | |
|---|---|---|---|---|---|---|---|---|---|
| | | | | % | Units | % | Units | % | Units |
| Op. WIP | 12,000 | Op.WIP | 12,000 | 100 | 12,000 | 100 | 12,000 | 100 | 12,000 |
| Introdu-ced | 52,000 | Compl-eted | 42,000 | 100 | 42,000 | 100 | 42,000 | 100 | 42,000 |
| | | Cl.WIP | 10,000 | 80 | 8,000 | 40 | 4,000 | 40 | 4,000 |
| | 64,000 | | 64,000 | | 62,000 | | 58,000 | | 58,000 |

**Statement of Cost**

| Element of Cost | Cost (Rs.) | Equivalent Production (units) | Cost per unit (Rs.) |
|---|---|---|---|
| Material | $3,000 + 28,000 = 31,000$ | 62,000 | 0.50 |
| Labour | $3,200 + 20,000 = 23,200$ | 58,000 | 0.40 |
| Overhead | $1,400 + 16,000 = 17,400$ | 58,000 | 0.30 |
| | Total $= 71,600$ | | 1.20 |

**Note:**

**In the average costing method the percentage of completion of the opening work-in-progress will not be given. The degree of completion of opening work-in-progress is not considered for calculating the value of closing work-in-progress.**

**Statement of Apportionment of Cost**

| Particulars | Rs. |
|---|---|
| Opening Work-in-progress = 3000 + 3200 + 1400 | 7,600 |
| Units Completed and Transferred | |
| (42,000 + 12,000 ) x 1.20 | |
| i.e., 54,000 x 1.20 | 64,800 |
| Closing Work-in-progress | |
| Material 8000 x 0.50 = 4,000 | |
| Labour 4000 x 0.40 = 1,600 | |
| Overhead 4000 x 0.30 = 1,200 | 6,800 |
| | 71,600 |

**Process A Account**

| Particulars | Units | Rs. | Particulars | Units | Rs. |
|---|---|---|---|---|---|
| To Opening WIP | 12,000 | 7,600 | By Completed and Transferred (42000+12,000) @ Rs 1.20 | 54,000 | 64,800 |
| ,, Material | 52,000 | 28,000 | | | |
| ,, Labour | | 20,000 | | | |
| ,, Overhead | | 16,000 | ,, Closing WIP | 10,000 | 6,800 |
| | 64,000 | 71,600 | | 64,000 | 71,600 |

## (c) LIFO METHOD

**Illustration: 17**

The costing records of a manufacturing company show the following information for the month of April 2011:

| | |
|---|---|
| Opening Work-in-progress | 7,000 Units |
| Units introduced | 39,000 |
| Units Completed and Transferred to Process II | 37,000 |
| Closing work-in-progress | 9,000 Units |

Cost incurred for the month are as follows:

| | Rs. |
|---|---|
| Direct Material | 46,320 |
| Direct Labour | 30,080 |
| Factory Overhead | 22,560 |

The Opening work-in-progress contains,

| | Rs. |
|---|---|
| Direct Material | 6,000 |
| Direct Labour | 5,000 |
| Factory Overhead | 4,000 |

The opening work-in-progress constitutes 80% of material and 30% of labour and overhead. The closing work-in-progress also constitutes 80% of material and 30% of labour and overhead.

Prepare Statement of Equipment production, Statement of cost, Statement of apportionment of cost and Process I Account by adopting LIFO method of inventory valuation.

***Solution:***

**Statement of Equivalent Production**

| Input | Units | Output | Units | Material | | Labour | | Overhead | |
|---|---|---|---|---|---|---|---|---|---|
| | | | | % | Units | % | Units | % | Units |
| Op. WIP | 7,000 | Units Completed | 37,000 | 100 | 37,000 | 100 | 37,000 | 100 | 37,000 |
| Units Introduced | 39,000 | Closing WIP: | | | | | | | |
| | | i. of Op. WIP | 7,000 | - | - | - | - | - | - |
| | | ii. New units | 2,000 | 80 | 1,600 | 30 | 600 | 30 | 600 |
| | 46,000 | | 46,000 | | 38,600 | | 37,600 | | 37,600 |

**Statement of Cost**

| Element of Cost | Cost (Rs.) | Equivalent Production (units) | Cost per unit (Rs.) |
|---|---|---|---|
| Material | 46,320 | 38,600 | 1.20 |
| Labour | 30,080 | 37,600 | 0.80 |
| Overhead | 22,560 | 37,600 | 0.60 |
| | 98,960 | | 2.60 |

**Statement of Apportionment of Cost**

| Particulars | | | Rs. |
|---|---|---|---|
| Opening work-in-progress | = | 6,000 + 5,000 + 4,000 | 15,000 |
| Completed and Transferred | = | 37,000 x 2.60 | 96,200 |
| Closing Work-in-progress: | | | |
| Material 1,600 x 1.20 | = | 1,920 | |
| Labour 600 x 0.80 | = | 480 | |
| Overhead 600 x0.60 | = | 360 | 2,760 |
| (For 2,000 units) | | | |
| For 7,000 units of Op. WIP (due to LIFO) method) | | Total = 15,000 + 2,760 = 17,760 | |
| Total Cost as per statement of cost = 96,200 + 2,760 | | | |
| | | | 98,960 |

**Process I Account**

| Particulars | Units | Rs. | Particulars | Units | Rs. |
|---|---|---|---|---|---|
| To Op.work-in-progress | 7,000 | 15,000 | By Process II A/c Transfer @ Rs 2.60 | 37,000 | 96,200 |
| ,, Material | 39,000 | 46,320 | ,, Closing work-in-progress | 9,000 | 17,760 |
| ,, Labour | | 30,080 | | | |
| ,, Overhead | | 22,560 | | | |
| | 46,000 | 113,960 | | 46,000 | 113,960 |

## 4. Process Costing with Opening and Closing Work-in-Progress and with Process losses or gains

Process account may contain process loss or gain in addition to opening and closing work-in-progress. The units of normal loss will be eliminated for calculating equivalent units. If normal loss realised due to sale of scrap, then it is credited in the process account. The process account may contain either abnormal loss or gain. Units of abnormal loss will be converted into equivalent units just like work-in-progress.Units of abnormal gain are like the completed units and hence,it need not be converted into equivalent units. While calculating the total equivalent units for material, labour and overhead, the equivalent units of abnormal loss should be added. If there is abnormal gain, then the units of abnormal gain should be deducted.

**Illustration: 18**

Prepare Statement of equivalent production, Statement of cost, Statement of apportionment of cost and Process X Account from the following costing information:

Units introduced 54,000 units valued at Rs. 156,600

| | |
|---|---|
| Direct wages | Rs. 73,640 |
| Production overhead | Rs. 62,400 |

The following futher information are also given:

(i) Opening work-in-progress is 6,000 units valued as Rs 9000. Degree of completion of opening work-in-progress -Material 100%, Labour 40% and Overhead 30%.

(ii) The units completed and transferred to next process is 51,000. Normal loss is 5% of the input including the opening work-in-progress.

(iii) The units scrapped is 5000 and the degree of completion of the scrapped units is Material 100%, Labour 80% and Overhead 60%. The scrap is sold @ Rs.2.00 per unit.

(iv) Closing work-in-progress is 4,000 units and the degree of completion of the closing work-in-progress is Material 80%, Labour 60% and Overhead 40%.

Adopt FIFO method of valuation.

***Solution:***

**Statement of Equivalent Production**

| Input | Units | Output | Units | Material % | Material Units | Labour % | Labour Units | Overhead % | Overhead Units |
|---|---|---|---|---|---|---|---|---|---|
| Op. WIP Units | 6,000 | Op.WIP Units | 6,000 | - | - | 60 | 3,600 | 70 | 4,200 |
| Introduced | 54,000 | Completed | 45,000 | 100 | 45,000 | 100 | 45,000 | 100 | 45,000 |
| | | Cl.WIP | 4,000 | 80 | 3,200 | 60 | 2,400 | 40 | 1,600 |
| | | Normal Loss (5%) | 3,000 | - | - | - | - | - | - |
| | | Abnormal Loss | 2,000 | 100 | 2,000 | 80 | 1,600 | 60 | 1,200 |
| | 60,000 | | 60,000 | | 50,200 | | 52,600 | | 52,000 |

**Statement of Cost**

| Element of Cost | Cost (Rs.) | Equivalent Production (units) | Cost per unit (Rs.) |
|---|---|---|---|
| Material : 156,600<br>Less : Sale of Scrap<br>3,000 x 2 = 6,000 | 150,600 | 50,200 | 3.00 |
| Labour | 73,640 | 52,600 | 1.40 |
| Overhead | 62,400 | 52,000 | 1.20 |
| | 286,640 | | 5.60 |

**Note: (i)** Since the method of valuation is FIFO, the value of opening work-in-progress is treated by taking the incomplete portion of work, in calculating the equivalent units. Hence, the material has no units, labour has 60% (100-40) and overhead has 70% (100-30).

**(ii)** Sale of scraped units are applied only for Normal loss and the percentage of completion of the Abnormal loss.

### Statement of Apportionment of Cost

| Particulars | | | Rs. |
|---|---|---|---|
| **(i) Units Completed and Transferred:** | | | |
| Opening work-in-progress (already completed) | | 9,000 | |
| Op.work-in-progress: (Completed in process) | | | |
| Material | -- | | |
| Labour 3,600 x 1.40 = | 5,040 | | |
| Overhead 4,200 x 1.20 = | 5,040 | 10,080 | |
| Units produced in the process 45,000 x 5.60 = | | 252,000 | 271,080 |
| **(ii) Abnormal Loss:** | | | |
| Material 2,000 x 3.00 = | 6,000 | | |
| Labour 1,600 x 1.40 = | 2,240 | | |
| Overhead 1,200 x 1.20 = | 1,440 | | 9,680 |
| **(iii) Closing Work-in-progress:** | | | |
| Material 3,200 x 3.00 = | 9,600 | | |
| Labour 2,400 x 1.40 = | 3,360 | | |
| Overhead 1,600 x 1.20 = | 1,920 | | 14,880 |

### Process X Account

| Particulars | Units | Rs. | Particulars | Units | Rs. |
|---|---|---|---|---|---|
| To Op.Work -in-progress | 6,000 | 9,000 | By Normal Loss A/c @ Rs.2 | 3,000 | 6,000 |
| ,, Material | 54,000 | 156,600 | ,, Completed & Transferred to next Process | 51,000 | 271,080 |
| ,, Labour | | 73,640 | ,, Abnormal loss A/c | 2,000 | 9,680 |
| ,, Overhead | | 62,400 | ,, Closing Work-in-progress | 4,000 | 14,880 |
| | 60,000 | 301,640 | | 60,000 | 301,640 |

**Workings:**

(i) Units Completed and Transferred = 51,000 Units
Units Produced in the process = 51,000 - 6,000
= 45,000 Units

(Completed and Transferred - Op.WIP )

(ii) Units Scrapped = 5,000 Units
Normal Loss (5% of 60,000) = 3,000 Units
Abnormal Loss = 2,000 Units

**Illustration: 19**

Prepare a Statement of equivalent production, Statement of cost, Statement of apportionment of cost and Process I Account from the following information.

| | |
|---|---|
| Units introduced 45,000 valued as | Rs.230,900 |
| Direct wages | Rs.78,800 |
| Factory Overhead | Rs.60,450 |

Opening work-in-progress is 5,000 units valued as Rs.17,500 The degree of completion of Op.WIP is Material 100%, Labour 60% and Overhead 30%.

The units completed and transferred to next process is 37,000. Normal loss is 4,000 units and the scrap of normal losss realised Rs.3 per unit.

Closing Work-in-progress is 6,000 units. The degree of completion of closing work-in-progress is Material 80%, Labour 40% and Overhead 30%. Also calculate the value of Opening Work-in-progress.

***Solution:***

**Statement of Equivalent Production**

| Input | Units | Output | Units | Material % | Material Units | Labour % | Labour Units | Overhead % | Overhead Units |
|---|---|---|---|---|---|---|---|---|---|
| Op.WIP Units | 5,000 | Op.WIP | 5,000 | - | - | 40 | 2,000 | 70 | 3,500 |
| Introduced | 45,000 | Units Completed | 37,000 | 100 | 37,000 | 100 | 37,000 | 100 | 37,000 |
| | | Cl.WIP | 6,000 | 80 | 4,800 | 40 | 2,400 | 30 | 1,800 |
| | | Normal Loss | 4,000 | - | - | - | - | - | - |
| | | | 52,000 | | 41,800 | | 41,400 | | 42,300 |
| | | Less : Abnormal Gain | 2,000 | 100 | 2,000 | 100 | 2,000 | 100 | 2,000 |
| | 50,000 | | 50,000 | | 39,800 | | 39,400 | | 40,300 |

**Statement of Cost**

| Element of Cost | Cost (Rs.) | Equivalent Production (units) | Cost per unit (Rs.) |
|---|---|---|---|
| Material 230,900 | | | |
| Less: | | | |
| Sale of scrap 12,000 | 218,900 | 39,800 | 5.50 |
| Labour | 78,800 | 39,400 | 2.00 |
| Overhead | 60,450 | 40,300 | 1.50 |
| | 358,150 | | 9.00 |

**Statement of Apportionment of Cost**

| Particulars | | | Rs. |
|---|---|---|---|
| **(i) Units Completed and Transferred:** | | | |
| Opening Work-in-progress (Already completed) | | 17,500 | |
| Op.WIP - Completed during the process | | | |
| Material | | | |
| Labour = 2,000 x 2.00 = | 4,000 | | |
| Overhead = 3,500 x 1.50 = | 5,250 | 9,250 | |
| Units Produced in the process = 37,000 x 9 = | | 333,000 | 359,750 |
| **(ii) Closing Work-in-progress:** | | | |
| Material = 4,800 x 5.50 = | 26,400 | | |
| Labour = 2,400 x 2.00 = | 4,800 | | |
| Overhead = 1,800 x 1.50 = | 2,700 | | 33,900 |
| **(iii) Abnormal Gain:** 2,000 x 9 | | | 18,000 |

**Process I Account**

| Particulars | Units | Rs. | Particulars | Units | Rs. |
|---|---|---|---|---|---|
| To Op. WIP | 5,000 | 17,500 | By Normal Loss A/c @ Rs.3 | 4,000 | 12,000 |
| ,, Material | 45,000 | 230,900 | ,, Units Completed & Transferred to Process II | 42,000 | 359,750 |
| ,, Labour | | 78,800 | ,, Closing WIP | 6,000 | 33,900 |
| ,, Overhead | | 60,450 | | | |
| ,, Abnormal Gain | 2,000 | 18,000 | | | |
| | 52,000 | 405,650 | | 52,000 | 405,650 |

**Abnormal Gain Account**

| Particulars | Units | Rs. | Particulars | Units | Rs. |
|---|---|---|---|---|---|
| To Normal Loss Realisation @ Rs.3 | 2,000 | 6,000 | By Process I A/c. | 2,000 | 18,000 |
| ,, Costing Profit & Loss A/c | | 12,000 | | | |
| | 2,000 | 18,000 | | 2,000 | 18,000 |

## VIII. INTER PROCESS PROFIT

Some concerns follow the practice of transferring the output of one process to the next process at a price which includes profit, instead of cost price. This profit is called Inter-Process profit. Since the profit is charged in each process, the transfer to finished goods account will be at an inflated price which includes cost of processes and all the inter process profit. Hence, the profit on sales is the profit realised at the finished stock account and all the inter process profits. The closing stock should also be valued at cost plus profit. But in the first process account the closing stock should be at cost price.

In order to show the inter-process profit, the process account should be prepared with three columns each for the debit side and for the credit side. The three columns represent cost, profit and total.

**Illustration: 20**

XYZ & Co. Ltd manufactures a product named 'X' which passes through three processes I, II and III. The information related to these processes for the month of October 2011 are as follows:

| | Process I | Process II | Process III |
|---|---|---|---|
| | Rs. | Rs. | Rs. |
| Direct Material | 14,000 | 17,000 | 15,000 |
| Direct wages | 8,000 | 15,000 | 13,000 |
| Factory Overhead | 7,000 | 5,000 | 9,000 |
| Stock as on 31st October 2011 | 5,000 | 6,000 | 11,000 |

The production of Processes I & II are transferred to the next process for a profit @ 25% on the transfer price. The sale of finished goods is Rs.125,000 and the stock of finished goods as an 31st October 2011 is Rs.20,000. The output transferred from the Process III to the Finished goods account is for a profit @ Rs 25% on the cost of production.

Prepare process accounts and find out the profit earned during the month October 2011.

***Solution:***

**Process I Account**

| Particulars | Total Rs. | Cost Rs. | Profit Rs. | Particulars | Total Rs. | Cost Rs. | Profit Rs. |
|---|---|---|---|---|---|---|---|
| To Material | 14000 | 14,000 | - | By Process II Transfer | 32,000 | 24,000 | 8,000 |
| ,, Wages | 8,000 | 8,000 | - | | | | |
| ,, Overhead | 7,000 | 7,000 | - | | | | |
| | 29,000 | 29,000 | | | | | |
| Less: | | | | | | | |
| Closing Stock | 5,000 | 5,000 | | | | | |
| | 24,000 | 24,000 | - | | | | |
| To Profit (25/75x24000) | 8000 | | 8,000 | | | | |
| | 32000 | 24,000 | 8,000 | | 32,000 | 24,000 | 8000 |

Value of closing stock = (2,90,000 / 29,000) x 5,000 = Rs.500.

**Process II Account**

| Particulars | Total Rs. | Cost Rs. | Profit Rs. | Particulars | Total Rs. | Cost Rs. | Profit Rs. |
|---|---|---|---|---|---|---|---|
| To Process I A/c | 32,000 | 24,000 | 8,000 | By Process III Transfer | 84,000 | 55,696 | 28,304 |
| ,, Material | 17,000 | 17,000 | - | | | | |
| ,, Labour | 15,000 | 15,000 | - | | | | |
| ,, Overhead | 5,000 | 5,000 | - | | | | |
| | 69,000 | 61,000 | 8,000 | | | | |
| Less: Closing Stock | 6,000 | 5304 | 696 | | | | |
| | 63,000 | 55,696 | 7,304 | | | | |
| To Profit (25/75 x 63,000) | 21,000 | - | 21,000 | | | | |
| | 84,000 | 55696 | 28304 | | 84,000 | 55696 | 28,304 |
| To Stock b/d | 6,000 | 5,304 | 696 | | | | |

$$\text{Value of Closing Stock (cost)} = \frac{61,000 \times 6,000}{69,000} = \text{Rs.}5,304$$

**Process III Account**

| Particulars | Total Rs. | Cost Rs. | Profit Rs. | Particulars | Total Rs. | Cost Rs. | Profit Rs. |
|---|---|---|---|---|---|---|---|
| To Process II A/c | 84,000 | 55,696 | 28,304 | By Finished Stock A/c | 137,500 | 84,269 | 53,231 |
| ,, Material | 15,000 | 15,000 | - | | | | |
| ,, Labour | 13,000 | 13,000 | | | | | |
| ,, Overhead | 9,000 | 9,000 | | | | | |
| | 121,000 | 92,696 | 28,304 | | | | |
| Less: Closing Stock | 11,000 | 8,427 | 2,573 | | | | |
| | 110,000 | 84,269 | 25,731 | | | | |
| To Profit (25/100 x110,000) | 27,500 | - | 27,500 | | | | |
| | 137,500 | 84,269 | 53,231 | | 137,500 | 84,269 | 53,231 |
| To Stock b/d | 11,000 | 8427 | 2,573 | | | | |

$$\text{Value of Closing Stock (cost)} = \frac{92,696 \times 11,000}{121,000}$$

$$= \text{Rs.}8,427$$

**Finished Stock Account**

| Particulars | Total Rs. | Cost Rs. | Profit Rs. | Particulars | Total Rs. | Cost Rs. | Profit Rs. |
|---|---|---|---|---|---|---|---|
| To Process III A/c | 137,500 | 84,269 | 53,231 | By Sales | 125,000 | 72,012 | 52,988 |
| Less: Closing Stock | 20,000 | 12,257 | 7,743 | | | | |
| | 117,500 | 72,012 | 45,488 | | | | |
| To Profit | 7,500 | - | 7,500 | | | | |
| | 125,000 | 72,012 | 52,988 | | 125,000 | 72,012 | 52,988 |
| To Stock b/d | 20,000 | 12,257 | 7,743 | | | | |

$$\text{Value of Closing Stock (cost)} = \frac{84{,}269 \times 20{,}000}{137{,}500}$$

$$= \text{Rs.}12{,}257$$

**Illustration: 21**

A product manufactured by a company passes through 2 different processes, A and B. The data related to these processes for the month August 2011 are as follows:

| | Process A Rs. | Process B Rs. | Finished Stock Rs. |
|---|---|---|---|
| Opening stock | 6000 | 13,000 | 25,000 |
| Material | 17,500 | 19,000 | |
| Labour | 15,000 | 20,000 | |
| Production Overhead | 7,500 | 3,000 | |
| Stock as on 31st August 2011 | 7,300 | 12,500 | 27,500 |
| Inter-process profit included in Op.stock | - | 2,350 | 4,500 |

The following further details are also given:

(i) Sales during the month is Rs.145,000.

(ii) Output of Process A is transferred to Process B at 10% profit on transfer price

(iii) Output of Process B is transferred to finished goods at 25% profit on transfer price.

(iv) Finished stock is valued at the price on the basis of the output transferred from Process B to Finished Goods Account.

Prepare Process Accounts and Finished goods Account.

***Solution:***

**Process A Account**

| Particulars | Total Rs. | Cost Rs. | Profit Rs. | Particulars | Total Rs. | Cost Rs. | Profit Rs. |
|---|---|---|---|---|---|---|---|
| To Opening Stock | 6,000 | 6,000 | - | By Process B A/c (Transfer) | 43,000 | 38,700 | 4,300 |
| ,, Direct Material | 17,500 | 17,500 | - | | | | |
| ,, Direct Wages | 15,000 | 15,000 | - | | | | |
| | 38,500 | 38,500 | - | | | | |
| Less: Closing Stock | 7,300 | 7,300 | - | | | | |
| | 31,200 | 31,200 | | | | | |
| To Production Overhead | 7,500 | 7,500 | | | | | |
| | 38,700 | 38,700 | | | | | |
| ,, Profit (10/90 x38,700) | 4,300 | | 4,300 | | | | |
| | 43,000 | 38,700 | 4,300 | | 43,000 | 38,700 | 4,300 |

**Process B Account**

| Particulars | Total Rs. | Cost Rs. | Profit Rs. | Particulars | Total Rs. | Cost Rs. | Profit Rs. |
|---|---|---|---|---|---|---|---|
| To Opening Stock | 13,000 | 10,650 | 2,350 | By Finished Stock A/c (Transfer) | 114,000 | 79,698 | 34,302 |
| ,, Process A A/c | 43,000 | 38,700 | 4,300 | | | | |
| ,, Direct Material | 19,000 | 19,000 | - | | | | |
| ,, Direct Wages | 20,000 | 20,000 | - | | | | |
| | 95,000 | 88,350 | 6,650 | | | | |
| Less: Closing Stock (Profit = $\frac{6,650 \times 12,500}{95,000}$) | 12,500 | 11,652 | 848 | | | | |
| | 82,500 | 76,698 | 5,802 | | | | |
| To Pro. OH | 3,000 | 3,000 | - | | | | |
| ,, Profit (25/75 x 85,500) | 85,500 | 79,698 | 5,802 | | | | |
| | 28,500 | - | 28,500 | | | | |
| | 114,000 | 79,698 | 34,302 | | 114,000 | 79,698 | 34,302 |

**Finished Goods Stock Account**

| Particulars | Total Rs. | Cost Rs. | Profit Rs. | Particulars | Total Rs. | Cost Rs. | Profit Rs. |
|---|---|---|---|---|---|---|---|
| To Opening Stock | 25,000 | 20,500 | 4,500 | By Sales | 145,000 | 80,375 | 64,625 |
| ,, Process B A/c (Transfer) | 114,000 | 79,698 | 34,302 | | | | |
| | 139,000 | 100,198 | 38,802 | | | | |
| Less: Closing Stock | 27,500 | 19,823 | 7,677 | | | | |
| (Profit = $\frac{38,802 \times 27,500}{139,000}$) | 111,500 | 80,375 | 31,125 | | | | |
| To Profit | 33,500 | - | 33,500 | | | | |
| | 145,000 | 80,375 | 64,625 | | 145,000 | 80,375 | 64,625 |

## IX. JOINT PRODUCT AND BY-PRODUCT

## JOINT PRODUCT

The processing of one raw material or combination of raw materials, may give two or more finished products of equal importance. These products are called joint products. For example, in the oil refinery, products like petrol, oil, gasoline, kerosene and lubricating oil are produced by processing of crude oil.

Joint products are manufactured by incurring common expenses in the different processes. These expenses must be apportioned among the different products in order to find out the cost of production separately and to know the individual profit for the joint products.

### Methods of allocation of Joint Costs

Joint expenses of the joint products can be apportioned by any of the following methods:

1. Average Cost Method
2. Physical Quantity Method
3. Sales Value Method
4. Weighted Average Cost Method

### 1. Average Cost Method

In this method, the average unit cost of product should be multiplied by the number of units produced for different joint products. Average unit cost of production is the total cost divided by the number of units of all joint products produced.

**2. Physical Quantity Method**

In this method, each element of cost is separated by the quantity of the material. The quantity of the material may either be in number of units or weight. For example, if quantity produced of joint products X, Y and Z are 2,000; 3,000 and 5,000 respectively then the costs should be apportioned in the ratio 2:3:5 for the products X,Y and Z

**3. Sales Value Method**

The basis of the apportionment of joint cost in this method is the sales value. Each element of cost is divided by the total sales value and multiplied by the individual sales value of the joint products.

**4. Weighted Average Cost Method**

In this method, a weight may be assigned to joint products, according to the importance and consumption of costs, for apportioning the joint cost. For example, quantity produced of joint products A, B and C are 1,000; 1,500 and 2,000 respectively. If weights assigned to these products are 3, 4 and 2 for A, B and C respectively, then the basis of apportionment of the joint costs is

1,000 x 3 : 1,500 x 4 : 1,000 x 4 i.e, 3 : 6 : 4.

This method is also called Survey Method.

**Illustration: 22**

A company produces 4 joint products A,B,C and D with the help of one raw material. The data related to the production for 3 months ended April, 2011 are as follows:

| | Rs. |
|---|---|
| Direct Material | 80,000 |
| Direct Wages | 70,000 |
| Factory Overhead | 35,000 |
| Administration Overhead | 25,000 |

Sales for the period are as follows:

| Joint Products | Number of units | Selling price per unit (Rs.) |
|---|---|---|
| A | 10,000 | 13.00 |
| B | 8,000 | 10.00 |
| C | 5,000 | 4.00 |
| D | 2,000 | 5.00 |

Prepare Cost Statement on the basis of (i) Allocation of costs by number of units and (ii) Allocation of costs by sales value.

***Solution:***

**Statement of Sales**

| Joint Products | Number of units | Selling price per unit (Rs.) | Sales value Rs. |
|---|---|---|---|
| A | 10,000 | 13 | 130,000 |
| B | 8,000 | 10 | 80,000 |
| C | 5,000 | 4 | 20,000 |
| D | 2,000 | 5 | 10,000 |
| Total | 25,000 | | 240,000 |

**Statement of Apportionment of Joint Costs**
**(On the basis of number of units)**

| Particulars | Joint Products | | | | Total (Rs.) |
|---|---|---|---|---|---|
| | A (Rs.) | B (Rs.) | C (Rs.) | D (Rs.) | |
| Material | 32,000 | 25,600 | 16,000 | 6,400 | 80,000 |
| Labour | 28,000 | 22,400 | 14,000 | 5,600 | 70,000 |
| Factory Overhead | 14,000 | 11,200 | 7,000 | 2,800 | 35,000 |
| Administration Overhead | 10,000 | 8,000 | 5,000 | 2,000 | 25,000 |
| Total Cost | 84,000 | 67,200 | 42,000 | 16,800 | 210,000 |

Ratio of apportionment = 10,000 : 8000 : 5000 : 2000
= 10 : 8 : 5 : 2

**Statement of Apportionment of Joint Costs**
**(On the basis of sales value)**

| Particulars | Joint Products | | | | Total (Rs) |
|---|---|---|---|---|---|
| | A (Rs) | B (Rs) | C (Rs) | D (Rs) | |
| Material | 43,333 | 26,667 | 6,667 | 3,333 | 80,000 |
| Labour | 37,917 | 23,333 | 5,833 | 2,917 | 70,000 |
| Factory Overhead | 18,958 | 11,667 | 2,917 | 1,458 | 35,000 |
| Administration Overhead | 13,542 | 8,333 | 2,083 | 1,042 | 25,000 |
| Total Cost | 113,750 | 70,000 | 17,500 | 8,750 | 210,000 |

Ratio of Apportionment = 130,000 : 80,000 : 20,000 : 10,000 :
= 13 : 8 : 2 : 1

**Illustration: 23**

Prepare a Statement of Apportionment of costs on the basis of number of units and sales value for three joint products X , Y and Z from the following particulars:

| | Rs. |
|---|---|
| Carriage inwards | 2,000 |
| Direct Labour | 28,000 |
| Production Overhead | 20,000 |
| Administration Overhead | 21,000 |

**Sales:**

X 800 units @ Rs.80 per unit

Y 700 units @ Rs.70 per unit

Z 500 units @ Rs.60 per unit.

The expected profit of the company is 25% on cost.

***Solution:***

| **Total Sales value** | | | **Rs.** |
|---|---|---|---|
| X | 800 x 80 | = | 64,000 |
| Y | 700 x 70 | = | 49,000 |
| Z | 500 x 60 | = | 30,000 |
| | Total | | 143,000 |
| Total Profit | (25 / 125) x 143,000 | = | 28,600 |
| | Total Cost | = | 114,400 |

**Less: Joint Costs (excluding Direct Material):**

| | | |
|---|---|---|
| Carriage inwards | 2,000 | |
| Direct Labour | 28,000 | |
| Production Overhead | 20,000 | |
| Administration Overhead | 21,000 | 71,000 |
| Direct material | | 43,400 |

**Statement of Apportionment of Cost (On the basis of No.of units)**

| Particulars | Joint Products (Rs.) | | | Total(Rs) |
|---|---|---|---|---|
| | X | Y | Z | |
| Direct Material | 17,360 | 15,190 | 10,850 | 43,400 |
| Carriage Inwards | 800 | 700 | 500 | 2,000 |
| Direct Wages | 11,200 | 9,800 | 7,000 | 28,000 |
| Production Overhead | 8,000 | 7,000 | 5,000 | 20,000 |
| Administration Overhead | 8,400 | 7,350 | 5,250 | 21,000 |
| Total | 45,760 | 40,040 | 28,600 | 114,400 |

Basis of Apportionment X, Y, Z = 800 : 700 : 500
(No. of units) = 8 : 7 : 5

**Statement of Apportionment of Cost**
**(On the basis of sales value)**

| Particulars | Joint Products (Rs.) | | | Total |
|---|---|---|---|---|
| | X | Y | Z | Rs. |
| Direct Material | 19,424 | 14,871 | 9,105 | 43,400 |
| Carriage Inwards | 895 | 685 | 420 | 2,000 |
| Direct Wages | 12,531 | 9,595 | 5,874 | 28,000 |
| Production Overhead | 8,952 | 6,852 | 4,196 | 20,000 |
| Administration Overhead | 9,399 | 7,196 | 4,405 | 21,000 |
| Total | 51,201 | 39,199 | 24,000 | 114,400 |

Basis of Apportionment X, Y, Z = 64,000 : 49,000 : 30,000
= 64 : 49 : 30

**Illustration: 24**

The cost data related to the production of three products named, A, B and C for the month April 2006 are as follows:

| | Rs. |
|---|---|
| Direct Material | 7,000 |
| Direct Wages | 5,000 |
| Fixed Overhead | 4,000 |
| Variable Overhead | 3,000 |

**Sales:** A 500 kgm @ Rs.22
B 300 kgm @ Rs.20
C 200 kgm @ Rs.35

Calculate the cost and profit for each product on the basis of (i) Weight (ii) Sales value and (iii) Weight for Marginal cost and Contribution for Fixed cost.

***Solution:***

Joint Cost for A, B, and C

| | | Rs. |
|---|---|---|
| Material | | 7,000 |
| Labour | | 5,000 |
| Fixed Overhead | | 4,000 |
| Variable Overhead | | 3,000 |
| | | 19,000 |
| Sales: A | 500 x 22 | 11,000 |
| B | 300 x 20 | 6,000 |
| C | 200 x 35 | 7,000 |

| | |
|---|---|
| | 24,000 |
| Profit | 5,000 |

Variable Cost (or Marginal cost) = 7,000 + 5,000 + 3,000

= Rs.15,000

Contribution = Sales - Variable Cost

= 24,000 - 15,000 = Rs.9,000

**Statement of Apportionment of Cost**
**(On the basis of weight)**

| Particulars | Joint Products | | | Total Rs. |
|---|---|---|---|---|
| | A Rs. | B Rs. | C Rs. | |
| Sales | 11,000 | 6,000 | 7,000 | 24,000 |
| Less: Total Cost | 9,500 | 5,700 | 3,800 | 19,000 |
| Profit | 1,500 | 300 | 3,200 | 5,000 |

Ratio of Apportionment: A, B, C = 500 : 300 : 200 = 5 : 3 : 2

**Statement of Apportionment of Cost (On the basis of Sales value)**

| Particulars | Joint Products | | | Total Rs. |
|---|---|---|---|---|
| | A Rs. | B Rs. | C Rs. | |
| Sales | 11,000 | 6,000 | 7,000 | 24,000 |
| Total Cost | 8,708 | 4,750 | 5,542 | 19,000 |
| Profit | 2,292 | 1,250 | 1,458 | 5,000 |

Ratio of Apportionment: A, B, C = 11,000 : 6,000 : 7,000

= 11 : 6 : 7

**Statement of Apportionment of Cost (On the basis of Weight, for Marginal Cost and Contribution for Fixed Cost)**

| Particulars | Joint Products | | | Total |
|---|---|---|---|---|
| | A Rs. | B Rs. | C Rs. | Rs. |
| Sales | 11,000 | 6,000 | 7,000 | 24,000 |
| Less: Marginal Cost (Weight basis) | 7,500 | 4,500 | 3,000 | 15,000 |
| Contribution | 3,500 | 1,500 | 4,000 | 9,000 |
| Less: Fixed Cost (Contribution basis) | 1,555 | 667 | 1,778 | 4,000 |
| Profit | 1,945 | 833 | 2,222 | 5,000 |

Ratio of weight A, B, C = 5 : 3 : 2

Ratio of Contribution A, B, C = 3,500 : 1,500 : 4,000

= 7 : 3 : 8

**Process Account and Apportionment of Joint Costs**

The joint cost of the joint products may be apportioned after completing one or two processes. For example, in the first process all the elements of costs are debited to find out the total cost of transfer to the next process. In the next process, the joint expenses and the transfer cost of the previous process would be apportioned among the joint products by suitable basis of apportionment.

**Illustration: 25**

A manufacturing company is producing 3 joint products by two processes.The joint products are produced in the second process. The data for the month of May 2011 of the manufacturing company are as follows:

| | Process I Rs. | Process II Rs. |
|---|---|---|
| Direct Material | | |
| 2,000 units @ Rs.2 per unit | 40,000 | - |
| Direct Wages | 22,500 | 27,000 |
| Factory Overhead | 27,000 | 9,000 |

Normal loss for process I is 15% and scrap value of loss is Rs.1.50 per unit. Output in Process I are sold as X @ Rs.9 per unit, Y @ Rs.8 per unit and Z @ Rs.10 per unit. Output of Process I are transferred to Process II for X - 8,000, Y - 6,000 and Z - 4,000 units.

Prepare Process I Account, Process II Account, Abnormal gain account and Normal loss account on the basis of apportionment of joint cost by number of units and sales value.

***Solution:***

**Process I Account**

| Particulars | Units | Rs. | Particulars | Units | Rs. |
|---|---|---|---|---|---|
| To Direct Material | 20,000 | 40,000 | By Normal | | |
| ,, Direct Wages | | 22,500 | Loss 15% | 3,000 | 4,500 |
| ,, Factory | | 27,000 | @ Rs.1.5 | | |
| Overhead | | | ,, Process II | | |
| ,, Abnormal gain | | | @ Rs.5 | 18,000 | 90,000 |
| @ Rs.5 | 1,000 | 5,000 | | | |
| | 21,000 | 94,500 | | 21,000 | 94,500 |

**Abnormal Gain Account**

| Particulars | Units | Rs. | Particulars | Units | Rs. |
|---|---|---|---|---|---|
| To Normal Loss A/c @ Rs.1.50 | 1,000 | 1,500 | By Process I A/c | 1,000 | 5,000 |
| ,, Costing P & L A/c | | 3,500 | | | |
| | 1,000 | 5,000 | | 1,000 | 5,000 |

**Normal Loss Account**

| Particulars | Units | Rs. | Particulars | Units | Rs. |
|---|---|---|---|---|---|
| To Process I A/c | 3,000 | 4,500 | By Abnormal Gain A/c | 1,000 | 1,500 |
| | | | ,, Sales | 2,000 | 3,000 |
| | 3,000 | 4,500 | | 3,000 | 4,500 |

**Process II Account**

(Apportionment of Joint Cost on the basis of number of units)

| Particulars | Joint Products | | | Total Rs. |
|---|---|---|---|---|
| | X Rs. | Y Rs. | Z Rs. | |
| Sales | 72,000 | 48,000 | 40,000 | 160,000 |
| Process I Account | 40,000 | 30,000 | 20,000 | 90,000 |
| Direct Wages | 12,000 | 9,000 | 6,000 | 27,000 |
| Factory Overhead | 4,000 | 3,000 | 2,000 | 9,000 |
| Total Cost | 56,000 | 42,000 | 28,000 | 126,000 |
| Profit | 16,000 | 6,000 | 12,000 | 34,000 |

Basis of Apportionment : X, Y, Z = 8000 : 6000 : 4000
= 4 : 3 : 2

**Process II Account**

(Apportionment of joint Cost on the basis of Sales value)

| Particulars | Joint Products | | | Total Rs. |
|---|---|---|---|---|
| | X Rs. | Y Rs. | Z Rs. | |
| Sales | 72,000 | 48,000 | 40,000 | 160,000 |
| Process I Account | 40,500 | 27,000 | 22,500 | 90,000 |
| Direct Wages | 12,150 | 8,100 | 6,750 | 27,000 |
| Factory Overhead | 4,050 | 2,700 | 2,250 | 9,000 |
| Total Cost | 56,700 | 37,800 | 31,500 | 126,000 |
| Profit | 15,300 | 10,200 | 8,500 | 34,000 |

Basis of Apportionment : X, Y, Z = 72,000 : 48,000 : 40,000

= 9 : 6 : 5

**Workings:**

Cost per normal unit in Process I Account

$$= \frac{40{,}000 + 22{,}500 + 27{,}000 - 4{,}500}{20{,}000 - 3000}$$

$$= \frac{85{,}000}{17{,}000} = \text{Rs.}5$$

**Illustration: 26**

X,Y, Z Co.Ltd produces 4 products namely A,B,C,D. The cost of manufacturing these products are as follows:

| | | | | |
|---|---|---|---|---|
| Output (in kgm) | 10,000 | 9,000 | 4,000 | 2,000 |
| Cost after split-of points(Rs.) | 21,000 | 18,000 | 6,000 | 8,000 |
| Sales per unit (Rs.) | 10 | 8 | 6 | 7 |

The total cost before the split off point amounted to Rs 126,000. If the products are sold at the split off point without further processing the selling price per unit are A @ Rs.7, B @ Rs.6, C @ Rs.4 and D @ Rs.5

Prepare a Statement of cost and profit if the products are sold after further processing (apportion the joint cost on the basis of sales value) and a Statement of cost and profit if the products are sold at split-off point.

***Solution:***

**(i) Statement of Cost and Profit**

(if the products are sold after further processing)

| Particulars | Joint Products | | | | Total |
|---|---|---|---|---|---|
| | A Rs. | B Rs. | C Rs. | D Rs. | Rs. |
| Cost before split-off point | 60,000 | 43,200 | 14,400 | 8,400 | 126,000 |
| Cost after split off point | 21,000 | 18,000 | 6,000 | 8,000 | 53,000 |
| Total Cost | 81,000 | 61,200 | 20,400 | 16,400 | 179,000 |
| Profit | 19,000 | 10,800 | 3,600 | (2,400) | 31,000 |
| Sales | 100,000 | 72,000 | 24,000 | 14,000 | 210,000 |

Basis of Apportionment:

A,B,C,D = 100,000 : 72,000 : 24,000 : 14,000
= 50 : 36 : 12 : 7

**(ii) Statement of Cost and Profit**
(if the products are sold at the point of separation)

| Particulars | Joint Products | | | | Total Rs. |
|---|---|---|---|---|---|
| | A Rs. | B Rs. | C Rs. | D Rs. | |
| Cost upto the point of separation | 60,000 | 43,200 | 14,400 | 8,400 | 126,000 |
| Costing Profit | 10,000 | 10,800 | 1,600 | 1,600 | 24,000 |
| Sales | 70,000 | 54,000 | 16,000 | 10,000 | 150,000 |

## BY - PRODUCTS

In the process of a raw material or combination of raw materials in some manufacturing concerns, an additional product may be produced, in addition to the main product. This additional product is called By-product. Some by- products require further processing before it is sold. For example in the manufacturing of sugar, a by product alcohol can be manufactured by processing the waste.

### Accounting Treatment of by - product

The accounting treatment of the by product depends upon the economical value of the by product and the policy of the management. The following are the different accounting treatments.

**1. Treatment of sale of by - product as other income :**

In this method the income from the sale of by product is treated as a miscellaneous income, which is transferred to the Profit and Loss account. This is just like the treatment of the sale of scrap in the job order costing.

**2. Treatment of sale of by - product as a deduction from the cost of main product**

In this method the sale of by product is credited in the process account so that the cost of production of the main product is reduced to that extent. If there are joint products in the process then the sales realised is allocated on the basis of joint cost method.

**3. Treatment of sale of by-product which requires further processing**

If the by product requires further processing after it is separated from the main product, then the cost of further processing is deducted from the sales value. The balance amount is transferred as a profit, to profit and loss account. In this method, pre-separation cost is not charged as a cost of the by- product.

**Illustration: 27**

A company manufactures a product named X. In the process of waste of X, it also produces two by products, $A_1$ and $A_2$. The costing information related to the manufacturing of these main and by products are as follows:

| | X | $A_1$ | $A_2$ |
|---|---|---|---|
| Sales (Rs.) | 130,000 | 40,000 | 30,000 |
| Cost after separation : | | | |
| Labour (Rs.) | - | 8,000 | 4,000 |
| Overhead (Rs.) | - | 2,000 | 2,000 |
| Estimated selling expenses as a percentage of sales value | 10% | 10% | 10% |
| Estimated profit as a percentage of cost of production | | 25% | 20% |

Total cost upto the separation point is Rs.120,000. Assume that there is no opening and closing stock.

Prepare a Statement of Apportionment of Cost and Statement of Profit and Loss Account.

***Solution:***

**Statement of Apportionment of Joint Costs**

| Particulars | | | By Products | |
|---|---|---|---|---|
| | | | $A_1$ Rs. | $A_2$ Rs. |
| Sales | | | 40,000 | 30,000 |
| **Less:** Net Profit | | | | |
| $A_1$ = 40,000 x (25 / 125); | | | | |
| $A_2$ = 30,000 x (20 / 120) | | | 8,000 | 5,000 |
| Total Cost of sales | | | 32,000 | 25,000 |
| **Less:** Selling expenses @ 10% on sales | | | 4,000 | 3,000 |
| Total Cost | | | 28,000 | 22,000 |
| **Less:** Cost after separation: | | | | |
| Labour | 8000 | 4000 | | |
| Overhead | 2000 | 2000 | 10,000 | 6,000 |
| Total Cost upto separation | | | 18,000 | 16,000 |

Total Cost upto separation for product X

= 120,000 - (18,000+16,000)

= 120,000 - 34,000 = Rs.86,000

**Statement of Cost and Profit**

| Particulars | Main Product X Rs. | By Products $A_1$ Rs. | By Products $A_2$ Rs. |
|---|---|---|---|
| Share of upto-separation cost | 86,000 | 18,000 | 16,000 |
| After separation costs | - | 10,000 | 6,000 |
| Cost of production | 86,000 | 28,000 | 22,000 |
| Selling overhead (10% of sales) | 13,000 | 4,000 | 3,000 |
| Cost of sales | 99,000 | 32,000 | 25,000 |
| Costing profit | 31,000 | 8,000 | 5,000 |
| Sales | 130,000 | 40,000 | 30,000 |

Note: The cost of by-products $A_1$ and $A_2$ upto separation are calculated by deducting the cost after separation from the cost of sales. The cost of sales is calculated by deducting profit from sales. The cost upto separation is added with the cost after separation to find out the total cost of production.

**Illustration: 28**

A company produces a product 'X' and in the process of production it also produces two by - products $B_1$ and $B_2$. The costing information for the month of May 2011 of the company are as follows:

| | Joint Expenses Rs. | X Rs. | Separate Expenses $B_1$ Rs. | Separate Expenses $B_2$ Rs. |
|---|---|---|---|---|
| Material | 60,000 | - | 12,000 | 11,000 |
| Labour | 13,000 | - | 8,000 | 5,000 |
| Overhead | 7,000 | - | 6,000 | 2,000 |
| Selling expenses | | 5,000 | 4,000 | 3,000 |
| Selling price per unit | | | 80 | 60 |
| Estimated profit (loss) per unit | | | (10) | 15 |

The main product is sold for a profit @ 20% on cost. The output of the company is 1,000 units of X, 700 units of $B_1$ and 800 units of $B_2$.

Prepare a Statement of cost and profit on the basis of reverse cost method of accounting for by-product.

***Solution:***

**Statement of Apportionment of Joint Costs**

| Particulars | By-products | |
|---|---|---|
| | $B_1$ Rs. | $B_2$ Rs. |
| Sales | 56,000 | 48,000 |
| **Less:** Estimated profit | | 12,000 |
| **Add:** Estimated Loss | 7,000 | |
| Cost of Sales | 63,000 | 36,000 |
| **Less:** Selling Expenses | 4,000 | 3,000 |
| Cost of Production | 59,000 | 33,000 |
| **Less:** Cost after separation | 26,000 | 18,000 |
| Cost before separation (Joint Cost) | 33,000 | 15,000 |

(i) Total Cost before separation:

| | | Rs. |
|---|---|---|
| Material | | 60,000 |
| Labour | | 33,000 |
| Overhead | | 7,000 |
| Total | | 100,000 |
| **Less:** Joint Costs of $B_1$ | 33,000 | |
| $B_2$ | 15,000 | 48,000 |
| Share of Joint Cost for X | | 52,000 |

(ii) After Separation Cost:

| | $B_1$ Rs. | $B_2$ Rs. |
|---|---|---|
| Material | 12,000 | 11,000 |
| Labour | 8,000 | 5,000 |
| Overhead | 6,000 | 2,000 |
| | 26,000 | 18,000 |

**Note:**

Joint cost is Rs.1,00,000. In order to find out the pre-separation cost for the main product X, the pre-separation cost of By-products $B_1$ and $B_2$ should be calculated. The total of pre-separation cost should be deducted from the total pre-separation (Joint) cost to know the pre-separation cost of the main product X. The pre-separation cost is calculated by deducting the estimated profit and all the post separation cost from the sales.

**Statement of Cost and Profit**

| Particulars | Main Product X (Rs.) | By - Product $B_1$ | By - Product $B_2$ | Total Rs. |
|---|---|---|---|---|
| Pre-Separation Cost | 52,000 | 33,000 | 15,000 | 100,000 |
| After - Separation Cost: | | | | |
| Material | - | 12,000 | 11,000 | 23,000 |
| Labour | - | 8,000 | 5,000 | 13,000 |
| Overhead | - | 6,000 | 2,000 | 8,000 |
| Cost of Production | 52,000 | 59,000 | 33,000 | 144,000 |
| **Add:** Selling Expenses | 5,000 | 4,000 | 3,000 | 12,000 |
| Cost of Sales | 57,000 | 63,000 | 36,000 | 156,000 |
| Costing Profit or Loss (X = 20/100 x 57,000) | 11,400 | (7,000) | 12,000 | 16,400 |
| Sales | 68,400 | 56,000 | 48,000 | 172,400 |

## EXERCISE

**I. Choose the correct answer for the following:**

1. Normal process loss is adjusted with the
   (i) Cost of production (ii) P &-L A/c (iii) Overhead (iv) Fixed cost
2. The loss caused due to unexpected condition is called
   (i)Normal loss (ii) Abnormal loss (iii) Gross loss (iv) Net loss
3. The loss which could not be avoided is called
   (i) Abnormal loss (ii) Gross loss (iii) Net loss (iv) Normal loss
4. If the output in a process is in excess of the expected output after adjusting the normal loss is known as
   (i) Abnormal loss (ii) Cost of production
   (iii) Abnormal gain (iv) Normal loss
5. Abnormal loss is the difference between the actual loss and
   (i) Normal loss (ii) Net loss (iii) Net Profit (iv) Gross profit
6. The value of abnormal loss is debited in the
   (i) Process account (ii) Costing Profit and Loss Account
   (iii) Income & Expenditure Account (iv) Cost Sheet
7. Equivalent production units are calculated in process account due to (i) Editing (ii) Cost centre (iii) Cost unit (iv) Work-in-progress
8. When two or more products of equal importance are simultaneously produced, the products are called
   (i) By-products (ii) Joint products
   (iii) Quality products (iv) Discounted products

9. One or more products of relatively small value which are produced simultaneously are called
   (i) Joint products (ii) Co-products
   (iii) By-products (iv) Discounted products
10. The method of costing adopted for products which undergo different stages of production is called
   (i) Marignal costing (ii) Standard costing
   (iii) Budgeting (iv) Process costing

[Ans:1. (i) 2. (ii) 3. (iv) 4. (iii) 5. (i) 6. (ii) 7. (iv) 8. (ii) 9. (iii) 10.(iv)]

**II. Answer the following questions:**

11. What is process costing? State the procedures for preparing process costing.
12. Define process costing. Distinguish between process costing and job costing.
13. Define process loss. Distinguish between normal loss and abnormal loss.
14. What is abnormal gain? Explain the treatment of abnormal gain in process account and costing profit & loss account
15. Define equivalent production. State the procedures for converting the incompleted units into completed units.
16. What is Joint products? Distinguish between joint products and by-products
17. Define joint products. Explain the accounting procedures of joint products in process costing
18. Define By-producsts. State the accounting procedures of By-products in process costing.
19. Explain the treatment of opening work-in-progress and closing work-in-progress in process costing.
20. Explain the treatment of post separation cost and pre-separation cost.
21. Enumerate the different methods of valuation of work-in-progress in process costing.
22. Write short notes of the following:
   (i) Normal loss (ii) Abnormal loss (iii) Abnormal gain
   (iv) Work-in-progress (v) Equivalent production (vi) Split of point
   (vii) Pre-separation cost (viii) Post separation cost (ix) Joint product
   (x) By-product (xi) Process costing (xii) Inter process profit
23. A product manufactured by MN&Co. undergoes three different processes. The expenses incurred for these processes are stated as follows:.

| | Process I | Process II | Process III |
|---|---|---|---|
| | Rs. | Rs. | Rs. |
| Material consumed | 32,000 | 21,000 | 19,000 |
| Direct wages | 30,000 | 23,000 | 17,000 |
| Direct expenses | 17,000 | 14,000 | 10,000 |

The indirect expenses amounted to Rs 42,000 should be apportioned on the basis of wages. The total quantity produced was 1,000 units.

Prepare process accounts and find out the cost of each process of manufacture and also calculate the cost per unit of the product.

[Ans: Rs.97,000; Rs.168,800; Rs.225,000; Rs.225]

24. Prepare process cost accounts from the following data:

| | Process A | Process B | Process C |
|---|---|---|---|
| Direct material (Rs.) | 45,000 | 41,000 | 31,500 |
| Direct wages (Rs.) | 32,500 | 30,500 | 18,500 |
| Factory overhead (Rs.) | 17,500 | 15,500 | 16,000 |
| Number of units produced | 30,000 | 34,000 | 35,000 |
| Stock as on 1st October 2011 (units) (From preceeding process) | | 5,000 | 4,000 |
| Stock as on 31st October 2011 (units) (From preceding process) | | 3,000 | 5,000 |

Assume that the increase of output in subsequent process is due to additional material.

[Ans: Rs.9,500; Rs.19,7850; Rs.248,800, Rs.3.17; Rs.5.54; Rs.7.11]

25. K Ltd. provided the following information related to the manufacturing in Process A.

Material consumed 3,200 units @ Rs.8. Direct wages Rs.18,500, Direct expenses Rs.12,500.The normal loss is 8% of input. The Scrap in the process was sold @ Rs.2.40 per unit. The net production in the process is 2,700 units.

Prepare process I Account and find out the cost per unit of Transfer to process II Account.

[Ans: Rs. 17.138; Rs.46,274]

26. Prepare Process X Account from the following information. 3,000 units were introduced @ Rs.70 per unit to the Process X. Material cost Rs.43,000, Labour Cost Rs.37,000, Factory Overhead Rs.19,000. The net output is 2,850 units. The normal process loss is @ 10% of the input. The normal loss realised Rs.7,000 by sale of scrap.

[Ans: Rs.2,850 units @ Rs.111.852; Rs.318,778; Abnormal gain 150 units, Rs.16,778 ]

27. The product manufactured by X Ltd passes through three different processes. The details of the expenses incurred in these processes are as follows:

| | Process A | Process B | Process C |
|---|---|---|---|
| Direct Material consumed (Kgm) | 20,000 | 13,000 | 12,000 |
| Material Cost per Kgm (Rs.) | 3 | 5 | 6 |
| Direct wages paid (Rs.) | 41,000 | 47,500 | 39,500 |
| Manufacturing expenses (Rs.) | 22,000 | 24,500 | 18,500 |
| Production (in Kgm) | 17,000 | 26,000 | 33,950 |

In the process of production, 3% of the total weight in each process is lost and 7%, 8% and 9% of Process K , M and N respectively became scrap. The scrap of Process K, M and N are sold @ Rs.2.50, Rs.2.00 and Rs.3.00 per kgm respectively.

Prepare the process accounts.

[Ans: Rs.6,639; 10.28; 11.518; Abnormal loss Rs.6,638; Rs.7,146; Abnormal gain Rs.5,759]

28. MWD & Co. Ltd produces a product with the help of three processes. The following are the information available in the cost records of the company:

| | Process X | Process Y | Process Z |
|---|---|---|---|
| Materials (Rs.) | 7,600 | 6,000 | 4,400 |
| Wages (Rs.) | 5,400 | 3,000 | 2,600 |
| Normal Loss as a percentage of input | 12 % | 15 % | 10 % |
| Value of scrap per kgm (Rs.) | Nil | 3 | 4 |
| Output (Kgm) | 700 | 480 | 552 |

In the Process X 800 Kgm were introduced @ Rs.13 per kgm. Factory overhead absorbed is 70 % on direct wages.

Prepare process accounts, abnormal loss account and abnormal gain account.

[Ans: Rs.33.84; Rs.57.94; Rs.84.35; Abnormal loss A Rs.6,091; B Rs.6,663; Abnormal gain C Rs.10,122]

29. K Ltd manufactured a product by two different processes. The following are the expenses and other costing information connected with the two processes:

The input of material in Process A is 40,000 units valued at Rs.240,000. The other expenses are,

| | Process A | Process B |
|---|---|---|
| Other materials (Rs.) | 80,000 | 44,000 |
| Direct wages (Rs.) | 33,000 | 25,000 |
| Manufacturing expenses (Rs.) | 18,000 | 15,000 |
| Output (in units) | 35,000 | 36,040 |
| Stock of Finished Product (in units) | | |
| 1st October 2011 | 5,000 | 7,000 |
| 30th October 2011 | 3,000 | 4,000 |

The wastage in the process of manufacturing is 10% in Process A and 8% in Process B. The wastage of material is calculated as a percentage to the input of material in each process. The wastage was sold @ Rs.4 per unit and @ Rs.2 per unit for Processes A and B respectively.

The stock as on 1st October 2011 is valued @ Rs.4.50 and Rs.7 per unit for Process A and B respectively. Prepare Process Accounts and Process Stock Accounts. Assume that the stock and the Transfer are valued on the basis of weighted average stock method.

[Ans: ProcessA: Ab.Normal loss Rs.9,861; Cl.Stock Rs.27,573; Transfer Rs.340,066; Process B: Ab.gain Rs.24,568; Cl.Stock Rs.45,698; Finished stock Rs.446,016.]

30. A product named 'T' manufactured by MW & Co. Ltd. passes through three different processes namely I,II and III. The expenses incurred for these processes are as follows:

| | Process I | Process II | Process III |
|---|---|---|---|
| Input of material @ Rs.20 (units) per unit | 9,000 | - | - |
| Other material cost (Rs.) | 32,500 | 17,000 | 23,000 |
| Direct wages (Rs.) | 14,500 | 12,000 | 10,000 |
| Loss of weight (as a percentage to input) | 15% | 12% | 10% |
| Sale of scrap (due to loss of weight) per unit (Rs.) | 5 | 7 | 8 |
| Selling price per unit (Rs.) | 35 | 50 | 80 |

Manufacturing expenses is 80% of direct wages. The general management expense is Rs.20,000 and selling expense is Rs.10,000 30% of the output of Process I, 20% of the output of Process II and the entire output of Process III are sold.

Prepare Process accounts, Process Stock accounts and Profit and Loss account.

[Ans: Rs.30.31; Rs.41.68; Rs.57.51; Profits Rs.10,785; Rs.7,825; Rs.76,322]

31. X Ltd is producing a product C by three processes namely X, Y and Z. Process Z produces a by - product in addition to the product C. The by- product is further processed in Process M to get a new product called by - product 'ZC'. The information available in the costing records of the company for the month February 2011 are as follows.

| | Process X | ProcessY | Process Z |
|---|---|---|---|
| Direct material introduced 60,000 units @ Rs.5 (Rs.) | 300,000 | - | - |
| Direct materials added (Rs.) | 40,000 | 34,000 | 21,000 |
| Direct wages (Rs.) | 30,000 | 17,000 | 13,000 |
| Direct expenses (Rs.) | 11,000 | 9,000 | 8,000 |
| Standard Normal loss as a percentage of input | 8% | 12 % | 10% |
| Realisation of normal loss by sale of scrap per unit @ (Rs.) | 2 | 3 | 4 |
| Output (in units) | 53,000 | 49,000 | 42,000 |

Production Overhead amounted to Rs.45,000 which was absorbed as a percentage on direct wages. The processing cost of by - product 'XC' is Rs.6 per unit. The output of the by-product is 4000 units. Selling expenses for product ZC is @ Rs.2 per unit. The selling price of Product ZC is Rs.20 per unit.

Prepare Process X, Y, Z and M accounts.

(Adapted: ICWAI )

[Ans: Rates Rs.7.14; Rs.9.26; Rs.10.92; Abnormal loss X Rs.15,699; Z Rs.22,932; Abnormal gain Y Rs.21,854]

32. Prepare Statement of equivalent production, Statement of cost and Process D Account from the following.

| | |
|---|---|
| Material introduced in the process (units) | 15,000 |
| Units completed and Transferred | 12,000 |

**Process Cost:**

| | |
|---|---|
| Material | Rs.33,120 |
| Labour | Rs.29,610 |
| Overhead | Rs.22,080 |

Degree of completion of closing work-in-progress

Material 80%; Labour 70%; Overhead 60%.

[Ans: Rate per unit Rs.2.30; Rs.1.60; Eq. units 14,400;14,100 13,800; Cl. WIP Rs.12,810; Transfer Rs.72,000]

33. K Ltd manufactures a product with the help of two processes namely M and N. The incompleted units in Process M at the end of the month are 20,000 units. The incompleted units constitute 100% of material, 70% of labour and 60 % of factory overheads.

The information related to these two processes for the month April 2011 are as follows:

| | **Process M** | **Process N** |
|---|---|---|
| Direct material (Rs.) | 160,000 | 130,000 |
| Direct wages (Rs.) | 59,200 | 80,000 |
| Factory overhead (Rs.) | 79,200 | 55,000 |
| Input (units) | 80,000 | 60,000 |

Assume that the input received by the process N is consumed completely and there is no closing work-in-progress. Completed units of Process M are transferred to Process N.

Prepare necessary Cost statements and find out the Cost per unit in Process B.

(ICWAI - Adapted)

[Ans: Eq.Units 80,000; 74,000; 72,000: Cl.Wip.Rs.64,400; Transfer Rs.2,34,000; Cost per unit Rs.8.32]

34. M Ltd. manufactured a product by two processes, namely H & N. The expenses incurred for the month August 2011, related to process H are as follows:

| | Rs. |
|---|---|
| Input of material 5,000 units | 200,000 |
| Additional direct material | 26,400 |
| Direct labour | 176,500 |
| Works overhead | 105,000 |

The normal loss is estimated as 8% of the input. The units produced and transferred to process N is 16,000. The incomplete units are 1,500. The stage of completion of incomplete units of Material 60%, Labour 50% and Overhead 40%. The Scrap in the process are sold @ Rs.4 per unit.

Prepare a Statement of equivalent production, Statement of cost, Statement of apportionment and Process H Account.

[Ans: Eq. units 17,800; 17,650; 17500. Cl. WIP Rs.21,900; Abnormal loss Rs.25,200; Transfer Rs.4,48,000]

35. H Ltd. manufactures a product named 'X' through two processes. The expenses incurred for manufacturing the product for the month April, 2011 are as follows:

| | Process A | Process B |
|---|---|---|
| Direct Material (Rs.) | 193,500 | - |
| Direct Labour (Rs.) | 113,700 | 66,560 |
| Factory Overhead (Rs.) | 75,000 | 32,920 |
| Units received in process (units) | 40,000 | 35,000 |
| Completed and transferred (units) | 35,000 | 33,000 |
| Remaining in process at the end (units) | 2,000 | 1,800 |
| Normal Loss in process (units) | 1,300 | 1,000 |

Production remaining in the process is completed to the extent of Material 100%, Direct Labour 60% and Factory overhead 40%. Prepare necessary ledger accounts and find out the cost per unit in each process. [Ans: A: Eq.units 28,700; 37,900; 37,500. Cl.WIP Rs.15,200; Ab.loss Rs.17,000; Transfer Rs.350,000. B: Eq.units 34,000; 33,280; 32,920; Cl. WIP Rs.21,409; Ab.gain Rs.10,635; Transfer Rs.438,706]

36. RLtd. manufactures a product named KH. The expenses incurred for the month August 2011, related to process N are as follows:

| | |
|---|---|
| Opening Work-in-progress | Nil. |
| Units introduced 30,000 units @ | Rs.7 per unit |
| Direct Material | Rs.68,400 |
| Direct Labour | Rs.128,500 |
| Overheads | Rs.74,700 |

Normal Loss is 10% of the input. Closing Work-in-progress is 4,000 units. The Work-in-progress completed to the extent of material 100%, Labour 80%, and Overhead 60%. The degree of completion of abnormal loss is material 60% and labour and overhead 50%.

The output of the process is 22,000 units. Normal Loss realised @ Rs.4 per unit due to the sale of scrap. The units of abnormal loss are sold @ Rs.2 per unit. Prepare Process N Account, Statement of Equipment Production, Statement of Cost and Abnormal Loss account. [Ans: Eq.units 26,600; 25,700; 24,900; Cl. WIP Rs.63,200; Ab.loss Rs.10,000; Transfer Rs.396,000]

37. KX& Co.Ltd. manufactures a product named 'T' and the expenses incurred for manufacturing the product for the month September, 2011 are as follows:

| | |
|---|---|
| Material | Rs. 22,500 |
| Labour | Rs. 17,800 |
| Overhead | Rs. 8,400 |
| Opening Work-in-progress 900 units @ | Rs. 10 |
| Units introduced to the process | 6,000 |

| | |
|---|---|
| Transfer to next process (units) | 5,300 |
| Closing Work-in-progress (units) | 1,200 |

Degree of completion of opening WIP

| | |
|---|---|
| Material | 100% |
| Labour | 50% |
| Overhead | 20% |

Degree of completion of closing WIP

| | |
|---|---|
| Material | 90% |
| Labour | 60% |
| Overhead | 40% |

Adopt the FIFO method of valuation of material.

Prepare the Statement of equivalent production, Statement of apportionment of cost and Process Account.

[Ans: Op.WIP Rs.1,956;Cl.WIP Rs.5,780; Transfer Rs.71,924]

38. GT& Co.Ltd manufacturer of a product named 'X' provides the following information for the month April, 2011 as follows:

| | |
|---|---|
| Opening WIP | 10,000 units |
| Units Introduced | 90,000 units |
| Units Completed for Transfer | 85,000 units |
| Closing WIP | 15,000 units |

Cost incurred for the months are

| | Rs. |
|---|---|
| Material | 40,000 |
| Labour | 28,000 |
| Overhead | 19,000 |

The Opening WIP constitutes the following expenses.

| | Rs. |
|---|---|
| Material | 4,000 |
| Labour | 3,000 |
| Overhead | 1,000 |

Closing work-in progress constitutes Material 60%,Labour 50% and Overhead 40%.

Prepare a Statement of equivalent production, Statement of cost, and Process A account by Average costing method.

[Ans: Rates Rs.0.404; Rs.0.288; Rs.0.189; Op.WIP Rs.8,000;
Cl.WIP Rs.6,900; Transfer Rs.88,100]

39. M Ltd manufactures a product named 'H' and the expenses incurred for manufacturing the product for the month November, 2011 are as follows:

| | |
|---|---|
| Opening Work-in-progress | 8,000 Units |
| Units introduced | 50,000 Units |
| Units Completed and Transferred | |

| | |
|---|---|
| to Process II | 47,000 Units |
| Closing work-in-progress | 11,000 Units |

Cost incurred for the month are as follows.

| | Rs. |
|---|---|
| Direct Material | 62,520 |
| Direct Labour | 40,960 |
| Factory Overhead | 35,840 |

The Opening work-in-progress contains

| | Rs. |
|---|---|
| Direct Material | 7,000 |
| Direct Labour | 6,000 |
| Factory Overhead | 5,000 |

The Opening work-in-progress constitutes 70% of material and 40% of labour and overhead. The closing work-in-progress also constitutes 70% of material and 40% of labour and overhead.

Prepare Statement of Equipment production, Statement of cost, Statement of apportionment of cost and Process I Account by adopting LIFO method of inventory valuation.

[Ans: Rate Rs.1.20; Rs.0.80; Rs.0.70; Eq. Units 52,100; 51,200; 51,200; Op. WIP Rs.18,000; Cl. WIP Rs.22,320; Transfer Rs.135,000]

40. A manufacturing company provides the following costing information. Opening work-in-progress is 8,000 units valued as Rs.21,000. Degree of completion of opening work-in-progress -Material 100%, Labour 60% and Overhead 40%.

| | |
|---|---|
| Units introduced is 72,000 units valued at | Rs. 272,000 |
| Direct wages | Rs. 195,900 |
| Production overhead | Rs. 96,000 |

The units completed and transferred to next process is 63,000. Normal loss is 5% of the input including the opening work-in-progress. The units scrapped is 7,000 and the degree of completion of the scrapped units is Material 100%, Labour 70% and Overhead 40%. The scrap is sold @ Rs.3 per unit. Closing work-in-progress is 10,000 units and the degree of completion of the closing work-in-progress is Material 70%, Labour 50% and Overhead 30%. Adopt FIFO method of valuation. Prepare Statement of equivalent production, Statement of cost, Statement of apportionment of cost and Process I Account.

[Ans: Rate Rs.4; Rs.3; Rs.1.50. Eq. units 65,000; 65,300; 64,000. Op.WIP Rs.21,000; Cl.WIP Rs.47,500; Ab. loss Rs.20,100; Transfer Rs.505,300]

41. KT Ltd., provides the following information related to a process for the month September,2011.

| | |
|---|---|
| Units introduced 30,000 valued as | Rs. 123,000 |
| Direct wages | Rs. 80,640 |
| Factory overhead | Rs. 45,720 |

Opening work-in-progress is 4,000 units valued as Rs.19,000. The degree of completion of Op.WIP is, Material 100%, Labour 70% and Overhead 40%.

The units completed and transferred to next process is 27,000. Normal loss is 3,000 units and the scrap of normal loss realised Rs.2 per unit.Closing Work-in-progress is 5000 units.The degree of completion of closing work-in-progress is material 80% Labour 40% and Overhead 20%. Prepare a Statement of equivalent production, Statement of cost, Statement of apportionment of cost and Process I Account.

[Ans: Rate Rs.4.50; Rs.3.20; Rs.1.80; Eq.units 26,000; 25,200; 25,400; Op.WIP Rs.27,160. Cl. WIP Rs.26,200; Ab.gain Rs,9,500; Transfer Rs.2,45,660]

42. H Ltd manufactures a product named 'X' which passes through three processes A, B and C. The information related to these processes for the month of April 2011 are as follows:

| | Process A | Process B | Process C |
|---|---|---|---|
| | Rs | Rs | Rs |
| Direct Material | 24,000 | 25,000 | 14,000 |
| Direct wages | 21,000 | 7,000 | 12,000 |
| Factory Overhead | 19,000 | 15,000 | 10,000 |
| Stock as on 31st April 2011 | 8,000 | 7,000 | 13,000 |

The production of each process is transferred to the next process for a profit @ 20% on the transfer price. The sale of finished goods is Rs.230,000 and the stock of finished goods as on 31st April 2011 is Rs.32,000. The output transferred from the Process C to the Finished goods account is for a profit @. 20% on the cost of production. Prepare process accounts and find out the profit earned during the month April 2011.

[Ans: Profits Rs.14,000; Rs.46,550; Rs.90,871; Rs.104,016]

43. KTS manufactures a product which is processed through 2 different processes, namely X and Y. The data related to these processes for the month June 2011 are as follows:

| | Product X | Product Y | Finished Stock |
|---|---|---|---|
| | Rs. | Rs. | Rs. |
| Opening stock | 14,000 | 17,000 | 20,000 |
| Material | 22,000 | 25,000 | |

| | | | |
|---|---|---|---|
| Labour | 21,000 | 18,000 | |
| Production Overhead | 9,000 | 8,000 | |
| Stock as on 31st June2011 | 15,500 | 13,500 | 27,000 |
| Inter-process profit included in op.stock | | 3,500 | 4,000 |

Sales during the month is Rs.175,000. Output of Process X is transferred to Process Y at 25% profit on transfer price and output of Process Y is transferred to Finished goods at 20% profit on transfer price. Finished stock is valued at the price on the basis of the output transferred from Process Y to Finished goods account.

Prepare Process Accounts and Finished goods Account.

[Ans: Profit X Rs.16,833; Y Rs.48,763; Finished stock Rs.74,203]

44. Z Ltd., produces 4 joint products namely A,B,C and D with the help of one raw material. The following are the data related to the production of these products for 3 months ended March, 2011.

| | Rs. |
|---|---|
| Direct Material | 120,000 |
| Direct Wages | 90,000 |
| Factory Overhead | 54,000 |
| Administration Overhead | 60,000 |

Sales for the period are as follows11

| Joint Products | Number of units | Selling price per unit (Rs.) |
|---|---|---|
| A | 12,000 | 15 |
| B | 10,000 | 12 |
| C | 6,000 | 8 |
| D | 2,000 | 6 |

Prepare Cost Statement on the basis of allocation of costs by (i) number of units and (ii) sales value.

[Ans: (i) Rs.129,600; Rs.108,000; Rs.64,800; Rs.21,600 (ii) Rs.162,000; Rs.108,000; Rs.43,200; Rs.10,800]

45. X Ltd provided the following information related to the production of 3 joint products namely A,B,C in the month of September,2011.

| | |
|---|---|
| Carriage inwards | 4,000 |
| Direct Labour | 37,000 |
| Production Overhead | 29,000 |
| Administration Overhead | 20,000 |

**Sales:**

| | |
|---|---|
| A | 1500 units @ Rs.60 per unit |
| B | 1000 units @ Rs.40 per unit |
| C | 600 units @ Rs.50 per unit. |

The expected profit of the company is 20% on cost. Prepare Statement of apportionment of costs on the basis of (i) number of units and (ii) sales value

[Ans: (i) Rs.58,064; Rs.38,710; Rs.23,226 (ii) Rs.67,501; Rs.30,000; Rs.22,499]

46. GC Ltd provides the following information related to the production of 3 joint products namely R,C,L in the month of October,2011.

| | Rs. |
|---|---|
| Direct Material | 15,000 |
| Direct Wages | 14,000 |
| Fixed Overhead | 11,000 |
| Variable Overhead | 10,000 |

**Sales:**

| | |
|---|---|
| X | 800 kgm @ Rs.30 |
| Y | 700 kgm @ Rs.40 |
| Z | 500 kgm @ Rs.30 |

Calculate the cost and profit for each product on the basis of (i) Weight (ii) Sales value and (iii) Weight for marginal cost and contribution for Fixed cost.

[Ans: (i) Cost Rs.20,000; Rs.17,500; Rs.12,500; Profit Rs.4,000; Rs.10,500; Rs.2,500 (ii) Cost Rs.17,910; Rs.20,896; Rs.11,194; Profit Rs.6,090; Rs.7,104; Rs.8,806 (iii) Profit Rs.5,100; Rs.8,712; Rs.3,188]

47. T Ltd.,a manufacturing company, is producing 3 joint products namely, X,Y and Z by two processes. The joint products are produced in the second process. The data for the month of November 2011 are as follows:

| | Process A Rs. | Process B Rs. |
|---|---|---|
| Direct Material | | |
| 25,000 units @ Rs.3 per unit | 75,000 | - |
| Direct Wages | 37,000 | 20,000 |
| Factory Overhead | 28,000 | 12,000 |

Normal loss for process A is 10% and scrap value of loss is Rs.2 per unit. Output in Process A are sold as 10,000 units of X @ Rs.10 per unit; 8,000 units of Y @ Rs.9 per unit and 6,000 units of Z @ Rs.8 per unit. Prepare Process A Account ; and Statement of cost and profit of Process B on the basis of apportionment of joint cost by (i) number of units and (ii) sales value.

[Ans: (i) Profit Rs.26,667; Rs.13,333; Rs.4000 (ii) Rs.20,000; Rs.14,400; Rs.9,600]

48. X Ltd., produces 4 products namely A, B, C and D The cost of manufacturing these products are as follows:

| | A | B | C | D |
|---|---|---|---|---|
| Output (in units) | 18,000 | 11,000 | 6,000 | 5,000 |
| Cost after split-of points(Rs.) | 72,000 | 40,000 | 25,000 | 13,000 |
| Sales per unit (Rs.) | 12 | 10 | 8 | 7 |

The total cost before the split off point amounted to Rs 180,000. If the products are sold at the split off point without further processing the selling price per unit are A @ Rs.5, B @ Rs.6, C @ Rs.5 and D @ Rs.4. Prepare a Statement of cost and profit if the products are sold after further processing (apportion the joint cost on the basis of sales value) and a Statement of cost and profit if the products are sold at split-off point.

[Ans: (i) Proft Rs.18,000; Rs.26,000; Rs.5,000; Rs.7,000 (ii) Profit Rs.48,939; Rs.21,589; Rs.1,875; Rs.6,597]

49. D Ltd. manufactures a product named X. In the process of waste of X, it also produces two by products namely, L and V. The costing information related to the manufacturing of these main and by products are as follows:

| | A | B | C |
|---|---|---|---|
| Sales (Rs.) | 150,000 | 120,000 | 90,000 |
| Cost after separation: | | | |
| Labour (Rs.) | - | 40,000 | 38,000 |
| Overhead (Rs.) | - | 20,000 | 17,000 |
| Estimated selling expenses as a percentage of sales value | 12% | 8% | 8% |
| Estimated profit as a percentage of cost of production | 20% | 25% | |

Total cost upto the separation point is Rs.110,000. Assume that there is no opening and closing stock.Prepare a Statement of apportionment of cost and Statement of Profit and Loss Account.

[Ans: Profit Rs.72,200; Rs.20,000; Rs.15,000: Cost upto separation Rs.30,400; Rs.9,800; Rs.59,800]

50. XYZ Ltd. produces a product named 'T' and in the process of production it also produces two by – products namely, A and B. The costing information for the month of July 2011 of the company are as follows:

| | Joint Expenses Rs. | Separate Expenses T Rs. | A Rs. | B Rs. |
|---|---|---|---|---|
| Material | 90,000 | - | 21,000 | 19,000 |
| Labour | 64,000 | - | 7,000 | 14,000 |
| Overhead | 16,000 | - | 12,000 | 8,000 |
| Selling expenses | | 30,000 | 10,000 | 9,000 |
| Selling price per unit | | | 90 | 70 |
| Estimated profit (loss) per unit | | | 14 | (12) |

The main product is sold for a profit @ 25% on cost. The output of the company is 1,200 units of X, 800 units of A and 1,000 units of B. Prepare a Statement of cost and profit on the basis of reverse cost method of accounting for by-product.

[Ans: Proft Rs.39,300; Rs.11,200; Rs.(12,000); Pre-separation cost Rs.1,27,200; Rs.20,800; Rs.32,000]

51. A manufacturing company named, XYZ Ltd. produces a product 'A' In the process of production it also produces two by – products namely, $A_1$ and $A_2$. The costing information for the month of November 2011 of the company are as follows:

| | Joint Expenses Rs. | Separate Expenses A Rs. | $A_1$ Rs. | $A_2$ Rs. |
|---|---|---|---|---|
| Material | 210,000 | - | 34,000 | 22,000 |
| Labour | 120,000 | - | 20,000 | 19,000 |
| Overhead | 80,000 | - | 17,000 | 10,000 |
| Selling expenses | | 40,000 | 15,000 | 11,000 |
| Selling price per unit | | | 20 | 17 |
| Estimated profit (loss) per unit | | | (2) | 3 |

The main product is sold for a profit @ 20% on sales. The output of the company is 20,000 units of A, 9,000 units of $A_1$ and 10,000 units of $A_2$. Prepare a Statement of cost and profit on the basis of reverse cost method of accounting for by-product.

[Ans: Proft Rs.65,000; Rs.(18,000); Rs.30,000; Pre-separation cost Rs.220,000; Rs.112,000; Rs.78,000]

# CHAPTER VIII

# OPERATING OR SERVICE COSTING

Operating Costing is a method of costing applied to undertakings which render services (Eg) Transport Companies, Hospital, Canteen, Boiler House etc. Undertakings which render services do not manufacture any tangible products. The services rendered by these establishments may either be internal or external. Internal services mean the services rendered by one department to other department or departments within the same organisation. For example, Boiler House or Canteen may be a separate department in an organisation and it may be rendering services to the personnel and the work of other departments. External service means the services rendered by the service department to different customers, as a department in an organisation or as a separate business establishment. Examples of the establishments providing services to customers are Transport Companies, Hospitals, Electricity Board, etc.

**Cost Unit for Operating Costing**

The determination of cost unit for operating costing is a complicated task since two or more cost units are available in operating costing. For example, in Transport Costing, cost unit is cost per running hour or cost per trip. Hence, the cost unit can be determined as per the requirement by the suppliers or customers. The most common types of cost units are (i) Per km for Passenger Transport (ii) Per patient or per bed or per operation for Hospital (iii) Per room for lodge (iv) Per meal for Canteen (v) Per kilowatt hour in Power House (vi) Per km or per tonne km for Goods Transport.

**Application of operating costing**

Operating costing is applied to all types of service organisation. But the most common types of organisations which apply operating costing are as follows,

1. Transport
2. Power House
3. Canteen.

**1. Transport Costing**

Transport Costing is applied to Transport Undertakings like Road Transport, Railways, Airways and Water Transport. The cost units in Transport Costing are per km, per tonne km, and per trip.

**Ascertainment of Transport Cost**

Transport companies are maintaining 'log sheet' to record the expenses incurred and for the receipts. The log sheet should be prepared daily. It contains information like passenger or weight carried, distance covered, starting time, returning time, petrol and oil used. The information in the log sheet is used to calculate the cost per tonne or cost per tonne km.

**Composition of Transport cost**

The transport cost consists of the following costs.

**(a) StandingCharges**

Standing Charges are otherwise called fixed charges. These charges should be incurred whether the transport is operated or not. The important standing charges are as follows.

(i) Insurance
(ii) License Fees
(iii) Taxes
(iv) Supervisor's Salary
(v) Garage Rent
(vi) Administrative Expense
(vii) Wages for driver, conductor and cleaner, if paid on monthly basis
(viii) Depreciation

**(b) Operating and Running Charges**

These charges are variable in nature and are not incurred when the vehicles are not in operation. The important Operating and Running charges are as follows.

(i) Petrol or Diesel
(ii) Oil and Grease.
(iii) Depreciation if charged on the basis of km run
(iv) Wages for driver conductor and cleaner if not paid on monthly basis.

**(c) Maintenance Charges**

Maintenance Charges are semi-variable in nature. These charges are incurred to keep the vehicle in good running condition. The important maintenance charges are as follows.

(i) Repair and maintenance.
(ii) Tyres, tubes and battery.
(iii) Cost of spares
(iv) Garage charges

(v) Water service

(vi) Painting

**Illustration: 1**

Calculate the cost per km of the vehicle for a transport company for the year 2011 from the data given below:

| | | Rs. |
|---|---|---|
| Cost of the vehicle | | 280,000.00 |
| Driver's Salary per month | | 4,000.00 |
| Cleaner's Salary per month | | 3,000.00 |
| Road license per year | | 3,600.00 |
| Insurance for one year | | 2,100.00 |
| Garage rent per month | | 1,200.00 |
| Maintenance and depreciation for tyres | per km | 0.80 |
| Cost of diesel per litre | | 30.00 |
| Kilometers run per litre | 10 kms | |
| Estimated life of the vehicle | 3 00,000 kms | |
| Kilometers run for the year | 30,000 kms | |
| Estimated scrap value of the vehicle | Rs.70,000 | |

***Solution:***

**OPERATING COST SHEET**

| Particulars | Cost per km Rs. | Total cost Rs. |
|---|---|---|
| **Fixed Expenses:** | | |
| Driver's Salary @ Rs.4,000 p.m. | 1.60 | 48,000 |
| Cleaner's Salary @ Rs.3,000 p.m. | 1.20 | 36,000 |
| Road license for one year | 0.12 | 3.600 |
| Insurance for one year | 0.07 | 2,100 |
| Garage rent @ Rs.1,200 p.m. | 0.48 | 14,400 |
| | 3.47 | 104,100 |
| **Variable Expenses:** | | |
| Cost for dieseal $\left[\frac{30,000}{10} \times 30\right]$ | 3.00 | 90,000 |
| Depreciation for the Vehicle $\left[\frac{(280,000-70,000) \times 30,000}{300,000}\right]$ | 0.70 | 21,000 |
| Maintenance & Depreciation for tyre (30,000 x .80) | 0.80 | 24,000 |
| | 4.50 | 135,000 |
| | 7.97 | 239,100 |

**Illustration: 2**

A transport company is running 7 buses between two villages. The distance between these two villages is 40 kms. The seating capacity of each bus is 50 passengers. Following are the details relating to the cost for running the 7 vehicles for the month June 2011.

| | Rs. |
|---|---|
| Salary for one driver per month | 4,800 |
| Salary for one conductor per month | 3,600 |
| Wages for one Cleaner for the month | 2,300 |
| Cost of diesel per litre | 30 |
| Repairs & Maintenance for the 7 vehicles | 12,000 |
| Insurance for one vehicle for one year | 4,000 |
| Road tax paid per quarter for one vehicle | 2,000 |
| Depreciation charged for the 7 vehicles | 18,000 |
| Total garage rent for the month | 6,000 |
| Kms run per litre per vehicle - 4 | |

The company has 14 drivers, 14 conductors and 7 cleaners. Each bus was operated four round trips per day. Assume that all the 7 buses were operated on all the days of the month. Actual passengers carried were 80% of the seating capacity. Calculate the cost per Passenger – km.

***Solution:***

**OPERATING COST STATEMENT**

| Particulars | Amount Rs. | Amount Rs. |
|---|---|---|
| **Fixed Expenses:** | | |
| Salary to the drivers (14 x 4,800) | | 67,200 |
| Salary to the Conductors (14 x 3,600) | | 50,400 |
| Salary to the Cleaners (7 x 2,300) | | 16,100 |
| Insurance $\left[\frac{4,000}{12} \times 7\right]$ | | 2,333 |
| Road Tax $\left[\frac{2,000}{3} \times 7\right]$ | | 4,667 |
| Garage Rent | | 6,000 |
| | | 146,700 |
| **Variable Expenses:** | | |
| Diesel Charges (40 x 2 x 4 x 30 x 30 x 7/4) | 5,04,000 | |
| Repairs and Maintenance | 12,000 | |
| Depreciation | 18,000 | 534,000 |
| Total Expenses | | 6,80,700 |

Calculation of cost per Passenger-km

Passenger – km = 40 x 2 x 4 x 7 x 50 x 30 x 80/100

[40 kms, 2 to and fro, 4 trips, 7 vehicles, 50 passengers for 30 days]

= 26,88,000

$$\text{Cost per Passenger - km} = \frac{6,80,700}{26,88,000} = \text{Rs.}0.25 \text{ paise}$$

**Note:** The cost per passenger kilometre is calculated by dividing the total cost with the effective passenger kilometres.The effective passenger kilometre is calculated by multiplying the one way distance with two and then with four since the bus operated four round trips in a day. Then it would be multiplied with the number of buses and with their seating capacity. From this, the number of days run in the month should be multiplied. Again, from this, the percentage of actual passengers carried should be multiplied to know the effective passenger kilometre.

**Illustration: 3**

The information relating to two different vehicles namely X and Y operated by a Transport Company are stated as follows:

| | | X | Y |
|---|---|---|---|
| Cost of the Vehicle | Rs. | 200,000 | 2,20,000 |
| Estimated life of the vehicle | Kms | 3,00,000 | 2,50,000 |
| Road license | Rs. | 4,200 | 4,200 |
| Insurance for one year | Rs. | 4,000 | 4,500 |
| Garage rent for one year | Rs. | 4,000 | 5,000 |
| Driver's wage per hour | Rs. | 20 | 20 |
| Cleaner's wage per hour | Rs. | 15 | 15 |
| Repairs and maintenance per km. | Rs. | 0.20 | 0.20 |
| Tyre charge per km. | Rs. | 0.25 | 0.25 |
| Kms run for one year | Kms. | 30,000 | 25,000 |
| Cost of diesel per litre | Rs. | 30 | 30 |
| Km run per litre | Kms. | 12 | 15 |
| Average Km per hour | Kms. | 30 | 40 |
| Depreciation charges per annum on the cost of the vehicle | | 10% | 10% |

Calculate the cost per running kilometre.

***Solution:***

**OPERATING COST STATEMENT**

| Particulars | Vehicle X Rs. | Vehicle Y Rs. |
|---|---|---|
| **Fixed Cost:** | | |
| Road license | 4,200 | 4,200 |
| Insurance | 4,000 | 4,500 |
| Garage rent | 4,000 | 5,000 |
| Depreciation for the vehicle | 20,000 | 22,000 |
| Fixed cost per annum | 32,200 | 35,700 |
| Kms run per annum | 30,000 | 25,000 |
| Fixed cost per km | 1.073 | 1.428 |
| **Variable cost:** | | |
| Diesel Cost | | |
| $\frac{30,000}{12} \times 30$; $\frac{25,000}{15} \times 30$ | 75,000 | 50,000 |
| Driver's wage | | |
| $\frac{30,000}{30} \times 20$; $\frac{25,000}{40} \times 20$ | 20,000 | 12,500 |
| Cleaner's wage | | |
| $\frac{30,000}{30} \times 15$; $\frac{25,000}{40} \times 15$ | 15,000 | 9,375 |
| Repairs & maintenance | 6,000 | 5,000 |
| Tyre charges | 7,500 | 6,250 |
| Variable cost per annum | 123,500 | 83,125 |
| Km run per annum | 30,000 | 25,000 |
| Variable cost per Km | 4.117 | 3.325 |
| Fixed cost per km | 1.073 | 1.428 |
| Total cost per km | 5.19 | 4.75 |

**Illustration: 4**

Joyce & Company Pvt.Ltd, run the following fleet of buses within the limit of a city.

| | Carrying Capacity |
|---|---|
| 8 Buses | 45 Passengers |
| 10 Buses | 50 Passengers |
| 10 Buses | 40 Passengers |

The records of the company revealed that each bus runs for 12 trips in a day. The distance in each trip was 6 kms. On an average 70% of the seats are occupied. Four buses were usually kept away from road daily on an average basis, for the purpose of repairs and maintenance.

The following expenses were related to the month of April,2011

| | Rs. |
|---|---|
| Road tax for one year per vehicle | 3,000 |
| Insurance per annum for all the vehicle | 62,000 |
| Salary per month for the Office Manager | 6,000 |
| Salary per month for Asst. Managers (3) @ | 5,000 |
| Salary per month for Supervisors (4) @ | 4,000 |
| Salary per month for Drivers (35) @ | 3,900 |
| Salary per month for Cleaners (35) @ | 3,000 |
| Salary per month for Clerks (5) @ | 3,200 |
| Consumable stores for the month | 51,000 |
| Diesel for the month | 3,90,000 |
| Lubricant oil for the month | 65,800 |
| Depreciation charge for tyres and tubes for the month | 58,000 |
| Depreciation for the vehicles for the month | 60,000 |
| Miscellaneous expenses | 24,800 |
| Garage rent for the month | 22,500 |

Calculate the cost per passenger km.

***Solution:***

**OPERATING COST SHEET**

| **Particulars** | **Rs.** | **Rs.** |
|---|---|---|
| Fixed Expenses: | | |
| Road Tax $\frac{3,000 \times 28}{12}$ | 7,000 | |
| Insurance $\frac{62,000}{12}$ | 5,167 | |
| Depreciation for the vehicles | 60,000 | |
| Salary for the Office Manager | 6,000 | |
| Salary for the Asst. Manager | 15,000 | |
| Salary for the Supervisor | 16,000 | |
| Salary for the Drivers | 136,500 | |
| Salary for the Cleaners | 105,000 | |
| Salary for the Clerks | 16,000 | |
| Garage Rent | 22,500 | 389,167 |
| **Variable Expenses:** | | |
| Diesel | 390,000 | |
| Lubricant Oil | 65,800 | |
| Tyre Charges | 58,000 | |
| Consumable Stores | 51,000 | |
| Miscellaneous Expenses | 24,800 | 589,600 |
| Total Expenses | | 978,767 |

Effective passenger kms. 16,32,960

Hence, cost per passenger km. = 978,767/ 16,32,960 = Rs.0.599

[Calculation of Effective Passenger Kms.

Effective Passenger Kms. = 8 x 45 x 12 x 6 x 30 x 70/100 +
10 x 50 x 12 x 6 x 30 x 70/100 +
10 x 40 x 12 x 6 x 30 x 70/100
= 5,44,320 + 7,56,000 + 6,04,800
= 19,05,120

**Less:** 1/7 (4/28) for repairs = 2,72,160
= 16,32,960 ]

**Note:** The effective passenger kilometre is calculated by multiplying number of buses in different category with number of trips and with number of kilometer in each trip. Then it would be multiplied with the number of days run in the month. Again it would be multiplied with the seating capacity and the average seat occupied. The average seat occupied is mentioned in percentage. In this illustration it is stated as 70%. The passenger kilometres so calculated for the three different categories of the buses are added to find out the total gross passenger kilometres run. The passenger kilometres for the 4 buses which are not operated in a month due to maintenance should be calculated proportionately and deducted from the gross total to find out the effective passenger kilometre.

**Illustration: 5**

The information given below are available in the records of KT Transport Company, with a fleet of 20 taxies.

| | Rs. |
|---|---|
| Cost of each taxi | 200,000 |
| Salary of manager p.m | 4,000 |
| Salary of accountant p.m | 3,900 |
| Salary of driver p.m per taxi | 3,700 |
| Salary of cleaner p.m. (2 Cleaners) each | 2,500 |
| Salary of mechanic p.m | 3,000 |
| Annual tax per taxi | 3,200 |
| Garage rent p.m | 4,000 |
| Insurance premium per annum | 3% |
| Annual repairs per taxi | 6,000 |

On an average the taxi run 5,000 kms in a month of which 10% run empty. The total life of a taxi is 30,000 kms. Diesel consumption is 20 kms per litre. The cost of petrol is Rs.40 per litre. Oil and other expenses are Rs.130 per 1,000 km. Prepare the Cost Sheet and calculate the cost of running a taxi per km.

***Solution:***

**OPERATING COST SHEET**

| Particulars | Rs. | Rs. |
|---|---|---|
| **Fixed Expenses:** | | |
| Salary of Manager | 4,000 | |
| Salary of Accountant | 3,900 | |
| Salary of Cleaner (2 x 2,500) | 5,000 | |
| Salary of Mechanic | 3,000 | |
| Salary of Driver (20 x 3,700) | 74,000 | |
| Garage Rent | 4,000 | |
| Road Tax $\frac{(3,200 \times 20)}{12}$ | 5,333 | |
| Insurance Premium $\frac{(200,000 \times 20 \times 3)}{12 \times 100}$ | 10,000 | 109,233 |
| **Variable Expenses:** | | |
| Petrol Charges $\frac{(5,000 \times 20 \times 40)}{20}$ | 200,000 | |
| Oil & Other expenses $\frac{(130 \times 5,000 \times 20)}{1000}$ | 13,000 | |
| Repairs & Maintenance $\frac{(6,000 \times 20)}{12}$ | 10,000 | 223,000 |
| Total Expenses | | 332,233 |
| Effective Kms $\frac{(90 \times 5,000 \times 20)}{100}$ | 90,000 | |
| Cost per km | | 3.69 |

**Illustration: 6**

The following information are obtained from the books of Mr.Y, owner of a transport vehicle, for the month April 2011.

| | Rs. |
|---|---|
| Cost of the bus | 2,00,000 |
| Depreciation @ 10% p.a. | |
| Road Tax p.a | 6,000 |
| Expenses for Permit & F.C. p.a. | 2,400 |
| Insurance p.a. | 7,200 |
| Salary of cleaner p.m. | 2,600 |
| Salary of driver p.m. | 4,900 |
| Salary of part-time accountant p.m. | 2,200 |
| Diesel consumption - 4 kms per litre | |
| Cost of diesel per litre | 30 |
| Lubricant oil cost per 100 km | 50 |
| Repairs and maintenance p.m. | 1,000 |
| Garage rent p.m. | 1,200 |

The bus is operated in three different routes in a month. The distance covered by the bus in the first route is 120 kms one way, for the first 12 days in the month. For the next 12 days in the month, it is operated in another route covering a distance of 100 kms in one way. For the remaining days the bus is operated to a distance of 150 kms in two ways. The bus returns to the garage in all the days of the month.

Assume that in April the bus runs all the 30 days and the seating capacity occupied in the first route is 80%, in the second route is 70%,and in the third route is 100%. The seating capacity of the bus for the passengers is 60.

Calculate the bus fare to be charged to the passengers to earn a profit of 25% on the total revenue. Assume that the passenger tax is 20% of the total revenue.

***Solution:***

**OPERATING COST STATEMENT**

| Particulars | Rs. | Rs. |
|---|---|---|
| **Fixed Expenses:** | | |
| Road Tax (6000/12) | 500 | |
| Permit (2400/12) | 200 | |
| Insurance (7200/12) | 600 | |
| Driver's Salary | 4,900 | |
| Cleaner's Salary | 2,600 | |
| Salary for Part-time Accountant | 2,200 | |
| Garage rent | 1,200 | 12,200 |
| **Variable Expenses:** | | |
| Diesel Charges (6180 x 30/4) | 46,350 | |
| Lubricant Oil (6180x50)/100 | 3,090 | |
| Repairs & Maintenance | 1,000 | |
| Depreciation (200000 x 10) / (100x12) | 1,667 | 52,107 |
| | | 64,307 |
| Passenger Tax | | 23,384 |
| Total Expenses | | 87,691 |
| Add: 25% Profit on revenue | | 29,231 |
| Total revenue | | 116,922 |
| Total passenger - kms 293,040 | | |
| Cost per passenger-kms 116,922/293,040 = Rs.0.40 | | |
| One-way fare in the first route - 0.40 x 120 | | 48 |
| One-way fare in the second route - 0.40 x 100 | | 40 |
| One-way fare in the third route - 0.40 x 75 | | 30 |

**Workings:**

(1) Calculation of the total-km run:

| | | |
|---|---|---|
| 1st route 120 x 12 x 2 | = | 2,880 |
| 2nd route 100 x 12 x 2 | = | 2,400 |
| 3rd route 150 x 6 | = | 900 |
| Total km run in the month | = | 6,180 |

(2) Calculation of the passenger – kms.:

| | | |
|---|---|---|
| 1st route $\frac{120 \times 12 \times 2 \times 60 \times 80}{100}$ | = | 1,38,240 |
| 2nd route $\frac{100 \times 12 \times 2 \times 60 \times 70}{100}$ | = | 1,00,800 |
| 3rd route $\frac{150 \times 6 \times 60 \times 100}{100}$ | = | 54,000 |
| Total passenger kms. | = | 2,93,040 |

(3) Calculation of Passenger – tax:

In order to calculate the passenger tax, assume total revenue as '$x$'

Hence, passenger tax $= \frac{20x}{100} = x/5$

Profit $= \frac{25x}{100} = x/4$

Total cost excluding the tax = Rs.64,307

$\therefore x = 64{,}307 + \frac{x}{5} + \frac{x}{4}$

$x - \frac{x}{5} - \frac{x}{4} = 64{,}307$

$\frac{20x - 4x - 5x}{20} = 64{,}307$

$\frac{11x}{20} = 64{,}307$

$x = \frac{64{,}307 \times 20}{11} =$ Rs.116,922

Passenger – tax $= 116{,}922 \times \frac{20}{100} =$ Rs.23,384

Profit $= 116{,}922 \times \frac{25}{100}$

= Rs.29,231

## 2. POWER HOUSE COSTING

Power house costing is otherwise called as Boiler house costing. Power house is a service department for generation of electricity. Cost unit in the production of steam is "per lb" and for generation of electricity is

' per Kilowatt'. Hence, the composite cost units are ' per lb hour' and 'per kilowatt hour'. The electricity generated by the power house is used by the factory and other departments of the organisation.The departments share the expenses of power generation on the basis of the consumption of power in the respective departments.

**Composition of power house cost**

The power house cost consists of the following types of costs.

a) Fixed Charges - (i) Rent, (ii) Insurance, (iii) Depreciation for building, (iv) Depreciation for plant
b) Fuel - (i) Coal , (ii) Oil
c) Labour – (i) Coal Handlers, (ii) Ash Removers
d) Water Charges – (i) Purchasing cost, (ii) Softening Cost,
e) Maintenance Charges - (i) Boiler, (ii) Meters, (iii) Softening Plant, (iv) Coal breakers, (v) Furnace.
f) Indirect Labour - (i) Supervisor, (ii) General Labour, (iii) Cleaners, (iv) Sweepers
g) Indirect Material - (i) Small tool, (ii) Service material

**Illustration: 7**

M Ltd provides the following information connected with the generation of electricity during the month June 2011.

Coal consumed during the month, 1500 tonnes @ Rs.50; Oil 12 tonnes @ Rs 400; Water 8,000 gallons; Pumping charges Rs.4 per 100 gallons; Handling charges of fuel @ Rs.0.80 per tonne; Ash removal charges, 200 tonnes @ Rs.0.50 per tonne; Repairs and maintenance of Generating Plant Rs 4200 ; Share of total administrative charges of Rs.6,000 is 20%.

Salaries and wages to the staff of the power house: 2 Foremen @ Rs.2,000 p.m; 5 Mechanics @ Rs.1,500 p.m; 6 Workmen @ Rs.1,000 p.m;

Depreciation for Steam Boiler @ 10%; Generator @ 8% and Building @ 9% Value of Steam Boiler Rs.30,000; Generator Rs.1,80,000 and Building Rs.2,16,000.

Recovery on account of sale of ash 180 tonnes @ Rs.2 per tonne and cost of steam supplied to Manufacturing Shop, 200 tonnes @ Rs.3 per hundred tonnes

The Power House generated 2,00,000 units (gross) of electricity and the loss due to leakage is 2,000 units.

Prepare the operating cost statement and find out the cost per unit of electricity generated.

**Solution:**

## OPERATING COST STATEMENT

| Particulars | Rs. | Rs. |
|---|---|---|
| **Material:** | | |
| Coal (1,500 x 50) | 75,000 | |
| Handling charges of fuel (1,500 x 0.80) | 1,200 | |
| Oil (12 x 400) | 4,800 | |
| Water: Pumping Charges (80 x 4) | 320 | |
| Ash removal charges (200 x 0.50) | 100 | 81,420 |
| **Wages and Salaries:** | | |
| Foremen (2 x 2000) | 4,000 | |
| Mechanics (5 x 1500) | 7,500 | |
| Labours (6 x 1000) | 6,000 | 17,500 |
| **Depreciation:** | | |
| Steam Boiler (10 x 30,000) / (12 x 100) | 250 | |
| Generator (8 x 1,80,000) / (12 x 100) | 1,200 | |
| Building (9 x 2,16,000) / (12 x 100) | 1,620 | 3,070 |
| Repairs and Maintenance | | 4,200 |
| Administrative Charges (20 x 6,000) / 100 | | 1,200 |
| **Total** | | 1,07,390 |
| Less: Recovery on account of sale of ash (180 x 2) | 360 | |
| Cost of steam supplied (200 x 3) | 600 | 960 |
| Total cost of generation of electricity | | 1,06,430 |

Actual units of electricity generated = 2,00,000 – 2,000 = 1,98,000

Cost per unit of electricity generated $= \dfrac{106,430}{198,000}$ = Rs. 0.54

## 3. CANTEEN COSTING

The function of canteen in a company is of providing meals, snacks and tea at subsidised rate to the employees. The subsidy is provided by the employer of the concern. The total cost of operating the canteen is ascertained and from that the subsidy is deducted. This amount is deducted from the sales to find out the profit or loss of the canteen. The canteen costing method can be applied to hotels, restaurants and motels.

**Composition of Canteen Costing:**

The canteen cost consists of the following costs.

a) Provisions

(i) Vegetable, (ii) Eggs, (iii) Milk, (iv) Fish, (v) Grocery items like rice, flour, oil, sugar, tea, coffee, etc.

b) Wages and salary
   (i) Cooks, (ii) Assistants, (iii) Waitresses, (iv) Porters and (v) Supervisors

c) Services
   (i) Gas, (ii) Electricity, (iii) Steam

d) Consumable Stores
   (i) Cutlery, (ii) Crockery, (iii) Glassware, (iv) Brushes, (v) Cleaning Material, (vi) Washing-up-cloths.

e) Overheads
   (i) Insurance, (ii) Depreciation, (iii) Rent and Rates.

**Illustration: 8**

Prepare an operating cost statement and find out the profit or loss of the canteen run by XYZ Co.Ltd, from the following particulars.

**(a) Purchase for the month April 2009**

(i) Rice 150 kgs @ Rs.12
(ii) Spices 5 kgs @ Rs.40
(iii) Potato 60 kg @ Rs.7
(iv) Mutton 20 kg @ Rs.110
(v) Green Vegetable 40 kg @ Rs.6
(vi) Tea 10 kg @ Rs.120
(vii) Milk 200 litres @ Rs.10
(viii) Flour 70 kg @ Rs.9
(ix) Dal 40 kg @ Rs.15
(x) Grocery Rs.750
(xi) Chicken 60 kg @ Rs.40
(xii) Ghee 20 kg @ Rs.40
(xiii) Coffee 3 kg @ Rs.150
(xiv) Sugar 30 kg @ Rs.15

**(b) Other Expenses**

(i) Gas and fuel Rs.800
(ii) Salary for cook Rs.1,200
(iii) Wages to assistant and waiters Rs.1,100
(iv) Supervisors salary Rs.1,500
(v) Crockery and glassware Rs.250

(c) Depreciation for furniture and utensils @ 10% p.a. Value of furniture and utensils Rs.24,000

(d) Sale of coupons 1,200 @ Rs.10 per coupon

(e) Subsidy for the Canteen is 50% of the total cost.

(f) Stock of material

| | Opening Stock Kgms. | Closing Stock Kgms. |
|---|---|---|
| Tea | 2 | 3 |
| Flour | 8 | 12 |

***Solution:***

## OPERATING COST STATEMENT

| Particulars | | | Rs. | Rs. |
|---|---|---|---|---|
| **Provisions:** | | | | |
| Rice (150 x 12) | | | 1800 | |
| Flour: Op. Stock | 8 | | | |
| Add: Purchase | 70 | | | |
| | 78 | | | |
| Less: Cl. Stock | 12 | (66 x 9) | 594 | |
| Spices | | (5 x 40) | 200 | |
| Dal | | (40 x 15) | 600 | |
| Potato | | (60 x 7) | 420 | |
| Grocery | | | 750 | |
| Mutton | | (20 x 110) | 2,200 | |
| Chicken | | (60 x 40) | 2,400 | |
| Green Vegetable | | (40 x 6) | 240 | |
| Ghee | | (20 x 40) | 800 | |
| Tea: Op. Stock | 2 | | | |
| Add: Purchase | 10 | | | |
| | 12 | | | |
| Less: Cl. Stock | 3 | (9 x 120) | 1,080 | |
| Coffee | | (3 x 150) | 450 | |
| Milk | | (200 x 10) | 2,000 | |
| Sugar | | (30 x 15) | 450 | |
| | | | | 13,984 |
| **Labour Charges:** | | | | |
| Salary for cook | | | 1,200 | |
| Wages to asssistants and waiters | | | 1,100 | |
| Salary to supervisor | | | 1,500 | |
| | | | | 3,800 |
| **Other Expenses:** | | | | |
| Gas and Fuel | | | 800 | |
| Crockery and Glassware | | | 250 | |
| Depreciation: | | (2400 x 10/100 x 1/12) | 200 | |
| | | | | 1,250 |
| Total Cost | | | | 19,034 |
| Less: Subsidy | | | | 9,517 |
| Actual Cost | | | | 9,517 |
| Sales (1,200 x 10) | | | | 12,000 |
| Profit from Canteen | | | | 2,483 |

## EXERCISE

**I. Choose the correct answer for the following:**

1. The method of costing applied to undertakings which render services is called
   (i) Operating costing (ii) Operation costing
   (iii) Output costing (iv) Process costing
2. In transport costing Insurance paid is a
   (i) Running charges (ii) Variable cost
   (iii) Standing charge (iv) Selling cost
3. Petrol expense in transport costing is
   (i) Fixed cost (ii) Running charge
   (iii) Standing charge (iv) Administration overhead
4. The method of costing applied for generation of electricity is known as
   (i) Canteen costing (ii) Transport costing
   (iii) Contract costing (iv) Power House costing
5. The profit for a canteen in a company is the difference between sales and
   (i) Expenses (ii) Expenses minus Subsidy
   (iii) Expenses plus Subsidy (iv) Expenses and Loss

[Ans: 1. (i) 2 (iii) 3 (ii) 4 (iv) 5 (ii)]

**II. Answer the following:**

6. Define operating costing. Give an outline of the application of operating costing.
7. What is service costing? State the procedures for the preparation of transport costing.
8. Define Service costing. Explain the procedures for the preparation of power house costing.
9. Define service costing. State the procedures for the preparation of canteen costing.
10. What is canteen costing? Explain the different type of expenses involved in canteen costing.
11. The information related for maintaining a vehicle by a company for the year 2010 are stated as follows:

| | Rs. |
|---|---|
| Cost of the vehicle | 300,000 |
| Driver's Salary per month | 4,000 |
| Cleaner's Salary per month | 3,000 |
| Road license per year | 4,500 |
| Insurance for one year | 4,100 |
| Garage rent per month | 800 |

| | |
|---|---|
| Maintenance and depreciation for tyres per km | 0.50 |
| Cost of diesel per litre | 36.50 |

Kilometers run per litre was - 10 kms
Estimated life of the vehicle - 250,000 kms.
Kilometer run for the year - 32,000 kms.
Estimated scrap value of the vehicle - Rs.20,000

Calculate the cost per km of the vehicle.

[Ans: Rs.3.19; Rs.6.21; Rs.9.40]

12. MWD Transporting company is running 8 buses between two villages. The distance between these two villages is 50 kms. The details relating to the costs for running the 8 vehicles for the month October 2011 are stated as follows:

| | Rs. |
|---|---|
| Salary for one driver per month | 3,500 |
| Salary for one conductor per month | 2,500 |
| Wages for one cleaner for the month | 1,500 |
| Cost of diesel per litre | 32 |
| Repairs & Maintenance for the 8 vehicles | 6,400 |
| Insurance for one vehicle for one year | 4,800 |
| Road tax paid per quarter for one vehicle | 3,900 |
| Depreciation charged for the 8 vehicles | 14,000 |
| Total garage rent for the month | 7,500 |

Kms run per litre per vehicle – 4.5 .The Company is having 16 drivers, 16 conductors and 8 cleaners. Each bus was operated in three round trips per day. Assume that all the 8 buses were operated on all the days of the month. Actual passengers carried were 90% of the seating capacity. The seating capacity of each bus is 45 passengers. Calculate the cost per Passenger – km.

[Ans: Rs.129,100; Rs.549,467; 30,13,200 Kms; Rs.0.04;Rs.0.18; Rs.0.22]

13. The costing information related to two different vehicles namely A and B are stated as follows:

| | | A | B |
|---|---|---|---|
| Cost of the Vehicle | Rs. | 250,000 | 3,20,000 |
| Estimated life of the vehicle | Km | 3,20,000 | 3,10,000 |
| Road license | Rs. | 4,200 | 4,200 |
| Insurance for one year | Rs. | 2,500 | 3,500 |
| Garage rent for one year | Rs. | 8,000 | 12,000 |
| Drivers wages per hour | Rs. | 20 | 20 |
| Cleaners wages per hour | Rs. | 5 | 5 |
| Repairs and Maintenance per km | Rs. | 0.20 | 0.30 |

| | | | |
|---|---|---|---|
| Tyre charge per km | Rs. | 0.60 | 0.50 |
| Km run for one year | Km. | 28,000 | 30,000 |
| Cost of diesel per litre | Rs. | 30 | 30 |
| Km run per litre | Km. | 14 | 15 |
| Average Km per hour | Km. | 32 | 32 |
| Depreciation charges per annum on the cost of the vehicle | | 10% | 10% |

Calculate the cost per running kilometer

[Ans: A Rs.1.42; Rs.3.72; Rs.5.14; B Rs.1.72; Rs.3.58; Rs.5.30]

14. W.Doyle & Co.Ltd. run the following fleet of buses within the limit of a city.

| | Carrying capacity |
|---|---|
| 10 Buses | 50 Passengers |
| 13 Buses | 45 Passengers |
| 17 Buses | 42 Passengers |

Each bus runs for 10 trips in a day and the distance in each trip was 6 kms. On an average 80% of the seats are occupied. For the purpose of repairs and maintenance, 7 buses were usually kept away from road daily on an average basis.

The following expenses are related to the month of April,2010

| | Rs. |
|---|---|
| Salary per month for the Office Manager | 5,000 |
| Salary per month for Asst. Manager (3) @ | 3,800 |
| Salary per month for Supervisors (4) @ | 3,000 |
| Salary per month for Drivers (35) @ | 3,000 |
| Salary per month for Cleaners (35) @ | 2,500 |
| Salary per month for Clerks (5) @ | 2,000 |
| Road tax for one year per Vehicle | 2,500 |
| Insurance per annum for all the vehicles | 60,000 |
| Consumable stores for the month | 24,000 |
| Diesel for the month | 420,000 |
| Lubricant oil for the month | 44,000 |
| Depreciation charge for tyre & tubes for the month | 42,000 |
| Depreciation for the vehicles for the month | 60,000 |
| Miscellaneous expenses | 34,000 |
| Garage rent for the month | 10,000 |

Calculate the cost per passenger km.

[Ans: Rs.0.41; Rs.314,233; Rs.564,000]

15. KT Transporting Company owned a fleet of 20 taxis. On an average the taxi run 5,000 kms in a month of which 15% run empty. The total life of a taxi is 250,000 kms. Petrol consumption is 12 kms per litre. The cost of petrol is Rs.40 per litre. Oil and other expenses are Rs.200 per 1,000 kms.The following are the further information connected with the operating of the taxies.

| | Rs. |
|---|---|
| Cost of each taxi | 260,000 |
| Salary of manager p.m | 5,000 |
| Salary of accountant p.m | 4,000 |
| Salary of driver p.m per taxi | 3,500 |
| Salary of cleaner p.m. (2 Cleaners) each | 3,000 |
| Salary of mechanic p.m | 3,200 |
| Annual tax per taxi | 4,000 |
| Garage rent p.m | 12,000 |
| Insurance premium per annum - 2% | |
| Annual repairs per taxi | 12,000 |

Prepare the Cost Sheet and calculate the cost of running a taxi per km.

[Ans: Km rate Rs.7.07; Passager km rate Rs.7.76]

16. G Ltd provides the following information for the month November 2011 with respect to the operation of a transport bus.

| | Rs. |
|---|---|
| Cost of the bus | 12,00,000 |
| Depreciation @ 10% p.a. | |
| Road Tax p.a | 12,000 |
| Expenses for Permit & F.C. p.a. | 30,000 |
| Insurance p.a. | 13,000 |
| Salary of Cleaner p.m. | 5,000 |
| Salary of driver p.m. | 6,000 |
| Salary of part-time accountant p.m. | 3,000 |
| Diesel Consumption is 4 km per litre | |
| Cost of diesel per litre | 34 |
| Lubricant oil cost per 100 km | 220 |
| Repairs and maintenance p.m. | 19,000 |
| Garage rent p.m. | 2,000 |

The bus is operated in three different routes in a month. The distance covered by the bus in the first route is 140 kms one way for the first 8 days in the month. For the next 10 days in the month, it is operated in another route covering a distance of 120 kms in one way. For the remaining days the bus is operated to a distance of 100 kms in one way. The bus returns to the garage in all the days of the month.

The bus runs all the 30 days in November and the seating capacity occupied in the first route is 100%, in the second route is 90%, and in the third route is 80%. The total seating capacity of the bus for the passenger is 50.

Calculate the bus fare to be charged to the passengers to earn a profit of 25% on the total revenue. Assume that the passenger tax is 10% of the total revenue.

[Ans: Revenue Rs.192,171; Expenses Rs.20,583; Rs.104,328; Rs.124,911; Profit Rs.48,043; Tax Rs.19,217]

17. Joyce & Co provides the following information connected with the generation of electricity during the month June 2011. Salaries and wages to the staff of the power house: 4 Foremen @ Rs.8,000 p.m; 5 Mechanics @ Rs.6,000 p.m; 6 Workmen @ Rs.4,000 p.m. Coal consumed during the month, 2000 tonnes @ Rs.200, Oil 12 tonnes @ Rs 4000; Water 8,000 gallons and the pumping charge is Rs.30 per 100 gallons; Handling charges of fuel @ Rs.40 per tonne; Ash removal charges, 200 tonnes @ Rs.5 per tonne; Repairs and maintenance of Generating Plant Rs.17,000; Share of total administrative charges of Rs.40,000 is 20%.

Depreciation for Steam Boiler @ 8%; Generator @ 6% and Building @ 4% Value of Steam Boiler Rs.100,000; Generator Rs.2,60,000 and Building Rs.300,000. Recovery on account of sale of ash 2,000 tonnes @ Rs 20 per tonne and cost of steam supplied to Manufacturing Shop, 50,000 tonnes @ Rs.40 per hundred tonnes

The Power House generated 4,00,000 units (gross) of electricity and the loss due to leakage is 4,000 units.

Prepare the operating cost statement and find out the cost per unit of electricity generated.

[Ans: Rs.10,77,367; Rs.10,17367; Rs.2.57]

18. Alfa Canteen provides the following particulars for operating a canteen for the month October 2011:

| **Stock of material** | **Opening Stock Kgms.** | **Closing Stock Kgms.** |
|---|---|---|
| Tea | 2 | 3 |
| Flour | 8 | 3 |
| Rice | 20 | 25 |

**Purchases:**

| | |
|---|---|
| (i) Rice 200 kgs @ Rs.13 | (viii) Flour 80 kgs @ Rs.12 |
| (ii) Spices 8 kgs @ Rs.38 | (ix) Dal 50 kgs @ Rs.24 |
| (iii) Potato 50 kgs @ Rs.10 | (x) Grocery Rs.2,000 |
| (iv) Mutton 30 kgs @ Rs.180 | (xi) Chicken 50 kgs @ Rs.42 |
| (v) Green Vegetable 60 kgs @ Rs.10 | (xii) Ghee 22 kgs @ Rs.50 |
| (vi) Tea 14 kgs @ Rs.150 | (xiii) Coffee 3kgs @ Rs.200 |
| (vii) Milk 900 litres @ Rs.11 | (xiv) Sugar 30kgs @ Rs.20 |

**Other Expenses:**

(i) Gas and fuel Rs.1,200
(ii) Salary for cook Rs.3,000
(iii) Wages to assistant and waiters Rs.5,000
(iv) Supervisors salary Rs.3,500
(v) Crockery and glassware Rs.1,250

Depreciation for furniture and utensils @ 12% p.a. Value of furniture and utensils Rs.50,000. Sale of coupons 4,000 @ Rs.9 per coupon. Subsidy for the canteen is 50% of the total cost.

Prepare an operating cost statement and find out the profit or loss for the canteen.

[Ans: Rs.46,795; Rs.23,398; Profit Rs.12,602]

19. The information relating to two different vehicles namely A and B operated by a Transport Company are stated as follows:

| | | A | B |
|---|---|---|---|
| Cost of the Vehicle | Rs. | 300,000 | 2,50,000 |
| Estimated life of the vehicle | Kms | 2,00,000 | 2,80,000 |
| Road license | Rs. | 6,000 | 6,000 |
| Insurance for one year | Rs. | 7,000 | 7,000 |
| Garage rent for one year | Rs. | 8,000 | 5,000 |
| Driver's wage per hour | Rs. | 30 | 30 |
| Cleaner's wage per hour | Rs. | 15 | 15 |
| Repairs and Maintenance per km | Rs. | 0.50 | 0.40 |
| Tyre charge per km | Rs. | 0.30 | 0.30 |
| Kms run for one year | Kms | 40,000 | 32,000 |
| Cost of diesel per litre | Rs. | 30 | 30 |
| Km run per litre | Kms. | 14 | 13 |
| Average Km per hour | Kms. | 32 | 32 |
| Depreciation charges per annum on the cost of the vehicle | | 10% | 10% |

Calculate the cost per running kilometre.

[Ans: Rs.5.98; Rs.5.64]

20. The following information are obtained from the books of of Mr.X, owner of a transport vehicle, for the month November 2011.

| | Rs. |
|---|---|
| Cost of the bus | 4,00,000 |
| Depreciation @ 10% p.a. | |
| Road Tax p.a | 7,000 |
| Expenses for Permit & F.C. p.a. | 4,000 |
| Insurance p.a. | 7,500 |
| Salary of cleaner p.m. | 3,500 |
| Salary of driver p.m. | 5,000 |
| Salary of part-time accountant p.m. | 2000 |
| Diesel consumption 4 kms per litre | |
| Cost of diesel per litre | 32 |
| Lubricant oil cost per 100 km | 40 |
| Repairs and maintenance p.m. | 1200 |
| Garage rent p.m. | 1500 |

The bus is operated in three different routes in a month. The distance covered by the bus in the first route is 100 kms one way for the first 10 days in the month. For the next 11 days in the month, it is operated in another route covering a distance of 110 kms in one way. For the remaining days the bus is operated to a distance of 140 kms in two ways. The bus returns to the garage in all the days of the month.

Assume that in November the bus runs all the 30 days and the seating capacity occupied in the first route is 90%, in the second route is 100%, and in the third route is 80%. The seating capacity of the bus for the passengers is 55.

Calculate the bus fare to be charged to the passengers to earn a profit of 20% on the total revenue. Assume that the passenger tax is 25% of the total revenue.

[Ans: Revenue Rs.138,856; Expenses Rs.76,371; Profit Rs.48,043; Tax Rs.19,217; Rates: Rs.0.405; Rs 40.50; Rs 44.55; Rs.56.70]

# CHAPTER IX

# COST LEDGER ACCOUNTING

There are two types of accounting systems adopted in companies to record the costing transactions. They are (i) Non-integral or Non-integrated Accounting system and (ii) Integral or Integrated Accounting system. Non-integrated accounting system is otherwise called as Cost Ledger Accounting. In this system separate accounts are maintained for cost and financial transactions. But in the Integrated Accounting system cost and financial transactions are integrated and one account system is followed for both cost and financial transactions.

## Non - integrated Accounting or Cost Ledger Accounting system

In this system of accounting separate accounting is adopted for recording costing transactions. This system is operated under the principle of double entry system of accounting. Separate ledgers are maintained on the basis of the different functions performed in an organisation. In order to complete the double entry system separate control accounts are maintained for respective ledger accounts.

## Cost Ledgers

The following are the important cost ledgers maintained by a company

1. Cost Ledger
2. Stores Ledger
3. Work-in-progress Ledger and
4. Finished Goods Ledger

### 1.Cost Ledger

This is the primary ledger. This ledger contains all the impersonal accounts. These accounts contain respective control accounts so that the cost ledger will self balance by itself.

### 2.Stores Ledger

This ledger contains separate accounts for the different types of stock of raw material

### 3.Work-in-progress Ledger

This ledger contains different accounts related to the different jobs which are in the process of completion.

### 4.Finished Goods Ledger.

This ledger contains separate accounts for the different types of finished goods.Cost ledger is the primary ledger and other ledgers are called the subsidiary ledger. In order to maintain clarity and accuracy, the subsidiary ledgers are maintained. Moreover it helps for handling numerous transactions.

**Control Accounts**

Control accounts are maintained for completing the double entry system. The balance of different accounts maintained in different subsidiary ledgers like Stores Ledger, Work-in-progress Ledger and Finished Goods Ledger are posted to the respective control accounts. Hence, all accounts in the Cost Ledger are having respective control accounts. It helps for easy identification of total of different types of expenses for a year in order to plan and control the different cost. The important Control Accounts are stated as follows.

**1.General Ledger Adjustment Account.**

This account is otherwise called as Cost Ledger Control Account or Cost Ledger Control Account. This account makes the Cost Ledger as self- balancing. This account contains only impersonal accounts. The transactions related to income and expenses which affect both financial and cost accounts only are recorded in this account. The transactions which are purely costing nature will not be recorded in this account. The following examples clearly explain the nature of the Cost Ledger Control Account.

(i) Purchase of raw material: In this transaction receipt of material is related to cost accounts and the payment of cash is related to financial account i.e., payment of cash is recorded in Cost Ledger Control Account and the receipt of material is recorded in Stores Ledger Control Account.

(ii) Issue of direct material to factory: It is purely a costing transaction and it will affect only the Cost Books. The journal entry is Work-in-progress Ledger Control A/c Dr To Stores Ledger Control A/c.

(iii) Payment of salaries and wages: This transaction will affect both the Financial Books and Cost Books. For the financial aspect of the transaction, Cost Ledger Control A/c should be used. The journal entry is Wages Ledger Control A/c Dr. To Cost Ledger Control A/c.

**2. Stores Ledger Control Account.**

It may otherwise be called as Material Control Account. This account deals with the receipt and issue of raw material from the store and records the balance of stock of material. It should be debited for the total value of receipt of material through purchase, as well as returns from the production centre or maintenance department. It should be credited for the issue of material to production centre or maintenance department as well as return of material to the suppliers. The debit balance of this account represents the total stock of material (direct and indirect), in the store.

**3. Wages Control Account.**

This account deals with the payment of wages and salaries and its allocation to different departments. It should be debited for the total payment of wages and salaries for the year and credited for the allocation of wages and salaries to different departments like, Production, Administration and Selling & Distribution.For direct wages, the account should be credited with the Work-in-progress Ledger Control Accounts and for the indirect wages, the account should be credited with the respective Overhead Control Accounts like the Factory overhead control account,Administration overhead control account and Selling & Distribution overhead control account.

**4. Work-in-progress Ledger Control Account.**

This account reveals the total amount of Work-in-progress during a period. It should be debited for the opening balance of work-in-progress, direct material, direct labour, direct expenses and factory overhead absorbed. It should be credited for the total finished goods during the period. The debit balance will represent the value of job incompleted during the period.It is credited as the closing balance of work-in-progress during the period.

**5. Finished Goods Ledger Control Account.**

It is a record for the unsold stock kept in the company. It should be debited for the opening balance of the total finished goods for the year and credited for the finished goods sold during the period. Hence, it should be debited with Opening balance and Work-in-progress Ledger Control Account and credited with the Cost of Sales Account. The debit balance in this account shows the unsold finished goods.It is called the closing stock of finished goods during the period.

**6. Factory Overhead Control Account.**

This account deals with the total factory expenses. It should be debited with indirect material, indirect labour and indirect expenses and credited with overhead absorbed to production. For the factory overhead absorbed to production, this account should be credited by Work-in-progress Ledger Control Account. The balance in this account is called under - absorption or over - absorption (under-recovery or over-recovery).The debit balance is called under-absorption and the credit balance is called over-absorption.It should be transferred to Costing Profit and Loss Account.

**7. Administration Overhead Control Account.**

This account shows the administration overhead incurred and absorbed. It should be debited for all the administrative expenses and credited for the recovery of the administration overhead to the Finished Goods Control Account. The balance is called under-absorption or over-absorption The debit balance is called under-absorption and the credit balance is called over-absorption.It should be transferred to Costing Profit & Loss Account.

**8. Selling and Distribution Overhead Control Account.**

This account reveals the total selling and distribution overhead incurred and absorbed. It should be debited for all the selling and distribution expenses and credited for the absorption of the overhead to the Cost of Sales Account. The balance is called under-absorption or over-absorption. The debit balance is called under-absorption and the credit balance is called over-absorption.It should be transferred to Costing Profit and Loss Account.

**9. Cost of Sales Account.**

It is a record for the cost of the goods sold for the year. It should be debited with the Cost of Finished Goods sold and with the Selling and Distribution Overhead recovered. This account should be closed by transferring the balance to Sales Account.

**10. Sales Account**

This is also a subsidiary account used in the Cost Books. This account should be credited with the Cost Ledger Control Account for the amount of sales for the year and debited with the Cost of Sales Account for the cost of goods sold. The balance amount may either be a profit or loss . It should be transferred to Costing Profit and Loss Account.

**11. Costing Profit and Loss Account.**

This account contains the over-recovery or under- recovery of Overhead Control Accounts and the balance from the Sales Account. The balance amount in this account may either be profit or loss. This profit or loss can be reconciled with the profit or loss of the Financial Profit and Loss Account.

## Advantages of Cost Ledger Accounts

The following are the advantages of maintaining cost ledger.

i) It helps to calculate the total of different types of expenses in a year, so as to plan and control cost.

ii) It is possible to analyse the budgeted and actual cost, at different stages within very short period of time.

iii) It helps for fixing standard at different levels of cost of production.

iv) It helps for easy identification of favourable deviations in the actual cost from the standard in order to give proper incentives and rewards for those who performed efficiently.

## Journal Entries in the Cost Book

### Journal Entries Relating to Material

| | | |
|---|---|---|
| 1 | Material purchased for Stock | Debit Stores Ledger Control A/c<br>Credit Cost Ledger Control A/c |
| 2 | Material purchased for Special Jobs | Debit Work-in-progress Control A/c<br>Credit Cost Ledger Control A/c |
| 3 | Direct material issued to Production Centre | Debit Work-in-progress Control A/c<br>Credit Stores Ledger Control A/c |
| 4 | Indirect materials issued to the Production Centre | Debit Factory Overhead Control A/c<br>Credit Stores Ledger Control A/c |
| 5 | Indirect materials issued to the Administration Department | Debit Administration Overhead Control A/c<br>Credit Stores Ledger Control A/c |
| 6 | Indirect materials issued to the Selling and Distribution Department | Debit Selling and Distribution Overhead Control A/c<br>Credit Stores Ledger Control A/c |
| 7 | Material returned to Suppliers | Debit Cost Ledger control A/c<br>Credit Stores Ledger Control A/c |
| 8 | Direct materials returned from Production Centre to the Store | Debit Stores Ledger Control A/c<br>Credit Work-in-progress Ledger Control A/c |
| 9 | Indirect materials returned from Factory to Store | Debit Stores Ledger Control A/c<br>Credit Factory Overhead Control A/c |
| 10 | Indirect materials returned from Administration department to Store. | Debit Stores Ledger Control A/c<br>Credit Administration Overhead Control A/c |
| 11 | Indirect materials returned from Sales department to the Store | Debit Stores Ledger Control A/c<br>Credit Selling and Distribution Overhead Control A/c |
| 12 | Material transferred from one job to another job | Debit Transferee Job A/c<br>Credit Transferred Job A/c |

**Journal Entries relating to Wages and Salaries**

| | | |
|---|---|---|
| 13 | Wages & Salaries paid in total | Debit Wages Ledger Control A/c<br>Credit Cost Ledger Control A/c |
| 14 | Direct wages paid individually to Production | Debit Wages Ledger Control A/c<br>Credit Cost Ledger Control A/c |
| 15 | Indirect wages paid for Production separately | Debit Wages Ledger Control A/c<br>Credit Cost Ledger Control A/c |
| 16 | Indirect wages and salaries paid to Administration Department or Office | Debit Wages Ledger Control A/c<br>Credit Cost Ledger Control A/c |
| 17 | Indirect wages and salaries paid for Sales Department | Debit Wages Ledger Control A/c<br>Credit Cost Ledger Control A/c |
| 18 | Direct wages allocated to Production | Debit Work-in-progress Ledger Control A/c<br>Credit Wages Ledger Control A/c |
| 19 | Indirect wages allocated to Production | Debit Factory Overhead Control A/c<br>Credit Wages Ledger Control A/c |
| 20 | Indirect wages & salaries allocated to Administration | Debit Administration Overhead Control A/c<br>Credit Wages Ledger Control A/c |
| 21 | Indirect wages and salaries allocated to Sales Department | Debit Selling and Distribution Overhead Control A/c<br>Credit Wages Ledger Control A/c |

**Journal Entry for Direct Expenses**

| | | |
|---|---|---|
| 22 | Direct Expenses paid | Debit Work-in-progress Ledger Control A/c<br>Credit Cost Ledger Control A/c |

**Journal Entries relating to Overhead Absorbed**

| | | |
|---|---|---|
| 23 | Factory Overhead paid | Debit Factory Overhead Control A/c<br>Credit Cost Ledger Control A/c |
| 24 | Administration Overhead paid | Debit Administration Overhead Control A/c<br>Credit Cost Ledger Control A/c |

| | | |
|---|---|---|
| 25 | Selling and Distribution Overhead paid | Debit Selling and Distribution Overhead Control A/c<br>Credit Cost Ledger Control A/c |
| 26 | For Factory Overhead absorbed | Debit Work-in-progress Ledger Control A/c<br>Credit Factory Overhead Control A/c |
| 27 | For Administration Overhead absorbed | Debit Finished Goods Ledger Control A/c<br>Credit Administration Overhead Control A/c |
| 28 | For Selling and Distribution Overhead absorbed | Debit Cost of Sales A/c<br>Credit Selling and Distribution Overhead Control A/c |

**Journal Entries for Under and Over Absorption of Overheads**

| | | |
|---|---|---|
| 29 | For Under-absorption of Factory Overhead | Debit Costing Profit and Loss A/c<br>Credit Factory Overhead Control A/c |
| 30 | For Under-absorption Administration Overhead | Debit Costing Profit and Loss A/c<br>Credit Administration Overhead Control A/c |
| 31 | For Under-absorption of Selling & Distribution Overhead | Debit Costing Profit and Loss A/c<br>Credit Selling and Distribution Overhead Control A/c |
| 32 | For Over-absorption of Factory Overhead | Debit Factory Overhead Control A/c<br>Credit Costing Profit and Loss A/c |
| 33 | For Over-absorption of Administration Overhead | Debit Administration Overhead Control A/c<br>Credit Costing Profit and Loss A/c |
| 34 | For Over-absorption of Selling and Distribution Overhead | Debit Selling & Distribution Overhead Control A/c<br>Credit Costing Profit and Loss |

**Note:** The journal entries stated above are related to the actual and estimated costs incurred and apportioned to various cost centres and departments. Total of these costs should be transferred to respective major accounts as follows, to ascertain the costing profit.

**Journal Entries relating to the transfer of Total Costs to the respective accounts**

| | | |
|---|---|---|
| 35 | For Finished Goods produced | Debit Finished Goods Ledger Control A/c<br>Credit Work-in-progress Ledger Control A/c |
| 36 | For Cost of Goods Sold | Debit Cost of Sales A/c<br>Credit Finished Goods Ledger Control A/c |
| 37 | For Cost of Sales | Debit Sales A/c<br>Credit Cost of Sale A/c |
| 38 | For Profit on Goods Sold | Debit Sales A/c<br>Credit Costing Profit and Loss A/c |
| 39 | For the Credit balance in Costing Profit and Loss A/c | Debit Costing Profit and Loss A/c<br>Credit Cost Ledger Control A/c |
| 40 | For the Debit balance in the Costing Profit and Loss A/c | Debit Cost Ledger Control A/c<br>Credit Costing Profit & Loss A/c |
| 41 | For Repair Works on completion | Debit Respective Overhead Control A/c<br>Credit Repair Order A/c |
| 42 | Special Order completed and sold individually at factory cost | Debit Cost of Sales A/c<br>Credit Sales A/c |
| 43 | Special Order Completed and sold at total cost | Debit Cost Ledger Control A/c<br>Credit Sales A/c |

**Illustration: 1**

Journalise the following transactions in the cost books of D Ltd. for the month March 2011.

1. Material purchased for cash Rs.7,000
2. Material purchased on credit Rs.3,500
3. Material purchased on credit for special jobs Rs.4,000
4. Material issued to production centre (direct) Rs.2,600
5. Material issued to production centre (indirect) Rs.1,000
6. Stationeries issued to administration department Rs.600
7. Stationeries issued to sales department Rs.500
8. Material returned to the suppliers Rs.750
9. Material transferred from Job No 201 to Job No. 205 Rs.300
10. Indirect material returned from production centre to stores Rs.700

***Solution:***

**Journal Entries in the book of D Ltd**

| | Particulars | | Dr. Rs. | Cr. Rs. |
|---|---|---|---|---|
| 1 | Stores Ledger Control A/c | Dr. | 7,000 | |
| | To Cost Ledger Control A/c | | | 7,000 |
| | (Being material purchased for cash) | | | |
| 2 | Stores Ledger Control A/c | Dr. | 3,500 | |
| | To Cost Ledger Control A/c | | | 3,500 |
| | (Being material purchased on credit) | | | |
| 3 | Work-in-progress Ledger Control A/c | Dr. | 4,000 | |
| | To Cost Ledger Control A/c | | | 4,000 |
| | (Being material purchased on credit for special jobs) | | | |
| 4 | Work-in-progress Ledger Control A/c | Dr. | 2,600 | |
| | To Stores Ledger Control A/c | | | 2,600 |
| | (Being indirect material issued to the production centre) | | | |
| 5 | Factory Overhead Control A/c | Dr. | 1,000 | |
| | To Stores Ledger Control A/c | | | 1,000 |
| | (Being indirect material issued to the production centre) | | | |
| 6 | Administration Overhead Control A/c | Dr. | 600 | |
| | To Stores Ledger Control A/c | | | 600 |
| | (Being Stationeries issued to the sales department) | | | |
| 7 | Selling and Distribution Overhead Control A/c | Dr. | 500 | |
| | To Stores Ledger Control A/c | | | 500 |
| | (Being stationaries issued to the sales department) | | | |
| 8 | Cost Ledger Control A/c | Dr. | 750 | |
| | To Stores Ledger Control A/c | | | 750 |
| | (Being material returned to the suppliers) | | | |
| 9 | Job No. 205 A/c | Dr. | 300 | |
| | To Job No. 201 A/c | | | 300 |
| | (Being material transferred from Job N. 201 to Job No. 205) | | | |
| 10 | Stores Ledger Control A/c | Dr. | 700 | |
| | To Factory Overhead Control A/c | | | 700 |
| | (Being indirect material returned from the production centre to store) | | | |

**Illustration: 2**

Pass journal entries for the following transactions in the Cost books of X Ltd. for the month March 2011. The total wages and salaries after deducting the Employers Provident Fund, Income Tax, State Insurance of the company for the month amounted to Rs.17,800.

The total wages and salaries were as follows:

| | |
|---|---|
| Direct wages | Rs.8,000 |
| Direct factory wages | Rs.3,000 |
| Salaries for the Administration Department | Rs.3,800 |
| Salaries for the Sales Department | Rs.3,000 |

***Solution:***

**Journal Entries in the book of X Ltd**

| | Particulars | Dr. Rs. | Cr. Rs. |
|---|---|---|---|
| 1 | Wage Ledger Control A/c Dr.<br>To Cost Ledger Control A/c<br>(Being the total wages paid for the month December) | 17,800 | 17,800 |
| 2 | Work-in-progress Ledger Contol A/c Dr.<br>To Wages Ledger Control A/c<br>(Being the direct wages for production paid) | 8,000 | 8,000 |
| 3 | Factory Overhead Control A/c Dr.<br>To Wage Ledger Control A/c<br>(Being the indirect wages paid for the production) | 3,000 | 3,000 |
| 4 | Administration Overhead Control A/c Dr.<br>To Wage Ledger Control A/c<br>(Being the salaries for the administration department paid) | 3,800 | 3,800 |
| 5 | Selling and Distribution Overhead Control A/c Dr.<br>To Wage Ledger Control A/c<br>(Being the salaries for the sales department paid) | 3,000 | 3,000 |

**Illustration: 3**

Journalise the following transactions in the cost books of N Ltd. for the month February 2011.

| | | |
|---|---|---|
| 1. | Indirect material issued to the Factory | Rs. 7,250 |
| 2. | Indirect material issued to the Sales Department | Rs. 600 |
| 3. | Administration Overhead paid | Rs. 4,000 |
| 4. | Factory Overhead paid | Rs. 2,700 |
| 5. | Selling and Distribution Overhead paid | Rs. 3,000 |
| 6. | Indirect Wages allocated to Factory | Rs. 1,500 |

7. Salaries & Wages allocated to Administrative staff Rs. 7,000
8. Salaries & wages allocated to Sales Department Rs. 8,000

***Solution:***

**Journal Entries in the book of G Ltd.**

| | Particulars | Dr. Rs. | Cr. Rs. |
|---|---|---|---|
| 1 | Factory Overhead Control A/c Dr.<br>To Stores Ledger Control A/c<br>(Being issue of indrect material to factory) | 7,250 | 7,250 |
| 2 | Selling and Distribution Overhead Control A/c Dr.<br>To Stores Ledger Control A/c<br>(Being indirect material issued to the sales department) | 600 | 600 |
| 3 | Administration Overhead Control A/c Dr.<br>To Cost Ledger Control A/c<br>(Being the administration overhead paid) | 4,000 | 4,000 |
| 4 | Factory Overhead Control A/c Dr.<br>To Cost Ledger Control A/c<br>(Being the factory overhead paid) | 2,700 | 2,700 |
| 5 | Selling & Distribution Overhead Control A/c Dr.<br>To Cost Ledger Control A/c<br>(Being the selling & distribution overhead paid) | 3,000 | 3,000 |
| 6 | Factory Overhead Control A/c Dr.<br>To Wages Ledger Control A/c<br>(Being the indirect factory wages paid) | 1,500 | 1,500 |
| 7 | Administration Overhead Control A/c Dr.<br>To Wages Ledger Control A/c<br>(Being the Salaries allocated to Administration Department) | 7,000 | 7,000 |
| 8 | Selling and Distribution Overhead Control A/c Dr.<br>To Wages Ledger Control A/c<br>(Being the salaries for selling and distribution department allocated) | 8,000 | 8,000 |

Note: It is clear from the above journal entries that Cost Ledger Control account is credited for the cash paid for various expenses.

**Illustration: 4**

H Ltd provides the following particulars from the Cost Books for the financial year ending 31st March, 2011 with respect to the expenses incurred and the revenue from sales.

| | Rs. | Rs. |
|---|---|---|
| Balance in Stores Ledger Control A/c as on 1-4-2010 | 32,000 | |
| Balance in Work-in-progress Ledger Control A/c as on 1-4-2010 | 28,000 | |
| Balance in Finished Goods Ledger Control A/c as on 1-4-2010 | 50,000 | |
| Balance in Cost ledger Control A/c as on 1-4-2010 | | 1,10,000 |
| Material purchased (Direct) for cash | | 70,000 |
| Material purchased (Indirect) for credit | | 40,000 |
| Indirect material purchased for cash | | 26,000 |
| Direct material issued to factory | | 74,000 |
| Indirect material issued to factory | | 14,000 |
| Material (Direct) returned from factory to stores | | 2,000 |
| Material (Indirect) returned from factory to stores | | 1,000 |
| Material returned to suppliers | | 3,000 |
| Wages and salaries (direct) paid for production department | | 47,000 |
| Indirect factory wages paid | | 17,500 |
| Salary paid for the administrative staff | | 51,500 |
| Salary paid for sales department | | 29,000 |
| Factory indirect expenses paid | | 7,250 |
| Administration overhead paid | | 6,150 |
| Selling and distribution overhead paid | | 4,950 |
| Factory overhead absorbed | | 39,000 |
| Administration overhead absorbed | | 55,000 |
| Selling and distribution overhead absorbed | | 33,000 |
| Cost of the finished goods during the year | | 1,70,000 |
| Cost of goods sold | | 2,00,000 |
| Cash sales | | 1,70,000 |
| Credit sales | | 70,000 |

**Journalise the above transactions in the cost books. Also prepare the necessary ledger accounts for the year ended 31st March 2011.**

***Solution:***

**Journal entries in the book of H Ltd**

| | Particulars | Dr. Rs. | Cr. Rs. |
|---|---|---|---|
| 1 | Stores Ledger Control A/c Dr.<br>To Cost Ledger Control A/c<br>(Being the purchase of direct and indirect materials for cash and for credit) | 1,36,000 | 1,36,000 |
| 2 | Work-in-progress Ledger Control A/c Dr.<br>To stores Ledger Control A/c<br>(Being the issue of direct material to factory) | 74,000 | 74,000 |
| 3 | Factory Overhead Control A/c Dr.<br>To Stores Ledger Control A/c<br>(Being the indirect material issued to factory) | 14,000 | 14,000 |
| 4 | Stores Ledger Control A/c Dr.<br>To Work-in-progress Ledger Control A/c<br>To Factory Overhead Control A/c<br>(Being the return of direct and indirect materials to stores) | 3,000 | 2,000<br>1,000 |
| 5 | Cost Ledger Control A/c Dr.<br>To Stores Ledger Control A/c<br>(Being the return of material to suppliers) | 3,000 | 3,000 |
| 6 | Wage Ledger Control A/c Dr.<br>To Cost Ledger Control A/c<br>(Being wages & salaries, paid for factory administration and sales department) | 145,000 | 145,000 |
| 7 | Work-in-progress Ledger Control A/c Dr.<br>To Wages Ledger Control A/c<br>(Being direct wages paid for factory) | 47,000 | 47,000 |
| 8 | Factory Overhead Control A/c Dr.<br>To Wages Ledger Control A/c<br>(Being the indirect wages paid for factory) | 17,500 | 17,500 |
| 9 | Administration Overhead Control A/c Dr.<br>To Wages Ledger Control A/c<br>(Being the salary paid for administrative staff) | 51,500 | 51,500 |
| 10 | Selling and Distribution Overhead Control A/c Dr<br>To Wages Ledger Control A/c<br>(Being the salaries paid for Sales Department) | 29,000 | 29,000 |

| | | | |
|---|---|---|---|
| 11 | Factory Overhead Control A/c Dr.<br>To Cost Ledger Control A/c<br>(Being the fatory overhead paid) | 7,250 | 7,250 |
| 12 | Administration Overhead Control A/c Dr.<br>To Cost Ledger Control A/c<br>(Being the administration overhead paid) | 6,150 | 6,150 |
| 13 | Sellilng and Distribution Overhead Control A/c Dr.<br>To Cost Ledger Control A/c<br>(Being the selling and distribution overhead paid) | 4,950 | 4,950 |
| 14 | Work-in-progress Ledger Control A/c Dr.<br>To Factory Overhead Control A/c<br>(Being the factory overhead absorbed) | 39,000 | 39,000 |
| 15 | Finished Goods Ledger Control A/c Dr.<br>To Administration Overhead Control A/c<br>(Being the administration overhead absorbed) | 55,000 | 55,000 |
| 16 | Cost of Sales A/c Dr.<br>To Selling and Distribution Overhead Control A/c<br>(Being the selling and distribution overhead absorbed) | 33,000 | 33,000 |
| 17 | Finished Goods Legder Control A/c Dr.<br>To Work-in-progress Ledger Control A/c<br>(Being the total finished goods transferred to finished goods ledger control account) | 1,70,000 | 1,70,000 |
| 18 | Cost of Sales A/c Dr.<br>To Finished Goods Ledger Control A/c<br>(Being the total cost of sales debited) | 2,00,000 | 2,00,000 |
| 19 | Sales A/c Dr.<br>To Cost of Sales A/c<br>(Being the total cost of sales transferred to sales account) | 2,33,000 | 2,33,000 |
| 20 | Cost Ledger Control A/c Dr.<br>To Sales A/c\<br>(Being the goods sold for cash and for credit) | 2,40,000 | 2,40,000 |
| 21 | Sales A/c Dr.<br>To Costing Profit and Loss A/c<br>(Being the profit on sales credited) | 7,000 | 7,000 |

| | | | |
|---|---|---|---|
| 22 | Factory Overhead Control A/c Dr.<br>To Costing Profit and Loss A/c<br>(Being the over-absorption of factory overhead credited) | 3,550 | 3,550 |
| 23 | Costing Profit and Loss A/c Dr.<br>To Administration Overhead Control A/c<br>To Selling & Distri. Overhead Control A/c<br>(Being the under absorption of overheads transferred to costing profit and loss account) | 3,600 | 2,650<br>950 |

## Ledger Accounts in the Book of H Ltd

### STORES LEDGER CONTROL ACCOUNT

| Particulars | Rs. | Particulars | Rs. |
|---|---|---|---|
| To Balance b/d | 32,000 | By Work-in-progress Ledger Control A/c | 74,000 |
| „ Cost Ledger Control A/c | 1,36,000 | „ Factory Overhead Control A/c | 14,000 |
| „ Work-in-progress Ledger Control A/c | 2,000 | „ Cost Ledger Control A/c | 3,000 |
| „ Factory Overhead Control A/c | 1,000 | „ Balanced c/d | 80,000 |
| | 1,71,000 | | 1,71,000 |

### WAGES LEDGER CONTROL ACCOUNT

| Particulars | Rs. | Particulars | Rs. |
|---|---|---|---|
| To Cost Ledger Control A/c | 1,45,000 | By Work-in-progress Ledger Control A/c | 47,000 |
| | | „ Factory Overhead Control A/c | 17,500 |
| | | „ Administration Overhead Control A/c | 51,500 |
| | | „ Selling and Distribution Overhead Control A/c | 29,000 |
| | 1,45,000 | | 1,45,000 |

## FACTORY OVERHEAD CONTROL ACCOUNT

| Particulars | Rs. | Particulars | Rs. |
|---|---|---|---|
| To Stores Ledger Control A/c | 14,000 | By Stores Ledger Control A/c | 1,000 |
| „ Wages Ledger Control A/c | 17,500 | „ Work-in-progress Ledger Control A/c | 39,000 |
| „ Cost Ledger Control A/c | 4,950 | | |
| „ Overhead Suspense A/c | 3,550 | | |
| | 40,000 | | 40,000 |

## WORK -IN-PROGRESS LEDGER CONTROL ACCOUNT

| Particulars | Rs. | Particulars | Rs. |
|---|---|---|---|
| To Balance b/d | 28,000 | By Stores Ledger Control A/c | 2,000 |
| „ Stores Ledger Control A/c | 74,000 | „ Finished Goods Ledger Control A/c (Balancing figure) | 1,70,000 |
| „ Wages Ledger Control A/c | 47,000 | „ Balance c/d | 16,000 |
| „ Factory Overhead Control A/c | 39,000 | | |
| | 1,88,000 | | 1,88,000 |

## ADMINISTRATION OVERHEAD CONTROL ACCOUNT

| Particulars | Rs. | Particulars | Rs. |
|---|---|---|---|
| To Wages Ledger Control A/c | 51,500 | By Finished Goods Control A/c | 55,000 |
| „ Cost Ledger Control A/c | 6,150 | „ Overhead Suspense A/c | 2,650 |
| | 57,650 | | 57,650 |

## SELLING AND DISTRIBUTION OVERHEAD CONTROL A/C

| Particulars | Rs. | Particulars | Rs. |
|---|---|---|---|
| To Wages Ledger Control A/c | 29,000 | By Cost of Sales A/c | 33,000 |
| „ Cost Ledger Control A/c | 4,950 | „ Overhead Suspense A/c | 950 |
| | 33,950 | | 33,950 |

## OVERHEAD SUSPENSE ACCOUNT

| Particulars | Rs. | Particulars | Rs. |
|---|---|---|---|
| To Administration Overhead Control A/c | 2,650 | By Factory Overhead Control A/c | 3,550 |
| ,, Selling and Distribution Overhead Control A/c | 950 | ,, Costing Profit & Loss A/c | 50 |
| | 3,600 | | 3,600 |

## FINISHED GOODS LEDGER CONTROL ACCOUNT

| Particulars | Rs. | Particulars | Rs. |
|---|---|---|---|
| To Balance b/d | 50,000 | By Cost of Sales A/c | 2,00,000 |
| ,, Work-in-progress Ledger Control A/c | 1,70,000 | ,, Balance c/d | 75,000 |
| ,, Administration Overhead Control A/c | 55,000 | | |
| | 2,75,000 | | 2,75,000 |

## COST OF SALES ACCOUNT

| Particulars | Rs. | Particulars | Rs. |
|---|---|---|---|
| To Finished Goods Ledger Control A/c | 2,00,000 | By Sales A/c | 2,33,000 |
| ,, Selling and Distribution Overhead Control A/c | 33,000 | | |
| | 2,33,000 | | 2,33,000 |

## SALES ACCOUNT

| Particulars | Rs. | Particulars | Rs. |
|---|---|---|---|
| To Cost of Sales A/c | 2,33,000 | By Cost Control Ledger A/c | 2,40,000 |
| ,, Costing Profit and Loss A/c | 7,000 | | |
| | 2,40,000 | | 2,40,000 |

## COSTING PROFIT AND LOSS ACCOUNT

| Particulars | Rs. | Particulars | Rs. |
|---|---|---|---|
| To Overhead Suspense A/c | 50 | By Sales A/c | 7,000 |
| ,, Cost Ledger Control A/c | 6,950 | | |
| | 7,000 | | 7,000 |

## COST LEDGER CONTROL ACCOUNT

| Particulars | Rs. | Particulars | Rs. |
|---|---|---|---|
| To Sales A/c | 2,40,000 | By Balance b/d | 1,10,000 |
| ,, Stores Ledger Control A/c | 3,000 | ,, Stores Ledger Control A/c | 1,36,000 |
| ,, Balance c/d | 1,71,000 | ,, Wages Ledger Control A/c | 1,45,000 |
| | | ,, Factory Overhead Control A/c | 4,950 |
| | | ,, Administration Overhead Control A/c | 6,150 |
| | | ,, Selling and Distribution Overhead Control A/c | 4,950 |
| | | ,, Costing Profit & Loss A/c | 6,950 |
| | 4,14,000 | | 4,14,000 |

## TRAIL BALANCE

| Particulars | Dr. Rs. | Cr. Rs. |
|---|---|---|
| Stores Ledger Control A/c | 80,000 | |
| Work-in-progress Ledger Control A/c | 16,000 | |
| Finished Goods Ledger Control A/c | 75,000 | |
| Cost Ledger Control A/c | | 1,71,000 |
| | 1,71,000 | 1,71,000 |

**Illustration: 5**

The following information are related to the cost records of a manufacturing company for the year ended 31st March 2011. Prepare necessary accounts in Cost Ledger.

| | Opening Balance Rs. | Closing Balance Rs. |
|---|---|---|
| Work-in-progress Ledger Control A/c | 4,000 | 3,700 |
| Stores Ledger Control A/c | 7,800 | 6,000 |
| Finished Goods Ledger Control A/c | 10,000 | 12,000 |

| Transactions for the year are as follows: | Rs. |
|---|---|
| Material purchased | 78,000 |
| Direct wages paid | 33,000 |
| Indirect wages paid for factory | 21,000 |
| Salaries paid to administration staff | 32,000 |

| | |
|---|---|
| Salaries paid for the sales department | 11,000 |
| Factory overhead paid | 7,000 |
| Administration overhead paid | 5,700 |
| Selling and distribution overhead paid | 3,200 |
| Factory overhead absorbed to production | 27,500 |
| Administration overhead absorbed | 38,000 |
| Selling and distribution overhead absorbed | 15,000 |
| Sales | 2,10,000 |

***Solution:***

## COST LEDGER

### STORES LEDGER CONTROL ACCOUNT

| Particulars | Rs. | Particulars | Rs. |
|---|---|---|---|
| To Balance b/d | 7,800 | By Work-in-Progress Ledger Control A/c (Balancing figure) | 79,800 |
| „ Cost Ledger Control A/c | 78,000 | By Balance c/d | 6,000 |
| | 85,800 | | 85,800 |

### WAGES LEDGER CONTROL ACCOUNT

| Particulars | Rs. | Particulars | Rs. |
|---|---|---|---|
| To Cost Ledger Control A/c | 97,000 | By Work-in-progress Ledger Control A/c | 33,000 |
| | | „ Factory Overhead Control A/c | 21,000 |
| | | „ Administration Overhead Control A/c | 32,000 |
| | | „ Selling and Distribution Overhead Control A/c | 11,000 |
| | 97,000 | | 97,000 |

### FACTORY OVERHEAD CONTROL ACCOUNT

| Particulars | Rs. | Particulars | Rs. |
|---|---|---|---|
| To Wages Ledger Control A/c | 21,000 | By Work-in-progress Ledger Control A/c | 27,500 |
| „ Cost Ledger Control A/c | 7,000 | „ Overhead Suspense A/c | 500 |
| | 28,000 | | 28,000 |

## ADMINISTRATION OVERHEAD CONTROL ACCOUNT

| Particulars | Rs. | Particulars | Rs. |
|---|---|---|---|
| To Wages Ledger Control A/c | 32,000 | By Finished Goods Ledger Control A/c | 38,000 |
| „ Cost Ledger Control A/c | 5,700 | | |
| „ Overhead Suspense A/c | 300 | | |
| | 38,000 | | 38,000 |

## SELLING AND DISTRIBUTION OVERHEAD CONTROL A/C

| Particulars | Rs. | Particulars | Rs. |
|---|---|---|---|
| To Wages Ledger Control A/c | 11,000 | By Cost of Sales A/c | 15,000 |
| „ Cost Ledger Control A/c | 3,200 | | |
| „ Overhead Suspense A/c | 800 | | |
| | 15,000 | | 15,000 |

## WORK -IN-PROGRESS LEDGER CONTROL ACCOUNT

| Particulars | Rs. | Particulars | Rs. |
|---|---|---|---|
| To Balance b/d | 4,000 | By Finished Goods Ledger Control A/c (Balancing figure) | 140,600 |
| „ Stores Ledger Control A/c | 79,800 | | |
| „ Wages Ledger Control A/c | 33,000 | „ Balance c/d | 3,700 |
| „ Factory Overhead Control A/c | 27,500 | | |
| | 144,300 | | 144,300 |

## FINISHED GOODS LEDGER CONTROL ACCOUNT

| Particulars | Rs. | Particulars | Rs. |
|---|---|---|---|
| To Balance b/d | 10,000 | By Cost of Sales A/c (Balancing figure) | 176,600 |
| „ Work-in-progress Ledger Control A/c | 1,40,600 | „ Balance c/d | 12,000 |
| „ Administration Overhead Control A/c | 38,000 | | |
| | 1,88,600 | | 1,88,600 |

## COST OF SALES ACCOUNT

| Particulars | Rs. | Particulars | Rs. |
|---|---|---|---|
| To Finished Goods Ledger Control A/c | 176,600 | By Sales A/c | 191,600 |
| ,, Selling and Distribution Overhead Control A/c | 15,000 | | |
| | 1,91,600 | | 191,600 |

## SALES ACCOUNT

| Particulars | Rs. | Particulars | Rs. |
|---|---|---|---|
| To Cost of Sales A/c | 191,600 | By Cost Control Ledger A/c | 2,10,000 |
| ,, Costing Profit and Loss A/c | 18,400 | | |
| | 2,10,000 | | 2,10,000 |

## OVERHEAD SUSPENSE ACCOUNT

| Particulars | Rs. | Particulars | Rs. |
|---|---|---|---|
| To Factory Overhead Control A/c | 500 | By Administration Overhead Control A/c | 300 |
| ,, Costing Profit & Loss A/c | 600 | ,, Selling and Distribution Overhead Control A/c | 800 |
| | 1,100 | | 1,100 |

## COSTING PROFIT AND LOSS ACCOUNT

| Particulars | Rs. | Particulars | Rs. |
|---|---|---|---|
| To Cost Ledger Control A/c | 19,000 | By Sales A/c | 18,400 |
| | | ,, Overhead Suspence A/c | 600 |
| | 19,000 | | 19,000 |

**Note:** Costing Profit and Loss account shows a balance of Rs.19,000 due to the difference between the sales and actual cost. The estimated overheads and actual overheads are adjusted in the Overhead Suspense account.

## COST LEDGER CONTROL ACCOUNT

| Particulars | Rs. | Particulars | Rs. |
|---|---|---|---|
| To Sales A/c | 2,10,000 | By Balance b/d (4,000 + 7,800 + 10,000) | 21,800 |
| ,, Balance c/d (3,700 + 6,000 + 12,000) | 21,700 | ,, Stores Ledger Control A/c | 78,000 |
| | | ,, Wages Ledger Control A/c | 97,000 |
| | | ,, Factory Overhead Control A/c | 7,000 |
| | | ,, Administration Overhead Control A/c | 5,700 |
| | | ,, Selling and Distribution Overhead Control A/c | 3,200 |
| | | ,, Costing Profit & Loss A/c | 19,000 |
| | 231,700 | | 231,700 |

## TRAIL BALANCE

| Particulars | Dr. Rs. | Cr. Rs. |
|---|---|---|
| Work-in-progress Ledger Control A/c | 3,700 | |
| Finished Goods Ledger Control A/c | 12,000 | |
| Stores Ledger Control A/c | 6,000 | |
| Cost Ledger Control A/c | | 21,700 |
| | 21,700 | 21,700 |

Note: Trial Balance is a proof to know whether the calculations are correct or not. Only four accounts will show balances and all other accounts are adjusted with these four accounts.Since Work-in-progress Ledger Control account, Finished Goods Ledger Control account, Stores Ledger Control account are related to assets, these accounts show debit balances.The effects of these accounts make the Cost Ledger Control account to show credit balance and the credit balance would be equal to the total of the all debit balances related to inventory.

## EXERCISE

**I. Choose the correct answer for the following:**

1. Cost Ledger accounting is otherwise called as
   (i) Non-integrated accounting (ii) Integrated accounting
   (iii) Stores Ledger accounting (iv) FOH accounting
2. Separate accounts are maintained for cost and financial accounts in
   (i) Integrated Accounting (ii) Cost Accounting
   (iii) Financial Accounting (iv) Non-Integrated Accounting
3. One accounting system is followed for cost and financial accounts in
   (i) Non-Integrated Accounting (ii) Integrated Accounting
   (iii) Overhead (iv) Direct Cost
4. Cost Ledger Control Account is otherwise called as
   (i) Finished Goods Ledger Account (ii) Stores Ledger Account
   (iii) General Ledger Adjustment Account (iv) WIP Account
5. Factory overhead absorbed is debited in
   (i) Work-in-progress Account (ii) Stores Ledger Account
   (iii) Finished Goods Account (iv) Cost of Sales Account
6. Administration overhead absorbed is debited in
   (i) Stores Ledger Account (ii) Finished Goods Account
   (iii) Work-in-Progress Account (iv) Cost of Sales Account
7. Selling and Distribution overhead is debited in
   (i) Sales Account (ii) Work-in-progress Account
   (iii) Cost of Sales Account (iv) Finished Goods Account

[Ans: 1 (i); 2 (iv); 3 (ii); 4 (iii); 5 (i); 6 (ii); 7 (iii)]

**II. Answer the following:**

8. Define Cost Ledger Accounting. What are the advantages of Cost Ledger Accounting?
9. Distinguish between Integrated Accounting System and Non-integrated Accounting System.
10. State the importance and merits of Cost Ledger Accounting.
11. Explain the different types of Control Accounts in the Cost Ledger.
12. Enumerate Cost Ledger and Control Accounts.
13. Distinguish between Work-in-progress Ledger Account and Finished Goods Account.
14. Write short notes of the following:
    (i) Work-in-progress Account (ii) Finished Goods Account
    (iii) Cost of Sales Account (iv) Cost Ledger Control Account
    (v) Integrated Accounting (vi) Non-Integrated Accounting
15. Journalise the following transactions in the cost books of KC Ltd.. for the month April, 2011.

    1. Material purchaed for cash Rs.27,000

2. Material purchased on credit Rs.30,000
3. Material purchased on credit for special jobs Rs.24,000
4. Material issued to production centre (direct) Rs.22,500
5. Material issued to production centre (indirect) Rs. 7,000
6. Stationeries issued to administration department Rs.12,000
7. Stationeries issued to sales department Rs. 7,500
8. Material returned to the suppliers Rs. 3,500
9. Material transferred from Job No.209 to Job No.215 Rs. 5,300
10. Indirect material returned from production centre to store Rs.2,700

16. G Ltd. provides the following transactions from the cost books for the month September 2011. The total wages and salaries after deducting the Employers Provident Fund, Income Tax, State Insurance for the month amounted to Rs.87,500.

The total wages and salaries were paid as follows:

| | |
|---|---|
| Direct wages | Rs. 25,000 |
| Direct factory wages | Rs. 18,000 |
| Salaries for the Administration Department | Rs. 33,500 |
| Salaries for the Sales Department | Rs. 11,000 |

Pass journal entries.

17. Journalise the following transactions in the books of KLtd. for the month November, 2011.
    1. Indirect material issued to the Factory Rs, 37,500
    2. Indirect material issued to the Sales Department Rs. 7,500
    3. Administration Overhead paid Rs. 24,000
    4. Factory Overhead paid Rs. 12,000
    5. Selling and Distribution Overhead paid Rs. 13,000
    6. Indirect Wages allocated to Factory Rs. 11,500
    7. Salaries & Wages allocated to Administrative staff Rs. 17,000
    8. Salaries & wages allocated to Sales Department Rs. 18,000

18. Journalise the following transactions in the cost books of C Ltd. for the month November, 2011.
    1. Material purchased for cash Rs. 12,000
    2. Material purchased on credit Rs. 7,000
    3. Material purchased on credit for special jobs Rs. 6,000
    4. Material issued to production centre (direct) Rs. 14,500
    5. Material issued to production centre (indirect) Rs. 4,000
    6. Stationeries issued to administration department Rs. 3,000
    7. Stationeries issued to sales department Rs. 3,500
    8. Material returned to the suppliers Rs. 1,500
    9. Material transferred from Job No. 220 to Job No. 222 Rs. 1,700
    10. Indirect material returned from production centre to store Rs. 1,000

19. MH Ltd. provides the following transactions from the cost books for the month September 2011. The total wages and salaries after deducting the Employers Provident Fund, Income Tax, State Insurance for the month amounted to Rs.130,500.

    The total wages and salaries were paid in the following form.

    | | |
    |---|---|
    | Direct wages | Rs. 40,000 |
    | Direct factory wages | Rs. 30,500 |
    | Salaries for the Administration Department | Rs. 47,500 |
    | Salaries for the Sales Department | Rs. 12,500 |

    Pass journal entries.

20. Journalise the following transactions in the books of NLtd. for the month October 2011.

    | | |
    |---|---|
    | 1. Indirect material issued to the Factory | Rs, 46,500 |
    | 2. Indirect material issued to the Sales Department | Rs. 11,500 |
    | 3. Administration Overhead paid | Rs. 39,000 |
    | 4. Factory Overhead paid | Rs. 32,000 |
    | 5. Selling and Distribution Overhead paid | Rs. 29,000 |
    | 6. Indirect Wages allocated to Factory | Rs. 44,500 |
    | 7. Salaries & Wages allocated to Administrative staff | Rs. 49,000 |
    | 8. Salaries & wages allocated to Sales Department | Rs. 31,000 |

21. The following information are collected from the cost books of D Ltd for the financial year ending 31st March, 2011.

    | | Rs. | Rs. |
    |---|---|---|
    | Balance in Stores Ledger Control A/c as on 1-4-2010 | 55,000 | |
    | Balance in Work-in-progress Ledger Control A/c as on 1-4-2010 | 44,000 | |
    | Balance in Finished Goods Ledger Control A/c as on 1-4-2010 | 99,000 | |
    | Balance in Cost ledger Control A/c as on 1-4-2010 | | 1,98,000 |
    | Material purchased (Direct) for cash | | 130,000 |
    | Material purchased (Indirect) for credit | | 70,000 |
    | Indirect material purchased for cash | | 46,000 |
    | Direct material issued to factory | | 94,000 |
    | Indirect material issued to factory | | 33,000 |
    | Material(Direct) returned from factory to stores | | 9,000 |
    | Material (Indirect) returned from factory to stores | | 7,000 |
    | Material returned to suppliers | | 10,000 |
    | Wages and salaries (direct) paid for production department | | 47,000 |

| | |
|---|---|
| Indirect factory wages paid | 35,500 |
| Salary paid for the administrative staff | 75,500 |
| Salary paid for sales department | 60,000 |
| Factory indirect expenses paid | 11,000 |
| Administration overhead paid | 14,000 |
| Selling and distribution overhead paid | 17,500 |
| Factory overhead absorbed | 50,000 |
| Administration overhead absorbed | 95,000 |
| Selling and distribution overhead absorbed | 63,000 |
| Cost of the finished goods during the year | 2,70,000 |
| Cost of goods sold | 2,20,000 |
| Cash sales | 3,00,000 |
| Credit sales | 50,000 |

Journalise the above transactions in the cost books and prepare the necessary ledger accounts for the year ended 31st March 2011.

(Ans: Costing profit Rs.43,000; Balance (debit) Rs.80,000; Rs.71,000; Rs.54,000; Credit Rs.205,000)

22. MW Ltd provides the following information from the cost records for the year ended 31st March 2011. Prepare necessary accounts in Cost Ledger.

| | Opening Balance Rs. | Closing Balance Rs. |
|---|---|---|
| Work-in-progress Ledger Control A/c | 21,000 | 30,500 |
| Stores Ledger Control A/c | 23,700 | 26,900 |
| Finished Goods Ledger Controls A/c | 32,500 | 39,700 |

| Transactions for the year are as follows: | Rs. |
|---|---|
| Matcrial purchased | 132,000 |
| Direct wages paid | 64,000 |
| Indirect wages paid for factory | 32,000 |
| Salaries paid to administration staff | 93,000 |
| Salaries paid for the sales department | 78,000 |
| Factory overhead paid | 26,000 |
| Administration overhead paid | 19,900 |
| Selling and distribution overhead paid | 17,400 |
| Factory overhead absorbed to production | 47,500 |
| Administration overhead absorbed | 103,000 |
| Selling and distribution overhead absorbed | 81,000 |
| Sales | 4,00,000 |

(Ans: Proft Rs.54,400; WIP Rs.230,800; Cost of Sales Rs.425,600)

23. The following information are collected from the cost books of M Ltd for the financial year ending 31st March, 2011.

| | Rs. | Rs. |
|---|---|---|
| Balance in Stores Ledger Control A/c as on 1-4-2010 | 75,000 | |
| Balance in Work-in-progress Ledger Control A/c as on 1-4-2010 | 90,000 | |
| Balance in Finished Goods Ledger Control A/c as on 1-4-2010 | 130,000 | |
| Balance in Cost ledger Control A/c as on 1-4-2010 | | 2,95,000 |
| Material purchased (Direct) for cash | | 150,000 |
| Material purchased (Indirect) for credit | | 90,000 |
| Indirect material purchased for cash | | 54,000 |
| Direct material issued to factory | | 143,000 |
| Indirect material issued to factory | | 43,000 |
| Material(Direct) returned from factory to stores | | 7,000 |
| Material (Indirect) returned from factory to stores | | 5,000 |
| Material returned to suppliers | | 9,000 |
| Wages and salaries (direct) paid for production department | | 52,000 |
| Indirect factory wages paid | | 44,500 |
| Salary paid for the administrative staff | | 97,500 |
| Salary paid for sales department | | 87,000 |
| Factory indirect expenses paid | | 19,000 |
| Administration overhead paid | | 21,000 |
| Selling and distribution overhead paid | | 22,500 |
| Factory overhead absorbed | | 90,000 |
| Administration overhead absorbed | | 125,000 |
| Selling and distribution overhead absorbed | | 80,000 |
| Cost of the finished goods during the year | | 3,90,000 |
| Cost of goods sold | | 4,20,000 |
| Cash sales | | 5,00,000 |
| Credit sales | | 85,000 |

Journalise the above transactions in the cost books and prepare the necessary ledger accounts for the year ended 31st March 2011.

(Ans: Costing Proft Rs.65,000; Balances SLC Rs.6,000; WIP Rs.7,000; FGLC Rs.45,000)

24. B Ltd provides the following information from the cost records for the year ended 31st March 2011. Prepare necessary accounts in Cost Ledger.

| | Opening Balance Rs. | Closing Balance Rs. |
|---|---|---|
| Work-in-progress Ledger Control A/c | 54,000 | 60,500 |
| Stores Ledger Control A/c | 67,500 | 71,500 |
| Finished Goods Ledger Controls A/c | 92,500 | 100,000 |

Transactions for the year are as follows:

| | Rs. |
|---|---|
| Material purchased | 147,000 |
| Direct wages paid | 112,000 |
| Indirect wages paid for factory | 55,000 |
| Salaries paid to administration staff | 134,000 |
| Salaries paid for the sales department | 110,000 |
| Factory overhead paid | 47,000 |
| Administration overhead paid | 32,000 |
| Selling and distribution overhead paid | 25,000 |
| Factory overhead absorbed to production | 139,000 |
| Administration overhead absorbed | 134,000 |
| Selling and distribution overhead absorbed | 122,000 |
| Sales | 5,90,000 |

[Ans: Costing profit Rs.4,000; Rs.357,500; Cost of sales Rs.519,000; OH Supense A/c Rs.3,000 (dt.)]

25. N Ltd. provides the following transactions from the cost books for the month December 2011. The total wages and salaries after deducting the Employers Provident Fund, Income Tax, State Insurance for the month amounted to Rs.291,000.

The total wages and salaries were paid in the following form:

| | |
|---|---|
| Direct wages | Rs. 90,000 |
| Direct factory wages | Rs. 60,000 |
| Salaries for the Administration Department | Rs. 75,500 |
| Salaries for the Sales Department | Rs. 65,500 |

Pass journal entries.

26. Journalise the following transactions in the books of C Ltd. for the month October 2011

| | |
|---|---|
| 1. Indirect material issued to the Factory | Rs. 37,500 |
| 2. Indirect material issued to the Sales Department | Rs. 17,500 |
| 3. Administration Overhead paid | Rs. 44,000 |
| 4. Factory Overhead paid | Rs. 42,000 |
| 5. Selling and Distribution Overhead paid | Rs. 33,000 |
| 6. Indirect Wages allocated to Factory | Rs. 29,500 |
| 7. Salaries & Wages allocated to Administrative staff | Rs. 55,000 |

# CHAPTER - X

# INTEGRATED ACCOUNTING SYSTEM

It is compulsory for business units to prepare Profit and Loss Account and Balance Sheet according to Companies Act 1956. Big business units are also preparing cost accounts though it is not compulsory according to any Act. These companies are maintaining separate set of books or one set of book for recording the financial transactions and cost transactions. If separate set of books are maintained, it is called non-integrated accounting system. If one set of book is maintained for both financial transactions and cost transactions, it is called Integrated Accounting System. The accounts in this system are called Integrated Accounts.

**Meaning and Definition**

The Institute of Chartered Accountants of India defined Integrated Accounts as, a single system of double entry book-keeping, which combines both cost and financial accounts. This system provides full information regarding cost as well as financial accounting. It provides details of the total cost of each job, standard cost, variance, marginal cost, abnormal losses and gain, in addition to Profit and Loss account and the Balance Sheet.

**Advantages:**

1. Integrated Accounts eliminate the need for reconciling Cost Accounts with Financial Accounts. Under integrated accounts there is no need for reconciliation since only one Profit and Loss account is prepared.
2. Duplication of work is avoided in the system of accounting. It will reduce the cost of clerical work.
3. This system enables a check on the correctness of the cost as well as financial data.
4. This system provides full accounting information to the management and to the management accountant.
5. It facilitates for the adoption of mechanised accounting.
6. Reports to management and the outsiders can be easily prepared since all the accounting information are available in one set of books.

**Principles involved in the Integrated Accounting system**

The basic principles of the Integrated Accounting system are outlined as follows.

**1. Degree of Integration**

The company should first of all decide about the degree of integration. Some business establishments may integrate the accounts upto the stage of prime cost or factory cost. But most of the business concerns prefer to integrate the cost accounts and financial accounts completely.

**2. Control Accounts.**

In addition to the financial records the following Cost Control Accounts should be maintained keeping in view of the degree of integration.

1. Stores Ledger Control Account.
2. Wages Ledger Control Account.
3. Factory Overhead Control Account.
4. Administration Overhead Control Account.
5. Selling and Distribution Overhead Control Account.
6. Work-in-progress Ledger Control Account.
7. Finished Goods Ledger Control Account.

Cost Ledger Account or General Ledger Adjustment account is replaced by other Financial Ledger Accounts like

1. Sundry Debtors Account or Bought Ledger Control Account or Total Debtors Account.
2. Sundry Creditors Account or Sales Ledger Control Account or Total Creditors Account.
3. Assets Account (Individual Assets Account should be opened.)
4. Outstanding Expenses Account and Outstanding Income Accounts.
5. Expenses paid in Advance Account and Income received in Advance Accounts.
6. Share Capital and Reserve Accounts.

**3. Third Entry Method**

Third Entry is not a part of the double entry system of book keeping. It is an explanatory in the Integrated Accounting system. Cost Ledger Account should be used in this regard. The Cost Ledger Control Account should be debited or credited depending upon the nature of the transaction. For example, when any expenditure relating to cost is incurred this account should be debited besides the usual debit and credit. The total cost shown in this account should be analysed with the items in the Store Ledger, Factory Overhead, Administration Overhead and Selling and Distribution Overhead Control Accounts. The credit in this ledger should be done with the Finished Goods Ledger Control Account and Profit and Loss Account.

**Examples**

1. Factory Overhead paid Rs. 2,000

The journal entry is

| | | |
|---|---|---|
| Factory Overhead Control A/c | Dr. 2,000 | |
| To Cost Ledger Control A/c | | 2,000 |

2. Wages paid Rs. 4,000

The journal entry is

| | | |
|---|---|---|
| Wages Ledger Control A/c | Dr. 4,000 | |
| To Cost Ledger Control A/c | | 4,000 |

## Distinction between Interlocking and Integration of Accounting system

If separate sets of books are maintained for recording the Costing and Financial transactions, then these two books, should be "interlocked" by maintaining Control Accounts. Both in the Cost Ledger and Financial Ledger, the Control Accounts should be operated. It may be called Cost Ledger Control Account or Financial Ledger Control Account or General Ledger Adjustment Account. In order to complete the double entry, without using the Ledger Accounts of Cost in Financial Books and Ledger Accounts of Financial in Cost Books, this Control Accounts should be used. But Integration is entirely different concept. Both Financial Books and Cost Books are combined together and only one set of book is maintained which will provide the information of both cost and financial nature. In this system, the Cost Ledger Control Account is totally eliminated.

## Journal Entries

In Non-integrated system of accounting separate set of journal entries are recorded for Financial accounts and Cost accounts. Some transactions are of purly financial nature which will be recorded only in Financial account.(Eg.) Purchase of fixed assets, Interest received,etc. Some transactions are of purely costing nature which will be recorded only in Cost account. (Eg.) Direct material issued to factory,Factory overhead absorbed,etc. Most of the transactions are of financial and cost nature which are to be recorded in Financial and Cost accounts.(Eg.) Purchase of material,Wages paid, Sale of goods,etc.

But in Integrated accounting system, the cost accounts and financial accounts are integrated and one set of account is maintained. Usual method of passing journal entires should be done. But the Cost Ledger Control account should not be maintained. Instead of that (This account is maintained in non-integrated accounting system to record the financial aspect of the transactions) the respective financial accounts should be debited or credited.

(Eg.) Purchase of material Rs. 50,000 is recorded as

| | | | |
|---|---|---|---|
| Stores Ledger Control A/c | Dr. | 50,000 | |
| To Cash A/c | | | 50,000 |

In non-integrated account system it is recorded as

| | | | |
|---|---|---|---|
| Store Ledge Control A/c | Dr. | 50,000 | |
| To Cost Ledger Control A/c | | | 50,000 |

The journal entries in Non-integrated accounting system and Integrated accounting systems are separately stated as follows.

### 1. Non-Integrated System

| Sl. No. | Particulars | Non-Integrated system | |
|---|---|---|---|
| | | Financial Books | Cost Books |
| 1. | Material purchased for cash | Purchase A/c Dr.<br>To Cash A/c | Stores Ledger Control A/c Dr.<br>To Cost Ledger Contl.A/c |
| 2. | Material purchased on credit | Purchase A/c Dr.<br>To Creditors A/c | Stores Ledger Control A/c Dr.<br>To Cost Ledger Control A/c |
| 3. | Material purchased for Specific job for cash | Purchase A/c Dr.<br>To Cash | Work-in-Progress Ledger Control A/c Dr.<br>To Cost Ledger Control A/c |
| 4. | Material purchased for specific job on credit | Purchase A/c Dr.<br>To Creditors A/c | Work-in-progress Ledger Control A/c Dr.<br>To Cost Ledger Control A/c |
| 5. | Direct material Issued to production centre | No entry | Work-in-progress Ledger Control A/c Dr.<br>To Stores Ledger Control A/c |
| 6. | Indirect material issued to production centre | No entry | Factory Overhead Control A/c Dr.<br>To Stores Ledger Control A/c |
| 7. | Indirect material issued to To Administration | No entry | Administration Overhead Control A/c Dr.<br>To Stores Ledger Control A/c |
| 8. | Indirect material issued to Selling and Distribution | No entry | Selling and Distribution Overhead Control A/c Dr.<br>To Stores Ledger Control A/c |
| 9. | Material returned to Supplier | Creditors A/c Dr.<br>To Purchases A/c | Cost Ledger Control A/c Dr.<br>To Stores Ledger Control A/c |
| 10. | Direct material returned from production centre to store | No entry | Stores Ledger Control A/c Dr.<br>To Work-in-progress Ledger Control A/c |

| Sl. No. | Particulars | Non-Integrated system | |
|---|---|---|---|
| | | Financial Books | Cost Books |
| 11. | Indirect material returned to store | No entry | Stores Ledger Control A/c Dr.<br>To Respective Overhead Control A/c |
| 12. | Material transferred from one job to another job | No entry | Transferee job A/c Dr.<br>To Transfer job A/c |
| 13. | Total wages and salaries paid | Wages & Salaries A/c Dr.<br>To Cash A/c | Wages Ledger Control A/c Dr.<br>To Cost Ledger Control A/c |
| 14. | Direct wages allocated to production | No entry | Work-in-progress Ledger Control A/c Dr.<br>To Wages Ledger Control A/c |
| 15. | Indirect wages allocated to production | No entry | Factory Overhead Control A/c Dr.<br>To Wages Ledger Control A/c |
| 16. | Indirect wages allocated to Administration Department | No entry | Administration Overhead Control A/c Dr.<br>To Wages Ledger Control A/c |
| 17. | Indirect wages allocated To Selling and Distribution Dept. | No entry | Selling and Distribution Overhead Control A/c Dr.<br>To Wages Ledger Control A/c |
| 18. | Direct expenses paid | Expenses A/c Dr.<br>To Cash A/c | Work-in-progress Ledger Control A/c Dr.<br>To Cost Ledger Control A/c |
| 19. | Factory overhead paid | Factory expenses A/c Dr.<br>To Cash A/c | Factory Overhead Control A/c Dr.<br>To Cost Ledger Control A/c |
| 20. | Administration overhead paid | Administration expenses A/c Dr.<br>To Cash A/c | Administration Overhead Control A/c Dr.<br>To Cost Ledger Control A/c |
| 21. | Selling and Distribution overhead paid | Sales expenses A/c Dr.<br>To Cash A/c | Selling and Distribution Overhead Control A/c Dr.<br>To Cost Ledger Control A/c |
| 22. | Factory overhead absorbed | No entry | Work-in-progress Ledger Control A/c Dr.<br>To Factory Overhead Control A/c |
| 23. | Administration overhead absorbed | No entry | Finished Goods Ledger Control A/c Dr.<br>To Administration Overhead Control A/c |

| Sl. No. | Particulars | Non-Integrated system | |
|---|---|---|---|
| | | Financial Books | Cost Books |
| 24. | Selling and Distribution overhead absorbed | No entry | Cost of Sales A/c Dr.<br>To Selling and Distribution Overhead Control A/c |
| 25. | Under- absorption of overhead | No entry | Costing Profit & loss A/c Dr.<br>To Respective Overhead Control A/c |
| 26. | Over-absorption of overheads | No entry | Respective Overhead Control A/c Dr.<br>ToCosting Profit & Loss A/c |
| 27. | Total Finished Goods during the year | No entry | Finished Goods Ledger Control A/c Dr.<br>To Work-in-progress Ledger Control A/c |
| 28. | Cost of Goods Sold | No entry | Cost of Sales A/c Dr.<br>To Finished Goods Ledger Control A/c |
| 29. | Cost of Sales | No entry | Sales A/c Dr.<br>To Cost of Sales A/c |
| 30. | Cash Sales | Cash A/c Dr.<br>To Sales A/c | Cost Ledger Control A/c Dr.<br>To Sales A/c |
| 31. | Credit Sales | Debtors A/c Dr.<br>To Sales A/c | Cost Ledger Control A/c Dr.<br>To Sales A/c |
| 32. | Credit Balance in Costing Profit & Loss A/c | No entry | Costing Profit & Loss A/c Dr.<br>To Cost Ledger Control A/c |
| 33. | Debit Balance in Costing Profit & Loss A/c | No entry | Cost Ledger Control A/c Dr.<br>To Costing Profit & Loss A/c |
| 34. | Purchase of Fixed Assets | Fixed Assets A/c Dr.<br>To Cash A/c | No entry |
| 35. | Rent paid | Rent A/c Dr.<br>To Cash A/c | No entry |
| 36. | Interest Received | Cash A/c Dr.<br>To Interest A/c | No entry |
| 37. | Profit or Loss on Sales | No entry | Sales A/c Dr.<br>To Costing Profit& Loss A/c (For Profit); (or)<br>Costing Profit & Loss A/c Dr.<br>To Sales A/c (For Loss ) |

## 2. Integrated Accounting system

| Sl. No. | Particulars | Integrated system |
|---|---|---|
| 1. | Material purchased for cash | Stores Ledger Control A/c Dr.<br>To Cash A/c |
| 2. | Material purchased on credit | Stores Ledger Control A/c Dr.<br>To Creditors A/c |
| 3. | Material purchased for specific job for cash | Work-in-Progress Ledger Control A/c Dr.<br>To Cash A/c |
| 4. | Material purchased for specific job on credit | Work-in-progress Ledger Control A/c Dr.<br>To Creditors A/c |
| 5. | Direct material issued to production centre | Work-in-progress Ledger Control A/c Dr.<br>To Stores Ledger Control A/c |
| 6. | Indirect material issued to production centre | Factory Overhead Control A/c Dr.<br>To Stores Ledger Control A/c |
| 7. | Indirect material issued to Administration | Administration Overhead Control A/c Dr.<br>To Stores Ledger Control A/c |
| 8. | Indirect material issued to Selling & Distribution | Selling & Distribution Overhead Control A/c Dr.<br>To Stores Ledger Control A/c |
| 9. | Material returned to Supplier | Creditors A/c Dr.<br>To Stores Ledger Control A/c |
| 10. | Direct material returned from production centre to store | Stores Ledger Control A/c Dr.<br>To Work-in-progress Ledger Control A/c |
| 11. | Indirect material returned to store | Stores Ledger Control A/c Dr.<br>To Respective Overhead Control A/c |
| 12. | Material transferred from one job to another job | Transferee job A/c Dr.<br>To Transfer job A/c |
| 13. | Total Wages and Salaries paid | Wages Ledger Control A/c Dr.<br>To Cash A/c |
| 14. | Direct wages allocated to production | Work-in-progress Ledger Control A/c Dr.<br>To Wages Ledger Control A/c |
| 15. | Indirect wages allocated to production | Factory Overhead Control A/c Dr.<br>To Wages Ledger Control A/c |
| 16. | Indirect wages allocated to Administration Department | Administration Overhead Control A/c Dr.<br>To Wages Ledger Control A/c |
| 17. | Indirect wages allocated to Selling and Distribution Dept. | Selling and Distribution Overhead Control A/c Dr.<br>To Wages Ledger Control A/c |

| Sl. No. | Particulars | Integrated system |
|---|---|---|
| 18. | Direct expenses paid | Work-in-progress Ledger Control A/c Dr.<br>To Cash A/c |
| 19. | Factory overhead paid | Factory Overhead Control A/c Dr.<br>To Cash A/c |
| 20. | Administration overhead paid | Administration Overhead Control A/c Dr.<br>To Cash A/c |
| 21. | Selling and distribution overhead paid | Selling and Distribution Overhead Control A/c Dr.<br>To Cash A/c |
| 22. | Factory overhead absorbed | Work-in-progress Ledger Control A/c Dr.<br>To Factory Overhead Control A/c |
| 23. | Administration overhead absorbed. | Finished Goods Ledger Control A/c Dr.<br>To Admin. Overhead Control A/c |
| 24. | Selling and Distribution overhead absorbed | Cost of sales A/c Dr.<br>To Selling and Distribution Overhead Control A/c |
| 25. | Under- absorption of overhead | Profit & Loss A/c Dr.<br>To Respective Overhead Control A/c |
| 26. | Over-absorption of overheads | Respective Overhead Control A/c Dr.<br>To Profit & Loss A/c |
| 27. | Total Finished Goods during the year | Finished Goods Ledger Control A/c Dr.<br>To Work-in-progress Ledger Cont. A/c |
| 28. | Cost of Goods Sold | Finished Goods Ledger Control Dr.<br>To Cost of Sales A/c |
| 29. | Cost of Sales | Sales A/c Dr. To Cost of Sales A/c |
| 30. | Cash Sales | Cash A/c Dr. To Sales A/c |
| 31. | Credit Sales | Debtors A/c Dr. To Sales A/c |
| 32. | Credit Balance in Costing Profit & Loss A/c | No entry |
| 33. | Debit Balance in Costing Profit & Loss A/c | No entry |
| 34. | Purchase of Fixed Assets | Fixed Assets A/c Dr.<br>To Cash A/c |
| 35. | Rent paid | Rent A/c Dr.<br>To Cash A/c |
| 36. | Interest received | Cash A/c Dr.<br>To Interest A/c |
| 37. | Profit or Loss on Sales | Sales A/c (For profit) Dr.<br>To Profit & Loss A/c<br>Profit & Loss A/c Dr.<br>To Sales A/c (For loss) |

**Illustration: 1**

Journalise the following transactions in the Integrated Ledger Accounts of K Ltd.

| | Rs. |
|---|---|
| Material purchased for cash | 19,750 |
| Material purchased on credit | 21,500 |
| Wages paid | 17,750 |
| Productive wages | 10,000 |
| Unproductive wages | 7,750 |
| Material (Direct) issued to factory | 25,000 |
| Indirect material issued to factory | 3,000 |
| Factory overhead paid | 9,250 |
| Administration overhead paid | 6,500 |
| Selling and Distribution overhead paid | 4,250 |
| Factory overhead absorbed to production | 18,000 |
| Administration overhead absorbed | 4,000 |
| Selling and Distribution overhead absorbed | 5,000 |
| Finished Goods during the period | 45,000 |
| Cash sales | 34,000 |
| Credit sales | 37,000 |

***Solution:***

**Journal Entries in the Book of K Ltd.**

| Particulars | | Dr. (Rs.) | Cr. (Rs.) |
|---|---|---|---|
| Stores Ledger Control A/c | Dr. | 41,250 | |
| To Cash A/c | | | 19,750 |
| ,, Creditors A/c | | | 21,500 |
| (Being the purchase of material) | | | |
| Wage Ledger Control A/c | Dr. | 17,750 | |
| To Cash | | | 17,750 |
| (Being wages paid) | | | |
| Work-in-progress Ledger Control A/c | Dr. | 10,000 | |
| To Wages Ledger Control A/c | | | 10,000 |
| (Being direct wages allocated to production) | | | |
| Factory Overhead Control A/c | Dr. | 7,750 | |
| To Wages Ledger Control A/c | | | 7,750 |
| (Being indirect wages allocated to production) | | | |
| Work-in-progress Ledger Control A/c | Dr. | 25,000 | |
| To Stores Ledger Control A/c | | | 25,000 |
| (Being direct material issued to production) | | | |
| Factory Overhead Control A/c | Dr. | 3,000 | |
| To Stores Ledger Control A/c | | | 3,000 |
| (Being indirect material issued to production) | | | |

| Particulars | | Dr. (Rs.) | Cr. (Rs.) |
|---|---|---|---|
| Factory Overhead Control A/c | Dr. | 9,250 | |
| To Cash A/c | | | 9,250 |
| (Being factory overhead paid) | | | |
| Administration Overhead Control A/c | Dr. | 6,500 | |
| To Cash A/c | | | 6,500 |
| (Being administration overhead paid ) | | | |
| Selling and Distri. OH. Control A/c | Dr. | 4,250 | |
| To Cash A/c | | | 4,250 |
| (Being the selling and distri.overhead paid) | | | |
| Work-in-progress Ledger Control A/c | Dr. | 18,000 | |
| To Factory Overhead Control A/c | | | 18,000 |
| (Being factory overhead absorbed) | | | |
| Finished Goods Ledger Control A/c | Dr. | 45,000 | |
| To Work-in-progress Ledger A/c | | | 45,000 |
| (Being finished goods transferred) | | | |
| Finished Goods Ledger Control A/c | Dr. | 4,000 | |
| To Admin. Overhead Control A/c | | | 4,000 |
| (Being the admini. overhead absorbed) | | | |
| Cost of Sales A/c | Dr. | 5,000 | |
| To Selling & Distri. OH Control A/c | | | 5,000 |
| (Being the selling and distri. oh. absorbed) | | | |
| Costing Profit & Loss A/c | Dr. | 4,500 | |
| To Factory overhead control A/c | | | 2,000 |
| ,, Administration overhead control A/c | | | 2,500 |
| (Being underabsorption of oh. debited in P&L A/c) | | | |
| Selling an Dist. OH Control A/c | Dr. | 750 | |
| To Costing Profit & Loss A/c | | | 750 |
| (Being over absor. of oh. credited in P & L a/c) | | | |
| Cost of Sales A/c | Dr. | 49,000 | |
| To Finished Goods Ledger Control A/c | | | 49,000 |
| (Being the total finished goods for the period transferred to Cost of Sales A/c) | | | |
| Sales A/c | Dr. | 54,000 | |
| To Cost of Sales A/c | | | 54,000 |
| (Being Cost of Sales transferred to Sales a/c) | | | |
| Cash A/c | Dr. | 34,000 | |
| Debtors A/c | Dr. | 37,000 | |
| To Sales A/c | | | 71,000 |
| (Being goods sold for cash and credit) | | | |
| Sales A/c | Dr. | 17,000 | |
| To Costing Profit & Loss A/c | | | 17,000 |
| (Being profit on sales credited in P & L A/c) | | | |

**Illustration: 2**

Following are the opening balances of DLtd in the Integrated Ledger Accounts.

| | Dr. Rs. | Cr. Rs. |
|---|---|---|
| Stores Ledger Control A/c | 71,200 | |
| Work-in-progress Ledger Control A/c | 42,800 | |
| Finished goods Ledger Control A/c | 69,500 | |
| Bank A/c | 21,000 | |
| Cash A/c | 11,000 | |
| Debtors A/c | 28,500 | |
| Land & Buildings A/c | 230,000 | |
| Plant & Machinery A/c | 470,000 | |
| Provision for depreciation of Plant & Machinery A/c | | 78,000 |
| Creditors A/c | | 92,000 |
| Share Capital A/c | | 700,000 |
| Reserves and Surplus A/c | | 74,000 |
| | 944,000 | 944,000 |

The transactions during the year are as follows:

| | Rs. |
|---|---|
| Material purchased for credit | 179,000 |
| Material issued to production | 187,000 |
| Material issued to maintenance department in production | 21,000 |
| Material (direct) returned from production | 5,750 |
| Material returned to suppliers | 11,750 |
| Carriage inwards | 7,250 |
| Carriage outwards | 12,500 |
| Production wages paid | 117,250 |
| Production salaries and indirect wages | 37,500 |
| Administration salaries | 77,750 |
| Salaries paid for sales department | 62,500 |
| Accrued wages and salaries at the end of the year | 12,250 |
| Production (indirect) expenses paid by cheque | 19,500 |
| Administration overhead paid by cheque | 15,250 |
| Selling indirect expenses paid by cheque | 10,200 |
| Distribution expenses paid by cheque | 6,800 |
| Payment to trade creditors by cheque | 198,000 |
| Cheques received from trade debtors | 210,000 |
| Discount allowed | 9,850 |

| | |
|---|---|
| Discount received | 27,750 |
| Factory overhead absorbed | 87,000 |
| Administration overhead absorbed | 91,500 |
| Selling and Distribution overhead absorbed | 95,000 |
| Provision for depreciation on plant & machinery | 42,000 |
| Provision for bad and doubtful debts | 25,000 |
| Bad Debts written off | 11,000 |
| Finished goods during the year | 390,000 |
| Cost of goods sold for the year | 480,000 |
| Cash Sales | 370,000 |
| Credit Sales | 300,000 |

Prepare the necessary ledger accounts in the Integrated Books for the year ending 31st March 2011.

***Solution:***

**Integrated Ledger Accounts**

**STORES LEDGER CONTROL A/c**

| Particulars | Rs. | Particulars | Rs. |
|---|---|---|---|
| To Balance b/d | 71,200 | By Work-in-progress Ledger Control A/c | 187,000 |
| To Creditors | 179,000 | By Factory Overhead Control A/c | 21,000 |
| To Work-in-progress Ledger Control A/c | 5,750 | By Creditors A/c | 11,750 |
| | | By Balance c/d | 36,200 |
| | 255,950 | | 255,950 |

**WAGES LEDGER CONTROL A/c**

| Particulars | Rs. | Particulars | Rs. |
|---|---|---|---|
| To Cash | 2,82,750 | By Work-in-progress Ledger Control A/c | 1,17,250 |
| To Wages outstanding | 12,250 | By Factory Overhead Control A/c | 37,500 |
| | | By Administration Overhead Control A/c | 77,750 |
| | | By Selling and Distribution Overhead Control A/c | 62,500 |
| | 2,95,000 | | 2,95,000 |

## FACTORY OVERHEAD CONTROL A/c

| Particulars | Rs. | Particulars | Rs. |
|---|---|---|---|
| To Stores Ledger Control A/c | 21,000 | By Work-in-progress Ledger Control A/c | 87,000 |
| To Carriage Inwards A/c | 7,250 | | |
| To Wages Ledger Control A/c | 37,500 | | |
| To Bank A/c | 19,500 | | |
| To Overhead Suspense A/c | 1,750 | | |
| | 87,000 | | 87,000 |

## ADMINISTRATION OVERHEAD CONTROL A/c

| Particulars | Rs. | Particulars | Rs. |
|---|---|---|---|
| To Wages Ledger Control A/c | 77,750 | By Finished goods Ledger Control A/c | 91,500 |
| To Bank A/c | 15,250 | By Overhead Suspense A/c | 1,500 |
| | 93,000 | | 93,000 |

## SELLING AND DISTRIBUTION OVERHEAD CONTROL A/c

| Particulars | Rs. | Particulars | Rs. |
|---|---|---|---|
| To Wages Ledger Control A/c | 62,500 | By Cost of Sales A/c | 95,000 |
| To Carriage Outwards A/c | 12,500 | | |
| To Bank A/c | 17,000 | | |
| To Overhead Suspense A/c | 3,000 | | |
| | 95,000 | | 95,000 |

## WORK-IN-PROGRESS LEDGER CONTROL A/c

| Particulars | Rs. | Particulars | Rs. |
|---|---|---|---|
| To Balance b/d | 42,800 | By Stores Ledger Control A/c | 5,750 |
| To Stores Ledger Control A/c | 187,000 | By Finished Goods Ledger Control A/c | 390,000 |
| To Wages Ledger Control A/c | 117,250 | By Balance c/d | 38,300 |
| To Factory Overhead Control A/c | 87,000 | | |
| | 434,050 | | 434,050 |

## FINISHED GOODS LEDGER CONTROL A/c

| Particulars | Rs. | Particulars | Rs. |
|---|---|---|---|
| To Balance b/d | 69,500 | By Cost of Sales A/c | 480,000 |
| To Work-in-progress Ledger Control A/c | 390,000 | By Balance c/d | 71,000 |
| To Administration Overhead Control A/c | 91,500 | | |
| | 551,000 | | 551,000 |

## COST OF SALES A/c

| Particulars | Rs. | Particulars | Rs. |
|---|---|---|---|
| To Finished Goods Ledger Control A/c | 4,80,000 | By Sales A/c | 575,000 |
| To Selling and Distribution Overhead Control A/c | 95,000 | | |
| | 575,000 | | 575,000 |

## SALES A/c

| Particulars | Rs. | Particulars | Rs. |
|---|---|---|---|
| To Cost of Sales A/c | 5,75,000 | By Cash A/c | 3,70,000 |
| To Profit & Loss A/c | 95,000 | By Debtors A/c | 3,00,000 |
| | 6,70,000 | | 6,70,000 |

**OVERHEAD SUSPENSE A/c**

| Particulars | Rs. | Particulars | Rs. |
|---|---|---|---|
| To Administration Overhead Control A/c | 1,500 | By Factory Overhead Control A/c | 1,750 |
| To Profit & Loss A/c | 3,250 | By Selling and Distribution Overhead Control A/c | 3,000 |
| | 4,750 | | 4,750 |

**DEBTORS A/c**

| Particulars | Rs. | Particulars | Rs. |
|---|---|---|---|
| To Balance b/d | 28,500 | By Bank A/c | 210,000 |
| To Sales A/c | 300,000 | By Bad Debts written off A/c | 11,000 |
| | | By Discount allowed A/c | 9,850 |
| | | By Balance c/d | 97,650 |
| | 328,500 | | 328,500 |

**CREDITORS A/c**

| Particulars | Rs. | Particulars | Rs. |
|---|---|---|---|
| To Bank A/c | 198,000 | By Balance b/d | 92,000 |
| To Stores Ledger Control A/c | 11,750 | By Stores Ledger Control A/c | 179,000 |
| To Discount received A/c | 27,750 | | |
| To Balance c/d | 33,500 | | |
| | 271,000 | | 271,000 |

**CASH A/c**

| Particulars | Rs. | Particulars | Rs. |
|---|---|---|---|
| To Balance b/d | 11,000 | By Carriage inwards A/c | 7,250 |
| To Sales A/c | 370,000 | By Carriage outwards A/c | 12,500 |
| | | By Wages Ledger Control A/c | 2,82,750 |
| | | By Balance c/d | 78,500 |
| | 381,000 | | 381,000 |

**BANK A/c**

| Particulars | Rs. | Particulars | Rs. |
|---|---|---|---|
| To Balance b/d | 21,000 | By Factory Overhead Control A/c | 19,500 |
| To Debtors A/c | 210,000 | By Administration Overhead Control A/c | 15,250 |
| To Balance c/d (Overdraft) | 18,750 | By Selling and Distribution Overhead Control A/c | 17,000 |
| | | By Creditors A/c | 198,000 |
| | 249,750 | | 249,750 |

**CARRIAGE INWARDS A/c**

| | | | |
|---|---|---|---|
| To Cash A/c | 7,250 | By Factory Overhead Control A/c | 7,250 |

**CARRIAGE OUTWARDS A/c**

| | | | |
|---|---|---|---|
| To Cash A/c | 12,500 | By Selling and Distribution Overhead Control A/c | 12,500 |

**DISCOUNT ALLOWED A/c**

| | | | |
|---|---|---|---|
| To Debtors A/c | 9,850 | By Profit & Loss A/c | 9,850 |

**DISCOUNT RECEIVED A/c**

| | | | |
|---|---|---|---|
| To Profit & Loss A/c | 27,750 | By Creditors A/c | 27,750 |

**WAGES OUTSTANDING A/c**

| | | | |
|---|---|---|---|
| To Balance c/d | 12,250 | By Wage Ledger Control A/c | 12.250 |

**PROVISION FOR BAD AND DOUBTFUL DEBTS A/c**

| | | | |
|---|---|---|---|
| To Balance c/d | 25,000 | By Profit & Loss A/c | 25,000 |

**PROVISION FOR DEPRECIATION ON PLANT AND MACHINERY A/c**

| | | | |
|---|---|---|---|
| To Balance c/d | 120,000 | By Balance b/d | 78,000 |
| | | By Profit & Loss A/c | 42,000 |
| | 120,000 | | 120,000 |

**PLANT AND MACHINERY A/c**

| | | | |
|---|---|---|---|
| To Balance b/d | 470,000 | By Balance c/d | 470,000 |

## SHARE CAPITAL A/c

| | | | |
|---|---|---|---|
| To Balance c/d | 700,000 | By Balance b/d | 700,000 |

## RESERVES AND SURPLUS A/c

| | | | |
|---|---|---|---|
| To Balance c/d | 112,150 | By Balance b/d | 74,000 |
| | | By Profit & Loss A/c | 38,150 |
| | 112,150 | | 112,150 |

## PROFIT AND LOSS A/c

| Particulars | Rs. | Particulars | Rs. |
|---|---|---|---|
| To Discount allowed A/c | 9,850 | By Sales A/c | 95,000 |
| To Bad Debts written off | 11,000 | By Overhead Suspense A/c | 3,250 |
| To Provision for Bad Debts | 25,000 | | |
| To Provision for Depreciation A/c | 42,000 | By Discount received A/c | 27,750 |
| To Reserve & Surplus A/c | 38,150 | | |
| | 1,26,000 | | 1,26,000 |

## BALANCE SHEET
### for the year ended 31st March 2011

| Liabilities | Rs. | Assets | | Rs. |
|---|---|---|---|---|
| Share Capital | 7,00,000 | Land and Building | | 2,30,000 |
| Reserve and Surplus | 1,12,150 | | | |
| Creditors | 33,500 | Plant and | | |
| Wages outstanding | 12,250 | Machinary - | 4,70,000 | |
| Bank overdraft | 18,750 | Less: Provision for | | |
| | | Depreciation | 1,20,000 | 3,50,000 |
| | | Cash | | 78,500 |
| | | Debtors | 97,650 | |
| | | Less: Provision | 25,000 | 72,650 |
| | | Finished goods | | 71,000 |
| | | Work-in-progress | | 38,300 |
| | | Stores | | 36,200 |
| | 8,76,650 | | | 8,76,650 |

**Illustration: 3**

Prepare integrated ledger accounts and Balance Sheet from the following information related to the year ending 31st March 2011 of MLtd.

**Balances as on 31st March 2010**

| Particulars | Rs. | Rs. |
|---|---|---|
| Share Capital | | 4,00,000 |
| Profit &loss A/c | | 92,000 |
| Stores Ledger Control A/c | 22,000 | |
| Work-in-Progress A/c | 15,500 | |
| Finished Goods Control A/c | 20,000 | |
| Plant & Machinery A/c | 1,80,000 | |
| Land & Building A/c | 2,50,000 | |
| Cash A/c | 13,500 | |
| Debtors A/c | 8,000 | |
| Creditors A/c | | 17,000 |
| | 5,09,000 | 5,09,000 |

Transactions during the year are as follows:

| | Rs. |
|---|---|
| Material purchased (40% credit purchase) | 60,000 |
| Material issued to factory | 49,000 |
| Indirect material issued to factory | 14,000 |
| Stationary issued to office from store | 4,000 |
| Direct wages paid | 43,000 |
| Direct expenses paid | 10,000 |
| Indirect wages paid for factory | 17,000 |
| Salary paid to administration department | 56,000 |
| Salary paid to selling department | 42,000 |
| Factory overhead paid | 11,000 |
| Administration expenses | 14,000 |
| Selling expenses | 15,000 |
| Income Tax paid | 22,000 |
| Value of finished goods during the year | 1,32,000 |
| Cost of goods sold | 2,00,000 |
| Cash sales | 2,10,000 |
| Credit sales | 1,20,000 |
| Cash received from debtors | 1,05,000 |
| Cash paid to creditors | 30,000 |
| Rent received | 25,000 |
| Purchase of machinery on 1st January 2011 | 20,000 |

Provision for depreciation on Plant & Machinery is 10% per annum.

***Solution:***

## Integrated Ledger Accounts of M Ltd. for the year ended 31st March 2011

### Stores Ledger Control A/c

| Particulars | Rs. | Particulars | Rs. |
|---|---|---|---|
| To Balance b/d | 22,000 | By Work-in-progress Ledger Control A/c | 49,000 |
| To Cash A/c | 36,000 | By Factory Overhead A/c | 14,000 |
| To Creditor Control A/c | 24,000 | By Administration Overhead Control A/c | 4,000 |
| | | By Balance c/d | 15,000 |
| | 82,000 | | 82,000 |

### Wages Ledger Control A/c

| Particulars | Rs. | Particulars | Rs. |
|---|---|---|---|
| To Cash A/c | 1,58,000 | By Work-in-progress L.C.A/c | 43,000 |
| | | By Factory Overhead A/c | 17,000 |
| | | By Administration Overhead A/c | 56,000 |
| | | By Selling and Distribution Overhead A/c | 42,000 |
| | 1,58,000 | | 1,58,000 |

### Factory Overhead Control A/c

| Particulars | Rs. | Particulars | Rs. |
|---|---|---|---|
| To Stores Ledger Control A/c | 14,000 | By Work-in-progress A/c | 42,000 |
| To Wages Ledger Control A/c | 17,000 | | |
| To Cash A/c | 11,000 | | |
| | 42,000 | | 42,000 |

### Selling & Distribution Overhead Control A/c

| Particulars | Rs. | Particulars | Rs. |
|---|---|---|---|
| To Wages Ledger Control A/c | 42,000 | By Cost of Sales A/c | 57,000 |
| To Cash A/c | 15,000 | | |
| | 57,000 | | 57,000 |

**Administration Overhead Control A/c**

| Particulars | Rs. | Particulars | Rs. |
|---|---|---|---|
| To Stores Ledger Control A/c | 4,000 | By Finished Goods Ledger Control A/c | 74,000 |
| To Wages Ledger Control A/c | 56,000 | | |
| To Cash A/c | 14,000 | | |
| | 74,000 | | 74,000 |

**Work-in-progress Ledger Control A/c**

| Particulars | Rs. | Particulars | Rs. |
|---|---|---|---|
| To Balance b/d | 15,500 | By Finished Goods Ledger Control A/c | 132,000 |
| To Stores Ledger Control A/c | 49,000 | | |
| To Wage Ledger Control A/c | 43,000 | | |
| To Factory Overhead Control A/c | 42,000 | By Balance c/d | 27,500 |
| To Cash A/c | 10,000 | | |
| | 159,500 | | 159,500 |

**Finished Goods Ledger Control A/c**

| Particulars | Rs. | Particulars | Rs. |
|---|---|---|---|
| To Balance b/d | 20,000 | By Cost of Sales A/c | 200,000 |
| To Work-in-progress Ledger Control A/c | 132,000 | By Balance c/d | 26,000 |
| To Administration Overhead Control A/c | 74,000 | | |
| | 226,000 | | 226,000 |

**Cost of Sales A/c**

| Particulars | Rs. | Particulars | Rs. |
|---|---|---|---|
| To Finished Goods Ledger Control A/c | 200,000 | By Sales A/c | 2,57,000 |
| To Selling & Distribution Overhead Control A/c | 57,000 | | |
| | 2,57,000 | | 2,57,000 |

**Sales A/c**

| Particulars | Rs. | Particulars | Rs. |
|---|---|---|---|
| To Cost of Sales A/c | 2,57,000 | By Cash A/c | 2,10,000 |
| ,, Costing Profit & Loss A/c | 73,000 | ,, Debtors Ledger Control A/c | 1,20,000 |
| | 3,30,000 | | 3,30,000 |

**Land and Buildings A/c**

| Particulars | Rs. | Particulars | Rs. |
|---|---|---|---|
| To Balance b/d | 2,50,000 | By Balance c/d | 2,50,000 |

**Debtors Control A/c**

| Particulars | Rs. | Particulars | Rs. |
|---|---|---|---|
| To Balance b/d | 8,000 | By Cash A/c | 105,000 |
| To Cost of Sales A/c | 120,000 | By Balance c/d | 23,000 |
| | 128,000 | | 128,000 |

**Creditors Control A/c**

| Particulars | Rs. | Particulars | Rs. |
|---|---|---|---|
| To Cash A/c | 30,000 | By Balance b/d | 17,000 |
| To Balance c/d | 11,000 | By Stores Ledger Control A/c | 24,000 |
| | 41,000 | | 41,000 |

**Plant & Machinery A/c**

| Particulars | Rs. | Particulars | Rs. |
|---|---|---|---|
| To Balance b/d | 180,000 | By Provision for Depreciation (18000+20000x10/100x3/12) | 18,500 |
| To Cash A/c | 20,000 | By Balance c/d | 181,500 |
| | 200,000 | | 200,000 |

**Provision for Depreciation A/c**

| Particulars | Rs. | Particulars | Rs. |
|---|---|---|---|
| To Plant & Machinery A/c | 18,500 | By Profit & Loss A/c | 18,500 |

**Rent A/c**

| Particulars | Rs. | Particulars | Rs. |
|---|---|---|---|
| To Profit & Loss A/c | 25,000 | By Cash A/c | 25,000 |

**Income Tax A/c**

| Particulars | Rs. | Particulars | Rs. |
|---|---|---|---|
| To Cash A/c | 22,000 | By Profit & Loss A/c | 22,000 |

**Cash A/c**

| Particulars | Rs. | Particulars | Rs. |
|---|---|---|---|
| To Balance b/d | 13,500 | By Stores Ledger Control A/c | 36,000 |
| To Sales A/c | 210,000 | By Wages Ledger Control A/c | 158,000 |
| To Rent A/c | 25,000 | By WIP Ledger Control A/c | 10,000 |
| To Debtors Control A/c | 1,05,000 | By Factory Overh. Control A/c | 11,000 |
| | | By Administration Overhead Control A/c | 14,000 |
| | | By Selling & Distribution Overhead Control A/c | 15,000 |
| | | By Creditors Control A/c | 30,000 |
| | | By Income Tax paid | 22,000 |
| | | By Plant & Machinery A/c | 20,000 |
| | | By Balance c/d | 37,500 |
| | 353,500 | | 353,500 |

**Profit & Loss A/c**

| Particulars | Rs. | Particulars | Rs. |
|---|---|---|---|
| To Income Tax A/c | 22,000 | By Balance b/d | 92,000 |
| To Provision for Depreciation A/c | 18,500 | By Sales A/c | 73,000 |
| To Net Profit | 149,500 | By Rent A/c | 25,000 |
| | 1,90,000 | | 1,90,000 |

**Balance Sheet as on 31st March 2011**

| Liabilities | Rs. | Assets | | Rs. |
|---|---|---|---|---|
| Share Capital | 4,00,000 | Land & Building | | 250,000 |
| Profit & Loss A/c | 149,500 | Plant & Machinery | 2,00,000 | |
| Creditors | 11,000 | Less: Depreciation | 18,500 | 181,500 |
| | | Stock | | |
| | | Finished Goods | 26,000 | |
| | | Work-in-progress | 27,500 | |
| | | Raw Material | 15,000 | 68,500 |
| | | Debtors | | 23,000 |
| | | Cash | | 37,500 |
| | 5,60,500 | | | 5,60,500 |

## EXERCISE

**I. Choose the correct answer for the following:**

1. In integrated accounting one set of book in maintained for financial transactions and
   (i) Accounting transactions (ii) Material transactions
   (iii) Costing transactions (iv) Inventery transactions
2. Integration is done through
   (i) Control accounts (ii) Inventory accounts
   (iii) Work -in-progress (iv) Contribution
3. For purchase of material, cost ledger control account should be
   (i) Debited (ii) Credited (iii) Added (iv) Deducted
4. Balance in Overhead Suspense account is transfered to
   (i) Balance Sheet (ii) Overhead control account
   (iii) Cost Sheet (iv) Proft and Loss account
5. Cost of sales account is debited in
   (i) Sales account (ii) Purchase account
   (iii) Wages account (iv) Administration Overhead account
6. Work-in-progress account is debited in
   (i) Sales account (ii) Purchase account
   (iii) Finished goods account (iv) Cost of sales account
7. Administration overhead account is debited in
   (i) Cost of sales account (ii) Sales account
   (iii) Factory overhead account (iv) Finished goods account

[Ans: 1. (iii) 2 (i) 3 (ii) 4 (iv) 5 (i) 6 (iii) 7 (iv)]

## II. Answer the following:

8. Define Integrated Accounting. State the advantages of Integrated Accounting System.
9. What is Integrated Accounting System? Explain the principles involved in the Integrated Accounting System.
10. Define Integrated Accounting. Distinguish between Inter Locking and Integration of Accounting System.
11. Journalise the following transactions in the Integrated Ledger Accounts of X Ltd.

| | Rs. |
|---|---|
| Material purchased for Cash | 65,400 |
| Material purchased on Credit | 32,600 |
| Wages paid | 42,000 |
| Productive Wages | 25,000 |
| Unproductive Wages | 17,000 |
| Direct Material issued to Factory | 54,000 |
| Indirect Material issued to Factory | 21,000 |
| Factory Overhead paid | 19,500 |
| Administration Overhead paid | 34,750 |
| Selling & Distribution Overhead paid | 31,250 |
| Factory Overhead recovered | 60,000 |
| Administration Overhead recovered | 33,000 |
| Selling & Distribution Overhead recovered | 32,000 |
| Finished Goods during the period | 150,000 |
| Cash Sales | 200,000 |
| Credit Sales | 50,000 |

12. Journalise the following transactions in the Integrated Ledger Accounts

| | Rs. |
|---|---|
| Material purchased for Cash | 50,000 |
| Material purchased on Credit | 30,000 |
| Wages paid | 27,000 |
| Productive Wages | 15,000 |
| Unproductive Wages | 12,000 |
| Direct Material issued to Factory | 45,000 |
| Indirect Material issued to Factory | 20,000 |
| Factory Overhead paid | 10,500 |
| Administration Overhead paid | 24,500 |
| Selling & Distribution Overhead paid | 30,500 |
| Factory Overhead recovered | 60,000 |
| Administration Overhead recovered | 30,000 |
| Selling & Distribution Overhead recovered | 29,000 |
| Finished Goods during the period | 100,000 |
| Sales | 190,000 |

13.KMLtd provided the following information from the Integrated Ledger Accounts.

**Balances as on 1st April 2010**

| Particulars | Dr. Rs. | Cr. Rs. |
|---|---|---|
| Stores Ledger Control A/c | 31,000 | |
| Work-in-progress Ledger Control A/c | 24,500 | |
| Finished Goods Ledger Control A/c | 35,000 | |
| Land & Building A/c | 250,000 | |
| Plant & Machinery A/c | 200,000 | |
| Provision for Depreciation on Plant & Machinery | | 35,000 |
| Bank A/c | 24,000 | |
| Cash A/c | 18,000 | |
| Debtors A/c | 26,000 | |
| Share Capital A/c | | 500,000 |
| Reserves & Surplus A/c | | 49,000 |
| Creditors A/c | | 24,500 |
| | 608,500 | 608,500 |

The transactions during the year are as follows:

| | Rs. |
|---|---|
| Material purchased (50% Cash purchase) | 90,000 |
| Material issued to production | 81,000 |
| Material issued to maintenance department in production | 12,000 |
| Direct material returned from factory to store | 6,000 |
| Materials returned to supplier | 7,000 |
| Production wages | 89,000 |
| Production indirect wages | 32,000 |
| Salaries for Administration Department | 110,000 |
| Sales Department salaries | 76,000 |
| Carriage inwards | 6,400 |
| Carriage outwards | 7,600 |
| Salaries and wages outstanding for the year | 9,500 |
| Indirect expenses paid for production by cheque | 14,500 |

| | |
|---|---|
| Administration overhead paid by cheque | 21,500 |
| Selling and distribution overhead paid by cheque | 19,500 |
| Payment to creditors by cheque | 42,000 |
| Cash received from debtors | 198,000 |
| Discount allowed | 7,500 |
| Discount received | 8,600 |
| Provision for depreciation on Plant & Machinery | 20,000 |
| Provision for bad and doubtful debts | 14,000 |
| Bad debts written off | 8,000 |
| Factory overhead absorbed | 64,000 |
| Administration overhead absorbed | 134,000 |
| Selling and distribution overhead absorbed | 102,000 |
| Finished goods during the year | 232,500 |
| Cost of goods sold for the year | 360,000 |
| Cash Sales | 350,000 |
| Credit Sales | 200,000 |

Prepare necessary ledger accounts in the Integrated Books for the year editing 31st March, 2011.

(Ans: Net profit for current year Rs.47600; B/S total Rs.687,000)

14. Prepare Integrated Ledger accounts and Balance sheet for the year ended31st March 2011, from the following information of a manufacturing company.

**Balances as on 31st March 2010**

| Particulars | Rs. | Rs. |
|---|---|---|
| Share Capital | | 700,000 |
| Profit & Loss Account | | 120,000 |
| Creditors | | 29,000 |
| Stores Ledger Control A/c | 49,500 | |
| Work-in-progress Ledger Control A/c | 52,000 | |
| Finished Goods Ledger Control A/c | 63,000 | |
| Plant & Machinery A/c | 300,000 | |
| Land & Building A/c | 320,000 | |
| Cash A/c | 27,000 | |
| Debtors A/c | 37,500 | |
| | 849,000 | 849,000 |

Transactions during the year are as follows.

| | Rs. |
|---|---|
| Material purchased for cash | 110,000 |
| Material purchased on credit | 40,000 |
| Material issued to Factory | 97,000 |
| Indirect material issued to Factory | 32,000 |
| Indirect material issued to Office | 10,000 |
| Direct wages paid | 82,000 |
| Direct expenses paid | 34,000 |
| Indirect wages paid for Factory | 55,000 |
| Administration Salary | 92,000 |
| Salary for Selling & Distribution Department | 84,000 |
| Factory Overhead paid | 19,000 |
| Administration expenses | 21,000 |
| Selling expenses | 18,000 |
| Income Tax paid | 20,000 |
| Rent received | 48,000 |
| Value of Finished Goods during the year | 331,000 |
| Cost of Goods sold | 467,000 |
| Cash Sales | 400,000 |
| Credit Sales | 240,000 |
| Cash received from debtors | 250,000 |
| Cash paid to creditors | 49,000 |
| Purchase of Machinery on 1st July 2010 | 40,000 |

Provision for depreciation on Plant & Machinery is 10% per annum.

(Ans: Net profit for current year Rs 67,000; Balance of Cash A/c Rs 101,000; B/S total Rs.9,07,000).

15. Journalise the following transactions in the Integrated Ledger Accounts of K Ltd.

| | Rs. |
|---|---|
| Material purchased for Cash | 99,000 |
| Material purchased on Credit | 85,000 |
| Direct Wages paid | 50,000 |
| Indirect Wages paid for Factory | 25,000 |
| Salary for Administration department | 45,000 |
| Salary for Selling department | 30,000 |
| Direct Material issued to Factory | 80,000 |
| Indirect Material issued to Factory | 60,000 |
| Factory Overhead paid | 21,000 |
| Administration Overhead paid | 35,000 |

| | |
|---|---|
| Selling & Distribution Overhead paid | 34,000 |
| Factory Overhead recovered | 115,000 |
| Administration Overhead recovered | 75,000 |
| Selling & Distribution Overhead recovered | 70,000 |
| Finished Goods during the period | 350,000 |
| Cash Sales | 500,000 |
| Credit Sales | 120,000 |

16. Journalise the following transactions in the Integrated Ledger Accounts

| | Rs. |
|---|---|
| Material purchased for Cash | 150,000 |
| Material purchased on Credit | 130,000 |
| Wages paid | 66,000 |
| Productive Wages | 44,000 |
| Unproductive Wages | 22,000 |
| Direct Material issued to Factory | 120,000 |
| Indirect Material issued to Factory | 75,000 |
| Factory Overhead paid | 25,500 |
| Administration Overhead paid | 33,500 |
| Selling & Distribution Overhead paid | 29,500 |
| Factory Overhead recovered | 120,000 |
| Administration Overhead recovered | 30,000 |
| Selling & Distribution Overhead recovered | 34,000 |
| Finished Goods during the period | 360,000 |
| Sales | 550,000 |

17. Journalise the following transactions in the Integrated Ledger Accounts

| | Rs. |
|---|---|
| Material purchased for Cash | 70,000 |
| Material purchased on Credit | 50,000 |
| Wages paid | 25,000 |
| Productive Wages | 15,000 |
| Unproductive Wages | 10,000 |
| Direct Material issued to Factory | 65,000 |
| Indirect Material issued to Factory | 35,000 |
| Factory Overhead paid | 15,000 |
| Administration Overhead paid | 39,000 |
| Selling & Distribution Overhead paid | 36,000 |
| Factory Overhead recovered | 64,000 |
| Administration Overhead recovered | 34,000 |
| Selling & Distribution Overhead recovered | 33,000 |
| Finished Goods during the period | 144,000 |
| Sales | 320,000 |

# CHAPTER XI

## RECONCILIATION OF COST AND FINANCIAL ACCOUNTS

Companies may maintain Cost Accounting in addition to the Financial Accounting. The profit or loss shown by these two accounting systems will not be same due to different treatment of various expenses and revenues.In order to know the accuracy of these two systems of accounts, the profit or loss shown by the two accounts should be reconciled. Hence, reconciliation may be defined as a process of compiling and ascertainment of reasons for the disagreement of the two profits or losses.

**Reasons for the difference in profit or loss of cost accounting and financial accounting systems**

The reasons for the difference in profits or losses are as follows.

1. Transactions appearing only in Financial Accounts
2. Transactions appearing only in Cost Accounts
3. Transactions appearing in both Cost and Financial Accounts with different values.

**1. Transactions appearing only in Financial Accounts**

The transactions appearing only in the financial accounts are classified into purely financial charges, purely financial incomes and appropriations of profits. The profit shown by financial accounting will be less than the profit of the cost accounting due to the purely financial charges and appropriations of profit. But the profit under financial accounting will be more due to the purely financial incomes.

**(i) Expenses treated only in financial books.**

The total of these expenses will reduce the profit in the financial accounting which will not reduce the costing profit. The important expenses debited only in the financial books are stated as follows.

(a) Losses in sale of fixed assets like Plant & Machinery, Land & Building, Furniture & Fittings and Investments.

(b) Interest on bank loan, debentures, mortgages etc.

(c) Fines and penalties payable

(d) Compensation payable under law

(e) Expenses for transfer of shares

(f) Loss due to the replacement of assets

(g) Expenses of capital nature like repairs and maintenance of fixed assets

(h) Discount on issue of shares or debentures

**(ii) Income treated only in financial books.**

(a) Profit on sale of fixed assets like Plant & Machinery, Land & Building, Furniture & Fittings and Investments.

(b) Interest received on bank deposits

(c) Rent received from buildings except of the sub leasing of business premises. (Rent due to the sub leasing of business premises should also appear in Cost Accounts.)

(d) Premium on issue of shares or debentures

(e) Receipt of transfer fees

(f) Interest received on Investments

(g) Dividends received from shares

(h) Commission and Brokerage received

**(iii) Appropriations of profit.**

(a) Income tax and other taxes

(b) Sinking Fund

(c) Writing-off of goodwill, underwriting commission, preliminary expenses etc.

(d) Donation

(e) Provision of dividends for equity and preference shares.

(f) Additional provision for depreciation on fixed assets and for bad and doubtful debts.

**2. Transactions appearing only in Cost Accounts**

The important transactions appearing only in cost accounts are stated as follows

(a) Rent charges for the own building

(b) Interest on capital employed

(c) Charging depreciation even though the book value of the asset is nil

**3. Transactions appearing both in cost and financial accounts with different values:**

**a) Under or over absorption of overheads**

In financial accounts the expenses actually spent should alone be taken into account. But cost account is based on estimates. The over estimation or under estimation of indirect expenses may be the reason for the treatment of expenses in cost books and financial books with different values. The estimation may be called in costing term as absorption or recovery. Costing profit would be less than actual (less than financial profit) because of over-absorption. Like that, it will be more than actual (or more than what shown in the financial profit) because of under-absorption.

**b) Valuation of stock**

In financial accounting the stock is valued on cost price or market price whichever is lower. But in cost accounting different methods are adopted for valuation of stock of Raw material, Work-in-progress and Finished goods. Raw material is valued on the basis of method of issue of material (FIFO, LIFO etc.). Work-in-progress is valued on the basis of prime cost or work cost or cost of production. Finished goods are valued on the basis of cost of production. This is the reason for the treatment of opening and closing stock at different values in financial account and cost account.

**c) Different methods of charging depreciation**

In financial accounting depreciation is calculated on the basis of straight line method or diminishing balance method. But in cost accounting depreciation is calculated on the basis of machine hour or production hour or production unit method. Hence, the depreciation is treated at different values in financial account and cost account.

**Illustration: 1**

The Net Profit shown by the financial accounts of a manufacturing company for the year ended 31st March 2011 is Rs.122,500. The Profit disclosed by the Costing profit and loss account for the year is Rs.105,000. The reasons for the difference in profit are stated as follows:

| | Rs. |
|---|---|
| Factory overhead over-recovered | 7,500 |
| Administration overhead under-recovered | 4,500 |
| Selling and distribution overhead under-recovered | 6,000 |
| Profit on sale of Fixed assets | 14,500 |
| Provision for Income Tax in Financial Account | 10,000 |
| Bank interest (Credit) | 12,000 |
| Depreciation charged to Financial Account | 15,000 |
| Depreciation recovered in Cost Account | 12,500 |
| Under-valuation of closing stock in Cost Account | 6,500 |

Prepare a Reconciliation Statement and verify the result.

***Solution:***

**Reconciliation Statement**

| Particulars | Rs. | Rs. |
|---|---|---|
| Profit as per Cost Account | 1,05,000 | |
| **Add:** Under-valuation of closing stock in cost account | 6,500 | |
| Over-recovery of factory overhead | 7,500 | |
| Profit on sale of fixed asset | 14,500 | |
| Bank interest | 12,000 | |

| Particulars | Rs. | Rs. |
|---|---|---|
| **Less:** Under-recovery of administration overhead | | 4,500 |
| Under-recovery of selling and distribution overhead | | 6,000 |
| Under charging of depreciation in cost account | | 2,500 |
| Provision for income tax | | 10,000 |
| | 1,45,500 | 23,000 |
| | | 1,22,500 |
| Net Profit as per financial account | | |

**Illustration: 2**

Prepare a Reconciliation Statement from the particulars given below:

| | Rs. |
|---|---|
| Factory overhead under-absorbed | 9,000 |
| Administration overhead over-absorbed | 5,500 |
| Selling and distribution overhead under absorbed | 3,900 |
| Income tax provided in Financial Account | 22,000 |
| Interest received recorded in Financial Account | 15,000 |
| Stock adjustment (Debit in Financial Account) | 4,000 |
| Depreciation charged in Financial Account | 14,000 |
| Depreciation charged in Cost Account | 17,500 |
| Value of opening stock in Cost Account | 21,500 |
| Value of opening stock in Financial Account | 18,500 |
| Value of closing stock in Cost Account | 44,500 |
| Value of closing stock in Financial Account | 40,000 |
| Preliminary expenses written off in financial account | 12,000 |
| Loss on sale of fixed assets recorded in financial account | 9,500 |
| Provision for bad and doubtful debts in financial account | 11,000 |
| Interest on capital charged in Cost Account | 19,000 |
| Obsolescence loss charged in Financial Account | 6,500 |
| Commission received recorded in Financial Account | 9,500 |
| Net loss as per Cost Account | 55,500 |
| Net loss as per Financial Account | 82,400 |

***Solution:***

**Reconciliation Statement**

| Particulars | Rs. | Rs. |
|---|---|---|
| Net Loss as per Cost Account | 55,500 | |
| **Add:** Over-valuation of closing stock in cost account | 4,500 | |
| Under-absorption of factory overhead | 9,000 | |
| Under-absorption of selling overhead | 3,900 | |
| Loss on sale of fixed asset | 9,500 | |

| | | |
|---|---|---|
| Income tax provided in financial account | 22,000 | |
| Stock adjustment | 4,000 | |
| Preliminary expenses written off | 12,000 | |
| Provision for bad and doubtful debts | 11,000 | |
| Obsolescence loss | 6,500 | |
| **Less:** Over-absorption of administration overhead | | 5,500 |
| Bank interest | | 15,000 |
| Over charging of depreciation in cost account | | 3,500 |
| Over valuation of opening stock in cost account | | 3,000 |
| Insterest on capital charged in cost account | | 19,000 |
| Commission received | | 9,500 |
| | 1,37,900 | 55,500 |
| Net loss as per financial account | | 82,400 |

**Illustration: 3**

D Ltd provides the following information for the year ended 31[st] March 2011.

| | Rs. |
|---|---|
| Opening stock of material as per Financial records | 37,000 |
| Opening stock of material as per Cost records | 35,000 |
| Closing Stock of material as per Financial records | 27,000 |
| Closing Stock of material as per Cost records | 22,000 |
| Purchase of material | 67,500 |
| Direct wages | 44,000 |
| Indirect wages | 34,000 |
| Direct expenses | 19,000 |
| Indirect expenses | 10,000 |
| Administration expenses | 30,000 |
| Selling expenses | 20,000 |
| Bad debts written off | 9,500 |
| Profit on sale of fixed assets | 11,500 |
| Interest on overdraft | 4,000 |
| Interest on capital charged only in cost account | 9,000 |
| Commission received | 7,000 |
| Depreciation charged in financial account | 12,500 |

Factory overhead recovered is 80% on direct wages. Administration overhead recovered is 20% on works cost. Selling and distribution overhead recovered is 10% on cost of production. Sale is Rs.290,000. Calculate the financial profit and costing profit and reconcile these profits by preparing a Reconciliation Statement.

***Solution:***

### Cost Sheet

| Particulars | Rs. | Rs. |
|---|---|---|
| Opening stock of material | 35,000 | |
| **Add:** Purchases | 67,500 | |
| | 1,02,500 | |
| **Less:** Closing stock of material | 22,000 | |
| Material consumed | | 80,500 |
| Direct wages | | 44,000 |
| Direct expenses | | 19,000 |
| Prime cost | | 1,43,500 |
| Factory Overhead (80% on Direct wages) | | 35,200 |
| Works cost | | 1,78,700 |
| Administration Overhead (20% on works cost) | | 35,740 |
| Cost of Production | | 2,14,440 |
| Selling and distribution overhead (10% on cost of production) | | 21,444 |
| Interest on capital | | 9,000 |
| Cost of sales | | 2,44,884 |
| Profit | | 45,116 |
| Sales | | 2,90,000 |

### Trading and Profit and Loss Account for the year ending 31st March 2011

| Particulars | Rs. | Particulars | Rs. |
|---|---|---|---|
| To Opening stock | 37,000 | By Sales | 2,90,000 |
| ,, Purchases | 67,500 | ,, Closing stock | 27,000 |
| ,, Wages | 44,000 | | |
| ,, Direct expenses | 19,000 | | |
| ,, Gross profit | 1,49,500 | | |
| | 3,17,000 | | 3,17,000 |
| To Factory expenses (34,000 + 10,000) | 44,000 | By Gross profit | 1,49,500 |
| ,, Administration expenses | 30,000 | ,, Commission received | 7,000 |
| ,, Selling expenses | 20,000 | ,, Profit on sale of fixed assets | 11,500 |
| ,, Depreciation | 12,500 | | |
| ,, Bad debts | 9,500 | | |
| ,, Interest on overdraft | 4,000 | | |
| ,, Net profit | 48,000 | | |
| | 1,68,000 | | 1,68,000 |

**Reconciliation Statement**

| Particulars | Rs. | Rs. |
|---|---|---|
| Profit as per Cost Account | 45,116 | |
| **Add:** Under-charging of closing stock in cost account | 5,000 | |
| Over-absorption of administration overhead | 5,740 | |
| Over-absorption of selling overhead | 1,444 | |
| Interest on capital charged in cost account | 9,000 | |
| Commission received | 7,000 | |
| Profit on sale of fixed assets | 11,500 | |
| **Less:** Under-absorption of factory overhead | | 8,800 |
| Under-charging of opening stock in cost account | | 2,000 |
| Bad Debts | | 9,500 |
| Depreciation | | 12,500 |
| Interest on overdraft | | 4,000 |
| | 84,800 | 36,800 |
| Net profit as per financial account | | 48,000 |

**Illustration: 4**

A manufacturing company provides the following information for the year ended 31st March 2011 in order to prepare the statements showing profits in cost account and financial account. Also prepare a statement of reconciliation of the two profits.

| | Rs. |
|---|---|
| Direct materials | 29,000 |
| Direct wages | 22,500 |
| Direct expenses | 14,250 |
| Sales | 1,25,000 |

Factory overhead absorbed is 100% on direct wages, administration overhead absorbed is 20% on works cost and selling and distribution overhead absorbed is 10% on works cost. The actual overhead expenses are as follows:

| | Rs. |
|---|---|
| Factory overhead | 24,000 |
| Administration overhead | 18,000 |
| Selling and distribution overhead | 8,000 |

***Solution:***

**Statement of Cost**

| Particulars | Rs. |
|---|---|
| Direct material | 29,000 |
| Direct wages | 22,500 |
| Direct expenses | 14,250 |
| Prime Cost | 65,750 |
| Factory overhead (100% on Direct wages) | 22,500 |
| Works Cost | 88,250 |
| Administration Overhead (20% on works cost) | 17,650 |
| Cost of production | 1,05,900 |
| Selling and Distribution overhead (10% on works cost) | 8,825 |
| Cost of Sales | 1,14,725 |
| Profit | 10,275 |
| Sales | 1,25,000 |

**Profit and Loss Account**

| Particulars | Rs. | Particulars | Rs. |
|---|---|---|---|
| To Material | 29,000 | By Sales | 1,25,000 |
| ,, Wages | 22,500 | | |
| ,, Direct expenses | 14,250 | | |
| ,, Factory expenses | 24,000 | | |
| ,, Administrative expenses | 18,000 | | |
| ,, Selling and Distribution expenses | 8,000 | | |
| ,, Net Profit | 9,250 | | |
| | 1,25,000 | | 1,25,000 |

**Reconciliation Statement**

| Particulars | Rs. | Rs. |
|---|---|---|
| Net profit as per Cost Account | 10,275 | |
| Add: Over absorption of selling and distribution overhead | 825 | |
| Less: Under absorption of factory overhead | | 1,500 |
| Under adsorption of administration overhead | | 350 |
| | 11,100 | 1,850 |
| Net profit as per Financial Account | | 9,250 |

**Illustration: 5**

The following information are collected from the books of WD Ltd. for the year ending 31st March 2011.

| | |
|---|---|
| Opening stock of material as per cost account | 19,850 |
| Opening stock of material as per financial account | 18,000 |
| Closing stock of material as per cost records | 27,800 |
| Closing stock of material as per financial records | 26,000 |
| Material purchased | 59,650 |
| Direct wages paid | 29,700 |
| Direct expenses paid | 18,900 |
| Indirect factory expenses paid | 21,250 |
| Indirect administrative expenses paid | 17,300 |
| Indirect selling and distribution expenses paid | 15,950 |
| Travelling fees paid | 7,200 |
| Bad debts | 750 |
| Bank interest received | 2,000 |
| Dividend received | 4,750 |
| Bank charges | 1,250 |
| Sales | 2,40,000 |

Factory overhead recovered is @ 100% on direct wages. Administration overhead recovered is @ 20% on works cost. Selling and distribution overhead under-recovered is Rs.2,950

Prepare the Trading and Profit & Loss account and find out the net profit as per financial records. Also prepare the Cost Sheet and ascertain the costing profit and prepare the Reconciliation Statement to reconcile the profits.

***Solution:***

**Cost Sheet**

| Particulars | Rs. | Rs. |
|---|---|---|
| Opening stock of material | 19,850 | |
| Add: Purchases | 59,650 | |
| | 79,500 | |
| Less: Closing stock of material | 27,800 | |
| Material consumed | | 51,700 |
| Direct wages | | 29,700 |
| Direct expenses | | 18,900 |
| Prime cost | | 1,00,300 |
| Factory overhead (100% on Direct wages) | | 29,700 |
| Works cost | | 1,30,000 |

| | | |
|---|---|---|
| Administration Overhead (20% on works cost) | | 26,000 |
| Cost of Production | | 1,56,000 |
| Selling and distribution overhead (15,950-2,950) | | 13,000 |
| Cost of sales | | 1,69,000 |
| Profit | | 71,000 |
| Sales | | 2,40,000 |

**Trading and Profit and Loss account for the year ending 31st March 2011**

| Particulars | Rs. | Particulars | Rs. |
|---|---|---|---|
| To Opening stock | 18,000 | By Sales | 2,40,000 |
| ,, Purchases | 59,650 | ,, Closing stock | 26,000 |
| ,, Wages | 29,700 | | |
| ,, Direct expenses | 18,900 | | |
| ,, Gross profit | 1,39,750 | | |
| | 2,66,000 | | 2,66,000 |
| To Factory Expenses | 21,250 | By Gross Profit | 1,39,750 |
| ,, Administrative expenses | 17,300 | ,, Dividend received | 4,750 |
| ,, Selling and distribution expenses | 15,950 | ,, Bank interest | 2,000 |
| ,, Transfer fees paid | 7,200 | | |
| ,, Bad debts | 750 | | |
| ,, Bank charges | 1,250 | | |
| ,, Net profit | 82,800 | | |
| | 1,46,500 | | 1,46,500 |

**Reconciliation Statement**

| Particulars | Rs. | Rs. |
|---|---|---|
| Profit as per Cost Account | 71,000 | |
| **Add:** Over-charging of opening stock in cost account | 1,850 | |
| Over-absorption of factory overhead | 8,450 | |
| Over-absorption of administration overhead | 8,700 | |
| Dividend received | 4,750 | |
| Bank interest | 2,000 | |
| **Less:** Under-absorption of selling and distribution overhead | | 2,950 |

| | | |
|---|---|---|
| Over-charging of closing stock in cost account | | 1,800 |
| Bad debts | | 750 |
| Transfer fees | | 7,200 |
| Bank charges | | 1,250 |
| | 96,750 | 13,950 |
| Net profit as per financial account | | 82,800 |

**Illustration: 6**

H Ltd. engaged in the manufacturing and selling of two products, namely A and B. The following particulars are related to the cost in the manufacturing of the two products for the year ending 31st March 2011.

| | Product A Rs. | Product B Rs. |
|---|---|---|
| Material | 46,700 | 72,800 |
| Labour | 30,900 | 47,750 |
| Direct expenses | 25,950 | 32,850 |

Manufacturing overhead recovered is @ 70% on direct wages, office overhead absorbed is @ 30% on works cost and selling and distribution overhead recovered is @ 20% on works cost.

The actual overheads are as follows:

| | Product A Rs. | Product B Rs. |
|---|---|---|
| Manufacturing indirect expenses | 21,000 | 35,000 |
| Administrative expenses | 36,000 | 51,250 |
| Selling and distribution expenses | 30,000 | 35,200 |

During the year 1,000 units of product A are manufactured and sold @ Rs.250 per unit and 2,000 units of product B are manufactured and sold @ Rs.200 per unit.

Prepare the financial as well as cost statements and find out the profits under the two statements. Also prepare the reconciliation statement and ascertain the accuracy of the two sets of books.

***Solution:***

**Statement of Cost**

| **Particulars** | **Product A** | | **Product B** | |
|---|---|---|---|---|
| | **Per Unit Rs.** | **Total Rs.** | **Per Unit Rs.** | **Total Rs.** |
| Material | 46.70 | 46,700 | 36.40 | 72,800 |
| Wages | 30.90 | 30,900 | 23.88 | 47,750 |
| Direct expenses | 25.95 | 25,950 | 16.42 | 32,850 |
| **Prime Cost** | 103.55 | 103,550 | 76.70 | 153,400 |

| | | | | |
|---|---|---|---|---|
| Factory Overhead | 21.63 | 21,630 | 16.71 | 33,425 |
| **Works Cost** | 125.18 | 125,180 | 93.41 | 18,6825 |
| Administration Overhead | 37.55 | 37,554 | 28.02 | 56,047 |
| **Cost of Production** | 162.73 | 162,734 | 121.43 | 242,872 |
| Selling and distribution overhead | 25.04 | 25,036 | 18.68 | 37,365 |
| **Cost of Sales** | 187.77 | 187,770 | 140.11 | 280,237 |
| **Profit** | 62.23 | 62,230 | 59.89 | 119,763 |
| **Sales** | 250.00 | 250,000 | 200.00 | 400,000 |

**Total profit as per Cost Account**

| | Rs. |
|---|---|
| Product A | 62,230 |
| Product B | 119,763 |
| Total profit | 181,993 |

**Profit and Loss Account**

| Particulars | Rs. | Particulars | Rs. |
|---|---|---|---|
| To Material | 119,500 | By Sales | 650,000 |
| ,, Wages | 78,650 | | |
| ,, Direct expenses | 58,800 | | |
| ,, Manufacturing expenses | 56,000 | | |
| ,, Office expenses | 87,250 | | |
| ,, Selling and distribution expenses | 65,200 | | |
| ,, Net profit | 184,600 | | |
| | 650,000 | | 650,000 |

Note: The expenses of Product A and Product B are combined and given in the financial Profit and Loss account.

**Reconciliation Statement**

| Particulars | Rs. | Rs. |
|---|---|---|
| Profit as per financial account | 184,600 | - |
| **Add**: Under-absorption of manufacturing overhead in cost account | 945 | - |
| Under absorption of selling and distribution overhead | 2,799 | - |

| | | |
|---|---|---|
| **Less**: Over-absorption of Administration Overhead in cost account | | 6,351 |
| | 1,88,344 | 6,351 |
| Profit as per Cost Account | | 1,81,993 |
| | 1,88,344 | 1,88,344 |

**Illustration: 7**

NLtd. has provided the following information for the year ended 31st March 2011.

| | Cost Account Rs. | Financial Account Rs. |
|---|---|---|
| Opening Stock | | |
| Raw material | 17,200 | 16,600 |
| Work-in-progress | 19,500 | 20,000 |
| Finished goods | 18,750 | 15,500 |
| Closing Stock | | |
| Raw Material | 28,700 | 30,000 |
| Work-in-progress | 32,800 | 31,600 |
| Finished goods | 70,500 | 73,000 |

The following additional information are also provided from both set of books.

| | Rs. |
|---|---|
| Direct material | 90,000 |
| Direct wages | 62,000 |
| Indirect wages | 31,750 |
| Factory expenses | 42,700 |
| Administrative expenses | 30,250 |
| Selling expenses | 7,500 |
| Miscellaneous financial expenses | 12,000 |
| Obsolescence loss in fixed assets | 6,250 |
| Transfer fees | 750 |
| Bad debts | 1,575 |
| Interest and dividend received | 4,500 |
| Transfer to General Reserve | 15,000 |
| Rent received | 1,200 |
| Provision for dividend | 20,000 |
| Provision for taxation | 14,000 |
| Overheads recovered in Cost Account are, | |
| Factory | 75,000 |
| Administration | 28,000 |
| Selling and distribution | 11,000 |

| | |
|---|---|
| Sales | 2,80,000 |
| Last year profit | 22,000 |

Prepare Manufacturing, Trading and Profit and Loss Account; Profit and Loss Appropriation Account and Cost Sheet and calculate the profits in Financial account as well as in Cost account. Also prepare a reconciliation statement and verify whether the profits shown by the financial account and cost account are correct.

***Solution:***

**Manufacturing, Trading and Profit and Loss Account**

| Particulars | Amount Rs. | Particulars | Amount Rs. |
|---|---|---|---|
| To Opening stock | | By Closing stock: | |
| Raw material | 16,600 | Raw material | 30,000 |
| ,, Work-in-progress | 20,000 | Work-in-progress | 31,600 |
| ,, Purchase | 90,000 | ,, Balance transferred | |
| ,, Direct wages | 62,000 | to Trading A/c | 201,450 |
| ,, Indirect wages | 31,750 | | |
| ,, Factory expenses | 42,700 | | |
| | 263,050 | | 263,050 |
| To Opening finished stock | 15,500 | By Sales | 280,000 |
| ,, Balance transferred from Manufacturing A/c | 201,450 | ,, Closing finished stock | 73,000 |
| ,, Gross profit | 136,050 | | |
| | 353,000 | | 353,000 |
| To Administration expenses | 30,250 | By Gross Profit | 136,050 |
| ,, Selling expenses | 7,500 | ,, Interest &Dividend received | 4,500 |
| ,, Miscellaneous expenses | 12,000 | ,, Rent received | 1,200 |
| ,, Obsolescence loss | 6,250 | | |
| ,, Transfer fees | 750 | | |
| ,, Bad debts | 1,575 | | |
| ,, Prov. for taxation | 14,000 | | |
| ,, P&L Appropriation A/c | 69,425 | | |
| | 141,750 | | 141,750 |

## Profit and Loss Appropriation Account

| Particulars | Amount Rs. | Particulars | Amount Rs. |
|---|---|---|---|
| To General reserve | 15,000 | By Balance from Last Year | 22,000 |
| „ Provision for Dividend | 20,000 | „ Profit & Loss A/c | 69,425 |
| „ Balance to Balance Sheet | 56,425 | | |
| | 91,425 | | 91,425 |

## Cost Sheet

| Particulars | Rs. | Rs. |
|---|---|---|
| Opening stock of material | 17,200 | |
| Add: Purchase | 90,000 | |
| | 107,200 | |
| Less: Closing stock of Material | 28,700 | |
| Material Consumed | | 78,500 |
| Direct Wages | | 62,000 |
| **Prime Cost** | | 140,500 |
| Add: Factory Overhead obsorbed | | 75,000 |
| | | 215,500 |
| Add: Opening Work-in-progress | | 19,500 |
| | | 235,000 |
| Less: Closing work-in-progress | | 32,800 |
| **Works cost** | | 202,200 |
| Add: Administration Overhead | | 28,000 |
| **Cost of production** | | 230,200 |
| Add: Op. stock of finished goods | | 18,750 |
| | | 248,950 |
| Less: Cl. stock of finished goods | | 70,500 |
| **Cost of goods sold** | | 178,450 |
| Add: Selling and distribution overhead | | 11,000 |
| **Cost of sales** | | 189,450 |
| **Profit** | | 90,550 |
| **Sales** | | 280,000 |

**Reconciliation Statement**

| | Particulars | Rs. | Rs. |
|---|---|---|---|
| | Profit as per Cost Account | 90,550 | |
| Add: | Over-absorption of Factory overhead | 550 | |
| | Over-absorption of Selling and Distribution overhead | 3,500 | |
| | Over-charging of Op. stock in Cost Account | 3,350 | |
| | Under-charging of Cl. stock in Cost Account | 2,600 | |
| | Interest and dividend received | 4,500 | |
| | Rent received | 1,200 | |
| | Last Year Profit | 22,000 | |
| Less: | Under-absorption of Administration overhead | | 2,250 |
| | Miscellaneous financial expenses | | 12,000 |
| | Obsolescence loss | | 6,250 |
| | Transfer fees | | 750 |
| | Bad debts | | 1,575 |
| | Transfer to reserve | | 15,000 |
| | Provision for dividend | | 20,000 |
| | Provision for taxation | | 14,000 |
| | | 128,250 | 71,825 |
| | Profit as per Financial Account | | 56,425 |

**Preparation of Reconciliation Statement when Trading and Profit and Loss Account is given**

In this method expenses or income only meant for financial account can easily be identified from the Trading and Profit & Loss Account.The expenses or income meant only for cost account can be known from the adjustments.

**Illustration: 8**

The following is the Profit and Loss account of M Ltd. for the year ended 31[st] March 2011.

**Trading and Profit and Loss account for the year ended 31st March 2011.**

| Particulars | Amount Rs. | Particulars | Amount Rs. |
|---|---|---|---|
| To Op. stock | 37,500 | By Sales | 210,000 |
| ,, Purchase | 82,000 | ,, Cl. stock | 47,500 |
| ,, Wages | 61,500 | | |
| ,, Factory overhead | 22,750 | | |
| ,, Gross Profit | 53,750 | | |
| | 257,500 | | 257,500 |
| To Interest paid | 17,000 | By Gross Profit | 53,750 |
| ,, Administrative expenses | 14,500 | ,, Dividend received | 23,750 |
| ,, Selling expenses | 12,900 | ,, Commission received | 8,950 |
| ,, Bad debts | 1,450 | | |
| ,, Taxes paid | 9,700 | | |
| ,, Net Profit | 30,900 | | |
| | 86,450 | | 86,450 |

The Cost records show the following information:

| | Rs. |
|---|---|
| (i) Costing Profit | 12,000 |
| (ii) Factory overhead absorbed | 25,000 |
| (iii) Administration overhead absorbed | 15,000 |
| (iv) Selling and distribution overhead absorbed | 10,000 |
| (v) Op. Stock of material | 32,500 |
| (vi) Closing Stock of material | 45,000 |
| (vii) Charge an interest on capital | 17,000 |

Prepare the reconciliation statement and find out the accuracy of the accounts.

***Solution:***

**Reconciliation Statement**

| | Particulars | Rs. | Rs. |
|---|---|---|---|
| | Profit as per Cost account | 12,000 | |
| Add: | Over valuation of closing stock in financial account | 2,500 | |
| | Over-absorption of factory Overhead | 2,250 | |

| | | |
|---|---|---|
| Over-absorption of Administration overhead | 500 | |
| Interest on capital charged only in Cost account | 17,000 | |
| Dividend received | 23,750 | |
| Commission received | 8,950 | |
| Less: Over-charging of Op.stock in Financial A/c | | 5,000 |
| Under-absorption of Selling & distribution overhead | | 2,900 |
| Interest paid | | 17,000 |
| Bad debts | | 1,450 |
| Taxes paid | | 9,700 |
| | 66,950 | 36,050 |
| Profit as per Financial Account | | 30,900 |

**Illustration: 9**

From the following financial profit and loss account and the cost data, prepare a reconciliation statement for the year ending 31st March 2011.

**Trading and Profit and Loss Account**

| Particulars | Amount Rs. | Particulars | Amount Rs. |
|---|---|---|---|
| To Op. Stock | 21,800 | By Sales | 50,000 |
| ,, Purchases | 69,300 | ,, Closing Stock | 19,750 |
| ,, Wages | 41,750 | ,, Gross Loss | 82,550 |
| ,, Factory expenses | 19,250 | | |
| | 152,300 | | 152,300 |
| ,, Gross Loss | 82,550 | By Bank interest | 22,000 |
| ,, Administration expenses | 17,500 | ,, Dividend received | 20,000 |
| ,, Selling expenses | 9,850 | ,, Net Loss | 77,950 |
| ,, Obsolescence loss | 1,700 | | |
| ,, Loss on sale of furniture | 2,300 | | |
| ,, Transfer fees | 1,850 | | |
| ,, Taxes paid | 3,000 | | |
| ,, Bad debts | 1,200 | | |
| | 119,950 | | 119,950 |

The Cost records show the following information:

| | Rs. |
|---|---|
| Net Loss | 116,250 |
| Factory overhead absorbed | 18,000 |
| Administration overhead absorbed | 16,000 |
| Selling and distribution overhead absorbed | 12,000 |
| Opening stock of material | 22,000 |
| Closing stock of material | 20,000 |
| Interest on capital | 7,000 |

***Solution:***

**Reconciliation Statement**

| Particulars | Rs. | Rs. |
|---|---|---|
| Net Loss as per Cost Account | | 116,250 |
| **Add:** Under-absorption of Factory Overhead | 1,250 | |
| Under-absorption of Administration Overhead | 1,500 | |
| Obsolescence loss | 1,700 | |
| Loss on sale of furniture | 2,300 | |
| Transfer fees | 1,850 | |
| Taxes paid | 3,000 | |
| Bad Debts | 1,200 | |
| Over-Valuation of closing stock in Cost Account | 250 | 13,050 |
| | | 129,300 |
| **Less:** Over-absorption of Selling and Distribution Overhead | 2,150 | |
| Over-Valuation of opening stock in Cost Account | 200 | |
| Bank interest | 22,000 | |
| Dividend received | 20,000 | |
| Interest on capital | 7,000 | 51,350 |
| Net Loss as per Financial Account | | 77,950 |

**Illustration: 10**

The following particulars are relating to a manufacturing company for the year ended 31st March 2011. Prepare Memorandum Reconciliation Account.

| | Rs. |
|---|---|
| Profit as per Cost Records | 72,750 |
| Profit as per Financial Records | 86,800 |
| Over-absorption of factory overhead | 7,200 |
| Under-absorption of administration overhead | 4,750 |
| Over-absorption of selling and distribution overhead | 3,250 |
| Over-valuation of opening stock in cost records | 1,750 |
| Over-valuation of closing stock in cost records | 2,350 |
| Over-charging of depreciation in financial account | 2,750 |
| Goodwill written-off in financial account | 3,200 |
| Dividend received | 10,000 |
| Interest on capital charged only in cost account | 7,500 |
| Transfer fees charged in financial account | 1,750 |
| Preliminary expenses written off in financial account | 850 |

***Solution:***

**Memorandum Reconciliation Account**

| Particulars | Amount Rs. | Particulars | Amount Rs. |
|---|---|---|---|
| To Under-absorption of administration overhead | 4,750 | By Profit as per Cost Account | 72,750 |
| " Over-valuation of closing stock in cost A/c | 2,350 | " Over absorption of factory overhead | 7,200 |
| " Over-charging of depreciation in financial A/c | 2,750 | " Over absorption of selling and distribution overhead | 3,250 |
| " Goodwill written off | 3,200 | " Over-valuation of Op.stock in cost records | 1,750 |
| " Transfer fees | 1,750 | " Dividend received | 10,000 |
| " Preliminary expenses written off | 850 | " Interest on own Capital | 7,500 |
| " Net Profit as per financial account | 86,800 | | |
| | 102,450 | | 102,450 |

**Illustration: 11**

MH Ltd. provided the following particular relating to the cost and financial accounts for the year 2011. Prepare the Memorandum Reconciliation Account.

| | Rs. |
|---|---|
| Net Loss as per Cost Account | 52,750 |
| Net Loss as per Financial Account | 41,300 |
| Opening Stock valued in Financial Account | 17,800 |
| Opening Stock valued in Cost Account | 19,000 |
| Closing Stock valued in Financial Account | 21,700 |
| Closing Stock valued in Cost Account | 23,000 |
| Over-absorption of Factory Overhead | 8,700 |
| Under-absorption of Administration Overhead | 4,200 |
| Under-absorption of Selling and Distribution Overhead | 3,000 |
| Depreciation charged in Financial Account | 7,750 |
| Depreciation charged in Cost Account | 11,000 |
| Interest on Capital charged only in Cost Account | 8000 |
| Transfer fees | 750 |
| Bank Charges | 1,800 |
| Bad Debts | 950 |
| Goodwill written off | 2,200 |
| Preliminary expenses written off | 1,800 |
| Dividend received | 4,000 |
| Commission received | 2,300 |

***Solution:***

**Memorandum Reconciliation Account**

| Particulars | Amount Rs. | Particulars | Amount Rs. |
|---|---|---|---|
| To Net Loss as per Cost Account | 52,750 | By Over-absorption of Factory Overhead | 8,700 |
| ,, Under absorption of Administration Overhead | 4,200 | ,, Over-valuation of Op.Stock in Cost A/c | 1,200 |
| ,, Under-absorption of Selling and Distribution Overhead | 3,000 | ,, Over-charging of depreciation in Cost A/c | 3,250 |
| ,, Over-Valuation of Closing stock in Cost A/c | 1,300 | ,, Interest on capital | 8,000 |
| ,, Transfer fees | 750 | ,, Dividend received | 4,000 |
| ,, Bank Charges | 1,800 | ,, Commission received | 2,300 |
| ,, Bad Debts | 950 | ,, Net Loss as per Financial Account | 41,300 |
| ,, Goodwill written off | 2,200 | | |
| ,, Preliminary expenses written off | 1,800 | | |
| | 68,750 | | 68,750 |

**Preparation of Reconciliation Statement after the preparation of Control Accounts**

**Illustration: 12**

Following are the balances in the cost ledger as on 31st March 2010 of Alfa Co. Ltd.

| | Rs. | Rs. |
|---|---|---|
| Stores Ledger Control A/c | 21,700 | |
| Work-in-progress Ledger Control A/c | 18,700 | |
| Finished Goods Ledger Control A/c | 28,800 | |
| Cost Ledger Control A/c | | 69,200 |

Transactions for the year ended 31st March 2011 are as follows:

| | Rs |
|---|---|
| Purchase of Raw Material | 79,850 |
| Direct Wages | 80,500 |
| Indirect Wages | 61,750 |
| Factory Overhead | 61,800 |
| Administration Overhead | 40,900 |
| Selling and Distribution Overhead | 30,250 |
| Factory Overhead recovered | 120,000 |
| Administration Overhead recovered | 42,000 |
| Selling and Distribution Overhead recovered | 31,000 |
| Material issued to production | 90,000 |
| Material returned from production centre to store | 4,500 |
| Material purchased for specific job | 10,000 |
| Value of Work-in-progress as on 31st March 2011 | 8,700 |
| Value of Finished Goods as on 31st March 2011 | 12,000 |
| Sales during the year | 485,000 |

The Company's Balance sheet shows the value of stock as on 31st March,2010 as Rs.72,000 and the value of stock as on 31st March 2011 as Rs.21,000.

The following transactions are recorded only in the financial account.

| | Rs. |
|---|---|
| Obsolescence loss | 2,700 |
| Bad debts | 2,100 |
| Loss on sale of fixed assets | 5,000 |
| Dividend received | 10,000 |
| Bank Interest | 1,850 |

Prepare (i) the necessary Ledger Accounts in the Cost books (ii) Financial Profit & Loss A/c and (iii) The Reconciliation Statement.

***Solution:***

**Stores Ledger Control Account**

| Particulars | Rs. | Particulars | Rs. |
|---|---|---|---|
| To Balance b/d | 21,700 | By Work-in-progress | |
| „ Cost Ledger Control A/c | 79,850 | Ledger Control A/c | 90,000 |
| „ Work-in-progress | | „ Balance c/d | 16,050 |
| Ledger Control A/c | 4,500 | | |
| | 106,050 | | 106,050 |

**Wages Ledger Control Account**

| Particulars | Rs. | Particulars | Rs. |
|---|---|---|---|
| To Cost Ledger Control A/c | 142,250 | By Work-in-progress | |
| | | Ledger Control A/c | 80,500 |
| | | „ Factory Overhead | |
| | | Control A/c | 61,750 |
| | 142,250 | | 142,250 |

**Work-in-progress Ledger Control Account**

| Particulars | Rs. | Particulars | Rs. |
|---|---|---|---|
| To Balance b/d | 18,700 | By Stores Ledger | |
| „ Stores Ledger | | Control A/c | 4,500 |
| Control A/c | 90,000 | „ Finished Goods Ledger | |
| „ Wages Ledger Control A/c | 80,500 | Control A/c | |
| „ Cost Ledger Control A/c | 10,000 | (Balancing figure) | 3,06,000 |
| „ Factory Overhead | 120,000 | „ Balance c/d | 8,700 |
| Control A/c | | | |
| | 319,200 | | 319,200 |

**Finished Goods Ledger Control Account**

| Particulars | Rs. | Particulars | Rs. |
|---|---|---|---|
| To Balance b/d | 28,800 | By Cost of Sales A/c | 364,800 |
| „ Work-in-progress | 306,000 | „ Balance c/d | 12,000 |
| Ledger Control A/c | | | |
| „ Administration | 42,000 | | |
| Overhead Control A/c | | | |
| | 3,76,800 | | 3,76,800 |

**Factory Overhead Control Account**

| Particulars | Rs. | Particulars | Rs. |
|---|---|---|---|
| To Cost Ledger Control A/c | 61,800 | By Work-in-progress Ledger Control A/c | 120,000 |
| ,, Wages Ledger Control A/c | 61,750 | ,, Costing Profit & Loss A/c | 3,550 |
| | 123,550 | | 123,550 |

**Administration Overhead Control Account**

| Particulars | Rs. | Particulars | Rs. |
|---|---|---|---|
| To Cost Ledger Control A/c | 40,900 | By Finished Goods Ledger Control A/c | 42,000 |
| ,, Costing Profit & Loss A/c | 1,100 | | |
| | 42,000 | | 42,000 |

**Selling and Distribution Overhead Control Account**

| Particulars | Rs. | Particulars | Rs. |
|---|---|---|---|
| To Cost Ledger Control A/c | 30,250 | By Cost of Sales A/c | 31,000 |
| ,, Costing Profit and Loss A/c | 750 | | |
| | 31,000 | | 31,000 |

**Cost of Sales Account**

| Particulars | Rs. | Particulars | Rs. |
|---|---|---|---|
| To Finished Goods Ledger Control A/c | 364,800 | By Costing Profit & Loss A/c | 395,800 |
| ,, Selling & Distribution Overhead Control A/c | 31,000 | | |
| | 395,800 | | 395,800 |

[Note: The balance in the Cost of Sales Account is transferred to the Costing Profit and Loss Account to ascertain the costing profit.]

**Sales Account**

| Particulars | Rs. | Particulars | Rs. |
|---|---|---|---|
| To Costing Profit & Loss A/c | 485,000 | By Cost Ledger Control A/c | 485,000 |

**Cost Ledger Control Account**

| Particulars | Rs. | Particulars | Rs. |
|---|---|---|---|
| To Sales A/c | 485,000 | By Balance b/d | 69,200 |
| ,, Balance c/d | 36,750 | ,, Stores Ledger Control A/c | 79,850 |
| | | ,, Wages Ledger Control A/c | 142,250 |
| | | ,, Factory Overhead Control A/c | 61,800 |
| | | ,, Administration Overhead Control A/c | 40,900 |
| | | ,, Selling and Distribution Overhead Control A/c | 30,250 |
| | | ,, Work-in-Progress Ledger Control A/c | 10,000 |
| | | ,, Costing Profit & Loss A/c | 87,500 |
| | 521,750 | | 521,750 |

**Costing Profit and Loss Account**

| Particulars | Rs. | Particulars | Rs. |
|---|---|---|---|
| To Cost of Sales A/c | 395,800 | By Sales A/c | 485,000 |
| ,, Factory Overhead Control A/c | 3,550 | ,, Administration Overhead Control A/c | 1,100 |
| ,, Cost Ledger Control A/c (Costing Profit) | 87,500 | ,, Selling & Distribution Overhead Control A/c | 750 |
| | 486,850 | | 486,850 |

**Trial Balance**

| Particulars | Dr. (Rs.) | Cr. (Rs.) |
|---|---|---|
| Stores Ledger Control A/c | 16,050 | |
| Work-in-progress Ledger Control A/c | 8,700 | |
| Finished Goods Ledger Control A/c | 12,000 | |
| Cost Ledger Control A/c | | 36,750 |
| | 36,750 | 36,750 |

**Financial Profit and Loss Account**

| Particulars | Amount Rs. | Particulars | Amount Rs. |
|---|---|---|---|
| To Opening stock | 72,000 | By Sales | 485,000 |
| ,, Purchase | 79,850 | ,, Closing stock | 21,000 |
| ,, Wages | 80,500 | | |
| ,, Indirect wages | 61,750 | | |
| ,, Factory overhead | 61,800 | | |
| ,, Gross Profit | 150,100 | | |
| | 506,000 | | 506,000 |
| To Administration expenses | 40,900 | By Gross Profit | 150100 |
| ,, Selling and distribution expenses | 30,250 | ,, Divided received | 10,000 |
| ,, Obsolesence loss | 2,700 | ,, Bank interest | 1,850 |
| ,, Loss on sale of fixed asset | 5,000 | | |
| ,, Bad debts | 2,100 | | |
| ,, Net Profit | 81,000 | | |
| | 161,950 | | 1,61,950 |

**Recociliation Statement**

| Particulars | Rs. | Rs. |
|---|---|---|
| Profit as per Cost Account | 87,500 | |
| **Add:** Dividend received | 20,000 | |
| Bank Interest | 1,850 | |
| **Less:** Under valuation of opening stock in Cost A/c | | 2,800 |
| Over-valuation of closing stock in Cost A/c | | 15,750 |
| Obsolescense loss | | 2,700 |
| Bad debts | | 2,100 |
| Loss on sale of fixed assets | | 5,000 |
| | 109,350 | 28,350 |
| Profit as per Financial Account | | 81,000 |

Note: Over-absorption and under-absorption of overheads should not be taken into account since it has been been adjusted in the Costing Profit and Loss Account.

In the reconciliation statement the profit shown by the cost account is adjusted with purely financial and cost expenses and income, so as to derive the financial profit.It is proved from the reconciliation statement that the calculations are correct.

## EXERCISE

**I. Choose the correct answer for the following:**

1. Over-absorption of overhead in cost account is a
   (i) Profit (ii) Gross proft (iii) Profit or Loss (iv) Cost of sales
2. Under absorption of overhead in cost account is a
   (i) Proft or Loss (ii) Loss (iii) Cost of sales (iv) Prime cost
3. Profit on sale of fixed asset is a
   (i) Costing transaction (ii) Financial and costing transaction
   (iii) Financial transaction (iv) Personal transaction
4. In Reconciliation statement, over-valuation of opening stock in cost account is added with
   (i) Financial profit (ii) Gross profit (iii) Net profit (iv) Costing profit
5. In Reconciliation statement over-valuation of closing stock in cost account is added with
   (i) Costing profit (ii) Financial profit
   (iii) Gross profit (iv) Financial loss
6. For reconciliation, interest received is deducted with
   (i) Financial profit (ii) Costing profit (iii) Gross profit (iv) Net loss
7. In reconciliation, goodwill written off is deducted with
   (i) Fixed cost (ii) Variable cost (iii) Financial profit (iv) Costing profit

[Ans: 1. (i) 2. (ii) 3. (iii) 4. (iv) 5. (ii) 6. (i) 7. (iv)]

**II. Answer the following:**

8. What is Reconciliation Statement in cost accounting?
9. Define Reconciliation Statement for Cost Accounting and Financial Accounting.
10. What is Memorandum Reconciliation Account ?
11. State the procedure in the preparation of Reconciliation Statement.
12. The Net Profit shown by the financial accounts of a manufacturing company for the year ended 31st March 2011 is Rs.65,000. The Profit disclosed by the costing profit and loss account for the year was Rs.70,100. The reasons for the difference in profit are due the following facts:

| | Rs. |
|---|---|
| Factory Overhead Under-recovered | 3,700 |
| Administration Overhead Over-recovered | 2,500 |
| Selling and Distribution Overhead Under-recovered | 3,000 |
| Loss on sale of fixed asset | 4,500 |
| Provision for Income Tax in Financial Account | 6,000 |
| Bank Interest | 3,000 |
| Depreciation charged to Financial Account | 5,000 |

| | |
|---|---|
| Depreciation recovered in Cost Account | 2,700 |
| Under-valuation of Closing stock in Cost Account | 2,900 |

Prepare a Reconciliation Statement and verify the result.

13. Prepare a Reconciliation Statement from the particular given below:

| | Rs. |
|---|---|
| Factory Overhead over-absorbed | 4,000 |
| Administration Overhead under-absorbed | 2,500 |
| Selling and distribution overhead over absorbed | 3,100 |
| Income tax provided in Financial Account | 18,000 |
| Interest received recorded in Financial Account | 4,700 |
| Stock Adjustment (Debit in financial Account) | 1,800 |
| Depreciation charged in Financial Account | 7,000 |
| Depreciation charged in Cost Account | 9,500 |
| Value of Opening stock in Cost Account | 17,500 |
| Value of Opening stock in Financial Account | 20,500 |
| Value of Closing Stock in Cost Account | 34,500 |
| Value of Closing Stock in Financial Account | 39,000 |
| Preliminary expenses written off in financial account | 10,000 |
| Loss on sale of fixed assets recorded in financial account | 4,000 |
| Provision for bad and doutful debts in financial account | 9,000 |
| Interest on capital charged in Cost Account | 12,000 |
| Obsolescence loss charged to Financial Account | 2,500 |
| Commission received recorded in Financial Account | 5,500 |
| Net Loss as per Cost Account | 37,500 |
| Net Loss as per Financial Account | 52,000 |

14. XY & Co. Ltd provides the following information from the books of the company for the year ended 31st March 2011.

| | Rs. |
|---|---|
| Opening stock of material as per financial records | 17,000 |
| Opening stock of material as per Cost records | 15,000 |
| Closing Stock of material as per Financial records | 24,000 |
| Closing Stock of material as per Cost records | 20,000 |
| Purchase of material | 37,500 |
| Direct wages | 40,000 |
| Indirect wages | 24,000 |
| Direct expenses | 14,000 |
| Indirect expenses | 12,000 |
| Administration expenses | 27,000 |
| Selling expenses | 17,000 |

| | |
|---|---|
| Bad debts written off | 6,500 |
| Profit on sale of fixed asset | 7,500 |
| Interest on overdraft | 3,000 |
| Interest on capital charged only in cost account | 14,000 |
| Commission received | 5,000 |
| Depreciation charged in financial account | 9,500 |

Factory overhead recovered is 100% on direct wages. Administration overhead recovered is 20% on works cost. Selling and distribution OH recovered is 10% on works cost. Sale is Rs.210,000. Calculate the financial profit and costing profits and reconcile these profits by preparing the Reconciliation Statement.

(Ans: Costing Profit Rs.21,150; Financial Profit Rs.29,000)

15. K Ltd provides the following information for the year ended 31st March 2011.

| | Rs. |
|---|---|
| Direct material | 110,000 |
| Direct wages | 79,000 |
| Direct expenses | 21,000 |
| Sales | 370,000 |

Factory overhead absorbed is 50 % on Direct Wages, Administration Overhead absorbed is 20% on Works cost and Selling and Distribution overhead absorbed is 10% on Cost of production. The actual overheads are as follows:

| | Rs. |
|---|---|
| Factory overhead | 42,000 |
| Administration Overhead | 45,000 |
| Selling and distribution overhead | 32,000 |

Calculate the financial profit and costing profit. Also prepare a Reconciliation statement.

(Ans: Costing Profit Rs.40,660; Financial Profit Rs.41,000)

16. Calculate the Financial profit, Costing profit and a Statement of Reconciliation from the following information:

| | Rs. |
|---|---|
| Opening Stock of material as per Cost Account | 7,800 |
| Opening Stock of material as per Financial Account | 5,500 |
| Closing Stock of material as per Cost Account | 11,500 |
| Closing Stock of material as per Financial Account | 7,600 |
| Purchase of material | 32,000 |
| Direct wages | 40,000 |

| | |
|---|---|
| Direct expenses | 25,700 |
| Indirect Factory expenses | 20,000 |
| Administration expenses | 25,000 |
| Selling expenses | 22,000 |
| Transfer fees paid | 6,000 |
| Bad Debts | 2,000 |
| Dividend received | 10,000 |
| Bank Charges | 4,000 |
| Bank Interest received | 7,000 |
| Sales | 22,5000 |

Factory overhead recovered is 25% on prime cost, Administration overhead under-recovered is Rs.1,500 and Selling and distribution overhead recovered is 20% on cost of production.

(Ans: Costing profit Rs.55,800; Financial profit Rs.67,400)

17. Z. Ltd manufactures two products, namely Product A and Product B. The cost connected with the production of these products for the year ended 31st March 2011 are as follows:

| | Product A | Product B |
|---|---|---|
| | Rs. | Rs. |
| Material | 31,500 | 43,500 |
| Labour | 29,000 | 34,000 |
| Direct expenses | 14,000 | 17,000 |

Factory overhead recovered is 100 % on direct wages, Administration overhead recovered is 20 % on Factory cost and Selling and distribution overhead recovered is 10% on Cost of production.

The actual overhead are as follows:

| | Product A | Product B |
|---|---|---|
| | Rs. | Rs. |
| Manufacturing Indirect expenses | 30,000 | 35,000 |
| Administration expenses | 18,000 | 21,000 |
| Selling expenses | 15,000 | 18,000 |

The company produced and sold 8,000 units of Product A @ Rs.20 per unit and 6,000 units of Product B @ Rs.30 per unit.

Prepare the Trading and Profit & Loss Account, and Cost sheet and find out the financial as well as costing profits. Also prepare a Reconciliation Statement.

(Ans: Costing Profit Rs.33,760; Financial Profit Rs.34,000)

18. The following information are extracted from the books of a manufacturing company for the year ended 31[st] March 2011.

| | Cost A/c | Financial A/c |
|---|---|---|
| | Rs. | Rs. |
| Opening Stock: | | |
| Raw material | 7,800 | 5,400 |
| Work-in-progress | 11,600 | 14,000 |
| Finished stock | 22,000 | 21,000 |
| Closing Stock : | | |
| Raw material | 6,000 | 4,800 |
| Work-in-progress | 14,800 | 13,500 |
| Finished stock | 31,500 | 27,500 |

The information available in financial and cost records are as follows:

| | Rs. |
|---|---|
| Direct material | 56,500 |
| Direct wages | 50,000 |
| Direct expenses | 40,000 |
| Indirect wages | 23,500 |
| Factory expenses | 19,800 |
| Administrative expenses | 48,500 |
| Selling expenses | 39,000 |
| Miscellaneous financial expenses | 4,500 |
| Interest and Dividend received | 38,000 |
| Bad Debts | 3,500 |
| Transfer fees | 5,000 |
| Obsolescence loss on fixed assets | 6,500 |
| Transfer to reserve | 14,000 |
| Rent received | 21,000 |
| Provision for dividend | 18,000 |
| Provision for taxation | 12,000 |
| Profit as on 31[st] March 2010 | 19,500 |
| Sales | 375,000 |

Overheads recovered in Cost Account are as follows:

| | Rs. |
|---|---|
| Factory | 47,000 |
| Administration | 50,000 |
| Selling and distribution | 35,000 |

Calculate profits as per Financial Account and Cost Account. Also prepare a Reconciliation Statement.

(Ans: Costing Profit Rs.107,400; Financial Profit Rs.118,100)

19. The Trading and Profit and Loss Account of KMW & Co Ltd for the year ended 31st March 2011 is as follows:

**Trading and Profit & Loss A/c for the year ended 31st Mar.2011.**

| Particulars Rs. | Amount | Particulars Rs. | Amount |
|---|---|---|---|
| To Op.Stock | 31,500 | By Sales | 369,000 |
| " Purchases | 67,800 | " Closing Stock | 27,500 |
| " Wages | 62,000 | | |
| " Factory Overhead | 41,200 | | |
| " Gross Profit | 194,000 | | |
| | 396,500 | | 396,500 |
| To Administrative expenses | 87,500 | By Gross Profit | 194,000 |
| " Selling expenses | 76,500 | " Commission received | 8,000 |
| " Interest paid | 32,100 | " Dividend received | 22,000 |
| " Bad debts | 2,900 | " Rent received | 20,000 |
| " Taxes paid | 12,500 | | |
| " Net Profit | 32,500 | | |
| | 244,000 | | 244,000 |

The information available in the cost records are as follows:

| | Rs. |
|---|---|
| Costing Profit | 11,000 |
| Factory Overhead absorbed | 39,000 |
| Administrative overhead absorbed | 90,000 |
| Selling and distribution overhead absorbed | 80,000 |
| Interest on capital | 15,000 |
| Opening Stock of material | 30,000 |
| Closing Stock of material | 25,000 |

Prepare the Reconciliation statement and prove the accuracy of the accounts.

20. Prepare a Reconciliation Statement for the year ended 31st March 2011 from the following particulars:

**Trading and Profit & Loss Account as on 31st March 2011**

| Particulars | Rs. | Particulars | Rs. |
|---|---|---|---|
| To Op. Stock | 19,000 | By Sales | 99,500 |
| " Purchases | 72,000 | " Closing Stock | 24,000 |
| " Wages | 48,000 | " Gross Loss | 49,500 |
| " Factory expenses | 34,000 | | |
| | 173,000 | | 173,000 |

| | Rs. | | Rs. |
|---|---|---|---|
| To Gross Loss | 49,500 | By Profit on sale of machinery | 16,000 |
| ,, Administrative exp. | 74,800 | ,, Bank Interest | 21,000 |
| ,, Taxes paid | 11,500 | ,, Dividend received | 53,000 |
| ,, Transfer fees | 3,000 | ,, Rent received | 34,000 |
| ,, Selling expenses | 61,000 | ,, Net Loss | 87,000 |
| ,, Obsolescence Loss | 6,500 | | |
| ,, Bad Debts | 4,700 | | |
| | 211,000 | | 211,000 |

The following information are available in the cost records:

| | Rs. |
|---|---|
| Factory overhead absorbed | 37,000 |
| Administration overhead absorbed | 72,000 |
| Selling and distribution overhead absorbed | 60,000 |
| Interest on Capital | 8,000 |
| Opening stock of material | 21,000 |
| Closing stock of material | 27,500 |

[Ans: Net loss Rs.191,000]

21. Prepare a Memorandum Reconciliation Account from the following particulars:

| | Rs. |
|---|---|
| Profit as per Cost Account | 97,500 |
| Under-absorption of Factory overhead | 3,700 |
| Over-absorption of Administration overhead | 4,500 |
| Under-absorption of Selling and Distribution overhead | 6,000 |
| Under-valuation of opening stock in Cost Account | 2,800 |
| Under-valuation of closing stock in Cost Account | 4,000 |
| Goodwill written-off in Financial Account | 15,000 |
| Over-charging of deprecition in Financial Account | 3,700 |
| Dividend received | 12,000 |
| Interest on Capital charged only in Cost Account | 9,000 |
| Preliminary expenses written-off in Financial Account | 7,000 |
| Transfer fees charged in Financial Account | 3,500 |

[Ans: Financial proft Rs.85,300]

22. A manufacturing company provides the following information for the year ended 31st March 2011.

| | Rs. |
|---|---|
| Net Loss as per Cost Account | 28,500 |
| Opening stock valued in Financial Account | 7,500 |
| Opening stock valued in Cost Account | 10,000 |
| Closing stock valued in Financial Account | 14,500 |
| Closing stock valued in Cost Account | 17,000 |
| Under-absorption of Factory overhead | 7,500 |
| Over-absorption of Administration overhead | 4,600 |
| Over-absorption of Selling and distribution overhead | 5,400 |
| Interest on capital charged only in Cost Account | 7,500 |
| Transfer fees | 2,500 |
| Commission received | 8,500 |
| Dividend received | 27,500 |
| Goodwill written-off | 22,000 |
| Bad debts | 1,500 |
| Bank charges | 2,000 |
| Depreciation charged in Financial Account | 15,500 |
| Depreciation charged in Cost Account | 14,000 |
| Loss on sale of fixed asset | 5,500 |

Prepare Memorandum Reconciliation account and find out the Net Loss as per Financial Account.

[Ans: Rs.17,500]

23. MWD & Co Ltd provides the following information from books of account for the year ended 31st March 2011.

| Balances as on 1st April 2010 | Rs. |
|---|---|
| Stores Ledger Control A/c | 18,500 |
| Work-in-progress Ledger Control A/c | 24,000 |
| Finished Goods Ledger Control A/c | 32,000 |
| Cost Ledger Control A/c | 74,500 |

Transactions for the year ended 31st March 2011 are as follows:

| | Rs. |
|---|---|
| Purchase of raw material | 97,500 |
| Direct wages | 62,000 |
| Direct expenses | 24,000 |
| Indirect wages | 26,500 |
| Factory overhead | 29,000 |
| Administration overhead | 84,000 |

| | |
|---|---|
| Selling and distribution overhead | 70,000 |
| Factory overhead recovered | 59,000 |
| Administration overhead recovered | 82,000 |
| Selling and distribution overhead recovered | 77,500 |
| Material issued to production | 105,000 |
| Material returned from production centre to store | 7,500 |
| Material purchased for specific job | 8,000 |
| Value of work-in-progress as on 31st March 2011 | 26,000 |
| Value of Finished Goods as on 31st March 2011 | 30,000 |
| Costing Profit | 49,500 |

The Company's Balance Sheet shows the value of closing stock as on 1st April 2010 as Rs.77,000 and as on 31st March 2011 as Rs 79,000. The transactions recorded only in Financial Accounts are as follows:

| | Rs. |
|---|---|
| Loss on sale of furniture | 9,500 |
| Obsolescence Loss | 3,500 |
| Bad Debts | 4,000 |
| Dividend received | 15,000 |
| Bank Interest received | 4,000 |

Prepare (a) Necessary Ledger Accounts in Cost Books, (b) Financial Profit and Loss Account and (c) The Reconciliation Statement.

[Ans: Net profit Rs.54,500]

24. R Ltd provides the following information from books of account for the year ended 31st March 2011.

| Balances as on 1st April 2010 | Rs. |
|---|---|
| Stores Ledger Control A/c | 40,000 |
| Work-in-progress Ledger Control A/c | 35,000 |
| Finished Goods Ledger Control A/c | 55,000 |
| Cost Ledger Control A/c | 130,000 |

Transactions for the year ended 31st March 2011 are as follows:

| | Rs. |
|---|---|
| Purchase of raw material | 115,000 |
| Direct wages | 80,000 |
| Direct expenses | 32,000 |
| Indirect wages | 20,000 |
| Factory overhead | 39,000 |
| Administration overhead | 92,000 |
| Selling and distribution overhead | 80,000 |

| | |
|---|---|
| Factory overhead recovered | 62,000 |
| Administration overhead recovered | 87,000 |
| Selling and distribution overhead recovered | 86,000 |
| Material issued to production | 120,000 |
| Material returned from production centre to store | 7,000 |
| Material purchased for specific job | 10,000 |
| Value of Work-in-progress as on 31st March 2006 | 33,000 |
| Value of Finished Goods as on 31st March 2006 | 44,000 |
| Sales | 550,000 |

The Company's Balance Sheet shows the value of closing stock as on 1st April 2010 as Rs.136,000 and as on 31st March 2011 as Rs.115,000 The transactions recorded only in Financial Accounts are as follows:

| | Rs. |
|---|---|
| Loss on sale of machinery | 15,000 |
| Profit on sale of furniture | 5,000 |
| Bad debts | 6,000 |
| Dividend received | 20,000 |
| Bank Interest paid | 7,000 |

Prepare (a) Necessary Ledger Accounts in Cost Books, (b) Financial Profit & Loss Account and (c) The Reconciliation Statement.

[Ans: Costing profit Rs.69,000; Net profit Rs.58,000]

25. Prepare a Memorandum Reconciliation Account from the following particulars:

| | Rs. |
|---|---|
| Profit as per Financial Account | 150,000 |
| Over-absorption of Factory overhead | 7,700 |
| Under-absorption of Administration overhead | 5,500 |
| Over-absorption of Selling and Distribution overhead | 9,000 |
| Under-valuation of opening stock in Cost Account | 5,000 |
| Under-valuation of closing stock in Cost Account | 7,000 |
| Goodwill written-off in Financial Account | 25,000 |
| Over-charging of deprecition in Financial Account | 4,000 |
| Interest received | 14,000 |
| Interest on Capital charged only in Cost Account | 10,000 |
| Preliminary expenses written-off in Financial Account | 7,000 |
| Transfer fees charged in Financial Account | 4,500 |

[Ans: Financial proft Rs.53,300]

# CHAPTER XII

# MARGINAL COSTING

Marginal costing is a technique of analysing the changes of cost due to the changes is volume of production. The total cost of production may be classified into fixed cost and variable cost. The fixed cost remain constant upto certain level of production. The variable cost changes due to the changes in volume production. The variable cost is otherwise called as marginal cost. Hence,marginal costing analyses the relationship of the changes of variable cost due to changes in volume of production.

**Meaning of Marginal cost**

The Institute of cost and Management Accountants, London defines marginal cost as "the amount of a given volume of output by which aggregate costs are changed if the volume of output is increased by one unit".

Blocker and Weltmere define, "Marginal cost is the increase or decrease in total cost which results from producing or selling additional or fewer units of a product or from a change in the method of production or distribution such as the one of improved machinery,addition or exclusion of a product or territory or selection of an additional sales channel".

It is clear from the definitions that marginal cost means additional or difference in cost due to the increase or decrease of producing one unit from the normal production.

Marginal cost may be termed as the total variable cost. It includes the prime cost and variable overhead.

(Eg) Material cost per unit isRs 8, Labour cost per unit is Rs 5, Variable overhead is Rs 3 per unit and number of units produced is 500 units. The marginal cost may be calculated as

| | Per unit Rs. | Total Rs. |
|---|---|---|
| Direct Material | 8 | 4,000 |
| Direct Labour | 5 | 2,500 |
| Prime cost | 13 | 6,500 |
| Variable overhead | 3 | 1,500 |
| Marginal cost or variable cost | 16 | 8,000 |

**Marginal costing**

The Institute of Cost and Management Accountants, London defined Marginal costing as " The ascertainment of marginal cost and of the effect on profit of changes in volume or type of output by differentiating between fixed cost and variable cost".

It is clear from the definition that marginal costing is a technique of analysing the marginal (or variable) cost and profit in relation to the changes in volume of production.

**Characteristics of Marginal Costing**

The important characteristics of marginal costing are as follows.

1. The total cost of production is classified into fixed and variable cost. Hence, all the functional cost like production, administration and selling cost are grouped into fixed cost and variable cost.
2. It is a technique of costing which helps the management to take various managerial decisions.
3. The stock of finished goods and work-in-progress are valued at marginal cost.
4. The price of the product is determined on the basis of contribution.
5. The variable cost is considered as the important cost of the product.

**Assumptions of Marginal Costing**

The following are the important assumptions of marginal costing.

1. The functional element of cost like production, administration and selling and distribution costs should be classified into fixed and variable cost.
2. Variable cost per unit should remain constant. It varies according to the changes in volume of production.
3. Fixed cost remains constant for all the levels of production. Hence, fixed cost per unit varies.
4. The selling price per unit should remain constant at all levels of activity.
5. The volume of production should be the only factor of production which influences the cost.

**Advantages of Marginal Costing**

The following are the advantages of marginal costing.

1. It is simple to operate and easy to understand.
2. It helps the management to take various managerial decisions.
3. It facilitates to fix the prices.
4. Marginal costing technique can be applied for profit planning.
5. It facilitates for taking decision regarding the acceptance or rejection of a bulk order.

6. Marginal Costing helps the management to calculate the Break- even-point.
7. It facilitates the management to decide the optimum product mix, when the company is producing more than one product.

**Limitations of Marginal Costing**

The following are the important limitations of marginal costing.

1. Changes in the selling price affects the results of marginal costing.
2. The assumption that the fixed cost remain constant may not be always correct, since it may also vary due to various reasons.
3. Marginal costing technique excludes fixed cost for various managerial decisions.
4. The assumption that the variable cost per unit remains constant is practically not possible always. Increase in volume of production may reduce the variable cost per unit.
5. Marginal costing technique considers only the value of contribution for deciding the profitability of a product. It ignores the time factor. Product which gives maximum contribution is the best product compared to other, irrespective of the duration of production.

## Calculation of costing profit by absorption costing method and marginal costing method

**(a) Calculation of costing profit by Absorption Costing Method:**

**Statement of Cost**

| Particulars | Amount (Rs.) |
|---|---|
| Direct material | x x x |
| Direct wages | x x x |
| Direct expenses | x x x |
| PRIME COST | x x x |
| Add: Factory overhead | x x x |
| WORKS COST | x x x |
| Add: Adminstration overhead | x x x |
| COST OF PRODUCTION | x x x |
| Add: Selling & distribution overhead | x x x |
| COST OF SALES | x x x |
| COSTING PROFIT | x x x |
| SALES | x x x |

**(b) Calculation of Costing profit by Marginal cost method.**

A model of the Statement of cost under Marginal Costing Method is stated as follows.

**Statement of Cost**

| Particulars | | Amount Rs. | Amount Rs. |
|---|---|---|---|
| | **Sales** | | x x x |
| Less: | Variable cost: | | |
| | Direct material | x x x | |
| | Direct wages | x x x | |
| | Direct expenses | x x x | |
| | Variable Factory overhead | x x x | |
| | Variable Administration overhead | x x x | |
| | Variable selling and distribution overhead | x x x | x x x |
| | **Contribution** | | x x x |
| Less: | Fixed cost: | | |
| | Fixed Factory overhead | x x x | |
| | Fixed Administration overhead | x x x | |
| | Fixed Selling and distribution overhead | x x x | x x x |
| | **Costing Profit** | | x x x |

**Illustration: 1**

Prepare a statement of cost by

(a) Absorption costing method and

(b) Marginal costing method

| Particulars | Period-1 Rs. | Period-2 Rs. | Period-3 Rs. |
|---|---|---|---|
| Direct material consumed | 21,000 | 30,000 | 25,000 |
| Direct wages paid | 17,000 | 15,000 | 20,000 |
| Direct expenses | 7,000 | 5,000 | 6,000 |
| Sales | 1,30,000 | 1,25,000 | 1,50,000 |
| Factory overhead | 14,000 | 7,000 | 4,000 |
| Administration overhead | 17,000 | 15,000 | 18,000 |
| Selling & Distribution overhead | 10,000 | 8,000 | 11,000 |

10% of the administration overhead and 20% of the selling overhead are variable in nature.

**Solution:**

***(a) Statement of cost by Absorption Costing Method:***

| Particulars | Period 1 (Rs) | Period 2 (Rs) | Period 3 (Rs) |
|---|---|---|---|
| Direct material consumed | 21,000 | 30,000 | 25,000 |
| Direct wages | 17,000 | 15,000 | 20,000 |
| Direct expenses | 7,000 | 5,000 | 6,000 |
| Prime cost | 45,000 | 50,000 | 51,000 |
| Add: Factory overhead | 14,000 | 7,000 | 4,000 |
| Factory cost | 59,000 | 57,000 | 55,000 |
| Add: Administration overhead | 17,000 | 15,000 | 18,000 |
| Cost of production | 76,000 | 72,000 | 73,000 |
| Add: Selling & Distribution overhead | 10,000 | 8,000 | 11,000 |
| Cost of sales | 86,000 | 80,000 | 84,000 |
| Costing profit | 44,000 | 45,000 | 66,000 |
| SALES | 1,30,000 | 1,25,000 | 1,50,000 |

***(b) Statement of cost by Marginal Costing Method:***

| Particulars | Period 1 (Rs) | Peiord 2 (Rs) | Period 3 (Rs) |
|---|---|---|---|
| SALES | 1,30,000 | 1,25,000 | 1,50,000 |
| Less: Variable costs: | | | |
| Direct material | 21,000 | 30,000 | 25,000 |
| Direct wages | 17,000 | 15,000 | 20,000 |
| Direct expenses | 7,000 | 5,000 | 6,000 |
| Factory overhead | 14,000 | 7,000 | 4,000 |
| Variable Administration OH | 1,700 | 1,500 | 1,800 |
| Variable Selling & Distribution OH | 2,000 | 1,600 | 2,200 |
| Total variable cost | 62,700 | 60,100 | 59,000 |
| Contribution (Sales - V.C) | 67,300 | 64,900 | 91,000 |
| Less: Fixed cost | | | |
| Fixed Administration OH | 15,300 | 13,500 | 16,200 |
| Fixed Selling & distribution OH | 8,000 | 6,400 | 8,800 |
| Total fixed cost | 23,300 | 19,900 | 25,000 |
| Costing profit | 44,000 | 45,000 | 66,000 |

**Illustration: 2** A manufacturing company produces three products namely A,B and C. The information related to the production and sales of these products for 3 months ending 30th June 2011 are as follows:

| | | A | B | C |
|---|---|---|---|---|
| | | Rs. | Rs. | Rs. |
| Direct material | | 14,000 | 11,000 | 12,000 |
| Direct wages | | 13,500 | 10,500 | 11,500 |
| Factory overhead - | Fixed | 7,000 | 9,000 | 10,000 |
| | Variable | 5,000 | 4,000 | 6,000 |
| Administration overhead - | Fixed | 10,000 | 9,000 | 7,000 |
| | Variable | 7,000 | 4,000 | 5,000 |
| Selling and Distribution overhead- | | | | |
| | Fixed | 5,000 | 6,000 | 4,000 |
| | Variable | 4,500 | 3,500 | 2,500 |
| Sales | | 95,000 | 76,000 | 79,000 |

Prepare a statement of cost by (a) Marginal Costing method and (b) Absorption Costing method.

***Solution:***

**(a) Statement of Cost (Marginal Costing Method)**

| Particulars | Products | | | Total |
|---|---|---|---|---|
| | A Rs. | B Rs. | C Rs. | Rs. |
| Sales | 95,000 | 76,000 | 79,000 | 250,000 |
| Variable Costs: | | | | |
| Direct material | 14,000 | 11,000 | 12,000 | |
| Direct Wages | 13,500 | 10,500 | 11,500 | |
| Variable Overhead: | | | | |
| Factory | 5,000 | 4,000 | 6,000 | |
| Administration | 7,000 | 4,000 | 5,000 | |
| Selling and Distribution | 4,500 | 3,500 | 2,500 | |
| Marginal cost | 44,000 | 33,000 | 37,000 | 1,14,000 |
| Contribution | 51,000 | 43,000 | 42,000 | 1,36,000 |
| (Contribution = Sales-M.C) | | | | |
| Less: Fixed overhead | | | | |
| Factory | 7,000 | 9,000 | 10,000 | |
| Administration | 10,000 | 9,000 | 7,000 | |
| Selling and Distribution | 5,000 | 6,000 | 4,000 | |
| Total FOH | 22,000 | 24,000 | 21,000 | 67,000 |
| Profit: (Contribution - Fixed overhead) | 29,000 | 19,000 | 21,000 | 69,000 |

**(b) Statement of Cost**
**(Absorption Costing Method)**

| Particulars | | Products A Rs. | B Rs. | C Rs. | Total Rs. |
|---|---|---|---|---|---|
| Direct mateiral | | 14,000 | 11,000 | 12,000 | |
| Direct wages | | 13,500 | 10,500 | 11,500 | |
| Prime cost | | 27,500 | 21,500 | 23,500 | 72,500 |
| Factory overhead: | Fixed | 7,000 | 9,000 | 10,000 | |
| | Variable | 5,000 | 4,000 | 6,000 | |
| Works cost | | 39,500 | 34,500 | 39,500 | 113,500 |
| Administration overhead: | Fixed | 10,000 | 9,000 | 7,000 | |
| | Variable | 7,000 | 4,000 | 5,000 | |
| Cost of Production | | 56,500 | 47,500 | 51,500 | 155,500 |
| Selling and Distribution overhead: | | | | | |
| | Fixed | 5,000 | 6,000 | 4,000 | |
| | Variable | 4,500 | 3,500 | 2,500 | |
| Cost of Sales | | 66,000 | 57,000 | 58,000 | 181,000 |
| Costing Profit | | 29,000 | 19,000 | 21,000 | 69,000 |
| Sales | | 95,000 | 76,000 | 79,000 | 250,000 |

**Contribution:**

Contribution is the difference between sales and variable cost. Contribution includes Fixed cost and Profit or loss. Hence, contribution can be calculated by adding the profit with the Fixed cost or deducting loss with the Fixed cost.

Hence, Contribution = Sales - Variable Cost or,
= Fixed Cost $\pm$ Profit or Loss.

***Marginal Cost Equation***

The equation, Contribution = Sales - Variable cost is called Marginal Cost Equation. It helps to find out either Fixed Cost or Variable Cost, when other information of the equation are given.

***Profit/Volume Ratio***

Profit/Volume Ratio is the ratio between contribution and sales. It is otherwise called as 'Contribution ratio' or 'marginal ratio'.

$$\text{P/V Ratio} = \frac{\text{Contribution}}{\text{Sales}} \quad \text{or}$$

$$= \frac{\text{Sales - Variable Cost}}{\text{Sales}} \quad \text{or}$$

$$= \frac{\text{Fixed Cost + Profit}}{\text{Sales}} \quad \text{or}$$

$$= \frac{\text{Change in Profit or Contribution}}{\text{Change in Sales}}$$

Sales for an expected profit can be calculated by P/V Ratio through the following formula

$$\text{Expected Sales} = \frac{\text{Fixed Cost + Expected Profit}}{\text{P/V Ratio}}$$

## BREAK - EVEN ANALYSIS

Break - even analysis is a study of the relationship between Cost, Volume and Profit. In narrow sense, it is an analysis to know the level of production. In the broader sense, it is an analysis to find out the relationship between cost, volume and profit at different levels of sales or production.

***Break - even Point:***

Break - even Point may be defined as the point of sales volume at which the total revenue is equal to the total cost. At break - even point there will be neither profit nor loss. At this point the contribution is equal to fixed cost. Break - even point is otherwise called as 'Critical Point', or 'Equilibrium Point' or 'Balancing Point'.

Break - even point can be calculated through the following formula.

$$\text{Break - even Point (in units)} = \frac{\text{Fixed Cost}}{\text{Contribution per unit}}$$

$$\text{Break - even Point (in value)} = \frac{\text{Fixed Cost x Selling price per unit}}{\text{Contribution per unit}}$$

$$\text{Contribution} = \text{Sales - Variable Cost}$$

Through P/V Ratio, B.E.P can be calculated as,

$$\text{B.E.P.} = \frac{\text{Fixed Cost}}{\text{P/V Ratio}}$$

Break - even analysis also helps to find out the expected sales to earn a given profit.

$$\text{Expected Sales for an expected profit} = \frac{\text{Fixed Cost + Expected Profit}}{\text{Contribution per unit.}}$$

**B.E.P Chart**

Break - even chart is a graphical representation of the Break - even point. The Break - even point can be measured by a graph through the following procedures.

1. X axis should be denoted for number of units and Y axis for cost and revenue.
2. Number of units should be provided conveniently in the X axis and

the amount should be marked uniformly in Y axis through a common scale.

3. Mark the Fixed cost on the Y axis and draw a parallel line to X axis through the point.
4. Plot points in the graph for the total cost (Fixed cost + variable cost) at various levels of production. Join all the points to get a straight line from the point of fixed cost at Y axis. This is called total cost line.
5. Plot points in the graph for the sales value at different levels (units) of sales. Join the point from O of the graph to get a straight line. This is called sales line.
6. The sales line cuts at a point in the Total Cost line. This point is called Break – even point.
7. Draw a perpendicular line to X axis from this B.E.P. Measure the number of units in the X axis, where the perpendicular line cuts, to know the B.E.P. of sales in units.
8. Draw a perpendicular line to Y axis from the B.E.P and measure the value in the Y axis. This is called the B.E.P in Sales value.

**The model B.E.P chart is shown as follows:**

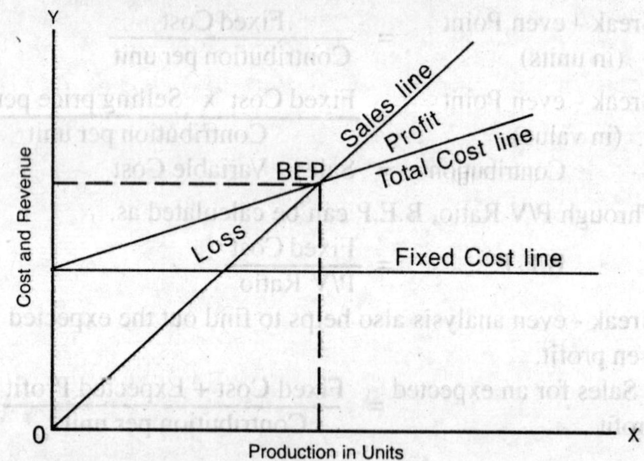


**Illustration: 3**

Calculate the profit earned by a company during the year 2011 from the following information:

| | |
|---|---|
| Fixed Cost | Rs.3,00,000 |
| Variable Cost | Rs.25 per unit |
| Selling Price | Rs.50 per unit |

Number of units produced 50,000.

***Solution:***

Sales = 50,000 x 50 = Rs.25,00,000

Fixed Cost = Rs.3,00,000

Variable Cost = 50,000 x 25 = Rs.12,50,000

S - V.C = F.C. + Profit

Profit = S - V.C - F.C

= 25,00,000 - 12,50,000 - 3,00,000

= Rs.9,50,000

**Illustration: 4**

Calculate (a) P/V ratio (b) Fixed Cost (c) Sales volume to earn a profit of Rs. 40,000.

Salcs Rs.2,00,000

Profit Rs.25,000

Variable Cost is 80% of sales.

***Solution:***

Sales = Rs.2,00,000

Variable Cost $= \frac{80}{100} \times 2,00,000 =$ Rs.160,000

(a) P/V Ratio $= \frac{\text{Sales - Variable Cost}}{\text{Sales}} \times 100$

$= \frac{200,000 - 160,000}{200,000} = 20\%$

(b) Contribution = Fixed Cost + Profit

Sales - Variable Cost = F.C. + Profit

200,000 - 160,000 = F.C. + 25,000

F.C. = 40,000 - 25,000

= Rs. 15,000

(c) P/V Ratio $= \frac{\text{Fixed Cost + Profit}}{\text{Sales}}$

Sales $= \frac{\text{F.C + Profit}}{\text{P/V Ratio}}$

$= \frac{15,000 + 40,000}{20\%}$

= Rs.2,75,000

**Illustration: 5**

The fixed cost for manufacturing 500 units of a product is Rs.2,000 per month and variable cost is Rs.10 per unit. Selling price is Rs.18 per unit.

Calculate the P/V ratio. If the selling price is reduced by 20%, find out the P/V ratio. Also calculate the number of units to be sold to earn the present total profit.

***Solution:***

Calculation of present P/V Ratio:

Sales = 500 x 18 = Rs.9,000

Variable cost = 500 x 10 = Rs.5,000

Contribution = Sales - Variable Cost = 9,000 - 5,000 = Rs.4,000

$$\text{P/V Ratio} = \frac{\text{Contribution x 100}}{\text{Sales}} = \frac{4000 \times 100}{9000} = 44.4\%$$

Profit = Contribution - Fixed Cost = 4,000 - 2,000 = Rs.2,000

Calculation of P/V Ratio when selling price is reduced by 20%

Selling price = 18 - 20% of 18 = 18 - 3.6 = Rs.14.40 per unit

Sales = 14.40 x 500 = Rs.7,200

Variable Cost = 500 x 10 = Rs.5,000

Contribution = 7,200 - 5,000 = Rs.2,200

$$\text{Contribution per unit} = \frac{2200}{500} = \text{Rs.}4.40$$

$$\text{P/V Ratio} = \frac{2200 \times 100}{7200} = 30.56\,\%$$

$$\text{Expected Sales to earn the present profit of Rs.2,000 is} = \frac{\text{Fixed Cost + Expected Profit}}{\text{Contribution per unit}}$$

$$= \frac{2000 + 2000}{4.4}$$

$$= \frac{4000}{4.4} = 909 \text{ units}$$

Expected Sales in value = 909 x 14.40 = Rs.13,089.60

**Illustration: 6**

From the following information find out (i) P/V ratio (ii) sales required to earn a profit of Rs.80,000. (iii) the profit if sales is Rs.2,00,000.

| Year | Sales Rs. | Profit Rs. |
|---|---|---|
| 2010 | 1,80,000 | 40,000 |
| 2011 | 2,40,000 | 64,000 |

***Solution:***

(i) $$\text{P/V Ratio} = \frac{\text{Changes in Profit}}{\text{Changes in Sales}}$$

Changes in Sales = 240,000 - 180,000 = Rs.60,000

Changes in Profit = 64,000 - 40,000 = Rs.24,000

$$\text{P/V Ratio} = \frac{24,000}{60,000} \times 100 = 40\%$$

(ii) $$\text{Contribution} = 180,000 \times 40\% = \frac{180,000 \times 40}{100} = \text{Rs.}72,000$$

Contribution = Fixed Cost + Profit

72,000 = F.C + 40,000

Fixed Cost = 72,000 - 40,000 = Rs.32,000

$$\text{Expected sales to earn profit of Rs 80,000} = \frac{\text{Fixed Cost + Expected Profit}}{\text{P/V Ratio}}$$

$$= \frac{32,000 + 80,000}{40\%}$$

$$= \frac{112,000 \times 100}{40}$$

= Rs.280,000

(iii) Calculation of profit when sales is Rs 200,000:

Contribution = 200,000 x 40%

= Rs 80,000

Contribution = F.C + Profit

80,000 = 32,000 + Profit

Profit = 80,000 - 32,000 = Rs.48,000

**Illustration: 7**

Calculate the break - even point in units and sales value from the following details:

| | |
|---|---|
| Production | 5,000 units |
| Total Fixed Cost | Rs.50,000 |
| Variable Cost | Rs.30 per unit |
| Selling Price | Rs.55 per unit |

***Solution:***

Sales = 5,000 x 50 = Rs.2,50,000

Variable Cost = 5,000 x 25 = Rs.1,25,000

Contribution per unit = Sales - V.C = 55 - 30 = Rs.25

$$\text{Break - even point} = \frac{\text{F.C}}{\text{Contribution per unit}}$$

$$= \frac{50,000}{25} = 2,000 \text{ units}$$

B.E.P in Sales value = 2,000 x 55 = Rs.1,10,000

**Illustration: 8**

Calculate break - even point in terms of sales value and in units. Also calculate the number of units to be sold to earn a profit of Rs.75,000.

| | |
|---|---|
| Fixed factory overheads | Rs.80,000 |
| Fixed selling overheads | Rs.20,000 |
| Variable manufacturing cost per unit | Rs.18 |
| Variable selling cost per unit | Rs.12 |
| Selling price per unit | Rs.50 |

***Solution:***

Fixed Cost = 80,000 + 20,000 = Rs.100,000

Variable Cost per unit = 18 + 12 = Rs.30

Sales = Rs.50

Contribution = S - V.C = 50-30 = Rs.20 per unit

$$\text{B.E.P.} = \frac{\text{Fixed Cost}}{\text{Contribution per unit}} = \frac{1,00,000}{20}$$

= 5,000 units

B.E.P in value = 5,000 x 50

= Rs.2,50,000

Number of units to be sold to earn a profit of Rs. 75,000

$$= \frac{\text{F.C+Expected Profit}}{\text{Contribution per unit}}$$

$$= \frac{100,000 + 75,000}{20}$$

$$= \frac{175,000}{20} = 8,750 \text{ units}$$

**Illustration: 9**

The following information are related to a manufacturing company:

| | | |
|---|---|---|
| Selling price per unit | - | Rs.60 |
| Fixed Cost | - | Rs.2,50,000 |
| Variable cost per unit: | | |
| Direct material | - | Rs.17 |
| Direct wages | - | Rs.4 |
| Variable overheads | - | 75% of direct wages. |

Calculate (i) P/V ratio (ii) Sales required to earn a profit of Rs.2,00,000 (iii) break - even sales with the help of P/V ratio.

***Solution:***

Sales = Rs.60 per unit

Variable cost per unit = 17 + 4 + (75% of Rs.4)

= 17 + 4 + (3/4 x 4)

= Rs.24

Contribution = S - V.C

= 60 - 24

= Rs.36 per unit

(i) P/V Ratio $= \frac{\text{Contribution}}{\text{Sales}} \times 100$

$= \frac{36}{60} \times 100 = 60\%$

(ii) Sales required to earn a profit of Rs.2,00,000

$= \frac{\text{F.C + Expected Profit}}{\text{Contribution per unit}}$

$= \frac{250{,}000 + 200{,}000}{36}$

$= \frac{4{,}50{,}000}{36}$

= 12,500 units

i.e., 12,500 x 60 = Rs.750,000 in value

(iii) B.E.P $= \frac{\text{F.C}}{\text{P/V Ratio}} = \frac{250{,}000}{60\%}$

$= \frac{250{,}000}{60} \times 100 =$ Rs.416,667

**Illustration: 10**

The fixed cost for manufacturing a product is Rs.1,20,000. The variable cost is 60% of sales. If sales is Rs.4,20,000 at 100% capacity, calculate the break - even point and percentage capacity at B.E.P. Also calculate the profit at 75% capacity.

***Solution:***

Variable cost = 60% of sales $= \frac{60}{100} \times 420{,}000$

= Rs.252,000

Contribution = 420,000 - 252,000 = Rs.168,000 (S - VC)

Fixed Cost = Rs.120,000

B.E.P $= \frac{\text{Fixed Cost}}{\text{P/V Ratio}}$

P/V Ratio $= \frac{\text{Contribution}}{\text{Sales}} \times 100$

$$= \frac{1,68,000}{4,20,000} \times 100 = 40\%$$

B.E.P. $= \frac{120,000}{40\%} = \frac{1,20,000 \times 100}{40}$

$= \text{Rs.}300,000$

Capacity $= \frac{100 \times 300,000}{420,000} = 71.4\%$

Sales at 75% of Capacity $= 420,000 \times \frac{75}{100}$

= Rs.315,000

Fixed Cost = Rs.120,000

Variable Cost = 60% x 315,000

= Rs.1,89,000

Total cost = 1,20,000 + 189,000

= Rs.3,09,000

Profit = Sales - Total Cost

= 315,000 - 309,000

= Rs.6,000

**Illustration: 11**

The sales of a company for 2 different periods are 10,000 units and 15,000 units, and the profits are Rs.25,000 and Rs.90,000. Calculate (i) Fixed cost (ii) Break - even point (iii) number of units to be sold to earn a profit of Rs.64,000. Assume selling price as Rs.50 per unit.

***Solution:***

P/V Ratio $= \frac{\text{Difference in Profit of two periods}}{\text{Difference in Sales of two periods}}$

$= \frac{90,000 - 25,000}{(15000 \times 50) - (10,000 \times 50)}$

$= \frac{65,000 \times 100}{250,000} = 26\%$

Contribution = (15,000 x 50) x 26/100

= Rs.195,000

Contribution = Fixed cost + Profit

195,000 = F.C + 90,000

(i) Fixed Cost = 1,95,000 - 90,000

= Rs.1,05,000

(ii) BEP $= \frac{\text{F.C}}{\text{P/V ratio}} = \frac{1,05,000}{0.26} = \text{Rs.}4,03,846$

(iii) Sales to earn a profit of Rs.64,000 $= \frac{\text{F.C + Expected Profit}}{\text{P/V Ratio}}$

$$= \frac{1,05,000 + 64,000}{26\%}$$

$$= \frac{169000 \times 100}{26}$$

= Rs.650,000

**Illustration: 12**

Calculate Break - even point from the following information:

| | |
|---|---|
| Sales | Rs.4,00,000 |
| Fixed Cost | Rs.1,50,000 |
| Variable cost | Rs.2,00,000 |

***Solution:***

$$\text{Break - even point} = \frac{\text{Fixed Cost x Sales}}{\text{Contribution}}$$

$$= \frac{1,50,000 \times 4,00,000}{4,00,000 - 2,00,000}$$

$$= \frac{1,50,000 \times 4,00,000}{2,00,000}$$

= Rs.3,00,000

**Illustration: 13**

A manufacturing company is providing the following information:

| | |
|---|---|
| Fixed expenses | Rs.300,000 |
| Selling price per unit | Rs.50 |
| Variable expenses - Material | Rs.12 per unit |
| Wages | Rs.8 per unit |

Draw a break - even chart and verify the result through a schedule. Aslo calculate the new break - even point if the selling price is reduced by 20%.

***Solution:***

| | | |
|---|---|---|
| Fixed Cost | = | Rs.300,000 |
| Variable cost per unit | = | Rs.20 |
| Selling price per unit | = | Rs.50 |
| Contribution | = | Selling perice- Variable cost |
| | = | 50 - 20 = Rs.30 |

$$\text{B.E.P.} = \frac{\text{Fixed Cost}}{\text{Contribution per unit}}$$

$$= \frac{3,00,000}{30} = 10,000 \text{ units}$$

**If selling price is reduced by 20%**

**Selling price per unit** = 50 - (20% of 50)

= 50 - 10 = Rs. 40

Contribution = 40 -20 = Rs.20 per unit

New B.E.P = $\frac{3,00,000}{20}$ = 15,000 units

**Calculation of Break - even Point**

| Units | Fixed Cost Rs. | Variable Cost (Rs. 20 per unit) Rs. | Total Cost Rs. | Sales at Rs.50 per unit Rs. | Sales at Rs.40 per unit Rs. |
|---|---|---|---|---|---|
| 7,000 | 300,000 | 140,000 | 440,000 | 350,000 | 280,000 |
| 8,000 | 300,000 | 160,000 | 460,000 | 400,000 | 320,000 |
| 9,000 | 300,000 | 180,000 | 480,000 | 450,000 | 360,000 |
| 10,000 | 300,000 | 200,000 | 500,000 | 500,000 | 400,000 |
| 11,000 | 300,000 | 220,000 | 520,000 | 550,000 | 440,000 |
| 12,000 | 300,000 | 240,000 | 540,000 | 600,000 | 480,000 |
| 13,000 | 300,000 | 260,000 | 560,000 | 650,000 | 520,000 |
| 14,000 | 300,000 | 280,000 | 580,000 | 700,000 | 560,000 |
| 15,000 | 300,000 | 300,000 | 600,000 | 750,000 | 600,000 |
| 16,000 | 300,000 | 320,000 | 620,000 | 800,000 | 640,000 |
| 17,000 | 300,000 | 340,000 | 640,000 | 850,000 | 680,000 |

It is clear from the above table that the B.E.P is 10,000 units when selling price is Rs.50 per unit, since total cost is equal to total sales at this point. When selling price is Rs.40 per unit B.E.P. is 15,000 units.

***B.E.P. Chart***

i) B.E.P. Chart when Selling Price is Rs.50.

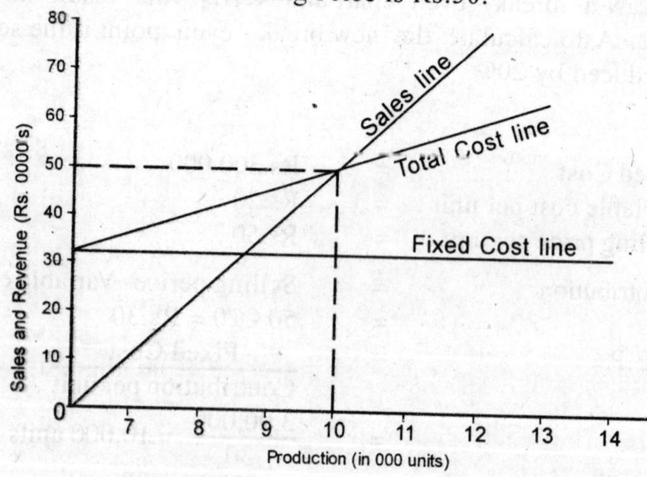

ii) B.E.P. Chart when Selling Price is Rs.40.

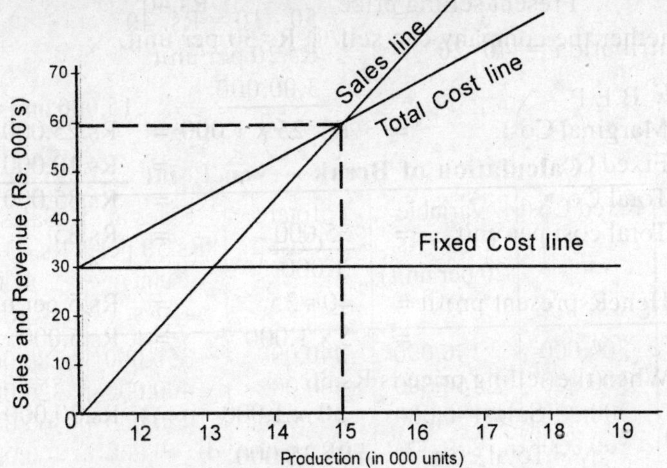


## Application of Break - even Analysis in Decision - Making

Marginal Costing and Break - even analysis help the management to take various managerial decisions, like profit planning, policy decision and control techniques.

The important managerial decisions which can be taken through Marginal Costing technique are stated as follows:

1. Pricing Decisions.
2. Decisions regarding the acceptance or rejection of foreign orders.
3. Profit Planning.
4. Problems of Key of Limiting Factor.
5. Make or Buy Decisions.
6. The effect of changes in selling price.
7. Selection of suitable sales mix.
8. Determination of optimum level of activity.
9. Measurement of performance.

### *1. Pricing Decisions*

Marginal costing technique assists the management in fixing prices. It suggests the management to fix price at least above the marginal cost.

**Illustration: 14**

Determine the minimum selling price from the following particulars:

| | |
|---|---|
| Marginal cost per unit | Rs.25 |
| Fixed Cost | Rs.10,000 |

Number of units sold 1,000
Present selling price Rs.40

State whether the company can sell @ Rs.30 per unit.

***Solution:***

| | | | | |
|---|---|---|---|---|
| Marginal Cost | = | Rs. 25 x 1,000 | = | Rs.25,000 |
| Fixed Cost | | | = | Rs.10,000 |
| Total Cost | | | = | Rs.35,000 |
| Total cost per unit | = | $\frac{35,000}{1,000}$ | = | Rs.35 |
| Hence, present profit | = | 40 - 35 | = | Rs.5 per unit |
| | = | 5 x 1,000 | = | Rs.5,000 |

When the selling price is Rs.30

| | | | | |
|---|---|---|---|---|
| Sales | = | 30 x 1,000 | = | Rs.30,000 |
| Total cost | = | Rs.35,000 | | |
| Loss | = | 35,000 - 30,000 | | |
| | = | Rs.5,000 | | |

If there is no sales then the company is facing a loss of Rs.10,000 in the form of Fixed Cost. It can be reduced to Rs.5,000, if selling price is @ Rs.30 per unit.

The minimum selling price should be at least Rs.35 to avoid the loss.

**2. Decisions regarding the acceptance of Bulk orders, Special orders, Additional orders and Export orders.**

The marginal costing technique is helpful for the management to take a decision regarding whether to accept or reject a foreign order or special order. When fixed cost for the period is spent then, the excess amount of marginal cost from the additional sales would be the profit of the company.

**Illustration: 15**

X Ltd. manufactures and sells 4,000 units of product 'X' @ Rs.20 per unit. The details regarding the cost of production are stated below:

| | Rs. |
|---|---|
| Direct material | 20,000 |
| Direct labour | 15,000 |
| Electricity | 5,000 |
| Miscellaneous expenses | 7,000 |
| Fixed Manufacturing expenses | 18,000 |
| Fixed Administration expenses | 12,000 |

The normal production capacity is 10,000 units per month. The company received an order of 6,000 units @ Rs.13 per month from a foreign market. Advise the management whether the order can be accepted or not.

***Solution:***

**Statement of the cost**

| Particulars | Unit Rate | Present capacity 40% (4,000 units) | Proposed capacity 60% (6,000 units) | Total |
|---|---|---|---|---|
| Sales (units) | - | 4,000 | 6,000 | 10,000 |
| Sales - value (Rs.) | 20 | 80,000 | 78,000 | 158,000 |
| Less: Variable cost | | | | |
| Material (Rs.) | 5 | 20,000 | 30,000 | 50,000 |
| Labour (Rs.) | 3.75 | 15,000 | 22,500 | 37,500 |
| Electricity (Rs.) | 1.25 | 5,000 | 7,500 | 12,500 |
| Miscellaneous Exp. | 1.75 | 7000 | 10,500 | 17,500 |
| (Rs.) | 11.75 | 47,000 | 70,500 | 117,500 |
| Contribution: (Rs.) | | | | |
| (Sales - Variable Cost) | 8.25 | 33,000 | 7,500 | 40,500 |
| Fixed cost (Rs.) | | 30,000 | - | 30,000 |
| Profit (Rs.) | | 3,000 | 7,500 | 10,500 |

The company should accept the order since it earns an additional amount of Rs.7,500 as profit. This is due to the fact that the additional order is within 100% capacity. If the order is from local market the order should not be accepted since it affects the local sales @ Rs.20 per unit.

### 3. *Profit Planning*

Profit planning means planning for future production to earn maximum profit. Marginal costing technique can be applied to determine the number of units to be produced in future to get maximum profit. The expected sales to earn a desired profit can be calculated though the following formula:

$$\text{Expected Sales} = \frac{\text{Fixed Cost + Expected Profit}}{\text{Contribution per unit}}$$

**Illustration: 16**

The details regarding the cost of manufacturing one unit of a product manufactured by KM & Co. Ltd. are as follows:

| | Rs. |
|---|---|
| Direct material | 18 |
| Direct labour | 13 |
| Variable overheads | 14 |
| | 45 |
| Fixed overheads | 30 |
| Profit | 25 |
| Selling price | 100 |

The capacity of the company is 30,000 units per month. The company has to reduce the selling price due to competition. Calculate the number of units the company should manufacture to earn the present profit if the selling price is reduced by 10% and 15% respectively. Assume that the present sales is 10,000 units.

***Solution:***

Fixed overhead = 30,000 x 30 = Rs.900,000

Contribution = Sales - Variable Cost

= 100 - (18 +13 + 14)

= Rs.55 per unit

Present profit = 10,000 x 25 = Rs.250,000

Calculation of expected sales when selling price is reduced by 10%

Selling price = 100 - 10% of 100 = Rs.90

Contribution = 90 - 45 = Rs.45 per unit

Expected sales = Fixed cost + Expected profit

$$= \frac{900,000 + 250,000}{45} = \frac{1150,000}{45} = 25,556 \text{ units}$$

Calculation of expected sales when selling price is reduced by 15%

Selling price = 100 - 15% of 100 = Rs.85

Contribution = 85 - 45 = Rs. 40

$$\text{Expected sales} = \frac{900,000 + 250,000}{40}$$

$$= \frac{11,50,000}{40} = 28,750 \text{ units}$$

## 4. *Problems of Key or Limiting Factor*

A limiting factor or key factor is a factor which restricts the company from earning profit. The limiting factor may be raw material, labour, electricity, finance, capacity of plant and sales. When a company is facing any of the limiting factor, the contribution per unit of the limiting factor should be the criterion to assess the profitability. The product which gives the highest contribution per unit of the limiting factor should be preferred. If the limiting factors are more than one, then all of them should be analysed.

**Illustration: 17**

A company is manufacturing two different products namely X and Y. The expenses for manufacturing the products are as follows:

| | Product X (Rs.) | Product Y (Rs.) |
|---|---|---|
| Materials: | | |
| 3 Kg @ Rs.10 | 30 | 50 |
| 5 Kg @ Rs.10 | | |
| Labour | 10 | 20 |
| Fixed cost | 15 | 8 |
| | 55 | 78 |
| Selling price | 73 | 105 |
| Profit | 18 | 27 |

The total number of units produced in a month are X 1,000 units and Y 1,500 units. The raw material is the key factor. Availability of raw material is 15,000 kgs.

Find out the product which gives the maximum profit through marginal costing techniques.

***Solution:***

| | Product X (per unit) Rs | Product Y (per unit) Rs |
|---|---|---|
| Selling price | 73 | 105 |
| Variable cost: | | |
| Material | 30 | 50 |
| Labour | 10 | 20 |
| | 40 | 70 |
| Contribution per unit (Sales - variable cost) | 33 | 35 |
| Contribution per 1 kg of material | 33/3 = Rs.11 | 35/5 = Rs.7 |

Though product Y gives more contribution per unit, product X is more profitable as per the material as key factor.

(Fixed Cost for X = 1,000 x 15; Y = 1,500 x 8)

**Proof:**

| | Product X | Product Y |
|---|---|---|
| **Maximum capacity** | **15,000 kgs** | **15,000 kgs** |
| **Material required per unit** | **3 kgs** | **5 kgs** |

Maximum capacity in Units $\frac{15,000}{3}$ = 5000 units; $\frac{15,000}{5}$ = 3000 units

| | | |
|---|---|---|
| Sales (Rs.) | 3,65,000 | 3,15,000 |
| Material (Rs.) | 150,000 | 1,50,000 |
| Labour (Rs.) | 50,000 | 60,000 |
| Fixed cost (Rs.) | 15,000 | 12,000 |
| Total cost | 2,15,000 | 2,22,000 |
| Profit | 1,50,000 | 93,000 |

### 5. *Make or Buy decisions*

The marginal costing technique helps the management to decide whether a product should be manufactured or bought from outside. The analysis of fixed cost and variable cost of manufacturing the product should be done in this regard. According to the marginal costing technique, it is advisable to produce the product if the marginal cost (variable cost ) is lower than the purchase price. It is advisable to buy the product if the purchase price is lower than the marginal cost. It is based on the technique that the fixed cost should be incurred whether the company manufacture the product or not during a period.

**Illustration: 18**

The cost of manufacturing a product is Rs.80 per unit. The product is available in the market @ Rs.75. Advise the management whether the product can be produced or bought from the market. Also suggest the management whether to make or buy if the purchasing price is reduced from Rs.75 to Rs.55.

The cost of manufacturing one unit of the product is material Rs.25; labour Rs.20, variable overhead Rs.15; and fixed cost Rs.20.

***Solution:***

| Marginal cost (variable cost) per unit | Rs. |
|---|---|
| Material | 25 |
| Wages | 20 |
| Variable overhead | 15 |
| Total | 60 |

It is advisable to produce the product when the purchase price is @ Rs.75 per unit, since the purchase price is more than the marginal cost.

When thepurchase price is reduced to Rs.55 per unit, it is advisable to buy the product since the purchase price is less than the marginal cost.

### 6. *The effect of changes in selling price*

The marginal costing technique analyses and measure the effect of changes in selling price.It helps to determine the new B.E.P. due to the changes in the selling price.

**Illustration: 19**

Calculate (i) P/V ratio, BEP and Margin of safety

(ii) The effect of 20% increase in selling price and

(iii) The effect of 20% decrease in selling price, from the following information

| | |
|---|---|
| Sales | Rs.4,00,000 |
| Variable cost | Rs.2,50,000 |
| Fixed cost | Rs.72,450 |

***Solution:***

(i) Sales = Rs.4,00,000

Variable cost = Rs.2,50,000

Fixed cost = Rs.72,450

Contribution = Sales - Variable cost

= 4,00,000 - 2,50,000 = Rs.1,50,000

$$\text{P/V Ratio} = \frac{\text{Contribution x 100}}{\text{Sales}} = \frac{1,50,000 \text{ x } 100}{4,00,000}$$

= 37.5%

$$\text{B.E.P} = \frac{\text{Fixed cost}}{\text{P/V Ratio}} = \frac{72,450}{37.5\%}$$

= Rs.1,93,200

Margin of safety = Present Sales - Sales at B.E.P

= 4,00,000 1,93,200 = Rs.2,06,800

(ii) The effect of 20% increase in selling price:

Sales = 4,00,000 + 20% of 4,00,000

= 4,00,000 + 80,000 = Rs.4,80,000

Contribution = 4,80,000 - 2,50,000 = Rs.2,30,000

$$\text{P/V ratio} = \frac{\text{Contribution x 100}}{\text{Sales}} = \frac{2,30,000 \text{ x } 100}{4,80,000}$$

= 47.92 %

$$\text{B.E.P} = \frac{\text{Fixed cost}}{\text{P/V ratio}} = \frac{72450}{47.92} \text{x100}$$

= Rs. 151,189

Margin of safety = 4,00,000 - 151,189 = Rs.248,811

(iii) The effect of 20% decrease in selling price:

Sales = 4,00,000 - 20% of 4,00,000

= 4,00,000 - 80,000 = Rs. 3,20,000

Contribution = 3,20,000 - 2,50,000 = Rs. 70,000

$$\text{P/V ratio} = \frac{\text{Contribution x100}}{\text{Sales}} = \frac{70,000 \text{ x } 100}{320,000}$$

= 21.88 %

$$\text{B.E.P} = \frac{\text{Fixed cost}}{\text{P/V ratio}} = \frac{72450}{21.88} \text{x100}$$

= Rs.331,124

When selling price is reduced by 20% there will not be any margin of safety units since the present sales is below the B.E.P. sales.Margin of safty is the sales above the B.E.P. sales.

### *7. Selection of suitable Product mix / Sales mix:*

Companies may manufacture more than one product. In such a situation the number of units of each product to be produced, to attain maximum profit should be determined. The composition of various products which gives the maximum contribution should be preferred. It is called the optimum product mix or sales mix. It can be determined through marginal costing principle.

**Illustration: 20**

A manufacturing company is providing the following information related to the month of December 2011.

| | Product X (Per unit) Rs. | Product Y (Per unit) Rs. |
|---|---|---|
| Direct material | 27 | 41 |
| Direct wages | 22 | 16 |
| Selling price | 70 | 80 |

Variable overhead is 50% of direct wages. Total fixed cost for manufacturing the two products is Rs.12,000.

Different Sales Mixes:

(i) 400 units of Product X and 600 units of Product Y

(ii) 600 units of Product X and 400 units of Product Y

(iii) 500 units of Product X and 500 units of Product Y

***Solution:***

**Statement of Cost**

| Particulars | Product X (per unit) Rs. | Product Y (per unit) Rs. |
|---|---|---|
| Selling Price | 70 | 80 |
| Variable Cost: | | |
| Material | 27 | 41 |
| Wages | 22 | 16 |
| Variable Overhead (50% of wages) | 11 | 8 |
| | 60 | 65 |
| Contribution (S - VC) | 10 | 15 |

**Calculation of profit for different sales mixes**

(i) ***400 units of product X and 600 units of product Y***

| | | | | Rs. |
|---|---|---|---|---|
| Contribution | X | = 400 x 10 | = | 4000 |
| | Y | = 600 x 15 | = | 9000 |
| Total | | | = | 13,000 |
| Fixed cost | | | | 12,000 |
| Profit | | | | 1,000 |

(ii) ***600 units of product X and 400 units of product Y***

| | | | | Rs. |
|---|---|---|---|---|
| Contribution | X | = 600 x 10 | = | 6,000 |
| | Y | = 400 x 15 | = | 6,000 |
| Total | | | = | 12,000 |
| Fixed cost | | | = | 12,000 |
| Profit | | | = | Nil |

(iii) ***500 units of product X and 500 units of product Y***

| | | | | Rs. |
|---|---|---|---|---|
| Contribution | X | = 500 x 10 | = | 5,000 |
| | Y | = 500 x 15 | = | 7,500 |
| Total | | | = | 12,500 |
| Fixed cost | | | = | 12,000 |
| Profit | | | = | 500 |

It is clear from the calculations that sales mix (i), ( i.e, 400 units of X and 600 units of Y) is more profitable.

### *8. Determination of Optimum Level of Activity*

The optimum level of activity can be determined through marginal costing principle. The contribution at different levels of activity should be calculated. The level of activity which gives the highest contribution is called optimum level of activity.

**Illustration: 21**

The details regarding the cost of one unit of a product manufactured by a company at 60% capacity are stated as follows:

| | Rs. |
|---|---|
| Material cost | 25 |
| Wages | 15 |
| Overhead | 20 (70% fixed) |

The number of units produced at 60% capacity is 12,000 units. The selling price is Rs. 75 per unit

The company has a plan to increase the capacity from 60% to 75% and 90% capacity. At 75% capacity the selling price is to be reduced by 10%. At 90% capacity the selling price is reduced by Rs.9/- per unit and the material cost is reduced by 10%.

Calculate the profit and break-even point at 75% and 90% capacities. Also state which one is optimum capacity.

***Solution:***

Number of units produced at 60% capacity = 12,000

Number of units produced at 75% capacity = $\frac{12,000}{60} \times 75$

= 15,000

Number of units produced at 90% capacity = $\frac{12,000}{60} \times 90$

= 18,000

Selling price at 60% capacity = Rs.75

Selling price at 75% capacity = 75 - 10 % of 75

= 75 -7.5

= Rs.67.50

Selling price at 90% capacity = 75 - 9

= Rs.66

Material cost at 90% capacity = 25 - 10% of 25

= Rs.22.50

**Statement of cost**

| Particular | 60% Capacity | | 75% Capacity | | 90% of capacity | |
|---|---|---|---|---|---|---|
| | Per unit | Total Rs. | Per unit | Total Rs. | Per unit | Total Rs. |
| Sales | 75 | 9,00,000 | 67.50 | 10,12,500 | 66 | 11,88,000 |
| Material | 25 | 3,00,000 | 25 | 3,75,000 | 22.5 | 4,05,000 |
| Wages | 15 | 1,80,000 | 15 | 2,25,000 | 15 | 2,70,000 |
| Variable Overhead | 6 | 72,000 | 6 | 90,000 | 6 | 1,08,000 |
| Total Variable Cost | 46 | 5,52,000 | 46 | 6,90,000 | 43.50 | 7,83,000 |
| Contribution (S - VC) | 29 | 3,48,000 | 21.50 | 3,22,500 | 22.50 | 4,05,000 |
| Fixed Overhead | 14 | 1,68,000 | 11.20 | 1,68,000 | 9.33 | 1,68,000 |
| Profit | 15 | 1,80,000 | 10.30 | 1,54,500 | 13.17 | 2,37,000 |

$$\text{Break-even point at 60\% capacity} = \frac{\text{Fixed Cost}}{\text{Contribution per unit}}$$

$$= \frac{1,68,000}{29} = 5,793 \text{ units}$$

$$\text{Break-even point at 75\% capacity} = \frac{1,68,000}{21.5} = 7,814 \text{ units}$$

$$\text{Break-even point at 90\% capacity} = \frac{1,68,000}{22.5} = 7,467 \text{ units}$$

It is advisable to maintain 90% capacity, since the total profit and contribution per unit is greater when compared to 75% capacity. When all the 3 capacities are compared the optimum level is 60% capacity since the contribution per unit is greater at this capacity.

*9. Measurement of performance*

The performance of various department can be measured through marginal costing technique. It helps to identify the departments which are performing efficiently and also to identify the products which are giving more profit so that the management can take necessary steps to increase the efficiency and profit.

**Illustration: 22**

**A manufacturing company is providing the following information, regarding the manufacturing of three different products.**

| Particulars | Product X Rs. | Product Y Rs. | Product Z Rs. |
|---|---|---|---|
| Selling Price | 100 | 80 | 50 |
| Direct Material | 45 | 25 | 10 |
| Direct Labour: | | | |
| Dept A | 18 | 14 | 7 |
| Dept B | 7 | 6 | 4 |
| Dept C | 5 | 5 | 4 |

The expenses towards overhead are stated below.

| | Dept A | Dept B | Dept C |
|---|---|---|---|
| Variable overhead (% on Direct Labour) | 50% | 60% | 40% |

Give your suggestions regarding the performance of the three products.

***Solution:***

***Statement of cost***

| Particular | Product X Rs. | Product Y Rs. | Product Z Rs. |
|---|---|---|---|
| Selling price | 100 | 80 | 50 |
| Direct Material | 45 | 25 | 10 |
| Direct Labour | 30 | 25 | 15 |
| Variable overhead | | | |
| Dept A | 9 | 7 | 3.50 |
| Dept B | 4.20 | 3.60 | 2.40 |
| Dept C | 2 | 2.00 | 1.60 |
| Total Marginal cost | 90.20 | 62.60 | 32.50 |
| Contribution | 9.80 | 17.40 | 17.50 |
| P/V Ratio | 9.8 | 21.75 | 35 |

$$\text{P/V Ratio} = \frac{\text{Contribution} \times 100}{\text{Sales}} \left[ \frac{9.8 \times 100}{100} : \frac{17.4 \times 100}{80} ; \frac{17.5 \times 100}{50} \right]$$

Out of the three products Z is considered as best since, it gives highest contribution and highest P/VRatio.

## MISCELLANEOUS ILLUSTRATIONS

**Illustration: 23**

Calculate (i) P/V Ratio (ii) Profit when sales is Rs.300,000 (iii) New BEP when selling price is increased by 30% (iv) New BEP when the selling price is reduced by 30% from the following information.

Fixed cost Rs.120,000; Sales Rs.160,000 at B.E.P.

***Solution:***

Contribution = Sales - Variable cost or Fixed cost + Profit

Since at BEP there is no profit or loss,

Contribution = Rs.1,20,000

Contribution = Sales - Variable cost

120,000 = 1,60,000 - V.C

V.C = 1,60,000 - 1,20,000 = Rs.40,000

(i.e., $\frac{40,000}{160,000}$ x 100 = 25% on sales)

(i) P/V Ratio = $\frac{\text{Contribution}}{\text{Sales}} = \frac{120,000}{160,000}$ x 100 = 75%

(ii) Contribution when sales is Rs. 3,00,000 = 300,000 x 75%
= Rs.2,25,000

Profit when sales is Rs. 3,00,000 = Contribution - Fixed cost
= 225,000 - 120,000
= Rs.105,000

(iii) Calculation of BEP when selling price is increased by 30%

Sales = Rs.3,00,000 + 30% of 3,00,000
= Rs.3,90,000

Variable cost = 25% of sales = $\frac{300,000 \times 25}{100}$
= Rs.75,000

Contribution = 3,90,000 - 75,000 = Rs.315,000

P/V Ratio = $\frac{C}{S} = \frac{315,000 \times 100}{390,000}$ = 80.77 %

New BEP = $\frac{\text{Fixed Cost}}{\text{P/V Ratio}} = \frac{120,000 \times 100}{80.77}$
= Rs.148,570

(iv) Calculation of New BEP when selling price is decreased by 30%

Sales = 3,00,000 - 30% of 300,000
= Rs.210,000

Variable cost = 25% of Sales = $\frac{3,00,000 \times 25}{100}$
= Rs.75,000

Contribution = 2,10,000 - 75,000 = Rs.1,35,000

$$\text{P/V Ratio} = \frac{C}{S} = \frac{1,35,000 \times 100}{2,10,000} = 64.29\ \%$$

$$\text{New BEP} = \frac{F.C}{\text{P/V Ratio}} = \frac{1,20,000 \times 100}{64.29}$$

$$= \text{Rs.}186,654$$

[It is assumed that variable cost is not changing due to the reduction or increase of selling price.]

**Illustration: 24**

The following data are related to a manufacturing company.

Fixed expenses Rs.80,000 Profit Rs.50,000 and Sales Rs.200,000

Calculate (i) P/V Ratio (ii) sales if the company incurred a loss of Rs.15,000 and (iii) the margin of safety when the profit is Rs.80,000 and Rs.1,00,000.

(Adapted: ICWAI Inter)

***Solution:***

(i) Contribution = Fixed Cost + Profit

$$= 80,000 + 50,000 = \text{Rs.}130,000$$

$$\text{P/V Ratio} = \frac{C \times 100}{S} = \frac{130,000 \times 100}{2,00,000} = 65\%$$

(ii) Contribution when the company incurred a loss of Rs.40,000 is,

Contribution = Fixed Cost - Loss

$$= 80,000 - 15,000 = \text{Rs.}65,000$$

$$\text{P/V Ratio} = \frac{C}{S}$$

$$65\% = \frac{65,000}{S}$$

$$S \times 65/100 = 65,000$$

$$S = \frac{65,000 \times 100}{65}$$

i.e., Sales = Rs.100,000

(iii) Margin of safety $= \frac{\text{Profit}}{\text{P/V Ratio}}$.

When, profit is Rs.80,000 Margin of safety $= \frac{80,000 \times 100}{65} = \text{Rs.}123,077$

When profit is Rs.100,000 Margin of safety $= \frac{1,00,000 \times 100}{65} = \text{Rs.}153,846$

**Illustration: 25**

A manufacturing company provides the following information related to the cost of production of product X

Cost of production per unit: Consumption of material Rs.25, wages Rs.20, variable overhead Rs.15 and fixed overhead Rs.25. The selling price per unit is Rs.100 and profit per unit is Rs.15. The present production of the company is 20,000 units of product X.

It was decided to reduce the selling price due to competition. If the company wants to maintain the same profit how many units it should produce when the selling price is reduced by (i) 15% and (ii) 25%

***Solution:***

Profit per unit = Rs.15

Profit for 20,000 units = 20,000 x 15

= Rs.300,000

(i) When selling price is reduced by 15%

Selling price = 100 - 15% of 100

= 100 - 15 = Rs. 85

$$\text{Expected sales} = \frac{\text{Fixed cost} + \text{Expected Profit}}{\text{Contribution per unit}}$$

Contribution = Sales - Variable cost

= 85 - (25 + 20 + 15)

= Rs.25 per unit

Expected profit = Rs.300,000

Fixed cost = 25 x 20,000 = Rs.5,00,000

$$\text{Expected sales} = \frac{500{,}000 + 300{,}000}{25}$$

$$= \frac{800{,}000}{25} = 32{,}000 \text{ units}$$

(ii) When selling price is reduced by 25%,

Selling price = 100 - 25% of 100

= 100 - 25 = *Rs. 75 per unit*

Contribution = Sales - Variable cost

= 75 - (25 + 20 + 15)

= 75 - 60 = Rs. 15 per unit

Expected profit = Rs.300,000

Fixed cost = Rs.500,000

$$\text{Expected sales} = \frac{\text{Fixed cost} + \text{Expected profit}}{\text{Contribution per unit}}$$

$$= \frac{5{,}00{,}000 + 3{,}00{,}000}{15}$$

$$= \frac{800{,}000}{15} = 53{,}333 \text{ units}$$

**Illustration: 26**

Cost data of a manufacturing company are as follows:

| | Rs. |
|---|---|
| Selling price | 30 per unit |
| Variable manufacturing cost | 15 per unit |
| Variable selling cost | 5 per unit |
| Fixed factory overhead | 100,000 per annum |
| Fixed selling overhead | 50,000 per annum |

Calculate: (i) Break - even point, (ii) Profit when sales in units are 20% above break - even point, (iii) Sales required to earn a profit of Rs.80,000 (iv) Sales required to earn a profit of 15% of sales.

***Solution:***

(i) Break - even point:

Contribution = Sales - Variable cost

= 30 - (15 + 5)

= 30 - 20 = Rs.10 per unit

Fixed cost = Fixed FOH + Fixed SOH

= 1,00,000 + 50,000 = Rs.150,000

$$\text{Break - even point} = \frac{\text{Fixed Cost}}{\text{Contribution per unit}}$$

$$= \frac{150,000}{10} = 15,000 \text{ units}$$

or 15,000 x 30 = Rs.4,50,000 in value

(ii) Calculation of profit when sales is 20% above BEP

BEP = 15,000 units

Sales above 20% of BEP= 15,000 + 20% of 15,000

= 18,000 units

Contribution per unit = Rs.10

Total Contribution = 18,000 x 10 = Rs.180,000

Profit = Contribution - Fixed Cost

= 180,000 - 150,000 = Rs.30,000

(iii) Expected sales for a profit of Rs. 80,000

$$\text{Expected sales} = \frac{\text{Fixed Cost + Expected Profit}}{\text{Contribution per unit}}$$

$$= \frac{150,000 + 80,000}{10} = \frac{230,000}{10}$$

= 23,000 units

= 23,000 x 30 = Rs.6,90,000

(iv) Expected Sales to earn a profit of 15% on sales.

Assume sales units as 'a'

| | | |
|---|---|---|
| Sales value | = | 30a |
| Profit | = | 30a x 15% = 4.5a |
| Sales | = | Total Cost + Profit |
| 30a | = | (20a + 150,000) + 4.5 a |
| 30a - 20a - 4.5a | = | 150,000 |
| 5.5a | = | 150,000 |
| a | = | $\frac{150,000}{5.5}$ = 27,273 units |

Expected Sales is 27,273 units x 30

= Rs.818,190 in value

**Illustration: 27**

XYZ Ltd. provides the following information from its cost records.

| | | | Rs. |
|---|---|---|---|
| Budgeted Sales: 10,000 units @ Rs.23 per unit | | | 230,000 |
| Budgeted Costs: | | | |
| Variable: | Direct material | 36,000 | |
| | Direct labour | 24,000 | |
| | Factory overhead | 20,000 | |
| | Administration overhead | 18,000 | |
| | Selling & distribution overhead | 12,000 | 110,000 |
| Fixed: | Factory overhead | 25,000 | |
| | Administration overhead | 29,000 | |
| | Selling & distribution overhead | 16,000 | 70,000 |
| Budgeted Profit | | | 50,000 |

Calculate Break - even point when

(i) Variable cost increased by 20%

(ii) Fixed cost increased by 20%

(iii) 20% increase in selling price

(iv) 20% increase in fixed overhead and 10% decrease in variable cost.

(Adapted Company Secretary Course)

***Solution:***

| | | |
|---|---|---|
| Sales | = | Rs.230,000 |
| Variable Cost | = | Material + Labour + VFOH +VAOH + VSDOH |
| | = | 36,000 + 24,000 + 20,000 + 18,000 + 12,000 |
| | = | Rs.1,10,000 |

Fixed Cost = FFOH + FAOH + FSDOH

= 25,000 + 29,000 + 16,000 = Rs.70,000

(i) B.E.P when variable cost increased by 20%

New variable cost = 110,000 + 20% of 110,000

= 110,000 + 22,000 = Rs.132,000

Contribution = Sales - Variable Cost

= 2,30,000 - 1,32,000 = Rs.98,000

$= \frac{98,000}{10,000}$ = Rs.9.8 per unit

B.E.P. $= \frac{\text{Fixed Cost}}{\text{Contribution per unit}} = \frac{70,000}{9.8}$

= 7,143 units

(ii) B.E.P. when Fixed Cost increased by 20%

New Fixed Cost = 70,000 + 20% of 70,000

= 70,000 + 14,000 = Rs.84,000

Contribution = Sales - V.C

= 230,000 - 110,000= Rs.120,000

$\frac{120,000}{10,000}$ = Rs.12 per unit

B.E.P. $= \frac{F.C}{C} = \frac{84,000}{12}$

= 7,000 units

(iii) B.E.P. when selling price increased by 20%

Actual selling price = Rs.23 per unit

New selling price = 23 + 20% of 23

= 23 + 4.60 = Rs.27.60 per unit

Variable cost per unit $= \frac{1,10,000}{10,000}$ = Rs.11

Contribution per unit = Sales - V.C

= 27.60 - 11 = Rs.16.60

B.E.P. $= \frac{F.C.}{C} = \frac{70,000}{16.60}$ = 4,217 units

(iv) BEP when Fixed cost increased by 20% and Variable cost decreased by 10%

New Fixed Cost = 70,000 + 20% of 70,000

= Rs.84,000

New variable cost = 110,000 - 10% of 110,000

= Rs.99,000

Contribution per unit $= \frac{\text{S - V.C}}{\text{No. of units}}$

$= \frac{230{,}000 - 99{,}000}{10{,}000}$

= Rs.13.10 per unit

B.E.P. $= \frac{\text{F.C}}{\text{C}} = \frac{84{,}000}{13.10}$

= 6,412 units

**[Illu]stration: 28**

The profit earned by a company is 12% on sales during 2010 and it is [15]% on sales during 2011. If the sales for 2010 is Rs.400,000 and 2011 is [Rs.]600,000; find out (i) P/V Ratio (ii) BEP (iii) Expected sales to earn a [pro]fit of Rs.120,000 (iv) The profit for sales of Rs.10,00,000.

***[Sol]ution:***

Sales in 2010 = Rs.4,00,000

Profit = 12%

$= \frac{400{,}000 \times 12}{100}$ = Rs.48,000

Sales in 2011 = Rs. 6,00,000

Profit = 15%

$= \frac{600{,}000 \times 15}{100}$ = Rs.90,000

(i) P/V ratio $= \frac{\text{Difference in profit}}{\text{Difference in sales}} \times 100$

$= \frac{90{,}000 - 48{,}000}{6{,}00{,}000 - 4{,}00{,}000} \times 100 =$ 21%

(ii) Calculation of BEP

P/V ratio $= \frac{\text{Contribution}}{\text{Sales}}$ or $\frac{\text{F.C + P}}{\text{S}}$

21% $= \frac{\text{Contribution}}{600{,}000}$

Contribution = 600000 x 0.21 = Rs.126,000

21% $= \frac{\text{F.C} + 90{,}000}{6{,}00{,}000}$

600000 x 0.21 = FC + 90,000

FC = 126,000 - 90,000 = Rs.36,000

(or, FC = C - P = 1,26,000 - 90,000 = Rs.36,000)

$$\text{BEP} = \frac{\text{Fixed Cost}}{\text{P/V ratio}}$$

$$= \frac{36{,}000}{0.21} = \text{Rs.}1{,}71{,}429$$

(iii) Expected sales $= \frac{\text{F.C + Expected Profit}}{\text{P/V Ratio}}$

$$= \frac{36{,}000 + 120{,}000}{0.21}$$

$$= \text{Rs.}7{,}42{,}857$$

(iv) Profit for Sales of Rs.10,00,000:

$$\text{P/V ratio} = \frac{\text{Contribution}}{\text{Sales}}$$

$$21\% = \frac{\text{Fixed cost + profit}}{\text{Sales}}$$

$$21\% = \frac{36{,}000 + P}{10{,}00{,}000}$$

$$36000 + P = 10{,}00{,}000 \times 0.21$$

$$\text{Profit} = 210{,}000 - 36{,}000$$

$$= \text{Rs.}1{,}74{,}000$$

**Illustration: 29**

A manufacturing company has to spent Rs.60,000 as fixed cost for a sales of Rs.1,80,000. If the profit earned is 20% of the sales, and the sales per unit is Rs.25, find out the (i) P/V ratio (ii) BEP (iii) Number of units of sales to earn a profit of Rs.50,000 (iv) The profit for the sales of Rs.4,00,000 (v) Estimated sales to earn a profit of 30% on sales.

***Solution:***

Fixed cost = Rs.60,000

Sales = Rs.180,000

Profit = 20% of sales

= Rs.36,000

Contribution = Fixed Cost + profit

= 60,000 +36,000

= Rs.96,000

or = S - V.C

96,000 = 180,000 - V.C

V.C = 180,000 - 96,000 = Rs.84,000

$$\text{No of units sold} = \frac{\text{Sales}}{\text{Selling price per unit}}$$

$$= \frac{180{,}000}{25} = 7{,}200 \text{ units}$$

Variable cost = Rs.84,000

Variable cost per unit $= \frac{84,000}{7,200}$ = Rs.11.67

Contribution per unit $= \frac{96,000}{7,200}$ = Rs.13.33

(i) P/V ratio $= \frac{\text{Contribution} \times 100}{\text{Sales}}$

$= \frac{96,000 \times 100}{180,000} = 53.33\%$

(ii) BEP $= \frac{\text{Fixed cost}}{\text{Contribution per unit}}$

$= \frac{60,000}{13.33}$ = 4,501 units

BEP in value = 4,501 x 25 = Rs.1,12,525

(iii) Estimated sales to earn a profit of Rs.50,000

$= \frac{\text{Fixed Cost + Estimated profit}}{\text{Contribution per unit}}$

$= \frac{60,000 + 50,000}{13.33}$ = 8,252 units

(iv) Estimated sales $= \frac{\text{(F.C + Estimated profit)} \times \text{Selling price per unit}}{\text{Contribution per unit}}$

4,00,000 $= \frac{(60,000 + \text{E.P.}) \times 25}{13.33}$

E.P. $= \frac{53,33,333 - 15,00,000}{25}$

Estimated profit $= \frac{38,33,333}{25}$ = Rs.1,53,333

[or]

P/V ratio $= \frac{\text{Fixed Cost + E.P}}{\text{Sales}}$

53.33% $= \frac{60,000 + \text{E.P}}{400,000}$

0.5333 x 4,00,000 = 60,000 + E.P

2,13,320 = 60,000 + E.P

E.P. = 2,13,333 - 60,000

= Rs.1,53,333

(v) Calculation of sales for profit of 30% on sales.

Profit $= 30\%$ on sales (Assume 'x' as sales)

$= \frac{30 \times x}{100} = 0.3x$

P/V ratio $= \frac{F.C + EP}{Sales} = \frac{60{,}000 \times .3x}{x}$

$53.33\%\, x = 60{,}000 + .3x$

$.5333\, x = 60{,}000 + .3x$

$.5333\, x - .3x = .3\, x = 60{,}000$

$.2333\, x = 60{,}000$

$x = \frac{60000}{.2333} = \text{Rs.}2{,}57{,}180$

Profit $= .3x$

$= .3 \times 2{,}57{,}180$

$= \text{Rs.}77{,}154$

**Illustration: 30**

A manufacturing company is earning 10% profit for a sales of Rs.2,00,000 with fixed cost Rs.50,000. Find out the (i) BEP units (ii) P/V ratio (iii) Estimated sales for a profit of Rs.1,00,000 (iv) Profit for sales of Rs.5,00,000 (v) Estimated sales to earn a profit of 15% on sales.

Assume that the number of units sold at present is 5,000.

***Solution:***

Sales $= \text{Rs.}2{,}00{,}000$

Profit $= \frac{2{,}00{,}000 \times 10}{100} = \text{Rs.}20{,}000$

Fixed cost $= \text{Rs.}50{,}000$

Contribution $=$ Fixed Cost + Profit $=$ S - V.C

$50000 + 20000 = 200{,}000 - V.C$

$70000 = 200{,}000 - V.C$

Variable cost $= 200{,}000 - 70{,}000 = \text{Rs.}1{,}30{,}000$

No. of units sold $= 5{,}000$

Selling price per unit $= \frac{200{,}000}{5{,}000} = \text{Rs.}40$

Variable cost per unit $= \frac{130{,}000}{5{,}000} = \text{Rs.}26$

Contribution per unit $= \frac{70{,}000}{5{,}000} = \text{Rs.}14$

(i) BEP units $= \frac{\text{Fixed cost}}{\text{Contribution per unit}}$

$= \frac{50{,}000}{14} = 3{,}571$ units

(ii) P/V ratio $= \dfrac{\text{Contribution x 100}}{\text{Sales}}$

$= \dfrac{70{,}000 \text{ x } 100}{2{,}00{,}000} = 35\%$

(iii) Estimated sales to earn a profit of Rs.1,00,000

$= \dfrac{\text{Fixed Cost + Expected profit}}{\text{Contribution per unit}}$

$= \dfrac{50000 + 100000}{14} = 10{,}714 \text{ units}$

i.e., 10,714 x 40 = Rs.4,28,560

(iv) Profit for sales of Rs.5,00,000

$= \dfrac{\text{(Fixed cost + Estimated profit) x Selling price per unit}}{\text{Contribution per unit}}$

[or]

P/V ratio $= \dfrac{\text{Contribution}}{\text{Sales}}$

35% $= \dfrac{\text{F.C + Profit}}{\text{Sales}}$

35% $= \dfrac{50{,}000 + P}{5{,}00{,}000}$

50000 + P = 5,00,000 x 0.35

50000 + P = 1,75,000

P = 1,75,000 - 50,000

Profit = Rs.1,25,000

(v) Estimated sales to earn a profit of 15% on sales.

Profit is 15% of Sales $= \dfrac{15 \text{ x } x}{100} = 0.15x$ (Assume $x$ as Sales)

P/V ratio $= \dfrac{\text{Fixed Cost + E.P}}{\text{Sales}}$

35% $= \dfrac{50{,}000 + 0.15x}{x}$

$0.35x - 0.15x$ = 50,000

$0.20\,x$ = 50,000

$x = \dfrac{50{,}000}{0.20} = \text{Rs.}2{,}50{,}000$

No. of units to be sold $= \dfrac{\text{Sales}}{\text{Sales per unit}} = \dfrac{250{,}000}{40} = 6{,}250 \text{ units}$

Profit = $0.15x$

= 0.15 x 2,50,000

= Rs.37,500

## EXERCISE

**I. Choose the correct answer for the following:**

1. The concept of marginal costing is based on
   (i) Fixed cost (ii) Standard cost (iii) Variable cost (iv) Prime cost
2. The difference in cost due to the increase or decrease of one unit from the normal production is known as
   (i) Marginal cost (ii) Budget (iii) Fixed cost (iv) Works cost
3. The difference between the selling price and the variable cost is called
   (i) Marginal cost (ii) Fixed cost (iii) Prime cost (iv) Contribution
4. The condition of no profit - no loss is known as
   (i) Mid point (ii) Break-even point (iii) Fixed point (iv) Starting point
5. The sales above Break-even point will give
   (i) Loss (ii) Costing loss (iii) Profit (iv) Fixed cost
6. The ratio between contribution and sales is called
   (i) Contribution ratio (ii) P/V ratio (iii) Sales ratio (iv) Profit ratio
7. The difference between actual sales and sales at break-even point is called
   (i) Margin of safety (ii) Margin of loss
   (iii) Sales margin (iv) Margin of contribution
8. Margin of safety is the ratio between profit and
   (i) B.E.P. (ii) P/V Ratio (iii) Sales ratio (iv) Current ratio
9. The factor which puts a limit on production and profit is known as
   (i) Sales factor (ii) Purchase factor (iii) Profit factor (iv) Key factor
10. A graphical representation of marginal costing is called
   (i) Break-even chart (ii) ABC chart (iii) VED chart (iv) LPP chart

[Ans: 1.(iii) 2. (i) 3. (iv) 4.(ii) 5. (iii) 6. (ii) 7. (i) 8. (ii) 9. (iv) 10. (i)]

**II. Answer the following:**

11. Define marginal costing. State the advantages and disadvantages of marginal costing.
12. What is marginal costing? State the assumptions of marginal costing.
13. State the procedures of preparing the statement of cost by marginal costing method.
14. Define B.E.P. State the procedures of preparing Break-even chart.
15. State briefly the important managerial decisions which can be taken through marginal costing technique.
16. Write short notes of the following.
   (i) BEP (ii) Marginal cost (iii) Marginal costing (iv) Break-even-point (v) P\V Ratio (vi) Marginal Costing Equation (vii) Contribution

17. Calculate BEP and P/V ratio from the following information

| | Rs. | | Rs. |
|---|---|---|---|
| Sales | 1,32,000 | Direct material | 27,500 |
| Direct wages | 18,300 | Variable overhead | 7,000 |
| Fixed cost | 20,000 | | |

(Ans: Rs.1,20,000; 1/6)

18. The cost data of a manufacturing company are as follows.
Selling price Rs.25 per unit; Variable cost Rs.5 per unit Fixed Cost Rs.80,000.
Calculate: (1) BEP in units and value (ii) Profit when sales is Rs.200,000 and (iii) Profit when sale is Rs.150,000
[Ans: (i) 4,000, Rs.100,000, (ii) Rs.60,000, (iii) Rs.25,000]

19. Calculate (i) P/V Rato (ii) Profit when sales is Rs.5,00,000 (iii) New Break-even point when the selling price is increased by 20% and (vi) New BEP when the selling price is reduced by 20%, from the following information:
Fixed cost Rs.1,50,000; BEP Rs.2,00,000
[Ans: (i) 75% (ii) Rs.225,000 (iii) Rs.189,466 (iv) Rs.218,182]

20. A manufacturing company is providing the following information for three months ending 31st December 2011.

| | |
|---|---|
| Direct material consumed | Rs.47,000 |
| Direct wages | Rs.35,000 |
| Direct expenses | Rs.12,000 |

Factory overhead absorbed is 80% of the direct material; Administration overhead absorbed is 40% of the works cost; Selling and distribution overhead absorbed is 10% of the cost of production. Costing profit is 20% on sales.
Prepare the cost statement by Absorption costing method and Marginal costing method.
[Ans: Costing profit Rs.50,666]

21. If the sales of a company is Rs.200,000, the profit is 25% on cost, fixed cost is Rs.75,000 and the number of units sold is 20,000,find out (i) BEP (ii) Sales to earn a profit of Rs.50,000 (iii) Margin of safety (iv) BEP when the selling price is reduced by 10%.
[Ans: (i) 13,043 units, Rs.130430 (ii) 21739 units (iii) Rs.69,570
(iv) 15,789 units, Rs.142,101]

22. A manufacturing company is providing the following information from its costing records. Fixed cost Rs. 60,000; Variable cost Rs. 40,000; Sales Rs. 120,000. Calculate (i) P/V Ratio (ii) The expected sales to earn a profit of Rs. 80,000 (iii) Profit when the sales is Rs. 300,000

(iv) BEP (v) New P/V Ratio and BEP when the selling price is increased by 10%.

[Ans: (i) 66.67% (ii) Rs.208,955 (iii) Rs.141,000 (iv) Rs.89,955 (v) 69.7%; Rs.86,083]

23. A manufacturing company is providing the profit and sales for two periods, as follows

| | Period I (Rs.) | Period II (Rs.) |
|---|---|---|
| Sales | 200,000 | 300,000 |
| Profit | 20,000 | 45,000 |

Find out the (i) P/V Ratio (ii) Sales to earn a profit of Rs.60,000 (iii) Profit when sales is Rs.700,000 (iv) BEP.

[Ans: (i) 25% (ii) Rs.360,000 (iii) Rs. 145,000 (iv) Rs.120,000]

24. X Ltd has to spend Rs.60,000 as fixed cost for a sales of Rs.180,000. If the profit earned is 20% on sales and the sales per unit is Rs. 25, find out (i) P/V Ratio (ii) BEP (iii) Number of units of sales to earn a profit of Rs. 50,000 (iv) Expected sales for a profit of 30% on sales.

[Ans: (i) 53.33% (ii) 4501; Rs.112,525 (iii) 8,252 units (iv) Rs.257,180]

25. A company is spending Fixed cost Rs.12 per unit, Direct material Rs.4 per unit, Direct wages Rs.4 per unit and Direct expenses Rs. 2 per unit at 100% capacity. At 80% capacity, the company is manufacturing and selling 8,000 units.

If the selling price per unit is Rs.25, find out

(i) How many units should be sold for break - even?

(ii) How many units should be sold for a profit of Rs.75,000?

(iii) How much sales to be done for 20% profit on sales?

If the demand of the product is 6,000 units, find out

(a) Selling price is to be charged per unit to break- even

(b) Selling price to earn a profit of Rs.50,000

(c) Selling price to earn a profit of 20% on sales

[Ans: (i) 8,000 units (ii) 13,000 units (iii) 12,000 units (a) Rs.30 (b) Rs.38.33 (c) Rs.37.50]

26. Calculate (a) P/V Ratio (b) Fixed cost (c) Sales to earn a profit of Rs.100,000 when, Sales is Rs.500,000; Profit is Rs.60,000; and Variable cost is 80% on sales.

[Ans:(a) 20% (b) Rs.40,000 (c) Rs.70,000]

27. The fixed cost for manufacturing 1,000 units of a product is Rs.8,000 and variable cost is Rs.12 per unit. Selling price is Rs.26 per unit. Calculate the P/V Ratio. If the selling price is reduced by 20% find out

the new P/V Ratio. Also calculate the number of units to be sold to earn the present total profit.

[Ans: 53.85%; 42.31%; 1591 units]

28. From the following information find out (i) P/V Ratio (ii) Sales required to earn a profit of Rs.150,000 (iii) Profit when sales is Rs.500,000.

| Year | Sales (Rs.) | Profit (Rs.) |
|---|---|---|
| 2010 | 200,000 | 35,000 |
| 2011 | 300,000 | 65,000 |

[Ans: 30%; Rs.583,333; Rs.125,000]

29. The fixed cost for manufacturing a product is Rs.75,000. The variable cost is 60% on sales. If sales is Rs.400,000 at 100% capacity, calculate the BEP and the percentage capacity at BEP. Also calculate the profit at 80% capacity.

[Ans: Rs.187,500; 46.88%; Rs.53,000]

30. K Ltd is providing the following information:

Fixed cost Rs.200,000; Selling price per unit Rs.40; Variable expenses - Material Rs.13 per unit; Wages Rs.7 per unit. Draw a Break - even chart and verify the result through a table. Also calculate the new BEP if the selling price is reduced by 10%.

[Ans: 10,000 units (Rs.400,000); 12,500 units (Rs.450,000)]

31. X & Co Ltd is working in 60% capacity and produces and sells 6,000 units @ Rs.20 per unit. The expenses in this regard are as follows: Administration overhead Rs.30,000; Selling and distribution overhead Rs.150,000; Direct material Rs.2 per unit; Direct wages Rs.2.50 per unit; Direct expenses Rs. 0.50 per unit; Variable manufacturing overhead Rs.2 per unit.

The company received an order for 4000 units @ Rs.9 per unit from a foreign country. Find out whether, it is advisable for the company to accept the order. In case, if it is advisable for the company calculate the total profit.

[Ans: Advisable; Rs.41,000]

32. G Ltd is manufacturing and selling 5,000 units of a product per month @ Rs.30 per unit. The company has to spend the following expenses in this regard.

Direct material Rs.26,000; Direct wages Rs.20,000; Carriage inwards Rs. 5000; Administration overhead Rs.30,000; Selling and distribution overhead Rs.20,000 (20% variable).

Find out the number of units the company has to sell to earn the present profit after reducing the selling price by 10% and by 15%.

Also prepare the statement of cost.

[Ans: Present profit Rs.34000; Expected Sales - 6,154 units; 6,957 units]

33. X Ltd is providing the following information in order to decide whether to manufacture or buy a product.Direct material Rs.7 per unit; Direct wages Rs.5 per unit; Direct expenses Rs.2 per unit; Variable overhead Rs.7 per unit; Selling price is Rs.30 per unit.Find out whether to manufacture or buy the product if the market price is (i)Rs.18.(ii)Rs.23

[Ans: (i) Buy (ii) Make]

34. AB Ltd is manufacturing two products namely X and Y and the details of the cost are as follows:

| | X | Y |
|---|---|---|
| | Rs. | Rs. |
| Selling price per unit | 40 | 50 |
| Direct material | 15 | 25 |
| 3 kgm @ Rs.5 for X | | |
| 5 kgm @ Rs.5 for Y | | |
| Direct wages per unit | 8 | 7 |
| Variable overhead per unit | 8 | 4 |
| Fixed cost | 4,000 | 5,000 |

The company manufactures 1,000 units of product X and 2,000 units of product Y. Suggest the management about the type of product to be manufactured more, by taking into account direct material as the constant factor. Also prepare a statement of cost.

[Ans: Contribution for X Rs.9,000; Y Rs.28,000; Contribution per unit of material consumed for X is Rs.3 and Y is Rs.2.80. Hence, X is preferred]

35. XYZ & Co Ltd is manufacturing and selling two products namely, A and B. The details of the cost are stated as follows:

| | A | B |
|---|---|---|
| | Rs. | Rs. |
| Selling price per unit | 30 | 25 |
| Dircct material per unit | 5 | 4 |
| Direct wages per unit | 6 | 5 |
| Direct expenses per unit | 4 | 5 |

The variable overhead is 100% of direct wages. The common fixed overhead is Rs.3,000. Advise the management, which of the following combination of production of products A and B will give maximum contribution and profit.

(i) 300 units of A and 300 units of B (ii) 400 units of A and 200 units of B (iii) 200 units of A and 400 units of B.

[Ans: (ii) is adviseable since total profit for (i),(ii) and (iii) are Rs.1500, Rs.1800 and Rs.1200 respectively]

36. A company wants to decide the optimum capacity among the different capacities of production as 60%, 80% and 90%. In this regard, the expenses incurred at 60% capacity are as follows.

    Direct material Rs.12,000; Direct wages Rs.9,000; Direct expenses Rs.3,000; Variable overhead 50% of the direct wages; Fixed overhead Rs.18,000.

    It is also given that the company is compelled to reduce the selling price by 5% at 80% capacity and by 10% at 90% capacity. It is also given that the company is manufacturing 6,000 units at 60% capacity, and the selling price is Rs.30 per unit at this capacity.

[Ans: Profits at 60%, 80% and 90% capacities are Rs.133,500,Rs.115,000 and Rs.101,250 respectively. 60% capacity is the optimum one]

37. Determine the minimum selling price, from the following:

    Marginal cost per unit Rs.40. Fixed cost Rs.50,000. Number of units sold is 2,000. Present selling price is Rs.80 per unit. State whether the company can sell the product @ Rs.60 per unit. What is the minimum selling price to prevent loss?

[Ans: No; Rs.65]

38. A Ltd is manufacturing and selling 5,000 units of a product @ Rs.30 per unit. The details regarding the cost of production are as follows. Direct material Rs.54,000; Direct labour Rs.30,000 Electricity Rs.7,000; Miscellaneous expenses Rs.5,000; Fixed manufacturing expenses Rs.20,000 and Fixed administration expenses Rs.40,000.

    The normal production capacity is 10,000 units per month. The company received an order for 4,000 units @ Rs.21 per unit from a foreign market. Advise the management, whether the order can be accepted or not.

[Ans: Accepted]

39. The details regarding the cost of manufacturing one unit of a product by X Ltd are as follows:

| | Rs. |
|---|---|
| Direct material | 20 |
| Direct labour | 15 |
| Variable overhead | 12 |
| Fixed overhead | 23 |
| Profit | 20 |
| Selling price | 90 |

The capacity of the company is 25,000 units per month. The company has to reduce the selling price due to competition. Calculate the number of units the company should manufacture to earn the present profit if the selling price is reduced by 8% and 10% respectively. Assume that the present sales is 12,000 units.

[Ans: 22,626 units; 23,824 units]

40. A company is manufacturing two different products namely A and B. The expenses connected with the manufacturing of the products are as follows:

| | Product A Cost per unit (Rs.) | Product B Cost per unit (Rs.) |
|---|---|---|
| Material | | |
| 7 kgm @ Rs.15 | 105 | |
| 4 kgm @ Rs.15 | | 60 |
| Labour | 60 | 30 |
| Fixed cost | 25 | 20 |
| | 190 | 110 |
| Selling price | 215 | 130 |
| Profit | 25 | 20 |

The total number of units produced in a month are A 2000 units and B 3000 units. The raw material is the key factor and the availability of raw material is 28,000 kgm. Find out the product which gives the maximum profit, through marginal costing technique.

[Ans: A gives maximum profit .But product B can be preferred as per the constraint factor i.e., Rs.7.10 and Rs.10]

41. The details regarding the cost of the unit of a product manufacturing by a company at 70% capacity are stated as follows:

| | Rs. |
|---|---|
| Material Cost | 50 |
| Wages | 20 |
| Overhead | 42 (60% Fixed) |

The number of units produced at 70% capacity is 1,400. The selling price is Rs.150 per unit. The company has a plan to increase the capacity from 70% to 80% and 90%. At 80% capacity the selling price is to be reduced by 10%. At 90% capacity the selling price is reduced by Rs.18 per unit and the material cost is reduced by 8%. Calculate the profit and BEP at 70%, 80% and 90% capacities. Also state which one gives the optimum capacity.

[Ans: Rs.53,630; Rs.42,320; Rs.53,280; BEP - 556; 727; 717]

42. XY Ltd is manufacturing two products namely A and B and the details of the costs are as follows:

| | A | B |
|---|---|---|
| | Rs. | Rs. |
| Selling price per unit | 90 | 70 |
| Direct material | 40 | 32 |
| 5 kgm @ Rs.8 for A | | |
| 4 kgm @ Rs.8 for B | | |
| Direct wages per unit | 12 | 10 |
| Variable overhead per unit | 10 | 7 |
| Fixed cost | 40,000 | 30,000 |

The company manufactures 5,000 units of product A and 4,000 units of product B. Suggest the management about the type of product to be manufactured more, by taking into account direct material as the constraint factor. Also prepare a statement of cost.

[Ans: Contribution for A Rs.140,000; B Rs.84,000; Contribution per unit of material consumed for A is Rs.5.60 and B is Rs.5.25. Hence, A is preferred]

43. K Ltd is manufacturing and selling two products namely, X and Y. The details of the cost are stated as follows:

| | X | Y |
|---|---|---|
| | Rs. | Rs. |
| Selling price per unit | 50 | 40 |
| Direct material per unit | 9 | 8 |
| Direct wages per unit | 8 | 7 |
| Direct expenses per unit | 7 | 6 |

The variable overhead is 100% of direct wages. The common fixed overhead is Rs.7,000. Advise the management, which of the following combination of production of products X and Y will give maximum contribution and profit.

(i) 500 units of X and 500 units of Y (ii) 600 units of X and 400 units of Y (iii) 400 units of X and 600 units of Y.

[Ans: (ii) is adviseable since total profit for (i),(ii) and (iii) are Rs.7,000, Rs.7,600 and Rs.6,400 respectively]

44. Determine the minimum selling price, from the following:

Marginal cost per unit Rs.90. Fixed cost Rs.150,000. Number of units sold is 5,000. Present selling price is Rs.140 per unit. State whether the company can sell the product @ Rs.110 per unit. What is the minimum selling price to prevent loss?

[Ans: No. Rs.120]

# CHAPTER XIII

# STANDARD COSTING

Standard costing means the method of determining the cost in advance. It is otherwise called as predetermined cost. It helps to control the cost so as to achieve maximum profit. Standard costing helps for managerial planning and decision making. In addition to this, it is possible to compare the actual performance with the expected standard performance. If the actual performance is below standard performance, necessary control measures can be taken by the management. Hence, it facilitates for the improvement in the organisation and the performance of employees.

## Meaning and definitions of Standard Cost and Standard Costing

### Standard Cost

Standard cost means predetermined cost.

According to the **Chartered Institute of management Accountants**, London, Standard cost means a predetermined cost which is computed in advance of production on the basis of specification of all the factors affecting cost and used in standard costing.

According to **Eric L.Kohler**, Standard cost is a forecast or predetermination of what actual cost should be under projected conditions, serving as a cost control and as a measure of production efficiency or standard of comparison when ultimately aligned against actual cost.

According to **T.Lucy** Standard cost is a target cost which should be attained. The build up of a standard cost is based on sound technical and engineering studies.

Hence, it is clear from the definitions that the standard cost is a predetermined cost. The cost is determined in advance for every stage of cost on the basis of past experience and the rate of growth of technological development.

### Standard costing

Standard costing is the process of preparing standard cost. It also involves the measurement and analysis of variance of actual cost and standard cost. In this way, it is possible to apply effective control measures to correct the deviations and to achieve maximum efficiency.

The **Chartered Institute of Management Accountants,** London defines Standard costing as the preparation and use of standard costs, their comparison with actual cost and analysis of variances to their causes and points of evidence.

Hence, Standard costing includes the following functions.

(i) Determination of standard cost

(ii) Measurement and recording of actual cost

(iii) Calculation of variations by comparing the actual cost with standard cost

(iv) Analysis of variances from standard cost in order to find out the reasons in the variations for the purpose of corrective action.

**Historical Costing and Standard Costing**

The important differences between historical costing and standard costing are as follows.

(i) Historical costs are the costs which are already incurred. It is a method of recording the cost after they are incurred. But standard cost is a predetermined cost. Standard costing is the method of calculating the standard cost.

(ii) In historical costing it is not possible to measure the efficiency of operation. But in standard costing the efficiency of operation can be measured by comparing the standard cost with actual cost.

(iii) Cost control measures are not possible in historical costing. But standard costing provides information for cost control measures.

(iv) Historical cost data are used for standard cost. But standard cost data have no value for the historical costing.

**Standard Costing and Budgetary Control**

The purpose of Standard costing and Budgetary control are same. Both of them are important tools for managerial planning and decision making.Hence the ideas, approaches and techniques adopted in Standard costing and Budgetary control are more or less same.In spite of their similarities there are some differences in Standard costing and Budgetary control. The important differences are stated as follows.

(i) The scope of budgeting is broad whereas the scope of standard costing in narrow. Budgeting is prepared for the operation of the business as a whole. But Standard costing is prepared only for the manufacturing section of the business.

(ii) Budgeting is concerned with the total activities of the organisation. Hence, there is no division of cost in budgeting. But in Standard costing each element of cost like material, labour and overhead are estimated and analysed.

(iii) Budgeting emphasises more on planning than control whereas standard costing emphasises more on control than on planning.

**Advantages of standard costing**

The important advantages of standard costing are as follows.

(i) Standard costing improves the efficiency of the employees in an organisation. The motivation for the employees to perform above the standard increases the efficiency.

(ii) It is possible to identify the area where performance is below standard so as to take corrective control measures.

(iii) It helps to compare the performance of one period to another and of one division to another division.

(iv) Standard costing facilitates for the determination of wage structure and incentive schemes.

(v) Standard costing provides information for fixing prices of the products.

(vi) Standard costing helps for cost reduction in every stage of production.

(vii) It provides information for the preparation of budgeting and for budgetary control.

(viii) It facilitates for the inventory control. It helps for the correct valuation of inventory like raw materials, work-in- progress and finished goods.

**Limitations of Standard Costing**

The important limitations of standard costing are stated as follows.

(i) Standard costing is expensive for companies to adopt. It is possible only for large scale enterprises to adopt standard costing system.

(ii) It is not possible to adopt standard costing method for all manufacturing companies. The companies which are producing non standard products could not adopt standard costing.

(iii) It is difficult to estimate the cost in future since future is uncertain.

(iv) The employees may oppose through trade unions for the adoption of standard costing.

(v) Standard costing focuses on cost per unit . But correct estimation of fixed cost per unit is not possible.

## VARIANCE ANALYSIS

An analysis about the actual cost and standard cost is called variance analysis. Variance is the difference between the actual and standard cost. When the actual cost is less than the standard cost then the variance is called " Favourable variance' and when the actual cost is greater than standard cost then the variance is called unfavorable variance."

The variances may be classified as

I Material Cost variance

II Labour Cost variance

III Overhead Variance

IV Sales Variance

# I. MATERIAL COST VARIANCE

Material cost variance is the difference between actual cost of material and the standard cost of material.

Material cost variance can be classified as follows.

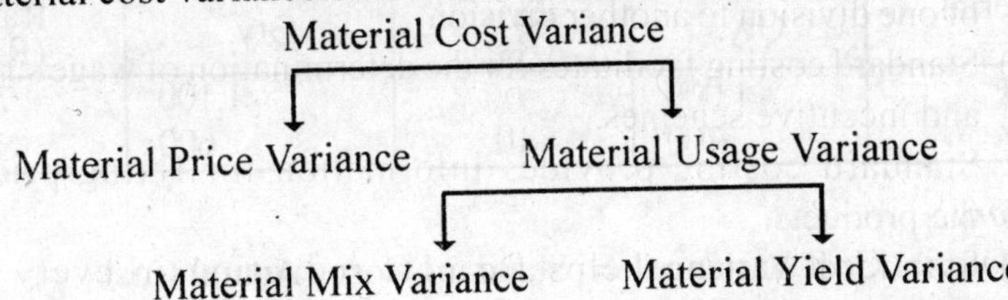


**1.Material Cost Variance**

Material cost variance is the difference between the standard cost of material and the actual cost of material . It may be calculated as follows.

Material Cost Variance = Standard Cost of Material–Actual Cost of Material

(or)

(Standard Qty. x Std.Price) – (Actual Qty. x Actual Price)

**2.Material Price Variance**

Material Price Variance = (Std.Price – Actual Price) x Actual Quantity

**3.Material Usage Variance**

Material Usage Variance is otherwise called as Material Quantity variance. It may be calculated as follows.

Material Usage Variance = (Standard Quantity – Actual Quantity) x Standard Price.

**4.Material Mix Variance**

Material Mix Variance = (Revised Standard Quantity – Actual Quantity) x Standard Price.

$$\text{Revised Std. Quantity} = \frac{\text{Std.Quantity of a material x Total Actual Qty.}}{\text{Total Std. Qty. of material}}$$

**5.Material Yield Variance**

Material Yield Variance = (Actual Yield – Standard Yield) x Standard Material Price per unit.

Standard Yield = Standard output for actual mix

Actual Yield = Actual output

Standard Material Cost per unit = Total cost of Standard mix at standard price / Net Standard output

**Relations between the various Material Cost variances**

1. Material Cost Variance = Material Price Variance + Material Quantity Variance
2. Material Quantity Variance = Material Mix Variance + Material Yield Variance

**Illutration: 1**

Calcualte Material Cost Variance, Material Quantity Variance and Material Price Variance from the following:

| Material | Standard | | Actual | |
|---|---|---|---|---|
| | Qty. | Rate (Rs.) | Qty. | Rate (Rs.) |
| X | 1,000 | 6 | 1,100 | 7 |
| Y | 700 | 10 | 600 | 8 |

***Solution:***

Material Cost Variance = Standard Cost - Actual Cost

Material X = (1000 x 6) - (1100 x 7) = Rs.1700 (Adverse)

Material Y = (700 x 10) - (600 x 8) = Rs.2200 (Favourable)

Total Material Cost Variance = 2200 - 1700 = Rs. 500 (F)

Material Price Variance = Actual Quantity (Std. Price - Actual Price)

Material X = 1100 (6 - 7) = Rs.1100 (Adverse)

Material Y = 600 (10 - 8) = Rs.1200 (Favourable)

Total MPV = 1200 - 1100 = Rs.100 (Favourable)

Material Quantity Variance = Std Price x (Std Quantity - Actual Quantity)

Material X = 6 (1000 - 1100) = Rs.600 (Adverse)

Material Y = 10 (700 - 600) = Rs.1000 (Favourable)

Total MQV = 1000 - 600 = Rs.400 (Favourable)

**Verification:**

Material Cost Variance = MPV + MQV = 100 + 400 = Rs.500 (Favourable)

**Illutration: 2**

XY & Co Ltd. purchased 2,500 units of a material for Rs.5,000. The standard material required for producing 1 tonne of the final product is 30 units. The standard price of the material is Rs.1.75 per unit. The stocks of material in the beginning and at the end are 700 units and 1,300 units respectively. Actual production is 75 tonnes. Calculate material cost variance, material price variance and material usage variance.

***Solution:***

Actual production = 75 tonnes

Standard units for 1 tonne = 30

Standard units for 75 tonnes = 75 x 30 = 2,250

Standard price per unit = Rs.1.75

Actual price per unit = $\frac{5000}{2500}$ = Rs.2

Material Consumed:

Opening Stock of material = 700

Add: Purchase = 2500

3200

Less: Closing stock of material = 1300

Actual Quantity = 1,900

Material Cost Variance = (SQ x SP ) – ( AQ x AP)

= (2250 x 1.75) – (1900 x 2)

= 3937.50 – 3800 = Rs.137.50 (F)

Material Price Variance = AQ (SP- AP)

= 1900 (1.75 -2)

= 1900 x 0.25 = Rs.475 (A)

Material Usage Variance = SP (SQ – AQ)

= 1.75 (2250 – 1900)

= 1.75 x 350 = Rs.612.50 (F)

**Verification:** MCV = MPV + MUV = - 475 +612.50 = Rs.137.50 (F)

**Illustration: 3**

X Ltd provided the following information from its costing records for the month of March 2011. The details regarding the standard cost of manufacturing 10 units of product A are as follows:

| Material | Qty (Kgm) | Unit Price (Rs.) | Value (Rs.) |
|---|---|---|---|
| K | 12 | 5 | 60 |
| M | 8 | 4 | 32 |
| Total | 20 | | 92 |

The actual cost for manufacturing 1000 units is as follows:

| Material | Qty (Kgm) | Unit Price (Rs.) | Value (Rs.) |
|---|---|---|---|
| K | 1700 | 4.50 | 7,650 |
| M | 700 | 5.00 | 3,500 |
| Total | 2,400 | | 11,150 |

Calculate material cost variance, material quantity variance, material price variance and material mix variance.

***Solution:***

Standard Quantity of Material K = 12/10 = 1.2 per unit

Standard Quantity of Material M = 8/10 = 0.8 per unit

Standard Quantity of Material K for 1000 units = 1.2x1000 = 1200 Kgm

Standard Quantity of Material M for 1000 units = 0.8 x 1000 = 800 Kgm

Revised standard Mix of Material K = (1200/2000) x2400 = 1440 Kgm

Revised standard Mix of Material M = (800/2000) x 2400 = 960 Kgm

(i) Material Cost Variance = (SQ x SP) – (AQ x AP)

Material K = (1200 x 5 ) – (1700 x 4.5)

= 6000-7650 = Rs.1650 (A)

Material M = ( 800 x 4 ) – (700 x 5)

= 3200 – 3500 = Rs.300 (A)

Total MCV = - 1650 – 300 = Rs.1950 (Adverse)

(ii) Material Quantity Variance = SP (SQ – AQ)

Material K = 5 (1200-1700) = 5 x 500 = Rs.2500 (A)

Material M = 4 (800-700) = 4 x 100 = Rs.400 (F)

Total MQV = -2500 + 400 = Rs.2100 (Adverse)

(iii) Material Price Variance = AQ (SP – AP)

Material K = 1700 (5 - 4.50)

= 1700 x 0.50 = Rs.850 (F)

Material M = 700 (4 - 5) = 700 x 1 = Rs.700 (A)

Total MPV = 850 – 700 = Rs.150 (Favourable)

(iv) Material Mix Variance = (Revised Standard Mix – Actual Mix) x Standard Price

Material K = (1440 – 1700) x 5

= 260 x 5 = Rs.1300 (A)

Material M = (960 – 700) x 4

= 260 x 4 = Rs.1040 (F)

Total MMV = -1300 + 1040 =Rs.260 (Adverse)

**Verification:** MCV = MQV + MPV = -2100 + 150

= Rs.1950 (A)

**Illustration: 4**

Calculate Material Cost Variance, Material Quantity Variance, Material Price Variance, Material Mix Variance and Material Yield Variance from the following particulars:

| Material | Standard | | | Actual | | |
|---|---|---|---|---|---|---|
| | Qty. | Rate (Rs.) | Amount (Rs.) | Qty. | Rate (Rs.) | Amount (Rs.) |
| A | 27,000 | 2.60 | 70,200 | 28,000 | 2.20 | 61,600 |
| B | 18,000 | 1.70 | 30,600 | 20,000 | 1.80 | 36,000 |
| Total | 45,000 | | 1,00,800 | 48,000 | | 97,600 |

Standard loss is 5 %

***Solution:***

(i) Material Cost Variance = Standard Cost– Actual Cost

= 100,800 – 97600 = Rs.3200(F)

(ii) Material Quantity Variance = SP (SQ – AQ)

Material A = 2.60 (27000 – 28000)

= 2.60 x 1000 = Rs.2600 (A)

Material B = 1.70 (18000 – 20,000)

= 1.70 x 2000 = Rs.3400 (A)

Total MQV = 2600 + 3400 = Rs.6000 (A)

(iii) Material Price Variance = AQ (SP – AP)

Material A = 28000 (2.60 – 2.20)

= 28000 x 0.40 = Rs.11200 (F)

Material B = 20,000 (1.70 – 1.80)
= 20000 x 0.10 = Rs.2000 (A)

Total MPV = 11,200 – 2000 = Rs.9200 (F)

(iv) Material Mix Variance = SP (RSM – ASM)

Material A = 2.60 (28,800 – 28,000)
= 2.60 x 800 = Rs.2080 (F)

Material B = 1.70 (19,200 – 20,000)
= 1.70 x 800 = Rs.1360 (A)

Total MMV = 2080 – 1360 = Rs.720 (F)

(v) Material Yield Variance = Std. Rate for actual outputx(AY- SY)
= 2.358 (42,750 – 45,600)
= 2.40 x 2850 = Rs.6,720 (A)

**Verification:** MCV = MPV+MQV = 9200 – 6000 = Rs.3200 (F)
MQV = MMV+MYV = 720 – 6720 = Rs.6000 (A)

**Workings:**

Revised Std. Mix (RSM): Material A = (27,000 / 45,000) x 48,000 = 28,800 units
Material B = (18,000 / 45,000) x 48,000 = 19,200 units
Total = 48,000 units

Standard output = Actual input – Std.Loss
= 48,000 – (5/100) x 48,000
= 48,000 – 2,400 = 45,600 units

Actual yield for Standard input = 45,000 – (5/100) x 45,000 = 42,750

Standard Rate for actual output = 1,00,800 / 42,750 = Rs.2.358

**Illustration: 5**

A manufacturing company provides that the standard cost for manufacturing 10 units of the finished product as follows:

| Material | Qty. | Rate (Rs.) | Amount (Rs.) |
|---|---|---|---|
| A | 150 | 5.00 | 750.00 |
| B | 175 | 6.00 | 1050.00 |
| C | 75 | 4.50 | 337.50 |
| Total | 400 | | 2137.50 |

Actual costs of manufacturing 100 units of finished products are as follows:

| Material | Qty. | Amount (Rs.) |
|---|---|---|
| A | 1,600 | 9,600 |
| B | 2,000 | 15,000 |
| C | 1,000 | 5,000 |
| Total | 4,600 | 29,600 |

Calculate (i) Material Cost Variance (ii) Material Quantity Variance (iii) Material Price Variance (iv) Material Mix Variance and (v) Material Yield Variance.

***Solution:***

Actual Price per unit of Material A = 9600 / 1600 = Rs.6

Material B = 15000 / 2000 = Rs.7.50

Material C = 5000 / 1000 = Rs.5

Revised Standard Quantity of Material A = (150 / 400) x 4600 = 1725units

Material B = (175 / 400) x 4600 = 2013 units

Material C = (75 / 400) x 4600 = 862units

Revised Standard output = (10/ 400) x 4600 = 115 units

Standard Rate = 2137.50 / 10 = Rs.213.75

(i) Material Cost Variance = Standard Cost – Actual Cost
= 21375 - 29600 = Rs.8225 (Adverse)

(ii) Material Quantity Variance = (SQ - AQ) x SR

Material A = (1500 - 1600) x 5 = 100 x 5
= Rs.500 (A)

Material B = (1750 - 2000) x 6 = 250 x 6
= Rs.1500 (A)

Material C = (750-1000) x4.50 = 250x4.50
= Rs.1125 (A)

Total = Rs.3125 (A)

(iii) Material Price Variance = (SP – AP) x AQ

Material A = (5 - 6)x1600 =1x1600
= Rs.1600(A)

Material B = (6 - 7.50) x 2000 = 1.50 x 2000 = Rs.3000 (A)

Material C = (4.50-5) x 1000 = 0.50x1000
= Rs.500 (A)

Total = Rs.5100 (A)

(iv) Material Mix Variance = (Revised Standard Mix – Actual Mix) x Standard Rate

Material A = (1725 - 1600) x 5 = 125 x 5
= Rs.625 (F)

Material B = (2013 – 2000) x 6 = 13 x 6
= Rs.78 (F)

Material C = (862 - 1000)x4.50=138 x4.50
= Rs.621 (A)

Total = Rs.82 (F)

Material Yield Variance = (Actual Yield – Revised Standard Yield) x Standard Rate for Actual output
= (100 – 115) x 213.75
= Rs.3206.25 (Adverse)

**Verification:** MCV = MQV + MPV=3125 + 5100
Rs.8225 (Adverse)

MQV = MMV + MYV=82 - 3206.25
= Rs.3124.25 (Adverse)

**Illustration: 6**

GR Ltd provides the following information from its costing records:

| Material | Standard | | | Actual | | |
|---|---|---|---|---|---|---|
| | Qty | Rate (Rs.) | Amount (Rs.) | Qty | Rate (Rs.) | Amount (Rs.) |
| A | 120 | 3 | 360 | 140 | 2.20 | 308 |
| B | 80 | 2 | 160 | 110 | 2.50 | 275 |
| Total | 200 | | 520 | 250 | | 583 |

The standard normal loss is estimated as 20%. Actual loss is 90 units.

Calculate all material cost variances.

***Solution:***

(i) Material Cost Variance = (Standard Qty. for Actual Production x S.P.) - (Actual Qty. x AP)

Material A = (120 x 3) - (140 x 2.20)
= 360 - 308 = Rs.52 (F)

Material B = (80 x 2) - (110 x 2.50)
= 160 - 275 = Rs.115 (A)

Total MCV = (52 - 115) = Rs.63 (A)

(ii) Material Price Variance = (SP – AP) x AQ

Material A = (3 - 2.20) x 140 = 0.80 x 140
= Rs.112 (F)

Material B = (2 - 2.50) x 110 = 0.50 x 110
= Rs.55 (A)

Total MPV = 112 - 55 = Rs.57 (F)

(iii) Material Quantity Variance = SP (SQ - AQ)

Material A = 3 (120 - 140) = 3 (-20)
= Rs.60 (A)

Material B = 2 (80 - 110) = 2 (-30)
= Rs.60 (A)

Total MQV = 60 + 60 = Rs.120 (A)

(iv) Material Mix Variance = (Revised Standard Mix – Actual Mix) x SP

$$\text{Revised std. mix of actual input} = \frac{\text{Std. Mix}}{\text{Total Std. input}} \times \text{Total Actual Input}$$

Material A = $\frac{120}{200}$ x 250 = 150 units

Material B = $\frac{80}{200}$ x 250 = 100 units

MMV: Material A = (150 - 140) x 3 = 10 x 3
= Rs.30 (F)

Material B = (100 - 110) x 2 = (-10) x 2
= Rs.20 (A)

Total MMV = 30 - 20 = Rs.10 (F)

(v) Material Yield Variance = (Std. loss on Actual Input-Actual Loss) x Average Std. Cost per unit of output
= (20% of 250 - 90) x $\frac{520}{(200 - 40)}$
= (50 - 90) x 3.25 = -40 x 3.25
= Rs.130 (A)

Verification: (i) MCV = MPV + MQV = 57 - 120
= Rs.63 (A)

(ii) MQV = MMV + MYV = 10 - 130
= Rs.120 (A)

## II. LABOUR COST VARIANCE

Labour cost variance analyses the actual cost of labour with the standard cost of labour.

The different types of labour variances are as follows.

1. Labour Cost Variance
2. Labour Rate Variance
3. Labour Efficiency Variance
4. Labour Mix Variance
5. Labour Yield variance
6. Idle Time Variance

### 1. Labour Cost Variance

The difference between the standard cost of labour and actual cost of labour is called Labour Cost Variance. It may be calculated as follows.

Labour Cost Variance = Standard Cost of Labour – Actual Cost of Labour ; (SC-AC)

(or) = (Std. Hours for actual output x Standard Rate) – (Actual Hours for Actual output x Actual Rate)
= [(SHxAQ)xSR]–[(AHxAQ)x AR]
= AQ [(SH x SR) – (AH x AR)]

**2. Labour Rate Variance**

It is also known as Labour Wage Variance.

Labour Rate Variance = Actual Hours (Standard Rate – Actual Rate); AH (SR – AR)

**3. Labour Efficiency Variance**

Labour Efficiency Variance is also known as Labour Time Variance.

Labour Efficiency Variance = Standard Rate (Standard Hours – Actual Hours); SR (SH – AH)

**4. Labour Mix Variance**

It is also known a Gang Composition Variance. It can be calculated when two or more types of labour cost are given. There are two different situations for the calculation of labour mix variance

**(a) Labour mix variance when both the Total Standard hours and Total Actual hours are equal; and the ratio of standard mix is different from the ratio of actual mix.**

Labour Mix Variance = Standard Rate (Standard Hours for Actual output – Actual Hours for Actual output)

**(b) Labour Mix Variance when the Total Standard hours and Total Actual hours are not equal; and the ratio of standard mix is different from the ratio of actual mix.**

Labour Mix Variance = Standard Rate (Revised Standard mix of actual hours–Actual mix of actual hours)

**5. Labour Yield Variance**

Labour Yield Variance = Standard Labour Cost per unit x (Standard Yield for Actual hours – Actual Yield)

**6. Idle Time Variance**

Idle time arises due to Machine break-down, Power failure, Strike, Shortage of raw material etc.

Idle Time Variance = Abnormal Idle Time x Standard Rate

**Illustration: 7**

Calculate Labour Cost Variance from the following:

| Particulars | Standard | Actual |
|---|---|---|
| Wage Rate per hour (Rs.) | 12 | 14 |
| Labour hours per unit | 4 | 3 |

The company produced 4,000 units during the period.

***Solution:***

Labour Cost Variance = AQ [(SH x SR) – (AH x AR)]
= 4,000 [(4 x 12) – (3 x 14)]
= 4,000 (48 – 42)
= 4,000 x 6= Rs.24,000(Favourable)

**Illustration: 8**

Calculate labour rate variance for actual output of 500 units.

| Particulars | Standard | Actual |
|---|---|---|
| Number of labour hours per unit | 3 | 3.5 |
| Wage rate per hour (Rs.) | 11 | 12 |

***Solution:***

Actual hours for one unit = 3.5
Actual hours for 500 units = 3.5 x 500 = 1750
Labour Rate Variance = AH (SR – AR)
= 1,750 (11 – 12)
= 1750 x 1
= Rs.1,750 (Adverse)

**Illustration: 9**

Calculate Labour Efficiency Variance from the following:

| Particulars | Standard | Actual |
|---|---|---|
| Wage rate per hour (Rs.) | 15 | 15.5 |
| Labour hours per unit | 3 | 2.5 |

Actual output 600 units.

***Solution:***

Standard hours for 600 units = 3 x 600 = 1,800
Actual hours for 600 units = 2.5 x 600 = 1,500
Labour Efficiency Variance = SR (SH – AH)
= 15 (1,800 – 1,500)
= 15 x 300 = Rs.4,500 (Favourable)

**Illustration: 10**

The standard labour cost of a product manufactured by X Ltd is stated as follows:

| Workers | Hours per unit of output | Hourly Rate Rs. | Amount Rs. |
|---|---|---|---|
| A<br>B | 12<br>8 | 12<br>10 | 144<br>80 |
| | 20 | | 224 |

The actual cost for producing 200 units is as follows:

| Workers | Hours | Hourly Rate Rs. | Amount Rs. |
|---|---|---|---|
| A<br>B | 2,500<br>1,500 | 13<br>9 | 32,500<br>13,500 |
| | 4,000 | | 46,000 |

Calculate (i) Labour Cost Variance (ii) Labour Rate Variance (iii) Labour Efficiency Variance (iv) Labour Mix Variance.

***Solution:***

(i) LCV = AQ [(SH x SR) – (AH x AR)]
A = 200 [(12 x 12) – (12.5 x 13)] = 200 (144 – 162.5)
= 200 x 18.5 = Rs.3,700 (Unfavourable)
B = 200 [(8 x 10) – (7.5 x 9)] = 200 (80 – 67.5)
= 200 x 12.5 = Rs.2,500 (Favourable)
LCV = -3700 + 2500 = Rs.1,200 (Unfavourable)

(ii) LRV = AH (SR – AR)
A = 2500 (12 – 13) = 2500 x 1 = Rs.2,500 (Unfavourable)
B = 1500 (10 – 9) = 1500 x 1 = Rs.1,500 (Favourable)
LRV = -2500 + 1500 = Rs.1,000 (Unfavourable)

(iii) LEV = SR ( SH – AH)
A = 12 (2400 – 2500) = 12 x 100 = Rs.1,200 (Unfavourable)
B = 10 (1600 – 1500) = 10 x 100 = Rs.1,000 (Favourable)
LEV = - 1200 + 1000 = Rs.200 (Unfavourable)

(iv) LMV = SR (SH – AH)
A = 12 (2400 – 2500) = Rs.1,200 (Unfavourable)
B = 10 (1600 – 1500) = Rs.1,000 (Favourable)
LMV = -1200 + 1000 = Rs.200 (Unfavourable)

When total standard hours are equal to total actual hours, then the LMV is equal to LEV.

Verification: LCV = LRV + LEV = 1000 + 200 = Rs.1,200 (U)

Workings:(a) AH per unit : A = 2,500 / 200 = 12.5
B = 1,500 / 200 = 7.5

(b) SH for 200 units: A = 12 x 200 = 2,400;
B = 8 x 200 = 1,600

**Illustration: 11**

XYZ Co. Ltd provided the following information from the costing records. Standard labour costs are as follows:

| Workers | Hours per unit | Hourly Rate Rs. | Amount Rs. |
|---|---|---|---|
| Male<br>Female | 5<br>3 | 20<br>18 | 100<br>54 |
| | 8 | | 154 |

Actual labour cost for 300 units are as follows:

| Workers | Hours | Hourly Rate Rs. | Amount Rs. |
|---|---|---|---|
| Male<br>Female | 1,710<br>990 | 17<br>15 | 29,070<br>14,850 |
| | 2,700 | | 43,920 |

Calculate (i) Labour Cost Variance (ii) Labour Rate Variance and (iii) Labour Efficiency Variance (iv) Labour Mix Variance.

***Solution:***

Standard hours for 300 units:

Male = 5 x 300 = 1,500
Female = 3 x 300 = 900
Total = 2,400

Revised Standard Hours:

Male = (1500 / 2400) x 2700 = 1,687.50
Female = (900 / 2400) x 2700 = 1,012.50
Total = 2,700.00

Standard Labour Cost for 300 units = 154 x 300 = Rs.46,200

(i) LCV = Standard Cost – Actual Cost
= 46,200 – 43,920 = Rs.2,280 (Favourable)

(ii) LRV = AH (SR – AR)
Male = 1710 (20 – 17) = 1710 x 3 = Rs.5,130 (Favourable)
Female = 990 (18 – 15) = 990 x 3 = Rs.2,970 (Favourable)
LRV = 5,130 + 2,970 = Rs.8,100 (Favourable)

(iii) LEV = SR (SH – AH)
Male = 20 (1,500 – 1,710) = 20 x 210 = Rs.4,200 (Unfavourable)
Female = 18 (900 – 990) = 18 x 90 = Rs.1,620 (Unfavourable)
LEV = 4,200 + 1,620 = Rs.5,820 (Unfavourable)

(iv) LMV = SR (RSH – AH)

Male = 20 (1,687.5 – 1,710) = 20 x 22.5 = Rs.450 (Unfavourable)

Female = 18 (1,012.5 – 990) = 18 x 22.5 = Rs.405 (Favourable)

LMV = 450 – 405 = Rs.45 (Unfavourable)

Verification: LCV = LRV + LEV = 8,100 – 5,820

= Rs.2,280 (Favourable)

**Illustration: 12**

Standard hours required for manufacturing 1 unit of a product is 12 hours @ Rs.10 per hour. If the company paid Rs.143,000 for manufacturing 1,000 units @ Rs.11 per hour, find out LCV, LRV and LEV.

***Solution:***

Standard hours for 1,000 units = 12 x 1,000 = 12,000

Actual hours for 1,000 units = 143,000 / 11 = 13,000

Actual hours for 1 unit = 13,000 / 1000 = 13

Standard Cost = 12,000 x 10 = Rs.120,000

SR = Rs.10; AR = Rs.11

LCV = Standard Cost – Actual Cost

= 120,000 – 143,000 = Rs.23,000 (Unfavourable)

LRV = AH (SR – AR) = 13000 (10 – 11) = 13000 x 1

= Rs.13,000 (Unfavourable)

LEV = SR (SH – AH) = 10 (12000 – 13000)

= 10 x 1000 = Rs.10,000 (Unfavourable)

LCV = LRV + LEV = 13000 + 10000

= Rs.23,000 (Unfavourable)

**Illustration: 13**

KM Ltd provided the following information related to the payment of wages.

| Particulars | Skilled Workers | Semi-Skilled Workers | Unskilled Workers |
|---|---|---|---|
| Standard number of workers in the gang | 20 | 20 | 10 |
| Standard rate per hour (Rs.) | 4 | 3 | 2 |
| Actual number of workers in the gang | 25 | 17 | 8 |
| Actual rate per hour (Rs.) | 5 | 2 | 3 |

The Company worked for 40 hours in the week and produced 1800 standard hours of work.

Calculate (i) Labour Cost Variance (ii) Labour Rate Variance (iii) Labour Efficiency Variance (iv) Labour Mix Variance and (v) Labour Yield Variance.

***Solution:***

Calculation of Labour Variances:

(i) LCV = Standard Labour Cost – Actual Labour Cost
= (1800/2000) x 6400 – 7320 = Rs.1,560 (Adverse)

(ii) LRV = AH (SR – AR)
Skilled = 1000 (4 – 5 ) = 1000 x 1 = Rs.1,000 (Adverse)
Semi–Skilled = 680 ( 3 -2) = 680 x1 = Rs.680 (Favourable)
Unskilled = 320 (2 – 3) = 320 x 1 = Rs.320 (Adverse)
LRV = -1000 – 320 + 680 = Rs.640 (Adverse)

(iii) LEV = SR (RSH – AH)
Skilled = 4 (720 - 1000) = 4 x 280 = Rs.1120 (Adverse)
Semi-Skilled = 3 (720 – 680) = 3 x 40 = Rs.120 (Favourable)
Unskilled = 2 (360 – 320) = 2 x 40 = Rs.80 (Favourable)
LEV = - 1120 + 120 + 80 = Rs.920 (Adverse)

(iv) LMV = SR (SH – AH)
Skilled = 4 (800 - 1000) = 4 x 200 = Rs.800 (Adverse)
Semi-Skilled = 3 (800 - 680) = 3 x 120 = Rs.360 (Favourable)
Unskilled = 2 (400 - 320) = 2 x 80 = Rs.160 (Favourable)
LMV = - 800 + 360 + 160 = Rs.280 (Adverse)

(v) LYV = SR (AY - SY)
= 3.20 (1800 - 2000) = 3.20 x 200 = Rs.640 (Adverse)
(SR = 6,400 / 2000 = Rs.3.20)

Verification:
LCV = LRV + LEV = 640 + 920 = Rs.1,560 (Adverse)
LEV = LMV + LYV= 280 + 640 = Rs.920 (Adverse)

**Workings:**

(a) Calculation of Standard and Actual Labour Cost:

| Labour | Standard | | | Actual | | |
|---|---|---|---|---|---|---|
| | Rate (Rs.) | Hours | Amount (Rs.) | Rate (Rs.) | Hours | Amount (Rs.) |
| Skilled | 4 | 20 x 40=800 | 3,200 | 5 | 25x40=1000 | 5,000 |
| Semi-skilled | 3 | 20 x 40=800 | 2,400 | 2 | 17x40 = 680 | 1,360 |
| Unskilled | 2 | 10 x 40=400 | 800 | 3 | 8 x 40 = 320 | 960 |
| Total | | 2,000 | 6,400 | | 2,000 | 7,320 |

(b) Calculation of Revised Standard hours:

Skilled workers = (800/2000) x 1,800 = 720 hours
Semi-skilled workers = (800/2000) x 1,800 = 720 hours
Unskilled workers = (400/2000) x 1,800 = 360 hours

[Note: Revised standard hour is considered as actual standard hour. Table (a) is related to Revised standard hours]

**Illustration: 14**

Calculate various Labour variances from the following information:

| Workers | Standard | | Actual | |
|---|---|---|---|---|
| | Number | Wage Rate per week (Rs.) | Number | Wage Rate per week (Rs.) |
| Male | 30 | 500 | 25 | 550 |
| Female | 20 | 400 | 20 | 425 |
| Children | 10 | 300 | 15 | 280 |
| | 60 | | 60 | |

The Standard time required for completing a job is 10 weeks and Actual time taken for completing the work is 8 weeks.

***Solution:***

**Calculation of Labour Variances**

| Workers | Standard | | | Actual | | |
|---|---|---|---|---|---|---|
| | Hours (weeks) | Weekly Rate (Rs.) | Total Wage (Rs.) | Hours (weeks) | Weekly Rate (Rs.) | Total Wage (Rs.) |
| Male | 30 x 10=300 | 500 | 150,000 | 25 x 8 =200 | 550 | 110,000 |
| Female | 20 x 10=200 | 400 | 80,000 | 20 x 8 =160 | 425 | 68,000 |
| Children | 10 x 10=100 | 300 | 30,000 | 15 x 8 =120 | 280 | 33,600 |
| Total | 600 | | 260,000 | 480 | | 211,600 |

Revised Standard hours: Male = (300 / 600) x 480 = 240
Female = (200 / 600) x 480 = 160
Children = (100 / 600) x 480 = 80
Total = 480

(i) LCV = SLC – ALC
= 260,000 - 211,600 = Rs.48,400 (Favourable)

(ii) LRV = AH (SR – AR)
Male = 200 (500 – 550)= 200 x 50 = Rs.10,000(Unfavourable)
Female = 160 (400 – 425)= 160 x 25 = Rs.4,000 (Unfavourable)
Children = 120 (300 – 280)= 120 x 20 = Rs.2,400 (Favourable)
LRV = - 10000 – 4000 + 2400 = Rs11,600 (Unfavourable)

(iii) LEV = SR (SH – AH)
Male = 500 (300 – 200)= 500 x 100= Rs.50,000 (Favourable)
Female = 400 (200 – 160)= 400 x 40 = Rs.16,000 (Favourable)
Children = 300 (100 – 120)= 300 x 20 = Rs.6,000 (Unfavourable)
LEV = 50000 + 16000 – 6000 = Rs.60,000 (Favourable)

(iv) LMV = SR (RSH – AH)

Male = 500 (240 – 200) = 500 x 40 = Rs.20,000 (Favourable)

Female = 400 (160 – 160) = 400 x 0 = Rs.0

Children = 300 (80 – 120) = 300 x 40 = Rs.12,000 (Unfavourable)

LMV = 20000 – 12000 = Rs.8,000 (Favourable)

(v) LYV = SR (AY – SY)

= 433.33 (600 – 480) = 433.33 x 120 = Rs.52,000 (Favourable)

(SR = 260000 / 600 = 433.33)

**Verification:**

LCV = LRV + LEV = -11,600 + 60,000 = Rs.48,400 (Favourable)

(or) = LRV + LMV + LYV

= - 11,600 + 8,000 + 52,000 = Rs.48,400 (Favourable)

LEV = LMV + LYV = 8000 + 52000 = Rs.60,000 (Favourable)

**Illustration: 15**

X Ltd provided the following information from the costing records.

| Workers | Standard | | Actual | |
|---|---|---|---|---|
| | Labour | Rate (Rs.) | Labour | Rate (Rs.) |
| A | 120 | 7 | 130 | 8 |
| B | 80 | 5 | 70 | 4 |

The company also provided that the Budgeted hours as 2,000, Actual hours as 1,800, Budgeted gross production 20,000 units, Standard loss 10%, Actual loss 1,500 units. Calculate all the labour variances.

***Solution:***

**Calculation of Standard and Actual Cost**

| Workers | Standard | | | Actual | | |
|---|---|---|---|---|---|---|
| | Hours | Rate Rs. | Amount Rs. | Hours | Rate Rs. | Amount Rs. |
| A | 240,000 | 7 | 16,80,000 | 234,000 | 8 | 1872,000 |
| B | 160,000 | 5 | 8,00,000 | 126,000 | 4 | 504,000 |
| Total | 400,000 | | 24,80,000 | 360,000 | | 23,76,000 |

Labour Cost Variance = Std. Cost for Actual Production - Actual Cost

$$= \frac{24,80,000}{18,000} \times 18,500 - 23,76,000$$

= 25,48,889 - 23,76,000 = Rs.172,889 (F)

Labour Rate Variance = Actual Hours (Std. Rate - Actual Rate)

A = 234,000 (7 - 8) = 234,000 x 1 = Rs. 234,000 (A)

B $= 126{,}000\,(5-4) = 126{,}000 \times 1 =$ Rs.126,000 (F)

LRV $= -234{,}000 + 126{,}000$ = Rs.108,000 (A)

Labour Efficiency Variance = SR(Std. Hours for actual output - Actual hours)

A $= 7\left[\dfrac{240{,}000}{18{,}000} \times 18500 - 234000\right]$

$= 7\,(246{,}667 - 234{,}000) = 7 \times 12{,}667$

= Rs.88,669 (F)

B $= 5\left[\dfrac{160{,}000}{18{,}000} \times 18500 - 126000\right]$

$= 5\,(164{,}444 - 126{,}000) = 5 \times 38{,}444$

= Rs. 192220 (F)

LEV $= 88{,}669 + 192{,}220$ = Rs.280,889 (F)

Labour Mix Variance = SR (Revised Std. Hours - Actual Hours)

A $= 7\left[\dfrac{240{,}000}{400{,}000} \times 360{,}000 - 234{,}000\right]$

$= 7\,(216{,}000 - 234{,}000) = 7 \times 18{,}000$

= Rs.126,000 (A)

B $= 5\left[\dfrac{160{,}000}{400{,}000} \times 360{,}000 - 126000\right]$

$= 5\,(144{,}000 - 126{,}000) = 5 \times 18{,}000$

= Rs.90,000 (F)

LMV $= -126{,}000 + 90{,}000$ = Rs.36,000 (A)

**Varification:** LCV = LRV + LEV

$= -108{,}000 + 280{,}889$ = Rs.172,889 (F)

**Illustration: 16**

The normal standard hours in a week of a company is 40 and the standard production is 5,000 units. The workers required for producing standard output are 20 skilled workers, 15 semi-skilled workers and 10 unskilled workers and they have to be paid @ Rs.7, Rs.5 and Rs.4 per hour respectively.

Actual production is 4500 units. Actual worker employed are 17 skilled workers, 16 semi-skilled worker and 12 unskilled worker and they are paid @ Rs.8, Rs.4 and Rs.3 per hour respectively. The abnormal idle time is 3 hours.

Calculate (i) Labour Cost Variance, (ii) Labour Rate Variance, (iii) Labour Efficiency Variance, (iv) Labour Mix Variance, (v) Labour Yield Variance and (vi) Idle Time Variance.

***Solution:***

**Calculation of Standard and Actual Cost**

| Workers | Standard | | | Actual | | |
|---|---|---|---|---|---|---|
| | Hours | Rate Rs. | Amount Rs. | Hours | Rate Rs. | Amount Rs. |
| Skilled | 800 | 7 | 5,600 | 680 | 8 | 5,440 |
| Semi-skilled | 600 | 5 | 3,000 | 640 | 4 | 2,560 |
| Unskilled | 400 | 4 | 1,600 | 480 | 3 | 1,440 |
| Total | 1800 | | 10,200 | 1800 | | 9,440 |

**Calculation of Labour Variance:**

(i) Labour Cost Variance = Std. Cost for Actual output - Actual Cost

$= \frac{10,200}{5,000} \times 4,500 - 9,440 = \text{Rs.}260\ (A)$

(ii) Labour Rate Variance = Actual Hours (Std. Rate - Actual Rate)

Skilled = 680 (7 - 8) = 680 x 1 = Rs.680 (A)

Semi-skilled = 640 (5 - 4) = 640 x 1 = Rs.640 (F)

Unskilled = 480 (4 - 3) = 480 x 1 = Rs.480 (F)

LRV = -680 + 640 + 480 = Rs.440 F)

(iii) Labour Efficiency Variance = SR (Std. hour for actual output - Actual hours for wage paid)

Skilled $= 7 \left[\frac{800}{5,000} \times 4500 - 680\right]$

= 7 (720 - 680) = 7 x 40 = Rs.280 (F)

Semi-skilled $= 5 \left[\frac{600}{5,000} \times 4500 - 640\right]$

= 5 (540 - 640) = 5 x 100= Rs.500 (A)

Unskilled $= 4 \left[\frac{400}{5,000} \times 4500 - 480\right]$

= 4 (360 - 480) = 4 x 120= Rs.480 (A)

LEV = 280 - 500 - 480 = Rs.700 (A)

Labour Efficiency Variance can be calculated by adjusting the Idle time also as follows:

Labour Efficiency Variance = SR (Std. hours for actual output - Actual hours worked)

(Actual hours = Normal hours - Idle time = 40 - 3 = 37)

Skilled = 7 [720 - (17 x 37)] = 7 (720 - 629)

= 7 x 91 = Rs.637 (F)

Semi-skilled = 5 [540 - (16 x 37)] = 5 (540 - 592)

= 5 x 52 = Rs.260 (A)

Unskilled = 4 [360 - (12 x 37)] = 4(360 - 444)

= 4 x 84 = Rs.336 (A)

LEV = 637 - 260 - 336 = Rs.41 (F)

(iv) Labour Mix Variance = SR (Revised Std. Hour - Actual Hour Worked)

Skilled $= 7\left[\frac{800}{1800} \times 1665 - (17 \times 37)\right]$

= 7 (740 - 629) = 7 x 111 = Rs.777 (F)

Semi-skilled $= 5\left[\frac{600}{1800} \times 1665 - (16 \times 37)\right]$

= 5 (555 - 592 ) = 5 x 37 = Rs.185 (A)

Unskilled $= 4\left[\frac{400}{1800} \times 1665 - (12 \times 37)\right]$

= 4 (370 - 444) = 4 x 74 = Rs.296 (A)

LMV = 777 - 185 - 296 = Rs.296 (F)

(Actual hours without idle time = 1800 - (45 x 3) = 1800 - 135 = 1665)

(v) Labour Yield Variance = Std. Rate per unit (Std. output for Actual Hours - Actual output)

= 2.04 (4625 - 4500) = 2.04 x 125 = Rs.255 (A)

[Std. Rate = 10200 / 5000 = Rs.2.04

Std.output for Actual Hour $= \frac{5000}{1800} \times 1665 = 4,625$ units]

(vi) Idle Time Variance = Idle hours x SR

Skilled = (17 x 3) x 7= 51 x 7 = Rs.357

Semi-skilled = (16 x 3) x 5= 48 x 5 = Rs.240

Unskilled = (12 x 3) x 4= 36 x 4 = Rs.144

ITV = 357 + 240 + 144 = Rs.741 (A)

Verification: (i) LCV = LRV + LEV = 440 - 700 = Rs.260 (A)

(ii) LEV = LEV + ITV = 41 - 741 = Rs.700 (A)

= LMV + LYV + ITV

= 296 - 255 - 741 = Rs.700 (A)

## III. OVERHEAD VARIANCE

Overhead means indirect cost. Indirect cost incurred in a concern may be classified on the basis of element wise, function wise and behaviour wise. Element wise, overhead constitutes indirect material, indirect labour and indirect expenses. Function wise, overhead included production overhead, administration overhead and selling and distribution overhead. Behaviour wise, overhead is classified as fixed and variable overheads.

Overhead Cost variance is the difference between the standard cost of overhead and the actual cost of overhead.

Overhead Cost Variance = Overhead recovered – Actual overhead incurred

Overhead Recovered = Standard hours for actual output x Standard overhead rate per hour.

(or) = Actual output x Standard overhead rate per unit

Overhead Cost variance is classified as follows:

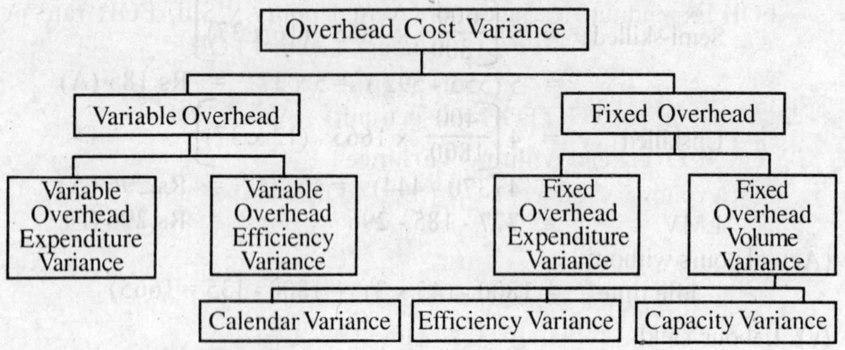


## A. VARIABLE OVERHEAD VARIANCE

Variable Overhead Variance is the difference between the standard variable overhead for actual output and the actual variable overhead.

VOH Variance = (Actual Output x Std. VOH rate per unit) – Actual Overhead.

(or)

(Std. VOH for actual hours x Std. VOH rate per hour) – Actual Overhead.

Variable overhead variance is classified as follows:

**1. Variable Overhead Expenditure Variance**

It is otherwise called as Variable Overhead Spending Variance or Variable Overhead Budget Variance.

VOH Expenditure Variance = (Actual hours x Std VOH rate per hour) - Actual VOH

(or)

(Actual Output x Std. VOH rate per unit) – Actual VOH

**2. Variable Overhead Efficiency Variance**

VOH Efficiency Variance = Std.Cost per hour x (Std. hours for actual output-Actual hours)

## B. FIXED OVERHEAD VARIANCE

Fixed overhead variance is the difference between Standard Fixed Overhead and the Actual Fixed Overhead.

FOH Variance = Fixed Overhead absorbed – Actual Fixed Overhead

(or)

(Std. hours for actual output x Std.FOH rate per hour) – Actual Fixed Overhead.

Fixed overhead variance is classified as follows.

**1. Fixed Overhead Expenditure Variance**

It is otherwise called as Fixed Overhead Spending Variance or Fixed Overhead Budget Variance.

FOH Expenditure Variance = (Actual hours x Std. FOH rate per hour) – Actual FOH

(or)

(Actual output x Std FOH rate per unit) – Actual FOH.

**2. Fixed Overhead Volume Variance**

FOH Volume Variance = Std. FOH rate per unit x (Budgeted production – Actual production)

(or)

Budgeted Fixed overhead based on Std. hours allowed by actual output - Budgeted Fixd overhead for actual output.

Fixed Overhead Volume Variance is classified as follows

**(a) Fixed Overhead Calendar Variance**

FOH Calendar Variance = Std. FOH rate per hour x (Budgeted hours – Revised budgeted capacity hours)

(or) = Std. FOH rate per unit x (Budgeted Quantity – Revised Quantity in terms of actual no.of days worked).

**(b) Fixed Overhead Efficiency Variance**

FOH Efficiency Variance = Std. FOH rate per hour x (Std. hours for actual production – Actual hours)

(or)

Std. FOH rate per unit x (Std. production as per actual time available – Actual production)

**(c) Fixed Overhead Capacity Variance**

FOH Capacity Variance = Std. FOH rate per hour x (Budgeted Capacity hours-Actual Capacity hours)

(or) = Std FOH rate per unit x (Revised budgeted units – Actual Capacity units)

The VOH Variances and FOH Variances are calculated either on the basis of hours or on the basis of number of units of production.

**Illustration: 17**

Calculate Variable Overhead Cost variances from the following information.

| Particulars | Budget | Actual |
|---|---|---|
| Labour hours | 500 | 480 |
| Output (units) | 200 | 160 |
| Variable Overhead (Rs.) | 2000 | 2400 |

***Solution:***

Standard VOH rate per hour = 2000/500 = Rs.4
Standard VOH rate per unit = 2000/200 = Rs.10
Standard hours based on actual output = 500/200 x 160 = 400 hours
Standard output based on actual hours = 200/500 x 480 = 192 units

**(a) VOH variances based on Hours:**

(i) VOH Variance = Std.VOH based on Actual hours – Actual VOH
= (400 x 4) – 2,400
= 1,600 – 2,400 = Rs.800 (A)

(ii) VOH Expenditure Variance = (Actual hours x Std.VOH Rate per hour) – Actual VOH
= (480 x 4) – 2,400 = 1,920 - 2,400
= Rs.480 (A)

(iii) VOH Efficiency Variance = Std VOH Rate (Standard hours for actual production -Actual hours)
= 4 (400 – 480) = Rs.320 (A)

**Verification:**

VOH Variance = VOH Exp. Variance+VOH Effy.Variance
= 480 + 320 = Rs.800 (A)

**(b) VOH variances based on Output:**

(i) VOH Variance = Standard VOH based on actual output per unit – Actual VOH
= (192 x 10) – 2,400
= 1,920 – 2,400 = Rs.480 (A)

(ii) VOH Expenditure Variance = (Actual output x Std. VOH Rate per output) – Actual VOH
= (160 x 10 ) – 2,400
= 1,600 - 2,400 = Rs.800 (A)

(iii) VOH Efficiency Variance = Std.VOH rate (Std. output for actual hours – Actual output)
= 10(192 – 160)
= **10 x 32 = Rs.320 (F)**

**Verification:**

VOH Variance = VOH Expenditure Variance + VOH Efficiency Variance.

= 800 – 320 = Rs.480 (A)

**Illustration: 18**

Calculate Variable Overhead variances from the following information.

| | Budgeted | Actual |
|---|---|---|
| Production (in units) | 4,000 | 3,500 |
| Man hours to produce above units | 40,000 | 36,000 |
| Variable overheads (Rs.) | 20,000 | 19,000 |

The standard time to produce one unit of the product is 10 hours.

***Solution:***

Standard VOH rate per hour = 20000/40000 = Rs.0.50

Standard VOH rate per unit = 20000/4000 = Rs.5

Standard VOH based on actual output = 3500 x 5 = Rs.17,500

Standard VOH based on actual hours= 36000 x 0.50 = Rs.18,000

Standard hours for actual output = 3500 x 10 = 35,000 hours

Standard output for actual hours = (4000/40000) x 36000 = 3,600 units

**(a) VOH variances based on Hours:**

(i) VOH Variance = Standard VOH based on Actual output – Actual VOH

= 17,500 – 19,000 = Rs.1,500 (A)

(ii) VOH Expenditure Variance = Std. VOH based on Actual hours – Actual VOH

= 18,000 - 19,000 = Rs.1,000 (A)

(iii) VOH Efficiency Variance = Std VOH Rate (Standard hours for Actual production - Actual Hours)

= 0.50 (35,000 – 36,000) = Rs.500 (A)

**Verification:**

VOH Variance = VOH Expenditure Variance + VOH Efficiency Variance

= 1,000 + 500 = Rs.1,500 (A)

**(b) VOH variances based on Output:**

(i) VOH Variance = Standard VOH based on actual hours – Actual VOH

= 18,000 – 19,000 = Rs.1,000 (A)

(ii) VOH Expenditure Variance = Standard VOH based on actual output – Actual VOH

= 17,500 – 19,000 Rs.1,500 (A)

(iii) VOH Efficiency Variance = Std.VOH rate per unit (Std.output for actual hours – Actual output)

= 5 (3600 – 3500) = 5 x100 =Rs.500(F)

**Verification:**

VOH Variance = VOH Expenditure Variance + VOH Efficiency Variance.

= 1500 – 500 = Rs.1,000 (A)

**Illustration: 19**

Calculate the Fixed overhead variances from the following:

| Particulars | Budget | Actual |
|---|---|---|
| Fixed Overhead (Rs.) | 30,000 | 35,000 |
| Output (units) | 15,000 | 14,000 |
| Working Days | 20 | 22 |

***Solution:***

Standard FOH rate per unit = 30,000/15,000 = Rs.2

(i) Fixed Overhead Variance = (Actual Output x Std.FOH rate) – Actual FOH

= (14,000 x 2) – 35,000

= 28,000 – 35,000 = Rs.7,000 (A)

(ii) FOH Expenditure Variance = Budgeted FOH – Actual FOH

= 30,000 – 35,000 = Rs.5,000 (A)

(iii) FOH Volume Variance = (Actual Output x Std.FOH rate)-Budgeted FOH

= (14,000 x 2) – 30,000

= 28,000 – 30,000 = Rs.2,000 (A)

(iv) FOH Capacity Variance = Std. FOH Rate(Budgeted Output -Actual Output)

= 2 (15,000 – 14,000)

= 2 x 1,000 = Rs.2,000 (A)

[Revised Budgeted Output = (15,000 /20) x 22 = 16,500]

(v) FOH Calendar Variance = Std FOH Rate (Budgeted Output - Revised Budgeted Output)

= 2 x (15,000 - 16,500) = Rs.3,000 (A)

(vi) FOH Efficiency Variance = Std. Rate x (Std. Output for Actual hours – Actual Output)

= 2 x (16,500 -14,000) = Rs.5,000 (A)

**Verification:** FOHV = FOHEV+FOHVV = 5,000 + 2,000 = 7000 (A)

FOH Eff. Variance = FOH Capa. V + FOH Cala. V

= 2,000 + 3,000 = Rs.5,000 (A)

## SALES VARIANCE

Sales Variance is the difference between Actual Sales and Budgeted Sales. It helps the management for making decision in future with respect to sales. It is possible for the management to take necessary steps if there is unfavorable sales variance. There are two methods for calculating sales variance.

They are
1. Profit Method or Sales Margin Method
2. Sales Value Method

### 1. Profit Method or Sales Margin Method

The following are the different Sales Variances under Profit Method.

(a) Total Sales Margin variance
(b) Sales Margin Variance due to Selling Price
(c) Sales Margin Variance due to Sales Volume
(d) Sales Margin Variance due to Sales Mixture
(e) Sales Margin Variance due to Sales Quantity

(a) Total Sales Margin Variance = Actual Profit – Budgeted Profit
(or) = (AP X AQ ) – ( BP X BQ)
(b) Sales Margin Variance due to Selling Price = AQ (ASP – BSP)
(c) Sales Margin Variance due to Sales Volume = BP ( AQ – BQ)
(d) Sales Margin Variance due to Sales Mixture = BP (AQ – RBQ)
(e) Sales Margin Variance due to Sales Quantity = BP (RBQ – BQ)

[Where AQ = Actual Quantity, BQ = Budgeted Quantity, AP = Actual Profit per unit, BP = Budgeted Profit per unit, ASP = Actual Selling Price per unit, BSP = Budgeted Selling Price per unit, RBQ= Revised Budgeted Quantity]

$$RBQ = \frac{\text{Individual Budgeted Quantity x Total Actual Quantity}}{\text{Total Budgeted Quantity}}$$

### 2. Sales Value Method

The following are the different sales variances under Sales Value method

(a) Total Sales Value Variance = Actual Sales – Budgeted Sales
(or) = (ASP X AQ) – (BSP X BQ)
(b) Sales Price Variance = AQ (ASP – BSP)
(c) Sales Volume Variance = BSP (AQ – BQ)
(d) Sales Mix Variance = BSP (AQ – RBQ)
(e) Sales Quantity Variance = BSP (RBQ – BQ)

[Where AQ = Actual Quantity, BQ = Budgeted Quantity, ASP = Actual Selling Price per unit, BSP = Budgeted Selling Price per unit, RBQ = Revised Budgeted Quantity.]

$$RBQ = \frac{\text{Individual Budgeted Quantity x Total Actual Quantity}}{\text{Total Budgeted Quantity}}$$

**Illustration: 20**

K Ltd. provided the following information from the costing records for the month March 2011.

| | Budgeted | Actual |
|---|---|---|
| Product: A Sales quantity | 3,000 | 3,500 |
| Selling price per unit (Rs.) | 60 | 65 |
| Product: B Sales quantity | 2,000 | 2,500 |
| Selling price per unit (Rs.) | 40 | 36 |

The cost of production for Product A and B are Rs.57 and Rs.33 respectively.

Calculate (i) Sales Margin Variance, (ii) Sales Price Variance (iii) Sales Volume Variance (iv) Sales Mix Variance and (v) Sales Quantity Variance by Sales Margin Method.

***Solution:***

Budgeted Profit per unit for Product A = 60 – 57 = Rs.3
Budgeted Profit per unit for Product B = 40 – 33 = Rs.7
Actual Profit per unit for Product A = 65 – 57 = Rs.8
Actual Profit per unit for Product B = 36 – 33 = Rs.3

(i) Sales Margin Variance = (Actual Quantity x Actual Profit per unit) – (Budgeted Quantity x Budgeted Profit per unit)

Product A = (3,500 x 8) – (3,000 x 3)
= 28,000 – 9,000 = Rs.19,000 (F)

Product B = (2,500 x 3) – (2,000 x 7)
= (7,500 – 14,000) = Rs.6,500 (A)

∴ SMV = 19,000 – 6,500 = Rs.12,500 (F)

(ii) Sales Price Variance = AQ (ASP – BSP)

A = 3,500 (65-60)
= 3,500 x 5 = Rs.17,500 (F)

B = 2,500 (36 – 40)
= 2,500 x 4 = Rs.10,000 (A)

∴ SPV = 17,500 - 10,000 = Rs.7,500 (F)

(iii) Sales Volume Variance = Budgeted Profit per unit (AQ – BQ)

A = 3 (3,500 – 3,000) = 3 x 500 = Rs.1,500(F)
B = 7 (2,500 – 2,000) = 7 x 500 = 3,500(F)

∴ SVV = 1,500 + 3,500 = Rs.5,000 (F)

(iv) Sales Mix Variance = Budgeted Profit per unit (AQ–RBQ)

$$\text{Revised Budgeted Quantity} = \frac{\text{Individual Budgeted Qty. x AQ}}{\text{Total Budgeted Qty.}}$$

A = (3,000/5,000) x 6,000 = 3,600

B = (2,000/5,000) x 6,000 = 2,400

Sales Mix Variance: A = 3 (3,500 – 3,600) = 3 x 100 = 300 (A)

B = 7 (2,500 – 2,400) = 7 x 100 = 700 (F)

∴ SMV = 700 – 300 = Rs.400 (F)

(v) Sales Quantity Variance = Budgeted Profit per unit (RBQ – BQ)

= 3 (3,600 – 3,000) = 3 x 600 = Rs.1,800 (F)

= 7 (2,400 – 2,000) = 7 x 400 = Rs.2,800 (F)

SQV = 1,800 + 2,800 = Rs.4600 (F)

**Verification:**

SMV = SPV + SVV

= 7,500 + 5,000 = Rs 12,500 (F)

SVV = SMV+SQV = 400 + 4,600 = Rs.5000(F)

SMV = SPV +SMV + SQV = 7500 + 400 + 4600

= Rs.12,500 (F)

**Illustration: 21**

G Ltd provided the following information from the costing records for the month April 2011.

| | | |
|---|---|---|
| Budgeted Sales | : | X 1,500 units @ Rs.7 per unit |
| | : | Y 2,500 units @ Rs.5 per unit |
| Actual Sales | : | X 1,000 units @ Rs.6 per unit |
| | : | Y 2,000 units @ Rs.8 per unit |

Calculate (i) Sales Value Variance (ii) Sales Price Variance (iii) Sales Volume Variance (iv) Sales Mix Variance and (v) Sales Quantity Variance by Sales Value Method.

***Solution:***

$$\text{Revised Standard Quantity (RSQ)} = \frac{\text{Individual BQ x Total AQ}}{\text{Total BQ}}$$

Product X = (1,500 / 4,000) x 3,000 = 1125

Product Y = (2,500 / 4,000) x 3,000 = 1875

3000

(i) Sales Value Variance = (AQ x ASP) – (BQ x BSP)

X = (1,000 x 6) – (1,500 x 7)

= 6,000 – 10,500 = Rs 4500 (A)

Y = (2,000 x 8) – (2,500 x 5)

= 16,000 – 12,500 = Rs.3,500 (F)

∴SVV = 4,500 – 3,500 = Rs.1,000 (A)

(ii) Sales Price Variance = AQ (ASP – BSP)

X = 1,000 (6 -7) = 1,000 x 1= Rs.1,000 (A)

Y = 2,000 (8-5) = 2,000 x 3 = Rs.6,000 (F)

∴ SPV = 6,000 – 1,000 = Rs.5,000(F)

(iii) Sales Volume Variance = BSP (AQ – BQ)

X = 7(1,000–1,500) = 7 x 500 =Rs.3,500(A)

Y = 5 (2,000 – 2,500) = 5 x 500=Rs.2,500(A)

∴SVV = 3,500 + 2,500 = Rs.6,000 (A)

(iv) Sales Mix Variance = BSP (AQ – RBQ)

X = 7(1,000 – 1,125)=7x125=Rs.875(A)

Y = 5(2,000–1,875) = 5 x125 =Rs.625 (F)

∴SMV = 875 – 625 = Rs.250 (A)

(v) Sales Quantity Variance = BSP (RBQ – BQ)

X = 7(1125–1500) = 7x375 = Rs.2,625 (A)

Y = 5(1875–2500) = 5 x 625 = Rs.3,125 (A)

∴SQV = 2625 + 3125 = Rs.5,750 (A)

**Verification:**

Sales Value Variance = SPV+SVV=5000–6000=Rs.1,000(A)

Sales Volume Variance = SMV+SQV=250+5750= Rs.6,000 (A)

Sales Value Variance = SPV+SMV+SQV=5,000 - 250 - 5,750 = Rs.1,000 (A)

**Illustration: 22**

Find out the sales variances from the following information:

Budgeted sales for the month of Feb. 2011 are stated as follows:

A 2,000 units @ Rs.5 per unit

B 5,000 units @ Rs.10 per unit

C 3,000 units @ Rs.25 per unit

Actual Sales are stated as follows:

A 1,800 units @ Rs.4 per unit

B 5,500 units @ Rs.13 per unit

C 3,200 units @ Rs.30 per unit

Cost of production A Rs.3 , B Rs.9 and C Rs.22 per unit.

***Solution:***

**I. Sales Margin Variance (Profit Method)**

**Standard Margin on Standard Mix**

| Products | Units | Rates (Rs.) | Amount (Rs.) |
|---|---|---|---|
| A | 2,000 | 2 | 4,000 |
| B | 5,000 | 1 | 5,000 |
| C | 3,000 | 3 | 9,000 |
| | 10,000 | | 18,000 |

Standard Margin per unit of Standard Mix = 18,000 /10,000 = Rs.1.80

**Standard Margin on Actual Mix**

| Products | Units | Rates (Rs.) | Amount (Rs.) |
|---|---|---|---|
| A | 1,800 | 2 | 3,600 |
| B | 5,500 | 1 | 5,500 |
| C | 3,200 | 3 | 9,600 |
| | 10,500 | | 18,700 |

Standard margin per unit of Actual Mix = 18,700/10,500 = Rs.1.781

**Actual Margin on Actual Mix**

| Products | Units | Rates (Rs.) | Amount (Rs.) |
|---|---|---|---|
| A | 1,800 | 1 | 1,800 |
| B | 5,500 | 4 | 22,000 |
| C | 3,200 | 8 | 25,600 |
| | 10,500 | | 49,400 |

1. Sales Margin Variance:

= [Actual Qty. x Actual Profit per unit] – [Standard Qty.x Budgeted profit per unit]

A = [1,800 x 1] – [2,000 x 2] = Rs.2,200 [A]
B = [5,500 x 4] – [5,000 x 1] = Rs.17,000 [F]
C = [3,200 x 8] – [3,000 x 3] = Rs.16,600 [F]
Total = Rs.31,400 [F]

2. Sales Margin Price Variance:

= Actual Qty. of Sales [Actual Price – Standard Price]

A = 1,800 [4 - 5] = Rs.1,800 [A]
B = 5,500 [13 – 10] = Rs.16,500 [F]
C = 3,200 [30 – 25] = Rs.16,000 [F]
Total = Rs.30,700 [F]

3. Sales Margin Volume Variance:

= Std. Margin per unit [Actual Sales – Budgeted Sales]

A = 2 [1,800 – 2,000] = Rs.400 [A]
B = 1 [5,500 – 5,000] = Rs.500 [F]
C = 3 [3,200 – 3,000] = Rs.600 [F]
Total = Rs.700 [F]

(i) Sales Margin Mix Variance:

= Budgeted Profit per unit [Actual Qty. – Revised Budgeted Qty.]

Revised Budgeted Qty:

A = (10,500/10,000) x 2,000 = 2,100 units
B = (10,500/10,000) x 5,000 = 5,250 units
C = (10,500/10,000) x 3,000 = 3,150 units
Total = 10,500 units

A = 2 [1,800 – 2,100] = Rs.600 [A]
B = 1 [5,500 – 5,250] = Rs.250 [F]
C = 3 [3,200 – 3,150] = Rs.150 [F]
Total = Rs.200 [A]

(ii) Sales Margin Qty. Variance:
= Budgeted Profit per unit [Revised Budgeted Qty–Budgeted Qty.]
A = 2[2,100 – 2,000] = Rs.200 [F]
B = 1[5,250 – 5,000] = Rs.250 [F]
C = 3[3,150 – 3,000] = Rs.450 [F]
Total = Rs.900 [F]

**Verification:**

SMV = SMPV + S.M.Vo.V
= 30,700[F]+700[F] = Rs.31,400 [F]
S.M.Vo.V = S.M.M.V + S.M.Q.V
= 200[A] + 900 [F] = Rs.700 [F]

## II. Sales Variances (Sales Value method)

1. Sales Value Variance = [Actual Qty. x Actual selling price per unit]–[Budgeted Qty x Budgeted selling price per unit]
A = [1,800 x 4] – [2,000 x 5] = Rs.2,800 [A]
B = [5,500 x 13] – [5,000 x 10] = Rs.21,500 [F]
C = [3,200 x 30] – [3,000 x 25] = Rs.21,000 [F]
Total = Rs.39,700 [F]

2. Sales Price Variance = Actual Qty [ Actual Rate – Std.Rate]
A = 1,800 [4-5] = Rs.1,800 [A]
B = 5,500 [13-10] = Rs.16,500 [F]
C = 3,200 [30-25] = Rs.16,000 [F]
Total = Rs.30,700 [F]

3. Sales Volume Variance = Standard Rate[Actual Qty– Budgeted Qty]
A = 5 [1,800 – 2,000] = Rs.1,000 [A]
B = 10 [5,500 – 5,000] = Rs.5,000 [F]
C = 25 [3,200 – 3,000] = Rs.5,000 [F]
Total = Rs.9,000 [F]

(i) Sales Mix Variance:
Std Rate [Actual Qty. – Revised Std. Qty.]
RSQ = Total Actual Mix of Sales x Standard Quantity
Total Standard mix of Sales:
A = (10,500/10,000) x 2,000 = 2,100 units
B = (10,500/10,000) x 5,000 = 5,250 units
C = (10,500/10,000) x 3,000 = 3,150 units
Total = 10,500 units

SMV: A = 5 [1,800 – 2,100] = Rs.1500 [A]
B = 10 [5,500-5,250] = Rs.2,500 [F]
C = 25 [3,200 – 3,150] = Rs.1,250 [F]
Total = Rs.2,250 [F]

(ii) Sales Qty. Variance: [Sub–volume variance]
= Std. Selling price [Revised Std. Sales Qty – Budgeted Sales Qty]
A = 5 [2,100 – 2,000] = Rs.500 [F]
B = 10 [5,250 – 5,000] = Rs.2,500 [F]
C = 25 [3,150 – 3,000] = Rs.3,750 [F]
Total = Rs.6,750 [F]

**Verification:**

Sales Variance = SPV + SQV
= 30,700 [F] + 9,000 [F] =Rs.39,700 [F]
SQV = S.M.V. + S.Q.V
= 2,250 [F] + 6,750 [F] = Rs.9,000 [F]

**Illustration: 23**

Calculate sales variances from the following:

| | | |
|---|---|---|
| Budgeted Sales | A | 10,000 units @ Rs.20 per unit |
| | B | 15,000 units @ Rs.30 per unit |
| Actual Sales | A | 12,000 units @ Rs.22 per unit |
| | B | 13,000 units @ Rs.33 per unit |

***Solution:***

Sales Value Variance = (AQ x ASP) - (BQ x BSP)
A = (12,000 x 22) - (10,000 x 20)
= 264,000 - 200,000 = Rs.64,000 (F)
B = (13,000 x 33) - (15,000 x 30)
= 429,000 - 450,000 = Rs.21,000 (A)
Total = 64,000 - 21,000 = Rs.43,000 (F)

Sales Price Variance = AQ (ASP - BSP)
A = 12,000 (22 - 20)
= 12,000 x 2 = Rs.24,000 (F)
B = 13,000 (33 - 30)
= 13,000 x 3 = Rs.39,000 (F)
Total = 24,000 + 39,000 = Rs.63,000 (F)

Sales Volume Variance = BSP (AQ - BQ)
A = 20 (12,000 - 10,000)
= 20 x 2,000 = Rs.40,000 (F)
B = 30 (13,000 - 15,000)
= 30 x 2,000 = Rs.60,000 (A)
Total = 60,000 - 40,000 = Rs.20,000 (A)

**Varification:**

Sales Value Variance = Sales Price Variance + Sales Volume Variance

= 63,000 - 20,000 = Rs.43,000 (A)

(Note: Since the total actual quantity and total budged quantity are equal, sales mix variance and sales quantity variance could not be calculated.)

## EXERCISE

**I. Choose the correct answer for the following:**

1. Predetermined cost is called
   (i) Budget cost (ii) Actual cost (iii) Standard cost (iv) Historical cost
2. Analysis of the deviation from actual and standard cost is called
   (i) Variance analysis (ii) Cost analysis
   (iii) Budget analysis (iv) Inventory analysis
3. If the actual cost is greater than standard cost it is known as
   (i) Favourable variance (ii) Budget
   (iii) Marginal cost (iv) Unfavourable variance
4. If the actual cost is less than the standard cost, it is known as
   (i) Unfavourable variance (ii) Favourable variance
   (iii) Cost centre (iv) Cost unit
5. Material usage variance is otherwise called as
   (i) Material mix variance (ii) Material price variance
   (iii) Material quantity variance (iv) Material cost variance
6. The difference between the standard labour hours specified for the output achieved and the actual labour hours spent is called
   (i) Labour efficiency variance (ii) Labour mix variance
   (iii) Labour cost variance (iv) Labour rate variance
7. The difference between the standard cost of material and actual cost of material is called
   (i) Labour cost variance (ii) Material cost variance
   (iii) Sales variance (iv) Material quantity variance
8. Variance is the difference between actual cost and
   (i) Budget (ii) Fixed cost (iii) Variable cost (iv) Standard cost
9. The difference between the budgeted fixed overhead and actual fixed overhead is called
   (i) Expenditure variance (ii) Variable overhead variance
   (iii) Volume variance (iv) Fixed overhead variance
10. The ratio between standard overheads and standard output is called
    (i) Volume variance (ii) Actual rate (iii) Standard rate (iv) Budget rate
    [Ans: 1. (iii) 2. (i) 3. (iv) 4. (ii) 5. (iii) 6. (i) 7. (ii) 8 (iv) 9 (iv) 10 (iii)]

**II. Answer the following:**

11. Define Standard Costing. Distinguish between Historical Costing and Standard Costing.

12. What is Standard Costing? Distinguish between Standard Costing and Budgetary Control.
13. Define Standard Costing.Explain the merits and demerits of standard costing.
14. Define Variance analysis. Explain the different types of Material Cost Variances.
15. Distinguish between Standard Costing and Variance Analysis. Explain the different types of Labour Cost Variances.
16. What is Variances analysis? Explain the different types of Labour Cost Variances.
17. Define Variance analysis. Explain the different types of Sales Variances.
18. Calculate Material Cost Variance, Material Price Variance and Material Quantity Variance from the following:

| | Material A | Material B |
|---|---|---|
| Actual Quantity | 300 | 600 |
| Standard Quantity | 240 | 680 |
| Actual Price per unit (Rs.) | 12 | 20 |
| Standard Price per unit (Rs.) | 14 | 19 |

19. M.Ltd spent on an average Rs.6,000 for producing 3,000 units. The standard material required for producing 100 units is 150 kgms. The standard price of the material is Rs.2.50 per kgm. The stock of material in the beginning and at the end are 300 kgms and 800 kgms respectively. Actual production is 4,200 units. Calculate the material cost variance material price variance and material usage variance.
20. G Ltd provided the following information from the costing records. The particulars about the production of 10 units of Product X are as follows:

| **Material** | **Qty.** | **Unit Price (Rs.)** | **Value (Rs.)** |
|---|---|---|---|
| A | 60 | 3 | 180 |
| B | 40 | 2 | 80 |
| Total | 100 | | 260 |

The actual cost of manufacturing 2000 units are as follows:

| **Material** | **Qty. (Kgm)** | **Unit Price (Rs.)** | **Value (Rs.)** |
|---|---|---|---|
| A | 2,500 | 2.70 | 6,750 |
| B | 1,400 | 3.00 | 4,200 |
| Total | 3,900 | | 10,950 |

Calculate material cost variance, material quantity variance, material price variance and material mix variance.

[Ans.: Rs.550 (A); Rs.650 (A); Rs.100 (F); Rs.160 (A)]

21. Calculate material cost variance, material quantity variance, material price variance, material mix variance and material yield variance from the following:

| Material | Standard | | | Actual | | |
|---|---|---|---|---|---|---|
| | Qty | Rate (Rs.) | Amount (Rs.) | Qty | Rate (Rs.) | Amount (Rs.) |
| X | 6,000 | 1.50 | 9,000 | 6,800 | 1.70 | 11,560 |
| Y | 2,500 | 2.20 | 5,500 | 2,400 | 2.10 | 5,040 |
| Total | 8,500 | - | 14,500 | 9,200 | - | 16,600 |

[Ans: Rs.2,100 (A); Rs.980 (A); Rs.1,120 (A); Rs.214 (F); Rs.1,194 (A)]

22. The following information are collected from XYZ Co.Ltd as on 31st March 2011. The standard cost of manufacturing 20 units and actual cost for 400 units are stated as follows:

| Material | Standard | | Actual | |
|---|---|---|---|---|
| | Qty. (Kgm) | Rate (Rs.) | Qty. (Kgm) | Rate (Rs.) |
| Q | 800 | 4,400 | 17,000 | 102,000 |
| R | 550 | 1,925 | 10,500 | 31,500 |
| L | 500 | 1,100 | 8,500 | 17,000 |
| Total | 1,850 | 7,425 | 36,000 | 150,500 |

Calculate all the possible material variances

[Ans: Rs. 200 (A); Rs.450 (A); Rs.1,550 (A); Rs.4,465 (A); Rs.4,015 (F)]

23. M Ltd provided the following information from its costing records with respect to the production of 500 units of product 'C'

| Material | Standard | | | Actual | | |
|---|---|---|---|---|---|---|
| | Qty. | Rate (Rs.) | Amount (Rs.) | Qty. | Rate (Rs.) | Amount (Rs.) |
| H | 350 | 2.40 | 840 | 340 | 2.50 | 850 |
| N | 450 | 1.60 | 720 | 480 | 1.20 | 576 |
| Total | 800 | - | 1,560 | 820 | | 1426 |

The standard normal loss is estimated as 10 %. Actual output is 702 units. Calculate all the material variances.

[Ans: Rs.134 (F); Rs.24 (A); Rs.150 (F); Rs.15 (F); Rs.39 (A)]

24. Calculate labour cost variances from the following:

| | Standard | Actual |
|---|---|---|
| Wage rate per hour (Rs.) | 20 | 22 |
| Labour hours per unit | 2 | 2.5 |

Production of the company is 5000 units

[Ans: Rs.75,000 (A); Rs.50,000 (A); Rs.25,000 (A)]

25. Calculate labour cost variance, labour efficiency variance and labour rate variance from the following:

| | Standard | Actual |
|---|---|---|
| Labour hours per 10 units | 5 | 4.5 |
| Labour rate per hour (Rs.) | 10.50 | 10.00 |

[Ans: Rs.7.50 (F); Rs.5.25 (F); Rs.2.25 (F)]

26. The standard labour cost of a product manufactured by G.R & Co.Ltd is stated as follows:

| Workers | Hours per unit of output | Hourly Rate Rs. | Amount Rs. |
|---|---|---|---|
| A | 8 | 20 | 160 |
| B | 4 | 18 | 72 |
| Total | 12 | - | 232 |

The actual cost for producing 500 units are as follows:

| Workers | Hours | Hourly Rate Rs. | Amount Rs. |
|---|---|---|---|
| A | 3,900 | 21 | 81,900 |
| B | 1,800 | 16 | 28,800 |
| Total | 5,700 | - | 110,700 |

Calculate (i) Labour Cost Variance (ii) Labour Rate Variance (iii) Labour Efficiency Variance and (iv) Labour Mix Variance.

[Ans: Rs.5,300 (F); Rs.5,600 (F); Rs.300 (A); Rs.200 (A)]

27. The following information are extracted from the book of KT & Co.Ltd Standard Labour Cost are as follows:

| Workers | Hours per unit | Hourly Rate Rs. | Amount Rs. |
|---|---|---|---|
| Male | 1.5 | 24 | 36 |
| Female | 2 | 20 | 40 |
| Total | 3.5 | - | 76 |

Actual labour cost for 400 units are as follows:

| Workers | Hours | Hourly Rate Rs. | Amount Rs. |
|---|---|---|---|
| Male<br>Female | 620<br>820 | 25<br>21 | 15,500<br>17,220 |
| Total | 1,440 | - | 32,720 |

Calculate all the labour cost variances .

[Ans: Rs.2,320 (A); Rs.880 (A); Rs.1,440 (A); Rs.12 (A)]

28. XY Ltd provided the following information related to the payment of wage.

| | Skilled workers | Semi-Skilled workers | Unskilled workers |
|---|---|---|---|
| Standard number of workers in the gang | 50 | 30 | 20 |
| Standard Rate per hour (Rs.) | 20 | 18 | 16 |
| Actual number of workers in the gang | 48 | 32 | 22 |
| Actual Rate per hour (Rs.) | 21 | 17 | 15 |

The company worked for 38 hours in the week and produced 3600 standard hours of work.

Calculate (i) Labour Cost Variance (ii) ) Labour Rate Variance (iii)Labour Efficiency Variance (iv) Labour Mix Variance (v) Labour Yield Variance.

[Ans.: (i) Rs.3,340 (A), (ii) Rs.152 (F), (iii) Rs.3,492 (A), (iv) Rs.228 (F), Rs.3,720 (A)]

29. Standand hours required for manufactaning 1 unit is 8 hours @ Rs.15 per hour.If the company paid Rs.238,000 for manufactaning 2,000 units @ Rs.14 per hour find out LCV,LRV and LEV

[Ans: Rs.2,000(F); Rs.17,000(F); Rs.15,000(A)]

30. Calculate all Labour Variances from the data provided by a manufacturing company.

| Workers | Standard | | Actual | |
|---|---|---|---|---|
| | Number | Rate per week Rs. | Number | Rate per week Rs. |
| Male<br>Female<br>Children | 40<br>30<br>20 | 200<br>600<br>500 | 35<br>28<br>22 | 250<br>630<br>490 |
| Total | 90 | - | 85 | - |

The standard time required for completing a job is 8 weeks and Actual time taken for completing the job is 7 weeks.

[Ans: LCV-Rs.10,522(A); LRV-Rs.16,590(A), LEV-Rs.6,068(F); LMV Rs.89,400(F), LYV- Rs.83,333(A)]

31. A company provided the following information from the costing records for the month October 2011.

Budgeted Sales : Product A 2,000 units @ Rs.10 per unit
: Product B 3,000 units @ Rs.14 per unit

Actual Sales : Product A 1,800 units @ Rs.12 per unit
: Product B 3,200 units @ Rs.15 per unit

Calculate (i) Sales Value Variance (ii) Sales Price Variance (iii) Sales Quantity Variance by Sales Value method.

[Ans: (i) Rs.7,600 (F); (ii) Rs.6,800 (F); (iii) Rs.800 (F)]

32. Calculate Variable overhead cost variances for a manufacturing company from the following information:

| **Particulars** | **Budget** | **Actual** |
|---|---|---|
| Labour hours | 700 | 680 |
| Output (units) | 400 | 430 |
| Variable Overhead (Rs.) | 4,200 | 4,500 |

[Ans: (i) Rs.882 (A); (Rs.1512 (A); (Rs.630 (F); (ii) Rs.1,512 (A); Rs.882 (A); Rs.630 (A)]

33. Calculate the Fixed overhead variances from the following:

| | Budget | Actual |
|---|---|---|
| Fixed Overhead (Rs.) | 60,000 | 55,000 |
| Output (units) | 8,000 | 7,500 |
| Working Days | 25 | 27 |

[Ans: Rs.1,250 (F); Rs.5,000 (F); Rs.3,750 (A); Rs.3,750 (A); Rs.4,800 (A); Rs.8,550 (A)]

34. X Ltd provided the following information from the costing records for the month March 2011.

| | | Budgeted | Actual |
|---|---|---|---|
| Product: A | Sales quantity | 5,000 | 4,500 |
| | Selling price per unit (Rs.) | 40 | 45 |
| Product: B | Sales quantity | 3,000 | 3,500 |
| | Selling price per unit (Rs.) | 20 | 18 |

The cost of production for Product A and B are Rs.40 and Rs.14 respectively.Calculate (i) Sales Margin Variance, (ii) Sales Price Variance (iii) Sales Volume Variance (iv) Sales Mix Variance and (v) Sales Quantity Variance by Sales Margin Method.

[Ans: Rs.24,500 (F); Rs.20,500 (F); Rs.4,000 (F); Rs.500 (F); Rs.3,500 (F) ]

35. N Ltd provided the following information from the costing records for the month April 2011.

Budgeted Sales : X 3,500 units @ Rs.10 per unit
: Y 4,000 units @ Rs.8 per unit
Actual Sales : X 3,800 units @ Rs.11 per unit
: Y 4,300 units @ Rs.7 per unit

Calculate (i) Sales Value Variance (ii) Sales Price Variance (iii) Sales Volume Variance (iv) Sales Mix Variance and (v) Sales Quantity Variance by Sales Value Method.

[Ans:Rs.4,900 (F); Rs.500 (A); Rs.5,400 (F); Rs.40 (F); Rs.5,360 (F)]

36. Find out the sales variances from the following information. Budgeted sales for the month of Feb 2011 are stated as follows:

A 4,000 units @ Rs.15 per unit
B 6,000 units @ Rs.13 per unit
C 5,000 units @ Rs.20 per unit

Actual sales are stated as follows:

A 3,800 units @ Rs.14 per unit
B 6,500 units @ Rs.15 per unit
C 4,200 units @ Rs.22 per unit

Cost of production: A Rs.9, B Rs.12, C Rs.18 per unit

[Ans: 1. Sales Margin Method: Rs.15,300 (F); Rs.17,600 (F); Rs.2,300 (A); Rs.968 (A); Rs.1,332 (A); Rs.1,332 (A); 2. Selling Price Rs.4,565 (A); Rs.17,600 (F); Rs.12,500 (A); Rs.4,565 (A); Rs.7,935 (A)]

37. The standard labour cost of a product manufactured by G.T & Co.Ltd is stated as follows:

| Workers | Hours per unit of output | Hourly Rate Rs. | Amount Rs. |
|---|---|---|---|
| X | 3 | 50 | 150 |
| Y | 2 | 40 | 80 |
| Total | 5 | - | 230 |

The actual cost for producing 1,000 units are as follows:

| Workers | Hours | Hourly Rate Rs. | Amount Rs. |
|---|---|---|---|
| X | 3,400 | 54 | 183,600 |
| Y | 2,200 | 38 | 83,600 |
| Total | 5,600 | - | 267,200 |

Calculate (i) Labour Cost Variance (ii) Labour Rate Variance (iii) Labour Efficiency Variance and (iv) Labour Mix Variance.

[Ans: Rs.37,200 (A); Rs.9,200 (A); Rs.28,000 (A); Rs.400 (A)]

38. The following information are extracted from the book of T & Co.Ltd Standard Labour Cost are as follows:

| **Workers** | **Hours per unit** | **Hourly Rate Rs.** | **Amount Rs.** |
|---|---|---|---|
| Male<br>Female | 5<br>4 | 40<br>30 | 200<br>120 |
| Total | 9 | - | 320 |

Actual labour cost for 2,000 units are as follows:

| **Workers** | **Hours** | **Hourly Rate Rs.** | **Amount Rs.** |
|---|---|---|---|
| Male<br>Female | 9,500<br>7,500 | 41<br>28 | 389,500<br>210,000 |
| Total | 17,000 | - | 599,500 |

Calculate all the labour cost variances .

[Ans: Rs.40,500 (F); Rs.5,500 (F); Rs.35,000 (F); Rs.560 (A)]

39. XY Ltd provided the following information from its costing records with respect to the production of 500 units of product 'C'

| Material | Standard | | | Actual | | |
|---|---|---|---|---|---|---|
| | Qty. | Rate (Rs.) | Amount (Rs.) | Qty | Rate (Rs.) | Amount (Rs.) |
| A | 1,200 | 5 | 6,000 | 1,400 | 4.50 | 6300 |
| B | 800 | 4 | 3,200 | 1,000 | 4.20 | 4200 |
| Total | 2,000 | - | 9,200 | 2,400 | | 10,500 |

The standard normal loss is estimated as 10 %. Actual output is 1800 units. Calculate all the material variances.

[Ans: Rs.1,300 (A); Rs.1,800 (A); Rs.500 (F); Rs.40 (F); Rs.1,840 (A)]

40. Calculate material cost variance, material quantity variance, material price varianceand material mix variance from the following:

| **Material** | **Standard** | | | **Actual** | | |
|---|---|---|---|---|---|---|
| | **Qty.** | **Rate (Rs.)** | **Amount (Rs.)** | **Qty.** | **Rate (Rs.)** | **Amount (Rs.)** |
| A<br>B | 10,000<br>5,000 | 9<br>7 | 90,000<br>35,000 | 9,500<br>4,500 | 8.40<br>7.20 | 79,800<br>32,400 |
| Total | 15,000 | | 125,000 | 14,000 | - | 112,200 |

[Ans: Rs.12,800 (F); Rs.8,000 (F); Rs.4,800 (F); Rs.334 (A);]

# Chapter XIV
# BUDGET AND BUDGETARY CONTROL

Budget is an important tool of planning and control of cost for the management. CIMA London defines budget as "a financial and / or quantitative statement prepared and appproved prior to a defined period time , of the policy to be pursued during that period for the purpose of attaining a given objective"Budgeting is the process of preparing the budget.

## Characteristics of a good budget

The following are the important characteristics of good budget

1. Persons at different levels of management should be involved in the preparation of budgets.
2. The targets of the budgets should be realistic.
3. The authority and responsibility should be clearly defined.
4. A good system of accounting should be followed.
5. The employees should be given education with regard to budget.
6. The actual results should be properly recorded for the purpose of performance appraisal.

## Budgetary Control

Budgetary control is the process of comparing the budgetary figures with the actual performance, for calculating variances, in order to control the variances.

**Brown and Howard** defined as "Budgetary control is a system of controlling costs which includes the preparation of budgets, co-ordinating the department and establishing responsibility, comparing actual performance with the budgeted and acting upon results to achieve maximum profitability.

**J.Batty** defines Budgetary control as "A system which uses budgets as a means of planning and controlling all aspects of producing and / or selling commodities and services".

According to **Welsch**, "Budgetary control involves the use of budget and budgetary reports throughout the period to co-ordinate, evaluate and control day-to-day operations in accordance with the goals specified by the budget"

It is clear from the definitions that budgetary control is a process of comparing the budget figures with actual figures. It helps to know the variances so that it can be controlled and also to plan for the future. Hence, the efficiency of the company can be improved through budgetary control.

## Objectives of Budgetary Control

The following are the important objectives of budgetary control.

1. To provide a detailed plan of action for a business over a period of time.
2. To co-ordinate all activities of the organisation.
3. To increase profitability and to eliminate waste.
4. To operate various cost centers and departments efficiently and economically.
5. To control the variances.
6. To fix responsibilities of various individuals in the organisation.

**Essentials of Budgetary Control**

The important essential steps for budgetary control are stated as follows.

**1. Organisation for Budgetary Control.**

A budget committee should be formed with heads of various departments as members. They should be entrusted to prepare the budgets. The Chief Executive should be in charge of overall budgetary system. A Budget Officer is the convener of the budget committee.He coordinates the different departments in the process of preparing budgets.

**2. Budget Centres**

A Budget centre is that part of the organisation for which the budget is prepared. (e.g.) departments. The establishment of various centres should be done as per the requirement of the organisation.

**3. Budget Manuals**

Budget manual is a written document which gives guidance to the functional managers about the procedures to be followed in the preparation of budgets. It contains the methods of preparation and execution of budgets. It defines the role of each individual in the preparation of budgets. It includes the details about the authority and responsibility of each functional heads. The budget manual should be very clear and there should not be any ambiguity in the expressions.

**4. Budget Officer**

The Budget Officer is appointed by the Chief Executive. He scrutinises all the budgets prepared by various functional heads. He can make necessary corrections in the budgets so prepared. He should compare the actual performance with budget. He should take necessary steps to rectify the variances. He also reports to the management about the various aspects related to budget.

**5. Budget Committee**

In business concerns, Budget Committee is formed to prepare the budget. The committee is responsible for the preparation and execution of budget with the Heads of various departments as its members.

### 6. Budget Period

There is no strict rule for the period of budget. The period depends upon the nature of the business and objectives of the company. It may be a very short period like one or two months, or a reasonably long period of one year. Normally the period of budget is one year. Companies prepare short term budgets to have effective control. Companies engaged in manufacturing of seasonal products definitely have to prepare short term budgets. Companies may prepare both short term and long term budgets at the same time. Short term budgets may be a supplement to the long term budget.

### 7. Key Factor or Limiting Factor

The factor which will limit the volume of production, at a particular point of time is called key factor or limiting factor.The factor may be demand for the product, availability of material, availability of technicians and other employees, capacity of plant and the availability of finance.Any of these factors may be a constraint for the smooth production.It may limit the quantity of production.It is the duty of the management to identify the key factor. The key factors must be considered for the preparation of budgets.

## Advantages of Budgetary Control

The important advantages of budgetary control are stated as follows.

1. The budgetary control helps in co-ordinating the activities of various departments.
2. It aims at maximisation of profits.
3. It helps in making suitable plans, policies and goals.
4. It helps in measuring the performance of managerial personnels, and thereby helps in improving their performance.
5. It measures the variances in all aspects and helps in identifying the reasons for the variances.
6. The planning of expenditure will be systematic and there will be economy in spending.
7. It creates budget consciousness among employees.

## Limitations of Budgetary Control

The limitations of budgetary control are stated as follows.

1. The future uncertainties affect the performance of budgetary control system.
2. It discourages efficient persons to perform more than expected.
3. The lack of co-ordination of various departments affects the performance of the budgetary control.
4. It may lead to conflicts among the managers of various departments.
5. Lack of support from top management affects the budgetary control system.

## Classification of Budgets

The budgets may be classified as follows.

**I. Classification on the basis of Time**

1. Long-term budgets
2. Short-term budgets
3. Current budgets

**II. Classification on the basis of Function**

1. Master budget.
2. Functional or Subsidiary budget.

**III. Classification on the basis of Flexibility**

1. Fixed budget
2. Flexible budget

### I. Classification on the basis of Time

#### 1. Long-term Budget

The period of long-term budget varies between five to ten years. It is based on long-term planning and prepared by top level management. Long term budgets are prepared for the management.(Eg) Capital expenditure, research and development etc.

#### 2. Short-term Budget

The period of short-term budget is one or two years. The consumer goods industries like textile, cotton ,sugar, coffee, cosmetics etc. prepare short-term budget.

#### 3. Current Budget

The period of current budget is generally of weeks or a month or few months.

### II. Classification on the basis of Function

1. Master Budget
2. Functional Budgets

The important functional budgets are as follows.

(i) Sales Budget
(ii) Production Budget
(iii) Cost of Production Budget
(iv) Purchase Budget
(v) Cash Budget
(vi) Capital Expenditure Budget

#### 1. Master Budget

The **Chartered Institute of Management Accountants** (CIMA) London defines the master budget as "the summary budget, incorporating its component functional budget, which is finally approved, adopted and employed". According to **ICWA London**, "The Master Budget is the summary budget incorporating its functional budgets".

It is clear from the definitions that master budget is a summary budget which includes all the functional budgets. This budget should be approved by the Budget Committee of the company.

**2. Functional Budget**

**(i) Sales Budget**

Sales Budget is a budget for forecasting the sales in future in terms of quantity and value. It is prepared on the basis of past sales, production capacity, report of salesmen, pricing policy and competition.

**(ii) Production Budget**

Production budget is a budget for forecasting the quantity of production for different types of products and for different periods. It is based on Sales Budget.

**(iii) Cost of Production Budget**

This budget forecasts the cost of production for different types of products of a company. A company may prepare separate budget for different elements of cost.

They are,

(a) Direct Material Budget
(b) Direct Labour Budget
(c) Factory Overhead Budget
(d) Administration Overhead Budget.
(e) Selling and Distribution Overhead Budget

**(a) Direct Material Budget**

It is otherwise called as Raw Material Budget . It is concerned with forecasting about the requirement of different types of raw materials and its value. This budget is based on the production budget, price of raw material, seasonal factors, inventory levels and storage facilities.

**(b) Direct Labour Budget**

This budget is concerned with the forecast of the requirement of different types of labourers in a company. It is also concerned with the cost of each type of labour. It explains the standard labour hours required for the estimated production and the estimated labour cost per hour for different types of labour.

**(c) Factory Overhead Budget**

This budget is prepared to forecast the indirect factory cost. It includes indirect material, indirect labour and indirect expenses to be incurred in the factory for certain level of production.

**(d) Administration Overhead Budget**

This budget is prepared to forecast the indirect administration cost. It includes indirect material, indirect labour and indirect expenses to be spent in the administration department in future.

**(e) Selling and Distribution Overhead Budget**

This budget is prepared to forecast the indirect selling and distribution cost. It includes indirect material, indirect labour and indirect expenses to be spent in the selling and distribution department in future.

**(iv) Purchase Budget**

Purchase Budget is prepared to find out the total cost of purchase in future.It involves the purchase of direct and indirect materials. Indirect materials are concerned with the materials used in Factory, Administration and Selling and Distribution departments.

**(v) Cash Budget**

Cash Budget is concerned with the inflow and outflow of cash in the budget period. This budget estimates the net cash flow in a concern. It facilitates the management to make necessary arrangements for the future cash requirements. This budget is prepared only after the preparation of all the functional budgets.

**(vi) Capital Expenditure Budget**

This budget is prepared to know the estimated expenditure on all fixed assets like Plant &Machinery, Land & Building and Furniture & Fittings during the budget period.

**III Classification on the basis of Flexibility**

**1. Fixed Budget**:

ICWA London defined "fixed budget is a budget which is designed to remain unchanged irrespective to the level of activity actually attained". It is related to a given level of activity and it is prepared before the budgeting of the financial year.

**2. Flexible Budget**:

A Flexible Budget is a budget for different levels of activities. Example for flexible budget is the budget for various capacity utilisations like 50%, 60%, 70%,100% etc. This budget is useful when the levels of activity in a company changes from time to time.

**Organisation of Budgetary Control**

There should be an organisation for the budget control. The organisation is headed by a Budget Officer. The budget officer is otherwise called as 'Budget Controller' or 'Budget Director'. The budget officer is appointed by the Chief Executive of the organisation of the company. He got the authority to prepare budget and to execute control, from the chief executive. He will prepare different types of budgets, as per the requirement of the company, in coordination with all the functional heads like, Sales Manager, Production Manager, Purchase Manager, Personal Manager and Accountant. All the functional heads together with the General Manager and the Budget Officer prepare the budgets meant for all departments. The function of the Budget Committee is to approve the individual budgets prepared by various functional heads, after making necessary corrections.

**Forecasts and Budget**

According to **Charted Institute of Management Accountants** (CIMA) London, forecast is ' a statement of probable events'. But budget has more meaning than forecast. Budget is a quantitative statement prepared for the future period. Forecast in the basic set up adopted in the preparation of budget. Hence the meaning of budget includes forecasting. The important differences between forecast and budget are stated as follows.

(i) Forecast is only an estimate of the future. But budget is concerned with what should be done in future.

(ii) In forecast there is no control required whereas budget is based on the control of deviations from the budgeted estimates.

(iii) Forecast is a general term which can be applied to any situation. But budget is concerned only with the financial aspect of the future expenses and income.

(iv) The process of forecast is over with the statement of probable events whereas the process of budget starts with forecast.

**Performance Budgeting or Responsibility Accounting**

Budget, nowadays focus on the performance of the employees in an organisation also. Budget in the past focused only on money concept. Performance budgeting is the process of preparing budget by associating money concept with the performance of the employees. In this type of budget the expenditure and income of the concern are related with specific responsibility centre. The budgeted expenses like purchase of material, wages, and other expenses are all related with respective responsibility centres. In this way the income like sales of different products and from different places are related with the respective responsibility centres. The centres should at least maintain the expected level of expenses and income specified in the budget. The reduction in cost or increase in income shows their good performance.

In order to measure the performance, the budget expenses and income should be compared with actual expenses and income with respect to each responsibility centres. This will help to create a competitive environment which will in fact improve the overall performance of the company.

## Zero Base Budgeting

Zero Base Budgeting (ZBB) was first used by U.S Department of Agriculture during 1961. The logical framework of it was developed during 1970 by Peter A Pyhrr. Hence, he is called as the father of Zero Base Budgeting .The Zero Base Budgeting got popularity when Mr.Jimmy Carter, President of U.S.A issued order to all the Federal Governments to use ZBB instead of the conventional budgeting. The State Government of U.S.A also adopted the ZBB.

In the Conventional budgeting, budgets are prepared by taking into account of previous year values as base.Increment to the previous year values are considered as the values of budget for current year. But the economical, social and financial conditions are changing day by day. Hence, the basis of previous year will not provide accurate data to suit the current situation. The inefficiencies and all defects of previous year are carried forward in the conventional budgeting. The new system named Zero Based Budgeting, provides solution for avoiding the defects in the conventional budgeting.

## Meaning of Zero Base Budgeting.

Zero Base Budgeting is a budget prepared by taking zero as base. Previous year data are not considered in the preparation of budget under this method.

According to Peter A. Pyhrr "An operating, planning and budgeting process which requires each manager to justify his entire budget requests in detail from scratch (hence, Zero-Basis). Each Manager state why he should spend any money at all.This approach requires that all activities be identified as decision packages which would be evaluated by systematic analysis"

It is clear from the statement of Peter A Pyhrr that the process of Zero Base Budgeting is

(i) Identification of all activities of the organisation as decision packages

(ii) Evaluation of the decision packages.

According to David Lieninger and Rolland C.Wong, "Zero Base Budgeting is a management tool which provides a systematic method for evaluating all operations and programmes current or new, allow for budget reductions and expansions in a rational manner and allows reallocation of source from low to high priority programme" It is clear from the definition that ZBB is concerned with periodical and systematic evaluation of all programmes of a company in order to improve the efficiency.

**Advantages of Zero Base Budgeting:**

The advantages of Zero Base Budgeting are stated as follows:

1. It considers all activities of an organisation as important and hence, focuses on the efficiency in the performance of these activities.
2. It helps for the systematic evaluation of different activities, so that mistakes if any can be rectified immediately.
3. It suggests alternative ways of doing a job every time when budget is prepared since Zero is taken as base.
4. It prevents the unnecessary expenditure in different activities of the organisation.
5. It helps to prepare various budgets on the basis of cost benefit analysis.
6. It gives proper direction to all managers to perform the activities in economical and efficient manner.

**1.Preparation of Sales Budget**

**Illustration: 1**

Doyle & Co. manufactures 2 types of products namely X and Y and sells them in Chennai and Mumbai markets. The following information are related to the year ending 31st March 2011.

| Markets | Product | Budgeted sales | Actual sales |
|---|---|---|---|
| Chennai | X | 600 @ Rs.12 | 800 @ Rs.12 |
| | Y | 500 @ Rs.35 | 400 @ Rs.35 |
| Mumbai | X | 900 @ Rs.12 | 120 @ Rs.12 |
| | Y | 700 @ Rs.35 | 500 @ Rs.35 |

Market studies reveal that product X is popular as it is under priced. It is observed if its price is reduced by Re.1 it will find a good market. On the other hand, product Y is over priced and it will get good market if the selling price is reduced to Rs.33. The management has agreed for this. The impact of the change in price is reported as follows:

| Product | Increase in sales over current budget | |
|---|---|---|
| | Chennai | Mumbai |
| X | +20% | +10% |
| Y | +25% | +5% |

In addition to this, the following additional sales above the estimated sales are possible with an intensive advertisement.

| Product | Chennai | Mumbai |
|---|---|---|
| X | 50 units | 70 units |
| Y | 60 units | 50 units |

Prepare a budget for sales by incorporating the above estimates.

***Solution:***

**SALES BUDGET**

| Area | Product | Budget for the current year | | | Actual Sales | | | Budget for the future period | | |
|---|---|---|---|---|---|---|---|---|---|---|
| | | Units | Price Rs. | Value Rs. | Units | Price Rs. | Value Rs. | Units | Price Rs. | Value Rs. |
| | X | 600 | 12 | 7,200 | 800 | 12 | 9,600 | 770 | 11 | 8,470 |
| | Y | 500 | 35 | 17,500 | 400 | 35 | 14,000 | 685 | 33 | 22,605 |
| Chennai | Total | 1,100 | | 24,700 | 1,200 | | 23,600 | 1,455 | | 31,075 |
| | X | 900 | 12 | 10,800 | 1,200 | 12 | 14,400 | 1,060 | 11 | 11,660 |
| | Y | 700 | 35 | 24,500 | 500 | 35 | 17,500 | 785 | 33 | 25,905 |
| Mumbai | Total | 1,600 | | 35,300 | 1,700 | | 31,900 | 1,845 | | 37,565 |
| | X | 1,500 | 12 | 18,000 | 2,000 | 12 | 24,000 | 1,830 | 11 | 20,130 |
| | Y | 1,200 | 35 | 42,000 | 900 | 35 | 31,500 | 1,470 | 33 | 48,510 |
| Total | | 2,700 | | 60,000 | 2,900 | | 55,500 | 3,300 | | 68,640 |

**Workings:**

| | X Units | Y Units |
|---|---|---|
| Budgeted Sales of Chennai: | 600 | 500 |
| Add: Increase | 120 (20%) | 125 (25%) |
| | 720 | 625 |
| Increase due to Advertisement | 50 | 60 |
| Total | 770 | 685 |
| Budgeted Sales of Mumbai: | 900 | 700 |
| Add: Increase | 90 (10%) | 35(5%) |
| | 990 | 735 |
| Increase due to Advertisement | 70 | 50 |
| Total | 1060 | 785 |

## 2. Preparation of Production Budget

### Illustration: 2

The following information are related to a company for 6 months ending 31st March 2011.

The units to be sold for the different months are,

| | |
|---|---|
| October 2010 | 4,000 |
| November 2010 | 4,500 |
| December 2010 | 4,800 |
| January 2011 | 5,000 |
| February 2011 | 5,500 |
| March 2011 | 6,200 |
| April 2011 | 7,000 |

Finished units equal to half the sales for the next month will be in stock at the end of each month including September 2010. Budgeted production for the year ending 31st March 2011 is 55,000 units. Budgeted material and labour cost per unit are Rs.12 and Rs.5 respectively. Total factory overhead absorbed is Rs.165,000.

Prepare production budget for each month and summarised production cost budget for six months ending 31st March 2011.

***Solution:***

**Production budget for 6 months from October 2010 to 31st March 2011**

| Months | Opening Stock (Units) | Sales (Units) | Closing Stock (Units) | Production (Units) |
|---|---|---|---|---|
| October 2010 | 2000 | 4000 | 2250 | 4250 |
| November 2010 | 2250 | 4500 | 2400 | 4650 |
| December 2010 | 2400 | 4800 | 2500 | 4900 |
| January 2011 | 2500 | 5000 | 2750 | 5250 |
| February 2011 | 2750 | 5500 | 3100 | 5850 |
| March 2011 | 3100 | 6200 | 3500 | 6600 |
| | | | **Total** | **31,500** |

Production = Sales + Closing sock – Opening stock

**Production Cost Budget for 6 months ending 31st March 2011 (for 31,500 units)**

| Particulars | Rate per unit Rs. | Amount Rs. |
|---|---|---|
| Direct Material | 12 | 378,000 |
| Direct Wages | 5 | 157,500 |
| Factory Overheads (165,000/55,000) | 3 | 94,500 |
| **Total** | | **630,000** |

**Illustration: 3**

A manufacturing company provided the following information about the manufacturing of two products namely, X and Y.

The budgeted sales in units are as follows:

| Months | Product X (Units) | Product Y (Units) |
|---|---|---|
| January | 120 | 40 |
| February | 132 | 52 |
| March | 124 | 60 |
| April | 152 | 64 |
| May | 160 | 68 |
| June | 160 | 80 |
| July - December @ | 200 | 100 |

The details of expense are as follows:

| | Product X Rs | Product Y Rs. |
|---|---|---|
| Direct Material per unit | 30 | 25 |
| Direct Wages per unit | 24 | 20 |
| Total Factory Overhead | 85,000 | 60,000 |
| Total Administration Overhead | 70,000 | 45,000 |
| Total Selling & Distribution Overhead | 60,000 | 50,000 |
| Selling price per unit | 70 | 110 |

It is assumed that (i) there is no work-in-progress at the end of any months and (ii) finished units equal to quarter the sales for the following months will be kept in stock.

Prepare a production budget and product cost budget for one year.

***Solution:***

**Production Budget**

| Months | Product X | | | | Product Y | | | |
|---|---|---|---|---|---|---|---|---|
| | Sales | Cl. Stock | Op. Stock | Production | Sales | Cl. Stock | Op. Stock | Production |
| January | 120 | 33 | 30 | 123 | 40 | 13 | 10 | 43 |
| February | 132 | 31 | 33 | 130 | 52 | 15 | 13 | 54 |
| March | 124 | 38 | 31 | 131 | 60 | 16 | 15 | 61 |
| April | 152 | 40 | 38 | 154 | 64 | 17 | 16 | 65 |
| May | 160 | 40 | 40 | 160 | 68 | 20 | 17 | 71 |
| June | 160 | 50 | 40 | 170 | 80 | 25 | 20 | 85 |
| July | 200 | 50 | 50 | 200 | 100 | 25 | 25 | 100 |
| August | 200 | 50 | 50 | 200 | 100 | 25 | 25 | 100 |
| September | 200 | 50 | 50 | 200 | 100 | 25 | 25 | 100 |
| October | 200 | 50 | 50 | 200 | 100 | 25 | 25 | 100 |
| November | 200 | 50 | 50 | 200 | 100 | 25 | 25 | 100 |
| December | 200 | 50 | 50 | 200 | 100 | 25 | 25 | 100 |
| | 2048 | | | 2068 | 964 | | | 979 |

Production = Sales + Closing stock - Opening stock

**Summarised Production Cost Budget**

| Particulars | Product X | | Product Y | | Total Rs. |
|---|---|---|---|---|---|
| | Cost / Unit Rs. | Amount Rs. | Cost / Unit Rs. | Amount Rs. | |
| Direct Material | 30 | 62,040 | 25 | 24,475 | 86,515 |
| Direct Wages | 24 | 49,632 | 20 | 19,580 | 69,212 |
| Factory Overhead | 41.10 | 85,000 | 61.29 | 60,000 | 145,000 |
| Works Cost | 95.10 | 196,672 | 106.29 | 104,055 | 300,727 |
| Administration Overhead | 33.85 | 70,000 | 45.97 | 45,000 | 115,000 |
| Cost of Production | 128.95 | 266,672 | 152.26 | 149,055 | 415,727 |
| Selling overhead | 29.01 | 60,000 | 51.07 | 50,000 | 110,000 |
| Cost of Sales | 157.96 | 326,672 | 203.33 | 199,055 | 525,727 |

## 3. Preparation of Material Budget

**Illustration: 4**

Prepare raw materials purchase budget from the following:

Materials (Units).

| | A | B | C | D | E | F |
|---|---|---|---|---|---|---|
| Estimated Stock on 1st Jan. 2011 | 20,000 | 5,000 | 12,000 | 18,000 | 10,000 | 15,000 |
| Estimated Stock on 31st January | 18,000 | 7,000 | 8,000 | 24,000 | 13,000 | 19,000 |
| Estimated Consumption | 90,000 | 45,000 | 30,000 | 110,000 | 80,000 | 130,000 |
| Standard Price per unit (Rs.) | 2 | 2.50 | 5 | 7 | 6 | 3 |

***Solution:***

**Raw Materials Purchase Budget for January 2011**

| Particulars | Cost of raw materials (Rs.) | | | | | |
|---|---|---|---|---|---|---|
| | **A** | **B** | **C** | **D** | **E** | **F** |
| Estimated Consumption (units) | 90,000 | 45,000 | 30,000 | 110,000 | 80,000 | 130,000 |
| Add: Estimated Stock on 31st Jan. | 18,000 | 7,000 | 8,000 | 24,000 | 13,000 | 19,000 |
| | 108,000 | 52,000 | 38,000 | 134,000 | 93,000 | 149,000 |
| Less: Estimated Stock on 1st Jan. | 20,000 | 5,000 | 12,000 | 18,000 | 10,000 | 15,000 |
| Estimated Purchase (Units) | 88,000 | 47,000 | 26,000 | 116,000 | 83,000 | 134,000 |
| Rate per Unit (Rs.) | 2 | 2,50 | 5 | 7 | 6 | 3 |
| Estimated Purchase (Rs.) | 176,000 | 117,500 | 130,000 | 812,000 | 498,000 | 402,000 |

**4. Preparation of Overhead Budget.**

**Illustration: 5**

The details of overhead of a Company named,K Ltd. at 70% capacity are stated as follows:

| Particulars | Rs. |
|---|---|
| **Variable Overheads:** | |
| Indirect Material | 14,000 |
| Indirect Wages | 17,500 |
| Indirect Expenses | 5,000 |
| **Fixed Overheads:** | |
| Salary | 40,000 |
| Insurance | 10,000 |
| Depreciation | 12,000 |
| **Semi-Variable overheads:** | |
| Repairs & Maintenance (90% Fixed and 10% Variable) | 15,000 |
| Electricity (60% Fixed and 40% Variable) | 20,000 |
| Supervisor's Salary (80% Fixed and 20% Variable) | 25,000 |
| **Total Overheads** | **158,500** |

Estimated direct labour hours are 140,000 at 70% capacity.

Prepare a Manufacturing Overhead Budget and find out the manufacturing overhead rates at 50 % and 80% capacities.

*Solution:*

**Manufacturing Overhead Budget**

| Particulars | Capacity | | |
|---|---|---|---|
| | **50% (Rs.)** | **70% (Rs.)** | **80% (Rs.)** |
| **Variable Overheads:** | | | |
| Indirect Material | 10,000 | 14,000 | 16,000 |
| Indirect Wages | 12,500 | 17,500 | 20,000 |
| Indirect Expenses | 3,571 | 5,000 | 5,714 |
| Repairs & Maintenance | 1,071 | 1,500 | 1,714 |
| Electricity | 5,714 | 8,000 | 9,143 |
| Supervisor's Salary | 3,571 | 5,000 | 5,714 |
| **Fixed Overheads:** | | | |
| Salary | 40,000 | 40,000 | 40,000 |
| Insurance | 10,000 | 10,000 | 10,000 |

| | | | |
|---|---|---|---|
| Depreciation | 12,000 | 12,000 | 12,000 |
| Repairs & Maintenance | 13,500 | 13,500 | 13,500 |
| Electricity | 12,000 | 12,000 | 12,000 |
| Supervisors Salary | 20,000 | 20,000 | 20,000 |
| **Total Overheads** | 1,43,927 | 1,58,500 | 1,65,785 |
| Estimated Direct Labour Hours | 1,00,000 | 1,40,000 | 1,60,000 |
| Overhead Rates (Rs.) | 1.44 | 1.13 | 1.04 |

## 5. Preparation of Cash Budget

Cash budget is prepared to know the net cash flow in future, by taking into consideration of cash inflow and cash outflow. There are three methods for preparing cash budgets. They are,

a. Receipts and Payment Method
b. Adjusted Profit and Loss Account Method, and
c. Balance Sheet Method

### (a) Receipts and Payments method

In this method, cash receipts and cash payments of various sources should be estimated for future. The cash receipts should include all the receipts of revenue and capital nature. The cash payment should include all the payments of revenue and capital nature. The cash budget will show the estimated closing balance of cash. It may be a debit balance or a credit balance.

**Illustration: 6**

Prepare a Cash Budget for 4 Months ending 30th April 2011 from the following information:

| Months | Sales Rs. | Purchase Rs. | Wages Rs. | Manuf. Expenses Rs. | Admin. Expenses Rs. | Selling Expenses Rs. |
|---|---|---|---|---|---|---|
| November 2010 | 50,000 | 13,000 | 4,000 | 1,500 | 1,700 | 1,000 |
| December 2010 | 60,000 | 15,000 | 5,000 | 2,000 | 1,800 | 1,200 |
| January 2011 | 55,000 | 14,000 | 4,500 | 1,600 | 1,750 | 1,100 |
| February 2011 | 70,000 | 20,000 | 6,000 | 2,200 | 1,900 | 1,300 |
| March 2011 | 75,000 | 22,000 | 7,000 | 2,400 | 2,050 | 1,400 |
| April 2011 | 80,000 | 24,000 | 8,000 | 2,600 | 2,200 | 1,500 |

**Additional Information:**

1. Balance of cash in hand on 1st Jan 2011 is Rs.40,000.
2. Tax of Rs.11,000 payable in the month of March.
3. A dividend of Rs.15,000 payable in the month of April.
4. Furniture worth Rs.8,000 to be purchased in the month of February.
5. A Machinery worth Rs.80,000 purchased on October 2010 and the payment is to be done on installment basis @ Rs.6,000 per month.
6. The creditors are allowing a credit of 2 months.
7. Wages are paid on the 1st of next month.
8. Lag in payment of manufacturing and selling expense is one month.
9. The customers are allowed a credit period of 2 months.
10. Lag in payment of administration expense is ½ month.

***Solution:***

**Cash Budget for 4 months ending 30th April 2011**

| Particulars | January Rs. | February Rs. | March Rs. | April Rs. |
|---|---|---|---|---|
| **Receipts:** | | | | |
| Balance b/d | 40,000 | 61,025 | 83,000 | 95,525 |
| Cash received from Drs. | 50,000 | 60,000 | 55,000 | 70,000 |
| **Total** | **90,000** | **121,025** | **138,000** | **165,525** |
| **Payments:** | | | | |
| Payemnt to Creditors | 13,000 | 15,000 | 14,000 | 20,000 |
| Wages payable | 5,000 | 4,500 | 6,000 | 7,000 |
| Manufacturing expenses | 2,000 | 1,600 | 2,200 | 2,400 |
| Administration expenses | 1,775 | 1,825 | 1,975 | 2,125 |
| Selling expenses | 1,200 | 1,100 | 1,300 | 1,400 |
| Tax payable | - | - | 11,000 | - |
| Dividend payable | - | - | - | 15,000 |
| Purchase of Furniture | - | 8,000 | - | - |
| Payment for purchase of Machinery | 6,000 | 6,000 | 6,000 | 6,000 |
| **Total** | **28,975** | **38,025** | **42,475** | **53,925** |
| **Closing Balance** | **61,025** | **83,000** | **95,525** | **111,600** |

**Illustration: 7**

Prepare a Cash Budget from the following data for 3 months ending 31st March 2011:

| Months | Sales Rs. | Purchase Rs. | Wages Rs. | Other Expenses Rs. |
|---|---|---|---|---|
| November 2010 | 160,000 | 90,000 | 20,000 | 26,000 |
| December 2010 | 210,000 | 110,000 | 30,000 | 42,000 |
| January 2011 | 230,000 | 100,000 | 60,000 | 35,000 |
| February 2011 | 250,000 | 160,000 | 75,000 | 50,000 |
| March 2011 | 240,000 | 130,000 | 59,000 | 34,000 |

Additional information.

1. Corporate Tax due on 31st March 2011 is Rs.35,000.
2. Interest to be received for investment is Rs.5,000 monthly.
3. Cash in hand on 1st January 2011 is Rs.7,000.
4. Dividend of Rs.15,000 to be paid during March.
5. 30% of the sales amount received in the month of sales, discount allowed 5%.The balance amount is paid equally in the following two months
6. Lag in payment of purchase 2 months.
7. 20% of the wages remain arrears and will be paid in the following month.
8. Other expenses are paid in the following month.

***Solution:***

**Cash Budget for the months from 1st January to 31st March 2011**

| Particulars | January Rs. | February Rs. | March Rs. |
|---|---|---|---|
| **Receipts:** | | | |
| Opening Balance | 7,000 | 21,050 | 34,300 |
| Receipts from Drs. and Cash Sales | 195,050 | 225,250 | 236,400 |
| Interest received | 5,000 | 5,000 | 5,000 |
| **Total** | **207,050** | **251,300** | **275,700** |
| **Payments:** | | | |
| Creditors | 90,000 | 110,000 | 100,000 |
| Wages | 54,000 | 72,000 | 62,200 |
| Other Expenses | 42,000 | 35,000 | 50,000 |
| Corporate Tax | - | - | 35,000 |
| Dividend | - | - | 15,000 |
| **Total** | **186,000** | **217,000** | **262,200** |
| **Closing Balance** | **21,050** | **34,300** | **13,500** |

**Workings:**

**(i) Calculation of receipts from Debtors and Sales:**

| | | Rs. |
|---|---|---|
| January: | Cash Sales (30% of Rs.230,000) | 69,000 |
| | Less: Discount @ 5% | 3,450 |
| | | 65,550 |
| | Add: 35% of Rs.210,000 (Sales of December 2010) | 73,500 |
| | 35 % of Rs.160,000 (Sales of November 2010) | 56,000 |
| | | 195,050 |
| February: | Cash Sales (30% of Rs.250,000) | 75,000 |
| | Less: Discount @ 5% | 3,750 |
| | | 71,250 |
| | Add: 35% of Rs.230,000 (Sales of January) | 80,500 |
| | Add: 35% of Rs.210,000 (Sales of December) | 73,500 |
| | | 225,250 |
| March: | Cash Sales (30% of Rs.240,000) | 72,000 |
| | Less: Discount @ 5% | 3,600 |
| | | 68,400 |
| | Add: 35% of Rs.250,000 (Sales of February) | 87,500 |
| | 35 % of Rs.230,000 (Sales of January) | 80,500 |
| | | 236,400 |

**(ii) Calculation of payment for wages**

| | | |
|---|---|---|
| January: | Wages of January 80 % of Rs.60,000 | 48,000 |
| | Arrear wage of December- 20 % of Rs.30,000 | 6,000 |
| | | 54,000 |
| February: | Wages of February 80 % of Rs.75,000 | 60,000 |
| | Arrear wage of January- 20%of Rs.60,000 | 12,000 |
| | | 72,000 |
| March: | Wages of March 80 % of Rs.59,000 | 47,200 |
| | Arrear wage of February- 20 % of Rs.75,000 | 15,000 |
| | | 62,200 |

**(b) Adjusted Profit and Loss Account method**

In this method, cash budget is prepared by taking into account of the opening balances of cash and bank, projected profit and loss account and the balances of the assets and liabilities. The balance of profit and loss account should be adjusted with non-operating items like depreciation , profit or loss on sale of fixed assets, etc. The cash inflow and outflow related to the capital items should be known by taking their differences between the opening and closing balances.

**Illutration: 8**

Prepare Cash Budget by Adjusted Profit and Loss Account method from the following:

**Balance Sheet as on 31st March 2010**

| Liabilities | Rs. | Assets | Rs. |
|---|---|---|---|
| Share Capital | 5,50,000 | Land & Building | 5,60,000 |
| Profit & Loss Account | 85,000 | Plant & Machinery | 2,40,000 |
| Reserve | 46,000 | Stock | 70,000 |
| Debenture | 1,00,000 | Debtors | 40,000 |
| Loan | 1,50,000 | Cash | 1,14,000 |
| Creditors | 85,000 | Interest prepaid | 4,000 |
| Bills payable | 17,000 | Bills receivable | 10,000 |
| Outstanding salary | 5,000 | | |
| | **10,38,000** | | **10,38,000** |

**Projected Trading and Profit and Loss Account as on 31st March 2011**

| Particulars | | Rs. | Particulars | Rs. |
|---|---|---|---|---|
| To Opening Stock | | 70,000 | By Sales | 3,90,000 |
| To Purchases | | 1,80,000 | By Closing Stock | 90,000 |
| To Wages | | 20,000 | | |
| To Gross Profit | | 2,10,000 | | |
| | | 4,80,000 | | 4,80,000 |
| To Salary | 50,000 | | By Gross Profit | 2,10,000 |
| Less: Outst.last yr. | 5,000 | | By Commission received | 55,000 |
| | 45,000 | | | |
| Add: Outstanding current year | 10,000 | 55,000 | | |
| To Telephone | | 5,000 | | |
| To Electricity | | 14,000 | | |
| To Interest | 15,000 | | | |
| Less: Prepaid current year | 6,000 | | | |
| | 9,000 | | | |
| Add: Prepaid - last year | 4,000 | 13,000 | | |

| | Rs. | | Rs. |
|---|---|---|---|
| To Administration expenses | 18,000 | | |
| To Depreciation | | | |
| Property 5% | 28,000 | | |
| Plant 10% | 20,000 | | |
| To Net Profit c/d | 1,12,000 | | |
| | **2,65,000** | | **2,65,000** |
| To Provision for Dividend | 40,000 | By Balance of Profit last year | 85,000 |
| To General Reserve | 30,000 | | |
| To Balance of Profit to be transferred to Balance Sheet | 1,27,000 | By Net Profit b/d | 1,12,000 |
| | **1,97,000** | | **1,97,000** |

Closing balances estimated: Loan Rs.1,80,000; Plant Rs.2,00,000; Debentures Rs.140,000; Creditors Rs.55,000; Debtors Rs.60,000; Bills Receivable Rs.8,000; Bills Payable Rs.10,000; Share Capital Rs.6,00,000.

***Solution:***

**Cash Budget**

| Particulars | Rs. | Rs. |
|---|---|---|
| Opening Balance as on 1st April 2010 | | 1,14,000 |
| Add: Net Profit for the year | 1,12,000 | |
| Depreciation (28,000 + 20,000) | 48,000 | |
| Decrease in Bills Receivable (10,000 - 8,000) | 2,000 | |
| Issue of Share Capital (600,000 - 550,000) | 50,000 | |
| Issue of Debentures (140,000 - 100,000) | 40,000 | |
| Increase in Salary Outstanding (10,000 - 5,000) | 5,000 | |
| Increase of Loan (180,000 - 150,000) | 30,000 | 2,87,000 |
| | | 4,01,000 |
| Less: Purchase of Plant (2,40,000 - 2,00,000 + Dep. 20,000) | 60,000 | |
| Increase in Stock (90,000 - 70,000) | 20,000 | |
| Increase in Debtors (60,000 - 40,000) | 20,000 | |
| Increase in Prepaid Interest (6,000 - 4,000) | 2,000 | |
| Decrease in Creditors (85,000 - 55,000) | 30,000 | |
| Decrease in Bills Payable (17,000 - 10,000) | 7,000 | 1,39,000 |
| Estimated Closing Balance of Cash | | **2,62,000** |

### (c) Balance Sheet Method

In this method, a projected Balance Sheet should be prepared with estimated assets and liabilities. The cash balance should not be projected. It should be ascertained from the balance of estimated assets and liabilities.

**Illutration: 9**

Prepare a cash budget on the basis of Balance Sheet metho... ... the following:

**Balance Sheet as on 31st March 2010**

| Liabilities | Rs. | Assets | Rs. |
|---|---|---|---|
| Share Capital | 6,00,000 | Freehold property | 5,00,000 |
| Profit & Loss Account | 85,000 | Plant & Machinery | 2,00,000 |
| General Reserve | 56,000 | Stock | 70,000 |
| Loan | 1,50,000 | Debtors | 40,000 |
| Creditors | 40,000 | Cash | 1,24,000 |
| Bills payable | 15,000 | Bills receivable | 10,000 |
| Salary outstanding | 4,000 | Prepaid interest | 6,000 |
| | **9,50,000** | | **9,50,000** |

**Adjustments:**

(1) Balance as an 31st March 2011 - Profit and Loss A/c Rs.1,70,000, Loan Rs.1,50,000; Creditors Rs.60,000; Debtors Rs.74,000; Salary Outstanding Rs 5,000; Stock Rs.60,000; General Reserve Rs.95,000

(2) Purchase of Furniture at the end of March 2011 Rs.20,000

(3) Depreciation for fixed assets @ 10% p.a.

(4) Plant to be purchased on 1st January 2011 for Rs.50,000.

***Solution:***

**Preparation of Cash Budget:**

**Budgeted Balance Sheet as on 31st March 2011**

| Liabilities | Rs. | Assets | | Rs. |
|---|---|---|---|---|
| Share Capital | 6,00,000 | Freehold Property | 5,00,000 | |
| Profit & Loss Account | 1,70,000 | Less: Depreciation | 50,000 | 4,50,000 |
| General Reserve | 95,000 | Plant & Machinery | 200,000 | |
| Loan | 1,50,000 | Add: Purchases | 50,000 | |
| Creditors | 60,000 | | 2,50,000 | |
| Outstanding Salary | 5,000 | Less: Depreciation | 21,250 | 2,28,750 |
| | | (20,000 + 1250) | | |

| | | | |
|---|---|---|---|
| | | Furniture | 20,000 |
| | | Stock | 60,000 |
| | | Debtors | 74,000 |
| | | Cash (Balancing Figure) | 247,250 |
| | **10,80,000** | | **10,80,000** |

**6. Preparation of Flexible Budget**

**Illustration: 10**

The information regarding the expenses of a company at 40% capacity are as follows:

| | Rs. |
|---|---|
| **Fixed expenses:** | |
| Salaries | 80,000 |
| Rent | 40,000 |
| Administrative expenses | 60,000 |
| Depreciation | 40,000 |
| **Variable expenses:** | |
| Material | 1,90,000 |
| Labour | 60,000 |
| Others | 30,000 |
| **Semi-Variable expenses:** | |
| Indirect Labour | 95,000 |
| Repairs & Maintenance | 75,000 |
| Electricity | 30,000 |

The estimated sales at various levels of capacity are,

Rs.8,00,000 at 40% Capacity
Rs.10,00,000 at 50% Capacity
Rs.12,00,000 at 60% Capacity
Rs.15,00,000 at 70% Capacity

The fixed expense will remain same till 100% capacity. Semi-variable expenses remain constant till 50% of capacity. It will increase by 15% between 50% and 65% capacity and further increased by 10% above 65% capacity.

Prepare a flexible budget and calculate the profit at various levels of capacities (40%, 50%, 60% and 70%)

***Solution:***

**Flexible Budget**

| Particulars | Capacity 40% Rs. | 50% Rs. | 60% Rs. | 70% Rs. |
|---|---|---|---|---|
| **Fixed Expenses:** | | | | |
| Salary | 80,000 | 80,000 | 80,000 | 80,000 |
| Rent | 40,000 | 40,000 | 40,000 | 40,000 |
| Administrative Expense | 60,000 | 60,000 | 60,000 | 60,000 |
| Depreciation | 40,000 | 40,000 | 40,000 | 40,000 |
| **Variable Expenses:** | | | | |
| Material | 190,000 | 237,500 | 285,000 | 332,500 |
| Labour | 60,000 | 75,000 | 90,000 | 105,000 |
| Others | 30,000 | 37,500 | 45,000 | 52,500 |
| **Semi Variables Expenses:** | | | | |
| Indirect Labour | 95,000 | 95,000 | 109,250 | 118,750 |
| Repairs & Maintenance | 75,000 | 75,000 | 86,250 | 93,750 |
| Electricity | 30,000 | 30,000 | 34,500 | 37,500 |
| **Total Cost** | **700,000** | **770,000** | **870,000** | **960,000** |
| **Profit** | **100,000** | **230,000** | **330,000** | **540,000** |
| **Estimated Sales** | **800,000** | **10,00,000** | **12,00,000** | **15,00,000** |

**Illustration: 11**

The following information are related to the budgeted production of 10,000 units of a product manufactured by X Ltd. The actual production during the period is 7,000 units. Calculate the budgeted cost per unit.

| | Rs. |
|---|---|
| Direct Materials | 125,000 |
| Direct Labour | 90,000 |
| Direct Expenses | 25,000 |
| Works Overhead (75% Fixed) | 160,000 |
| Administration Overhead (60% Fixed) | 120,000 |
| Selling Overhead (40% Fixed) | 100,000 |

***Solution:***

**Flexible Budget**

| Particulars | Production Cost for 10,000 Units | | Production Cost for 7,000 Units | |
|---|---|---|---|---|
| | Per Unit Rs. | Total Rs. | Per Unit Rs. | Total Rs. |
| Direct Material | 12.50 | 125,000 | 12.50 | 87,500 |
| Direct Wages | 9 | 90,000 | 9 | 63,000 |
| Direct Expense | 2.50 | 25,000 | 2.50 | 17,500 |
| **Prime Cost** | **24** | **240,000** | **24** | **168,000** |
| Works Overhead - Fixed | 12 | 120,000 | 17.14 | 120,000 |
| Variable | 4 | 40,000 | 4 | 28,000 |
| **Work Cost** | **40** | **400,000** | **45.14** | **316,000** |
| Administration Overhead-Fixed | 7.20 | 72,000 | 10.29 | 72,000 |
| Variable | 4.80 | 48,000 | 4.80 | 33,600 |
| **Cost of Production** | **52** | **520,000** | **60.23** | **421,600** |
| Selling overhead-Fixed | 4.00 | 40,000 | 5.71 | 40,000 |
| Variable | 6.00 | 60,000 | 6.00 | 42,000 |
| **Cost of Sales** | **62** | **620,000** | **71.94** | **503,600** |

**Workings:**

Works Overhead: (For10,000 units) Rs. 160,000

(Fixed 75% 120,000

Variable 25% 40,000)

Works Overhead: (For 7,000 units)

Fixed 75% = Rs. 120,000

Variable $\frac{40,000}{10,000} \times 7000$ = Rs. 28,000

Total = Rs 148,000

**7. Preparation of Master Budget**

**Illustration: 12**

K Ltd presents the following information as on 31st March 2011.

Sales Rs.5,00,000

Direct Material Cost - 20% of Sales

Direct Wages Rs.40,000

Direct Expenses Rs.50,000

Factory Overheads:

Supervisors Salary Rs.3,000 per month
Manager's Salary Rs.4,000 per month
Foreman's Salary Rs.1,500 per month
Light & Power Rs.10,000
Depreciation on Plant & Machinery Rs.15,000
Spare and Lubricating oil 1.5 % of Sales
Repairs & Maintenance 2% of Plant & Machinery

Administration overhead Rs.40,000 per year
Selling and distribution overhead Rs.30,000 per year.
Value of Plant & Machinery Rs.5,00,000

Prepare a Master Budget

***Solution:***

**Master Budget**

| Particulars | | | Rs. | Rs. |
|---|---|---|---|---|
| Sales | | | | 5,00,000 |
| Less: | Cost of Production | | | |
| | Direct Material | | 100,000 | |
| | Direct Wages | | 40,000 | |
| | Direct Expenses | | 50,000 | |
| | **Prime Cost** | | **1,90,000** | |
| Factory overhead: | | | | |
| Fixed: | Manager's Salary | 48,000 | | |
| | Supervisor's Salary | 36,000 | | |
| | Foreman's Salary | 18,000 | | |
| | Depreciation | 15,000 | 1,17,000 | |
| Variable: | Light & Power | 10,000 | | |
| | Spares & Lubricating Oil | 7,500 | | |
| | Repairs & Maintenances | 10,000 | 27,500 | |
| | **Works Cost** | | | **3,34,500** |
| | **Gross Profit** | | | **1,65,500** |
| Less: | Administration Overhead | | 40,000 | |
| | Selling & Distribution Overhead | | 30,000 | 70,000 |
| | **Net Profit** | | | **95,500** |

**8. Preparation of Performance Budgeting**

**Illustration: 13**

M Ltd provided the following information for the month of November 2011.

The budgeted sales is 20,000 units @ Rs.15 per unit. The fixed cost is estimated as Rs.95,000 and the variable cost is estimated as Rs.6 per unit. The company could able to produce only 18,000 units due to low demand in the market. Moreover, the variable cost per unit increased by Re.1 per unit, and the selling price increased by Rs.1.50 per unit. The company has to spend Rs. 5000 for research and development, in addition to the usual increase in the cost of production.

Prepare a Performance Budget and a Summary Report.

(Adapted: ICWA Inter)

***Solution:***

**Performance Budget**

| Particulars | Original Plan Rs. | Adjusted Plan Rs. | Actual Rs. |
|---|---|---|---|
| Sales | 300,000 | 270,000 | 297,000 |
| Variable Cost | 120,000 | 108,000 | 126,000 |
| Contribution | 180,000 | 162,000 | 171,000 |
| Fixed Cost | 95,000 | 95,000 | 100,000 |
| Profit | 85,000 | 67,000 | 71,000 |

**Summary Report**

| Particulars | Rs. |
|---|---|
| Budgeted Profit | 85,000 |
| Selling Price Variance | |
| [(18,000 x (16.5 - 15.00)] = 27,000 (Favourable) | |
| Variable Cost Variance | |
| [(18,000 x (6-7)] = 18,000 (Unfavourable) | |
| Fixed Cost Variance | |
| (95,000 - 100,000) = 5,000 (Unfavourable) | |
| Profit Volume Variance | |
| [(2,000 x (15-6)] = 18,000 (Unfavourable) | |
| | 14,000 |
| **Actual Profit** | **71,000** |

## EXERCISE

### I. Choose the correct answer for the following:

1. Budget is prepared for
   (i) Future period (ii) Present period
   (iii) Past period (iv) Any period
2. The document which explains the responsibilities of individuals, involved in the preparation of budget is called
   (i) Cost statement (ii) Profit statement
   (iii) Budget manual (iv) Fund flow statement
3. The consolidated summary of the various functional budgets is called
   (i) Budget committee (ii) Budget manual
   (iii) Master Budget (iv) Fixed Budget
4. The budget prepared for a given level of activity is known as
   (i) Variable budget (ii) Fixed budget
   (iii) Market budget (iv) Budget manual
5. A budget designed to change in accordance with the level of activity is
   (i) Flexible budget (ii) Master budget
   (iii) Fixed budget (iv) Budget manual
6. The budget which forecasts the total output of the organisation is called
   (i) Master budget (ii) Functional budget
   (iii) Fixed budget (iv) Production budget
7. The budget which estimates the total amount of capital required for acquiring fixed assets is called
   (i) Fixed Budget (ii) Capital Expenditure Budget
   (iii) Sales Budget (iv) Cash Budget
8. The budget which estimates the receipt and payment of cash is called
   (i) Cash budget (ii) Sales budget
   (iii) Production budget (iv) Master budget
9. Previous year data are not considered in
   (i) Master budget (ii) Fixed budget
   (iii) Zero-base budget (iv) Flexible budget
10. The process of preparing budget by associating money concept with the performance of employees is called
    (i) Performance Budgeting (ii) Zero-base Budgeting
    (iii) Master Budgeting (iv) Functional Budgeting

[Ans: 1.(i) 2.(iii) 3.(iii) 4.(ii) 5. (i) 6.(iv) 7.(ii) 8.(i) 9.(iii) 10.(i)]

### II. Answer the following:

11. Define budget. State the characteristics of a good budget.
12. What is budgetary control? State the objectives of budgetary control.
13. Define budgetary control. Explain the merits of budgetary control.
14. Explain the advantages and limitations of budgetary control.

15. Explain the different types of budgets.
16. Write short notes of the following:
    (i) Fixed budget (ii) Flexible budget
    (iii) Cash budget (iv) Overhead budget
    (v) Master budget (vi) Budget manual
17. X Ltd manufactures two type of products namely A and B and sells them in Mumbai and Delhi markets. The following information are related to the year ending 31st March 2011.

| Markets | Product | Budgeted Sales | Actual Sales |
|---|---|---|---|
| Mumbai | A | 2,000 Units@ Rs.11 | 1,800 Units@ Rs.11 |
| | B | 3,000 Units@ Rs.40 | 2,700 Units@ Rs.40 |
| Delhi | A | 1,000 Units@ Rs.11 | 1,300 Units@ Rs.11 |
| | B | 5,000 Units@ Rs.40 | 5,500 Units@ Rs.40 |

Market Report revealed that Product A is popular as it is under priced. If the price is reduced by Rs.1 it will get more sales. On the other hand, Product B is over priced and it is predicted that more sales is possible if the selling price is reduced to Rs.37. The management has agreed to give effect to the above price change.

On the above basis, the following estimates have been done by the Sales Manager.

| Products | % increase in sales over current budget | |
|---|---|---|
| | Mumbai | Delhi |
| A | 25% | 15% |
| B | 20% | 10% |

In addition to this, the following additional sales above the estimated sales are possible, with an intensive advertisement.

| Products | Mumbai | Delhi |
|---|---|---|
| A | 200 units | 100 units |
| B | 300 units | 500 units |

Prepare a Sales Budget

(Ans: Rs.35,3000; Rs.362,100; Rs.439,450)

18. The following information are related to a company for 6 months ending 31st March 2011. The units sold for different months are as follows:

| | |
|---|---|
| October 2010 | 6,000 |
| November | 7,000 |
| December | 7,500 |
| January 2011 | 8,000 |
| February | 9,200 |
| March | 10,000 |
| April | 12,000 |

Finished units equal to half the sales for the next months will be in stock at the end of each month including September 2010. Budgeted production for the year ending 31st March 2011 is 120,000 units. Material and labour cost per unit are Rs.15 and Rs.7 respectively. Total factory overhead absorbed is Rs.420,000.

Prepare Production Budget for each month and summarised Production Cost Budget for six months ending 31st March 2011.

(Ans: Rs.12,92,850)

19. Prepare a Production Budget for each month and Production Cost Budget for one year from the following information:

The budgeted sales in units are as follows:

| | Product A (Units) | Product B (Units) |
|---|---|---|
| January | 1,000 | 600 |
| February | 1,400 | 800 |
| March | 1,800 | 1,200 |
| April | 2,500 | 1,500 |
| May | 3,000 | 1,800 |
| June | 3,700 | 2,000 |
| July | 4,000 | 2,500 |

The details of expenses are as follows:

| | Product A Rs. | Product B Rs. |
|---|---|---|
| Direct Material per unit | 25 | 20 |
| Direct Wages per unit | 15 | 12 |
| Total Factory overhead | 240,000 | 200,000 |
| Total Selling & Distribution overhead | 200,000 | 170,000 |
| Selling price per unit | 80 | 75 |

It is assumed that (i) there is no work-in-progress at the end of any month (ii) forecasted units equal to one fourth of sales for the following month will be kept in stock.

(Ans: Rs.60.68; Rs.60.66)

20. Prepare Raw Material Purchase Budget from the following:

| Particulars | Materials (Units) | | | | | |
|---|---|---|---|---|---|---|
| | A | B | C | D | E | F |
| Estimated Stock on 1st January 2011 | 25,000 | 10,000 | 18,000 | 24,000 | 5,000 | 14,000 |
| Estimated Stock on 31st January 2011 | 22,000 | 12,000 | 13,000 | 30,000 | 9,000 | 20,000 |
| Estimated Consumption | 120,000 | 50,000 | 40,000 | 150,000 | 20,000 | 40,000 |
| Standard Price per unit (Rs.) | 4 | 6 | 8 | 5 | 3 | 2 |

(Ans: Rs.468,000; Rs.312,000; Rs.360,000; Rs.780,000; Rs.72000; Rs.29600)

21. Prepare a Cash Budget for 4 months ending 31st March 2011 from the following particulars:

| Months | Sales Rs. | Purchase Rs. | Wages Rs. | Salary Rs. | Manufacturing Expenses Rs. | Administrative Expenses Rs. |
|---|---|---|---|---|---|---|
| Sep. 2010 | 80,000 | 19,000 | 16,000 | 8,000 | 10,000 | 11,000 |
| Oct. 2010 | 110,000 | 20,000 | 20,000 | 12,000 | 11,600 | 19,000 |
| Nov. 2010 | 95,000 | 23,000 | 17,000 | 10,000 | 9,000 | 14,000 |
| Dec. 2010 | 100,000 | 27,000 | 21,000 | 9,000 | 12,000 | 15,000 |
| Jan. 2011 | 12,000 | 32,000 | 20,000 | 15,000 | 14,000 | 18,000 |
| Feb. 2011 | 140,000 | 40,000 | 42,000 | 14,000 | 16,000 | 19,000 |
| Mar. 2011 | 130,000 | 34,000 | 36,000 | 13,000 | 18,000 | 17,000 |

**Additional Information:**

1. Balance of Cash in hand on 1st December 2010 Rs.95,000.
2. Wages are paid in the 1st of next month.
3. Tax amounted to Rs.14,000, payable in the month of March.
4. A dividend of Rs.20,000 payable in the month of January
5. Furniture worth Rs.35,000 to be purchased in the month of December 2010.
6. A machine worth Rs.50,000 purchased in the month of September and the payment is to be made in instalment basis @ Rs.5,000 per month.
7. The Creditors are allowing a credit period of 3 months.
8. Lag in payments of Manufacturing and Selling expenses are two months.
9. The customers are allowed a credit period of 2 months.
10. Lag in payment of Administration expenses is ½ month.

(Ans: Cl.Cash balances: Rs.65,500; Rs.62,000; Rs.61,500; Rs.25,500)

22. Prepare a Cash budget from the following data for 3 months ending 31st March 2011.

| Months | Sales Rs. | Purchases Rs. | Wages Rs. | Other Expenses Rs. |
|---|---|---|---|---|
| Nov. 2010 | 300,000 | 190,000 | 60,000 | 20,000 |
| Dec. 2010 | 270,000 | 160,000 | 50,000 | 15,000 |
| Jan. 2011 | 290,000 | 180,000 | 55,000 | 21,000 |
| Feb. 2011 | 350,000 | 220,000 | 60,000 | 30,000 |
| Mar. 2011 | 400,000 | 250,000 | 80,000 | 40,000 |

**Additional information:**

1. Corporate tax due for 31st March 2011 is Rs.30,000
2. Interest to be received for investment @ Rs.15,000 monthly.
3. Dividend of Rs 25,000 to be paid during March 2011.
4. 40 % of the sales amount realised in the month and discount allowed was @5%. The balance amount realised equally in two subsequent months.
5. Lag in payment of purchase is 2 months.
6. 30 % of the wages remains arrear and will be paid in the following months.
7. Other expenses are paid in the following months.
8. Cash in hand on 1st January 2011 is Rs.60,000.

(Ans: Rs.183,200; Rs.343,700; Rs.459,700)

23. The information regarding the expenses of a company at 60 % capacity are given below:

| Particulars | Rs. |
|---|---|
| **Fixed expenses:** | |
| Salaries | 150,000 |
| Rent | 60,000 |
| Administration expenses | 90,000 |
| Depreciation | 50,000 |
| **Variable expenses:** | |
| Material | 200,000 |
| Labour | 120,000 |
| Others | 40,000 |
| **Semi-variable expenses:** | |
| Indirect Labour | 80,000 |
| Repairs & Maintenance | 70,000 |
| Electricity | 40,000 |

The estimated sales at various levels of capacity are,

Rs.12,00,000 at 60% capacity, Rs.14,00,000 at 70% capacity
Rs.16,00,000 at 80% capacity, Rs.18,00,000 at 90% capacity

The fixed expense will remain same till 100% capacity. Semi-variable expenses remain constant till 60 % capacity. It will increase by 20 % between 60 % to 70 % capacity and further increase by 15% when the capacity increases above 70 %. Prepare a Flexible budget and calculate the profit at various level of capacities (i.e., 60%,70%, 80% and 90%)

(Ans: Profit Rs.300,000; Rs.402,000;Rs.507,300; Rs.648,800)

24. The following information are related to the budgeted production of 20,000 units of a product by XYZ Co.Ltd. The actual production during the period is 15,000 units. Calculate the budgeted cost per unit.

| Particulars | Rs. |
|---|---|
| Direct Material | 20,000 |
| Direct Labour | 110,000 |
| Direct Expenses | 50,000 |
| Factory Overhead (80% fixed) | 190,000 |
| Administration Overhead (70% fixed) | 170,000 |
| Selling Overhead (50% fixed) | 90,000 |

(Ans: Cost of Sales Rs.8,10,000; Rs.686,500)

25. The details of overhead of a company at 60% capacity are stated as follows:

| | Rs. |
|---|---|
| **Fixed overheads:** | |
| Salary | 50,000 |
| Depreciation | 40,000 |
| Insurance | 15,000 |
| Rent | 30,000 |
| **Variable overheads:** | |
| Indirect material | 18,000 |
| Indirect wages | 22,000 |
| Indirect expenses | 12,000 |
| **Semi - variable overheads:** | |
| Electricity(70% fixed; 30% variable) | 21,000 |
| Supervisors Salary(80% fixed; 20%variable) | 32,000 |
| Repairs & Maintenance (90% fixed; 10% variable) | 24,000 |
| **Total overheads** | **2,64,000** |

Estimated direct labour hours are 1,20,000 at 60% capacity.

Prepare a Manufacturing Overhead Budget and find out manufacturing overhead rate at 60% and 80% capacities.

(Ans: Rs.264,000; Rs.275,183; Rs.286,367. Rates Rs.2.20; Rs.1.97; Rs.1.79)

26. Prepare a Cash Budget by Adjusted Profit and Loss Account method from the following:

**Balance Sheet as on 31st March 2010**

| Particulars | Rs. | Particulars | Rs. |
|---|---|---|---|
| Share Capital | 9,00,000 | Premises | 6,00,000 |
| Profit & Loss Account | 1,20,000 | Plant & Machinery | 4,80,000 |
| General Reserve | 80,000 | Stock | 1,30,000 |
| Debentures | 1,50,000 | Debtors | 82,000 |
| Creditors | 40,000 | Cash | 10,000 |
| Bills Payable | 14,000 | Bills Receivable | 5,000 |
| Interest outstanding | 6,000 | Prepaid rent | 3,000 |
| | 13,10,000 | | 13,10,000 |

**Projected Trading and Profit and Loss Account as on 31st March 2011**

| Particulars | | Rs. | Particulars | Rs. |
|---|---|---|---|---|
| To Opening Stock | | 1,30,000 | By Sales | 7,00,000 |
| ,, Purchase | | 1,90,000 | ,, Closing Stock | 1,50,000 |
| ,, Wages | | 50,000 | | |
| ,, Gross Profit c/d | | 4,80,000 | | |
| | | 8,50,000 | | 8,50,000 |
| To Salary | | 80,000 | By Gross Profit b/d | 4,80,000 |
| To Eelectricity | | 30,000 | By Commission received | 20,000 |
| To Telephone | | 20,000 | | |
| To Administration expenses | | 35,000 | | |
| To Rent | 32,000 | | | |
| Less: Prepaid current year | 5,000 | | | |
| | 27,000 | | | |
| Add: Prepaid last year | 3,000 | 30,000 | | |
| To Interest | 24,000 | | | |
| Less: Outstanding last year | 6,000 | | | |
| | 18,000 | | | |
| Add: Outstanding current year | 4,000 | 22,000 | | |
| Depreciation: Premises | | 30,000 | | |
| Plant & Machinery | | 20,000 | | |
| To Net Profit c/d | | 2,33,000 | | |
| | | 5,00,000 | | 5,00,000 |

| | | | |
|---|---|---|---|
| To Dividend paid<br>To General Reserve<br>To Balance of Profit to be transferred to Balance Sheet | 1,10,000<br>40,000<br><br>2,03,000 | By Balance of Profit last year<br>By Net Profit b/d | 1,20,000<br><br>2,33,000 |
| | **3,53,000** | | **3,53,000** |

Closing balances estimated: Debenture Rs.2,50,000; Bills Receivable Rs.12,000; Bills Payable Rs.17,000; Debtors Rs.75,000; Creditors Rs 35,000; Machinery Rs.5,00,000; Premises Rs.550,000.

(Ans: Rs.347,000)

27. Prepare a Cash Budget by Balance Sheet method from the following:

**Balance Sheet as on 31st March 2010**

| Liabilities | Rs. | Assets | Rs. |
|---|---|---|---|
| Share Capital | 5,00,000 | Land & Building | 5,00,000 |
| Profit & Loss Account | 2,10,000 | Plant & Machinery | 2,00,000 |
| General Reserve | 70,000 | Stock | 60,000 |
| Debentures | 1,00,000 | Debtors | 40,000 |
| Creditors | 48,000 | Cash | 1,24,000 |
| Interest outstanding | 12,000 | Bills Receivable | 10,000 |
| | | Commission outstanding | 6,000 |
| | **9,40,000** | | **9,40,000** |

**Adjustments:**

(i) Balances as on 31st March 2011 - Profit & Loss A/c Rs.2,50,000; General Reserve Rs.90,000; Debenture Rs.2,00,000; Stock Rs.110,000; Debtors Rs.98,000 ; Creditors Rs 40,000; Bills Receivable Rs.15,000; Bills Payable Rs.11,000; Outstanding Salary Rs.10,000.

(ii) Plant to be purchased on 1st July 2010 for Rs.70,000

(iii) Depreciation for fixed assets @ 10% p.a.

(Ans: Cash at the end Rs.373,250)

28. X Ltd. provided the following information as on 31st March 2011.

| | Rs. |
|---|---|
| Sales | 7,60,000 |
| Direct Material cost | 1,20,000 |

Direct Wages 70% of the cost of material
Direct Expenses 10,000
Factory Overheads:
Work Manager's salary Rs.5,000 per month
Supervisor's salary Rs.4,000 per month
Foreman salary Rs.3,000 per month
Light & Power 17,000
Depreciation on Plant & Machinery 20,000
Consumable stores 1.4% on sales
Repairs & Maintenance 2.5% of Plant & Machinery
(Value of Plant & Machinery Rs.4,00,000)
Administration overhead Rs.50,000 per year;
Selling and Distribution overhead Rs.45,000.

Prepare a Master Budget

(Ans: Estimated Net Profit Rs.249,360)

29. The information regarding the expenses of a company at 70 % capacity are given below:

| Particulars | Rs. |
|---|---|
| **Fixed expenses:** | |
| Salaries | 210,000 |
| Rent | 45,000 |
| Administration expenses | 110,000 |
| Depreciation | 60,000 |
| **Variable expenses:** | |
| Material | 140,000 |
| Labour | 105,000 |
| Others | 70,000 |
| **Semi-variable expenses:** | |
| Indirect Labour | 121,000 |
| Repairs & Maintenance | 187,000 |
| Electricity | 99,000 |

The estimated sales at various levels of capacity are,
Rs.12,60,000 at 60% capacity, Rs.14,70,000 at 70% capacity
Rs.16,80,000 at 80% capacity, Rs.18,90,000 at 90% capacity

The fixed expense will remain same till 100% capacity. Semi-variable expenses remain constant till 50 % capacity. It will increase by 10 % between 65 % to 70 % capacity and further increase by 20% when the capacity increases above 70 %. Prepare a Flexible budget and calculate the profit at various level of capacities (i.e 60%,70%, 80% and 90%)

(Ans: Profit Rs.195,000; Rs.323,000; Rs.406,600; Rs.571,600)

# Chapter XV

# SOCIAL COST BENEFIT ANALYSIS

The success of a business depends upon the effective utilisation of its resources to earn fair rate of return. Hence, the analysis of the viability of a business in providing fair rate of return is an essential factor. The viability normally means economical viability. It means whether the economical cost of inputs for land, labour and capital is properly compensated in the form of fair rate of return (maximum profit). Like that, the social viability (i.e. whether the social cost of a business is properly compensated in the form of social benefit) is also more essential factor. The social cost is the losses and inconveniences the society experienced due to the establishment of an industrial unit. Example, (i) The medical expenses of the people due to noise, water and air pollutions, (ii) Savings of the people which are provided to the industrial units as long-term and short-term loans. The benefits derived are the employment, corporate tax, quality products with cheap prices. Hence, the social viability of industrial unit is that the social benefits should be greater then the social cost. Hence, it is essential for the business units to measure the social cost benefit through social accounting.

## Social Accounting

The business units are more responsible to the society since it utilises the resources of the society. The aim of it is not only to satisfy the owners in providing maximum profit. But it is equally accountable to the society. The society is providing the land, labour and part of capital in the form of loan for the business units. Hence, it is a must for each of the units to ascertain to what extent it is providing benefits to the society. The extent of benefit can be known only through Social Accounting.

## Meaning and Definition of Social Accounting

Social Accounting is otherwise called as Social Responsibility Accounting or Socio-Economic Accounting or Social Reporting and Social Audit. It is a system of accounting related to the social welfare measures taken by company and the benefits derived out of it by the society. The concept of Social Accounting is well known through the following definition.

According to the **National Association of Accounts (NAA)** Committee, Social Accounting means "the identification, measurement, monitoring and reporting of the social and economic effects of an institution on society".

**Richard Dobbins** and **David Fanning** defined Social Accounting as "the measurement and reporting of information concerning the impact of an entity and its activities on society".

According to **F.E. Perry** "Social Accounting is the reporting of the cost incurred in employing with anti-pollution, safety and health and other societal beneficial requirements and, more generally the impact of business entity on the endeavour to project society its amenities and the environment".

It is clear from the definitions that social accounting means reporting of the information about the social welfare measures and its impact on the society.

## Meaning of Social Audit

The Social Audit is mostly considered as Social Accounting. These two terms are used interchangeably to give the same meaning. Social Audit can be differentiated to some extent from Social Accounting. Social Audit means the verification of the accounting system related to society. It is concerned with whether the objective of the company in providing the social welfare measures has been properly executed. It is also concerned with the impact of social welfare measures on the society (i.e., the benefits derived by the society) is properly reported or not.

## Objectives of Social Accounting

The important objective of Social Accounting are stated as follows,

(i) To earn a goodwill from the society.

(ii) To know the extent of social services done by the company.

(iii) To find out the impact of the social services rendered by the company.

(iv) To find out the expectation of the people for further improvement in the social services of the company.

(v) To determine the different methods of social services for a company.

## Approaches of Social Accounting

There are different approaches to Social Accounting, formulated by many experts in the field of accounting and social science. The important approaches to Social Accounting are stated as follows.

1. Classical Approach
2. Descriptive Approach
3. Net Contribution Approach
4. Social Indicator Approach
5. Integral Welfare Theoretical Approach
6. Linowes Operating Statement Approach
7. Multidimensional Statements Approach
8. Social Income Statement and Balance Sheet Approach

### 1. Classical Approach

According to classical approach the companies can maximise the profit within the legal and ethical boundaries. The functions of the company should be as per the rules and regulations of the various laws like MRTP Act, Companies Act 1956 etc. Also the activities are with of ethical and moral values. These are considered as the good things a company can do for the society.

### 2. Descriptive Approach

In this method the social activities performed by the company are presented in descriptive form along with the final accounts. The quantitative information about the social services are not presented in this method.

### 3. Net Contribution Approach

Net contribution, method is developed by Ralph W. Estes during 1972. In this method the Social Costs and Social Benefits are presented is an account form which is called Social Impact statement. This statement explains the details of social services of a company in quantitative manner. It helps for knowing the Social Surplus or Social Deficits. A model of the Social Impact Statement is stated as follows.

**Social Impact Statement**

| Social Benefits | Social Costs |
|---|---|
| I. Products and Services provided | (i) Goods and materials acquired |
| II. Payments to other elements of Society | (ii) Buildings and equipment purchased |
| (a) Employment provided | (iii) Labour and services used |
| (b) Payment for goods and other services | (iv) Discrimination |
| | (a) in hiring (external) |
| (c) Taxes paid | (b) in placement and promotion (internal) |
| (d) Contributions | (v) Work related injuries and illness |
| (e) Dividend and Interest paid | (vi) Public services and facilities used |
| (f) Loans and other payments | (vii) Other sources used |
| (g) Additional direct benefits to employees | (viii) Environmental damage: |
| | (a) Terrain damage |
| (h) Staff equipment and facilities | (b) Air pollution |
| (i) Services donated | (c) Water pollution |
| (j) Environmental improvements | (d) Noise pollution |
| (k) Other benefits | (e) Solid Waste |
| | (f) Visual and aesthetic pollution |
| | (g) Other environmental damage |
| | (ix) Payments from other elements of society |
| Total Social Benefits | (x) Other Costs |
| Social Surplus / Deficit (Net Contribution) | Total Social Costs |

It is clear from the statement that the debit side represents the social benefits and credit side represents the social costs. The Surplus or Deficit of Social Benefits can easily be ascertained through this statement.

**4. Social Indicator Approach**

This approach was developed by Lee Brummet during 1973. According to this approach, the performance of a company is measured through the economic and social information. He suggested the following method for the measurement of total performance of a company.

Total performance = Net Income ± Human Resource Contribution ± Public Contribution ± Environmental Contribution ± Product or Service Contribution

**5. Integral Welfare Theoretical Approach**

This method is suggested by P. Eichhorn during the year 1974. According to him the Social Costs and Social Benefits can be measured through the following statement.

**Model of the Corporate Social Auditing Statement**

| Social Costs | Social Benefits |
|---|---|
| **I. Producer's Surplus for** | **I. Consumer's Surplus for** |
| 1. Labour Performance | 1. Product A |
| 2. Fixed Assets | 2. Product B |
| 3. Materials | 3. Product C |
| 4. Capital | 4. Product D |
| 5. Entrepreneurial performance | |
| 6. Performances paid in advance | |
| **II. Value of Negative External Effect on** | **II. Value of Positive External Effect on** |
| 1. Employees | 1. Employees |
| 2. Population | 2. Population |
| 3. Companies | 3. Companies |
| 4. Public Entities | 4. Public Entities |
| **III.Net Social Benefits** | **III.Net Social Costs** |

It is clear from the statement that Net Social Cost and Net Social Benefit can only be ascertained through this method.

**6. Linowes Operating Statement Approach**

This approach is developed by D.F. Linowes. According to him the Social Cost Benefit analysis can be done through a statement called Socio-Economics Operating Statement (SEOS). This statement represents the social costs and social benefits. It should be presented along with the final accounts.

**7. Multidimensional Statements Approach**

According to this approach the financial statements should be prepared in multidimensional form so that it accomodates all the social costs and benefits. It suggests that all the social costs and social benefits should be measured in monetary terms.

**8. Social Income Statement and Balance Sheet Approach**

Abt Associates Inc. developed this approach. According to this approach, Social Cost Benefit analysis can be done by preparing Social Income statement and Social Balance Sheet. The Social Income statement is represented with social costs and benefits concerned with employees, community and general public. The Social Balance Sheet should contain human assets, social capital investment in buildings, equipments and other organisational assets.

## Social Accounting in India

The developed countries like U.S.A. and Britain have already adopted the Social Accounting practices. These countries make it compulsory to companies for preparing the Social Accounting. But in India there is no compulsion till now for the preparation of Social Accounting. The Companies Act 1956 has no provisions for the preparation of Social Accounting. But the Sachar Committee (1978) in its report felt the need for 'Social 'Disclosures' by the companies. In India, Tata Iron and Steel Company (TISCO) was the first company to prepare Social Accounting. But the first Social Accounting was subject for critision for its high descriptive nature and self projection of the company. At present many public sector companies like Oil India Ltd., ONGC, NTPC, Madras Refineries Ltd., BHEL, National Textile Corporation and Cement Corporation of India prepare Social Accounting. The Social Accounting is prepared in the form of Social Income Statement and Social Balance Sheet.

## Advantages of Social Accounting

The following are the advantages of Social Accounting.

(i) It improves the reputation of the company.

(ii) It increases the status and motivation of the employees.

(iii) The social organisations will be much satisfied about the company.
(iv) It helps for improving sales of the company.
(v) It facilitates for getting accurate market information from the public.
(vi) The Government will have much reputation about the company.
(vii) It helps for taking various policies and decision making by the management.
(viii) The owners of the company will have a good opinion about the management of the company.
(ix) It improves the rate of return on investment.

## EXERCISE

**I. Choose the correct answer for the following:**

1. The system of accounting related to Social Costs and Social Benefits is known as
   (i) Financial Accounting (ii) Cost Accounting
   (iii) Social Accounting (iv) Management Accounting
2. Identify the social cost from the following
   (i) Pollution (ii) Employment (iii) Profit (iv) Sales
3. Identify the social benefit from the following
   (i) Loss (ii) Pollution (iii) Purchase (iv) Employment
4. The verification of the accounting system related to the social activities of a company is called
   (i) Cost Audit (ii) Social Audit (iii) Financial Audit (iv) Editing

[Ans: 1. (iii); 2. (i); 3. (iv); 4. (ii)]

**II. Answer the following questions:**

1. Define Social Cost Benefit Analysis. State the advantages of Social Cost Benefit Analysis.
2. What is Social Accounting? State the merits of Social Accounting.
3. What is Social Accounting? State the objectives of Social Accounting.
4. Give a brief account of the difficult approaches to Social Accounting.
5. Define Social Accounting. Explain the Net Contribution Approach to Social Accounting.
6. Define Social Accounting. What is Integral Welfare Theoretical Approach to Social Accounting.
7. Write short notes of the following:
   (i) Cost Accounting (ii) Cost Audit (iii) Social Cost (iv) Social Benefit
   (v) Classical Approach to Social Accounting
   (vi) Descriptive Approach to Social Accounting
   (vii) Social Indicator Approach to Social Accounting

# Chapter XVI
# COST AUDIT

Cost Accounting system is developed during 1550s in order to reduce the cost of production to face the competition. The accuracy and efficiency of this system need to be examined. The process of examination of the accuracy and efficiency of this system is called Cost Audit. Though many companies adopted the Cost Accounting system and Cost Audit, there was no compulsion to maintain Cost Accounting and Cost Audit. Only during the year 1965 it is compelled to conduct Cost Audit for specified type of companies, through the amendment of Companies Act, 1956. Cost Audit was introduced in India through the recommendations of Vivian Bose Commission, Daphthary Shastri Committee and Sachar Committee. On the basis of the recommendations of these commissions, the Government of India notified 36 Cost Accounting Record Rules covering 54 industrial products.

## Meaning and Definitions of Cost Audit

Cost Audit is concerned with the examination of the accuracy of the records and system and Cost Auditing. The meaning is well known through the following definitions.

According to **Smith** and **Day** "Cost Audit means the detailed checking of the costing system, techniques and accounts to verify their correctness and to ensure adherence to the objective of cost accounting".

According to **I.G. Tikhe,** "Cost Audit means an examination of cost books, cost accounts, cost statements and subsidiary and prime documents with a view to satisfying the auditor that these represent a fair and true view of the cost of production".

The Institute of **Cost and Works Accountant** of London defines, "Cost Audit is the verification of the correctness of cost accounts and adherence to the cost accounting plans".

It is clear from the definitions that Cost Audit means the examination of the correctness of the cost accounts and cost statements with respect to the procedures and rules laid down by the Companies Act, 1956 and by the respective companies.

## Objectives of Cost Audit

The important objectives of Cost Audit are as follows.

1. To find out the accuracy of the cost accounting system maintained by the company.

2. To examine whether the principles of Cost Accounting system prescribed by the Companies Act 1956 and Institute of Cost and Works Accountant of India have been properly adopted.
3. To find out whether the rules and regulation of the company have been properly followed or not in the preparation of cost accounting.
4. To find out the defects in the cost accounting system followed by the company.
5. To identify and prevent the misappropriation and frauds committed by the managerial personnels.
6. To prevent the errors in the cost accounting system.
7. To find out whether the cost of production is determined correctly or not.
8. To examine whether the standard fixed and estimations are properly and genuinely done.
9. To find out whether the integration of Cost Accounting system with Financial Accounting system is properly done.
10. To give suggestions to the management for the improvement in the Cost Accounting system for better performance of the company.

**Aspects of Cost Audit**

The important aspects of Cost Audit are, (1) Proprietary Audit and (2) Efficiency Audit.

**1. Proprietary Audit**

Proprietary Audit is concerned with the audit of expenditure of a company. The audit related to the examination of whether the budgeted expenditure is optimum one and which provides good result; whether the expenditure is properly planned. It also analyses and suggests various methods of improving the return on investment through proper allocation of expenditure.

**2. Efficiency Audit**

Efficiency audit is concerned with the performance of the company. It is related to the review of the existing policies and procedures of the company. It examines the actual performance with the budgeted performance and find out various methods of improving the actual performance.

**Distinction between Cost Audit and Financial Audit**

The purpose of Cost Audit and Financial Audit are to examine the books and accounts and find out whether the records exhibit true and fair view of the information in the accounts. Though these two audits are technically same, there are few distinctions with respect to the objectives, approaches and procedures. The important distinctions of the Cost Audit and Financial Audit are stated as follows.

1. Financial Audit is compulsory for all companies as per the Companies Act, 1956. But Cost Audit is not compulsory for all type of company. Only specified companies with manufacturing or mining activities are required to maintain Cost Accounting records and subject for audit under Section 209 (i) (d) and Section 233-B of the Companies Act, 1956.
2. The main object of Financial Audit is to find out whether the Profit and Loss Account and Balance Sheet exhibit true and fair view of the affairs of the company. But the main object of Cost Audit is to find out whether the cost of product, prices or activity are proper and genuine.
3. Financial Audit is related to the verification of financial accounts and Cost Audit is related to the verification of cost accounts.
4. Financial Audit is conducted at the end of the financial year. But Cost Audit is conducted during the financial year. Hence, in Cost Audit, it is possible to prevent misappropriation and frauds before it happened.
5. Financial Audit examines only the accuracy about the profit of the company. But Cost Audit examines whether the resource of the company are properly utilised to earn maximum profit.
6. Financial Audit is not concerned with the reduction in cost of production. Cost Audit is concerned with the reduction of cost of production of the company.
7. Financial Auditor has to verify whether the closing stock is properly recorded and valued. But Cost Auditor has to examine more about the adequacy of the closing stock in addition to the proper valuation.
8. Financial Audit is not concerned about certain items like cost of capital which are concerned by Cost Audit. But Cost Audit is not concerned about certain items like deprecation which are considered by financial audit.
9. The Financial Auditor has to submit his report to shareholders of the company. But Cost Auditor has to submit his report to Board of Directors of the company.

## Advantages of Cost Audit

The important advantages of Cost Audit to Shareholders, Management, Employees, Government and Consumers are stated as follows.

### 1. Advantages to Shareholders:

Advantage of Cost Audit to shareholders are stated as follows.

(i) It helps for increasing the return on investment to shareholders.

(ii) It facilitates for proper maintenance of accounts.

(iii) It improves the overall performance of the company.

(iv) It highlights the misappropriation and frauds committed by the management.

**2. Advantages to Management:**

The advantages of Cost Audit to management are stated as follows.

(i) It suggests different methods of increasing the profit of the company.

(ii) It helps for improving the overall performance of the management.

(iii) It analyses the expenses and revenue of various periods and helps for managerial decision making.

(iv) It facilitate to find out the inefficiency in any section of the management so that corrective measures can be taken.

(v) It suggests different methods for improving the cost accounting system.

(vi) It exposes the misappropriation and frauds committed in the company.

(v) It suggests whether the standard fixed for all activities are genuine one.

**3. Advantages to Employees:**

The advantage of Cost Audit to employees are stated as follows.

(i) It helps to improve the performance of all the employees.

(ii) Cost audit helps to increase the profit of the company which facilitates for high wages and bonus.

(iii) Merits of the employees are properly recognised due to Cost Audit.

**4. Advantages to Government:**

The advantages of Cost Audit to Government are stated as follows.

(i) Cost Audit helps for fixing prices of commodities by the government.

(ii) Government can take various decisions regarding export and import of different commodities based on the Cost Audit Report.

(iii) It helps for policy decisions regarding tariffs.

(iv) It facilitates for deciding the concessions and subsidies for various industries.

(v) It helps for the revisions in the MRTP Act by the MRTP commission.

(vi) It helps for an indirect control by the Government to prevent misappropriation and frauds in companies.

(vii) It facilitates for the control of prices by efficient management of companies.

**5. Advantages to Consumers:**

The advantages of Cost Audit to consumers are stated as follows.

(i) Cost audit helps to provide quality products at cheaper prices to the consumers.

(ii) It improves the purchasing power of the consumers.

(iii) It improves the standard of living of consumers.

## Cost Audit Report

Cost Audit Report should be in accordance of the prescribed form of Cost Audit Report Rules 1968. It may be amended from time to time. A model of the Cost Audit Report is stated as follows.

### Model of Cost Audit Report

I / We .............. having been appointed as auditor(s) under Section 233-B of the Companies Act, 1956 (hereinafter referred to as the "Cost Auditor(s)" of Messrs .......... Ltd. (hereinafter referred to as the company) have examined the books of accounts prescribed under clause(d) of Sub-section (1) of section 209 of the said Act and other relevant records for the year ended ......... related to ............ maintained by the company and report, subject to my (our comments under the heading "Auditor's observations and conclusions, contained in the Annexure to this report, that.

(a) I / we have / have not obtained all the information and explanation which to the best of my / our knowledge and belief were necessary for the purpose of this audit;

(b) Proper cost accounting records as required under clause(d) of sub-section (1) of Section 209 of the Companies Act, 1956 (1 of 1956) have / have not been kept by the company;

(c) Proper returns adequate for the purpose of my / our cost audit have / have not been received from branches not visited by me / us.

(d) The said books and records give / do not give the information required by the Companies Act, 1856d in the manner so required; and

(e) in my / our opinion the company's cost accounting records have / have not been properly kept so as to give a true and fair view of the cost of production, processing, manufacturing or mining activities, as the case may be, and marketing of the product under reference.

The matters contained in the Annexure to this report form part of this report, which is also subject to my / our observations made therein.

Dated this .......... day of ......... 200 ........ at

Sd/-

(Cost Auditors)

The cost Audit Report should be submitted as per the Section 233-B of Companies Act, 1956 to the Board of Directors of the Company. The report must be sent to the Central Government within 120 days from the end of the financial year.

## EXERCISE

### I. Choose the correct answer from the following:

1. The process of verification of the correctness of cost accounts is called
   (i) Cost Audit (ii) Financial Audit (iii) Editing (iv) Ratio analysis
2. Cost Audit was introduced in India during
   (i) 1947 (ii) 1956 (iii) 1965 (iv) 1970
3. Cost Audit was introduced in India through the amendment in the
   (i) MRTP Act (ii) Companies Act, 1956 (iii) Contract Act (iv) Labour Act
4. The number of industrial products identified for maintaining Cost Accounting system during 1965 is
   (i) 84 (ii) 24 (iii) 74 (iv) 54
5. Cost Audit Report should be submitted to Board of Directors and
   (i) State Government (ii) Shareholders
   (iii) Central Government (iv) Financial Auditor

[Ans: 1. (i); 2. (iii); 3. (ii); 4. (iv); 5. (iii)]

### II. Answer the following questions:

1. Define Cost Audit. State the advantages of Cost Audit.
2. What is Cost Audit? Distinguish between Cost Audit and Financial Audit.
3. Define Cost Audit. State the objectives of Cost Audit.
4. What is Cost Audit? State the aspects of Cost Audit.
5. Define Cost Audit Report. State the objectives of Cost Audit.

